STOP YELLIN' BEN PIVAR

AND THE HORROR, MYSTERY AND ACTION-ADVENTURE FILMS OF HIS UNIVERSAL B-UNIT

THOMAS REEDER

BearManor Media

Albany, Georgia

Stop Yellin'
Ben Pivar and the Horror, Mystery, and Action-Adventure Films of His Universal B Unit
© 2011 Thomas Reeder
All rights reserved.

The quotes, narratives, and images used in this work are entirely for research purposes. Photographs illustrating this book belong to the author and other collections, except where otherwise indicated. No infringement on the rights of the individual copyright holders is intended.

All photos from the author's collection, unless otherwise noted.

No part of this book may be reproduced in any form or by any means, electronic, mechanical, digital, photocopying or recording, except for the inclusion in a review, without permission in writing from the the publisher.

Published in the USA by:
BearManor Media
PO Box 1129
Duncan, OK 73534-1129
www.BearManorMedia.com

ISBN: 1-59393-666-4
ISBN-13: 978-1-59393-666-2

Printed in the United States.

Design and Layout by Allan T. Duffin.

Table of Contents

Dedication	ix
Acknowledgements	xi
Introduction	xv
Prologue	xxi
1. The Grass is Always Greener on the Other Side of the Atlantic	1
2. Universal Pictures: Pit Stop at a Future Home	11
3. Hail Columbia	19
4. Production with New Independents: Grand National Pictures and Condor Productions (1937)	51
5. Production with Another New Independent: Republic Pictures (1938)	71
6. The Arlen-Devine Series, 1939-1941 (Part 1, the 1939-1940 Season)	79
7. The Other Films (1939-1940 Season)	129
8. The Arlen-Devine Series, 1939-1941 (Part 2, the 1940-1941 Season)	165
	199
9. The Mummy Returns	
10. An Unexpected "Horror"	209
11. The Arlen-Devine Series—Sans Arlen, 1941-1942	217
12. The Mummy Returns Yet Again	245
13. The Loose Ends of 1943, Adolf Included	253
14. The Inner Sanctum Mysteries (Part 1, 1943-1944)	281
15. Cheela Has a Makeover	299
16. The Mummy Overstays His Welcome	323
17. The Inner Sanctum Mysteries (Part 2, 1944-1945)	341
18. The Final Few: Two Noirs, Two Horrors, and One *Horror*	365
19. Edward Small's Small Reliance Pictures	409
20. The Syndicated Television Shows	429
21. The Final Years	445
22. Gone, But Forgotten: Pivar's Legacy	463
Filmography	465
Bibliography	503
Index	507

44. MED CLOSE SHOT OF DAISY
    Daisy approaches camera and comes to
    a stop, takes a cigarette from her
    handbag, and looks over her shoulder
    at . . .

45. LONG SHOT DOWN SIDEWALK   FOOTSTEPS
    The Creeper rounds the corner and
    slowly approaches.

46. MED CLOSE SHOT OF DAISY
    Daisy places the cigarette in her
    mouth, strolls out of frame right.

47. LONG SHOT DOWN SIDEWALK   FOOTSTEPS
    The Creeper continues his approach,
    moving forward from left and out of
    frame right.

48. MED SHOT OF ALLEY
    Daisy from behind, enters alley,
    stops and looks in her handbag for a
    match.

49. MED CLOSE SHOT OF SIDEWALK
    The Creeper strolls from left to
    right, camera pans as he enters   FOOTSTEPS
    alley and Daisy comes into view,
    still looking in her handbag. He
    comes to a stop.

                                          DAISY - Got a match, mister?

    Daisy looks up at the Creeper, the
    cigarette drops from her mouth as
    she recoils in horror.

                                          DAISY - No, wait . . . Don't touch me!

                                          CREEPER - Stop yellin'

                                          DAISY - I won't stop! You go away!

    Creeper moves forward, blocking
    Daisy from view.

                                          DAISY - screams

    Camera pans to their shadows on the
    wall as the Creeper strangles Daisy.

       . . . DISSOLVE TO

50. CLOSE SHOT OF "CITY MORGUE" SIGN

Dedication

To Lorie, Jan, and Neil,
for trusting me with their father's story.

Acknowledgments

A book of this sort cannot be written without the contributions of others, and I would be remiss if I didn't give credit where credit is due. First and foremost are Ben and Judy Pivar's three children, all of whom dug deep into their memories to provide the various reminiscences that follow. Neil, the oldest of the three, was unstinting and surprisingly candid with his comments, which were voluminous and invaluable; he was there at Universal, viewing things through a child's wide eyes. It was always a pleasure communicating with Neil, his dry wit and occasional sarcasm making his responses a delight to read. I don't think Neil realizes just what a funny guy he can be.

Oldest daughter Lorie Pivar Viner has only the dimmest recollections of Universal, not even five when her father's employment with the studio came to an abrupt end. Her recollections of her dad's later years in the fifties and early sixties were extremely informative, however, and her heartfelt retelling of the events leading up to his death was quite moving. I thank her for her openness and candor, and for taking that first call; her quiet encouragement was the impetus behind pursuing this project.

Youngest daughter Jan Pivar Dacri had the least time with her dad, his untimely death occurring when she was only thirteen. Her childhood memories of him are those of a loving daughter, tinged with nostalgia and loss. While all three children provided stills for use in this book, Jan provided an album's worth of priceless images.

Other relatives of Ben's were forthcoming with their thoughts and reminiscences of their long-dead relation. Niece Carol Pivar Miller, daughter of Ben's brother George, is a natural-born storyteller and keeper of the early family lore; she, too, provided some invaluable images from Ben's earliest years. Bette Marks, daughter of Judy's sister Libby Schonzeit Silverstein, was helpful not only with her memories but acting as conduit to her mom's comments as well; a nod to Bette's husband George is also in order. Shirley Karnes, daughter of Judy's oldest sister Anne, was extremely informative, having spent some time with Ben and Judy in the early forties while employed at Universal in the editorial department, followed by a lengthy post-war friendship after she and her husband moved to San Diego. Thanks to Hank Schonzeit as well, son of Judy's brother David and family historian of all things Schonzeit. Ben's grandson Derik Viner shared his knowledge of Ben's roots, passed on by grandmother Judy years earlier.

Andrew J. Fenady worked with Ben in the mid-fifties, and had a number of interesting stories to tell—and when it comes to storytelling, no one tops Andrew. Son Duke Fenady should also be mentioned for tirelessly acting as go-between. Ann Rutherford Dozier good naturedly took my calls, regaling me with stories about her starring role in *Inside Job*, Ben's last film at Universal, and about her career in general. Glenda Goldie Schoncite, wife of Ben's later partner Alvin Schoncite, helped fill in some blanks and confirm some suspicions.

Historian Tom Weaver was extremely generous with his willingness to let me quote from his numerous books, and prompt with responses to my various queries. Tom is second-to-none with his decades of interviews with dozens of Hollywood's movers and shakers, and if you haven't read any of his fascinating books, you should.

Ned Comstock, Senior Library Assistant and film archivist at the University of Southern California's Cinematic Arts Library, gets singled out for my "Good Guy of the Year" award for the immediate interest he took in my project, and the wealth of material he contributed from the library's Universal Collection. I can't thank him enough.

Additional thanks to the nameless but very helpful participants at the Salford City Council Discussion Forum; to Alexandra Grime, Curator of the Manchester Jewish Museum; and to Jim Episale at Unshredded Nostalgia (www.unshreddednostalgia.com), Brent Walker, Dr. Suzanne Holdcraft, Robert Connors, Jack Theakston, Steve Massa, Joan Myers, Anthony Osika, and Doug Kennedy, all of whom contributed in some fashion or other with the writing of this book. Film stills, posters, and lobby cards used as illustrations were generously provided by Diana R. Garcia of Heritage Auction Galleries (www.HA.com), Jerry Murbach at Doctor Macro's High Quality Movie Scans (www.doctormacro.com), and Boyd Magers at Western Clippings (www.westernclippings.com).

Thanks, one and all.

§

Introduction

Why Ben Pivar? Why, indeed. During the research and writing of this book I've been asked that question dozens of times, by friends, by Pivar co-workers, acquaintances, and relatives. Not to mention his children.

The easy, flippant answer was "If I don't write it, nobody else will."

Easy, but probably accurate. For Ben Pivar was a minor player in the film industry, little known to filmgoers and only slightly better known to a subset of industry insiders. Most of his career was spent at the second-tier, penny-pinching, mini-majors of Columbia and Universal, with snippets of employment shoehorned in at the doomed startup Grand National, the surprisingly resilient Republic, and Edward Small's long-lived, on-and-off independent Reliance Pictures. When film work evaporated, Pivar moved into the fledgling television industry, with only the occasional attempt to make a return to cinema. These latter attempts were sporadic, and in most instances abortive.

Mentions in the trades of Pivar's comings and goings were few and far between, more often than not buried far back in the pages, and brief in content. Like so many faceless workers in the industry, Pivar was known, if at all, simply as a name flashing by in a B movie's credits, albeit one that had "Producer" attached to it, alone or trailing "Associate" or "Executive."

So, why Ben Pivar? For one simple reason: Pivar's career affords us a snapshot of a segment of the industry that is frequently ignored, dismissed or, at best, given fleeting mention in the various histories of Hollywood, histories that concentrate on the glitz and glamour at the expense of the mundane and workaday. The annual schedules of these secondary studios were filled with lower-budget fare, the bread-and-butter films that kept the contract players and studio technicians busy, that helped to whittle away at each studio's overhead. Made on tight schedules and even tighter budgets, then rented to theaters for a flat rate or forced upon exhibitors as part of studio package deals, each release was almost guaranteed to turn a profit—a minimal profit, perhaps, but a profit nonetheless. This is more than could be said for the higher profile, costlier studio offerings that occasionally sacrificed earnings for short-lived prestige. The B films offered an extremely useful training ground for novice technicians and contract players alike, where rough edges and questionable performances could be tolerated given each film's throwaway status. And for fading former stars on the slippery slide to obsolescence, the B film offered a last bastion of employment, the opportunity to earn a few more dollars and one more credit before fading into obscurity. Requiring large doses of discipline and ingenuity on the part of the filmmakers, these things were cranked out seemingly overnight, reusing other productions' standing sets or frugally constructed new ones. They were pieced together from single takes even when flubbed lines or substandard action marred them. Their brief running times were padded with stock footage obtained from studio libraries or third-party purveyors, thereby reducing production costs. The bottom line was to keep the costs in check.

At this, Ben Pivar was second to none, and Universal was the studio at which he had the golden opportunity to demonstrate his considerable talent for making polyester purses out of sows' ears. As for stock footage, Pivar embraced the stuff, his years as an editor and his story-writing abilities affording him a unique talent for seamlessly integrating interesting stock into a new, coherent storyline. His workload at Universal grew over the years, his position advancing from associate to executive producer, his purview expanding from a sole action-adventure series to encompass a wide array of films of numerous genres, with serials and shorts thrown into the mix as well. Not to mention, of course, the numerous horror films for which he is occasionally remembered today. So prolific was his output as producer du jour and author of numerous storylines that Universal eventually insisted on, and Pivar complied with, the adoption of a pseudonym so that the Pivar name would seem something less than ubiquitous.

This book is intended primarily as a look at the B films of Ben Pivar and the conditions under which they were made, rather than an in-depth biography of the man himself. While his earliest films are touched upon, first as a film editor at Universal and Columbia and later as a production supervisor at Columbia, it is his later work with Grand National, Republic, and Reliance that is looked at in depth, with a concentration on his work at Universal during the period 1938-1946. These latter years were Pivar's most productive and rewarding, both creatively and financially.

They were probably his happiest years as well.

§

Introduction

There's no such thing as a "bad" movie. Really. Approached with an open mind and fair degree of tolerance, the viewer can find something worthwhile in any film. It may take some doing, but if you look hard enough and give it some thought, you'll soon find that there is a nugget or two, perhaps barely discernible, in even the so-called "worst" of films. It can be something as minor as an actor's momentary bit of business, the photographer's lighting of or camera placement for an individual shot, an imaginative use of sound, or the director's orchestration of some action. It could be some creative penny-pinching that evokes a setting with only a few minor pieces of furniture or other adornments, a clever use of rear-projection, the rare glass shot that turns a tiny stage into a huge outdoor arena, or some impeccably-chosen stock footage that blends seamlessly with the onscreen action—or lack thereof. Once you sign on to the notion that there's no such thing as a "bad" movie, you'll soon find that what previously may have been a painful viewing experience has now become a more worthwhile endeavor, almost a game of sorts. And it is an adherence to this credo that makes jumping headlong into the world of B films a much richer experience.

Let's clarify one point up front: These aren't the films embraced by film-lovers at large. You won't find any glossy coffee-table books for any of the B films, nor exhaustive biographies of the people in front of the cameras or behind the scenes. B movies inhabited a world all their own, separate and distinct from the bigger-budget, heavily-promoted, top-of-the-bill A films prominent in contemporary ads and reviews. You won't find any *Gone with the Wind*'s, *Casablanca*'s, or *The Wizard of Oz*'s here. The B film needs to be considered and accepted within the context of its peers only, with exceptions readily made for its more modest trappings, uneven cast, streamlined script, and hurried pace. When these films were originally released, theatergoers may have griped about these aspects, but they expected and demanded an evening's worth of entertainment. Along with the coming attractions, a newsreel, a cartoon, a short, and the headlining feature, the lower-half-of-the-bill B film went a long way toward filling out the program, or at least sixty minutes' worth of it.

More often than not, the B film provided unexceptional, undemanding, and passably acceptable entertainment, offering diversion comparable to that provided by the bulk of today's hour-long television programs. Many B films provided little more than an hour's worth of mind-numbing pap, be it a laughable horror film, a humorless comedy, an unengaging drama, or a claustrophobic musical. The B film was filler, pure and very simple. But then there was the occasional B film that rose above the crowd and offered something different, something engaging, something actually enjoyable. A clever script, some good performances, some stylish direction, or some evocative photography; any combination of these elements could result in a film that stood out from the crowd. The difference may have been obvious or barely perceptible, and in some rare instances resulted in a film deemed better than the program's headliner.

Ben Pivar thrived in this milieu, his ambitions modest, his offerings prodigious, his body of work a staggering number of modestly-budgeted films produced over a two-decade period. There was not a stinker in the bunch, the least memorable among them providing an acceptable hour's entertainment, and the best thoroughly engaging and undeniably entertaining.

Not surprisingly, few recognize his name today, and the numerous films he was responsible for during this period are for the most part hidden away in vaults or lost to the ages. And the obvious reason for this lack of access is that Pivar was involved with B movies; they were considered dispensable and, with few exceptions, no longer have an audience. Pivar's most prolific period spanned the late thirties through the mid-forties, when he served as one of the faceless powers in Universal's B unit. Pivar's production associates, all in positions similarly hidden from the public eye, included Morgan B. Cox, Oliver Drake, Howard Welsch, Paul Malvern, Jack Bernhard, Ken Goldsmith, Frank Shaw, Donald H. Brown, Will Cowan, and Marshall Grant.

The lack of availability of Pivar's films was not always the case, though, as a large number were readily available on television from the later fifties through the early seventies, when the B product that remained accessible on television were the comedy, horror, and, to a lesser extent, the mystery series. For example, a minor studio such as Monogram was represented only by its "East Side Kids" and "Bowery Boys" comedies, its "Charlie Chan" mysteries, and a handful of horror films. The televised offerings of Producers Releasing Corporation (PRC) consisted of less than a dozen horror thrillers. Larger studios such as Columbia had a few series such as the "Blondie" and "Crime Doctor" films that received the occasional airing.

And then there was Universal, whose B output was represented primarily through the horror film and a few borderline mysteries. Of the aforementioned associates of Pivar's, Malvern had some exposure through reruns of *The Mad Doctor of Market Street*, *House of Frankenstein*, and *House of Dracula*, Bernhard through *Man Made Monster* and *The Strange Case of Doctor Rx*, and Cox, Cowan, and Drake through their collaborations with Pivar on several films. But Pivar, with eighteen of his forty-eight credited films at Universal—primarily those of a horrific nature—shown repeatedly on TV, had the most extensive exposure of any of his former peers at Universal. Sadly, those days are gone, but fond memories of so much enjoyable, admittedly lightweight, entertainment warrants a look back at Pivar's career and the workings of the Universal B unit.

While it is his horror films for which he is most remembered, Pivar's best films were the small, modest mystery and crime thrillers that he produced sporadically during his eight years with the studio. *Framed*, *Double Alibi*, *Enemy Agent*, *Eyes of the Underworld*, *Blonde Alibi*, and *Inside Job* are all visually

Introduction

arresting and taut little thrillers that make the most of their limited budgets, lean but solid casts, and avoid (or minimize) the intrusive comic relief that permeates so many of Pivar's other films.

On March 7, 2010, the *82nd Annual Academy Awards®* Oscar presentation featured a tribute to horror films, a montage of the genre's most iconic moments and characters. Included was a brief clip of Lon Chaney, Jr., from the mummy sequel *The Mummy's Ghost*, decked out in rotting bandages, shuffling toward the camera with arm outstretched. As one of four sequels to the original Karloff classic of 1932, *The Mummy's Ghost* remains one of Pivar's most visible efforts over the years since it was released back in 1944. It is not a particularly good film, but the fleeting on-screen image was instantly recognizable; such is the power and resiliency of the image of Kharis, drummed into the public consciousness over the intervening years. Chaney grew to detest the character by the time he'd finished his third appearance in the fourth installment, but along with the wolf man it is the role for which he is most remembered today. Many a forgotten leading man in far more prestigious studios' films should be so lucky.

Consider this book a sincere attempt to rescue one of those faceless toilers from obscurity, to honor him for a job well done, and for the hours of modest entertainment he has provided over the years. And keep in mind that there were many more forgotten souls that took part in the industry, in all sorts of capacities. Most of the big players have already received their share of attention, and, in many instances, far too much attention. So let us now give one of the little guys his due.

§

Prologue

"This kid looks too young to be on a second career," thought Ben as he stared at the fast-talking fellow standing before him, surveying the stage building across the way as he spoke, on and on, about the attributes of Celotex. "*Avrom Goldbogen, eh? A Jew like me. Should think about changing his name; assimilate. Like everyone else in this town did. And maybe grow a moustache; add a few years to his impossibly young-looking face. Like I did.*"

Ben Pivar stood outside the editing room where he toiled, day in and day out, cutting whatever new Columbia feature was assigned him, assembly line-like. His brother Murray stood beside Avrom; took some time off from Universal to come over and introduce his new friend. Avrom was here on business, though. Studio boss Harry Cohn had just hired him and his new startup firm to soundproof two of the studio's stages. Sound films were sweeping over the industry like a tidal wave, and Columbia wanted to jump on board, and fast. Ben had already been told that he was going to have to learn the cutting of sound as well as its accompanying image, and the challenge was a welcome one. It would help break up some of the boredom that had quickly set in over the past two years of cutting footage, first, and briefly, at Universal, and now at Columbia. And when this Goldbogen fellow was finished here at Columbia, he claimed he had a follow-up assignment at Universal to convert one of their stages as well. Ben inhaled his cigarette's smoke, and then exhaled.

"Interesting racket, converting stages for sound; not much competition," thought Ben. Only one problem, as far as he could see it, and it was to his way of thinking a big one: "*What's he gonna do after all of the industry's stages were converted? Then what? Guess he'll find another line of work, a third career, whatever that would be."* Ben kept an easy smile on his face, inwardly thinking of the short-sightedness of the venture while this cocky little guy went on and on, never taking a breather from his seemingly endless chatter. *"Make some quick money, but then what? Making movies,"* thought Ben, *"now that's a job with a future, and there's a lot of money to be made. And I'm going to make it. Production supervision's my goal, and the bucks that go with it."*

Avrom's non-stop discourse continued as he and Murray wandered off, introductions now out of the way. Ben tossed the cigarette to the ground, snuffed it with the toe of his shoe. *"He should change his name,"* thought Ben as he reentered the editing building and rejoined his coworkers. *"Soundproofing. Can't imagine I'll ever see that guy again, once he's finished soundproofing all of this town's studios."* Ben resumed his work, already five minutes behind schedule.

Avrom faded from his mind almost instantly. It never occurred to him that Avrom would play a major role in his life a quarter century hence.

And not a pleasant one.

It could have happened something like that.

§

1 The Grass is Always Greener on the Other Side of the Atlantic

Benjamin Pivar was a secretive man.
Or so it seemed, but this reticence to discuss the past was more likely due to his overriding ambition and preoccupation with the future rather than by design. The past held little interest for him; the future was everything. After his arrival in Hollywood in 1927, little more would be said about his earliest days back in New York. Once his children were old enough to grasp and retain what they heard, all of their father's stories were of the present.

None of his three children have any knowledge of their father's youth and, more surprisingly, of his actual age or the year he was born. Christmas Day, 1900, was the date he would toss out when pressed, but no one knew whether or not this response was accurate, or if their father even knew the actual date. As son Neil put it, "We always knew that December 25 was questionable. I wonder why he didn't know his actual birthday. Moreover, I wonder why we don't know why he didn't know. I can't remember ever asking. Everyone was certain he was born in 1900. At one point, I had heard 1904."[1] Assuming that Ben knew his true birth date, he'd always play fast and loose with the facts, as did his siblings as well. It was, after all, merely a date.

Pivar displayed a seeming total lack of interest in the past; however, family was everything to him. He would keep in close contact with all of his surviving siblings throughout his life, and not just those who had relocated to the west coast. Unfortunately, however, Pivar's total disinterest in his pre-Hollywood days has resulted in a dearth of information regarding those earliest years back in New York. While those formative years no doubt had an impact on shaping the man that Pivar was to become, they remain for the most part a "closed book." Or, perhaps, a "book" with most of the pages torn from it. Sadly, what

---

[1] Neil Pivar correspondence with author, September 20, 2010.

little that's available regarding Pivar's youth is gleaned primarily from public documents and a smattering of personal reminiscences, the latter in most instances having to do with the Pivars in general rather than Ben specifically.

There is, of course, the possibility that Pivar *wanted* to forget the past, and carve out a new, unblemished future geographically removed from whatever unpleasantness he left behind. Unfounded conjecture, admittedly, but a possibility nonetheless. Regardless, Pivar made a name for himself out in Hollywood—reinvented himself, perhaps—and that is what he is known for to this day. And that is what this book is concerned with.

Benjamin Pivar was born to Adolphus and Hannah Marx[2] Pivar on March 23, 1901[3], the youngest child in a family with seven sons and two daughters. The Pivars lived at 175 Sussex Street, mid-way between Edward Street and Ellison Street[4] in the Grosvenor Ward section of the County Borough of Salford, a metropolitan borough of Greater Manchester. Located in the county of Lancashire in the northwest of England, Salford had at the time a population of 162,452. The Sussex Street home was one of a six-dwelling Victorian-era terraced housing estate, row house affairs built right up to the property line as homes for workers in the area's burgeoning textile industry.

When the 1901 England Census was conducted

Pivar's birthplace at 175 Sussex Street in Salford, circa 1901. Photo courtesy of Carol Pivar Miller.

---

[2] Spelled as *Marks* on some documents.

[3] *The Film Daily Yearbook of Motion Pictures*, 1942, and the *California Death Index, 1940-1997*, got it right, confirmed by his Salford birth certificate. Other sources vary and only add to the confusion: March 2 was given as the day in the *1945-46 International Motion Picture Almanac*, and 1902 in the *1936 Film Daily Production Guide and Directors' Annual*.

[4] "Slater's Manchester, Salford & Suburban Directory, 1903. Part 1: Topography & Street Directory," 515.

a month later, Ben's siblings were named as follows, from oldest to youngest: Eli, age sixteen; Levi, age fourteen; Gershon, age twelve; Joe, age ten; Jacob, age eight; Morris, age six, Dinah, age four, and Bertha, age two.[5] Adolph and Anna[6] (the names the parents commonly went by), demonstrably methodical in the spawning of children, were listed as age forty and thirty-seven, respectively. Neither parent was native to England, both born in Russia in the early 1860s. The couple had relocated to Germany where the three oldest sons were born, and eventually made their way to England sometime between late 1889 and 1891 where the rest of their brood was born and raised. Adolph was a schoolmaster by trade, while Anna stayed at home to keep house, have babies, and raise their children, with a considerable assist from their live-in sixteen-year-old domestic servant Amelia "Milly" Hyman.

Ben's oldest siblings had all attended Hebrew school at the Manchester Talmud Torah School on Bent Street, the school independent of the family's house of worship, The Manchester New Synagogue and Beth Hamedrash, located several blocks away on Cheetham Hill Road. Lessons cost 1d (one pence, or penny) a week, with classes two or three times a week after regular school and on Sunday mornings.

**The Manchester New Synagogue and Beth Hamedrash, circa 1901.
Photo courtesy of Carol Pivar Miller.**

An incident involving Gershon (later George) that occurred before the turn of the century demonstrates Anna's feisty, protective nature. George's daughter Carol retells the story, one she says her father repeated many times.

---

[5] *1901 Census for England*, March 31, 1901.

[6] *Annie* on some documents.

Stop Yellin'

My father—they all went to the same religious school. When he was a little boy he didn't quite know the prayer for the dead, which is called the Kaddish; that's what it's called in Hebrew. And so he made a mistake while he was saying it in Hebrew school after he was in school all day long. And the teacher-slash-Rabbi—which means *teacher*—came over and beat him, hit him, with a cane, or bamboo thing, something. Really hit him. Hit him, hit him, hit him. And he came home from school—there were a lot of children in this family, but he had a really wonderful mother, and father. Wonderful. And he told her—children don't always tell, but he did—he told what happened. The next day she went to the school, she came in front of the whole classroom and she said, 'Did you hit my Georgie?' And he apparently answered, 'Yes.' She took his cane, or ruler, or whatever it was—bamboo stick—and she said, 'Don't you ever hit my child again,' and began hitting him over his back. And that was really quite an amazing thing if you consider that back in those days, whatever the teacher said was law. That was in England. They had corporal punishment. Rules. And in the religious schools, beat the crap out of the kids. He didn't know the words for the prayer for the dead. Seven years old, come on.[7]

By the time of Ben's birth in 1901, his two oldest brothers had entered the workforce. Eli was employed in a Mackintosh factory, manufacturing the raincoats made of a waterproof rubberized cloth named after its Scottish inventor, Charles Macintosh; Levi worked as a clerk in a local warehouse. Yiddish was spoken, but only at home.

Adolph's true surname was Pivarnick, which he shortened to Pivar upon arriving in England. The 1901 Census records reflect this shortened name, but Pivarnick remained the family's legal surname. Both Pivar and Pivarnick would appear on various documents until the family emigrated to the United States in 1904, after which most of the family adopted the new surname. Second son Levi stubbornly resisted the change, retaining the Pivarnick appellation for the rest of his life. Father Adolph was indecisive, going by the Pivarnick surname as well after his arrival in the United States, but eventually abandoning it for the shorter Pivar.

At the time, Sussex Street extended from its junction with Lower Broughton Road and included what is now Cottenham Lane. Ellison Street no longer exists, but was the next street after Edward near the end of what was then Sussex Street, crossing the River Irwell on the Springfield Lane Bridge. The Sussex Street house was situated only a few blocks away from a tight loop in the Irwell known as the Anaconda Bend, which was prone to localized flooding. The

---

[7] Carol Pivar Miller interview with author, November 1, 2010.

Irwell separated Salford from Manchester proper, with the Sussex Street side primarily residential. A wall of factories fronted the river on the Manchester side, all contributing to the river's horribly polluted state at the time. Disastrous floods in 1946 alerted the city to the fact that steps had to be taken to avoid a devastating repeat, but it was not until 1963 that the decision was made to cut a channel between Broughton Bridge and Mary Street to bypass the bend and minimize the possibility of a recurrence. This reconfiguration of the river altered the makeup of the area, with Ellison Street eliminated.

Turn-of-the-century Salford was an important factory town and inland port. Cotton mills and textile processing predominated, and the completion of the Manchester Ship Canal in 1894 resulted in the area's development as a major inland port. Salford Docks alone provided employment to more than 3,000 laborers. Salford could lay claim to several world firsts, including the first unconditionally free public library, and the first street to be lit by gas. The growth of the working class had led to overpopulation, however, and increased foreign competition and regional transport infrastructure improvements soon led to a decline in the area's industrial activities, resulting in increased economic depression. It was a good time to depart for greener pastures for those who could afford to do so.

The family decided to emigrate to the United States three years after Ben's birth. Father Adolph and oldest son Eli were the first to head over, setting up a residence in downtown Manhattan at 58 Forsyth Street near Canal Street.[8] The rest of the family followed, sailing from Liverpool on August 30, 1904, on the S.S. *Baltic* (a mere two months after the new ship's maiden voyage), arriving at the port of New York on September 2.[9]

The children's names would be anglicized soon after the family's arrival in America. Eli now went by Edward, Levi became Louis, Gershon became George, Jacob was now Jack, Morris was now Maurice (although he'd come to be known by one and all as Murray), and Dinah would alternate between her given name and Diana. Bertha and Joe remained as Bertha and Joe.

Within two years the family had moved several blocks away to 254 Broome Street[10] in downtown Manhattan, a block over from Delancy Street. By 1909 they had relocated several blocks south to 173 Henry Street[11] near East Broadway, a three block walk from Adolph's business at 48 Canal Street[12] where

---

[8] *S.S. Baltic Manifest of Alien Passengers*, September 2, 1904.

[9] *Ibid.*

[10] *Bureau of Immigration and Naturalization Declaration of Intention*, November 28, 1906.

[11] *Bureau of Immigration and Naturalization Petition for Naturalization*, October 7, 1909.

[12] *New York City Directory, 1909.*

he specialized in women's shirtwaists. Within a year Adolph's business had moved to new quarters across town at 53 Walker Street.[13] Given his previous employment back in Salford in the garment industry, it is likely that eldest son Eli, now going by Edward, was a part of this business. By 1918, Adolph had relocated once again to 233 West 111th Street,[14] his last known residence in Manhattan.

The educational and employment status of the various family members for these early years is cloudy at best, with only random pieces of information surviving. Fifth son Jack, as Jacob was now called, did not attend college. By 1915 he was a co-owner of the Motion Picture Specialty Co. at 1402 Broadway, along with Joseph J. Murphy and William K. Hedwig.[15] Second son Levi, now going by Louis, was the only one of the siblings to have an advanced formal education, eventually acquiring a law degree. By 1916, Louis was the President of the Jireh Diabetic Food Company, whose principal office was up in northwest New York in Watertown, located in Jefferson County. Louis had the company's name legally changed to the Jireh Food Company, Incorporated,[16] neatly eviscerating the potentially off-putting "Diabetic" from its name. By 1918, Louis was head of Pivar & Company, a food distribution business located in Manhattan. Whether this was the evolution of Jireh or a whole new, family-owned business is unclear, but father Adolph and a number of Louis' siblings were by now involved as well.

**From left to right, Ben with brothers Murray and George, late teens.
Photo courtesy of Carol Pivar Miller.**

---

[13] *New York City Directory, 1910.*

[14] *New York City Directory, 1918.*

[15] *New York City Directory, 1915*, 1859.

[16] *Watertown Daily Times*, June 28, 1916, page unknown.

The 1918 *New York City Directory* has conflicting addresses associated with the business, giving both the Mecca Building at 1600 Broadway and another address blocks away downtown at 106 Seventh Avenue.[17] What's not clear is whether these were corporate office and distribution center addresses, or if one was Louis' private residence. The business eventually ended up at 110 Hudson Street.

Former schoolmaster Adolph had a love of mathematics and geometry, and would create involved puzzles for his children to unravel. When he'd oversee these gatherings, he'd assume the moniker "Pivarnickus."

> [Adolph] was very brilliant, he was like a mathematician—that I know, he had a reputation for being extremely smart ... I know that they used to have these ... gatherings, when they were all like young men, before they were all married, and they still were all in New York, before anyone went to California. This I remember my dad telling me, that they would have these gatherings, they and all their men friends—I don't know that women were ever involved—but people that they knew would all come to their home, to get together and have—it sort of sounds like Gertrude Stein—that kind of thing. [He] would come up with puzzles for them. You know in the Hebrew language, numbers and letters are the same ... and so you could do puzzles with words, and mathematically they were numbers, if you wanted to turn them into numbers—the letter "A"—Aleph— is "A," is "1." It would be like ABC is 123. He would have all of these wonderful puzzles for people to figure out, using either numbers or letters.[18]

By 1922, Louis was no longer a part of the family food business, having moved on to the vice presidency of Beth David Hospital. On June 6, 1922, just five days before the official announcement of his engagement to Ida Feinberg, thirty-five-year-old Louis attended a dinner of the hospital's Board of Directors. This was to celebrate the opening of the new $500,000 building constructed at 113th Street and Lexington Avenue, a project for which Louis was instrumental in raising funds and pushing to completion.[19] What should have otherwise been a pleasant evening turned out less so:

> [Louis] was very active politically, and they were opening a hospital—and the hospital was Beth [David] Hospital, the first one

---

[17] *New York City Directory, 1918*, 1532.

[18] Carol Pivar Miller interview with author, February 2, 2010.

[19] "Louis Pivarnick Dies On Eve of Marriage," *New York Times*, June 8, 1922, page unknown.

in New York—and he was very much involved in fundraising, and the political part of it, and in terms of—I think he was a lawyer for the hospital—put the whole thing together. Here's what happened: They had a big opening gala at the hospital, and it was all the dignitaries of New York City, including the mayor, and everyone, and all the doctors that were going to be working at the hospital, and my grandparents were there. He did not feel well during the evening—it was a big dinner—and, in fact, he was having severe pain, so they brought him into an examining room and discovered he was in the midst of an appendix attack—well, you can imagine in those days this was not a simple matter. He was the first patient ever to have been operated on in that hospital and he died, that night, in the hospital, first patient. It was really a most horrific tragedy—it sounds like a Greek tragedy, doesn't it? And they actually had to come out and make the announcement of what happened, and my grandparents were sitting there. People were waiting to hear how he was. And that's what happened to Louis Pivar.[20]

Third eldest son George served in the Army during World War I, but only briefly. In later years he would promote that he entered the armed forces under false pretenses, falsifying his age when he was only sixteen. A consistent fibber when it came to his age, George would have been at least twenty-eight when the United States entered the war. The truth finally came out, as his daughter Carol explained:

> He did not really serve, in that he never went overseas, because at some point when they were learning how to shoot, his rifle backfired, kicked backed, discharged improperly, and it shot backwards and he was hit right above the eye, and it was a big trauma, he had an injury. He was discharged right after that, probably the end of the war anyway. My father always sat, twisting his eyebrow, that eyebrow where he was shot ... when we finally got television he would always sit and twist his eyebrow, he always had a little scar there.[21]

As the youngest of nine children, Ben quietly grew up in the shadow of his older siblings. In 1919, the City College of New York established a School of Business and Civic Administration, offering an MBA program a year later. With high school finally behind him, Ben enrolled at the business school,[22] which

---

[20] Miller, *op cit.*

[21] *Ibid.*

[22] Terry Ramsaye, ed., *International Motion Picture Almanac, 1939-1940* (New York:

was renamed years later in 1953 as Baruch College of the City University of New York. This further, final educational pursuit and the full-time job that followed would keep Ben in the city—but not for too long, as we shall soon see.

§

Quigley Publishing Co.).

2 Universal Pictures: Pit Stop at a Future Home

Hollywood beckoned. Older brother Murray was probably the first to head out in 1925, but details of this westward migration are lost to time. Murray had taken a job in New York with Universal Film Manufacturing Company in 1917, and by 1922 was manager of Picture Art Sales Corp., Inc., a subsidiary set up to market packages of Universal's older product on a state rights basis.[1] Universal's home office occupied the entire third floor of New York City's ten-story Mecca Building at 1600 Broadway, located on the corners of 48th, Broadway, and Seventh Avenue.[2] (Pivar & Company food distributors was located in that same building,[3] and may very well have offered Murray his first exposure to Universal and the exotic-sounding business they were engaged in.) Much of Murray's time with Universal was spent in the editorial department, but by late 1923 he had been promoted to manager of supplies.[4] After several years of proving himself to his bosses, Murray was taken along with Carl Laemmle when he went out to the west coast in late October 1925. Murray was set up in the editorial department at Universal City,[5] and it wasn't long before he was promoted to department head. He served in that capacity

---

[1] "State Righters: Here's the Chance of a Lifetime," *Film Daily*, August 3, 1922, 4.
[2] Originally built in 1902 as the Studebaker Building, Studebaker had moved out in 1911 and the structure was converted to an office building. Over the years, Universal shared the building with numerous other businesses, a number of them in the film industry. Loew's International Corporation purchased the building in 1947, and in 2005 it was razed to make way for luxury condominiums.
[3] *New York City Directory, 1918*, 1532.
[4] "Changes in 'U' Personnel," *Film Daily*, November 2, 1923, 2.
[5] "Pivar Goes to Universal City," *Film Daily*, October 26, 1925, 2.

(with ever-expanding duties) for nearly three decades until his departure from the studio in 1949.

Carol Pivar Miller, daughter of Ben's older brother George, has a different take on the exodus to California: "[The family was] in the food business in Astoria and [knew] people from 'Biograph.' Voila! That's the connection."[6] Perhaps. There is mention in a biography of Murray that appeared in the *1930 Motion Picture News Blue Book* stating that he "[e]ntered pictures 17 yrs. ago through his brother,"[7] so perhaps he had a first, pre-Universal job with one of the other New York studios, with one of his older brothers—Louis?—greasing the path. Biograph had moved from its 14th Street location in Manhattan up to the Bronx in 1913, and Vitagraph had its studios in Queens, but Famous Players-Lasky wouldn't build its Astoria studio until 1920. If there was an earlier industry connection than Universal, we'll probably never know for certain.

At any rate, Murray ended up out in California and was soon settled in a stable and prominent position as editor-in-chief with Universal. Murray married a woman named Sue Cohen and they moved into a home at 1360 North Crescent Heights Boulevard in Los Angeles.[8] Their sole child, a daughter named Lois, was born at the end of the decade.

Carl Laemmle, Universal's German-born studio head, had his start in the film industry back in early 1906 with a string of Chicago-based storefront theaters. He expanded operations over the next two years to include a distribution exchange called The Laemmle Film Service, with offices in the western United States and Canada. As the largest picture exchange in the United States, it purchased film product from numerous sources, but eventually ran afoul of the Motion Picture Patents Company.

The Motion Picture Patents Company, or the "Trust" as it was more commonly known, was a combine of manufacturers who pooled all of their patents related to the production and projection of motion pictures. Production companies were licensed to use Trust equipment and film. Distributors and exhibitors were licensed to handle films made solely by the Trust's licensee companies, to use projectors manufactured by Edison, and to pay ongoing fees for the privilege; all others were threatened with patent infringement and the inevitable lawsuits that would go along with it. The goal was to eliminate the independent film producers and the roughly 1,000 independent exchanges and exhibitors functioning at that time.

---

[6] Carol Pivar Miller interview with author, February 3, 2010.

[7] *1930 Motion Picture News Blue Book* (New York: Motion Picture News, Inc., 1930), 202.

[8] *Fifteenth Census of the United States: 1930.*

Universal Pictures: Pit Stop at a Future Home

As the Trust's single biggest customer, Laemmle felt that he should be exempt from what he considered Draconian rules, regulations, and fees. He was not. Laemmle balked at the strong-arm tactics of the Trust, and pulled out in 1909. He formed the Independent Motion Picture Company (affectionately known as IMP) to produce his own films in New York, and began cranking out a slew of low-budget one- and two-reelers. Twelve of these were released in 1909, a hundred in 1910, and another hundred and twenty in 1911. First working out of a rented studio at 111 East 14th Street, production later moved uptown to 43rd Street and Eleventh Avenue.

The Trust's tactics were shady at best, imposing one unreasonable restriction after another on exhibitors, with the unstated goal of driving the little guys out of business. Laemmle exposed these tactics week after week in the trades, and his constant hammering resulted in the Trust's termination of each targeted tactic only to find Laemmle replacing the object of his wrath with another despised tactic. Among those implemented or proposed was a 10% fine on exhibitors for switching distributors; the reduction to a sole distributor per state; the forced increase of admissions to 10¢ even in the most rural and impoverished of areas; and the switch from an ongoing weekly fee to a single annual fee, to be paid up front. Noting the impact Laemmle's editorials were having on business and the resultant accompanying loss of revenues, the Trust attempted to break Laemmle under an avalanche of litigation. Two hundred and eighty-nine actions were brought against him over the course of three years, and at a cost to Laemmle of over $300,000. The Trust never anticipated what a formidable opponent he would be.

IMP merged in mid-1912 with several other independent companies operating outside of the Trust, and The Universal Film Manufacturing Company came to be. After an internal power struggle, Laemmle emerged as the new firm's president. Production moved to the west coast for California's optimum filming conditions, and to avoid the Trust's hired goons and lawyers who were sent out in waves to inhibit or terminate any sort of competition. By October 1915, the Trust had ceased to be a threat to the independents, weakened by its ongoing battles with Laemmle, and dealt a final deathblow by the federal court decision in *United States v. Motion Picture Patents Co.* citing illegal restraint of trade.

Universal's filmmaking operations were consolidated in the newly-built Universal City, a huge production facility constructed on the two-hundred-and-thirty-acre Taylor Ranch five miles north of Hollywood, California, across the Cahuenga Pass. Universal's corporate offices remained back in Manhattan at 1600 Broadway, where they shared the building with a growing number of motion picture-related businesses.

Universal's smoothly run assembly line approach to filmmaking generated a steady output of product, offering exhibitors an ongoing program of entertainment that consisted of shorts, newsreels, modest features, and the occasional serial. Unlike some of its competitors who owned hundreds of theaters in which to showcase their films, Universal did not, leaving the first-run theaters to others and concentrating on independently-owned neighborhood theaters and those in smaller or more rural towns. The downside to this approach was that by not controlling exhibition the profits were far smaller. Universal remained a minor player while its fully integrated competitors in the twenties—First National, Paramount, and MGM—had far greater returns on their product.

Into the twenties, Universal production chief Irving Thalberg promoted an increase in the production of more prestigious first-run films, and lobbied for the acquisition of theaters in which to showcase them. Laemmle reluctantly went along with the increase of A-class films—the von Stroheim troika *Blind Husbands* (1919), *The Devil's Passkey* (1920), and *Foolish Wives* (1922), and Wallace Worsley's *The Hunchback of Notre Dame* (1923) among them—but Laemmle's conservative streak made him balk at taking on a chain of theaters and the accompanying mortgage debt. Thalberg departed for Louis B. Mayer Productions in 1923 and MGM in 1924, and there was no further concerted effort to alter Universal's modus operandi until the late twenties.

Back in New York, Ben had taken a job as manager of the Motion Picture Specialty Co. after completing his schooling at the Business School of the City College of New York. His brother Jack's co-ownership of the firm no doubt greased the path for Ben's hiring. A later mini-bio named the business as Murphy and Co.,[9] so it is possible that brother Jack was no longer involved by the time Ben came on board, hired instead on his merits and, of course, his familial connection.

In the interim, Jack had married wife Yetta in 1917 and she gave birth to a son, Sidney, soon after. Jack became involved in the food industry some time in the twenties, although it is unknown—but probable—that it was the family-owned business. Jack came up with what seemed like a great business idea that ultimately fizzled and resulted in a career change. Jack's niece Carol explains:

> He was the only one who was moderately successful. Jack Pivar—this is his story. He had a scheme—listen to this one, 'cause he lost his shirt—and why he didn't get much assistance from his brothers—maybe they didn't have much money then, because it was early on. But when I was a child my Uncle Jack owned a candy store, in Astoria, New

---

[9] Jack Alicoate, ed., *The Film Daily Yearbook of Motion Pictures: 1936* (Fort Lee: J.E. Brulatour, Inc., 1937).

Universal Pictures: Pit Stop at a Future Home

York. I thought it was fabulous, you know, you could go there and have an ice cream cone, everything was free ... But what had happened to him, he was a very creative and artistic guy, he used to travel a lot, he went to South America ... I remember the story of him coming back with a parrot, its name was Esmeralda ... it's true. And my grandmother, they had to get rid of it [in August 1921[10]], because she got Parrot Fever from it. What happened to Jack was he was in the food business with his father and got into importing and then got into this big, big thing of bringing in refrigerated and frozen food ... He had a scheme for freezing orange juice—I believe it was orange juice—and he borrowed a fortune, and he never could pay it back because he lost his shirt like the character in *East of Eden* ... He lost everything, and he didn't have a penny and he, somehow—maybe somebody leant him some money—and he opened a candy store ... I said to [my brother]: "Didn't the family help him out after that?" because he was really, really poor. What my brother said is: "No, Jack would never take any money from anybody." Why he went and bought a candy store—who knows? And we thought it was great.[11]

Jack and his wife lived with his parents at the West 111th Street address in 1921, but it is not known whether they had from the time they were married, or if his failed business deal and resultant impoverishment forced them to move back home. By 1930 Jack, his wife, and their two children Sidney and Florence had moved to 18th Avenue in Brooklyn. By 1933 he was manager at Brooklyn's Emerson Food Packing Company,[12] and eventually acquired the candy store in Astoria.

The reasons behind Ben's decision to leave New York and head west to California are unknown, but older brother Murray's offer to give Ben a foothold in the flourishing motion picture industry most likely played a big part. Whatever the impetus, Ben packed his bags in early 1927 and headed out to Los Angeles, eventually taking a room at the DorElaine Apartments at 1516 North Normandie Avenue, just off West Sunset Boulevard. Murray took the "baby" of the family under his wing and hired Ben as an assistant editor.

---

[10] "PARROT, fine talker, with brass cage," classified ad in *New York Evening Telegram*, August 20, 1921, page unknown.

[11] Miller, *op. cit.*

[12] "Bandits Line Up 11, Rob Office of $800," *Brooklyn Daily Eagle*, March 12, 1933, A7

On-the-job training was the order of the day, and Ben learned the rudiments of cutting film and assembling a visually coherent storyline. After a brief apprenticeship, Murray decided that Ben was ready to advance to editor, keeping a watchful eye on his progress and correcting any missteps along the way. Murray was not about to turn his brother loose on any of the studio's higher-profile projects, instead assigning him to one of the many lowest-budget westerns that occupied a huge chunk of Universal's annual schedule. These westerns cost the studio the least in money, time, and manpower, so any screw-ups here would be of minor concern in the overall scheme of things.

Ben on the steps of the DorElaine Apartments. Photo courtesy of Jan Pivar Dacri.

Ben's first film as full-fledged editor was a modest western titled *The Clean-Up Man*, which he cut sometime in late summer or early autumn of 1927. *The Clean-Up Man* was directed by Ray Taylor, a relative newcomer who had helmed his first western a year earlier and had by then close to a dozen of these sagebrush quickies to his credit.

For those involved with the production of these low-budget westerns, it was a pressure-cooker, baptism-by-fire type atmosphere requiring an impossibly fast turnaround. Noted director Edgar G. Ulmer had his start directing some of these westerns for Universal, and had this to say about the experience in a February 1970 interview with Peter Bogdanovich:

> There were two Western streets—on the upper part of one, Willy [William Wyler] worked; on the lower part of the street, I worked. When Willy used the horses and the cowboys, I had to do close-ups for my picture. Then, when I ran out of close-ups, *I'd get the horses*. We each made twenty-four of those a year. We had the following schedule: Monday and Tuesday, you wrote your script and prepared the production; Wednesday and Thursday, you shot; Friday, you cut; and Saturday, you went to Tijuana gambling with the old man [Carl Laemmle].[13]

---

[13] Peter Bogdanovich, *Who the Devil Made It* (New York: Alfred A. Knopf, 1997), 567.

While Ulmer may have been referring to the studio's "Mustangs," two-reel western shorts filmed between 1925 and 1927 with budgets just cresting the two-thousand-dollar mark, it still provides a rough indication of the comparable time allotted a five-reel western. These longer films were Universal's "Blue Streak Westerns" series through 1926, after which they became part of the "Adventure Series."[14]

The Clean-Up Man follows the exploits of a road agent known as "The Hawk," and the poor innocent sap that is suspected of his crimes. "The Hawk" mingles with the townsfolk by day in his disguise as a peace-loving minister, committing his robberies by night. Ted Wells starred, a relative newcomer to films with only five previous westerns to his credit. Wells would plod on solely in westerns through the late forties, often without credit in bit parts, and almost as often anonymously as someone else's stunt double. Peggy O'Day costarred in what would be one of the last films in her brief nine-year career. Coincidentally (or maybe not), Wells' character's name of "Steve Banning" would resurface a dozen years later as Dick Foran's character's name in Pivar's *The Mummy's Hand* and its follow-up two years later, *The Mummy's Tomb*.

The Clean-Up Man was followed in quick succession by two more Ray Taylor-directed westerns, *Quick Triggers* and *Greased Lightning*. Fred Humes starred in the former as a ranch foreman who leads his men after a gang of cattle rustlers. *Quick Triggers* would be Humes' last in a staggering three-dozen western series churned out for Universal over a three-year period. Derelys Purdue costarred, taking a break from the endless series of "The Newlyweds" comedy shorts based on the comic strip by George McManus, creator of the more famous "Bringing Up Father" strip featuring Maggie and Jiggs. *Greased Lighting* had Ted Wells back in the lead as foreman of a ranch inherited by a city girl well out of her element, as portrayed by Betty Caldwell. Caldwell's career was one of those short-lived affairs, with fewer than a dozen films in a three-year period.

Now that Ben had some practical, hands-on experience in a craft essential to the filmmaking process, it would appear that Murray turned his kid brother loose to go out and find a job at a studio other than Universal. Why Ben departed from Universal after such a brief tenure is unknown, whether it was by choice, force, or the next step in a previously agreed upon course of action.

Ben picked up a one-picture stint as co-editor on the DeMille Pictures Corp. production *Midnight Madness*. Adapted from the play *The Lion Trap, a Comedy in Four Acts* by Daniel Nathan Rubin, this melodrama has star Jacqueline Logan marrying for money rather than love, then dragged by her "diamong king" husband from the comfort of their New York City digs to the wilds of

---

[14] George N. Fenin and William K. Everson, *The Westerns: From Silents to the Seventies* (New York: Penguin Books, 1973), 164.

South Africa. F. Harmon Weight directed, with Clive Brook costarring. Pivar and Harold McLernon wielded the shears, the finished film released through the Pathé Exchange the following year in March 1928.[15]

Ben was hired by Columbia late in 1927 and immediately put to work in the studio's editorial department. Ben had sold himself on words alone, as his three maiden efforts for Universal would not be released until the following year, the first in February 1928, the latter two in July, and his one-shot deal for DeMille in March. Columbia would be his home and the place where he fully learned his craft—both editing and production supervision—over the better part of the following decade. Pivar had left Universal behind.

But, as we shall see, not for good.

§

---

[15] "Midnight Madness," *Film Daily*, August 19, 1928, 7.

3 Hail Columbia

By comparison to Universal, Columbia Pictures Corporation was a newcomer to the industry. Formed late in 1920 by brothers Harry and Jack Cohn along with Jack's friend Joseph Brandt, the company was originally called the CBC Film Sales Corporation. The "CBC" came from the first initial of the three partners' last names—Cohn-Brandt-Cohn—but industry wits took to referring to the upstart little company as "Corned Beef and Cabbage." Understandably lacking a sense of humor where the prestige of their rapidly-expanding company was concerned, the owners effected the name change in 1926. This corresponded with the acquisition of the twenty-six-acre California Studios property at 1438 North Gower Street, and within a few more years additional space was added as independent studios were snapped up on Gower Street, Beachwood Drive, and Sunset Boulevard.

The company's origins were modest. The brothers had both previously worked for Universal, Jack since 1912 as a film editor, and more recently Harry, hired in 1918 as an administrative assistant. Not satisfied with working for others who reaped the rewards of the brothers' labors, the Cohns struck out on their own and put together two series of shorts. Harry was the creative force behind the immediately popular "Hall Room Boys" comedies based on the comic strip characters created by H.A. McGill. Jack was responsible for the "Screen Snapshots" series, a rambling weekly documentary of sorts featuring behind-the-scenes clips of Hollywood's most popular film stars. Funding for additional productions was acquired with the sales of the initial films in these two series, and upon their backs CBC was formed and grew.

It was not long before production was expanded from shorts to features, the first few years a cash flow balancing act. Harry made the films, while Jack settled in to the business end of the company. Former lawyer and third partner

Joe Brandt, an old friend of Jack's who'd worked with him at Universal from the very beginning, handled the new company's promotion and exploitation.

While Jack and Brandt remained behind in New York, Harry headed out to the west coast to make the films, originally working out of space rented from Wilnat Films at 6070 Sunset Boulevard. With the success and growth of the company came the establishment of its own film exchanges and the aforementioned acquisition of the California Studios on North Gower. Additional real estate would be added into the mix as the years went on, eventually encompassing an entire block.

Columbia had Universal in its sights, and tended to emulate that company's approach to production and distribution in its unstated goal of one day rivaling Universal's success. Although fewer in numbers annually—Columbia's mid-twenties output was roughly a third of Universal's—Columbia's films were designed to appeal to the broader mass audience. These films all belonged to one of three series, tagged as either a Columbia, Perfection, or Waldorf. Unlike Universal, however, these designations had little to do with the cost of the films in each of the series. Frugality ruled the studio, and profits were funneled into new productions rather than unneeded additional real estate, improved working conditions, or a stable of contract players. For the most part, actors and actresses were hired between contracts or on loan-out from the other studios. The decision was made early on not to acquire a chain of theaters, a move that proved beneficial with the coming Depression and much later on when the major studios were forced to split off their considerable theater holdings.

The studio continued to grow both in output and prestige, and by late 1927 was on the verge of acquiring the status of mini-major along side of Universal. Newly hired Frank Capra, a former writer for Mack Sennett and more recently writer-director for comedian Harry Langdon at First National, was to have his first film for Columbia released at the beginning of 1928. It would be the first of twenty-five films made for the studio over the next twelve years, and the beginning of an unparalleled string of successes that would bring fame, profits, and prestige to both Capra and the studio he worked for. It was during this period of growth that Ben Pivar entered into the fold as an assistant editor, and just about the same time that Capra was hired.

Pivar was put to work immediately cutting the Jack Holt melodrama *The Tigress*, directed by George B. Seitz. Released in October 1927, the story revolves around gypsy Mona (Dorothy Revier), intent in exacting revenge on Winston Graham (Holt), Earl of Eddington, whom she thinks is responsible for the murder of her father. As usual, love conquers hate, and jealous rival Pietro (Frank Leigh) is exposed as the real murderer. And dispatched.

Pivar continued in the editorial department for the next several years, fine-tuning his craft and receiving screen credit on another dozen films. Within a year he had advanced to the position of the studio's chief film editor,[1] although it's unclear just where this new position fell in the overall editorial department hierarchy. Few of Pivar's efforts as editor survive or are remembered today, and most were silents.

First released in 1928 was the weepy *Modern Mothers* (Director: Philip Rosen), with mamma Helene Chadwick attracting the interest of Douglas Fairbanks, Jr., the boyfriend of the daughter she left with relatives when an infant. *Name the Woman* (Erle C. Kenton) followed in May, Anita Stewart starring as the straying wife of a prosecuting attorney who risks both her and hubby's reputations when testifying at a sensational murder trial. Next in line came Dorothy Revier, good-girl school teacher by day, cabaret dancer by night, in the melodrama *Sinner's Parade* (John G. Adolfi), followed by Marceline Day as the woman of somewhat dubious virtue in the passion-in-the-tropics melodrama *Driftwood* (Christy Cabanne)

Sinner's Parade (1928), Pivar's third editing credit at Columbia.
Image courtesy of Heritage Auction Galleries, Ha.com.

Two more Pivar-credited films were released in November. Jacqueline Logan played the fur-coveting wife and Theodore von Eltz her more fiscally responsible hubby in the comedy of fur-errors *Nothing to Wear* (Erle C. Kenton), followed at the end of the month by Marceline Day playing a college dropout and Ralph Forbes the lawyer (and former lover) who defends her in

---

[1] "Pivar Named Chief Editor," *Film Daily*, June 28, 1928, 3.

a sensational murder trial in another Christy Cabanne-directed melodrama, *Restless Youth*. Director Cabanne would resurface in Pivar's career eleven years later at Universal in a fruitful producer-director relationship that would yield more than a dozen additional films—but more on that in a later chapter.

Wrapping up 1928 was *Object - Alimony* (Scott R. Dunlap) in December, with Lois Wilson the abandoned mother-to-be whose pitiful story is turned into a bestseller by a sympathetic writer. Her husband sees the play made from the book and, typical of these things, sees the error of his ways and returns to her forgiving embrace. Sandwiched in among these films was the higher-profile Frank Capra-directed melodrama *Submarine*, with Jack Holt and Ralph Graves butting heads over Holt's wife Dorothy Revier. When Graves' sub sinks, guess who has to come to the rescue? Good guess. Pivar reportedly assisted Arthur Roberts with the editing of this one, with only Roberts receiving screen credit.

1929 opened with two final silents. *Behind Closed Doors* (Roy William Neill) was the Virginia Valli espionage tale involving the delivery of a secret document, and the attempts of a spy known only as "The Eagle" to intercept it. *The Eternal Woman* (John P. McCarthy) followed with Argentina-born Olive Borden seeking revenge for the murder of her father, coming to suspect her new lover as the culprit.

The release of Warner Brothers' partial talkie *The Jazz Singer* in October 1927 had caught the industry off guard, and the film's subsequent success forced the other studios to take notice that sound films with dialog—even if only *intermittent* scenes with dialog—might very well be

Pivar assisted with the editing of Frank Capra's *Submarine* (1928), without credit. Image courtesy of Heritage Auction Galleries, Ha.com.

here to stay. Fox was one of the first to follow suit using its new Movietone system, with Paramount and MGM both committing to the conversion to sound as well. Columbia, however, cautious as ever when it came to spending hard-earned cash, was one of the last studios to make the leap. Capra's aforementioned *Submarine* was the studio's first "sound" film, but that was limited to a music score and the occasional sound effect.

Pivar's *The Bachelor Girl* (Richard Thorpe) was another of Columbia's early semi-sound efforts, with a recorded music score and sound effects, but now with some recorded dialog as well. Jacqueline Logan starred as the so-called bachelor girl, who stupidly helps to advance her shiftless and ungrateful boyfriend's career, and compounds her naiveté by actually believing he'll change his ways years later when she is a success and he is a flop. Pivar's uncredited apprenticeship on *Submarine* would have given him the experience and confidence to undertake the cutting of this early exercise with sound-on-film.

Jacqueline Logan and William Collier face off in the semi-sound *The Bachelor Girl* (1929).
Image courtesy of Heritage Auction Galleries, Ha.com.

The musical semi-comedy *Broadway Scandals* (George Archainbaud) has a complete soundtrack, one of three musicals churned out by Columbia that same year. Lovers Sally O'Neil and Jack Egan attempt to resuscitate their old vaudeville act, with slinky musical star Carmel Myers threatening to divert Egan's attentions. Pivar co-edited with Leon Barsha, an editing newcomer with only one previous credit.

**Pivar's first all-sound editing effort *Broadway Scandals* (1929).
Image courtesy of Heritage Auction Galleries, Ha.com.**

For *Flight*, director Frank Capra reunited Jack Holt and Ralph Graves as US Marines in yet-another romantic triangle, this time with Lila Lee the nurse they both lust after. It is Holt's turn to be rescued by Graves after he is injured battling rebels down in Nicaragua. Gene Milford and uncredited newcomer Murray Wright helped edit the film along with first-credited Pivar. Wright, too, would play a major role in Pivar's films for Universal, as we'll soon see.

While he was not at Columbia editing film, Pivar would spend some of his free time in his room at the DorElaine Apartments on North Normandie Avenue. This was a sizeable structure housing more than fifty tenants along with its manager, his wife, and their two children. Located a healthy six-mile haul from Pivar's previous employer Universal, it was in much closer proximity to Columbia's studios at less than a mile-and-a-half. Pivar's fellow tenants came from all walks of life and a divergent mix of occupations. As one would expect, a number of them were affiliated with the film industry in one capacity or another, and most at the very lowest levels. Fifty-one-year-old Adrienne D'Ambricourt was the most successful thespian in residence in 1930, a character actress who'd graced the casts of films at MGM, Paramount,

Famous Players, United Artists, and several lesser studios, and would continue to take roles right up to her death at age eighty. The other actors and actresses were far less successful: Boris Charsky had only two credits by this time, and no more to follow; wife Sonia may have been an actress in name only; and the oddly-named Theodore Glaesel was a Dane and actor-wannabe who, while having a name suspiciously similar to that of Dr. Seuss, was not, nor did he have any locatable film credits. Film producer Howard C. Brown had a single credit over at Poverty Row studio Tiffany-Stahl, Daniel D. Seitz served as an accountant in another studio's bookkeeping department, Yoselia F. Borowsky was a studio artist, and David Miller was editor of a fan magazine. Hollywood's so-called "royalty" lived elsewhere.

Pivar's film credits evaporate for about a year and a half from later 1929 to early 1931. Due to the dearth of surviving Columbia studio records and Harry Cohn's stinginess with film credits, documentation of Pivar's involvement with the studio's output is incomplete at best. Let it suffice to say that *Flight* was Pivar's last known effort as an editor.

Brother Murray's allegiances during this period are somewhat cloudy. It was announced back in October 1928 that he had signed a new five-year contract with Universal[2] as editor-in-chief, but a year later in October 1929 it was reported that he was joining Columbia, and that Del Andrews had succeeded him as editor-in-chief at Universal.[3] Within a half year, however, it was announced that Murray was *returning* to Universal, and that Ben had replaced his brother as editorial supervisor at Columbia.[4] The reasons for Murray's move from Universal to Columbia and back again, and how he managed to get out of that five-year contract with Universal may never be known for certain. And did Murray's position with Columbia during that half-year stay temporarily alter Ben's role with the company, or had Murray assumed the position of another who had previously been Ben's superior? Regardless, it appears to have been a big promotion for Ben, and the second in a series of promotions at Columbia over the following five years.

El Código Penal
(Director: Phil Rosen; Released February 19, 1931)

According to his brief biography in the *International Motion Picture Almanac, 1939-40*, Pivar was subsequently promoted to a series of positions with long-winded titles, first to Supervisor of American Production, followed by

---

[2] "Pivar Signs New Contract," *Film Daily*, October 14, 1928, 8.

[3] "Andrews 'U' Editor," *Film Daily*, October 25, 1929, 4.

[4] "Brother Vice Brother," *Variety*, March 19, 1930, 12.

Production Executive in Charge of Foreign Production, and finally the oddly-titled Supervisor to Associate Producer of American Production.[5] Whether these titles are all accurate or a casualty of a sleepy-eyed proofreader is debatable, but the second, "Foreign Production" title no doubt applies to his first known production credit. This was for the Spanish-language version of director Howard Hawks' *The Criminal Code*, titled *El Código Penal*; both based on Martin Flavin's successful Broadway play of 1929-1930. Directed by Phil Rosen, *El Código Penal* starred a young Argentinean actor named Barry Norton, with Carlos Villarias in the Walter Huston role of the prison's warden. Villarias is most remembered today for the title role in the Spanish-language version of *Dracula*, under the shortened name of Carlos Villar. Norton, after a successful career in the United States in silents, had switched over to Spanish-language remakes due to his thick accent. Norton appeared in the Spanish-language *Dracula* as well, in the David Manners role of Jonathan Harker, altered slightly to Juan Harker. *El Código Penal* had its Mexico City premiere in February 1931, with New York and Los Angeles premieres the following month.

The Buck Jones Westerns

Pivar supervised a series of Buck Jones westerns as well during this period, although you won't find his name in the credits of any of them. As with most other Columbia films made around this time, Harry Cohn reserved the sole credit of producer for himself, and would continue to do so into the mid-thirties.

Buck Jones was an extremely popular star who had been in the business from the early teens, reportedly getting a start at Universal as a five-dollar-a-day stuntman and bit player. He eventually ended up at Fox in 1920, soon after starring in westerns a notch below (if only in budget) those of Fox's biggest western star, Tom Mix. Jones was being built up as a potential replacement for Mix, should the latter's ongoing salary increase demands some day prove too onerous for the studio to stomach. Jones became such a success that in 1928 he decided to leave Fox and set up his own production company. After the failure of that venture and the follow-up failure of an ambitious traveling Wild West show, Jones appeared as the feature attraction in the Robbins Brothers Circus. While that latter stint proved a success, it did little to restore the large sums blown on his two failed ventures. Deciding that it was time to reline his emptied pockets, Jones headed back to Hollywood to attempt to reclaim his position as one of the leading screen stars in westerns.

---

[5] Terry Ramsaye, ed., *International Motion Picture Almanac, 1939-40* (New York: Quigley Publishing Co.)

Western star Buck Jones, with Columbia 1930-1934. Pivar oversaw these films during the 1931-1932 season.
Photo courtesy of Jerry Murbach at Doctor Macro's High Quality Movie Scans, www.doctormacro.com.

With the advent of sound, Hollywood had given up on westerns, if only temporarily. The earliest sound films were confined to soundstages where the immobile, soundproof booth-relegated cameras sat aimed at small groups of actors hovering around and speaking into hidden stationary microphones. The "blimping" of cameras by resident photographer Joseph Walker afforded some camera mobility, as did the mounting of microphones on movable booms, but the great outdoors was plagued with the uncontrollable extraneous noise of the wide open expanses. *In Old Arizona* (1929; Irving Cummings) and *The Virginian* (1929; Victor Fleming) proved that outdoor shooting could be accomplished, and effectively so, but at a cost of time and labor. By mid-1930, however, most of the technical difficulties had been overcome, and the ever-popular western was ready for a comeback.[6]

Jones contracted with producer Sol Lesser's Beverly Productions for a series of low-budget westerns for release through Columbia. Jones' $300-per-week compensation for these was a major step down from the $3,500 per week during his heyday back in the twenties, but monetary losses from bad investments left him with little recourse. Lesser delivered eight of these during the 1930-1931 season, after which Columbia took over control of production and Lesser moved on. Jones made close to two dozen films over the next three years for Columbia, all but two of them his popular westerns. Pivar was

---

[6] Elena Boland, "Westerns Stage Comeback," *Los Angeles Times*, May 4, 1930, B11.

assigned to supervise the first round for the 1931-1932 season, and most likely several more after these with *White Eagle*, the eleventh, probably the last.

Jones was a striking figure on film, and extremely likable. With his rugged good looks, appropriate attire (none of those gaudy Tom Mix duds, thank goodness), and impressive riding capabilities, Jones certainly looked the part. His willingness to be the butt of jokes and take part in humorous scenes, coupled with his adequate delivery of lines in a voice that fit the previously silent image, resulted in a renewed popularity with filmgoers. These were low-budget B programmers, for sure, but fast-moving, tautly directed, and handsomely photographed programmers that put much of the sagebrush competition to shame. Low-budget specialist D. Ross Lederman directed Pivar's first, *Branded* (1931), as well as many of the Pivar-supervised Jones westerns to follow; *Branded* was Lederman's second directorial effort for Columbia under a new five-year contract. Western veteran Lambert Hillyer, whose roots reached back to the late teens directing the likes of William S. Hart, Tom Mix, and Jones, handled all but one of the rest of the Pivar-supervised westerns. Titles of some of the other productions that followed in 1931 included *Border Law* (Louis King), *Range Feud* (Lederman) with young co-star John Wayne, and *Deadline* (Hillyer); in 1932 *Ridin' for Justice* (Lederman), *One Man Law* (Hillyer), *South of the Rio Grande* (Hillyer), *Hello Trouble* (Hillyer), *McKenna of the Mounted* (Lederman), *White Eagle* (Hillyer), and the contemporary crime story *High Speed* (Lederman).

Branded is typical of the Columbia westerns overseen by Pivar. Tom Dale (Buck Jones) and his Swedish pal Olaf (John Oscar) stumble across a stage robber (Wallace McDonald) shortly after he has committed a robbery. He escapes, but they retrieve the money. A hastily assembled posse comes across the two of them and, thinking they are the robbers, arrests them. Soon after, Tom and Olaf manage to escape the Falls City jail and head for the Dale Ranch in Prestonville that Tom has learned he has inherited. On the way they befriend and hire a cowhand, not realizing that he was the robber of the stage.

Neighboring ranch owner Lou Preston (Ethel Kenyon) wants to buy Tom's ranch from him, but he refuses. Her ranch manager, Joe Moore (Al Smith), is a dishonest soul who intends to get the ranch the hard way. To that end he and his buddy Tex sucker Tom into buying some cattle that they've appropriated from the Preston Ranch, then convince Lou that Tom's a cattle rustler. He is told to leave town that night, or they'll be back with the sheriff come morning. Tom doesn't leave, of course, and the group arrives the next day. Unfortunately for Moore, Tom has in the meantime acquired documentary evidence, and hog-tied Tex as backup. The sheriff acquits Tom of any guilt, and Lou realizes that Moore is nothing more than a crook. She fires him.

Later, Moore receives a wanted poster with Tom and Olaf's pictures on it. He quickly assembles a posse, with plans to shoot and kill Tom and Olaf. Lou overhears their plan and runs for help from the sheriff. Moore's posse chases down Tom, Olaf, and their cowhand friend, and a shootout ensues. Moore sneaks up behind Tom but is seen by the cowhand, who moves into place and takes the bullet for his new friend. Mortally wounded, he manages to shoot and kill Moore. The rest of the posse overpowers Tom and is about to lynch him when the sheriff arrives with his posse, Lou, and one of the fellows from the robbed stage. Near death, the cowhand admits to the robbery, and his former victim verifies his story. Tom is absolved of all wrongdoing, and comforts his dying friend with a cigarette. Or tries to; his wounded friend dies before he can light it. Tom and Lou embrace for the fadeout.

This is a good-looking film for its minor budget, with nicely chosen outdoor locations, effective staging by director Lederman, and some pleasing photography by Benjamin Kline and Elmer Dyer, both old hands at this sort of thing. The film benefits from a number of visually striking compositions and well thought out camera placements. There are a handful of day-for-night shots during Tom's initial pursuit by a posse that are positively stunning and would not have looked out of place in a John Ford effort, the wide open vistas dominated by a sky full of ominously billowing clouds. Programmer westerns rarely look better than this.

The sound is sufficiently clear and the acting typical, with some actors handling their roles flawlessly—Kenyon and Smith are both quite good—while others suffer from awkward delivery and clumsy movements. One of the film's minor problems is the plethora of actors with moustaches, which leads to some character identity confusion in some of the longer shots, and as with many rushed B's there are a whole lot of long shots. John Oscar, as Jones' Swede companion, taps into his inner "El Brendel," and on that level is rather good, if somewhat goofy. He gets to mangle a few little ditties, humorous in their lyrics and his "singing." There's some appealing low-key comedy, most of it courtesy of Oscar, but Jones is not above taking part at times either, most prominently in a well-worn running gag involving Tom's real name—Cuthbert Chauncy Dale—that works here to harmless effect. All in all, *Branded* provides an enjoyable hour or so of entertainment, regardless of how familiar some of the storyline may seem.

High Speed (1932), one of Jones' occasional non-westerns, is a slick-looking crime drama that takes place on and around the racetrack. Race driver Paul Whipple is mortally wounded during a race, and on his deathbed convinces his mechanic Bill Toomey (Jones) to take care of his crippled son Buddy (uncredited Mickey Rooney, in those days billed as Mickey McGuire). Whipple also gives Bill his blessing to take over piloting the race cars owned by Preston (William Walling). When Bill crashes during his first race, he is unfairly blamed with un-sportsman-like conduct and suspended from racing for a year; any hopes of winning a big purse to go toward medical treatment for Buddy are dashed.

Bill joins the police force and is partnered with Ham (Ward Bond). He eventually uncovers a gambling racket led by gangster Tony Orlando, who is behind the sabotaging of various racers' cars. By film's end, Bill rounds up all of the crooks, race car owner Preston's business manager (Wallace MacDonald) included. Bill wins the big race, and wins the love of Preston's daughter Peggy (Loretta Sayers). And, assumedly, uses the purse to restore Buddy's ability to walk.

Photographer Ted Tetzlaff does excellent work here, with extensive location shooting and absolutely no bogus-looking rear projection. The car race sequences are all the more exciting for it, and several car chase scenes set on the streets of Los Angeles benefit as well. Jones clicks as the hero of the piece, although in an early scene where he is well dressed he looks like he is going to burst out of his suit. Sayers is adequate as the love interest, but MacDonald is unexpressive as the duplicitous business manager. Rooney, just turned eleven when *High Speed* was filmed, gives a surprisingly natural performance, and one can see why he had a long, successful career ahead of him. In later years, Pivar used to tell his kids about the time he interviewed Rooney for a film role early in the young actor's career. Rooney was so short that he had to stand on the chair to see Pivar sitting on the other side of the desk.[7] In all likelihood that would have been for his role in this Buck Jones non-western, since it is the only known film the two were involved with. Rooney's only other feature for Columbia during the period of Pivar's employment was *Blind Date* (1934; Roy William Neill), and while this film has not been associated with Pivar it doesn't rule out involvement on some level or other. It is also possible that Rooney did not get some other role he was interviewed for.

By this time the Pivar family had split up geographically, with several remaining on the east coast while the others migrated to the west coast. Murray, of course, had settled in at Universal and Ben had followed. Brother Ed had moved out to Los Angeles where he opened a men's shop that eventually evolved into the Edward's Men's Store chain that thrived up until his death in the mid-fifties. Pivar's parents had relocated, moving into a house in Los Angeles at 5979 Franklin Avenue. Sisters Dinah and Bertha ended up in California as well.

Jack remained behind in New York, as did third oldest brother George. George got into the importing business, traveling all over Europe in his quest for velvets, ribbons, and trimmings to ship back to the States. Raised in England and relocated to the United States when he was in his mid-teens, George

---

[7] Lorie Pivar Viner interview with author, April 27, 2009.

"always had an English accent—not a real British [accent], but there was always that little sense of it."[8] Louis, of course, had passed on back in 1922, and the fate of fourth-oldest brother Joe, who was a member of the exodus from England back in 1904, remains unknown. While Ben was supervising the Buck Jones films at Columbia later in the 1931-1932 season, his mother Anna took ill and died on August 15, 1932.[9] Anna's body was assumedly shipped back east for burial, as would her husband Adolph's several years later.

Pivar was reported to have relinquished the supervision of the Jones westerns to George B. Seitz in late 1932, to focus on a series of six romantic action melodramas for the upcoming season.[10] Seitz was to finish the balance of the season's eight films, with the tentatively titled *Reckless Romance* his first.[11] Whether or not this actually came to pass for Seitz is in question since production-supervision credits are nil, and Seitz's name pops up instead as director of several of the later Jones westerns. Louis Sarecky was named as supervisor of the Jones films in early January 1933,[12] but it is not unlikely that the actual supervisory position ended up in western producer Irving Briskin's hands. The ongoing lack of credits for the Columbia releases only adds to the confusion.

Anna Pivar, early 1930s. Photo courtesy of Carol Pivar Miller.

The American Film Institute's online film catalog[13] credits Pivar with the supervision of two more Buck Jones westerns released in 1934, *Man Trailer* (Lambert Hillyer) and *The Fighting Ranger* (George B. Seitz), both filmed a year prior to their eventual release. These were remakes of Jones' earlier Columbia features *The Lone Rider* (1930) and *Border Law* (1931), respectively. Jones remained at Columbia to finish up the 1933-1934 season, after which

---

[8] Carol Pivar Miller interview with author, February 2, 2010.

[9] *Variety*, August 23, 1932, page unknown.

[10] "Seitz to Be Supervisor," *Los Angeles Times*, October 2, 1932, B17.

[11] "Hollywood: Seitz On Jones Films," *Variety*, September 20, 1932, 6.

[12] "Hollywood," *Variety*, January 10, 1933, 27.

[13] www.afi.com

he moved over to Universal where he continued acting, now assuming the production chores as well.

As for Pivar, this period from 1932 into 1935 remains as a mostly undocumented black hole. In the same article that named Louis Sarecky as the new supervisor of the Jones westerns, it stated that he was replacing Pivar who had resigned as a Columbia supervisor. Pivar, it reported, was heading over to K.B.S. Productions to produce westerns.[14] When this did not pan out, Pivar hooked up with producer Phil Goldstone and spent several months in story preparation, but this too fell through.[15] In mid-1933, Pivar headed back to Universal in the capacity of associate producer and went on salary on Friday, July 7.[16] He was assigned to something tentatively titled *Two Sons*, an original story by Harrison Jacobs to be adapted by Frances Hyland.[17] It appears that this film never made it past the planning stages.

Filmed in 1933, *The Fighting Ranger* (1934) was a remake of Jones' 1931 *Border Law*. Image courtesy of Heritage Auction Galleries, Ha.com.

King of the Wild Horses (Director: Earl Haley; Released November 10, 1933)

By August 1934 Pivar was back at Columbia. Re-signed as a supervisor,[18] Pivar resumed oversight of a string of films, albeit *sans* credit. One film we know about was filmed in later 1933, which would suggest that his one-picture deal with Universal was a brief one. This was the western *King of the Wild Horses* (Earl Haley) featuring silent screen star Rex, the Wonder Horse, with Lady co-starring as his love interest (I guess you'd call it); Pivar and George Seitz co-supervised. In films since 1924 when he—Rex—made his debut in Hal Roach's

---

[14] *Variety*, op. cit.

[15] "Ben Pivar Joins U as Goldstone Deal Sours," *Variety*, June 6, 1933, 23.

[16] "Pivar, U Associate," *Variety*, July 11, 1933, 7.

[17] "Ben Pivar Joins U as Goldstone Deal Sours," op. cit.

[18] "Contracts," *Variety*, November 13, 1934, 21.

The King of the Wild Horses (Fred Jackman), this assumed remake would prove to be Rex's swan song.

The plot entails a scheme to steal thousands of horses from a Navajo tribe in Arizona, with Wallace MacDonald playing the bad guy and a horse named Marquis playing the bad stallion. *Daily Variety*'s reviewer had mixed feelings about the results, and showed a decided preference for the acting abilities of the onscreen equine players: "Rex has lost none of his ability in talkers. He snorts, laughs and utters his battle cry while fighting villains, rescuing the girl, or tromping on his rival…It is only when the two-legged actors get between [the horses] and the camera that the plot's shaky structure wobbles … Production is gained in a big Navajo pow-wow. Dialog and its delivery is wooden-Indian. Photography veers from so-so to very good."[19]

According to press information, the film—working title *Wild Horse Stampede*—was shot entirely on location at Navajo and Hopi reservations in Arizona, with several Indian ceremonies recorded on film and a "cast" of nearly two thousand Indian extras.[20] This would be the last starring role for Rex, a somewhat temperamental four-legged actor who by several accounts had the disconcerting habit of going after cast and crew alike to display his momentary displeasure.

In 1935 Pivar became an associate producer at Columbia, a position he held until late 1936 or early 1937 working out of Columbia's Sunset Studios near Vermont and Sunset. One of the perks of this promotion, coupled with Cohn's recent loosening of restrictions on producers' credits, was that Pivar now received credit in the trades for his work, if not always

With *King of the Wild Horses* (1934), star Rex "The Wonder Horse" would cap a decade-long career, both in film and attacking crew members. Image courtesy of Heritage Auction Galleries, Ha.com.

---

[19] "King of Wild Horses," *Daily Variety*, October 31, 1933, 3.

[20] Alan Gevinson, ed., *The American Film Institute Catalog of Motion Pictures Produced in the United States: Within Our Gates: Ethnicity in American Feature Films, 1911-1960* (University of California Press, 1997).

onscreen. A studio publicity close-up of a dapper-looking Pivar accompanied full-page promotional pieces in *Boxoffice* for some of the later releases.

His first project, based on his own original story titled *Crimson Orchid*, doesn't appear to have been made.[21] After this false start, Pivar was responsible for such films as *Air Hawks* (1935; Albert Rogell; based on Pivar's unpublished story *Air Fury*) and *After the Dance* (1935; Leo Bulgakov), both *sans* onscreen credit. *Too Tough to Kill* (1935; D. Ross Lederman), *The Lone Wolf Returns* (1935; Roy William Neill) and *Trapped by Television* (1936; Del Lord) followed with Robert North as executive producer. Pivar finally received screen credit for the last two of these, and those that followed: *Two-Fisted Gentleman* (1936; Gordon Wiles), *The Man Who Lived Twice* (1936; Harry Lachman), *End of the Trail* (1936; Erle C. Kenton), and *Come Closer, Folks* (1936; D. Ross Lederman), all with recently-promoted Irving Briskin as executive producer overseeing Pivar's work. Several of these films were of a fantastic nature, with the lethal electrical ray in *Air Hawks*, the television apparatus of *Trapped by Television*, and the facial and mental retooling resultant from the brain operations of *The Man Who Lived Twice* all foreshadowing the more vivid horrors yet to come at Universal several years hence.

The studio publicity portrait of Pivar that accompanied Columbia's promotional pieces in the trades. Photo courtesy of Neil Pivar.

Air Hawks
(Director: Albert Rogell; Released June 1, 1935)

Director Albert Rogell, a seasoned vet of the industry from the (and his) mid-teens, was at the helm for *Air Hawks*, the first film where Pivar received any sort of publicity, if only in the trades and not on screen. Rogell had an endless string of western shorts and features to his credit from 1921 on, switching over to programmer features of varying genres with the coming of sound. His work on *Air Hawks* is solid if uninspired, resulting in a dispensable action-adventure yarn more likely to appeal to the gee-whiz kids in the audience than their parents. Or maybe not.

---

[21] *Daily Variety*, January 10, 1935, 3.

Consolidated Airlines bigwig Martin Drewen (Robert Middlemass) wants to take over mail route competitor ITL (Independent Transcontinental Lines), but ITL owner Barry Eldon (Ralph Bellamy) won't sell. Crooked Victor Arnold (Douglass Dumbrille) makes a suggestion to Drewen: He has been working with German Professor Shulter (Edward Van Sloan) at the supposedly deserted Mountain View Inn. Shulter has perfected some stolen plans for an electronic ray that will destroy bridges and most anything else it is aimed at—including airplanes. If Arnold can come up with the money for a full-size working model, Shulter could shoot ITL's planes out of the sky and put them out of business. Drewen takes this colorful plan to his boss, an unseen character referred to only as "The Chief," and he OKs it.

It isn't long before three of ITL's planes have been shot down, resulting in two deaths—Eldon's brother-in-law included—and one hospitalization. ITL's planes are declared unsafe and the government steps in to investigate. Several agents confide to Eldon their suspicions that Shulter may be involved, his theft of the plans years earlier known to them. His commercial planes grounded, Eldon announces a record-breaking cross-country flight that he plans to make in his new experimental airplane.

In the meantime, Eldon has run into and started an affair with Renee Dupont (Tala Birell), a singer at Arnold's nightclub. Newspaper reporter Tiny Davis (Victor Kilian) grows suspicious about the goings-on at the Mountain View Inn, and some poking around yields a phone number. He takes this to his friend Eldon who quickly ties it to Arnold and Renee. His suspicions aroused, Eldon breaks into Arnold's office and discovers a map of the ITL route that flies over the Mountain View Inn, near where the three planes were brought down. He also finds evidence of Arnold's involvement with Shulter, which he takes with him.

When Arnold gets wind of Eldon's discoveries and theft, he sets in motion a plan to lure Eldon to his death. Renee, who hasn't before realized what a crook Arnold is, alerts Eldon. Eldon comes up with a plan, and postpones his cross-country flight. Enlisting Renee's aid, he has her return to Arnold with the stolen evidence, claiming she has retrieved it. Arnold is elated, and she suggests a weekend getaway to Canada where they can fly in Arnold's plane. Once they board, though, Arnold finds that Eldon is his pilot, and that he is a prisoner at Tiny's gunpoint. Eldon announces that they have only three parachutes, that he is going to fly over the dangerous route, and that he has placed large "ITL" labels on the plane. Once they are airborne, Renee and Tiny parachute out of the plane after a panicky Arnold has admitted his complicity. Eldon flies low over Shulter's truck bearing the electric ray and drops several bombs on it, blowing it to smithereens.

Returning to land, a defeated Arnold squeals all to the police. Drewen is arrested, and "The Chief" turns out to be Eldon's old friend and hoped-for investor Holden (Wyrley Birch). Holden shoots himself before they can arrest him. Renee and Eldon end up together as a couple, and his new experimental plane has in the meantime been proven successful; with an assist from one of Eldon's buddies, celebrity pilot Wiley Post flew it cross-country without Eldon's knowledge, and set a new record.

Kid stuff, but well-done kid stuff, and the production values are high. Ralph Bellamy is sufficiently earnest in the lead, with Tala Birell his exotic opposite as the singer of questionable allegiances. Victor Kilian's reporter is your film version standard, fast-talking but none-too-bright. Douglass Dumbrille is his usual unctuous self, with Columbia stock players Robert Middlemass and Wyrley Birch rounding out the villainous portion of the cast. An uncredited Edward Van Sloan looks at home in his basement laboratory, lit from below to accentuate his madness, all sorts of Ken Strickfaden-looking electrical devices zapping away around him. His electronic ray gun and the tricked-out truck it resides in look convincing enough, but the pressurized outfits that Post and his co-pilot (Robert Allen) wear for their cross-country flight look downright silly. And whoever (Pivar?) came up with the bright idea of putting air ace Wiley Post in a small role as himself should have checked first to see if he had even a modicum of acting talent, because he didn't. The eye-patch looks cool, though; kind of like the Hathaway Shirt Man crossed with the Pillsbury Dough Boy.

One-eyed Wiley trumps the *Air Hawks* (1935) stars in this misleading poster. Image courtesy of Heritage Auction Galleries, Ha.com.

**After the Dance
(Director: Leo Bulgakov; Released July 26, 1935)**

The musical drama *After the Dance* followed in August 1935, with unjustly convicted George Murphy escaping from prison. He is taken in by a dancer (Nancy Carroll), and they end up forming a dance team. At the height of their success, however, her jealous boyfriend (Jack La Rue) reveals Murphy's identity to the police.

Daily Variety's unnamed reviewer summed it up thusly: "This one has no names, uses trite story and makes no pretensions, but is well and sincerely played, carefully directed and enlivened with agreeable song and dance to accomplish what it apparently was content to reach, a satisfactory dual program spot ... Miss Carroll performs with easy grace and nice restraint and shows to advantage in smart dances with Murphy, whose hoofing is first class but singing just average ... Leo Bulgakov does a careful, workmanlike job of directing, maintaining good pace and handling character and situation for all value provided by Harrison Jacobs' story and Harold Shumate's screenplay, which, while familiar in plot, has bright spots of incident and detail. Bruce Manning's added dialog has legitimate show world ring."[22]

The gig's up for *After the Dance* (1935) stars Nancy Carroll and George Murphy.
Image courtesy of Heritage Auction Galleries, Ha.com.

Too Tough to Kill
(Director: D. Ross Lederman; Released November 23, 1935)

D. Ross Lederman handled the direction of the drama *Too Tough to Kill*, having made a break from western-helming purgatory several years earlier. In this one, engineer Victor Jory is sent to the southwest to find out what is impeding the progress of a tunnel's construction. Aided by female reporter Sally O'Neil and her photographer (Johnny Arthur), he exposes and gets rid of the criminals responsible for the holdup.

---

[22] "After the Dance," *Daily Variety*, November 4, 1935, 3.

Pivar between takes, mid-thirties. Photo courtesy of Jan Pivar Dacri.

Motion Picture Daily's reviewer tagged it as "an action love drama," but seemed unmoved by whatever sparks were generated in the Jory-O'Neil matchup, commenting that "[t]here is perhaps sufficient suspense to intrigue the general run of audiences, although the love interest is meager."[23] The plot device of imbedded saboteurs from another construction company could serve as a virtual blueprint for some of Pivar's storylines in his upcoming Richard Arlen-Andy Devine and Andy Devine-Leo Carrillo series at Universal circa 1939-1942, and screenwriter Griffin Jay would in several instances be the author of those later scripts as well. "Hey, Griff, remember that story we did back in '35 with the saboteurs and the jinxed tunnel? How about we redo it at a lumber camp?" Or something like that.

The Lone Wolf Returns
(Director: Roy William Neill; Released December 31, 1935)

The cops are on the alert for notorious international jewel thief Michael Lanyard (Melvyn Douglas) when *The Lone Wolf Returns* to New York. This results in an uncomfortably close call while in the midst of the theft of the famous Bancroft pearls. Eluding bungling police Detective Benson (Robert Emmet O'Connor) and his men, Lanyard ducks into a masquerade party hosted by socialite Marcia Stewart (Gail Patrick). He is surprised to find rival jewel thief Liane Mallison (Tala Birell) and her partner-in-crime husband (Henry Mollison) in attendance, the Mallsions having befriended Marcia with the goal of stealing her valuable jeweled pendant. Lanyard and Marcia fall for each other in record time, and he now determines to go straight for the love of this good woman.

Liane and Mallison inform their ruthless boss Morphew (Douglass Dumbrille) of Lanyard's presence on the scene, so he sets up a meeting with his perceived competitor. When now-retired Lanyard refuses Morphew's offer of participation in the theft for a percentage of the take, Morphew moves to eliminate him from the picture. Anticipating this reaction, Lanyard has arranged with his gentleman butler Jenkins (Raymond Walburn) to have the

---

[23] "Too Tough to Kill," *Motion Picture Daily*, December 5, 1935, 2.

police raid the place. In the commotion that follows, Lanyard escapes with Marcia who is downstairs in the nightclub below Morphew's office.

Undaunted, Morphew steals Marcia's pendant and frames Lanyard, leaving Marcia despondent over her lover's apparent duplicity. Detective Crane (Thurston Hall), lured out of retirement to go after his former arch nemesis, attempts to arrest Lanyard. Lanyard insists on his innocence and asks for freedom until midnight to prove so. Crane refuses, but Lanyard gets the upper hand and locks him in a closet. Working with Jenkins, Lanyard comes up with a plan to locate Morphew's apartment and find the pendant, which is hidden in the fireplace mantle. Lanyard orchestrates events so that the pendant is returned to Crane along with enough evidence to arrest the trio of crooks.

Crane, appreciative of Lanyard's efforts, squares things with Marcia and Chief of Detectives McGowan (Robert Middlemass). Lanyard and Marcia are reunited, and he proposes with a diamond ring—one that he's actually paid for!

Released at the end of 1935, *The Lone Wolf Returns* is an enjoyably unassuming little film. Smoothly unobtrusive direction by old pro Roy William Neill yields on-screen results sufficiently handsome to belie its modest budget. Douglas is letter-perfect as the unflappable Lone Wolf, a role he was born to play. Raymond Walburn provides stiff-upper-lip support as his fussy but resourceful gentleman butler, and Gail Patrick is competent but unremarkable as Lanyard's socialite lover; few sparks there. As for the trio of rival thieves, Birell is sexy if occasionally unintelligible, Mollison amusingly pompous while repeatedly dissed by his cohorts, and Dumbrille achingly familiar in his stock hood-with-breeding character. Thurston Hall is a standout as the flower-loving retired detective, with O'Connor amusing as the ineffectual detective he replaces, and Middlemass solid as their blustery boss. All in all, a good if somewhat low-wattage cast.

Reviews were for the most part favorable: "Gags are hilarious and novel, dialog sparkles, characters take a new slant out of the old ruts," raved *Daily*

The Lone Wolf Returns (1935) was popular in overseas markets, including Belgium ... Image courtesy of Heritage Auction Galleries, Ha.com.

Variety, "a topnotch script which holds pace, hilarity and suspense in mixing nifty lines, smoothly developed incident and entertaining character clash ... the picture has been given nice mounting and smart cutting."[24] *Motion Picture Daily* was more succinct: "The story is well conceived, acted and directed,"[25] and *Film Daily* concurred, deeming it "an entertaining program number principally on the basis of a little freshness in handling and the work of an able cast."[26] *The Hollywood Reporter* provided a dissenting opinion, saying that while "all decked out in evening clothes with quite professional smartness, it does not succeed in being either credible or particularly interesting."[27]

... and Sweden. Image courtesy of Heritage Auction Galleries, Ha.com.

The reviews, however, were unanimous in their praise for director Roy William Neill. *The New York Herald Tribune* gushed that "Mr. Neill presents his story with such freshness it almost achieves the deft touch of a Vandyke [sic] or a Capra. It is gay and lilting in its rapid pace, and it bends to the director's humor as a weed in the wind."[28] *Daily Variety*'s positive review went on to state that "Roy William Neill sets himself a new par with practically flawless direction ... Director Neill [has] come through with about his best job to date, one to make him a contender in the ranks of light comedy meggers."[29] *Harrison's Reports* weighed in on the film in general with the stuffy assertion that "[b]ecause of the robberies it is unsuitable for children, adolescents, or Sundays. Adult entertainment."[30]

Oh, how the times have changed.

---

[24] "The Lone Wolf Returns," *Daily Variety*, January 14, 1936, 3.

[25] "The Lone Wolf Returns," *Motion Picture Daily*, January 15, 1936, 12.

[26] "The Lone Wolf Returns," *Film Daily*, February 4, 1936, 10.

[27] "The Lone Wolf Returns," *Hollywood Reporter*, January 14, 1936, 3.

[28] "The Lone Wolf Returns," *New York Herald Tribune*, February 3, 1936, 7.

[29] *Daily Variety*, op. cit.

[30] "The Lone Wolf Returns," *Harrison's Reports*, January 18, 1936, page unknown.

Hail Columbia

Trapped By Television
(Director: Del Lord; Released June 16, 1936)

Television broadcasting, then in its embryonic stage and three years away from its introduction to the public at the 1939 World's Fair, was the subject of the enjoyable *Trapped By Television*. Inventor Fred Dennis (Lyle Talbot) has developed broadcasting and receiving apparatus, but lacks the funds for a cathode ray tube, his system's sole missing piece. Acme bill collector Rocky O'Neil (Nat Pendleton) has a love of science that compels him to forget about Fred's debt and join forces with him. Money hungry marketer Bobby Blake (Mary Astor) talks Fred into letting her manage and promote his invention, promising to raise funds for its completion. Meanwhile, Frank Griffin (Marc Lawrence), who has posed as aide to Paragon Broadcasting's top inventor Paul Turner (Wyrley Birch), kidnaps and murders Turner and appropriates his plans for a broadcasting system. With Turner's disappearance, company president John Curtis (Thurston Hall) is convinced by his assistant Standish (Robert Strange) of the need to put out bids for outside development of a broadcasting system. Standish is in cahoots with Griffin, and they plan to orchestrate it so that Paragon will unknowingly buy its own system, and at an inflated price.

Pivar on the Columbia lot, mid-thirties. Photo courtesy of Neil Pivar.

Bobby convinces Curtis and Paragon's Board of Directors to meet to preview Fred's now-completed system. Standish gets wind of this and manages to sabotage the demonstration, leaving everyone convinced that Fred's system is a sham. Standish and Griffin now think that Fred is no longer a threat, but are soon shocked to find that Fred has rebuilt it. Bobby cons the Board into another meeting where they'll be forced to watch a broadcast from Fred's lab. Griffin and another hood go up to the lab to destroy the broadcasting device, while Standish waits outside. Fred defends his invention with his fists, and the fight is broadcast back to the assembled Board. Rocky rushes to Fred's assistance and the hoods are overpowered and arrested. Paragon is now more than willing to back Fred's new system.

Mary Astor, near the start of a new two-year contract with Columbia, commented on the experience several decades later: "It paid well, but it meant constant work on a great many insignificant pictures. I worked on three and even four at a time, meaning retakes on one, costumes for two coming up, 'art' and publicity for current production. On very rare occasions I had a week or two weeks off. It was dull …"[31] *Trapped By Television* was one of her first for the studio, and she handles her part with ease in spite of the appearance of slumming in a production like this.

Pendleton steals the show as the tough-talking, *Popular Mechanics*-addicted bill collector, and provides the film's biggest laughs with his dimwitted cockiness. Talbot is likable but wimpy in the lead role, weighed down by his character's insufferably boyish enthusiasm. As Astor's wisecracking assistant Mae Collins, pretty B actress Joyce Compton manages to dominate the scenes shared with her higher-profile star. An uncredited Marc Lawrence is the film's cookie-cutter crook, two-dimensional aside from his amusing habit of blowing darts at a dartboard.

Noted silent and sound comedy-short director Del Lord handled the chores on *Trapped By Television*, injecting a fair amount of energy into this wittily-scripted comedy tinged with moments of action and violence. This was only the second feature he had directed since his start in 1920, with only eleven more features in the years to follow. While his work here is fine, it is in the direction of shorts where he really shines. Production values are decent if unspectacular, with veteran cinematographer Allen G. Seigler's camerawork a notch or two above the norm. James Sweeney's editing is underwhelming, particularly in the leaden fight scene near the film's end; blame for that should be shared, though.

Budget cutting is evident, with several invention-construction montages to kill screen time and none-too-convincing rear projection for scenes set at a big football game. The climactic car chase is expertly done, and while Del Lord was a master of filmic car chases and general all-around vehicular mayhem, these shots look as though they may have been lifted from some earlier, higher-budget production. Whatever the case, a number of these shots would reappear repeatedly twenty-five years later as stock inserts in the popular 1930s-based television show *The Untouchables*.

The New York Times called *Trapped By Television* "a breezy, illogical concoction of comedy and melodrama. For its lighter moments, we are indebted to Nat Pendleton, who contributes a delightfully amusing performance even though he must wrestle with some fairly inane dialogue."[32] *Variety* was less enthused, calling it an "ordinary melodrama lacking name draw and handicapped by tedious early performances."[33] Lyle Talbot? Lacking name

---

[31] Mary Astor, *My Story: an Autobiography* (Garden City, New York: Doubleday & Company, Inc., 1959), 164.

[32] T.M.P., "Trapped By Television," *New York Times*, June 15, 1936, 24.

[33] "Trapped By Television," *Variety*, June 17, 1936, 23.

draw? Not if you were a regular attendee of filmdom's cinematic underbelly, the B film.

Soon after *Trapped By Television*'s shooting wrapped in April, Irving Briskin was promoted to executive producer in charge of all class B westerns and action films. He replaced Robert North, who was promoted to executive producer of class A productions. Pivar continued on as associate producer under Briskin, along with John Decker and Ralph Cohn.[34]

Two-Fisted Gentleman
(Director: Gordon Wiles; Released August 15, 1936)

"His Wife Was His Manager … And He Couldn't Manage Without Her!" The comedy *Two-Fisted Gentleman* (pre-release title: *The Fighter*), filmed in June and released two months later, has fight promoter's daughter Ginger Roberts (June Clayworth) unsuccessfully attempting to convince daddy to give pig-headed hamburger stand waiter Mickey Blake (James Dunn) a shot in the ring. Ginger takes over management when daddy dies in an auto accident, and the fighters all walk, refusing to be managed by a woman. This gives Blake his big chance, and he wins his maiden fight. Blake and Ginger marry. After several lows and highs, success goes to Blake's head, his romantic interests wander to society girl June Prentice (Muriel Evans), and he goes soft. Disgusted, Ginger leaves him. Blake's career crumbles, but later on Ginger gives him one last chance to prove himself in the ring, which he does. As one would expect, Blake and Ginger are reunited.

Reviewers dismissed the results. *The New York World-Telegram* called it "ten rounds of moralizing."[35] *Variety* dismissed it as a "routine fight story … In most all respects, including story, direction, production, comedy and cast, 'Two-Fisted' is ordinary."[36] *The New York Times* focused on the film's familiar plot, a remake of Columbia's Ben Lyon-Constance Cummings starrer *The Big Timer* (1932; Edward Buzzell). Rookie screenwriter Tom Van Dycke retooled the Robert Riskin original. "We forget what it was called the last time Columbia filmed it," complained *New York Times* reviewer Frank S. Nugent, "but 'Two-Fisted Gentleman' is the same old story about the young middleweight who could not stand prosperity … Altogether a picture of decidedly juvenile appeal."[37]

As for Pivar, *Two-Fisted Gentleman* was notable in that his name and photo accompanied its promotion in the trades, a first for him. Pivar's publicity

---

[34] "Irv Briskin Moved Up," *Variety*, May 27, 1936, 5.

[35] "Two-Fisted Gentleman," *New York World-Telegram*, August 24, 1936, 13.

[36] "Two-Fisted Gentleman," *Variety*, August 26, 1936, 20.

[37] Frank S. Nugent, "The Screen," *New York Times*, August 24, 1936, 11.

photo was prominent in the full-page piece that appeared in *Boxoffice* midway through the film's production. Cast and crew, a plot summary, suggestions for promotional tie-ins, and assorted suggestions for ad lines were included. John Gallaudet and Victor Kilian are listed fourth and fifth in the cast, but their participation in the finished film has not been confirmed, suggesting that they were replaced by others during the film's production. Noble "Kid" Chisel was one of several real-life boxers with uncredited bits in this film, and would reappear several years later to greater advantage in Pivar's *The Leather Pushers*.

The Man Who Lived Twice
(Director: Harry Lachman; Released October 13, 1936)

The Man Who Lived Twice was a decided change of pace for Pivar, an intriguing if wholly implausible tale of an on-the-lam murderer, Slick Rawley (Ralph Bellamy), who stumbles into the Baldwin Medical College to hide, and hears Dr. Schuyler (Thurston Hall) give a lecture on his radical new experiments to remove brain tumors that result in "certain criminal types." Rawley convinces the doctor to use him as a human guinea pig, and undergoes a brain operation that removes his homicidal tendencies, mellows the fellow, and leaves him with no memory of his former life and misdeeds; as an added plus the doctor cleans up the fellow's hideously scarred face. With this new face and identity as James Blake, ten years pass and he quickly rises to the top of the medical profession, a respected and eminent physician committed to social and prison reform. Dr. Schuyler does everything in his power to help Blake succeed, while hiding his sordid past and identity from him. As far as Blake knows, he always has been Blake, only now with a severe case of amnesia regarding his past.

Blake's past catches up with him as his distinctive voice and well-known habit of twirling his keychain conspire to reveal his true identity. When former girlfriend Peggy Russell (Isabel Jewell) recognizes his voice, she decides that he is an easy mark and should be robbed. She convinces Rawley's old buddy and partner-in-crime Gloves Baker (Ward Bond) to rob Dr. Blake, but in the midst of the robbery he, too, comes to realize that Blake is his old friend. Blake, wanting to help others to avoid lives of crime, hires Gloves as his driver, oblivious of their past association. Schuyler knows otherwise; he takes Gloves into his confidence and has the fellow swear he will keep Blake's past as Slick Rawley from him.

Peggy flips out over this turn of events, and confronts Blake with a blackmail demand of $5,000 or she will reveal his past identity as Rawley to Homicide Inspector Logan (Willard Robertson). It was Logan's partner who Rawley murdered ten years earlier, and Rawley's capture has been his single-minded obsession ever since. Blake still has no idea what Peggy is talking about, so he sends her packing. She heads straight for Logan and spills.

With all of this incessant yammering about his past, though, Blake begins to doubt his true identity. He confronts Schuyler, who eventually breaks down and reveals all. Logan arrives to make his arrest just as Schuyler's confession has finished, and a now thoroughly demoralized Blake willingly gives himself up.

A sensational, headline-making trial follows, and Blake's old friend Judge Treacher (Henry Kolker) steps down from the bench to defend him. Peggy and Gloves are subpoenaed as witnesses for the prosecution, but then Gloves finds that she was the one who ratted out his old buddy. Devoted friend to the end, Gloves drives their speeding car into a tree, killing the two of them and thereby preventing their testimony. In spite of an ongoing series of impassioned pleas from the medical profession, prison reformers, and numerous others that Blake should be set free, he is found guilty—and just as quickly pardoned by the governor. There is the usual happy ending where he and Janet Haydon (Marian Marsh), the homeless waif he took in as his secretary, are to be married.

Homicidal maniac Ralph Bellamy, pre-makeover, menaces Marian Marsh in *The Man Who Lived Twice* (1936).
Don't look for this shot in the film; you won't find it.

In the dual role of hideously scarred Slick Rawley and the post-operation, good-looking James Blake, Bellamy steals the show with a satisfying performance that peaks with the realization of the monster he once was. As for his pre-surgery makeup as the scarred and disfigured Rawley, Bellamy is totally unrecognizable both in face and voice. Supporting performances are commendable as well, with Bond giving a convincingly moving performance as Rawley's dedicated and supportive friend. Jewell is delightfully brassy as Rawley's cold-hearted former girl, and Marsh, while charming, has a backseat role that only occasionally allows her to swoon over her benefactor or slip into histrionics over his potential fate at the hands of the law. Robertson stands out as the doggedly determined cop, with Hall and Kolker doing their usual solid turns in their supporting roles as doctor and judge.

This is a slick-looking film. Director Harry Lachman keeps things moving at a speedy clip, and in conjunction with photographer James Van Trees and editor Byron Robinson turns out a couple of atypically fast-paced sequences.

The wonders of cosmetic surgery, on display in *The Man Who Lived Twice* (1936). Thurston Hall administers a polygraph test to Ralph Bellamy to see if he remembers his criminal past, as Nana Bryant looks on.

The opening scene is a particular standout: Rawley, interrupted mid-robbery by the police, beats a hasty retreat through the city's alleys while the cops pursue him in a hail of back-and-forth gunfire. All shot in medium-to-close setups from numerous angles in stark, shadowy lighting, and with rapid-fire cutting from shot-to-shot, the result is an exhilarating opening sequence that leaves the viewer breathless. A later scene where Rawley escapes from his hideout with the law hot on his heels is almost as good. The rest of the film is handled in a matter-of-fact fashion, with a handful of scene-compacting montages to keep things moving.

As a whole, however, the film's success was undercut by an abrupt, contrived ending, as reviewers were quick to point out: "Producers have tried to work up this hoax to a climactic pitch, but it drops with a thud when the only solution they can offer to such an impossible situation is to have the jury find an innocent man guilty as the law requires, but recommend his pardon as a citizen now useful to society."[38] "Although it has some lively and exciting moments, pithy speeches and expert performances … its direction is uneven and its denouement slovenly. The result is a good idea gone wrong."[39]

They should have sent him to Old Sparky.

End of the Trail
(Director: Erle C. Kenton; Released October 31, 1936)

It was a return to a western of sorts with *End of the Trail*, based on the Zane Grey novel *Outlaws of Palouse* that takes place during and after the Spanish-American War. Rivals Dale Brittenham (Jack Holt) and Bob Hildreth (Guinn Williams) both fall for nurse Belle (Louise Henry) while recuperating from war-related injuries in Cuba. Returning home, Hildreth resumes his former job as deputy, but Brittenham cannot find work. Resorting to cattle rustling, Brittenham eventually saves enough money to purchase the local saloon, but soon finds that Belle will have nothing to do with him until he reforms. When Belle's younger brother (John McGuire) is murdered, Brittenham takes the law into his own hands and shoots the killer. Hildreth is forced to arrest his old friend, who is sentenced to hang. Brittenham goes to the gallows for his efforts, proudly waving goodbye to his friends on his way.

The critics, or at least the ones that bothered to take the time to view it, liked this effort: "An exceptionally good Zane Grey Western," decreed *Select Motion Picture*, "that includes realistic scenes of the battle of San Juan Hill and the usual quota of cattle rustling, hard riding and thrilling adventure … The

---

[38] "The Man Who Lived Twice," *Hollywood Reporter*, October 19, 1936, 3.

[39] William Boehnel, "The Man Who Lived Twice," *New York World-Telegram*, October 12, 1936, 10.

direction is smooth, the photography excellent and the acting exceptionally good."[40] *Philadelphia Exhibitor* gave a positive review as well: "For the most part heavy drama, with some comedy intervals, ending with Holt heading toward the noose ... should give patrons practically everything they are seeking."[41]

On a whim, director Erle C. Kenton pulled a "Hitchcock," donning makeup and appearing in a small role as Teddy Roosevelt.

Come Closer, Folks
(Director: D. Ross Lederman; Released November 24, 1936)

D. Ross Lederman was again pressed into service to direct *Come Closer, Folks*, a return to comedy co-written by Pivar's *Trapped By Television* team of Lee Loeb and Harold Buchman. Department store owner Elmer Woods (Gene Lockhart) takes notice of the sales skills of con man and street hawker Jim Keene (James Dunn), and offers him a job as salesman. Keene quickly rises to the store's position of assistant manager, and convinces Elmer's homely daughter Peggy (Marian Marsh) to purchase miscellaneous substandard merchandise at inflated prices; the difference in cost ends up in his pockets. With Keene's encouragement Peggy remodels the store to attract new customers, and remodels herself into a good-looking babe in the process. Keene falls for her, sees the error of his ways, and cancels the standing junk order. His sordid past is eventually exposed to Peggy, and the business is nearly ruined when customers demand their money back on their worthless purchases. Keene comes up with a promotional scheme that saves the business and wins back the customers, and Elmer reveals to Peggy that it was Keene's idea. Peggy forgives Keene and the two are reunited for the standard happy ending.

Ben off set and still single, mid-thirties. Photo courtesy of Jan Pivar Dacri.

"Save for the pleasant people in it, who make the film seem considerably more entertaining than it actually is, there is nothing to recommend ...

---

[40] "End of the Trail," *Select Motion Picture*, October 1, 1936, 9.

[41] "End of the Trail," *Philadelphia Exhibitor*, October 1, 1936, 34.

[The film is] loaded down with musty prattle and complications that are embarrassing for their lack of ingenuity ... [A] clumsy and feeble little comedy drama,"[42] stated reviewer William Boehnel, whom I sense did not care for the film. *Variety*'s reviewer was slightly more enthusiastic, rating the film "never more than casually diverting. It is of minor box office value ... The plot is equaled in its inconsistency only by the triteness of the dialog ..."[43] Another *Variety* reviewer disagreed, calling *Come Closer, Folks* "good clean comedy, well suited for any type of audience. There are plenty of laughs through the whole picture ... James Dunn as the fast-talking racket salesman is right in character and does a swell job."[44] *The Hollywood Reporter* concurred: "... a more than ordinarily worthy representative of its class, packing some rollicking comedy and cleverly-constructed farce situations, with which the majority of the cast do first-rate."[45]

Produced in August and early September 1936, and released in November, *Come Closer, Folks* would be Pivar's last effort for Columbia. He had by now gained solid experience as an associate producer, and was marketable as such; he could hawk his wares elsewhere.

And so he did.

§

---

[42] "William Boehnel, "Come Closer, Folks," *New York World-Telegram*, November 23, 1936, 21.

[43] "Come Closer, Folks," *Variety*, November 25, 1936, 15.

[44] "Come Closer, Folks," *Daily Variety*, November 28, 1936, 3.

[45] "Come Closer, Folks," *Hollywood Reporter*, November 28, 1936, 3.

4 Production with New Independents: Grand National Pictures and Condor Productions (1937)

Late in 1936, Pivar moved over to Grand National Films, Inc., and assumed the position of associate producer at George A. Hirliman's Condor Productions. The reason behind his decision to leave Columbia, the studio he'd been affiliated with for the past nine years, may have been financial, with notions of marrying and settling down to a more stable life. On the other hand, he too may have run afoul of Columbia's dictatorial president Harry Cohn, as so many others had before him, and would continue to do so after Pivar's departure. Another possibility is that Cohn's twenty-two-year-old nephew Ralph, fresh out of Cornell, had been placed in executive producer Irving Briskin's B unit in 1936 as an associate producer,[1] so perhaps Pivar feared that nepotism would rear its head and he would be crowded out or shunted off to a less-desirable position. Regardless, it was a fresh start for Pivar with a pair of promising young concerns. Placed on the payroll in late December 1936, Pivar's first film was to be something tentatively titled *Black Ivory*.[2] It doesn't appear to have gotten beyond the planning stages.

Former film salesman and film exchange manager Edward L. Alperson organized Grand National Pictures in the spring of that same year. Setting himself up as president, Alperson signed a ten-year lease for the Santa Monica Boulevard-based Hollywood studios of the by-then-defunct Educational Films, renaming it Grand National Studio.[3] Grand National strived to offer a wide variety of fare, with the earliest releases hitting screens later in 1936, produced by Hirliman, B.F. Zeidman, Zion Myers, and the German-born Alexander

---

[1] Bernard F. Dick, *The Merchant Prince of Poverty Row: Harry Cohn of Columbia Pictures* (Lexington: The University Press of Kentucky, 1993).

[2] *Daily Variety*, November 25, 1936, page unknown.

[3] Charles C. Cohan, "Film Studios to Expand," *Los Angeles Times*, January 17, 1937, C1.

brothers, Arthur and Max. Grand National had their shot at the big time when Alperson managed to sign Jimmy Cagney after the popular actor walked out of Warner Brothers during a contract dispute. Cagney's first vehicle, *Great Guy* (1936; John G. Blystone), was a success in spite of the fact it had a rather cut-rate look compared to the slicker Warners' output. Grand National's first fiscal year, which ended April 3, 1937, was somewhat less than rosy, with a net loss of $636,201.79 after all charges, including organization and other corporate expenses, on gross film rentals of $1,205,652.[4]

The studio quickly acquired *Angels with Dirty Faces* as a follow-up for Cagney, paying author Rowland Brown $30,000 for the rights. Cagney's brother Bill was scheduled to produce, with Pivar acting as associate producer, and Brown himself directing; filming was to commence in February 1938.[5] It did not happen, though. The decision was made to back-burner the property, and Cagney was reassigned to the musical *Something to Sing About* (1937; Victor Schertzinger). Not a wise move, as it turned out, costing the none-too-well-established studio a crippling $900,000, only to flop at the box office; it was one of the primary causes of the studio's eventual demise. *Angels with Dirty Faces*, needless to say, never came about at Grand National. With contractual disputes ironed out with Warners, Cagney relieved the ailing Grand National of their $150,000 obligation and headed back to his rightful home.[6] Grand National quickly sold the *Angels* rights to Warners, where it was Cagney's second starring vehicle upon his return. The previously announced collaborators were all replaced by others. But we're getting ahead of ourselves here.

The Gold Racket
(Director: Louis G. Gasnier; Released April 10, 1937)

Condor Pictures Corp. came into being mid-December 1936, the result of a merger of the interests and capital of several companies and financial organizations. George Hirliman's Hirliman Productions was one of these merging companies, along with M.H. Hoffman's Liberty Pictures; Hirliman was named president, and Hoffman vice president and executive producer. Deals were struck to produce films for release through several companies, Grand National and RKO among them.[7] One of the new company's eye-catching claims was that it was going to film sixteen of its upcoming releases in "natural

---

[4] "GN Reports Loss of $636, 201 In '36," *Hollywood Reporter*, June 12, 1937, 1.

[5] Edwin Schallert, "'The Letter' to Be Filmed Again with Isa Miranda Playing Lead," *Los Angeles Times*, January 1, 1938, A7.

[6] "Cagney to Report to 'Boy Meets Girl,'" *New York Times*, January 14, 1938, page unknown.

[7] "Independent Producers Merge for New Firm," *Boxoffice*, December 19, 1936, 13.

colors," a process modestly tagged as Hirlacolor and for which he sought patents on some sort of "camera device."[8] On display in Hirliman's *Captain Calamity*, Hirlacolor's "natural colors" were in reality somewhat less than natural, looking more like the two-color Cinecolor process used in a number of films several years prior to this. Two of the films announced for upcoming production were *Gold*, to co-star Conrad Nagel and Eleanor Hunt, and *Love Takes Flight*, an Anne Morrison Chapin story to be directed by Nagel in the touted new color process. Ben Pivar was assigned to associate produce both of these, with release through Grand National.[9]

**Eleanor Hunt and Conrad Nagel, as government agents Alan O'Connor and Bobbie Reynolds, in a posed shot for *Bank Alarm* (1937), the fourth and final series entry.
Image courtesy of Heritage Auction Galleries, Ha.com.**

Gold was the third in a four-film series following the exploits of government agents Alan O'Connor and Bobbie Reynolds, as portrayed by Conrad Nagel and Eleanor Hunt, respectively. *Yellow Cargo*, the first in the series in November 1936, had the intrepid duo on the trail of a ring of smugglers sneaking Chinese

---

[8] Edwin Schallert, "The Pageant of the Film World," *Los Angeles Times*, March 16, 1936, 13.

[9] "Newly-Set Condor Pictures Corp. Will Stress Color Films," *Boxoffice*, December 26, 1936, 8.

aliens into the country, with *Navy Spy* following in March 1937. Both were written and directed by former silent film star and stage presence Crane Wilbur, with release through Grand National. *Bank Alarm* would be the fourth and final entry in the series in June 1937, following on the heels of *The Gold Racket*, the title finally assigned for *Gold* by the time production finished on February 20, 1937;[10] both were to be directed by Louis J. Gasnier. *The Gold Racket* went into release a month later, on April 10, 1937.

The Gold Racket chronicles the smuggling of gold from Mexico into the United States; an illegal act made extremely profitable after President Roosevelt had the price of gold raised from $20.67 an ounce to $35 back in 1934. Department of Justice agents attempt to crack down on the smugglers, but after one of them is killed in San Diego and two more killed in a car crash following a running gun battle, the Bureau of Investigation assigns agent Alan O'Connor (Nagel) to the case. O'Connor uses the analysis of a gold bar recovered earlier to track the smugglers to the small Mexican town of Los Moradas, where he hangs out at Café La Tarantella, a small club owned by expat Scotty Summers (Fuzzy Knight).

Convincing Scotty that they'd met before years earlier, O'Connor suggests that he bring in a singer named Dixie to fill out his musical act. Dixie is in actuality O'Connor's partner Bobbie Reynolds (Hunt), and her job is to infiltrate a pair of tough customers who frequent the bar. O'Connor, having spotted one of them flaunting a gold nugget, is convinced they are part of the ring. When the smugglers get wind of agents on their trail, they quickly smuggle a final load of gold out of the country by plane. A mine in the small Californian town of Winton is its intended destination, where it will be processed and distributed that very same day. Or at least that's the plan; O'Connor and Reynolds head for Winton and, backed by a small army of agents, intercept the plane as it lands and arrest its occupants. They round up the remaining gang members after a brief gun battle inside the mine.

The Gold Racket is a decent little action piece with some occasional humor thrown in to keep things light and breezy. "Strictly routine G-man stuff," concluded the *Brooklyn Daily Eagle*.[11] *The New York Times* agreed, declaring it a "melodrama just saved from banality by a fresh topical twist."[12] *The Hollywood Reporter* was more objective in its favorable review: "The G-man versus G-girl formula for this series of action mellers is proving an effective one, capable of engaging variations. The two characters, played with ingratiating assurance by Conrad Nagel and Eleanor Hunt, should grow in popularity. Made on a very

---

[10] "'Racket' Finishes Today," *The Hollywood Reporter*, February 20, 1937, 2.

[11] J.W., "Brooklyn Strand," *Brooklyn Daily Eagle*, August 20, 1937, 26.

[12] J.T.M., "The Screen," *New York Times*, August 2, 1937, 10.

limited budget allowance, the pictures doubtless fill the needs of the action houses on the fringe, for which they are obviously designed."[13]

Nagel, *The Gold Racket*'s star, was in the sunset of his career as a matinee idol. A nineteen-year veteran of the industry, Nagel would soldier on for another thirty years in film, radio, and television. He is at turns charming and sufficiently rugged throughout the film's brief sixty-six-minute running time, although the charm comes across as somewhat forced at times. At forty, he looks older than his chronological age.

Co-star Hunt is a likeable presence, witty and comfortable with her flirtatious banter with Nagel, although seen to best advantage in *Yellow Cargo*, the first in the series, where she poses throughout as a wise-cracking newspaper reporter. She demonstrates a decent singing voice in a short number with Fuzzy Knight, Julie Cruze's "I'd Like to Be the Buttons on Your Vest." Hunt cuts a fine figure in long- and medium-shot, but her looks suffer in the occasional close-up that shows off her slightly bugged-eyes, high cheekbones, and pronounced overbite. A former Ziegfeld Follies girl, Hunt had appeared in film since 1930. After two stunningly unsuccessful marriages, Hunt hooked up with hubby number three in June 1935, who just happened to be Hirliman himself;[14] one suspects she did not have to lobby very hard to be awarded the lead role in his new series. After these four series entries and one other for her husband's company (*We're in the Legion Now*, 1936), the couple separated late in 1938.[15] No hard feelings, it would seem, as Hunt managed one last film for Hirliman in 1941, the Louis Gasnier-directed drama *Stolen Paradise*. With this, Hunt's career in the industry came to an end, and not with a bang.

Fuzzy Knight steals the show as club owner Scotty Summers, providing whatever genuine laughs there are in a film otherwise short on laughs. A former vaudevillian and performer in stage musicals, he was spotted by actress Mae West and tapped to appear in her 1933 *She Done Him Wrong* in the small role of Ragtime Kelly. In *Racket*, Knight helps to pad out the film with a few well-integrated musical numbers, "Broken Down Mama" the film's highlight, relatively speaking. Silent comedian Jack Duffy is on hand as well, once again in his toothless, old geezer getup as a taxi driver desperate for customers in the sleepy little mining town of Winton.

Director Louis Gasnier does a workmanlike job, but his best days were behind him in the silent era. He had started out in France directing short comedies for Pathé, many of which starred the famous comedian Max Linder. Pathé sent him to the States in 1912 to head up its operations there, where he was responsible for a number of very popular serials (including *The Perils of*

---

[13] "Nagel, Hunt Make Fine Sleuth Team," *Hollywood Reporter*, April 21, 1937, 3.

[14] "Eleanor Hunt Weds Hirliman," *Los Angeles Times*, June 16, 1935, 21.

[15] "Ex-Follies Beauty and Mate Separate," *Los Angeles Times*, November 23, 1938, A2.

Pauline in 1914) and dozens of features throughout the teens and twenties. His career faded as the thirties drew to an end, his last film the aforementioned Hunt starrer *Stolen Paradise* in 1941 when Gasnier was sixty-six. Gasnier's reported difficulty with the English language, occasionally requiring the presence of an on-set dialog coach, may have had something to do with *Racket's* occasional stilted-sounding dialog. His direction here is adequate, however, and a notch or two above Crane Wilbur's direction on the series' previous two films. *Variety* seemed content with his efforts, though, stating that the "direction of Louis Gasnier keeps the picture moving along at a good pace, assuring its success in theaters which go for the action stuff."[16]

Conrad Nagel and Eleanor Hunt mean business in *The Gold Racket* (1937). Image courtesy of Heritage Auction Galleries, Ha.com.

The Gold Racket has the usual B film ragged edges, with stage-bound exterior sequences notable for totally blank backgrounds, whole sequences set in Mexico with nary an exterior street shot to establish location and hotel rooms more suitable to Los Angeles than a tiny backwater Mexican village, and occasional rough continuity where the action in one shot fails to match that of the next. These awkward cuts probably were more a function of single-take economics than a comment on editor Robert Jahn's capabilities, working here under the supervision of future director Joseph H. Lewis. The ubiquitous stock footage was in play as usual, although the running gun battle between two cars that end up crashing off the side of a hill is surprisingly energetic and exciting, and a good lift from elsewhere. Fortunately, the jarring microphone boom shadows that kept cropping up in series opener *Yellow Cargo* are absent here. Mack Stengler's cinematography, here as in the rest of the series, is satisfactory if unremarkable, less fluid perhaps than in *Yellow Cargo*, but without that film's trembling camera movements in those same shots. The story itself is chock full of all sorts of implausible situations and coincidences, but no more than the usual B film where haste is *de rigueur* to keep things moving and come to a conclusion in about an hour. And just how much gold can a creaky biplane

---

[16] "The Gold Racket," *Variety*, August 4, 1937, 19.

with two husky passengers carry and still manage to get off the ground? Never mind.

Nagel and Hunt display an easy and likeable rapport throughout the series, with their romantic involvement occasionally bubbling to the surface. *The Hollywood Reporter* complimented the leads: "Nagel is good. His G-man has dignity, force and ease. Miss Hunt is an engagingly merry foil for his seriousness. She injects a grand gusto into the most serious situations but makes it evident that as a detective she is not missing a trick."[17] One might question why Nagel's agent would so unhesitatingly assign his girl the task of seducing Steve (Frank Milan), the pilot hired by the gang to fly gold out of the country. She takes her assignment in stride, and soon has the poor sap mooning over her and compromising the gang's efforts. When Steve is shot during the climatic gun battle, it would seem that Hunt's character had actually fallen for the guy as she kneels over his corpse, fighting back tears, mumbling, "He was a nice kid." Nice in what ways we'll never know, but it is clear that she always gets her man.

Love Takes Flight
(Director: Conrad Nagel; Released August 13, 1937)

Pivar's next assignment for Condor was the romantic drama *Love Takes Flight*, first announced in December 1936 as one of Hirliman's color productions, to be helmed by actor (and first-time director) Conrad Nagel.[18] A month later, however, the still-in-the-planning-stages film was abandoned as a color feature and scheduled for the more prosaic black and white. Condor's explanation for this change: "It was felt that the story could be more suitably presented in the normal photographic medium despite recent progress in color."[19] That, or it was simply the less expensive option. Mervin Houser was brought in to rewrite[20] what was felt to be an unacceptable script, with older brother Lionel assisting. The film was ready to roll three months later, with Bruce Cabot signed for the lead and director Nagel slated for a small acting part in the film as well.[21] Pre-production was briefly interrupted when Nagel took a short break

---

[17] "Nagel, Hunt Make Fine Sleuth Team," *Hollywood Reporter*, April 21, 1937, 3.

[18] "Newly-Set Condor Pictures Corp. Will Stress Color Films," *Boxoffice*, December 26, 1936, 8.

[19] Edwin Schallert, "No Color for 'Love Takes Flight,'" *Los Angeles Times*, January 19, 1937, 8.

[20] "Houser Vamps 'Flight,'" *Hollywood Reporter*, March 23, 1937, 3.

[21] "Two Way Chore for Nagel," *Boxoffice*, April 17, 1937, 52.

to bury his father,[22] with actual filming of *Love Takes Flight* underway on May 11, 1937.[23] Nagel's small role in the film fell by the wayside, as it turned out.

Pivar looks on as *Love Takes Flight* director Conrad Nagel contemplates hitting someone with his script. Photo courtesy of Jan Pivar Dacri.

Pivar took a short break from his production duties on April 22, 1937, to marry Judith Schonzeit. Services were held at his parents' Franklin Avenue home in Los Angeles, with ceremonies performed at his dying father's bedside by Rabbi Benjamin Marcus.[24] Abandoning his former residence at 6154 Glen Tower Street, Ben and Judith—whom everyone called Judy—moved into

---

[22] "Nagel Funeral Services," *Hollywood Reporter*, April 16, 1937, 2.

[23] "Edwin Schallert, The Pageant of the Film World," *Los Angeles Times*, May 11, 1937, 10.

[24] "Film Producer Weds Designer," *Los Angeles Times*, April 24, 1937, A3. The actual marriage certificate gives April 29 as the couple's wedding date, with Rabbi Marcus certifying that he was the person who performed the ceremony on this date. Since both the *Los Angeles Times* and *Variety* ran articles on the marriage a week earlier, it's clear that a ceremony took place at that earlier date. Whether this is an instance of a religious ceremony followed a week later by a civil ceremony is unclear, as Rabbi Marcus performed both. Perhaps a "rushed" ceremony for Ben's dying father's benefit before a license could be obtained. Or it could simply be a typo. The explanation is lost to the ages.

a home on Beachwood Drive. This was in the Hollywood Hills, just below the famous HOLLYWOOD sign on Mt. Cahuenga (which at the time still said HOLLYWOODLAND; the last four letters would not be removed until 1949). Work always came first, so the young couple postponed their honeymoon until after production of *Love Takes Flight* was completed. The wedding's timing was fortuitous, as Ben's father Adolph died several days later of stomach cancer. His body was shipped back to New York for burial.[25]

Judy, thirteen years Ben's junior, was born and raised in Brooklyn, New York. The youngest of nine children, her siblings were (from oldest to youngest) Anne, Sam, Ina, Ruth, Hyman, Debbie, Libby, and David. Parents Wolfe and Jennie Weiner Schonzeit were both Russia-born immigrants, Wolf a kosher butcher who owned his own store on Division Avenue around the corner from the family's Keap Street residence. Judy, a seamstress back in New York, had traveled west to Los Angeles in 1933 to help her older sister Ina after the birth of Ina's first son Carl. Ina's husband Gerson "Gus" Barth was a sales representative for Agfa Film Corp. whom Ina had met when he was in the Catskills on business. Gus and Ben Pivar were friends, and when Judy accompanied Gus and Ina to an elegant dinner party, Gus introduced Judy to Ben; the romance blossomed from there. The rest, as they say, is history.

Back to *Love Takes Flight*. Neil "Brad" Bradshaw (Cabot) is a hotshot pilot for American Airlines, and while he is fond of air hostess and good friend Joan Lawson (Beatrice Roberts), he has a reputation as a ladies' man. Joan, of course, is head over heels for Brad, but keeps her rather obvious feelings to herself (and a small army of coworkers). Brad's goal is to quit the airline, buy a small airplane, and be the first to fly non-stop from California to Manila in the Philippines; Joan is to be his right-hand (wo)man. Big-time film producer David Miller (Edwin Maxwell) spots Joan during a flight to the West Coast and immediately offers her a job as lead in his upcoming film *Sky Fever*. Swellheaded actress Diana Audre (Astrid Allwyn) was supposed to have the lead, but she has balked at co-starring with

Ben's father Adolph, early 1930s. Photo courtesy of Carol Pivar Miller.

---

[25] "Pivar Burial East," *Hollywood Reporter*, April 30, 1937, 9.

an inexperienced new actor, so this move will supposedly teach her a lesson. Joan decides to not accept the offer, preferring to stay near her love's side.

Bruce Cabot looks like he can't make up his mind, here with *Love Takes Flight* costar Astrid Allwyn (1937). Image courtesy of Heritage Auction Galleries, Ha.com.

Meanwhile, airline publicity director Spud Johnson (John Sheehan) hooks up Brad with actress Audre, who has demanded to be flown back to Los Angeles from New York in spite of a raging storm. Their plane goes down and they are assumed dead, but they eventually turn up on a mountainside in Arizona, alive, well, and in love. Audre suggests that Brad be made her male lead in *Sky Fever*, and the studio, sensing a great publicity gimmick, agrees.

Brad goes on to become a big star, leaving a heartbroken Joan behind. Concentrating on flying to assuage her broken heart, Joan soon becomes a famous aviatrix, aided at every step by Spuds who feels guilty over being the cause of Brad and Joan's "breakup." Joan eventually announces that she is going to fly solo to Manila herself, and no one can talk her out of it—not even Brad who's urged to do so. Brad stows away on her plane, and is instrumental in the success of the flight to Manila, bailing out before she lands so that she can claim the glory. Instead, Joan fesses up to the press, and then heads home to whimper over the loss of Brad, whom she thinks perished when he bailed out. He did not and, realizing his love for her, heads to her home just in time for a fade-out kiss.

Production with New Independents

Released to theaters on August 13, 1937, Grand National offered exhibitors a promotional angle of somewhat questionable taste:

> Because of recent interest in the loss of Amelia Earhart and the record-breaking Polar flight by the Soviet fliers, the aviation angles in this picture are particularly timely. Use tearsheets describing the two happenings in a lobby display board.[26]

Evidently a month earlier three Soviet airmen had made a 5,700-mile Moscow-to-California trans-Polar flight, breaking the previously-set record for a non-stop distance flight by roughly sixty miles.[27] I remember learning about Earhart and Lindbergh in elementary school, but my teachers were mum about the Soviet achievement. What a surprise.

American Airlines cooperated with the making of *Love Takes Flight*, their logo prominent on the various airplanes and uniforms worn by the airline's "employees." American Airlines helped promote the film by showing scenes from the production in the airline's various offices, offering visitors free transportation to and from its flying fields.[28]

For the most part, the performances in *Love Takes Flight* are uniformly good. The role of "Brad" Bradshaw fits Cabot like a well-worn glove, and in spite of the fact that the character is bull-headed, cocky, and occasionally insensitive, it is still difficult to resist Cabot's roguish, "bad boy" charm. Too bad Pivar did not spring for a (more competent?) makeup artist to deal with Cabot's obtrusive five o'clock shadow. Born with the fifty-cent moniker Etienne Pelissier Jacques de Bujac, Cabot wisely changed his name and broke into film after meeting RKO producer David O. Selznick at a party. Cabot landed the plum role of Jack Driscoll in the huge hit *King Kong* (1933), his fourth credited film and his first as lead. But in spite of the film's huge success, stardom eluded Cabot. A solid supporting player, however, Cabot plodded on in the industry right up until his death in 1972, leaving an impressive tally of over one hundred films in his resume.

Cabot's love interest is played by Beatrice Roberts, a several-time beauty pageant contestant in the mid-1920s and, believe it or not, for a brief time the fourteen-year-old bride of Robert L. Ripley, of *Ripley's Believe It or Not!* fame. In film since 1933 in a series of uncredited roles, a two-year stint with MGM led to more of the uncredited same in spite of the fact that she was reportedly studio head Louis B. Mayer's landing pad. The last of the MGM roles was a bit in *Sinner Take All* (1936) starring Bruce Cabot, so *Flight's* two leads had at least

---

[26] "Exploitips," *Boxoffice*, August 7, 1937, 24.
[27] "Russians Set Mark On Flight to U.S.," *New York Times*, July 14, 1937, page unknown.
[28] "Airline Tieup Sells 'Love Takes Flight,'" *Boxoffice*, August 7, 1937, 36.

a passing acquaintance. MGM loaned Roberts to Condor for this production,[29] and it must have become evident that her future with MGM was somewhat less than promising. She bolted from MGM soon after, landing in the care of Hirliman and several other low-budget producers. Roberts is fine here in the feminine lead, only the third film in which she received credit and a prominent role.

Astrid Allwyn, with three-dozen films behind her, gives an assured performance as the haughty prima donna Diana Audre. Grady Sutton is somewhat wasted in the minor role of Donald, the poor sap who hasn't a chance in hell in his pursuit of Audre's affections. John Sheehan, however, shines as the anything-goes publicity director "Spud" Johnson, a heavy-drinking, alimony-avoiding bumbler who seemingly has nothing more than Joan Lawson's success as his goal in life. In film since 1914 and with well over one hundred credits to show for it, Sheehan provides whatever laughs are to be found in *Flight*, with perhaps a chuckle or two reserved for Sutton's sad sack character. Silent comedian Jack Duffy is once again thrown a bone in a blink-or-you'll-miss-it bit as a bartender phoning in a plane crash.

Conrad Nagel had his directorial debut with *Love Takes Flight*, and for that matter his directorial swansong as well. And it shows. There is not a single camera movement in *Flight*, and it is a shame that cinematographer Mack Stengler did not care enough to suggest otherwise, or did so and was summarily ignored. The biggest "problem" with the various performances, if you want to call it that, stems from Nagel's inadequate coverage; mismatched cuts abound. These result in some rather jarring cuts from shot-to-shot, with smiles turning to frowns, and actors' motions and placement shifting. Perhaps editor Tony Martinelli could have done a better job at matches, but with more experienced editor Robert Crandall supervising and looking over his shoulder, I suspect there simply was not the footage needed to bridge the numerous gaps. It was, after all, a second feature, so the prevailing wisdom may have simply been, "Who cares?" Nagel later dismissed the film as "Just a quickie, but good experience."[30] *New York Times* critic Bosley Crowther was singularly unimpressed with Nagel's efforts, writing off the film with the snide comment that "it is reasonable to assume that his familiarity as an actor with platitudinous plots has finally bred contempt."[31] Ouch. *Daily Variety* was merciless in its review, singling out Nagel's direction and the production as a whole for withering comment: "[T]he direction of Conrad Nagel, who tries megging for the first time, has all the earmarks of a backyard amateur's job …

---

[29] "Condor Tests Roberts," *Hollywood Reporter*, April 19, 1937, 2.

[30] Alma Whitaker, "Dr. Faust Reviews New Incarnation," *Los Angeles Times*, August 28, 1938, C1.

[31] Bosley Crowther, "Love Takes Flight," *New York Times*, September 27, 1937, 24.

Production with New Independents

The production side is an obvious attempt to escape as much as possible set construction by utilizing airports and stock shots. The result is a hodge-podge of stuff that bores the audience stiff."[32] On the other hand, *The Hollywood Reporter* gave the film a glowing review: "This is A grade in B pictures, ingeniously written, cleverly directed, lacking only the bigger names and higher polish of fatter funds to rate the upper half ... The first credit citation goes to Conrad Nagel, who in his maiden effort as a director, turns in a fine piece of work. He gets full value out of every situation and the ability of each player, keeps his story moving and properly punctuated with laughs and excitement ... George Hirliman and Ben Pivar have done a competent production job."[33] One man's opinion.

Condor Productions found itself in a precarious financial state by the middle of 1937, and fears grew that the company would not be able to meet its contractual agreements to deliver completed films on time, if at all; renewal of a contract for the Nagel-Hunt series was one casualty of this growing concern.[34] The industry as a whole was in the midst of a production slump, with economic measures taken by studios across the board as producers debated the seriousness of the situation. As a result, belts were tightened and lavish spending came to a halt, if only temporarily. The more worrisome and less financially stable producers simply cut costs across the board. Grand National made the decision to avoid more costly literary purchases, turning to the acquisition of pulp fiction for their story ideas—as if anyone would notice.[35]

As Condor's outstanding debts to executives, employees, film labs, sound recording studios, and other involved parties continued to mount, it became obvious that steps would need to be taken to shore up the ailing company. An effort was underway by Lester Cowan and Condor stockholders to reorganize the company under the name Hollywood Pictures and assume the ailing company's assets, liabilities, and contractual commitments to both Grand National and RKO. The rug was temporarily pulled out from under Cowan when a trio of creditors, including Pivar, writer Frank Gay, and cinematographer Albert Wetzel, brought an involuntary bankruptcy petition against Condor seeking permission to reorganize the company.[36] Federal court Justice Cosgrove denied the threesome's request, and approved the petition

---

[32] "Love Takes Flight," *Daily Variety*, August 18, 1937, 39.

[33] "Nagel Clicks First Time As Director," *Hollywood Reporter*, July 28, 1937, 3.

[34] "Condor Woe No Threat to Grand National Lineup," *Boxoffice*, September 4. 1937, 42.

[35] Ivan Spear, "Economy Wave Calling Halt to Lavish Studio Spending," *Boxoffice*, November 20, 1937, 4.

[36] "Assets Receiver Studies Condor Financial Setup," *Boxoffice*, December 4, 1937, 46; Ivan Spear, "Producer Barks Ground in Court," *Boxoffice*, December 11, 1937, 72.

for Condor's reorganization submitted by Clinton Miller, recently appointed trustee by Condor stockholders.[37] Pivar, Gay, and Wetzel did not give up on their petition, and were soon joined by another creditor, Consolidated Film Industries, Inc.[38] George Hirliman, who in the interim had resigned from Condor and moved over to Republic, was approached to return to his former position in hopes of returning the company to some semblance of health. He agreed, Republic extended him a leave of absence, and Condor had a new lease on life.[39] Pivar's petition was thrown out of court. Condor managed to limp along for another year or so, but had gone belly-up by the end of 1940.

Mr. Boggs Steps Out
(Director: Gordon Wiles; Released November 12, 1937)

With Condor on shaky ground, Pivar moved over to Zion Myers' production unit in June to assume production duties on the Stuart Erwin vehicle *Face the Facts*. Originally scheduled to start filming back on May 15,[40] the troubled production had run into some problems, a suitable producer not the least of them. Pivar was brought in to replace Richard Rowland in that capacity, who had in turn earlier replaced producer Andrew L. Stone,[41] who had stepped in when Douglas MacLean stepped out.[42] Rowland, hired away from Paramount back in January, had yet to produce a film at Grand National in spite of the announcement of several different assignments in the interim, and his replacement on *Face the Facts* was reportedly due to a conflict in schedules with *Painter in the Sky*, another film he was to produce.[43] This sounded reasonable, but a follow-up story two weeks later stated that Rowland's contract with Grand National had been torn up by mutual agreement.[44] Rowland moved on to Edward Small Productions at United Artists.

Face the Facts was to be based on an original *Saturday Evening Post* magazine story written by Clarence Budington Kelland. Kelland was an extremely prolific writer, turning out some sixty novels and more than 200 short stories during the course of his long career, the latter appearing primarily in the pages of *The*

---

[37] "Bankruptcy Actions Knot Independents," *Boxoffice*, January 1, 1938, 46.
[38] "Tentative Plan to Condor Creditors," *Boxoffice*, January 8, 1938, 74.
[39] "Production Tangle Ending for Condor," *Boxoffice*, January 15, 1938, 35.
[40] Edwin Schallert, "Erwin Set as 'Small Town Boy,'" *Los Angeles Times*, March 19, 1937, 17.
[41] Edwin Schallert, "The Pageant of the Film World," *Los Angeles Times*, April 30, 1937, 10.
[42] "Films Debated," *Los Angeles Times*, February 15, 1937, 10.
[43] "Pivar Takes the Reins on 'Face the Facts,'" *Boxoffice*, July 17, 1937, 38.
[44] "Rowland and GN Split by 'Mutual Agreement,'" *Boxoffice*, July 31, 1937, 36.

Saturday Evening Post and *The American*.⁴⁵ Kelland's stories had been the basis for numerous screenplays over the previous twenty years, Frank Capra's *Mr. Deeds Goes to Town* a year earlier perhaps the most popular adaptation. While *Facts* was struggling to make it into production, two other Kelland stories were being readied for the screen at other studios: *Mr. Dodds Takes the Air* at Warners, and *Stand-In* at United Artists.

Pivar hired screenwriter Aben Kandel to provide additional dialog for Richard English's script, with production of *Face the Facts* scheduled to commence once star Erwin had finished filming *I'll Take Romance* at Columbia.⁴⁶ English had been brought in earlier to replace Arnold Belgard,⁴⁷ who had in turn replaced original scripters Betty Laidlaw and Robert Lively, first assigned to the project back in April.⁴⁸ Sidney Algier, a former silent-era assistant director and second-unit director who had become a production manager with the coming of sound, had been hired in that latter capacity for this film,⁴⁹ but was switched over to Hirliman's *Wallaby Jim of the Islands* when production was delayed; Harold Lewis was brought on as his replacement. *Wallaby* would turn out to be Algier's last film.

Direction of *Face the Facts* had originally been assigned to aforementioned producer Andrew L. Stone,⁵⁰ but by May had been reassigned to Alexis Thurn-Taxis.⁵¹ This would have been Thurn-Taxis' maiden effort, but he was soon replaced and would not have another chance at direction until 1942 when he cranked out a series of four quickies for Producers Releasing Corporation, followed by a position as associate producer at Universal. Thurn-Taxis was the American-born son of Alexander Prince of Thurn and Taxis, a nephew of the slain Empress Elizabeth of Austria. Thurn-Taxis had a colorful past, serving as former chief of staff for Milan Stefanic of the French army, and later as aide to White Russian Admiral Kolchak; he was among the first to enter Ekaterinburg in Siberia to obtain facts surrounding the slaughter of the Russian Imperial family. Leaving the military behind, Thurn-Taxis changed his name to the more user-friendly "Cliff Wheeler," produced a few Broadway shows, and obtained a job at Universal in the mid-twenties through former Yale classmate and

---

⁴⁵ "Clarence Budington Kelland, Prolific Author, Is Dead at 82," *New York Times*, February 19, 1964, page unknown.

⁴⁶ "Kandel Writing Dialog For GN 'Face the Facts,'" *Hollywood Reporter*, August 21, 1937, 2.

⁴⁷ "Belgard on 'Facts,'" *Hollywood Reporter*, June 4, 1937, 9.

⁴⁸ "Laidlaw, Lively Collab On GN 'Facts,'" *Hollywood Reporter*, April 9, 1937, 2.

⁴⁹ "Algier Named Manager," *Boxoffice*, May 29, 1937, 70.

⁵⁰ *Ibid.*

⁵¹ "Pictures in the Making: Starting," *Boxoffice*, May 29, 1937, 79.

prominent director Rex Ingram. Returning to Europe with the advent of sound, Thurn-Taxis was forced to return to the United States for political reasons, and reassumed his original name.[52]

Silent comedian Glenn Tryon was briefly slated to direct,[53] but the assignment ended up with Ewing Scott. This did not pan out, either; Scott was involved in an auto accident that damaged his knee, necessitating an operation. Complications set in, a follow-up operation was scheduled, and Scott was yanked from the production with vague assurances that he'd get to helm Erwin's next film;[54] it did not happen.

Gordon Wiles, a competent director with only a handful of films to his credit, was ultimately signed to serve in that capacity, having proved his worth to Pivar the year before at Columbia with *Two-Fisted Gentleman*. Formerly a painter and illustrator, Wiles' industry start was in 1931 as an art director, winning an Oscar for his first assignment, William K. Howard's *Transatlantic*. After a dozen or so more assignments, Wiles graduated to direction in 1935 and was responsible for some reasonably stylish efforts, but eventually ended back in art direction and production design. Wiles died comparatively young, not reaching fifty.

Filming of *Face the Facts* began on Friday, September 3,[55] with Hungarian-born cinematographer and seasoned pro John Stumar behind the camera, the film now going by the rather curious title of *Mr. Boggs Buys a Barrel*. By the time it was released in November, the title had been tweaked slightly to *Mr. Boggs Steps Out*.

Mr. Boggs Steps Out is a delightfully charming comedy about bean-counting contest winner Oliver Boggs (Stuart Erwin) who heads to Peckham Falls, Vermont, to satisfy his life-long desire to own a cooperage. Discovering that the sleepy little town suffers from what he calls "industrial anemia," Boggs hopes to rejuvenate the business with the collapsible barrel invented by the absent-minded father Angus Tubbs (Spencer Charters) of love interest Oleander Tubbs (Helen Chandler), both of whom work by his side at the cooperage. Morton Ross (Tully Marshall), the owner of the town's pickle factory, is planning to sell out to Mammoth Packing Company representative Dennis Andrews (Walter Byron), which will leave a majority of the town's workers without jobs. Ross tells Boggs he'll invest in his barrel if and when Boggs can demonstrate its

---

[52] Hans J. Wollstein, "Alexis Thurn-Taxis," *Allmovie* <http://www.allmovie.com/artist/alexis-thurn-taxis-114149> (December 30, 2010)

[53] "Rowland Takes Stone's Reins on GN's 'Facts,'" *Hollywood Reporter*, May 28, 1937, 2.

[54] "Ewing Scott Drops Meg On Grand National 'Facts,'" *Hollywood Reporter*, August 3, 1937, 17.

[55] "Grand National Resumes with Three for Cameras," *Hollywood Reporter*, August 31, 1937, 5.

monetary value, compelling Boggs to set out on a city-to-city trek to try to drum up interest. With no success, as it turns out.

On the *Mr. Boggs Steps Out* (1937) set, Pivar admires the lengthy list of actor Tully Marshall's (right) previous stage and screen appearances, awarded on the fiftieth anniversary of Marshall's first Broadway appearance. Photo courtesy of Jan Pivar Dacri.

Boggs eventually manages to sway Ross into keeping his factory running and investing in Boggs' barrels. He convinces him with a demonstration of how wood aging improves taste, inundating the poor fellow with a bunch of silly slogans ("Food in wood tastes pretty good!"). Undaunted, Andrews connives to gain control of the collapsible barrel patent by tricking Angus into signing a personal contract with him. Just when it looks like Ross is out of the picture and all is lost for the good people of Peckham Falls, Boggs announces that he had registered the patent in Oleander's name, not Angus'. The ending, not too surprisingly, is a happy one, and Boggs even gets to punch Andrews in the deal!

Boggs is without question the best of Pivar's three films for Grand National, a slickly made and handsome production that only rarely displays any hints of a lower budget. Stumar's camera setups are well chosen and adroitly fluid, the convincingly lived-in looking sets lit skillfully and properly for a change, and no boom mike shadows. Director Wiles, his direction solid but unobtrusive, elicits uniformly pleasing performances from the film's fine cast, keeping the story flowing and the viewer's interest on high for the feature's brief sixty-eight minutes. Even the editing is seamless for a welcome change, with a decent little montage thrown in as Boggs wearily travels from city-to-city in the futile search for a buyer for his barrels.

Erwin, who had bought out the remainder of his contract with MGM earlier in the year to freelance,[56] was the perfect choice for the lead. As Boggs, he gives a welcome variation of the amiable oaf character he'd portrayed in his two previous films, *Small Town Boy* and *Dance Charlie Dance* (both 1937), and a slew of others before those. As the *Los Angeles Times* reviewer put it, "Stuart Erwin at last comes into his own in a role in which his naturalness, humor and a certain integrity of personality as well as of characterization find full play. 'Stu' has played bungling saps aplenty, roles that were about as true to life as a tin minnow; but in this picture he has a chance to play an earnest, characterful youth who is unconsciously funny, yet likable and believable."[57]

Mr. Boggs Steps Out (1937). Image courtesy of Heritage Auction Galleries, Ha.com.

Helen Chandler is delightfully feisty as Boggs' co-worker, in love with him but frustrated with his infatuation with Toby Wing's character Irene Lee. Former stage actress Chandler, in films for a decade before this and most notably perhaps in Tod Browning's *Dracula* (1931), failed to click with audiences and returned to the stage with the completion of *Boggs*, her final screen performance. Walter Byron is adequately slimy as the financier out to gain control of the barrel patents, and Toby Wing comfortable in the role of the sexy but shallow rich girl Boggs is head over heels for; she is easy on the eyes, too. Milburn Stone is sufficiently threatening and solid looking in the small role of a rabble-rousing worker trying to incite his co-workers to violence. The bulk of the remaining cast is comprised of a bunch of seasoned old-timers, including Tully Marshall, Spencer Charters, Otis Harlan, and Otto Hoffman. The delightful cast had been assembled by Grand National's

---

[56] "Stuart Erwin East for Airer After MGM Split," *Hollywood Reporter*, March 16, 1937, 6.

[57] "Stu Erwin Scores as 'Mr. Boggs,'" *Los Angeles Times*, November 15, 1937, A9.

casting director Vance Carroll, hired in May to function in that capacity for all of GN's affiliated producers; previously each had to scramble to pull together casts for each new production.[58]

Pivar, needing the collapsible barrel around which the plot centers, reportedly invented one himself and intended to have it patented. He promoted his invention by claiming that these new barrels could be shipped back to the owner at one-fifth the freight charge of a regular barrel.[59] A search of the US Patent and Trademark Office's issued patents does not turn up any such patent, however, suggesting that either his application was rejected or, more likely, the report itself was just another instance of promotional ballyhoo.

Pivar was scheduled to produce Stu Erwin's second film for Grand National, tentatively titled *Signals Over*. Based on a story written by Dudley Earle and adapted for the screen by Richard English,[60] *Signals Over* was eventually shelved, and Erwin abandoned Grand National.

Grand National was in desperate trouble by the beginning of 1938. Cagney had secured release from his contract, Edward L. Alperson had been unsuccessful in obtaining new financing for the company, and filming had ground to halt with *The Shadow Murder Case* (released in 1938 as *International Crime*) the only film produced over the previous three months. With the completion of his trio of films and the loss of the *Angels with Dirty Faces* gig, Pivar deserted the ailing Grand National for the healthier Republic Pictures. Fellow producer David Diamond left the studio as well, leaving Bennie Zeidman and Bud Barsky as the studio's sole remaining producers, both dormant.[61] Grand National finally succumbed to its financial troubles, with Alperson resigning from the sinking ship in February 1939, the studio liquidated a year later.[62]

§

---

[58] "Carroll GN Caster for All Producers," *Hollywood Reporter*, May 27, 1937, 1.

[59] E.V. Durling, "On the Side," *Los Angeles Times*, September 30, 1937, A1.

[60] "Pivar Reins 'Signals,'" *Hollywood Reporter*, September 17, 1937, 3.

[61] "Production Future at GN is Blurred," *Boxoffice*, January 15, 1938, 44.

[62] Ted Okuda, *Grand National, Producers Releasing Corporation, and Screen Guild/Lippert: Complete Filmographies with Studio Histories* (Jefferson, NC: McFarland & Company, Inc., 1989).

5 Production with Another New Independent: Republic Pictures (1938)

Republic Pictures Corporation came into being in May 1935, when Herbert J. Yates, head of Consolidated Film Laboratories, decided to foreclose on a number of defaulting motion picture companies, merging them into a single operating unit. The affected companies were M.H. Hoffman's Liberty Pictures, A.W. Hackel's Supreme Pictures, Larry Darmour and Phil Goldstone's Majestic Pictures, Nat Levine's Mascot Pictures, and Monogram Pictures, co-owned by Trem Carr and W.L. Johnston. (Monogram Pictures was reinstated as an independent production company two years later as a result of irresolvable disagreements between Carr and Johnston on one side, and Yates on the other.)[1]

Initial releases that same year were both second feature B westerns (*Westward Ho!* with John Wayne, followed by cowboy wannabe Gene Autry singing his way through *Tumbling Tumbleweeds*), but within a year the studio was averaging a film per week: fifty releases in 1936, sixty-nine releases in 1937, and fifty-one releases in 1938. These were all B quality, a public-friendly mix of westerns, serials, dramas, musicals, and series entries. A few more years would elapse before the occasional A feature would be thrown into the mix, a number of these the unfortunate, big-budget but money-losing vehicles starring Yates' future wife Vera Hruba Ralston.

The Great Wall Street Scandal

The Great Wall Street Scandal was announced within days of the notorious headline-making Wall Street scandal involving former New York Stock

---

[1] Len D. Martin, *The Republic Pictures Checklist, 1935-1959* (Jefferson, NC: McFarland & Company, Inc., 1998).

Newlyweds Ben and Judy at home, 1938. Photo courtesy of Jan Pivar Dacri.

Exchange president Richard Whitney. Born into a wealthy, upper-crust family in Boston, Whitney and his older brother George had relocated to New York City in 1910, Richard eventually establishing his own bond brokerage company Richard Whitney & Co. George obtained a prominent position with Morgan Bank, funneling a lot of business in Richard's direction. Richard purchased a seat at the NYSE and within years was elected to the Board of Governors, eventually named vice president, and finally president of the Exchange.

While widely believed to be a brilliant financier, Richard had engaged in a number of highly speculative investments and had suffered considerable losses. In an attempt to keep things afloat, Whitney borrowed large sums of cash from brother George and a number of wealthy friends. This was not enough, and after tapping out all legally available loans, Whitney turned to the illegal, embezzling large amounts from the NYSE's gratuity fund and the New York Yacht Club, where he served as treasurer. Nor was family immune from his predatory acts, either; he stole $800,000 in bonds from his father's estate. Whitney's illegal activities were eventually found out, and on March 10, New York County District Attorney Thomas E. Dewey charged him with embezzlement.[2] Whitney's arrest made headlines nationwide, and within ten days Republic Pictures made the hurried announcement regarding plans to film the story as *The Great Wall Street Scandal* with Neil Hamilton as the lead.[3]

Pivar was handed this story as his first production assignment only days after joining Republic in mid-March.[4] He went to work assembling a team, doling out screenwriting chores to thirty-one-year-old Russia-born Alex Gottlieb and thirty-year-old Norman Burnstine, both of whom had just successfully collaborated on the scripts for Republic's *Arson Gang Busters* and *Invisible*

---

[2] Thomas E. Dewey, "Text of Dewey's Report to Court Reviewing the Causes of Whitney's Failure," *New York Times*, April 10, 1938, page unknown.

[3] Louella O. Parsons, "Louis Bromfield's Epic of India Set for Screening," *Schenectady Gazette*, March 21, 1938, 4

[4] "Pivar Moves to Rep," *Variety*, March 23, 1938, 11.

Enemy. Production was to commence on April 20,⁵ by which time Whitney's trial in New York had concluded and sentencing taken place. Republic's plans for filming Whitney's story eventually fizzled out, and the project was shelved. Whitney ended up in Sing Sing with a five-year sentence, having squandered more than $5½ million dollars of other people's money.⁶

Judy feeds the wild animals at Yosemite, early 1938.
Photo courtesy of Jan Pivar Dacri.

Love is a Fable

Love is a Fable was first announced during its preparatory stages back in June 1937. It was reported that writer Edmund Seward had returned to Republic after a short illness to write the original screenplay; Leonard Fields was named as producer.⁷ The studio revealed ongoing attempts to lure actress Nancy Carroll back to the screen for the lead role after a three-year absence.⁸ "Edmund" Seward, as his name was misspelled in the trades, was thirty-year-old Edmond Seward, comparatively new to screenwriting with only a few other credits to his name: an initial effort for Fox Film back in 1934, a pair of Australian-made films released in 1936 (one in which he had a starring role as well) and *The Duke Comes Back* for Republic which he'd just completed to their

---

⁵ "Scripters," *Boxoffice*, April 9, 1938, 41.

⁶ Hugh O'Connor, "Whitney & Co. Loss is Put at $2,655,000," *New York Times*, April 28, 1938, 29.

⁷ "Seward Vamps 'Fable,'" *Hollywood Reporter*, June 4, 1937, 10.

⁸ Harriet Parsons, "Sir Walter Scott Classic Likely Screen Material," *Schenectady Gazette*, July 20, 1937, 15.

apparent satisfaction. Fields was fresh from his associate producer role on the soon-to-be-released *All Over Town* for the same studio.

By mid-September production was scheduled to begin on October 1, but with only two weeks remaining it still needed to be cast.[9] Plans fell through when the script was deemed unsuitable, and the film was temporarily shelved until the following March. Production chores were then reassigned to Sol Siegel, with Richard English brought in to rework the script.[10] Fields licked his wounds and headed over to Sol Lesser Productions to produce *Peck's Bad Boy with the Circus*, released at the end of 1938. Seward, similarly dumped from the project, moved on to co-write the script for Max and Dave Fleischer's feature-length *Gulliver's Travels* (1939), followed by sporadic work throughout the forties, with a final credit on *Bela Lugosi Meets a Brooklyn Gorilla* (1952) where he provided additional dialog for Tim Ryan's script.

Siegel, a real company man in the busiest sense of the word, was new to this genre of film, having produced an endless string of Joseph Kane-directed B westerns over the past year, with several fifteen-chapter serials co-directed by William Witney thrown into the mix. English had written the story or screenplay for three previous Republic releases over the past two years (*Bulldog Edition* in 1936, and *Larceny on the Air* and *All Over Town* in 1937). The project foundered, and Pivar, freed up while production of *The Great Wall Street Scandal* was on hiatus, was brought in at the end of March[11] to replace Siegel, whose assembly-line talents were needed elsewhere. The script was once again reassigned, this time to Matthew Webster and George Yates.[12] This duo was similarly green to screenwriting: Webster had only written stories upon which three films had been made, one each at Paramount, Universal, and most recently for Republic; Yates had a sole screenwriting credit under his belt, the Republic serial *The Lone Ranger* (1938). After some fitful attempts to rejuvenate the production, nothing more was heard of this film—or at least under this title.

On Official Duty *and* Lady Mouthpiece

George Yates was assigned in May to do a treatment of a film tentatively titled *On Official Duty* as well, another project Pivar was to oversee.[13] Whether or not this was ever made is unknown, and may have become *The Mysterious Miss*

---

[9] "Leonard Fields Will Can 2 for Republic," *Boxoffice*, September 18, 1937, 88.
[10] "Scripters," *Boxoffice*, March 19, 1938, 43.
[11] *Daily Variety*, April 1, 1938, 4; April 19, 1938, 5.
[12] "Scripters," *Boxoffice*, April 30, 1938, 102.
[13] *Daily Variety*, May 20, 1938, 10.

X (1939; Gus Meins) for which Yates received original story credit, and that was ultimately associate produced by Herbert Schlom.

Lady Mouthpiece is a mystery. While it was credited to Pivar after the fact,[14] no mention of a film bearing this title has been found in the trades, nor did Republic have a release with this title. In fact, the fate of these last three films is a mystery. Any of them may have taken on a new title some time during preparation or production after Pivar's departure from Republic, or may have been shelved altogether. A search through Republic's releases for 1938 and 1939 and their accompanying synopses[15] does not reveal any obvious on-screen fates for these films (aside from the aforementioned *The Mysterious Miss X*), but that doesn't rule out that one or more of them actually made it to the screen in one form or another. Let it suffice to say that Pivar received credit for having some involvement in the preparation of these titles.

Regardless, Pivar's association with Republic was a brief one, and after only three months he was released from his production contract in June 1938. Creative differences on *The Great Wall Street Mystery* [sic] were cited as the reason behind the split.[16]

On a more positive note, Judy gave birth to the couple's first child within a few weeks of the split from Republic. Son Neil was born to them on July 3, 1938, and had this to say about the background of the name his parents chose for him:

> I don't think my name relates to anyone, but who knows. I was told that my name is a transliteration from the Hebrew name Naftali. They wanted to name me Wolf, after my maternal grandfather, but he was still alive when I was born. My mother told me that Adolph was another consideration. Fortunately for me, Hitler was making world headlines about that time. I wonder what my life would have been like being Jewish with the name Adolph.[17]

In retrospect, the choice was probably a judicious one.

---

[14] *The International Motion Picture Almanac, 1939-1940*, 499; *The Great Wall St. Scandal* and *Love is a Fable* are listed as well, Pivar's three sole credits for 1938.

[15] Len D. Martin, *The Republic Pictures Checklist, 1935-1959* (Jefferson, NC: McFarland & Company, Inc., 1998).

[16] "Pivar Leaves Rep," *Variety*, June 15, 1938, 2.

[17] Neil Pivar correspondence with author, August 20, 2010.

Stop Yellin'

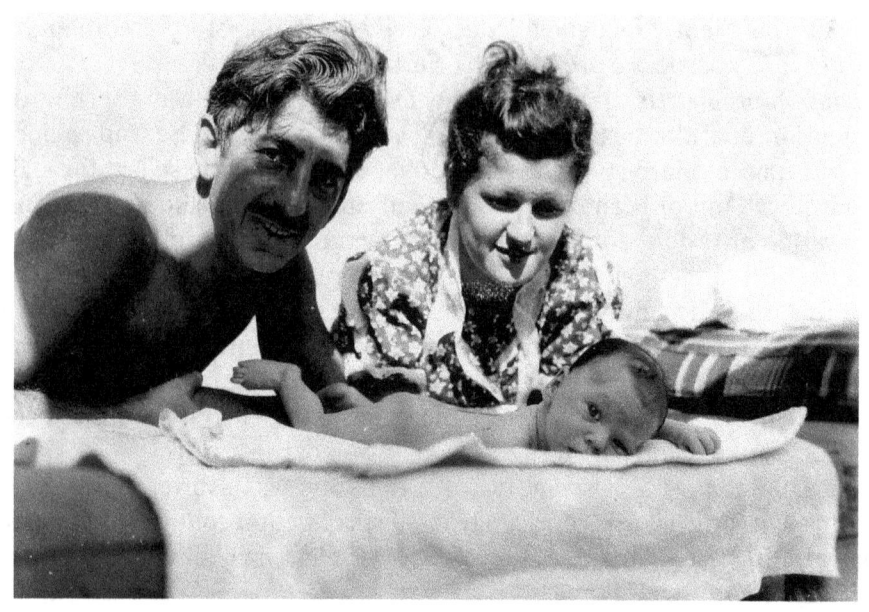

Son Neil, born July 3, 1938, now six weeks old.
Photo courtesy of Jan Pivar Dacri.

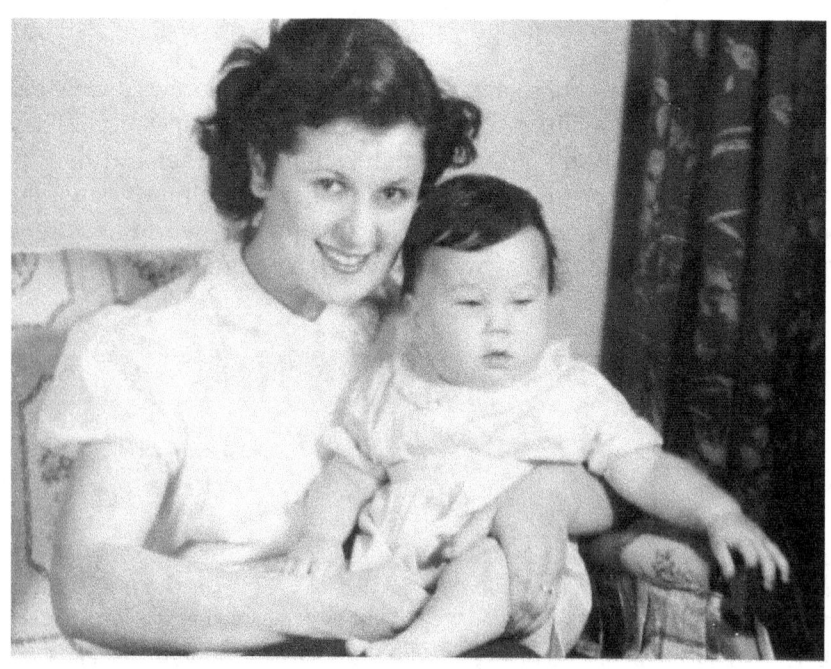

Judy with son Neil. Photo courtesy of Jan Pivar Dacri.

Production with Another New Independent

Of Judy's eight siblings, two of them—Ina and Sam—had relocated from the east coast to Los Angeles; the other six remained behind in New York. Older sister Libby, five years Judy's senior and a teacher in the New York City school system, had married fellow teacher Paul Silverstein in 1934. After Judy gave birth to Neil, Libby took leave of her husband and headed out to California to give her sister a hand with the newborn. It was the only time that she'd venture west for another fifty-eight years, when she'd head back west to live with her daughter.

Now with both a wife and child to support, Pivar felt it was time to settle down into more permanent, steady-paying employment. To that end, negotiations were entered into for a solid position back with Universal, ushering in the promise of a brighter, more secure, future both at home and within the industry.

§

6 The Arlen-Devine Series, 1939-1941 (Part 1, the 1939-1940 Season)

During the latter half of the 1930s, approximately two-thirds of the product churned out in Hollywood (and other, less exotic, locations) was of B quality, with budgets at the majors ranging from $50,000 to $200,000, and frequently less with the minors and independents. Described in show-business parlance as "good for duals and nabes" (double bills and neighborhood houses), the B's were a commodity that the vast majority of filmgoers had come to expect, but only a smaller number readily welcomed.[1] In spite of the public's occasionally disparaging remarks concerning the quality of the B's, the theaters featuring double bills consistently did better business than those with single features. The production of B's was a flourishing business, and Pivar—at home in this segment of the industry—wanted to flourish with it.

Not that the B's were without vociferous detractors—they were plentiful. In March of 1939, Dr. Ray Lyman Wilbur, Stanford University president and head of the National Motion Picture Research Council, went on record as saying the council opposed double feature programs. Stating that "diversified programs made it unlikely that both features of a double bill would be of 'family' suitability," Wilbur went on to say that "[i]t is quite clear that the motion pictures have a number of inadequacies, particularly in relation to children and the effects, good and bad, upon them. Recent studies seem to indicate many films are shown that certainly cannot be classified as appropriate for all members of the family."[2] Another instance where "recent studies" were referred to, but left unnamed.

---

[1] Douglas W. Churchill, "Hollywood from A to Z," *New York Times*, March 14, 1937, X3.

[2] "Against Double Features," *New York Times*, March 8, 1939, page unknown.

Stop Yellin'

In 1937, a survey was conducted among the filmgoers of St. Louis. 310,000 ballots were distributed to the patrons of four first-run theaters and twenty-seven neighborhood theaters, with 19%—roughly 59,000—ballots filled out and returned. The results revealed that the patrons of first-run theaters were in favor of single bills by a margin of two-to-one, while the subsequent run theatergoers preferred double bills by a margin of four-to-one.[3] Or, put another way, the more affluent theatergoers were more selective, while the common folk simply wanted an evening's entertainment. The sentiments of the denizens of St. Louis, while interesting, did not necessarily reflect the pulse of the country as a whole.

James Roosevelt, a motion picture executive employed by Samuel Goldwyn and the oldest son of then-President Franklin D. Roosevelt, spoke of the "'evils' of double features" to a group of educators with the National Education Association. He emphasized his disapproval of the double bill, and threw in so-called "bargain nights" at the movies for good measure. And for some added Brownie points with his employer, said that Samuel Goldwyn was a "lone wolf" in Hollywood when it came to opposition to double features.[4]

Which brings us to Samuel Goldwyn, a long-time foe of the double bill and its resultant "cheapening" of the Hollywood product ("a major menace to the industry," he railed).[5] On May 15, 1940, Goldwyn and famed pollster Dr. George Gallup announced at a press conference a poll to be conducted by the latter's American Institute of Public Opinion to determine the popularity of the double feature. The sample size of 1,100 respondents included children ages six and older, with interviewing conducted nationwide over the following three months. Goldwyn went into this with a less-than-open mind, stating that even if the poll went against his opinions, his mind was made up, bluntly stating that "I am not going to change my policy."[6] The results were announced on August 9, 1940: 57% preferred single features, and 43% double features. When asked their feelings on the subject if *both* films were good, however, 66% approved of the double bill. The double feature was preferred primarily by New Englanders, by those teenaged or younger, and by lower income groups. Among the double bill advocates, three primary reasons were given for their preference: 1) more product for the money; 2) if one film stinks, the other film is likely to be good (or at least offer some variety); and 3) gives attendees a chance to "kill more time."[7]

---

[3] "First-Run Patrons Favor Single Bills in St. Louis," *Hollywood Reporter*, October 9, 1937, 7.

[4] "James Roosevelt in Talk," *New York Times*, July 6, 1939, page unknown.

[5] "Film Survey to Be Taken," *New York Times*, May 16, 1940, page unknown.

[6] "Goldwyn-Gallup Poll," *Motion Picture Herald*, May 18, 1940, 9.

[7] "57% of Movie Fans Favor Single Film," *New York Times*, August 9, 1940, page

THE ARLEN-DEVINE SERIES, PART I (1939-1940)

Meanwhile over at Universal Pictures, several decades of growth and comparative stability had come to an end. Back in 1929, Carl Laemmle awarded son Carl Jr. a twenty-first birthday present to beat all twenty-first birthday presents, the position of production chief at the studio. Born in 1908, Carl Jr. finished high school at age fifteen and immediately went to work at the studio. Within a few years Junior was writing and producing more than forty entries in the popular (and profitable) "The Collegians" series of two-reel comedies, spanning four years of the characters' lives and adventures at college. And then Junior's twenty-first birthday arrived, along with his promotion. Carl Sr. headed off to Europe, leaving Junior to read and buy stories, hire actors and directors, and supervise the studio's productions.[8] In the interim Carl Sr. had finally broken down and taken on the acquisition of several hundred smaller theaters, but Carl Jr. dumped them as soon as the studio was faced with the expensive prospect of wiring them for sound.

Junior Laemmle had instituted a policy with a thrust toward more prestige productions, cutting back dramatically on the studio's output of shorts and programmers—another, less pejorative name for the lowly B's. The studio had undergone a major $1,500,000 overhaul at the end of the twenties with the construction of three new soundstages, three projection theaters, a state of the art lab for handling both sound and silent film, along with improved dressing rooms, property rooms, and several other affiliated structures. Additionally, six new Movietone trucks were equipped to facilitate location shoots.[9] The success of *All Quiet on the Western Front* (1930; Lewis Milestone) and the Paul Whiteman musical *King of Jazz* (1930; John Murray Anderson) contributed to the decision to reduce the feature output for the 1930-1931 season to twenty A-class films, down from the previous year's fifty, with a comparable budget of $12,000,000 meaning a greater expenditure per film. Program pictures were to be eliminated.[10]

Unfortunately, the critical and comparative financial success of such prominent films as the musical *Broadway* (1929; Paul Fejos) and the aforementioned *All Quiet on the Western Front* and *King of Jazz* were compromised by a sales and distribution setup not geared to yield maximum results from first-run releases of this sort. Coupled with a number of expensive failures and the company's expansion plans, Universal's cash reserves were depleted, and obtaining loans of any size grew increasingly difficult in those early days of the Depression. Production was scaled back and budgets cut,

---

unknown.

[8] "Film Chiefs Cement Dynasties," *Los Angeles Times*, December 14, 1930, B22.

[9] "Universal Plans Changes," *Los Angeles Times*, June 28, 1929, A10.

[10] "Universal to Boost Budget," *Los Angeles Times*, May 2, 1930, A16.

with a return to the bread-and-butter programmer fare the studio was better equipped to deal with, and more comfortable producing.

While Universal lost money in 1930, it made a modest profit in 1931, faring better than most of its competitors. The success of Junior Laemmle's horror films, such as *Dracula* (1931; Tod Browning), *Frankenstein* (1931; James Whale), *The Mummy* (1932; Karl Freund), and *The Old Dark House* (1932; James Whale) gave the studio a signature genre, but Universal lost money again in 1932—but not nearly as much as most of its competitors, MGM the sole exception. Twenty-six pictures were planned for the 1932-1933 season, and Laemmle Sr. spoke as though these were still the prestige pictures Junior had pushed for: "There is no profit in cheap pictures. We realize that truly great pictures are the only productions that net profits and whatever a fine, outstanding picture costs is money well spent. We are eliminating waste in energy as well as money so that more dollars may be available for actual picture making."[11]

Universal limped along through 1933, showing a comparatively modest loss for that year. Production was increased to a planned thirty-six features for the 1933-1934 season,[12] and 1934 marked a turnaround with a very modest profit of $238,792 for the year.[13] Laemmle Jr. decided the time was right to expand the studio's genre offerings beyond the well-received horror output. Forty-two features were planned for the 1935-1936 season, and along with the westerns and melodramas were a number of prestige pictures, Junior's new focus on "musical comedy farces and romantic dramas with operatic stars in the leading roles."[14] This did not turn out as planned.

In November 1935, the costly production of several of the studio's more lavish A's—James Whale's remake of *Show Boat*, James Cruze's *Sutter's Gold*, and Walter Lang's *Love Before Breakfast*—had put a serious crimp in the company's cash flow.[15] Laemmle Jr.'s contention that the studio's bread-and-butter lower-cost productions would cover overhead was dashed when box-office receipts were less than expected. Cash reserves were quickly depleted due to rapidly mounting preproduction costs. Laemmle Sr. took out a loan for $750,000 from an investment group headed by former RKO and Paramount producer (of programmers) Charles Rogers, and British financier and Wall St. concern Standard Capital Company president J. Cheever Cowdin. Laemmle put up a chattel mortgage on the studio's forthcoming product, and as personal

---

[11] "Laemmle Tells Plans for Year," *Los Angeles Times*, May 18, 1932, A8.

[12] "Universal Sets Larger Output," *Los Angeles Times*, July 1, 1933, A5.

[13] "Stocks Slip Off Sharply," *Los Angeles Times*, March 13, 1935, 14.

[14] "Film Budget Given Boost," *Los Angeles Times*, June 7, 1935, A12.

[15] "Universal Studio Sale Forecast," *Los Angeles Times*, November 2, 1935, 1.

security his own controlling stock interest in Universal. Further financial problems resulted in another $300,000 loan in February 1936, and after some wheeling and dealing, the investors called their option on March 14. Everything went to Standard Capital for a paltry $5,500,000, and the Laemmle dynasty came to an end with a whimper. (Carl Laemmle would die from a heart attack three-and-a-half years later at age seventy-two.) An executive purge ousted the last of his many relatives, Laemmle Jr. included. Charles Rogers set himself up as executive vice president in charge of production, the position formerly held since 1929 by Laemmle Jr. Robert H. Cochrane, vice president of Universal since its founding back in 1912, was promoted to president of the parent company,[16] with his former annual salary of $33,533 increased to $91,000.[17]

Rogers announced that the Warners' system of front office domination would be put into effect, with supervisors and directors forbidden to make changes in scripts and production plans once they'd been approved by the executives. News trends would govern the B film themes, and little latitude would be allowed in the making of films costing less than $350,000; "indulgence" would mark the executives' attitude toward "more pretentious offerings."[18] Cowdin made no bones about the new direction in which Universal was headed: "Certain persons, veterans in motion picture production, have always claimed that the industry is more of an art than a business and could never be conducted successfully on straight business lines. We are proving that it can."[19]

A half year later, Rogers announced in no uncertain terms that Universal would "not produce any more Class B films."[20] Those "pretentious offerings" proved to be few and far between, and the cessation of "Class B" films ephemeral; the lower-budget programmer continued to dominate with only a few exceptions (the popular Deanna Durbin vehicles), and not too much financial success. The year ending October 29, 1937, showed a net loss, after amortization of fixed assets, of $1,084,998; 1938 fared somewhat better, with a loss of only $591,178.

Another executive purge followed at the end of 1937. On November 30, Robert H. Cochrane was unceremoniously ousted from his position as president, even though he had a contract that was supposed to run until April 1941; he did not go quietly. Former RKO theater executive Nate Blumberg

---

[16] "Studio Sold By Laemmle," *Los Angeles Times*, March 15, 1936, 1.

[17] "Universal's Aide Picked," *Los Angeles Times*, May 8, 1936, 13.

[18] W. Douglas Churchill, "'Yellow Peril' Threatens Hollywood," *New York Times*, May 10, 1936, X3.

[19] Wesley Smith, "The March of Finance," *Los Angeles Times*, October 23, 1936, 19.

[20] "Universal Studio Adopts Highest Picture Standard," *Los Angeles Times*, January 27, 1937, A1.

was brought in to succeed Cochrane as president.[21] Several months later, on May 19, 1938, Charles Rogers "retired" from his position as vice president in charge of production, replaced by yet-another RKO theater executive, Cliff Work.[22] These purges went beyond the executive level, affecting employees in all departments. Other studios suffered similar layoffs and firings as well, due in no small part to an industry-wide production lull.[23]

Only nine days earlier, Rogers—blissfully unaware of his upcoming "intention" of retiring—made an announcement at the annual Universal sales convention regarding the company's newly revised approach to production for the upcoming 1938-1939 season's forty feature films and twelve westerns. He stated that "the hard-and-fast production schedule [is] an outmoded and dangerous procedure for any studio" and that Universal's schedule would be kept flexible at all times "so that we may obtain stories and personalities that meet the public taste."[24] And while Rogers was no longer around to see it, this new approach was more successful, for by the end of October 1939, Universal was showing its first net profit in years—$1,153,321—and by the end of October 1940, showed a net profit of $2,390,772.[25] It was into this era of low-budget prosperity that Ben Pivar became affiliated with the studio.

The choice, of course, was a logical one. Pivar had by now a dozen years of experience with various studios' lower-budget films, three of them in the editing departments of Universal and Columbia followed by production chores at Columbia, Universal (briefly), Grand National and, as mentioned earlier, aborted ones at Republic. Corner-cutting and tight schedules were the working norm for most of his career to date, so the new position was a savvy choice on Universal's part. Pivar could crank out workmanlike programmer fare on shoestring budgets, and had an editor's eye for integrating stock footage when needed. And, as it turned out, he could write as well, or at least had a fertile enough mind to conjure up sufficiently imaginative plotlines for more experienced writers to build from and flesh out. It was a good fit, and it probably did not hurt that older brother Murray was firmly entrenched as supervisor of Universal's editing department, a position he'd held since the mid-twenties. Murray's position had been further strengthened during the studio's latest purge of employees, when censorship department head Lillian

---

[21] "Universal Chief Ousted," *Los Angeles Times*, December 1, 1937, 12.

[22] "Shake-up Ousts Chief at Universal," *Los Angeles Times*, May 20, 1938, 1.

[23] "The Doctor Called Too Late in MPAC Case," *Boxoffice*, July 9, 1938, 26.

[24] "Universal Plans 40 Feature Films," *New York Times*, May 11, 1938, page unknown.

[25] "$2,390,772 Earned By Film Company," *New York Times*, January 29, 1941, page unknown.

The Arlen-Devine Series, Part I (1939-1940)

Russell was dumped and her department—albeit a small one—was merged with Pivar's.[26] The two brothers were once again working under the same roof.

Hired as both an associate producer and writer, Pivar and fellow scribe Maurice Tombragel were given their first assignment, which tied in with the company's belt-tightening: write a dozen action-filled scenarios that could be filmed on a shoestring budget, creating plotlines with Universal's extensive stock footage library in mind, utilizing as much existing footage as could logically (and, in some instances, illogically) be incorporated. This approach, of course, would reduce the number of shots that would need to be staged and filmed, ideally those of a spectacular and otherwise costly nature. We'll probably never know if they were intrigued by the challenge of their new assignment, but Pivar and Tombragel went to work knocking out a bunch of storylines built around available stock footage.

In February 1939, Universal announced the teaming of rugged action star and new hire Richard Arlen with comedic character actor Andy Devine in a new action-adventures series based on these stories. This series would be an addition to the unspecified number of smaller-budget features already on the season's schedule, separate and apart from the forty-four "large-scale productions" planned for the upcoming 1939-1940 season. Funding for this new series would be covered in part by the additional $5,000,000 increase in budget over the previous year.[27]

Seven outdoor productions were initially planned for the Arlen-Devine co-starrers, to be filmed between April 1, 1939, and April 1, 1940, with budgets of approximately $160,000.[28] Studio-owned stories were to be selected from a number of well-known authors, including Jack London, Earl Derr Biggers, W.R. Burnett, Courtney Riley Cooper, and Peter B. Kyne—or at least that's what the press release claimed—and new hire Pivar was assigned to oversee production as associate producer.[29] Arlen's contract with Universal committed him to six films per year, allowed him to appear in films for other companies during breaks from his Universal commitments,[30] and provided an annual salary in the neighborhood of $90,000, with four months vacation.[31] Arlen's compensation was in the ballpark of other Universal contractees, such as Charles Winninger and Edgar Bergen at $82,000 and $90,416, respectively (for the previous fiscal

---

[26] "The Doctor Called Too Late in MPAC Case," *Boxoffice*, July 9, 1938, 26.

[27] "Universal Boosts Budget to Make 44 Feature Films," *Los Angeles Times*, April 17, 1939, 18.

[28] "'U' Starting Season Sans Pact Change," *Boxoffice*, March 18, 1939, 14.

[29] "Screen News Here and in Hollywood," *New York Times*, February 11, 1939, 18.

[30] "Arlen's Agreement," *Los Angeles Times*, December 3, 1938, A7.

[31] Hedda Hopper, "Hedda Hopper's Hollywood," *Los Angeles Times*, August 13, 1940, 9.

year), although roughly a third less than W.C. Fields' $115,000, and half that of Universal's highest paid star Deanna Durbin's $174,916.[32]

While employment at Universal would seem to be a step down from Arlen's "glory days" back at Paramount, and the estimated $200,000-per-year income he'd been used to during those years,[33] the reality is that Arlen's once-promising career had given way to a string of programmers in the early thirties, settling into somewhat of a rut in the four years following the termination of his Paramount contract. Arlen's youthful good looks had evolved into that of a ruggedly handsome middle age, and while he was still a dependable box-office draw, his days as a matinee idol were well behind him. Not a bad situation, though, in the world of B films, where name recognition coupled with an appeal that could now straddle several generations all played in Arlen's favor. And while Arlen's natural, surgery-free looks might not strike twenty-first-century eyes and their expectations of cookie-cutter good looks as anything out of the ordinary, to late 1930s eyes he was still considered quite handsome; to paraphrase Norma Desmond, "They had faces then."

Born September 1, 1900, in Charlottesville, Virginia, and soon after relocated to St. Paul, Minnesota, Arlen—whose real name was Richard Van Mattimore—served in Canada's Royal Air Force during World War I, but never saw combat. After brief stints as sportswriter for the *Duluth Tribune*, swimming instructor, and laborer in Texas oil fields, Arlen eventually headed west to Los Angeles. There he found occasional employment in a few uncredited bit parts in film, a sole lead role in *Vengeance of the Deep* (1923), and as a motorcycle messenger for a film lab. This last position led to his "discovery" by studio executives at Paramount, the acquisition of his screen name, and a lengthy business relationship that resulted in over sixty films. Among these were William Wellman's *Wings* (1927) and *Beggars of Life* (1928); Merian C. Cooper, Lothar Mendes, and Ernest B. Schoedsack's *The Four Feathers* (1929); Victor Fleming's *The Virginian* (1929); and Erle C. Kenton's *Island of Lost Souls* (1932). With the completion of his last film, *Ready for Love*, and the expiration of his final contract on September 26, 1934, Arlen's eleven-year association with Paramount came to an end,[34] or at least for the time being.

Arlen bounced around from studio to studio over the next five years, starring in films of varying stature at 20th Century-Fox, Edward Small's Reliance Pictures (releasing through United Artists), Sol Lesser's Principal

---

[32] "Louis Mayer's $688,369 Pay Check Leads Nation," *Los Angeles Times*, July 1, 1940, 1.

[33] "Richard Arlen, Actor, Dies; Star of First Oscar Film," New York Times, March 29, 1976, page unknown.

[34] Philip K. Scheuer, "Richard Arlen Winding Up Record Sojourn," *Los Angeles Times*, August 29, 1934, 19.

The Arlen-Devine Series, Part I (1939-1940)

Productions (releasing through Columbia and, later, 20th Century-Fox), MGM, Columbia, and Republic. After filming an oater for Fox and a G-man crime story for Reliance, Arlen signed with producer Sol Lesser for eight pictures adapted from novels by the then-popular author Harold Bell Wright.[35] Wright was the best-selling author of his day, and the first reportedly to have sold over a million copies of a single novel. The resulting films—*The Calling of Dan Matthews* (1935), *The Mine With the Iron Door* (1936), and *Secret Valley* (1937)—were sufficiently popular that Lesser announced in March 1937 a fourth film to co-star Arlen with new hire and baseball great Lou Gehrig. Tentatively titled *The Trail Blazers*, it was scheduled to go into production at the conclusion of the baseball season.[36] Arlen wanted out of the contract and obtained a release, citing his desire for more important parts and more time to prepare for shooting.[37] Lesser hoped to renegotiate and lure him back, but his hopes were dashed with the announcement in April that Arlen had signed a long-term contract with Columbia.[38] Lesser scrambled and quickly signed radio personality and singing cowboy Smith Ballew, who went to work immediately upon completion of his contract with RKO at the end of May 1937; the film was ultimately released as *Rawhide* (1938). Arlen's first under his Columbia contract, a romantic comedy mystery announced as *Park Avenue Dame*[39] but finally released as *Murder in Greenwich Village* (1937), was followed by a second film.

During the break between contracts, Arlen went on location for a starring role in the Gaumont-British production *The Great Barrier*. After interiors were filmed in England by directors Geoffrey Barkas and Milton Rosmer, location filming followed in Canada. *The Great Barrier*—released in the US as *Silent Barriers*—was a western of sorts that chronicled the building of the Canadian Pacific Railway through the Rocky Mountains in the 1880s, and the hardships encountered. There was talk of Arlen's involvement in a second British production, a drama about the French Foreign Legion to be filmed on location in Morocco, but this project never came to fruition.[40]

By mid-1938, Arlen's personal life was in disarray. After almost twelve years of marriage to actress Jobyna Ralston (his co-star in the film *Wings*), the

---

[35] Edwin Schallert, "Richard Arlen Will Portray Harold Bell Wright Hero in Lesser Pictures," *Los Angeles Times*, August 7, 1935, 12.

[36] Edwin Schallert, "Gehrig to Star With Dick Arlen," *Los Angeles Times*, March 4, 1937, 15.

[37] "Arlen Gets Release From Lesser Pact," *Hollywood Reporter*, March 19, 1937, 1.

[38] Philip K. Scheuer, "Arlen Signs Contract," *Los Angeles Times*, March 11, 1937, C4.

[39] Philip K. Scheuer, "Arlen Assigned," *Los Angeles Times*, May 2, 1937, C1.

[40] Edwin Schallert, "England Will Lure Arlen Again," *Los Angeles Times*, September 29, 1936, 15.

two separated in July with three-and-a-half-year-old son Rickey remaining with his mother. At the time Arlen indicated that the separation had come as a complete surprise to him. He claimed that he was notified by their joint business manager that the former couple would take up separate residences. "The news was rather stunning to me," said Arlen. Ralston remained in their North Hollywood home,[41] and Arlen moved into their newly-built ranch home in the San Fernando Valley, which he named Breezy Top Ranch.[42] After seven years of separation, Ralston was finally granted a divorce on charges of desertion, painting a slightly different version of the events of 1938: "He left me. He just packed his clothes and said he was leaving."[43] Regardless of where the truth lies, Arlen remarried a year later—his third go at it—and remained married to the same woman until his death in 1976.

With the separation, Arlen was eager to acquire another studio contract and the security that came along with it. The success of *The Great Barrier* eventually led to contract talks with British producer Alexander Korda in 1938. Sportsman Arlen took some time off from the industry to fish in Mexican waters on his boat the *Dijo*, keeping in touch with his manager regarding the progress of those talks.[44] Playwrights Ben Hecht and Charles MacArthur approached Arlen around this time with the prospect of a role in a Broadway play planned for the upcoming season.[45] Nothing came of the contract, and nothing came of the Broadway play. Arlen was left looking for a new prospect.

Around this same time, gravel-voiced thirty-seven-year-old comedic character actor Andy Devine was one of the more popular and sought-after figures in film.[46] A former college and semi-pro football player, Flagstaff, Arizona-born Devine headed to Hollywood in the mid-1920s, finding mostly uncredited bit parts throughout the end of the decade. A pair of Universal serials followed in early 1931, and company executives took note of his acting abilities. He eventually landed a plum role in Universal's 1931 gridiron film *The Spirit of Notre Dame*, his former experience on the field lending added

---

[41] "Richard Arlen and Wife Part," *Los Angeles Times*, July 16, 1938, A1.

[42] Read Kendall, "Around and About in Hollywood," *Los Angeles Times*, November 21, 1938, 24.

[43] "Richard Arlen Divorced," *New York Times*, September 5, 1945, 19.

[44] Read Kendall, "Arlen Awaits Word on Contract," *Los Angeles Times*, August 8, 1938, A18.

[45] Read Kendall, "Arlen May Accept Offer for Play," *Los Angeles Times*, October 5, 1938, 11.

[46] His distinctive voice reportedly the result of a childhood accident: the roof of his mouth was punctured by a curtain rod, and the slow-healing wound altered his voice permanently. While there were a few other versions of how Devine acquired his distinctive gravely wheeze, this was the one reported most often.

credibility to his performance. Carl Laemmle, Jr., and the other studio heads were sufficiently impressed with his work, and immediately signed him up for another film, and to a contract as well.[47]

Devine starred or co-starred in more than fifty films over the next eight years before his teaming with Arlen. Almost half of them were loan-outs to other studios, including Warner Brothers, Paramount, MGM, 20th Century-Fox, and RKO, as well as to indies Selznick International (the William Wellman-directed *A Star is Born*, 1937) and Walter Wanger Productions (John Ford's classic *Stagecoach*, 1939); both independents released through United Artists. An informal survey among casting directors was conducted in 1938 asking who their favorite "go-to" supporting players were: Devine tied for ninth place, with Mischa Auer, Beulah Bondi, Walter Connolly, Edward Everett Horton, Jean Hersholt, Donald Meek, Alan Mowbray, and Frank Morgan topping the list.[48] Given the quirky-type roles Devine usually played, some of these "winners" would never have been any sort of serious competition; Devine's charm was unique, his services always in demand.

In August 1937, the upcoming Broadway production of John Steinbeck's *Of Mice and Men* was slated to star actor Victor McLaglen in the role of "Lennie." Hollywood became interested in the play, and it was assumed that McLaglen would be awarded the filmed role as well. Assumptions were turned on their heads, however, when it was reported that Devine would play "Lennie" to Burgess Meredith's "George" in the film to be directed by Lewis Milestone for producer Hal Roach.[49] The role, of course, eventually went to Lon Chaney, Jr., who gave one of the best performances of his career. As for the Broadway play, it ran at New York's *Music Box Theater* for two-hundred-and-seven performances from November 1937 through May 1938, with Broderick Crawford appearing in the role of Lennie.[50] McLaglen starred in Roach's *Captain Fury* instead, released a half-year before the Steinbeck film—a peace offering, perhaps?

At Universal, the success of Devine's *The Spirit of Notre Dame* led to another football-themed film the following year, 1932's *The All-American*. This film is notable in that it is the first to co-star Devine and Arlen as the two leads, with Arlen on rare loan-out from Paramount; this only happened three other times during his eleven-year association with the studio. And now, seven years later, the two actors were to be re-teamed.

---

[47] Grace Kingsley "Andy Devine Signs," *Los Angeles Times*, September 24, 1931, A9.

[48] "Unstarred Favorites Named by Directors," *Boxoffice*, July 9, 1938, page unknown.

[49] Philip K. Scheuer, "Devine Likely for 'Of Mice and Men,'" *Los Angeles Times*, August 25, 1937, A18.

[50] "News of the Stage," *New York Times*, May 21, 1938, page unknown.

Stop Yellin'

Arlen reported to Universal studios in early February 1939,[51] but did not have a whole lot to do until the initial entry's production was to commence April 1.[52] The scheduled starting date was delayed for a week, however, because Devine had to fulfill a previous loan-out commitment at Paramount. As a result, Arlen made a hasty trip over to Columbia for a starring role opposite Rochelle Hudson in the low-budget feature *Missing Daughters*; filming of this Columbia programmer began the week of February 20,[53] with release three months later.

As previously mentioned, Pivar's charge with this series—indeed for most of the films he was to make for Universal—was to incorporate as much stock footage as possible from Universal's vast film library, thereby imparting the appearance of production values not actually covered in each film's modest budget. Heavy utilization of stock footage was a time-honored approach to keeping costs down, but in the wrong hands could result in a schizophrenic on-screen mess. This, of course, depended on the studio and the time and care "lavished" on a given production, with wildly varying results that could be slickly incorporated and visually seamless, or clumsy, slap-dash efforts. The potential problems with this approach were numerous: marrying new footage with older footage shot at a different camera speed; older footage of poor visual quality due to age, abuse, or differing film stock; poorly matched shots where the action or lighting in one shot fails to dovetail with the next; characters appearing out of nowhere and disappearing just as quickly; occasionally recognizable actors from other, older films; and awkward, occasionally absurdist dialog introduced solely to account for the on-screen incongruities to follow. Rear screen projection might place crisply focused foreground actors and props in front of grainy background action, lessening or totally destroying the sought-after on-screen "reality." Happily, Universal was one of the slicker studios when it came to the creative and comparatively convincing use of older footage, but they had their unfortunate moments as well.

While the inclusion of stock footage may be blatantly obvious to today's viewers of these films, this is due in part to the familiarity of the reused footage. Nighttime shots of police cars and gangsters' cars careening through city streets have been used and reused so many times in films and older television series that their presence draws attention to itself. Films originally released in the thirties and forties became part of numerous film packages released to television, affording the interested viewer the opportunity to watch and rewatch these films repeatedly from the 1950s on. While not as prevalent as they were in the fifties and sixties, older films remain readily available to this

---

[51] Read Kendall, "Arlen Returns," *Los Angeles Times*, February 16, 1939, A17.

[52] "Pivar Signed to Produce Seven Arlen Starters," *Boxoffice*, February 18, 1939, 60-A.

[53] Edwin Schallert, "Movieland Jottings and Castings," *Los Angeles Times*, February 17, 1939, 15.

day at various cable outlets such as Turner Classic Movies, and on release to DVD. It was a totally different situation back when the films were first released. Looked upon as a dispensable medium, a given film saw a brief release and then, with only a few exceptions, shelved. Or, in the most egregious instances, destroyed. If a patron failed to see a film upon its initial release, in most instances that was the sole opportunity unless it made a follow-up appearance at a second-run theater or on a Saturday matinee. As a result, any footage lifted from a film and reused a number of years later could, if handled properly, appear as new footage, its previous use having faded from memory. Pivar's *Legion of Lost Flyers* is a perfect example of this, with its voluminous use of footage from the seven-year-old *Air Mail* so skillfully and seamlessly integrated that only those who saw the earlier film might recognize the inserted footage. Even that is doubtful in that the average viewer would have seen literally hundreds of other films during that seven-year gap, rendering recognition of the random piece of older film close to nil.

    Pivar knew that the best way to ensure the seamless and convincing incorporation of older stock footage into any given film would require that he have a competent director who would keep this eventual celluloid marriage foremost in mind, supported by an experienced cinematographer who could light and shoot footage that would best match and cut with the stock footage. And, equally important, an editor who would instinctively know exactly which library footage would best integrate with the new material, when and where to cut, and just how long to retain any one length of footage. For this latter position Pivar got just the man he wanted, an experienced editor named Maurice E. Wright.

    Pivar had known Wright for the past ten years, since Pivar's work as editor on Frank Capra's airborne epic *Flight* back at Columbia in 1929; uncredited newbie Wright had assisted Pivar with the cutting. Wright quickly became a full-fledged editor at Columbia where he worked on several dozen films, including a handful of the Buck Jones westerns that Pivar supervised. During his stint at Columbia, Wright also became one of the go-to editors for Capra's early thirties films, handling the chores on *Ladies of Leisure*, *Rain or Shine* (both 1930), *Dirigible*, *The Miracle Woman* (both 1931), *Forbidden*, and *American Madness* (both 1932). Nearly forty years later, Wright commented on the value of this association: "Frank Capra is not only an actor's director, but he is a great technician as well," he declared. "It was not unusual for Capra to shoot much more film than he could possibly use in order to allow for the development of a picture with editing. For example, more than a million feet of film were shot to make *Dirigible* as compared with two hundred thousand to four hundred thousand feet for an average picture. And even this much must be edited down to about ten thousand feet in the final version seen by viewers. In looking at the 'dailies,' Capra considered everything that had been filmed and then chose the best of all."[54]

This certainly was not standard operating procedure at the otherwise tight-with-a-buck Columbia, nor would it be later on at Universal. Whether Wright's assignment to the Capra Columbians was at Capra's request or the whims of the studio is unknown, but if it was the former you would not know it from Capra's 1971 autobiography, *The Name Above the Title*, where in typical fashion the egotistical, then-retired director failed to mention the poor fellow's name or modest contributions even once in that weighty tome's 495 pages (Gene Havlick, Wright's successor as Capra's "golden boy" editor, managed a whopping three mentions). Oh, the indignities suffered by the weary troops.

Wright left Columbia in 1933 and after a three-film stint for Fox hooked up with Universal in 1934, where he cut several dozen more films over the next five years before Pivar was hired by the studio. Two of these, coincidentally, were for Ben's brother Murray, who served in the capacity of associate producer for a short while in 1935: *Storm Over the Andes* and *Chinatown Squad*. The former of these happened to be directed by seasoned veteran Christy Cabanne as well, the director to whom Wright was about to become closely associated; Cabanne would direct and Wright would edit the first five films of Pivar's new Arlen-Devine series. It would quickly prove to be a good working relationship, with Wright's experience and comfort functioning within time and budgetary constraints a big plus.

Mutiny on the Blackhawk
(Director: Christy Cabanne; Released August 1, 1939)

Filming of the first in the series finally commenced in late April, the initial entry of what would eventually grow to a fourteen-picture series produced by Pivar. The first seven of these were announced by general sales manager William A. Scully at the 1939 annual sales convention as "seven outdoor dramas," along with forty features, seven Johnny Mack Brown westerns, four serials, thirteen two-reel and forty-three one-reel subjects.[55] Series titles were eventually announced in the trades two months later,[56] although these would undergo significant changes or be scrapped altogether in the ensuing months: *Mutiny on the Blackhawk* and *Man from Montreal* survived as listed; *Air Express* and *Steel* would become *Legion of Lost Flyers* and *Hot Steel*, respectively; and *Way*

---

[54] "Frank Capra Film Festival at L.A. Museum," *Pasadena Star-News*, August 1, 1971, page unknown.

[55] "Universal Lists 40 Feature Films," *New York Times*, April 18, 1939, page unknown.

[56] "7 Productions with Richard Arlen—Andy Devine," full-page ad in *Boxoffice*, June 17, 1939, 15.

of the West, *Raging Rivers*, and *Sea Patrol* would fall by the wayside, replaced with new storylines altogether. The ad was, in fact, already out of date when it appeared; *Dark Empire*, later to be renamed *Tropic Fury*, had been announced as the second in the series two weeks earlier.[57]

Pivar had pieced together a short story he titled *In Old California*, written with available stock footage in mind, an action that may very well have worked to the completed film's detriment. Screenwriter Michael L. Simmons adapted, having left his former haunts at Columbia to pen this and the following entry in the series. *Boxoffice* magazine attributed the original story to author Harold Bell Wright,[58] but this credit is doubtful.

In Old California began filming on Wednesday, April 26, 1939, with a ten-day shooting schedule and a projected budget of $73,000, less than half the $160,000 per film stated in Universal's promotional materials a mere month before. Three days of sunlight were required for exterior scenes, which they managed to squeeze in around foggy working conditions. In order to stay on schedule, three nights of work were required lasting until approximately 10:00 p.m. each night. Filming wrapped late in the day Saturday, May 6—six-day work weeks were the norm back then—right on schedule. The film discarded its somewhat colorless working title during post-production, acquiring the more action-promising *Mutiny on the Blackhawk*. If this new label was intended to evoke fond memories of the MGM Gable-Laughton spectacular of four years earlier, the similarity ended there, with Pivar's low-rent *Mutiny on the Blackhawk* a far cry from the classic *Mutiny on the Bounty*.

A (slightly) more elaborate musical score than usual was planned for recording the week of May 22, but was delayed by a week when the facilities were needed for director Rowland V. Lee's *The Sun Never Sets*. The completed film was previewed on June 6 and shipped on June 13. With the enhanced score, more complex editing than initially anticipated, some extra royalties and other delayed charges, the final budget came in at $78,000, $5,000 over the projected budget. This final cost included the studio's customary 25% overhead.

The two leads made an attractive team. Arlen, with his youthful good looks (although pushing forty when the series started), could play the rugged action hero in his sleep, but was equally adept at handling the occasional comedic role as well. Devine was Devine, the big husky lug who was there primarily for comedic relief even when the film itself was not a comedy—and that's what the audiences wanted and expected.

---

[57] "Cabanne on 'Dark Empire,'" *Boxoffice*, June 3, 1939, 36.
[58] "Arlen Starter Set," *Boxoffice*, February 25, 1939, 40.

Stop Yellin'

At the helm of *Mutiny on the Blackhawk* was veteran director Christy Cabanne, a position he would fill for the remainder of the series' first-season offerings as well. A graduate of the US Naval Academy at Annapolis, Cabanne had a brief career in the Navy before entering film as an actor for D.W. Griffith at Biograph in 1910. Promoted to Griffith's assistant, Cabanne eventually moved into direction under Griffith's supervision in 1913. This association served him well, opening doors at studios, including Majestic, Mutual, Metro, Goldwyn, Columbia, and Robertson-Cole, for numerous projects of varying prestige throughout the silent era, directing the likes of the Gish sisters, Douglas Fairbanks, and Francis X. Bushman. With the coming of sound, however, Cabanne's career had taken somewhat of a dive, relegated to quickies at such Poverty Row studios as Monogram, Tiffany, and Mascot, with the occasional borderline-prestigious project at RKO and a sole effort for Universal in mid-1937. This latter film, announced as *Detective Crane* but released as *The Westlake Case*, was the first in what was to be a new series that petered out after another two entries.[59] But now the fifty-one-year-old director was faced with an opportunity to inject some life into his foundering career, and he signed on. The teaming of Pivar and Cabanne was prominently announced in the trades.[60]

1840: With the ports of African slave trade closed, traders have turned to the islands of the South Pacific as a new source for human trafficking, smuggling their illicit cargo into the US. Military Intelligence assigns Army Captain Robert Lawrence (Richard Arlen) to investigate the problem at its source, the Sandwich Islands,[61] where the Kanakas natives are prime targets. Traveling incognito as a writer, Lawrence runs across the Captain (Noah Beery), his First Mate Blake (Guinn Williams), and crew of the *Blackhawk* hanging around a native village. He grows suspicious of their motives, especially when he notes that their ship is sitting so low in the water. When they leave, Lawrence stows away on the ship, but is discovered and put to work with the rest of the crew, who believe their cargo to be cocoa. They soon learn otherwise when they discover the hold filled with Kanakas slaves, but the heavily armed officers keep them at bay.

---

[59] "News of the Screen," *New York Times*, July 17, 1937, page unknown.

[60] Such as the half-page ad in *Boxoffice Records: Season 1938-1939*, 72.

[61] So named by British Captain James Cook on his third visit in 1778, in honor of his patron John Montagu, the fourth earl of Sandwich. The islands eventually acquired the native name Hawai'i. While the third time may have been the charm for Cook, the fourth wasn't; the natives killed him on his next visit. On an unrelated note, Montagu's love of meat between two slabs of bread provided the tasty assemblage its name for centuries to come.

The Arlen-Devine Series, Part I (1939-1940)

Slave-running Captain introduces undercover Army officer Lawrence to "Slim" in *Mutiny On the Blackhawk* (1939). Left to right: Noah Beery, Richard Arlen, Andy Devine, Mamo Clark, unidentified.

Taking a roundabout route to avoid the authorities, the ship's food and water soon run low, and only the officers are well fed. Crewmember Jock (Paul Fix) observes this and spreads the word amongst the starving crew. A fleeting moment of rebellious feelings is quickly stamped out when Jock is seized, whipped, and thrown overboard. Later on, though, when food and water run perilously low, the Captain decides that the entire human cargo—$20,000 worth—should be thrown overboard. Lawrence learns of this and tries to incite the crew to mutiny, but is forced to hide when he is ratted on by crewmember Coombs (Byron Foulger). Sneaking into the hold, he cuts the chains of the slaves, who revolt the next day as they are to be thrown overboard. The Captain and Blake are put in chains, and Lawrence's new friend and accomplice "Slim" Collins (Andy Devine) is made the new Captain. Lawrence tells the slaves' leader Woni (Mala) that they'll head back to the island where they can "take care" of their ruthless chief who sold them into slavery for gold. Slim finds a huge stockpile of weapons below deck, and realizes that the Captain was a gunrunner as well as a slave trader.

Stop Yellin'

Hawaiian beauty Mamo Clark and her friend dote on Andy Devine.

A desperate need of food forces them to land at the nearest coast, which turns out to be Southern California. There they find Fort Bailey, an outpost set up five years earlier on Mexican land by Sam Bailey (Thurston Hall) and his followers, who had come in search of gold. None was found, however, and Bailey and his new young Russian bride Tania (Sandra Kane) have frittered away supplies on endless parties. The residents of the fort tell Bailey they want to return east, which would make the Mexican garrison posted two days away at Simona very happy since Bailey has failed repeatedly to pay his taxes.

Lawrence, Slim, and the two hundred crewmen and slaves arrive looking for food and provisions, but Bailey and Tania nix this. One look and Bailey's daughter Helen (Constance Moore) falls for Lawrence, and convinces daddy to relent and give them all a meal. When Lawrence learns of the Mexican garrison, he borrows Helen's horse and rides to meet with the garrison's commanding officer, General Romero (Francisco Maran). Lawrence uses the thinly-veiled threat of two hundred armed men to coerce the fellow to agree to deliver the desperately needed supplies to the fort.

Tania is actually a spy for Romero, and she has gotten word to him that if he stonewalls Lawrence the rest of the fort's residents will return east. Lawrence returns to the fort and tells the residents that food is on its way, but the initial response of jubilation is cut short when a note arrives from Romero: Lawrence's visit was viewed as an unfriendly act, and coupled with the refusal to pay taxes the fort's residents must pack up and get out—or else. Instead, Lawrence has the slaves come over from the moored ship and set up shelters within the fort, their new home until supplies are secured. Bailey is not happy, and Tania takes off under the dark of night to inform Romero. He assembles his troops for the battle ahead.

Kit Carson (Richard Lane) arrives at the fort, and announces he is part of General Freemont's (Charles Trowbridge) unit stationed nearby. Lawrence knows Freemont, so he heads over and gets the needed supplies, ostensibly for his crew and slaves. Instead, he returns and gives it to the fort's collective

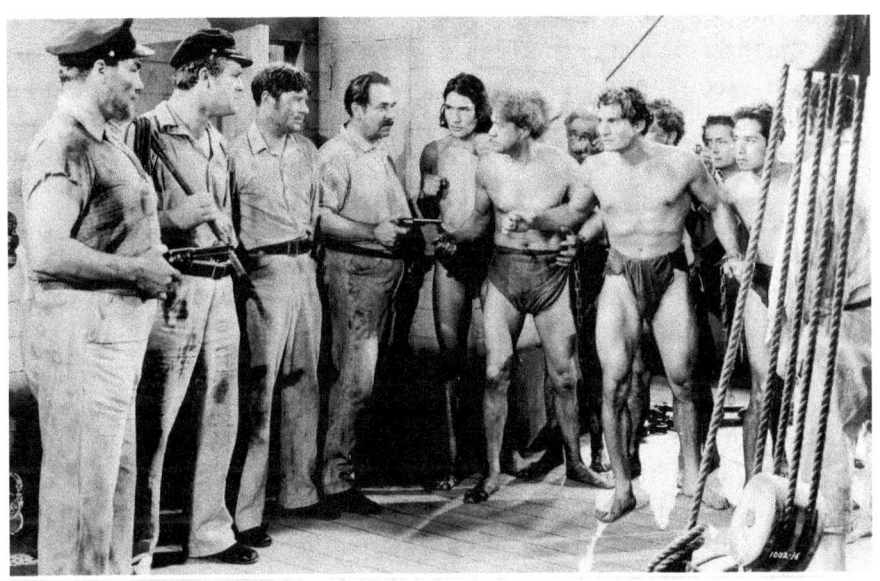

Noah Beery (center) and crew hold rebellious slaves at bay while helpless Richard Arlen looks on. De facto slave leader Mala at center, Guinn Williams second from left.

residents. When their feast is interrupted by the Mexican troops' approach, Lawrence reveals his true identity and rouses the bunch of them to action. Armed, and with boulder-and-log booby traps assembled high up on the cliffs, they await the Mexicans' arrival while a rider goes for support from Freemont. The Mexicans arrive and are held at bay until Freemont's troops arrive and drive them away. Woni is shot during the conflict, living long enough for Lawrence to promise the return of the surviving natives to their island. The American flag is hoisted over Fort Bailey.

Lawrence prepares to set sail back to the Sandwich Islands, and promises Helen that he'll return once he has fulfilled his promise to Woni. Instead, Helen insists on accompanying him on his voyage, marriage and babies her goal. Slim charges after them through the surf in a desperate attempt to escape the man-hungry widow (Mabel Albertson) who has had her eye on him.

The on-screen results look more like two films than one, the first half set aboard the *Blackhawk*, with its beleaguered slaves, and the second half concerning the protection of a colony of border settlers from the approaching Mexican troops. Stock footage was integrated as needed, with bits of director James Cruze's 1936 *Sutter's Gold* in evidence, and the latter part of the film incorporating liberal amounts of Napoleonic Alpine warfare footage from the 1933 Deutsche Universal-Film production *The Rebel* (1933; Luis Trenker). These later scenes were accompanied by the familiar "galloping" music of Franz von Suppé's 1866 "The Light Cavalry Overture," recognizable to viewers today as much from Warner Brothers cartoons as anywhere else. Film historian William K. Everson commented on the stock footage: "The unique photographic style of the latter doesn't entirely match, but is led up to by a quick insert of Andy Devine (new footage) asking his western confreres why they are wearing Tyrolean feathered hats. Not too convincingly, but quite effectively, they reply that when they go into battle they wear those hats to remind them of the old country!"[62] Everson's memory was slightly faulty here; Devine stops one of the colorfully dressed men and comments, "That's a cute suit. Where did you get it?" The response: "I'm a Swiss. Many of us came out with Mr. Bailey." Still, it gets the point across; creative connecting dialog at its best.

New York's *Brooklyn Eagle*, which tended to review films primarily for their entertainment value and with few pretensions, commented on the film's dual nature: "[The film] turns out to be a double feature all by itself. It would more appropriately be called 'Mutiny on the Blackhawk, and Here Comes the Army,' for its story is nearly parted in the middle, the first half being given over to dirty-work at sea, the second detailing a bang-up war in the Fort Bailey country near the Mexican border in the 1840s. But partitioned though it is, 'M on the B' is action every foot of the way and so adds up to something of a field day for the thriller fans."[63]

Howard Barnes of the *New York Herald Tribune* had a similar, albeit less positive, reaction: "The Rialto's patrons are not sticklers for dramatic sense, but even they are likely to be slightly baffled by the film. Something of a cross between 'Mutiny on the Bounty' and 'Man of Conquest,' the film skips blithely from maritime melodrama to Wild West shindigs with as little sustained continuity as any photoplay has had for some time … The narrative is really

---

[62] William K. Everson, "Movies Out of Thin Air: A Minor Art Form," *The New School Program Notes, Film Series 36: Program #3*, February 22, 1980.

[63] Herbert Cohn, "'Mutiny on Blackhawk' On B'klyn Strand Bill," *Brooklyn Eagle*, September 29, 1939, 13.

hit or miss. There is a certain amount of factual history in the show, but it is preposterously garbled."[64]

New York Times critic Bosley Crowther, on the other hand, remarked on the film's duality with his familiar condescending tone directed toward films of this sort: "... even considering the fact that 'Mutiny on the Blackhawk' is probably the first double feature to be combined into a single bill, it seems unnecessarily extended. 'We've got a long haul ahead of us,' said Guinn Williams, the First Mate, at the outset of the voyage. And he was referring just to the first half of the picture."[65]

Boxoffice was more succinct, simply calling it "a curious combination of rousing sea melodrama and an outdoor western."[66] *Variety* was a bit more charitable, commenting favorably on the leads' "individual efforts and several standout secondary performances," but singling out Simmons' uneven screenplay for criticism: "... the story never quite makes up its mind whether to be historic, romantic, outright western or a sea meller." Having said that, the reviewer complimented Cabanne's direction for making "some thin material seem worthwhile."[67]

While the critics may have felt indifferent toward the film, the public enjoyed it. One pleased exhibitor wrote to the *Motion Picture Herald* with his reaction to the first series offering: "We believe you will be surprised at the plot, action, and humor in this show. It is excellent, and did excellent business doubled with 'You're Not So Tough,' Universal. I believe that the program picture, well made, will show a more consistent profit for the subsequent run than the 'A' product...."[68]

Arlen and Devine provide the hoped-for enjoyable mix of personalities, and click as a team. Arlen handles all of the film's he-man chores, duking it out with Williams (and winning!), staring down Francisco Maran's cool Mexican general, and reducing Constance Moore to a quivering heap of lustful female flesh with one charming glance. (In a middle-aged man's fantasy world, Arlen almost always ends up with love interests half his age in this series.) Devine provides the somewhat dubious humor, running the gamut from amusing (his ongoing interplay with the widow, and her reminiscences of her former husbands: "Big strappin' fellows") to the infantile (his introductory tickling session; bopping

---

[64] Howard Barnes, "Mutiny on the Blackhawk," *New York Herald Tribune*, August 2, 1939, 14.

[65] Bosley Crowther, "The Screen," *New York Times*, August 2, 1939, 17.

[66] "Review Flashes: Mutiny on the Blackhawk," *Boxoffice*, June 17, 1939, 30-H.

[67] "Mutiny on the Blackhawk," *Variety*, August 9, 1939, 14.

[68] "What the Picture Did for Me," letter from William C. Clark, *Motion Picture Herald*, April 11, 1942, 50.

opponents on their heads during the otherwise straightforward and violent mutiny) to flat out unfunny. Cheap and easy laughs, all of 'em.

Joining Arlen and Devine in *Mutiny on the Blackhawk* was newcomer Constance Moore, a former band singer hired by Universal while still a teenager in 1937. She was part of the studio's "seven-year talent plan" implemented in late 1936 to provide potential stars for upcoming productions.[69] Moore appeared in several uncredited bit parts before moving up to romantic lead in a string of B's for directors including Joseph H. Lewis, S. Sylvan Simon, and James Whale. A series of low-budget musicals followed, interspersed with numerous bits and leads in B's as well as the occasional A, among these the George Marshall-directed W.C. Fields' classic *You Can't Cheat an Honest Man* (1939). At the end of her contract with Universal in 1940, Moore switched over to Paramount for a handful of films before eventually ending up in a number of musicals at Republic. Her film career ended with 1947's *Hit Parade of 1947*.

Veteran bad guy Noah Beery played the *Blackhawk's* villainous Captain. Born in 1884 and older brother to actor Wallace Beery, Noah had begun his stage career around the turn of the century, entering film in the later teens. More than a hundred films followed, with Beery quickly acquiring the reputation of the quintessential heavy in both westerns and dramas alike in films such as *The Mark of Zorro* (as Sergeant Gonzales), *The Sea Wolf* (as "Wolf" Larsen), and *Beau Geste* (as Sergeant Lejaune). After a smooth transition to sound, Beery continued on primarily in character roles, never attaining the success and popularity of his younger brother.

Actor Richard Lane was borrowed from MGM when production of *Stronger Than Desire* was delayed at that studio. Chosen for the smaller role of Kit Carson,[70] Lane had previous experience with director Cabanne in RKO's *The Outcasts of Poker Flats* (1937).

The rest of the cast was populated with dependables. Guinn Williams is quick with his fists and a frightening presence as the *Blackhawk's* ruthless First Mate, but there are several distracting moments when his lighter, more humorous, side threatens to creep in. Thurston Hall's Sam Bailey comes across like a blustery Edward Arnold—chosen for the role perhaps to match with *Sutter's Gold* stock footage inserts with glimpses of that film's star Arnold—and newcomer Sandra Kane is attractively calculating as Bailey's Russian bride; this was to be her sole film role. Hawaiian Mamo Clark is lovely in her

---

[69] "The company is selecting clever unknowns possessing the earmarks of ability to become star or featured players and signing them to seven-year contracts and then starting them on an intensive and continuous course of training." Wesley Smith, "The March of Finance," *Los Angeles Times*, October 23, 1936, 19.

[70] "Edwin Schallert, Richard Lane Will Portray Kit Carson," *Los Angeles Times*, May 3, 1939, A10.

tiny part as one of two native girls tickling a wildly-giggling Devine, and Mala is adequately stoical as the de facto leader of the freed slaves. Eddy Waller's parson keeps popping up in inserts praying to the Almighty, and, in retrospect, I guess it worked.

The marriage of new and stock footage is for the most part handled smoothly, resulting in a bigger-budget look from a small-budget production. There are some rough spots, though, that belie the process. New shipboard footage only uses rear-projection once or twice to show the sea and sky beyond, the bulk of the shots having that give-away blank "dead" sky beyond. These latter shots are jarring when intercut with stock footage displaying sea and sky and the great outdoors as backdrop. Some of that stock footage is quite spectacular, such as the natives diving into the sea one after another from high up on the *Blackhawk*'s masts, and the construction and unleashing of the five log-and-boulder devices on the unsuspecting and helpless Mexican troops far below. *Mutiny on the Blackhawk* was a fine introductory film for the new series, and delivered exactly what Universal had hoped for—a programmer with a near-A film look.

Tropic Fury
(Director: Christy Cabanne; Released October 13, 1939)

Universal was experiencing growth under its new management, with 2,500 employees on its payroll—an all-time high—and seven productions underway in May, the maximum number that studio facilities could accommodate. Close to a half-million dollars was being spent on new equipment and construction, with the goal to have nine films in production by July 1939; this, too, would be an all-time high for the studio.[71] Pivar's next with Arlen and Devine, tentatively titled *Dark Empire*, was scheduled as one of the additional two productions to be underway by that time, scheduled for a June 27 start.[72]

Arlen's mind was elsewhere during this period, preoccupied by two other events affecting his life. First was the requirement to attend a trial during the break between films, to act in his own defense against a suit brought by Sam Jaffe, Inc. theatrical agency for the collection of $19,600 in commissions.[73] This was put on a back burner, however, when the trial was postponed for three months when Arlen had to fly home to St. Paul, Minnesota, to be with his eighty-two-year-old mother, who was dying.[74]

---

[71] "Studio Adds to Payroll," *Los Angeles Times*, May 30, 1939, A18.

[72] "Cabanne on 'Dark Empire,'" *Boxoffice*, June 3, 1939, 36.

[73] "Richard Arlen Trial Delayed by Illness," *Los Angeles Times*, May 17, 1939, A3.

[74] "Arlen Flies to Side of Dying Mother," *Los Angeles Times*, May 10, 1939, A18.

Life was looking good for Pivar, with a young son, a lovely and socially active wife, and his new position with Universal that promised a long, comfortable, and secure future. Befitting his status as a full-fledged producer, Pivar purchased a new home at 10135 Valley Spring Lane for approximately $10,000. Built four years earlier in 1935 and located in the Toluca Lake section of Los Angeles, the 3,690-square-foot, four-bedroom, three-bath house was in close proximity to the Universal studios. Across the street was a golf course, beyond that a small shallow river, then the back lot of Universal studios. Aside from a few Pepper trees, the view of Universal from Pivar's home was unobstructed.

By the time it went into production on June 27, *Dark Empire* had acquired the name of the story it was based on, *Fury in the Tropics*, but would eventually be released in October as *Tropic Fury*. The story, an original co-authored by Pivar (uncredited) and Maurice Tombragel, and again written for the screen by Michael L. Simmons, is a grab-bag of clichés rolled into one big mindless adventure, complete with the missing professor who's been tortured into insanity, and the determined daughter on a relentless search to find him. Cabanne returned to direct.

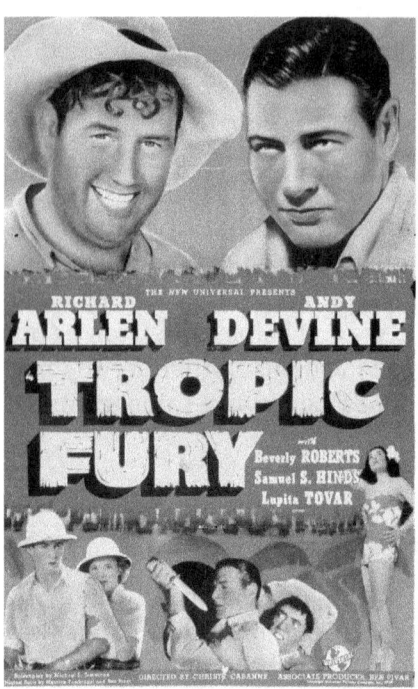

Universal didn't always go all out with their poster art and design for their B films. Image courtesy of Heritage Auction Galleries, Ha.com.

Ohio-based Waterford Rubber Company owner J.P. Waterford (Samuel S. Hinds) wants to set up a South American operation in the Amazon, selecting laboratory head Dan Burton (Richard Arlen) to head down to Guamao's interior to scout out suitable locations. Burton agrees to go, with the primary intention of finding out what happened to Dr. Taylor, sent down earlier and never heard from again.

Arriving in Guamao and trolling for guides, Burton finds the resident natives all terrified of heading up the Guamao River. Burton is told to go see a fellow named Gallon (Leonard Mudie), who has the inside track on hiring natives. Gallon was alerted to Burton's mission by a telegram sent by Thomas Snell (Milburn Stone), a plant back in the Waterford offices. Gallon introduces Burton to Judith Adams (Beverly Roberts), an archaeologist hoping to head up

The Arlen-Devine Series, Part I (1939-1940)

river as well, but tells Burton he can't help him. Soon after, a pair of thugs hired by Gallon attempt to poison Burton, but is thwarted when bartender Tynan "Tiny" Andrews (Andy Devine) spots them trying to spike Burton's drink. After a fight with Burton and Tiny, the battered thugs flee the bar and return to Gallon, telling him that Burton was killed so that they can collect their pay.

Gallon has his man Soledad (Adia Kuznetzoff) con a bunch of natives to go to work on the plantation of a brutal fellow named Scipio (Lou Merrill), turning them over to his henchman Hannibal (Noble Johnson) for the trip. Soledad tells Judith he'll take her up the river, planning to turn her over to Scipio as a present. Soledad wants to marry Scipio's daughter Maria (Lupita Tovar), and hopes that Scipio will look favorably upon the union as a result of this female offering. Arriving at the plantation, Scipio accepts Judith into his home, but whips Soledad for his impertinence when marriage to Maria is mentioned. Meanwhile, Burton has learned that Judith has headed up river, so he signs on to Hannibal's work crew in order to follow, convincing the now-jobless Tiny to join him.

It doesn't take long to realize that all the workers are essentially slaves to Scipio, whipped or locked in stocks if they fail to perform, and tracked by bloodhounds if they escape. (There's a grisly snippet of stock footage employed showing a bunch of hungry crocodiles chowing down on a hapless worker.) Scipio, a short fellow with a Napoleonic complex, tells Judith about "the Professor," a fellow who has lost his mind but still reads to Scipio. "The Professor" turns out to be the long-missing Dr. Taylor (Charles Trowbridge, who does "mad" rather well), and Judith is shocked when she sees him. Judith Adams, it turns out, is actually Judith Taylor, his daughter; her father's disappearance the real reason for her trip to Guamao. When Burton sees Judith with Scipio, he is convinced that she is part of Scipio's crooked setup.

Burton clandestinely documents the brutalities prevalent at the plantation, with the intention of eventually having Scipio arrested. Hannibal discovers Burton's notes and takes them to Scipio. Unable to read English, he turns to Judith who makes up a translation on the spot, promoting that Burton is nothing more than an insectologist. Scipio falls for this. Later, Burton stumbles across Judith searching Scipio's room, and the two quickly realize they both have the same goal of locating Dr. Taylor. Soledad sees them leave together and reports back to Scipio, who has "the Professor" brought in to reread Burton's notes. Which he does, and accurately, exposing Burton. Soon after, Burton and Judith grab Taylor and attempt to escape, but are captured by Gallon who is just now arriving at the plantation. Gallon, having thought Burton to be dead, is startled to see him alive and well. Scipio has Burton placed in the stocks.

Maria, who has grown fond of Burton, delivers a message to Tiny: "Today is the day." Word is quickly passed around among the workers, who organize and revolt. Burton is freed, Hannibal receives a machete to his skull, Soledad suffers a similar fate by ax, Scipio is shot dead, and Gallon is taken prisoner; the workers are now free. Cut to days later when Burton and Judith speak of marriage, as do Tiny and Maria. The plantation is rich with rubber trees, and an offer from Waterford to lease it from Maria is turned over to her husband-to-be Tiny, whose future now looks rosy. Dr. Taylor sits nearby, seemingly (and inexplicably) recovered from his former madness.

"A thousand dollar bill—torn in half—starts the strangest, most exciting story ever lived or played." Or so claimed Universal's publicity.[75] *Variety* was not impressed by the results, which the reviewer summarized as "pretty tepid stuff … Stereotype yarn has a few mild laughs, but lacks suspense or a moving climax. Direction is commonplace and the settings scarcely suggest authentic jungle atmosphere."[76] *The New York Times*, not too surprisingly, concurred, complaining that the film "contains all the stock inanities and insanities of the worst jungle fictions—the breezy young scientist in quest of rubber, the brutal nabob who rules a jungle-locked empire worked by impressed labor, the missing professor who has been tortured into lunacy and his beautiful daughter who has sought him with a heart full of woe. Mixed together they add up to practically nothing but a poor excuse for killing time."[77] And as negative as *The New York Times* review was, the *New York Herald Tribune* managed to "top" it in scathing fashion: "If Universal plans more pictures starring Richard Arlen and Andy Devine, something will have to be done to make them resemble entertainment … The sequences are slapped together hit or miss, creating the most miserable kind of unintentional humor. 'Tropic Fury' has little excuse for its existence."[78] Maybe in the big city, but in lots of places elsewhere they loved this stuff.

On the other hand, there were a number of reviewers who liked the film, or at least on its own low-budget terms. *The Hollywood Reporter* called it "an actionful melodrama that will fit neatly into the niche for which it is intended. Built solely for the action fans and Saturday matinee trade, picture romps through 62 minutes of suspenseful action in the jungles. Producer Ben Pivar has accounted on the screen for every dollar spent."[79] *Daily Variety* agreed: "Audiences craving melodrama in the raw will find 'Tropic Fury' to their liking. In addition to running heavy on dramatics, it also carries extensive load

---

[75] "Exhibitors' Sponsored Testimonial Pictures Delivered By Universal in August, September, and October," *Boxoffice*, August 26, 1939, 17.

[76] Hobe Morrison, "Tropic Fury," *Variety*, September 20, 1939, 12.

[77] Bosley Crowther, "The Screen: Four Films in Review," *New York Times*, September 8, 1939, 28.

[78] Robert W. Dana, "Tropic Fury," *New York Herald Tribune*, September 9, 1939, 8.

[79] "Tropic Fury," *Hollywood Reporter*, September 28, 1939, 4.

of action."[80] *Film Daily* was succinct in its appraisal: "Action story set in the tropics rates as popular entertainment."[81]

Devine's character was once again given a nickname, a trademark of sorts for the initial entries in the series, with each successive character name—Slim, Tiny, Beef, Bones, Guppy—a little bit goofier than the last. As the series grew in popularity, the scriptwriters—their collective imaginations no doubt spent by season's end—eventually settled on plain old "Andy," and stuck with it through the second season as well; Arlen's characters, too, came to be known simply as "Dick."

The daughter was portrayed by Beverly Roberts, a twenty-five-year-old actress who'd trained as a teen at Eva Le Gallienne's Civic Repertory Theatre company, and later under Maria Ouspenskaya. Spotted singing in a New York City club by a Warner Brothers talent scout, Roberts was signed to a contract in 1936 and starred in close to a dozen features before her contract's expiration in 1938. A handful of films followed at Columbia, Republic, and MGM before Universal signed her to play opposite Arlen in *Tropic Fury*, a reunion of sorts as they'd played opposite each other in the previous year's *Call of the Yukon* at Republic.

Milburn Stone, who has a tiny part in the film, was a minor actor who'd worked at practically every studio in Hollywood from the mid-thirties, appearing in roles both big and (mostly) small. His name misspelled twice in the opening and closing credits as *Milburne* Stone, this was his second film for Pivar, having effectively played a rabble-rousing striker a year-and-a-half earlier in *Mr. Boggs Steps Out*. Stone was to appear in eleven more Pivar productions over the next seven years, the bulk of them after Universal had signed him to a contract. Similarly, character actor Samuel S. Hinds, in roles of varying importance in well over one hundred films since 1932, also had a part in the film, and would appear in seven more Pivar productions in as many years. Pivar would borrow liberally from Universal's large roster of contract players for his other productions, frequently reusing those whom he was comfortable with and found to be competent and appropriate for the sort of film he was cranking out. Among these contractees were Eddy Waller and Eddie Chandler in eight films each, Frank Mitchell in six, Jack Arnold and Marc Lawrence in five each, Don Porter, Guinn Williams and Robert Armstrong in four films each, and the prizewinner, Wade Boteler, in a total of ten films. Not all of these appearances, it should be noted, were cited in the films' credits.

---

[80] "Tropic Fury," *Daily Variety*, September 28, 1939, 3.
[81] "Tropic Fury," *Film Daily*, September 8, 1939, 18.

Mexican-born actress Lupita Tovar rounded out the cast,[82] and in more ways than one. After appearing in several silents for Fox, Tovar appeared in a number of Spanish-language versions of films for several studios including Universal—George Melford's arguably better version of Tod Browning's 1931 horror sensation *Dracula* the most famous of these—before returning to Mexico for a string of features in the mid-thirties. *Tropic Fury* and RKO's *The Fighting Gringo* marked a return to film production here in the States, with a number of additional domestic productions up until her retirement from film in the mid-forties.

"[L]avishly-bedecked, star-studded, orchids-and-ermine world premieres," as *Boxoffice* called them, were in vogue in 1939, and new releases from two studios competed for attention on the evening of September 27. Warner Brothers trotted out their big-budget *The Private Lives of Elizabeth and Essex* at the Beverly Hills Theater, with an impressive lineup of luminaries in attendance. These included Bette Davis, Errol Flynn, Gary Cooper, Norma Shearer, Marlene Dietrich, Edward G. Robinson, John Garfield, Claudette Colbert, Douglas Fairbanks, Jr., and a bunch of lesser names, along with Warners' behind-the-scenes personnel and executives.

Slightly less—okay, *much* less—impressive was Universal's premiere of *Tropic Fury* in two Van Nuys theaters. Publicists made sure that the requisite floodlights and similar trappings were in place, but screwed up the arrangements for the "special" train chartered to haul invited guests from Hollywood to the San Fernando Valley; it was canceled at the last minute, leaving those invited guests to scramble for alternate transportation. The roster of attendees included Arlen, Devine, Mischa Auer, Hugh Herbert, Al Jolson, Marian Marsh, Bing Crosby, and Glenda Farrell, all honorary mayors of the various communities in which they resided.[83] A less impressive event, perhaps, but probably more fun.

Legion of Lost Flyers
(Director: Christy Cabanne; Released November 3, 1939)

The thoroughly enjoyable *Legion of Lost Flyers* went into production in August, a last-minute replacement for the previously scheduled third series entry, *Man from Montreal*.[84] Under Cabanne's direction, Arlen and Devine once again took on new occupations, playing pilot "Loop" Gillan and mechanic "Beef" Brumley,

---

[82] Edwin Schallert, "Lupita Tovar Joins 'Fury of Tropics,'" *Los Angeles Times*, June 19, 1939, A14.

[83] "Premieres Still Have Hold," *Boxoffice*, September 30, 1939, 38.

[84] Douglas W. Churchill, "Screen News Here and in Hollywood," *New York Times*, July 15, 1939, 14.

respectively. First-time screenwriter Maurice Tombragel adapted this Pivar original, cleverly constructing it to accommodate the stock footage already selected for incorporation. *Legion of Lost Flyers* is a poor-man's *Only Angels Have Wings*, with its well-worn hangar and planes set in mountainous Alaskan terrain near Fairbanks. Arlen is repeatedly required to perform miracles of landing and take-off, in treacherous canyons and without benefit of landing gear and the like; suspension of disbelief required in very large doses. Arlen managed to break a finger during shooting, but persevered to finish the film.[85] What a trouper.

Filming commenced on Wednesday, July 26, with a tight nine-day schedule and even tighter $68,750 budget. Numerous process shots (aka, rear projection) along with snow and fog effects contributed to the difficulty of the shoot, requiring cast and crew to continue working after dinner break six of the nine days. Filming wrapped at 11:30 p.m. on Thursday night, August 4—right on schedule. Editing took place the weeks of August 7 and 14, with the film's musical score recorded in a combined session on Monday, August 21. Its first preview followed on Wednesday, August 23, the completed film shipped to New York the following Wednesday; the final budget came in at $69,000. Working in close accord, Pivar and Cabanne once again demonstrated their ability to bring in a film on schedule and within, or close to, budget.

A small charter plane carrying five Acme Steel Mill executives loses its left motor and spirals earthward. All passengers are killed, but the pilot, believed to be internationally famous airman Gene "Loop" Gillan (Richard Arlen), bails out shortly before the crash and survives. Gillan's name is soon splashed over headlines nationwide as the man responsible, the pilot who "chickened out."

The Desert Airport up in northern Alaska is a refuge for pilots with a past who can't get jobs elsewhere. When the assembled group, which includes mechanic "Beef" Brumley (Andy Devine), radio operator Blinkey (David Willock), and pilots Frenchy (Leon Belasco), Jake Halley (Guinn Williams), and Smythe (Leon Ames), all read about their old associate Gillan, even this hardened bunch despise what he is reported to have done. All, that is, except for Beef, who doubts that the story is accurate. Jake and Beef have words over Gillan's alleged guilt, but boss Bill Desert (Theodor von Eltz) intervenes and sends them back to work.

Gillan arrives in a showy display of aerial maneuvers, but soon finds that he is not welcome. Beef convinces Desert to let him stay on, not as a pilot but as Beef's assistant mechanic. Gillan displays an inordinate amount of interest in Ralph Perry (William Lundigan), one of the airport's new pilots who is away on airport business. Beef is convinced that it was not Gillan who piloted and

---

[85] Hedda Hopper, "Hedda Hopper's Hollywood," *Los Angeles Times*, August 30, 1939, A14.

bailed out of the ill-fated plane, and says as much to Gillan, urging him to speak up to the others. Gillan tells him to drop it.

Ben and Judy (center and right) on the *Legion of Lost Flyers* set with unidentified friend, August 1, 1939. Photo courtesy of Jan Pivar Dacri.

Pilot Sam Bradford (Pat Flaherty) returns from a flight late one night, but has trouble landing due to the heavy fog. He crashes and dies, and both Desert and Gillan suffer burns to the arms in futile attempts to rescue the doomed pilot.

It is not long before Desert's younger girlfriend Paula Wilson (Anne Nagel) takes a liking to Gillan (don't they all?), who tries to keep her at arm's length out of respect for Desert. After she has given Gillan a ride into town, Jake makes some snide comments and he and Gillan get into a fistfight; Desert breaks up this altercation as well.

Perry returns to the airport, and is startled to see Gillan when he confronts him in the locker room. It was Perry, not Gillan, who had bailed out on the five executives, having replaced Gillan as pilot at the last minute. Gillan demands that Perry fess up to the other pilots, but when the cocky pilot refuses the two of them get into a violent fight. Desert breaks this one up as well, no doubt tiring of playing referee to this group of short-tempered "losers." Beef guesses the truth about Perry, and Gillan confirms it, but says it is his word against Perry's and no one would believe him at this stage.

Frenchy and Gillan have to fly out and hook up with young Freddy Sims (Jerry Marlow), whose plane broke down on a return trip from the Whitehead

Mining Co. with $18,000 in gold on board. When the two planes return, it is nighttime and snowing. Sims lands without mishap, but Perry grabs the radio and misguides Frenchy's plane into some power lines, hoping that Gillan will perish. Frenchy is injured in the crash and is hospitalized, but Gillan emerges with minor injuries. Desert says he is going to continue on to Fairbanks with the gold, and has Gillan prep the plane. Perry knocks Gillan cold and takes off with the plane, but he crashes into Gailwind Canyon. Declaring it inaccessible by plane, Desert calls for a rescue party, but it will be days before they'll be able to reach the injured pilot, and he'll die in the meantime.

Gillan takes matters into his own hands, forcing his way to a plane and taking off solo. He manages to land the plane in the canyon with only some minor damage. Perry tries to convince him that they should both make off with the gold, but Gillan ignores him and dumps him into the passenger seat. The takeoff is a touch-and-go effort with the wheels and axel damaged and the wings torn, but Gillan manages to get the plane into the air. Perry is terrified, and even more so when Gillan hands him the plane's radio and tells him he is going to stay up in the air until Perry radios a confession, or run out of fuel and crash while waiting. Watching the plane slowly falling apart around him, Perry radios in a full confession, absolving Gillan of all guilt. Perry chickens out once again, knocking Gillan cold and bailing out of the now-pilotless plane. The plane crashes, but Gillan survives; Perry is picked up by others. Beef brings Paula to the hospital to see Gillan, Paula "released" by Desert when he realized that she loves Gillan and not him.

Legion of Lost Flyers (1939). Image courtesy of Heritage Auction Galleries, Ha.com.

This is a good little film, due in no small part to the extensive aerial footage lifted from Universal's 1932 John Ford-directed drama *Air Mail*. The film's opening credits appear over point-of-view footage shot through a plane's windshield, flying low over snow-capped mountain peaks and pines. Soon after is the effective lead-up to the crash, with looming mountains viewed through the same windshield, growing closer and finally spinning dizzily out of control, followed by silence in the airport's radio room. There is much visually exciting aerial photography, with Sam's crash into the airfield's tower and the following conflagration handled nicely and rather spectacular looking. The miniatures, while nicely executed by in-house special-effects whiz John P. Fulton, occasionally fall short during the action. One such example takes place when Frenchy and Gillan's plane crashes into the power lines while landing, a visually convincing landscape that could pass for real up until the moment of the plane's impact when everything shakes—just like a miniature!

Much of the reused footage had been shot for the Ford mini-epic seven years earlier by German émigré Karl Freund, dictating the film's dark and oppressive visual style that had to be carefully matched by photographer John W. Boyle. The old and new footage blends seamlessly, both photographically and with Maurice Wright's tight editing. Compare this film to 20th Century-Fox's Sol Wurtzel-produced B *Tail Spin* released earlier in the year, and this film's virtues become all the more apparent. *Tail Spin* is well acted and sufficiently engaging, but its stage-bound artificiality and over abundance of unconvincing and washed-out looking rear projection is a distinct visual impediment, and like so many other of that studio's films there's simply too much talk and maudlin contrivance. *Legion of Lost Flyers* delivers the goods, and in a tight, action-packed package.

Devine is rather amusing here, and is participant in the film's one running gag. Prospector Petey (Eddy Waller) leaves his Eskimo bride Bertha (Edith Mills) in Beef's care while he is gone. Bertha drives Beef crazy, dogging his every step and with her fondness for motor grease. Beef continuously admonishes her for eating up his supplies—"Bad, bad girl!"—as if she is a disobedient pet. This sounds rather silly, but it is genuinely amusing, and Bertha's hang-dog look each and every time he yells at her is hilarious. Even a touch of the risqué is evident when Desert finds her undressing in the men's locker-room behind an oblivious Beef. "Ug" is her only response, and frequently so. *Variety* singled out newcomer Mills for the film's obligatory comic relief: "The Eskimo role, played by Edith Mills, calls for nothing more than 'ugh' and a couple of belches outside of the effective pantomime. Yen of the Esk for motor grease and the way she follows Devine around, dog-like, produces welcome surcease from the large amount of flying indulged, crashes, landings in bad weather, etc."[86] Mills would go on to play a variety of squaws and Indian women in a handful of films and TV shows over the next twenty years.

Love interest was supplied by recent Universal acquisition Anne Nagel, who would work for Pivar again in *Hot Steel*, *Mutiny in the Arctic*, and *Road Agent*. Nagel had appeared in uncredited bit parts from the early thirties at Fox and Paramount, but a contract with Warner Brothers in 1936 put her name before the public primarily in competently executed B's such as Noel M. Smith's *King of Hockey* (1936); Ray Enright's more prestigious *China Clipper* (1936) was the

---

[86] "Legion of Lost Flyers," *Variety*, November 1, 1939, 14.

happy exception. After Warners and, for that matter, the suicide of her husband, Nagel was all over the place in an endless succession of B's at Monogram and Republic, with an occasional return to Warners. Hooking up with Universal in 1939 was a fortuitous turn of events, as she had starring roles in nearly two-dozen features and several serials over the next three years. These were for the most part B's, but they were slickly-made Universal B's; *Legion of Lost Flyers* was among the first.

Also in the cast was former radio announcer William Lundigan, signed by Universal talent scouts in 1937. Lundigan finished off a two-year series of B's with this production, and then headed for greener pastures at Warners. Guinn "Big Boy" Williams, Ona Munson (fresh off of Victor Fleming's *Gone With the Wind*), Leon Ames, and Theodor Von Eltz round out the cast. Eltz's character was creatively named Bill Desert so that the *Air Mail* footage with its prominently labeled hanger—"Desert Airport"—would make sense in these frozen climes. Jack Carson has an amusing bit as the fast-talking, sensation-seeking, on-site radio announcer, providing local color to the final sequences, much to the annoyance of the airport staff.

The Hollywood Reporter's reviewer was underwhelmed by the results: "In an effort to provide audiences with tops in low-cost action pictures, producer Ben Pivar has overstepped the bounds of plausibility in trying to obtain highly suspenseful situations … Christy Cabanne's direction was handicapped by the material provided in Maurice Tombragel's screenplay of Ben Pivar's original story."[87] The *Motion Picture Herald*, on the other hand, gave *Legion* a generally favorable review, reporting that "the constant takeoffs and landings are pictorially exciting, if confusing to plot structure. The writers, Ben Pivar and Maurice Tombragel, have allowed their imaginations to soar. Action fans, however, should have a spine-tingling holiday." The review wraps up with some comments regarding the showing attended, which gives us a hint of the market for this series: "A packed audience of practically 99 and 9/10 per cent masculine constituency seemed to enjoy the aerial gymnastics in a thorough, if not fully credulous, manner."[88] One wonders if the other 1/10 per cent of the audience felt overwhelmed by the testosterone-heavy atmosphere. *Legion of Lost Flyers* saw release on November 3.

---

[87] "Arlen-Devine Hurt By Poor Material," *Hollywood Reporter*, March 12, 1940, 3.

[88] "Legion of Lost Flyers," *Motion Picture Herald*, November 4, 1939, 50.

Man from Montreal
(Director: Christy Cabanne; Released December 8, 1939)

After Devine's return from a loan-out to 20th Century-Fox for a part in Henry King's *Little Old New York*,[89] production of *Man from Montreal* commenced in September with the ubiquitous Cabanne directing. Location filming took place at Cedar Lake Camp near Big Bear in the San Bernardino Mountains, the popular film location a short two-hour drive from Los Angeles. Screenwriter Owen Francis adapted another Pivar original, and the plot, such as it is, has northwest Canada-based independent fur trapper Clark Manning (Arlen) arrested for unknowingly carrying stolen pelts. Not too surprisingly, Arlen's innocence is quickly established, a necessity in that there was only sixty-three minutes to wrap up loose ends.

Weighing in at 270 pounds, Devine, in his role as a Canadian Mounted Police constable, was required to do a lot of strenuous horseback riding. While this was not a problem for Devine, it reportedly was for the horses, with several replacements brought in after each new frantic call from Cabanne.[90] As one reviewer put it, "Andy, who seems to be gaining more weight every time you gaze upon him, fills out a uniform much in the manner of an elephant in khaki ..."[91]

Up in La Crosse, Canada, fur trapper Clark Manning (Richard Arlen, sporting a pencil-thin moustache) is in love with school teacher Myrna Montgomery (Kay Sutton), unaware that she is married to, rather than the sister of, mining engineer Ross Montgomery (Reed Hadley). Montgomery uses his business as a front for moving furs stolen by his trio of crooks led by Biff Anders (Joe Sawyer), and has Manning unwittingly take the stolen furs down river for him. When Manning is stopped by some constables and the stolen furs discovered, he plays dumb rather than implicating his girlfriend's brother. Not a wise move.

Manning's good friend and Canadian Mountain Police constable "Bones" Blair (Devine) overhears Ross and Myrna discussing their complicity in the thefts as well as their marital status, so he informs jailed Manning. Instead of taking Bones' advice and telling all to Captain Owens (Addison Richards), Manning decides to go it alone and breaks out of jail. Hearing of this, Ross has Anders shoot and kill Luther St. Paul (William Royle), another trapper who has voiced his suspicions of Anders' guilt to him. Evidence implicating Manning is left at the scene, leaving the fugitive wanted for murder as well as theft.

---

[89] Edwin Schallert, "Concentrates of the News," *Los Angeles Times*, August 2, 1939, 13.

[90] Hedda Hopper, "Hedda Hopper's Hollywood," *Los Angeles Times*, September 11, 1939, 8.

[91] "Furs and Murder," *Brooklyn Daily Eagle*, month and day unreadable, 1940, page unknown.

The Arlen-Devine Series, Part I (1939-1940)

Man from Montreal (1939).
Image courtesy of Heritage Auction Galleries, Ha.com.

Manning sneaks into Ross' home looking for evidence, but finds only the couple's marriage license. Ross and Myrna walk in on Manning, who manages to escape as Myrna heads out to alert the Mounties of Manning's presence. Both Bones and his younger sister Doris (Anne Gwynne), who's madly in love with Manning, want to help the fugitive, but the arrival of a constable results in Manning's arrest. Bones and Doris quickly hatch a plan: when he and the other constable are escorting Manning back to jail, Manning is able to dive off a cliff into the river below where Doris awaits with a canoe. Bones is suspended from duty, suspected of allowing Manning to escape.

Still pursued by constables, Manning takes refuge in Anders' mine, Anders and his two cohorts seemingly agreeable to helping him. Instead, they go get Ross and the four of them quickly work out a plan. They'll kill another trapper named Jacques (Eddy C. Waller) and steal his furs, assuming the locals will attribute the murder and theft to Manning. Manning will have "disappeared" for good, as their plan includes his murder as well.

Bones, meanwhile, has been visited by Manning, who has come to suspect Anders' complicity in the thefts. He instructs Bones to search Ross' office for evidence, and then returns to the mine. Bones finds some evidence, and overhears the gang's plans for the double murder. He alerts Captain Owens, who rounds up some constables and follows Bones to the mine. At the mine, Anders and his two cohorts have turned on Ross, realizing that he has been double-crossing them by selling furs and not splitting the receipts. A gun battle breaks out between Manning, who wants to keep Ross alive to testify, and the other gang members. Owens and his men arrive in time to rescue Manning and arrest the surviving gang members; they always get their man. Bones is reinstated as a constable, and Manning ends up with Bones' sister Doris.

One has to admire Pivar's use of stock footage in this film. There's an art of sorts to the seamless incorporation of third-party footage into a newly written story, and this is about as good as it gets. Bones and the other constable, on horseback, escort Manning through the woods and along cliffs, intercut with perfectly matching long shots from another source. Doris follows by canoe in the river below, her footage intercut as well with long shots of a canoeist navigating turbulent waters. It is such a perfect match that one must assume that Pivar studied the footage beforehand, and structured his story so that director Cabanne and photographer Milton Krasner could film and deliver multiple shots that editor Maurice Wright could later piece together with the older footage in such a way as to be virtually undetectable. They should give an Academy Award for this sort of creative cobbling! *Daily Variety* summed up Pivar's cost-cutting efforts with the throwaway "Ben Pivar never took his finger off the pulse of the budget."[92]

Man from Montreal garnered an atypically glowing review from *Variety* soon after its release in December: "Canadian Northwest Mounties are not new screen fare hence the producing of Ben Pivar, Christy Cabanne's direction and topnotch performances by Richard Arlen, Andy Devine and Anne Gwynne must be credited for this strong dual entry. It will prove a surprise package for exhibitors seeking to bolster duals." The reviewer went on to single out newcomer Gwynne: "Anne Gwynne, former bathing suit model, indicates considerable promise as a coming young actress in the role of Arlen's sweetheart."[93]

Twenty-year-old Texas-born Anne Gwynne, a former model with stage experience, was snapped up by Universal earlier in 1939, with a western and two "Baby Sandy" films under her belt before Pivar took her in. Billed as the "TNT" girl ("Trim, Neat, and Terrific"), she survived a series of bit parts in A's and leads in B's (including Pivar's *Road Agent* and *Weird Woman*) before eventually working her way down to freelancing in minor studios' B's.

Kay Sutton, whose film career was a comparatively brief one, played the film's other leading lady. Spent primarily at RKO from the mid-thirties until 1939 (and with a small role as a gangster's girlfriend in Cabanne's 1938 *This Marriage Business*), she then moved over to Republic to make the disaster quickie *S.O.S. Tidal Wave*. Several films followed for Universal, after which she

---

[92] "Man from Montreal," *Daily Variety*, May 15, 1940, 3.

[93] "Man from Montreal," *Variety*, February 28, 1940, 16.

The Arlen-Devine Series, Part I (1939-1940)

had some uncredited bit parts in films for the majors, and several leads at the minors. By the end of 1941 she'd retired from film, no doubt frustrated by her lack of success.

There's a chunky little kid named Tom Whitten in the film as well, who plays Captain Owens' son Brad. He spends most of his time decked out in a miniature constable suit, unconvincingly forcing out tears over Manning's plight. As Bones' young friend in the story, he looks like a pint-sized version of Andy Devine. A terrible actor, this appears to have been his sole film appearance—a wise decision on someone's part.

Danger on Wheels
(Director: Christy Cabanne; Released February 2, 1940)

Danger on Wheels, the fifth in the series, went before Elwood Bredell's cameras in October, released nationwide five months later in February 1940. Arlen and Devine co-starred as test car driver "Lucky" Larry Taylor and his mechanic "Guppy" Wexel, with newcomer Peggy Moran on board as love interest Pat O'Shea. Based on another Pivar original titled *Test Driver* and adapted for the screen by Maurice Tombragel, the story revolves around Atlas Motors test- (and stunt-) driver Taylor who, in spite of his skills behind the wheel, always seems to be rubbing someone the wrong way. *Danger on Wheels* is one of two Arlen-Devine films readily available today (*A Dangerous Game* is the other film) due to a failure on Universal's part to have its copyright renewed; it has entered the public domain and is now up for grabs.

Larry Taylor spends a lot of his time on the Atlas Motors proving grounds testing the firm's vehicles. Rules are rules, so he forces a trespassing young lady off the grounds, unaware that she is June Allen (Sandra King), daughter of Atlas Motors bigwig Lloyd B. Allen (Landers Stevens). The outraged girl demands that her father fire Taylor, but he instead gives Taylor a twenty-five-dollar raise due to the fellow's skills and importance to the company. Taylor makes a pass at Allen's secretary Patricia "Pat" O'Shea (Peggy Moran) on his way out, but she gives him the cold shoulder.

Taylor's mechanic buddy "Guppy" Wexel invites him back to his rooming house to see the new oil-burning motor that he and "Pop" O'Shea (Herbert Corthell) have been working on, much to O'Shea's daughter Pat's annoyance. Taylor is introduced to Eddie Dodds (John Holmes), the young fellow who is going to test drive the "O'Shea Special" at the upcoming Grover County Fair; the race car is outfitted with O'Shea's oil-burner. "Larry Taylor and His Stunting Daredevils" are to open at the fair.

On the day of the fair, Taylor puts on his show and Pat finds herself falling for the man she previously despised. Bruce Crowley (Jack Arnold), who is to drive Atlas Motors' "Atlas Special" in the upcoming twenty-lap race, has an intense dislike for Taylor, and the feeling is mutual. When Crowley urges his fellow drivers to mock Taylor and his crew, and then follows it up with some thrown food, a free-for-all breaks out. Boss Allen shows up and fires Crowley on the spot, and takes up Taylor on his offer to drive the "Atlas Special." Crowley, pissed off at being fired, coaxes his now-former fellow drivers to box in Taylor during the race so that he'll lose.

Which they do, but in the reckless maneuvering that follows the "O'Shea Special" crashes, killing young Eddie Dodds. No one seems to know for sure whether the crash was the result of faulty motor design on the O'Shea vehicle (it was), or foul driving on Taylor's part. Pat is convinced of the latter, and wants nothing more to do with Taylor in spite of the fact that he is eventually exonerated of all wrongdoing. Taylor is now free to drive the Atlas race car in the following week's international race. Unfortunately for Pop O'Shea, oil-burning engines are now banned from the event. Pop grows despondent over this turn of events, his young driver's death, and the puzzling failure of his engine. He climbs into bed and remains there in a lingering funk.

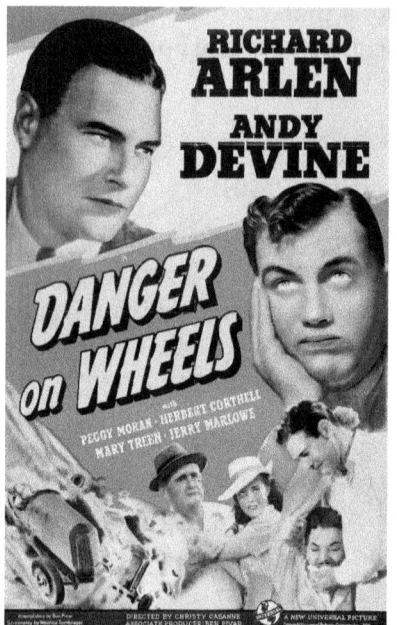

Danger on Wheels (1940). Image courtesy of Heritage Auction Galleries, Ha.com.

While testing some new shatterproof glass, Taylor realizes why the oil-burning engine failed. He goes to Allen and his associates at Atlas to convince them to back further development of the engine, which they reluctantly agree to. Approaching O'Shea with the prospect of letting Atlas buy in, O'Shea at first seems amenable to the idea. Pat quickly talks him out of it, convinced that Taylor is trying to pull one over on them.

Former Atlas employee Crowley has been hired to drive the O'Shea vehicle at the international classic, the vehicle now outfitted with a gas engine. Taylor comes up with a plan to demonstrate the viability of O'Shea's oil-burner, and enlists Guppy's aid. Right before the race, Taylor and Guppy sneak the oil-burning engine into the Atlas race car, having earlier taken care of the engine's one flaw. When Pat stumbles across them in the midst of the illegal transfer, Taylor has Guppy lock her in the back of an Atlas panel truck and take her away. The race soon begins with Taylor behind the wheel of the retrofitted Atlas car.

When Guppy runs a red light, two cops pull him over and discover Pat locked in the back of the truck. She attempts to explain what has happened

The Arlen-Devine Series, Part I (1939-1940)

and demands Guppy's arrest, but Guppy claims she is drunk. The cops decide to head to the racetrack to see if her story is true.

Taylor has been holding back during the first half of the race, but now opens her up, overtaking most of the other racers before running out of fuel. Making a quick pit stop, Taylor refuses assistance and fills the tank with some handy oil. Heading back on to the track, he refuses to stop when the true nature of his engine is revealed. Needless to say, Taylor wins the race.

The racing commission bans Taylor from any further racing, but he doesn't care; the value of the O'Shea oil-burning engine has been proven, and everyone is now happy, including Pop O'Shea who has finally gotten out of bed, and even Pat who has now come full circle in her feelings for Taylor. Taylor is promoted to manage the O'Shea wing of Atlas Motors, and tells Pat that they are going to be married.

The template for the Arlen-Devine series was by this time firmly established, although there would be exceptions with any given film. Stories were often set in unusual, frequently exotic locations, and/or would be centered on a unique business or industry. Generous amounts of stock footage, of course, helped place these backlot quickies into more visually interesting locales. Devine's buffoonery would surface with increasing regularity as the series progressed, although he was on occasion allowed the rare, serious role. Viewers were guaranteed at least one donnybrook per film, and often two or more, with manly Arlen slugging it out and Devine putting his size and girth behind his encounters. The odds would usually be stacked heavily against Arlen midway through the story, his character assumed guilty or complicit in some crime or otherwise unpleasant situation. But always the happy ending, his innocence established and a starlet half his age ending up in his arms.

Danger on Wheels is typical of the series: workmanlike direction by Cabanne that is unobtrusive but efficient, crisp photography by cinematographer Elwood "Woody" Bredell, competent acting from most participants, and solid-looking sets that actually look lived in. There's plenty of stock footage involved, with all but a single shot devoted to the automotive stunts and races. One of these is edge-of-the-seat material, a point-of-view shot through the windshield of a fast-moving car as it aims for and smashes into the front end of another parked vehicle. Editor Maurice Wright has done a solid job of integrating the stock and newly-filmed racing footage, with only the occasional rear-projected shot standing out as somewhat less than convincing. These latter shots are filmed so tightly on the participants, however, that only small surrounding areas are filled by the projected footage, lessening the negative visual impact.

As usual, there is enough humor interspersed throughout to balance the more dramatic scenes, some of which are quite strong with stock footage of limp bodies thrown from flaming crashes, to be carried away on stretchers. Devine, of course, provides the bulk of the lighter moments: mercilessly henpecked by fiancée Esme (established actress Mary Treen); yodeling at the top of his lungs so that no one will hear the yells of kidnapped Pat in the back of the panel truck; and his interaction with the two cops who arrest him, one personable (and ticklish!) and the other a humorless, by-the-book flatfoot. A race track announcer stands out as well, urging his radio listeners to buy a sponsor's ice cream, while swigging bottle after bottle of cold beer.

Universal contract player Peggy Moran was signed in 1939 after a part in Columbia's John Brahm-directed *Girls' School* (1938) and bits in MGM's Ernst Lubitsch comedy *Ninotchka* (1939) and a handful of other films following her first uncredited part in 1938. Roles in close to two-dozen B's kept her busy and in the public's eye through 1942 (including Pivar's *Alias the Deacon*, *Hot Steel*, *The Mummy's Hand*, and *Horror Island*), after which she went over to MGM for Frank Borzage's *Seven Sweethearts* in 1942 and Republic for Joseph Kane's *King of the Cowboys* in 1943, before retiring from film and marrying director Henry Koster. Of her performance in *Danger on Wheels*, *Variety* summed it up thusly: "Peggy Moran, new, but with plenty of possibilities, is an eye-filler and up to her job."[94] *The Hollywood Reporter* concurred, calling Moran "a pert and attractive heroine. Obviously, she is being groomed by Universal for more important assignments."[95] If that was Universal's intent, it did not pan out that way.

Danger on Wheels was advertised as featuring "Lucky" Teter and His Hell Drivers. Noblesville, Indiana's claim to fame, Earl "Lucky" Teter was a nationally-known automobile stunt driver who appeared regularly at state and county fairgrounds and race tracks with his troupe, performing all sorts of death-defying leaps over cars, crashes through burning walls of rubble, and other idiotically exciting stunts. Much of the stock footage used in *Danger on Wheels* was of various stunts performed by Teter, captured on film for Universal's use. Unfortunately, three months after the film's release, a suit was filed in Superior Court naming Universal Pictures Corp., Studebaker Sales Corporation, and not-so-"Lucky" Teter as defendants in a $100,000 damage suit. Earl Lester "Wild Bill" Simon, a stunt driver, charged that some of the footage used was of him and his assistants, taken at the Studebaker proving grounds in South Bend back in 1935.[96]

The film's problems did not end there. A year later a $30,000 plagiarism suit was filed against Universal Pictures Corp. by writer Ron Ferguson naming this same film. Ferguson claimed that he had submitted a story to the studio back in 1938 titled *Suicide Crew*, and that the story told in *Danger on Wheels* was

---

[94] "Danger on Wheels," *Variety*, April 17, 1940, 13.
[95] "Arlen-Devine Team In Good Thriller," *Hollywood Reporter*, May 20, 1940, 3.
[96] "File Universal Suit," *Motion Picture Herald*, May 11, 1940, 59.

the same as his original.⁹⁷ Universal countered, claiming theirs was an original written by Pivar. Ferguson's claims must have been sufficiently convincing, as the jury's verdict was in his favor and he was awarded $5,000 in damages.⁹⁸

"Lucky" Teter proved to be considerably less lucky than his on-screen incarnation. On July 6, 1942, Teter was killed while taking part in the last event at the Indiana State Fairgrounds, suffering a crushed chest and head injuries while attempting a 150-foot leap over a parked transport truck.⁹⁹

After the production of the first five of the series' entries was completed, a four-month break followed while production was halted. Two reasons were cited for this temporary action. First and foremost, Universal—and the industry, for that matter—was in the midst of stabilizing production and operational procedures due to the falloff of foreign sales resulting from the European War, now in its second month. The second, less-important, reason given was that the B film production schedule was ahead of itself for the season. Similar reasons were given over at Warner Brothers when production was temporarily suspended in Bryan Foy's B film unit, with all employees given four-to-six-week vacations.¹⁰⁰ During this halt in production, Devine was loaned out for roles at other studios willing to pay for his services. Paramount wanted him for the Jack Benny vehicle *Buck Benny Rides Again* (1940; Mark Sandrich) where Devine played himself, and Warner Brothers for comic support in the James Cagney-Pat O'Brien comedy *Torrid Zone* (1940; William Keighley). Arlen, on the other hand, was content to enjoy this brief respite from filmmaking; instead taking part in several charity golf events.

Hot Steel
(Director: Christy Cabanne; Released May 24, 1940)

Hot Steel followed upon the actors' return, heading into production on April 17. Christy Cabanne gravitated back to his usual post, having directed *Alias the Deacon* for Pivar in the interim (more on that film to follow). Screenwriter Clarence Upson Young, fresh off a trio of westerns for RKO, collaborated with Maurice Tombragel on adapting the latter's original story for the screen. Arlen starred as metallurgist Frank Stewart, Devine as sidekick and comic relief Matt Morrison, with Peggy Moran again costarring, this time as Devine's sister. Anne

---

[97] "Harold Lloyd's Mother Dies in Hollywood Home," *Altoona Mirror*, August 19, 1941, 19.

[98] "Plagiarism Suit Won by Writer," *Los Angeles Times*, August 23, 1941, 16.

[99] "'Lucky' Teter Dies in Crash at Indianapolis," *Daily Times-News*, July 6, 1942, 1. Teter's last name was misspelled in the press with an extra "e" as "Teeter" almost as often as it was spelled correctly.

[100] "Efforts for Stabilization Advance Waveringly," *Boxoffice*, October 21, 1939, 25.

Nagel was also on board to round out the distaff portion of the cast, and thirty-nine-year-old vaudevillian Joe Besser made his feature film debut in the small comedic role of Siggie. In spite of a satisfying effort on Besser's part, however, his contributions always seemed to be overshadowed by Devine whenever the two appeared together on screen.

Unemployed metallurgist Frank Stewart (Arlen) arrives in town and finds employment shoveling coal at the Arlington Steel Mills where his old buddy Matt Morrison (Devine) works. Stewart takes a room at the boarding house of Matt's widowed mother (Dorothy Vaughan), and it is love at first sight for Matt's younger sister Beatrice, aka Bebe (Peggy Moran); over time, Stewart falls for her as well. The other residents of the boarding house are co-worker and foreman Dave Martin (William Flynn) and his flirtatious wife Rita (Anne Nagel), co-worker Siggie Landers (Joe Besser), and the nosy, old, gossip-mongering spinster Elvira Appleby (Myra McKinney).

Mill owner Joe Farley (Wade Boteler) is faced with a daunting challenge: the government wants his mill to up its production of grade A steel ("the cream of the hearth") from their current 25% to a much higher, seemingly unobtainable, percentage, and he doesn't see how it can be accomplished. Inspired by an old superstition passed on by Matt's father about throwing a handful of BB's into each vat of molten steel, Stewart begins experimenting and comes up with a formula for purer steel. He presents his findings to mill owner Farley, who allows him some tonnage to experiment with. Farley's young metallurgist assistant George Barnes (Donald Briggs), secretly having an affair with Rita and hoping for a quick score so that he and Rita can skip town together, plots to steal the formula and sell it to a rival mill owner named Carlton (Edward McWade; misspelled in the credits as *Carleton*). He enlists Rita's aid to do the dirty work.

Martin has grown jealous of his wife Rita, who is always throwing herself at Stewart. Nice guy Stewart indulges her up to a point, but would never cheat on a fellow worker. Martin doesn't see it that way, though, and several fights break out between the two men. Rita takes advantage of this, stealing Stewart's detailed notes for the formula and a vial of the "pure" steel while the two men duke it out. Martin is knocked silly, but when he revives he sees Rita leaving with a man and, assuming it to be Stewart, follows. Confronting them, he finds the other man to be Barnes, and during a quick struggle Martin is killed. Later, when Martin's body is discovered, Stewart is assumed by almost everyone to be the murderer because of the bad blood between the two of them. Their suspicions seem to be confirmed when the incriminating vial of steel is found by Martin's body, dropped by Barnes during the struggle. Stewart is arrested by a police inspector (Robert Emmet O'Connor), but Farley's lawyer has him released on bail.

The Arlen-Devine Series, Part I (1939-1940)

When Matt gets promoted at the mill, coworker Storm Swenson (James Flavin) is apoplectic with anger figuring he should have gotten the promotion. Barnes uses this anger to his end, convincing the not-too-bright steelworker to act as the go-between in selling the stolen formula to competitor Carlton. Swenson agrees, promoting himself to Carlton as the man behind the formula. He then decides to double-cross Barnes by taking the larger cut. Stewart, meanwhile, clever guy that he is, connects news of Carlton's new steel formula with the theft of his formula and presents his suspicions to Farley. Together they confront Carlton, who eventually tells them it was Swenson who sold him the formula. As Farley's assistant, Barnes is privy to all of this, and learning of Swenson's double-cross shoots Swenson, who falls into a huge vat of molten steel.

Short-tempered steel mill worker James Flavin (center) thinks he should have gotten the promotion instead of Andy Devine (left) in *Hot Steel* (1940). Richard Arlen looks on with amusement.

Stewart's fertile brain now connects Swenson's death with all that has gone before. Suspecting Barnes, he makes a phone call to "Rita" and tells her to meet him at a prearranged location, throwing in enough worrisome comments so that Barnes, who is listening in, will grow concerned. Stewart rigs a dummy "Rita" to sit in her car and has Siggie drive it to the meeting place. Barnes drives by and opens fire, shooting what he believes to be Rita. The inspector and some cops are stationed nearby and observe this, arresting

STOP YELLIN'

Barnes shortly thereafter. When Rita learns of his attempt to murder her, she spills all regarding Barnes' plans. She is arrested as well for complicity.

A routine story placed in an interesting setting, *Hot Steel* benefits from its almost documentary-like detailing of how certain aspects of steel production take place. This is presented with oodles of intercut stock footage, but the matching sets are visually convincing and the transition from new to stock footage almost imperceptible. From what we see onscreen, it is evident this is a hot, dangerous, and physically demanding job.

Arlen smokes a pipe in this one; otherwise, he is much the same "character" populating the bulk of the series' films. Ditto for Devine, who shares the humor spotlight with Joe Besser. Anne Nagel is surprisingly sexy as Martin's tramp wife, and Peggy Moran is cute as always, perfect here as Devine's pouty "baby sister" Bebe who is determined to act "older," and be treated as such. The incessant squabbling between Bebe and brother Matt provides the film's humorous high-points, more so even than Matt's squabbling with snoopy boarder Elvira, and Bebe's squabbling with Rita. This is a squabble-filled film, or at least in the scenes set in the boarding house.

Variety was tepid in its reaction to the film: "Nothing of much consequence transpires in this steel mill actioner but nevertheless it moves along at a comfortable pace. As a dualer, okay."[101] *The Hollywood Reporter* was more upbeat about the results, saying that it "rates with the best of this series ... Christy Cabanne maintains a steady flow of action and good clean comedy in his direction ... Associate Producer Ben Pivar has balanced all of his ingredients to excellent effect."[102] *Hot Steel* went into release on May 24, 1940.

A rather curious incident occurred during the break between films, made more so by the fact that it initially went unreported. Arlen, debarking from a plane at Metropolitan Airport, was accosted and held at gunpoint for more than two hours. His assailant complained that Arlen had "broken up his home," and demanded $1,000 "to get out of town." Arlen claimed he responded by saying, "I don't know your wife, never met her, and don't know you." And then, somehow, he managed to escape from the unhinged fellow. The story would have ended there with the press and public none the wiser, except the fellow, a thirty-year-old named William Taite, was a persistent chap, and went for a second round two months later in mid-June. While golfing at the Wiltshire Country Club, Arlen was decked by Taite when the latter emerged from the bushes and attacked. Picking himself off the ground, Arlen was struck several more times before his slow-moving bodyguard and some caddies subdued the attacker and hauled him off to the police station. Arlen sustained a cut chin and

---

[101] "Hot Steel," *Variety*, June 26, 1940, 18.

[102] "Comedy Asset In Arlen-Devine Film," *Hollywood Reporter*, June 27, 1940, 3.

bruised forehead, and later told reporters of the original incident at the airport two months earlier.¹⁰³ Taite was charged with attempted extortion.

Arlen's initial assertions that he'd never before met Taite's wife came into question two days later, when he informed authorities he did not wish to press charges. This followed an appearance of Taite's estranged wife Evelyn at the District Attorney's office. While she stated that she was not reconciled with her husband and hoped to obtain a divorce, her comments suggested that extortion was not behind her hubby's actions: "You can say for me that my husband wasn't after money." She admitted that she had met Arlen in the ballroom of a Long Beach hotel, but refused further comment.¹⁰⁴ An interested public was left to scratch its collective head, read between the lines, and draw its own conclusions.

Black Diamonds
(Director: Christy Cabanne; Released July 16, 1940)

Announced in the trades in mid-March as Pivar's next assignment, *Black Diamonds* went into production on May 2, 1940,¹⁰⁵ and wrapped a short two weeks later; it was the seventh and final film of the series' first season. Arlen and Devine were paired with starlet Kathryn Adams and Mary Treen for this one, with Cabanne back again to direct. Screenwriter Clarence Upson Young returned as well, this time collaborating with Sam Robins in adapting Robins' original story. Robins' only previous experience was on a western released through Paramount, and Pivar's *Enemy Agent* (more on that film shortly).

Former executive vice president Charles Rogers had stated four years earlier that "News trends would govern the B film themes,"¹⁰⁶ and *Black Diamonds* is a perfect example of this approach to story construction. On January 10, 1940, a horrific explosion in West Virginia's Pond Creek No. 1 Mine resulted in the death of ninety-one coal miners, and was the worst disaster of its kind in that state in over a decade. The story made headlines nationwide, and dragged on for several days as rescue attempts were made and the body count grew.¹⁰⁷ With this disaster fresh in everyone's mind, Robins knocked out the basis for

---

¹⁰³ "Richard Arlen Injured by Surprise Attacker," *Los Angeles Times*, June 18, 1940, A1.

¹⁰⁴ "Arlen Refuses to Press Charges Against Assailant," *Los Angeles Times*, June 20, 1940, A3.

¹⁰⁵ "Pickup Shots Along Cinema Way," *Los Angeles Times*, May 1, 1940, A17.

¹⁰⁶ W. Douglas Churchill, "'Yellow Peril' Threatens Hollywood," *New York Times*, May 10, 1936, X3.

¹⁰⁷ George D. Turok, *A Guide to Historic Coal Towns of the Big Sandy River Valley* (University of Tennessee Press, 2004), 140-143.

a timely story, and with Young's assistance turned it into the screenplay that was filmed.

Bulletin reporter Walter Norton (Arlen), prepped for an assignment in Europe as a war correspondent, stops off in his coal-mining hometown of Redman to visit his family and friends before departing. He reunites with former girlfriend Linda Connor (Kathryn Adams), now a nurse at the town's hospital, and his old friend Tolliver (Andy Devine), an employee of the Redman Coal Mines. Tolliver and Norton's sister Nina (Mary Treen) are an on-again, off-again couple.

Cop James Norton is sidetracked by Kathryn Adams while Arlen looks on in *Black Diamonds* (1940). Image courtesy of Heritage Auction Galleries, Ha.com.

Norton is surprised to hear Linda's embittered father Archie (Cliff Clark) rail on about the lack of safety at the mines, Archie recently fired for provoking dissent among his fellow miners. When Norton's dad's legs are crushed in a mine explosion, Norton decides to investigate. He has Tolliver sneak him into the mine where he discovers that Archie's accusations are true. Brutish foreman Johnson (Pat Flaherty) confronts and slugs Norton, and fires Tolliver.

Norton confronts mine owner James Redman and on-the-take District Mining Inspector Mathews (Paul Fix) with his findings, but is rebuffed. Turning to the miners themselves and the town's newspaper editor, he finds that everyone is in fear for their jobs and livelihood, and unreceptive to anything he has to say.

When Linda discovers that her father is heading to the mine bearing dynamite, she goes to Norton for help. Norton follows Archie to the mine but is too late to stop him from blowing up the main shaft. The two are discovered and both arrested, Norton thought to have been in on the plot. The miners, fearing a loss of jobs, are ready to lynch the two of them. Their fears are unfounded, though, when Redman announces that he is reopening tunnel nine. Mining Inspector Matthews confronts Redman, telling him the tunnel is unsafe, but is promptly bribed to keep his mouth shut. Nina, Redman's secretary, overhears this along with Tolliver. They inform Linda, who informs Norton, still in jail for his assumed complicity in the bombing. Needing Norton's help, Linda devises a plan that has Norton hospitalized for a faked poisoning, then helps him to escape the police guard (James Norton) assigned to him at the hospital.

The Arlen-Devine Series, Part I (1939-1940)

Together they come up with another plan, this one to expose Redman. Nina and Tolliver break into his office and steal his dictation machine. Norton confronts Matthews and forces him into tunnel nine, and keeps him there while Tolliver lights some blasting dynamite; if the tunnel is truly safe, no one will get hurt by the blast. Knowing otherwise, Matthews panics and blurts out the cover-up, which is recorded on the hidden dictation machine. Johnson and his guards arrive and cut Norton's plan short, knocking Norton, Tolliver, and Matthews out cold. Sending the guards out, Johnson relights the dynamite with the intention of silencing the interlopers, once and for all. Johnson attempts to flee the tunnel but is stopped by the angry advancing miners, who want Norton and Tolliver. Matthews comes to and, realizing that the fuse has gone out, has a change of heart. He rushes forward and confronts the advancing miners, convincing them of the mine's lack of safety, his complicity in the cover-up with Redman, and Norton and Tolliver's innocence. Convinced, the angry miners shift their attention to Johnson, and haul him away to an uncertain fate.

Later, Linda and Nina dote on Norton and Tolliver, both hospitalized as a result of their beatings back at the mine. The town paper's editor arrives and displays his latest edition, which details the government takeover of the mine and the investigation into Redman's guilt. When Helen Martin, the unseen rival for Tolliver's affections and the target of much of Nina's jealousy and scorn, arrives to visit Tolliver, Nina hauls her out of the room and unleashes her off-camera fury on the poor girl.

Unlike some of the other entries in the series, *Black Diamonds* has a confined, low-budget look to it, with far too many interior scenes played in lackluster sets. There is plenty of humor (or what was intended as humor) courtesy of Devine and the towering Mary Treen, who make an amusing, perpetually combative couple. Separate them, or remove them from the scene altogether, however, and a lot of the jokes fall flat: the *Bulletin* secretary smoking Norton's cigar after he leaves, her initial pleasure turning to nausea; Tolliver confusing the mine guard with double-talk involving matches and cigarettes; Tolliver "singing" "Home On the Range" into the dictating device; the chastised cop ("I'm a bad, bad boy," a la Lou Costello); and Nina's off-screen, horrendous-sounding confrontation with Helen Martin. Curiously, Devine's character is listed as "Barney Tolliver" in the opening and closing credits, but in the film he is always referred to as "Tolliver Higgenbotham."

The *Los Angeles Times*' reviewer singled out Devine for kudos: "All the serious fol-de-rol [sic] is lightened by the comedy of Andy Devine and his girl friend. The humor is a bit infantile, but preview customers seemed to find it funny. And, of course, Andy really is one of the profession's real gifts to the screen, easy, spontaneously droll."[108] And as Arlen's girl Linda, Kathryn Adams impresses with her relaxed performance.

Burly forty-three-year-old actor Pat Flaherty plays the film's character of Johnson. A former athlete of some note, Flaherty was a pitcher for several minor league baseball teams back in the early twenties, followed by fourteen seasons of professional football with the New York Giants, Brooklyn Horsemen, and several other teams. Flaherty also managed to squeeze in some time as an amateur heavyweight boxer and wrestler.[109] He ventured into film back in the mid-thirties in a series of uncredited bits and character parts, usually pigeonholed into such roles as cops, detectives, thugs, prison guards, referees, bartenders, and the like due to his stocky build and tough, no-nonsense demeanor. Flaherty frequently functioned as a technical advisor as well, his baseball experience first coming into play for Edward Sedgwick's *Death on the Diamond* (1934), and in later years when he worked with Gary Cooper on his pitching for Sam Wood's *The Pride of the Yankees* (1942) and on Roy Del Ruth's *The Babe Ruth Story* (1948). Flaherty's First World War aviation experience lent some verisimilitude to his roles in films such as Howard Hawks' *Only Angels Have Wings* (1939) and Frank Borzage's upcoming *Flight Command* (1940). In addition to his role in *Black Diamonds*, Flaherty had previously appeared in Pivar's *Air Hawks* at Columbia, and in *Legion of Lost Flyers* and *Man from Montreal* as well.

Variety's reviewer regarded this film as one of the best of the series to date: "Richard Arlen and Andy Devine have been teamed up with excellent results in this melodrama of coal miners. It is the original direction and pace maintained by Christy Cabanne which gives the film its socko appeal. He's accorded the production a pace worthy of a better story."[110] *Boxoffice* was more succinct, calling the film an "action-melodrama of fair quality, giving a good account of itself as a low-budget endeavor." *Boxoffice* singled out Pivar's contributions to the finished film, saying that he "marshaled his production elements well."[111] *Black Diamonds* went into release July 16, 1940.

The success of the series' first seven entries ensured a second wave of films for the following season, and both Arlen and Devine were on board. Given the nature of the scripts and the comic-relief sidekick roles automatically assigned to Devine, Arlen was left to shoulder the leads. In spite of his likeable good nature and competency as an actor, the uneven scripts and often juvenile or ludicrous plotlines put him at a distinct disadvantage. This was unfortunate,

---

[108] "Film Holds Laughs, Thrills," *Los Angeles Times*, July 23, 1940, 13.

[109] Bob Ray, "Sports Soldier of Fortune Making Good as an Actor," *Los Angeles Times*, September 8, 1940, A14.

[110] "Black Diamonds," *Variety*, September 18, 1940, 14.

[111] Ivan Spear, "Spearheads," *Boxoffice*, July 27, 1940, 27.

for while others in the cast were usually recognized for their acting chops (or lack thereof), Arlen bore the brunt of criticism, often bordering on ridicule, primarily for the characterizations he was saddled with. Reviewers were quick to leap on him:

> *Mutiny on the Blackhawk*: "Arlen, as the navy captain entrusted with the secret mission of ferreting out slave-runners, survives his costume and some of the silly things he has to do."[112]
>
> *Tropic Fury*: "Richard Arlen gives a straight, if perfunctory performance, as the Rover Boy hero who saves the gal from a fate worse than death."[113]
>
> *Man from Montreal*: "Richard Arlen, having proved himself, can be forgiven one appearance such as this."[114]
>
> "Arlen is a bit stiff, but he's been through so much of this sort of thing that it is only natural he should take it in his stride. For a trapper he rates an extra pelt for keeping his hair and moustache in such fine trim and gloss."[115]
>
> *Hot Steel*: "Arlen's performance…is okay but too stolid. His stoicism endures through all happenings which makes for a patterned piece of acting that hardly excites."[116]
>
> *Black Diamonds*: "Richard Arlen struggles to make his role seem real."[117]

Regardless, the film-going public did not seem to care, and his popularity in these second-tier action-adventure type films remained undiminished.

§

---

[112] "Mutiny on the Blackhawk," *Variety*, August 9, 1939, 14.
[113] Hobe Morrison, "Tropic Fury," *Variety*, September 20, 1939, 12.
[114] "Whole Cast Sunk By Feeble Story," *Hollywood Reporter*, January 2, 1940, page unknown.
[115] "Man from Montreal," *Daily Variety*, May 15, 1940, 3.
[116] "Hot Steel," *Variety*, June 26, 1940, 18.
[117] "Film Holds Laughs, Thrills," *Los Angeles Times*, July 23, 1940, 13.

Stop Yellin'

7 The Other Films (1939-1940 Season)

While the Arlen-Devine series was Pivar's primary focus during the 1939-1940 season, he managed to squeeze in an additional six films, all of which went into theaters in the three-and-a-half-month period between the releases of series entries *Danger On Wheels* and *Hot Steel*.

Framed
(Director: Harold Schuster; Released February 23, 1940)

The first of these, the mystery *Framed*, was assigned to Pivar in September 1939. Based on Roy Chanslor's original story *Trouble Is My Middle Name*, Pivar tapped Harold Schuster, a comparative newbie at Universal, to direct. Frank Albertson had the lead as the wisecracking reporter around whom the story centers, and Pivar again enlisted Constance Moore as the female lead. Jerome Cowan was on hand as another reporter, this one rather slimy, with a solid supporting cast that included Robert Armstrong, Sidney Blackmer, Herbert Rawlinson, and the reliable Milburn Stone. Anne Gwynne was brought back as well for an uncredited, blink-and-you'll-miss-it bit part.

With a twelve-day shooting schedule, filming commenced on Monday, October 16, with the tentative title *Trouble's My Middle Name*. Early 8:00 a.m. starts each day necessitated only two nights of late filming, the first until 9:00 p.m. and the second until 10:00. Shooting wrapped right on schedule on Saturday, October 28, the film by now having undergone its title change. Scoring took place in a combined session on Saturday, November 18, with a first preview three weeks later during the week of December 11. The completed film shipped to New York on December 19, and was released theatrically the following year on February 23, 1940. *Framed* was brought in with a final cost of $73,000, a penny-pinching $6,000 under the approved budget of $79,000.

Stop Yellin'

Crime reporter Henry "Hank" T. Parker (Frank Albertson) has saved for ten years to retire to a cabin and write the "great American novel." Now that the big extortion story he broke is about to go to trial, he tells his city editor boss Skippy (Robert Armstrong) as much. Skippy begs him to stay, informing Hank that Walter Billings (Herbert Rawlinson), the key witness in the extortion trial of shady Tony Bowman (Sidney Blackmer), has gone missing. Hank balks at this, but when he receives a phone call from novice fellow reporter and socialite Monty de Granville (Jerome Cowan) saying he has heard where Billings is hiding, Hank reconsiders. Skippy's offer of a $500 bonus to "finish" the story is all it takes to change Hank's mind.

Meeting at the 44 Club, de Granville tells Hank that Billings is in Hotel McAdams room 313. Hank confronts Billings, who's at first reluctant to speak with Hank; Billings was the one who paid Bowman $5,000 "to keep that Miami thing quiet," and is annoyed that Hank had exposed him in the papers. Hank persists and finally convinces Billings to testify, but for naught when Billings gets shot. Hank finds Phyllis Sanderson (Constance Moore) in an adjacent room, and together they flee when curious bystanders approach the room.

Back at the 44 Club, Phyllis explains that she was Billings' secretary, and had just arrived with the tickets to Bermuda he had asked her to pick up. When it is announced on the club's radio that the cops are looking for Hank—they found his pistol and reporter's ID card at the murder scene—the couple flees once again. They head for Skippy's apartment, where Hank calls Skippy at the newsroom and fills him in on what has taken place. Hank realizes that someone lifted his pistol and ID card, and that the ID card he now carries is a substitute. He has the ID number checked, but it was one that was never issued. Not entirely trusting Phyllis, he calls de Granville and has him do a background check, the results of which allay Hank's fears about her.

Skippy arrives at the apartment, the cops close on his heels. The couple takes flight once again, taking refuge in a passing upholstery truck. They get off at the Marlborough Hotel where Hank approaches de Granville, asking him where he heard about Billings' hiding place. De Granville says he overheard hood Matthew Mattison (Milburn Stone) and his girl Goldie Green (Barbara Pepper) talking about it at the club. Hank goes and confronts Mattison, but the cops are lying in wait and he is forced to escape through a window. De Granville now joins Hank and Phyllis in their search, Hank telling him he'll make a real reporter out of him.

The cops are now on to Phyllis as well, issuing an all-points bulletin for the two of them; the city limits are blockaded and all vehicles checked. Hank purchases a used ambulance and has de Granville dress in an attendant's uniform and act as driver. The ruse works, and more than once. Hank searches out Goldie, but Bowman arrives while he is questioning her, so Hank is forced to flee for what seems like the hundredth time.

The Other Films (1939-1940 season)

Frank Albertson grills hood's moll Barbara Pepper in *Framed* (1940).

Phyllis now drops a bombshell: She claims that when she had entered Billings' hotel room right before he was murdered, she'd recognized the scent of perfume permeating the air: Joie de Vivre. Furthermore, it was the same perfume that she'd noticed down in Miami when she accompanied Billings on his visit to Bowman, back when the illegal transaction took place. Hank contacts Skippy, who manages to dig up the names of seven women who were seen with Bowman in Miami. Armed with a $90 bottle of Joie de Vivre for comparison's sake, Hank tracks down and visits the first five of them with no success. He hits the jackpot with number six, however, a nightclub singer named Gwen Porter (Judith Allen), who is wearing the same perfume. He gets her to admit that she lured Billings to the hotel where he was killed, but balks at answering any more questions. For naught as well, when a shadowy intruder shoots and kills her. Hank and the assailant engage in a struggle, the latter taking off and accidentally leaving his gun behind. Hank is reasonably sure it was Bowman.

Back in the ambulance, Hank has de Granville pull over so he can make a call to Bowman. He tells Bowman's butler to pass on the message that "Parker's getting warm." Hank then sets an elaborate scheme in motion. De Granville has left Phyllis in the ambulance while he goes to get a paper, and she takes off during his absence. She heads to Bowman's home and confronts him, telling him she was the one who shot Billings and now needs Bowman's help. Hank and de Granville head over to Bowman's hotel and enter through a window, but Hank soon finds himself held at de Granville's gunpoint. De Granville admits that he had killed Billings because he did not want his—de Granville's—racket blown during a trial. De Granville had switched Hank's pistol and ID card hoping to successfully frame him by luring him to the scene of the upcoming crime. Bowman enters the room, and it is revealed that he had only killed Gwen Porter to keep her from talking. Skippy and the cops break in, having been previously alerted by Hank. The cops make arrests, and Skippy gets photos for that night's edition. Hank explains that he had the ID number checked for the ID card immediately preceding the one planted on him, and it turned out to belong to de Granville. This was the tip-off.

Fellow reporter Jerome Cowan (left) turns out to be something less than a friend as he gets the drop on Frank Albertson in *Framed* (1940).

Hank calls fellow reporter Nick (Jack Arnold) and tells him to spread the word that he is now retiring for real and marrying Phyllis, and together they'll head to that cabin so he can write his novel. Phyllis chimes in that it will have a happy ending.

As a mystery, *Framed* is painless good fun if you are willing to suspend your disbelief for sixty-one minutes. The convoluted plot is burdened by far too many close calls, a perfume angle that's an enormous stretch in plausibility, and a guilty party whose identity remains unknown until the denouement for only the most oblivious of viewers. It is the uniformly good cast that carries the film, with Albertson breezy and self-assured in the lead, and Moore a charming presence; together they make an agreeable screen couple. Armstrong is a natural for the cynical, fast-talking, duplicitous city editor Skippy (why *Skippy?*), and Cowan a good choice as the socialite-turned-ineffectual reporter with a nasty secret to hide. Jack Arnold is priceless in a bit part as the bored, sleepy-eyed reporter Nick who never budges from his desk. Arnold, incidentally, initially appeared in films as Vinton Haworth, his birth name, alternating this with his adopted screen name of Jack Arnold. The latter name finally took hold and remained in use for nine years until he disappeared from the screen in 1943. Upon his return in 1950 he was now billed as Vinton Hayworth, a slight spelling variation of his surname and the name he used for a quarter century in numerous appearances on television. He died in 1970.

The film has its share of amusing moments, bolstered by screenwriter Roy Chanslor's dialog: A used car dealer listening to classical music on one of his cars' radios, taking part in an extremely animated way; our sham ambulance crew waving goodbye to their unsuspecting motorcycle police escorts; the elderly woman confronting de Granville in the ambulance, badgering him for information about the person in need of his services; Hank alternately sniffing the $90 perfume and the first five of Bowman's seven girls in an absurd effort to come up with a matching scent, with amusingly mixed results and no successes; and the multiple ambulance rides through the city, sirens blaring and driver de Granville grinning from ear-to-ear all the while. Rare was the Pivar film that did not leaven the drama with moments of whimsy or borderline slapstick.

Los Angeles Times reviewer Grace Kingsley was rather fond of the film, calling it "a delightfully fascinating story," with praise reserved for the film's leads: "[Albertson's] wisecracks are a large part of the amusing quality of the picture, and Albertson plays the role in completely believable fashion ... Constance Moore is a lovely heroine."[1] Ivan Spear had good things to say about *Framed* in *Boxoffice* as well: "'Framed' [is a] mystery-comedy that boasts snappy dialog, fast-paced action and a whirlwind climax, all keyed in the lighter vain. In its unassuming way, this should more than pass muster with audiences of all types. Producer Ben Pivar and Director Harold Schuster fulfilled their respective assignments with complete competency, while Roy Chanslor's original screenplay was well-contrived."[2] *The Hollywood Reporter*, true to form, dismissed the film out of hand as "a pretty feeble effort. We hesitate to say wasted effort, for there may be some who will find a modicum of entertainment in its familiar story." In fairness, though, the reviewer had nice things to say about the cast, Constance Moore in particular: "[She] steals

---

[1] Grace Kingsley, "Newspaper Story Shown," *Los Angeles Times*, May 24, 1940, 28.
[2] Ivan Spear, "Spearheads," *Boxoffice*, June 1, 1940, 29.

the picture ... Her unfailing charm and vivid personality are about the only thing the spectator will remember, or want to remember, 24 hours after seeing the picture." A few kind words were saved for co-star Albertson as well, whom the reviewer called "a pleasing juvenile, [who] works hard, but gets hopelessly lost in the holes in the story."[3]

Harold Schuster's work on *Framed* is solid if unremarkable, almost stylish in a modest sort of way. His body of work was generally a notch or two above many of his peers' efforts in terms of visuals, and Jerome Ash's fluid camerawork on *Framed* gives the completed film a visual boost. Iowa-born and University of Southern California-educated Schuster had entered the industry back in the twenties, serving in an array of capacities including script clerk, assistant cameraman, and uncredited extra before an extended stint in the editing department. Schuster performed his handiwork on over two-dozen films for Fox in the nine years that followed, most prominent of these being his first, F.W. Murnau's classic *Sunrise - A Song of Two Humans* in 1927. Schuster left the editing scissors behind in the mid-thirties and turned to direction, helming a trio of British productions before hooking up with Universal in 1938 where he directed another trio of films, *Swing That Cheer*, *Exposed* (both 1938), and *One Hour to Live* (1939) before Pivar assigned him to *Framed*.

Screenwriter Roy Chanslor, a thirty-nine-year-old former New York newspaper reporter, was a prolific writer of short stories and novels. Many of these were made into films over the years, some of which he adapted for the screen himself; *Framed* was one such venture. Perhaps the most famous of his novels reworked for the screen was *The Ballad of Cat Ballou*, a straightforward western that ended up as a comedy in director Elliot Silverstein's hands. Chanslor might have been upset at his novel's fate, but he was in no position to say as much; he died of a heart attack the year before *Cat Ballou*'s release in 1965.

Double Alibi
(Director: Philip Rosen; Released March 1, 1940)

Double Alibi, a murder mystery adapted from a Frederick C. Davis original titled *The Devil is Yellow*, followed on the heels of *Framed*. Chanslor scripted this one as well, with an assist from Harold Buchman and Charles Grayson. Pivar replaced the film's originally announced producer, Milton Schwarzwald, and Philip Rosen was hired to direct.[4] Pivar and Rosen had worked together

---

[3] "Constance Moore, Albertson Good," *Hollywood Reporter*, May 24, 1940, 3.
[4] "Adapts 'Devil is Yellow,'" *Boxoffice*, November 11, 1939, 107.

previously at Columbia when Pivar served as editor a decade earlier on the director's *Modern Mothers* (1928), and as producer on *El Código Penal* (1931).

Production commenced on Thursday, December 7, 1939, with a twelve-day shooting schedule and approved budget of $86,875. The film was announced in the trades under its interim title of *Devil in Uniform*[5] but referred to internally as *The Devil is Yellow*. Cast and crew toiled well into the night, finishing at 11:00 p.m. or later on seven of the production's twelve days, again finishing on schedule late on Wednesday night, December 20. With all of the exterior scenes set at night and most in rain, weather conditions for once were a minor consideration. Editing took place after Christmas, with an initial preview on Tuesday, January 30, 1940. The finished film was shipped to New York on Friday, February 2, with a final cost of $84,000. This was $4,000 under the final approved budget, which had been upped some time during production to $88,000. The film was released the following month with the more suitable title *Double Alibi*, which at least gave prospective patrons a hint of the film's genre.

Double Alibi (1940). Image courtesy of Heritage Auction Galleries, Ha.com.

Starring Wayne Morris and Margaret Lindsay, *Double Alibi* is a slick little thriller somewhat in the Hitchcock tradition, involving an innocent man wrongly accused of murder, and his desperate attempts to clear his name while all circumstantial evidence mounts against him. Although the plotline is at times predictable, it is structured by scripters Chanslor, Buchman, and Grayson, and directed by Philip Rosen in such a fashion as to make those deficiencies less apparent. The results are far better than the average film of its ilk.

Someone is digging a hole in Stephen Wayne's (Morris) ex-wife's basement, and when she goes down to check out the noise she is shot and killed. Captain Orr (James Burke) of the police happens to be passing by, spots a man fleeing across the yard, and shoots. The man drops his satchel when his left arm is shot, an unfortunate move in that his name, "Stephen Wayne," is monogrammed on

---

[5] "Megs 'Devil in Uniform'" *Boxoffice*, December 9, 1939, 88.

Stop Yellin'

the bag; an all-points bulletin is quickly issued. Wayne, unaware of his wife's murder and the identity of the fellow who shot him, heads to the police station to report his assault. Once there, though, he realizes that he is the assumed murderer, and makes a hasty departure. The drops of blood he inadvertently leaves behind alert the police to the stranger's identity.

Pursued, Wayne ducks into the offices of *The Chronicle*, and as B movie luck would have it is mistaken for a Pulitzer Prize-winning crime reporter named Chick Lester, due in that same day from Kansas City. Desperate, Wayne assumes the role. The paper's editor, Walter "Griff" Gifford (William Gargan), pairs Wayne with staff photographer Jeremiah "Jake" Jenkins (Roscoe Karns), sending them out to cover Wayne's ex-wife's murder. Meanwhile, Sue Carey (Lindsay), the paper's "Guide to Health" columnist, begs editor Griff to let her cover a real story. Griff, who's in love with Sue and unsuccessfully persists in proposing to her, tells her he'll give her the assignment if she'll marry him. No dice.

Arriving at his ex's house, Wayne and Jake meet the assembled reporters, homicide Inspector Early (Cliff Clark), and Captain Orr. Orr goes on to explain that he was first on the scene having heard two gunshots, and had shot at the fleeing suspect, Stephen Wayne. Orr sums it up tidily, saying it was premeditated murder on Wayne's part. Only one bullet is retrieved, however. Upstairs, Sue tries to gain entry to the crime scene to demonstrate her capabilities, in spite of her editor's refusal to give her the assignment. She sweet-talks patrolman Delaney (Emmet O'Connor) and manages to sneak in. When the group departs, Sue sends photographer Jake back to the paper to develop his plates, and it is obvious that she wants to be alone with Wayne.

Back at her apartment, Sue soon determines that Wayne is not Chick Lester, and she tricks him into admitting so. When he passes out, Sue discovers his bleeding wound, and while cleaning and patching it retrieves the second bullet. When Wayne awakens, she sarcastically tells him, "I'd do the same for a dog that was hurt." Wayne explains who he really is, and why he happened to be at his ex's house when the murder took place: He is an airplane engineer, divorced from his wife, and found himself in the wrong place at the wrong time when he responded to a panicked call from his ex. He also explains that the reason for the divorce is that his ex was messing around with a hood named Lenny Nolan, that Nolan and a partner, Dan Kraley, had stolen $40,000, and were both captured and imprisoned. Nolan is still in the clink, but Kraley has been released, supposedly gone straight, and is now a bartender. The $40,000 was never found. Sue, convinced of Wayne's innocence, is now determined to help him find the real killer and clear Wayne's badly-tarnished name.

Arriving back at *The Chronicle*, Sue and Wayne intercede when the real Chick Lester (Robert Emmett Kean) arrives. Wayne poses as the paper's editor Griff, and sends Lester to his hotel to rest up. Lester, dog-tired, leaps at the

The Other Films (1939-1940 season)

offer. Soon after, Sue finds that Nolan was released from prison that same day, so they head to Kraley's bar to question him about Nolan's whereabouts. Kraley feigns ignorance, so they follow him later on and determine where Nolan's room is. Entering the room along with Jake, they find a badly beaten Nolan lying on his bed. Then, like a bad penny, Orr shows up once again and finds them standing over Nolan's body. Orr is growing annoyed with Wayne, whom he still thinks is Chick Lester and sarcastically refers to as "Mr. Crime Expert." Orr calls for an ambulance while the trio takes off.

Wayne comes up with a theory: the $40,000 is buried in his ex's basement, newly-released Nolan went to retrieve it, Kraley had followed him there, and Wayne's ex was shot when she walked in on them. Pursuing this train of thought, Wayne, Sue, and Jake head back to the basement to see if the cash is buried there. Patrolman Delaney discovers them, so Sue and Jake lure him back upstairs for some photos, leaving Wayne alone to continue his pursuit. When Sue and Jake return to the basement, they find that Wayne has fled with the cash, and assume the worst. Sue reveals Wayne's true identity to Jake, and they both now realize what hot water they've gotten themselves into.

Wayne again confronts Kraley. Back at *The Chronicle*, Griff and the real Lester confront Sue, and she sheepishly reveals Wayne's true identity. A teletype comes in: Kraley has been shot dead, and "Lester" is the culprit. Assuming Wayne to be the murderer of his ex, he is now pegged with two murders.

Lester heads out to do what he does best, and while grilling Kraley's fellow bartender is told that Orr had shown up right after the bartender heard the shot that had killed Kraley. Wayne, his real identity exposed, heads to the hospital where the battered Nolan had been taken, but when he arrives in Nolan's room is confronted by a gun-wielding Orr. A cop outside the room hears a shot, and upon entering is informed by Orr that Wayne had just committed his third murder, killing Nolan. Wayne, now appearing to be in genuinely hot water, once again manages to escape.

Wayne sneaks into Sue's apartment, and he, now thought to be a multiple murderer, frightens her. He attempts to put her mind at ease, and says he is ready to give the police a full confession, but only after he receives an important call. When the call comes through, Wayne seems pleased with what he hears. Sue and Wayne head down to headquarters, and Lester and Jake show up as well.

In Inspector Early's office with Orr in attendance, Wayne gives his account of what has transpired over the last day or two. He reveals that ballistic tests performed by the police had tied together the three bullets retrieved from Wayne's ex, Kraley, and Nolan. He then further reveals that the bullet retrieved from his own arm—the one that Orr had said came from his gun—had been tested and came from that same gun as the other three. Orr, now exposed as the real guilty party who has ruthlessly killed to cover his tracks, attempts to escape at gunpoint; he is subdued and arrested. Wayne has, in the best B movie tradition, solved the crime, and tidily so.

And now the obligatory happy ending: Jake snaps a photo of Sue and Wayne embracing and kissing, and announces its intended caption: "Killer Turns Out to be Lady-Killer!"

Double Alibi is a taut little thriller that keeps the viewer guessing. Wayne's guilt seems increasingly likely as the two additional murders take place, the growing body of circumstantial evidence all pointing toward him. To the film's credit, less suspension of disbelief is required as the intriguing plot unfolds than with a number of other films in this vein.

Director Phil Rosen, a former cameraman in the teens who'd turn to direction in the twenties, saw his opportunities dwindle with the coming of sound, finding a home at lesser studios such as Tiffany, Columbia, Monogram, and several others. *Double Alibi* was only one of a couple of random assignments for Universal, and his work here is solid but never showy. Director of photography "Woody" Bredell, returning after his first stint for Pivar on *Danger on Wheels*, lends the visuals an element of class they might not have had in the hands of another, with his fluid, prowling camerawork, well-chosen angles, and atmospheric lighting all contributing to the overall mood. Bredell would be back for a pair of Pivar chillers over the following year, later building on the *noir*-ish look of his camera work for films such as the Robert Siodmak classics *Phantom Lady* (1944) and *The Killers* (1946). Editor Ted Kent, an eventual forty-year staple at Universal, does a crisply efficient job here, and is only required to resort to stock footage for several police mobilization montages.

The New York Times reviewer B.R. Crisler for once gave this one a pass, singling out the two young leads for praise: "A lean and laconic melodrama, beautified by the presence of Margaret Lindsay and rendered plausible even in its more implausible premises by a surprisingly effective performance on the part of Wayne Morris, 'Double Alibi ... is the cinematic answer to a pulpwood fictioneer's dream."[6] *The Hollywood Reporter* finally broke down and admitted liking one of Pivar's films, calling it "good action entertainment ... Philip Rosen's direction is mainly responsible for the exciting pace at which the story unfolds. Ben Pivar's production is satisfying, and Elwood Bredell's camera work adds to the picture's value."[7] *Daily Variety* concurred, crediting Pivar right out of the gate: "Ben Pivar has turned out a corking good crime picture in 'Double Alibi.'"[8]

Double Alibi grabs the viewer's attention at the get-go, with a wordless, moodily effective opening scene. It is nighttime and raining, and the camera

---

[6] B.R. Crisler, "The Screen," *New York Times*, March 11, 1940, 11.

[7] "Double Alibi," *Hollywood Reporter*, April 27, 1940, 3.

[8] "Double Alibi," *Daily Variety*, April 27, 1940, 3.

silently moves toward the Wayne home, the outside basement doors open. Inside, we watch the dirt pile up from a grave being carefully dug by a shadowy individual. Outside again we see a living room light snap on. Back inside moments later, the arrival of Mrs. Wayne provides the fresh hole with an occupant, and off we go. As staged by Rosen, and lighted and filmed by cinematographer Bredell, this visually arresting sequence sets the pace and mood for the taut little crime thriller that follows. The film has a number of clever little moments, both dramatic and humorous: Sue, discovering the blood-soaked bandage wrapped around unconscious Wayne's arm while a waltz plays merrily on the radio; the real Lester confronting the real Griff, neither believing nor accepting the other's identity; Jake belting out songs in the basement attempting to drown out Wayne's digging, only to have patrolman Delaney come down and request some good old Irish songs; the bloody, battered Nolan discovered lying in a heap on his bed in his seedy little hotel room; the chaotic, utterly convincing escape from Nolan's hospital room; and more.

Morris, on loan from Warner Brothers where he'd already established himself in lead roles in films such as Michael Curtiz's *Kid Galahad* (1937) and William Keighley's *Brother Rat* (1938), gives a solid performance as the hapless ex-hubby. Big and stocky, Morris gives a slow talking, almost lethargic delivery to his lines, lending to the credibility of an innocent deep in over his head in a situation he doesn't understand. Morris returned to Warners after completion of the film, and his career looked promising until a highly-decorated four-year stint as a Navy flier during the war brought his ascension in the industry to a grinding halt. The remainder of his career was spent in minor films, westerns, and television.

Co-star Lindsay had been scooped up by Universal in the early thirties, where the Dubuque-born actress was promoted as British born, a guise she was able to gracefully assume due to several years' previous speech and acting training, followed by work on the British stage. She moved over to Warner Brothers in 1933 where she dropped the British pretense and spent the next seven years in support of the company's leading stars or as lead in minor efforts, none of which fellow contractee Morris appeared in. *Double Alibi* was one of four efforts lensed for Universal in 1940 before she signed with Columbia. Her performance here is letter-perfect, her initial assertive, wise-cracking, tough-cookie persona as she confronts Griff reminiscent of (but not influenced by) Rosalind Russell's Hildy Johnson in *His Girl Friday* (Howard Hawks), released a mere two months earlier. Sue is eventually revealed to have a warmer, more personable, side, and Lindsay gives the character her all. It is a shame that Pivar did not use her again in another of his films, as she is very appealing and natural here. Lindsay's career lasted into the sixties, an impressive, if unremarkable, thirty-plus-year run.

Double Alibi's cast was rounded out by tough guy James Burke as the crooked police captain, the type of Irish cop role in which he excelled. Burke would move on to Columbia to co-star with Lindsay in their "Ellery Queen" series where he settled into the fits-like-a-glove role of police sergeant Velie. William Gargan, who'd been in the business since 1930 primarily in character roles, appears as *The Chronicle*'s hard-boiled but love-struck city editor. Coincidentally, Gargan would go on to star as Ellery Queen along with Lindsay and Burke in three of that series' entries, and would settle into television and radio work at the end of the decade. Unfortunately, throat cancer and the resultant removal of his larynx brought an abrupt end to these roles. Roscoe Karns' presence as the none-too-bright staff photographer provides occasional respite from the overall gloom of the story as a whole, and what would a Pivar film be without some comic relief? Emmet O'Connor is typecast as the sentimental Irish cop Delaney, a role he could handle in his sleep, and Pivar perennials Eddie Chandler and Wade Boteler are back for some minor bits as a patrolman and bartender, respectively.

Zanzibar
(Director: Harold Schuster; Released March 8, 1940)

Zanzibar is a true oddity for a feature, having more in common with the over-the-top, action- and peril-filled serials cranked out on a ongoing basis by Columbia, Republic, and—of course—Universal. Pivar must have reveled in cost-cutting glee with the prospect of a jungle-bound mini-epic, lining up all sorts of stock footage from jungle and south seas flicks from years gone by, Universal's own George Melford-directed *East of Borneo* (1931) and *East of Java* (1935) among them, while eyeing standing sets and back lot "jungles" for redressing and reuse. Curiously, *Zanzibar* was the one Pivar film from this era to receive the least advance publicity in the press—almost none, actually—with only occasional early mention under its working title of *The River of Missing Men*. Instead, it was sprung upon the public in all its unheralded glory, much to the delight of undemanding "children" of all ages.

Some background here to put the film's plot hinge—or should I say *MacGuffin?*—in proper perspective. The east coast African country now known as Tanzania was from the later 1800s until 1919 a German colony known as German East Africa. In 1891, a German battalion set out to suppress an uprising by the Hehe tribe and their leader, Chief Mkwawa. Mkwawa's army of nearly 3,000, armed solely with spears and clubs, managed to overpower the more sophisticated and better-equipped but woefully outnumbered German force, killing its commanding officer Emil von Zelewski in the process. The Germans, as would be expected, did not take this lightly, and three years later attacked and overwhelmed Mkwawa's fortress at Kalenga. Mkwawa managed

The Other Films (1939-1940 season)

to slip through their hands, form a small guerilla army, and continued to bedevil the Germans for another four years before he was cornered, alone except for a sole supporter. Choosing what he no doubt considered the lesser of two evils, Mkwawa put a bullet through his own head and ended it all. His jubilant pursuers beheaded the now-defenseless fellow, took his head—bullet and all—back to the Motherland as a keepsake, and quickly wrote a revisionist account of what had happened. Fast-forward to the end of World War I when the British decided to reward the Tanganyikans for their assistance during the war by having the skull returned, a symbol of sorts that German domination had come to an end, once and hopefully for all. This act was written into the 1919 Treaty of Versailles.

Zanzibar, an archipelago off the coast of Tanzania that has little to do with the film's plot but affords the film a recognizable name as its title, follows the exploits of famed explorer and big game huntress Jan Browning (Lola Lane). British government consul Michael Drayton (Lionel Pape) enlists her aid in recovering the skull of Mkwawa, known to be hidden in a temple in the interior of Africa. The quick explanation is that whoever possesses the skull will have control over the superstitious natives, and better the Brits than some nasty Axis country, right? She agrees, but shifty servant Aba (Abner Biberman) listens in, passing this information on to enemy agent Koski (Eduardo Ciannelli).

Browning sets sail on Captain Craig's ship along with her right-hand man Rhad Ramsey (Tom Fadden) and several other expedition members, with the pretense of capturing some wild animals. American Steve Marland (James Craig) stows away in the ship's hold, having convinced old friend Rhad to assist him in doing so after Browning's refusal to let him join the expedition. Koski is on board as well, now a crewmember due to some pulled strings by bribed Ship's Mate Simpson (Henry Victor). Browning discovers Marland not-so-hidden in the ship's hold, and after a half-hearted scolding reluctantly agrees to let him stay—not that she has much of a choice now that they are out at sea.

When the captain (Oscar O'Shea) discovers that Koski's papers are forged, Koski and Simpson overpower him. Left alone with the defenseless captain, Koski kills him and dumps his body out a window. The other passengers are unaware of what has taken place, and Koski is now in control of the boat.

Well, sort of; the boat sinks during a violent storm, and the rag-tag group of survivors—Browning, Marland, Rhad, Koski, Simpson, and hired help Bino (Clarence Muse) and Mayla (Ray Mala)—makes it to shore. Koski maintains a low profile, voting along with the others to put Browning in control of the group, quietly explaining to Simpson that he wants her to lead him to "something," no doubt the missing skull. Their situation looks perilous: they'll most likely perish during a five-day walk up the coast to the nearest port. Jan comes up with an alternative: head inland to the village of friendly chief Ali Muhammed (Robert C. Fischer), a two-day trek that's doable but fraught with wildlife risk.

Lola Lane reluctantly agrees to let not-so-well hidden stowaway James Craig stay on board in *Zanzibar* (1940).

Once there they will stock up and finish the trip by river. The group reluctantly agrees, well aware of the danger facing them.

Mayla's the first to perish, ending up as a tiger's meal. That night the group takes refuge in a bat-filled cave, keeping the hungry lions outside at bay with a hastily built fire. When Simpson forces Bino to head down to the stream for water, spiritual-singing Bino becomes the second casualty, this time at the paws of one of the assembled leopards. The next morning as their fire is about to peter out, the remaining survivors exit the cave from a cliff-side opening at its rear while Marland holds off the angry beasts with a succession of tossed flaming torches.

Jan leads them to the interior village, keeping mum about her goal of securing the skull housed nearby. She is greeted by Umboga (Everett Brown), who explains that Chief Ali Muhammed has been elevated to the position of Sultan. The Sultan is happy to see his old friend again, and has the group fed, clothed, and equipped with rifles. Later that night there's a semi-romantic interlude where Browning and Marland marvel at the beauty of the surroundings and the star-filled sky above, seemingly unfazed by the recent deaths of their two companions. They reveal to each other that they have ulterior motives for being there, but those motives remain unstated.

The Other Films (1939-1940 season)

The following day while the group heads out to capture some wild animals, Koski remains behind and attempts to convince the Sultan that Browning has retrieval of the skull as her real, unstated goal; Koski claims no personal interest in the skull. The Sultan doubts that his old friend would be up to such a nefarious deed, but he keeps a partially-open mind about it.

Meanwhile, Browning has the natives construct a series of traps, after which they set fire to the underbrush to drive out the animals lurking within. The fleeing animals are captured, and the group returns to the village with their impressive haul that includes lions, tigers, leopards, and zebras. That night Simpson taunts a caged lion, with the unintended result that the lion breaks loose from its cage, numerous other animals quickly following suit. Umboga is mauled in the wild melee that follows, but Marland manages to rescue him from certain death. The animals are rounded up and returned to their cages.

A nearby volcano that the natives call Rigadoon has begun to show signs of activity, and this has them spooked. They believe Mkwawa's spirit inhabits it—his headless body was tossed into it years earlier—and will unleash its fury if anyone dares to remove his skull from the temple-based shrine at its foot. The Sultan explains that the natives are distrustful of the white visitors, and shows them a ritual dance in progress. There is growing unrest, and the ritual dance always results in a human sacrifice, so he strongly encourages them to leave the next day. Realizing that it is now or never, Browning and Marland take a canoe down river to the shrine housing the skull. Koski informs the Sultan of their surreptitious trek, who is now finally convinced of Browning's ulterior motive. Angry natives are dispatched and greet the two adventurers when they arrive at the shrine

The two are unceremoniously hauled back to the village, and Marland and Rhad are tied to stakes to await their fate. It's ladies first here, and a nifty Jan-tied-to-a-tree-while-crocodiles-lick-their-lips scene follows. Umboga,

Lola Lane and James Craig, ready for action in front of a backdrop. *Zanzibar* (1940).

in a life-for-a-life gesture, reciprocates by cutting Marland loose. Marland asks Umboga to intercede with the angry natives in a desperate attempt to try to save Browning, but unfortunate Umboga becomes the next victim for his unwelcome efforts. Marland and Rhad release the wild animals from their cages and torch the village, which has the intended result of diverting the natives' attention. Browning is rescued in the nick of time, while the wild animals chow down on the fleeing, bloodthirsty (and now bloody) savages. Browning and her two companions escape the conflagration by boat, and head back to the shrine.

Koski and Simpson have taken advantage of the intended sacrifice of the trio to head for the shrine and collect Mkwawa's skull. As they take the box containing the skull from its perch, the volcano explodes, sending molten lava streaming toward the temple below. Browning, Marland and Rhad arrive and confront the thieves. Simpson shoots and wounds Rhad, who in turn shoots and kills Simpson. Marland and Koski struggle on the stone staircase and Koski falls to his death far below. With skull in hand, our trio of heroes escapes by boat as the jungle around them is destroyed by the volcano's fury. As Browning and Marland clutch, Rhad speaks to the skull he is holding: "Mack, when them two kids get married, you and me are going off on a bender."

A cheesy volcano dominates the poster for *Zanzibar* (1940). Image courtesy of Heritage Auction Galleries, Ha.com.

The film went before cameras on Tuesday, December 12, 1939, with an approved budget of $67,780 and eleven-day shooting schedule, optimistically set up to wrap early on the last working day before Christmas. Uncooperative weather conditions caused all sorts of problems, compounded by the need to match the production's overabundant use of stock footage, resulting in six days of late-night shooting out of the scheduled eleven. Pivar and director Harold Schuster managed to stick to the schedule, however, finishing up at 6:35 p.m. Saturday evening, December 23. As a result, cast and crew missed out on all of the studio's holiday festivities.

Editing of the newly-shot and stock footage was rushed through to try to keep costs down, even though it was anticipated that the film's release would be held back so as not to conflict with director James Whale's more elaborate production *Green Hell*. A very real possibility, since glimpses of the shrine on which Mkwawa's skull resides might reveal that it was one of Whale's more prestigious film's sets. The studio was pleased with the results, so the decision was made to enhance the production with a more elaborate musical score, recorded on Monday, January 29. The film was retagged *Zanzibar*, previewed on Friday, February 9, and shipped to New York on the 13th. The film's final cost came in at $77,000, $8,000 over the revised approved budget of $69,000.

Lola Lane, the oldest and arguably least attractive of the three Lane Sisters, is sufficiently rugged in the lead, tapping her inner "Osa Johnson" to get into the spirit of the role. Lola got her start in film in the late twenties, her younger sisters Rosemary and Priscilla following suit in the later thirties with contracts at Warner Brothers. A fourth, oldest sister, Leota, had made a couple of films early on with little success, soon abandoning any thoughts of stardom. Adhering to the old adage that the best defense is a good offense, Lola was quoted at the time of the film's release commenting on "too much glamour in the movies. I mean that the girls who insist upon looking beautiful and perfectly groomed regardless of the roles they are playing are actually inviting criticism."[9] Not to worry.

Co-star and relative newcomer James Craig lent his good looks and little else to the proceedings, giving a stilted performance and bellowing his lines in an annoyingly loud fashion; he is the weak-acting link in an otherwise respectable cast. Tom Fadden fluctuates between wisecracking sidekick and dependable, gun-toting ally. As Bino, Clarence Muse provides the remainder of the film's humorous asides, albeit of the era's "darkie" humor variety. Ciannelli and cohort Henry Victor supply the requisite menace. The natives, as one would expect, are of the Hollywood stereotypical cookie-cutter variety.

Harold D. Schuster returned to direct this hodge-podge of new and older footage, and the results are surprisingly good. After a few more films for Universal, Schuster returned to his old home 20th Century-Fox, eventually ending up in television in the fifties, with occasional films for Allied Artists thrown into the mix. *Zanzibar*'s far-fetched (but admittedly exciting) script was written by the dependable Maurice Tombragel, with an assist by Maurice Wright, the latter's only effort as a screenwriter and for once foregoing his editorial chores.

Milton Krasner was in charge of photography, shooting much of the film in well-chosen mid- and close-up shots, with a pleasing number of tracking shots. Much of this was filmed with an eye toward the eventual juxtaposition of his footage with that lifted from stock library sources, all pieced together by editor Milton Carruth. And there's a lot of it in this one, beginning with the

---

[9] "Coming from Lola We Can't Believe It," *Brooklyn Eagle*, March 3, 1940, 6.

spectacular storm sequence that scuttles the boat. Once on land, much of the jungle and village footage had seen previous screenings, with the latter pieces somewhat rougher visually but nicely integrated. Much of the animal footage is exciting stuff, perhaps more so for today's CGI-numbed audiences who aren't used to seeing the "real" thing. The climactic volcano footage, shot in miniature and lifted from *East of Borneo*, was convincingly executed and provides the film the appearance of a higher budget. Alas, the temple shrine at the foot of the volcano would look more at home in the Southeast Asian location of its parent film than in *Zanzibar*'s Africa.

Editor Carruth was by this time an old hand at this sort of thing, with such genre classics as *Dracula* (1931), *The Mummy* (1932), and *Dracula's Daughter* (1936) to his credit. An editor since the late twenties, Carruth had taken a two-year sabbatical when Universal had tried him out as a director, but after a handful of efforts in 1936 and 1937 had returned to the back room to resume his previous career. He would continue in that position for the next three decades. After cutting the high-profile James Stewart and Marlene Dietrich co-starrer *Destry Rides Again* (1939), however, *Zanzibar* must have seemed somewhat like cinematic slumming.

Said *Boxoffice* of the on-screen results following the film's release on March 8, 1940: "Herein is incorporated every known type of action, from shipwrecks and erupting volcanoes to weird native tortures, all of which have been blended into a satisfactory programmer for the neighborhood trade and Saturday matinee patrons."[10] Truer words were never spoken.

Exhibitors were happy with the results, and one overjoyed fellow wrote to the *Motion Picture Herald* with his praise: "Don't throw this one away. This is a jungle picture, full of action. They'll eat this up. The lions almost kill off the cast, it's melodrama, but they really come to see it. We originally had this booked for mid-week, but when we saw the trailer, we knew we had a good action picture and changed to Thursday-Friday-Saturday, with a western as double. I believe that any good action picture will do business anywhere, and most dramatic pictures are poison, generally, for small towns."[11]

Full disclosure here: the writer hailed from Pine Bluff, Arkansas.

Enemy Agent
(Director: Lew Landers; Released April 19, 1940)

Enemy Agent is another one of those spy adventures featuring the then-ubiquitous foreign agents from countries only hinted at but never named; the

---

[10] Ivan Spear, "Spearheads," *Boxoffice*, March 30, 1940, 81.
[11] "What the Picture Did for Me," letter from William C. Clark, *Motion Picture Herald*, April 11, 1942, 50.

finished film followed *Zanzibar* into theaters a month later on April 19. Lew Landers directed, with Edmund L. Hartman and Sam Robins adapting Robins' original story *Enemy Alien*. Co-starring Richard Cromwell and Helen Vinson, the Los Angeles-based story began filming on Monday, January 15, amidst much speculation that its title would need to be changed; Warner Brothers was about to release a Terry Morse-directed drama with the same title[12] co-starring Boris Karloff and Margaret Lindsay, adapted from Anthony Paul Kelly's play *Three Faces East*. The conflict was resolved at the end of January when Warners released their film as *British Intelligence*, retaining the *Enemy Agent* title solely for the British release. Universal's *Enemy Agent*, of course, required a title change when released in Great Britain, adopting the more awkward title *Secret Enemy*.

Budgeted at $72,000, with an eleven-day shooting schedule, production went smoothly and wrapped on schedule at 3:45 p.m. Friday, January 26, with only three short after-dinner evenings required for nighttime exteriors. The film's score was recorded in a combined session on Monday, February 12, with a first preview that Friday. The completed film came in within dollars of the approved budget. As released on April 19, 1940, *Enemy Agent* provides a reasonably enjoyable hour's diversion.

**Richard Cromwell might get top billing, but Robert Armstrong's agent dominates this poster for *Enemy Agent* (1940).
Image courtesy of Heritage Auction Galleries, Ha.com.**

---

[12] Edwin Schallert, "Spy Story with Los Angeles Locale Planned," *Los Angeles Times*, January 10, 1940, 13.

Stop Yellin'

When a turned Fulton Aircraft Company engineer fails in his attempt to smuggle the plans for the new flying fortress and its top-secret bombsight ("You could drop a bomb into a pickle barrel from five miles up"), head spy Dr. Jeffry Arnold (Philip Dorn) has him murdered. Arnold reassigns the task to Lester Taylor (Jack Arnold), a money-hungry draftsman at the plant. FBI agent Gordon (Robert Armstrong) is working with Lyman Scott (Russell Hicks), the plant's owner, to stop the outgoing flow of smuggled blueprints. They know that Evans, the murdered engineer, was responsible for some earlier thefts, and also know that the bombsight was his latest intended goal. Fellow engineer Jimmy Saunders (Richard Cromwell) is the only one with access to those specific blueprints, so they keep an eye on him.

All of the plant's personnel eat their meals at a neighborhood joint called "Irene's," and hostess Irene Hunter (Helen Vinson) is the object of Saunders' affections. When she backs out of a date with him to instead go out with Taylor, pretty waitress Peggy O'Reilly (Marjorie Reynolds), long adoring Saunders from afar, catches him on the rebound.

Using a state-of-the-1940s-art pocket watch camera, Taylor surreptitiously snaps photos of the blueprints that his "friend" Saunders is working on. When the plant goes into lockdown, Taylor ditches his camera in Saunders' locker, where it is soon found. Saunders is hauled in and grilled, but a lack of definitive evidence results in his release. The papers are full of stories about him and the government's suspicions, and Saunders soon finds himself out of a job and with nary a prospect. He turns to drink and his disposition turns sour.

Now that Saunders is down on his luck, only faithful Peggy stands by his side. Returning to his apartment in a drunken haze, Saunders finds Irene there moments after she is seen rifling through his desk. Viewer suspicion regarding her allegiances is aroused.

Dr. Arnold wants Saunders out of the way, so he arranges a "job" for him out in Kansas City where his two goons will arrange a car "accident." Taylor is given the task of telling Saunders about the new job. Taylor's not a particularly good spy, though, as he repeatedly brags to new girl Irene about how he is going to be rich soon and buy her expensive things; the more he drinks, the more he talks. True to form, he writes the address of the Kansas City company on the back of an old envelope that has his real name—Lionel Carter—and address typed on the reverse.

When he finally realizes he has been duped, Saunders heads over to Taylor's place and recovers the photo of the bombsight and an incriminating bankbook. Arnold's goon Baronoff (Abner Biberman) arrives with Taylor and they find Saunders there, but after a brief brawl Saunders manages to flee up the fire escape with pistol-wielding (and lousy shot) Baronoff hot on his heels. Saunders navigates a building-to-building leap, but Baronoff doesn't.

The Other Films (1939-1940 season)

Saunders flees in his car, hiding the blueprint and bankbook under the passenger seat. Pursuing cops overtake and arrest him, charging him with illegal entry. Peggy visits Saunders in jail, and he reveals to her all he knows about the spies and the fact that he has incriminating evidence. Peggy naively passes this information on to Irene, who makes a beeline for Saunders' apartment. Finding an auto storage receipt, she deduces the location of the hidden evidence, and soon the blueprint and bankbook are in her possession.

Taylor had earlier introduced Irene to Dr. Arnold at a swank nightclub, and while Arnold has growing doubts about Taylor's reliability and effectiveness, he is smitten with Irene. Irene now confronts Taylor and purrs her demand for $5,000 in exchange for the blueprint and bankbook. Taylor agrees, and is about to write a check when Gordon and some fellow agents arrive and haul him off. Irene avoids them by hiding in a closet.

Meanwhile, Saunders, having regained his freedom, learns that Irene has been snooping around his garaged car. When he checks to see if the blueprint and bankbook are still safely hidden, he finds the evidence removed. Saunders now suspects the worst of Irene.

Arnold has the luckless Saunders abducted and brought back to his home where he intends to learn by force the whereabouts of the hidden evidence. Saunders is knocked unconscious, and knocked unconscious a second time for good measure when one of the goons' enthusiasm gets the best of him. Irene shows up and confronts Arnold with inflated demands for the return of the blueprint and bankbook, now valued at $10,000. Saunders revives and overhears this, and is shocked by Irene's lack of patriotism. He gives her a good, hard slap, and she looks stunned. Arnold reluctantly agrees to her demands, but she says that she'll return the next day for the exchange since she has a bunch of friends waiting for her outside. The friends barge into the house, seemingly a bunch of drunken, high-spirited college kids. Their rowdiness increases, but Arnold and his associates are at a loss as to how to get rid of these nuisances. A spur-of-the-moment football game—you read that right—quickly escalates, and Arnold's associates are all tackled and relieved of their firearms. Agent Gordon now arrives, and the college students are revealed as fellow agents. And so is Irene, who has been working undercover all along. Saunders is relieved, not only to have been saved, but to learn of Irene's true nature as well. Arnold and his gang of spies are hauled off to jail.

Utilizing liberal amounts of footage from the 1937 serial *Radio Patrol* and other sources, *Enemy Agent* packs a lot of action and comparatively little comedy into its brief sixty-one minutes, culminating with the ludicrously amazing living room-based football game finale. So much for realism, but I guess contemporary audiences got a kick out of it. The film is montage-heavy, even more so than the average programmer, with a grand total of four montages. The first summarizes the destruction caused by various acts of sabotage; another gives a capsulated look at the nightclub whirlwind of the two couples on one particularly energetic evening; the third, the cascading newspaper headlines chronicling Saunders' supposedly nefarious deeds; and finally as Saunders plods on in his futile quest for work. All necessary, I suppose, to keep the film at its brief running time.

The film, unfortunately, is a disappointment, the potential of its premise compromised by a seeming disinterest on the part of the filmmakers. The editing is lackluster and strictly utilitarian, a fact driven home by the rooftop chase, a scene that should have had viewers on the edges of their seats, instead void of any excitement aside from that generated by the accompanying score. Jerome Ash's photography, workmanlike elsewhere, borders on the amateurish for this sequence. Director Landers could and should have done a better job setting up this and other action scenes, but it seems his mind and energies were elsewhere.

Daily Variety's somewhat less-than-enthusiastic reviewer commented on Landers' contributions, stating that he "didn't have much to work with in his direction but keeps things moving generally towards satisfactory conclusion." As for Pivar and the rest of his team, "Pivar's production is sufficient for picture's goal, as are other technical contributions."[13] *The Hollywood Reporter*'s reviewer felt more positively about the film, calling it "[f]ast-paced, well-directed and nicely played ... [with] plenty of zest and action ... Lew Landers did a lot with the script which was handed to him, particularly in the matter of establishing a tempo which never lets down, and in individual scene construction."[14]

Enemy Agent's cast is sufficiently good, and play their respective roles straight. As the hapless draftsman, young lead Richard Cromwell brought his boyish good looks and undeniable charm to the film. As written, though, his character is somewhat of a whiney wimp, and the diminutive Cromwell is not at all convincing in his several fistfights. Born Melvin Radabaugh and mercifully renamed by mogul Harry Cohn for his first starring feature at Columbia in 1931, Cromwell had made an immediate impression on audiences and critics alike in John G. Blystone's *Tol'able David*. His career was on the ascension throughout the thirties with work for a number of studios, Henry Hathaway's *The Lives of a Bengal Lancer* for Paramount (1935), William Wyler's *Jezebel* for Warners (1938), and John Ford's *Young Mr. Lincoln* (1939) among them. And then Cromwell's career took a nosedive, with a handful of films following for RKO, Monogram, PRC, and *Enemy Agent* for Universal. After a stint in the military, Cromwell effectively abandoned film, returning to his original passion for art.

Frits van Dongen, actor son of a Holland shipbuilder, had graduated to the big leagues of Austrian and German cinema with some degree of success.

---

[13] "Enemy Agent," *Daily Variety*, April 6, 1940, 3.

[14] "Direction, Acting Better Than Yarn," *Hollywood Reporter*, April 6, 1940, 3.

The Other Films (1939-1940 Season)

Frits beat a hasty retreat from that country as the Nazis gained power, lured to Universal by director Henry Koster, an old friend who had fled Vienna for Hollywood several years earlier.[15] Rechristened with the more marquee-friendly name of Philip Dorn, Universal kept him on a back burner for nearly a year while he studied English. His first two films stateside were for Pivar in roles where his noticeable accent made sense, here in *Enemy Agent* as the villain of the piece. Pivar retained his services for his next film as well, the topical *Ski Patrol*. As the head spy, Dorn's Jeffry Arnold is one of the film's strongest characters. Smooth but cold, Arnold delivers his orders to kill without batting an eyelash, occasionally "softening" them with his puckish sense of humor. Instructing his goons to arrange Saunders' car "accident" out in Kansas City, Arnold adds, "I'd be very pleased to give you the business, so that you can give him the business" with a touch of a smile. When his joke falls flat, he quickly acknowledges with a shrug that perhaps it was not so funny, resulting in one of the film's few humorous moments. It is Dorn who holds the film together, urbane but deliciously amoral as the head spy for a country that remains unnamed, but not in the fertile minds of viewers. Dorn's salary on *Enemy Agent* was $3,700.

Marjorie Reynolds comes off as chipper but somewhat goofy (and admittedly likable) as Peggy O'Reilly, the film's love interest. Her acting here is somewhat stilted and awkward, but in general she was a decent actress saddled with too many roles in minor films throughout the thirties and forties. Her starring role in Fritz Lang's excellent wartime thriller *Ministry of Fear* (1944) was one of a handful of exceptions resulting from a move to Paramount. Reynolds settled in television work in the fifties, most notably as William Bendix's long-suffering wife in the hit television series *The Life of Riley* (1953-1958).

Cute as a button Texas-born Helen Vinson rounds out the cast as the perky undercover agent waitress. Her still-evident Southern drawl and comparative maturity adds a layer of verisimilitude to her on-screen ruse, one that keeps the audience guessing through most of the film's brief hour. Jack La Rue is on board as a heavy, with Luis Alberni as the manager of Irene's, Milburn Stone as an aircraft company employee, Jack Carson as one of the FBI agent "college students," and an uncredited Henry Victor—*Freaks*' strongman Hercules— as Arnold's butler, following his *Zanzibar* performance.

Lew Landers, one of the industry's most prolific directors, does adequate but unremarkable work here. Landers started with Universal back in 1934 where he made a handful of serials and a trio of features, the Karloff-Lugosi horror fest *The Raven* (1935) among them; their credits listed him under his real name, Louis Friedlander. Moving over to RKO in 1936, he abandoned

---

[15] Frederick C. Othman, "Crisis in Hollywood Resulted From Russo-Finnish Peace Pact," *Daily Times-Bulletin*, March 23, 1940, 5.

his name and adopted the new moniker Lew Landers. Close to two-dozen programmers resulted over the next four years, after which Landers returned to Universal for another four films, *Enemy Agent* and the Pivar follow-up *Ski Patrol* among them. A stint at Republic followed before Landers was lured back to Universal in 1941 to helm Pivar's *Lucky Devils*. It was a one-shot deal, however, and Landers settled in at Columbia where he was responsible for a staggering number of B's into the fifties, with occasional side-treks to other studios, Monogram and PRC among them. Like so many other directors of second features, Landers ended up directing for television, where his time-proven ability to produce acceptable results under tight time constraints, modest budgets, and with a minimum of fuss was a necessity.

Edmund Hartmann, who throughout his career retained and dropped the final "n" from his surname with disconcerting regularity, had been writing scripts for programmers at RKO from the mid-thirties, finally hooking up with Universal in 1937. Over the next eight years Hartmann pounded out several dozen screenplays, demonstrating a knack for comedy that turned into a lengthy relationship generating stories and scripts for the popular team of Abbott and Costello. These included director Arthur Lubin's *Keep 'Em Flying* (1941) and *Ride 'Em Cowboy* (1942), and Jean Yarbrough's *In Society* (1944), *Here Come the Co-Eds*, and *The Naughty Nineties* (both 1945). Hartmann abandoned Universal and moved over to Paramount in 1947, putting his comedic abilities to work for Bob Hope. Hartmann's *Enemy Agent* co-scripter Sam Robins, this only his second effort, had a far shorter and significantly less distinguished career that lasted a brief four years. His films for Universal were probably the high point of his brief engagement in the industry, ending up writing for the Poverty Row studios of Monogram and PRC.

Ski Patrol
(Director: Lew Landers; Released May 10, 1940)

At the end of January 1940, Universal announced plans for a film ripped from the headlines, based on what came to be known as both the Winter War and the Russo-Finnish War. The Russians had invaded Finland back on November 30, 1939, in what was intended as a land grab after negotiations broke down over Soviet demands for territorial concessions. With three times as many troops as the Finns and countless more aircraft and tanks, the Russians assumed that it would only be a matter of weeks before the successful conclusion of their efforts. It didn't work out that way. Not only had the highest ranks of the Russian military been severely compromised by Stalin's purges, but they were faced with a total lack of infrastructure over which to move their forces. The Finns dug in and knew how to fight in the snow-covered forests, and the resultant Russian casualties were staggering.

The Other Films (1939-1940 season)

Popular opinion worldwide was with the underdog Finns, and executive producer Warren Douglas gave associate producer Pivar the assignment to knock out a film to capitalize on the public's interest in this ongoing conflict. Newcomer Paul Huston was engaged to write a script for a drama to be titled *Ski Patrol*, and popular actor Gary Cooper was optimistically sought for the lead.[16] Cooper's participation never panned out, so Pivar assigned his new find Philip Dorn to the lead, with Viennese import Luli Deste to play opposite him in a battle of the accents.

Deste had a handful of European films to her credit, and a couple of unremarkable efforts for Columbia since arriving in the United States—so unremarkable that she gave up and returned to Europe and the London stage. Universal Chairman of the Board J. Cheever Cowdin had seen one of her performances while on vacation there, decided she was right for his studio, and lured the hesitant actress back to Hollywood once more. Deste swore at the time that if things did not work out this time, she'd return to Europe for good. *Ski Patrol* afforded her a minor, comparatively thankless role where she is required to do little else than smile and look pretty. Seemingly a decent actress, she is wasted here. After a few more potboilers she stuck to her word.

Much was made in the press about this being Dorn's American debut, his smaller role in *Enemy Agent* evidently having gone unnoticed. With his rumbling bass voice, he is excellent as the small group's leader, convincingly conveying the commanding presence of a leader well respected by his troops. Director Lew Landers was brought back as well to oversee the filming. Pivar put prop men to work building gypsum "snow" drifts inside on one of Universal's soundstages, some of them mounted on rubber wheels so that they could be rearranged to represent different settings.[17]

Alas, timing is everything. The film was rushed into production with initial background footage shots to be filmed in the snows of the Sierras on March 11.[18] Finland is essentially a mountain-less country, but Pivar needed snow, and where else were they to find snow in California on such short notice? A day later, the Finns, finally overwhelmed by Soviet numbers and might, surrendered. The script was hastily revised so that the heroic Finns, who seemingly had the upper hand when Huston turned in his completed screenplay, would now philosophically accept their defeat at the hands of the Soviets, now portrayed as

---

[16] Douglas W. Churchill, "Screen News Here and in Hollywood," *New York Times*, February 1, 1940, 26.

[17] Frederick C. Othman, "Crisis in Hollywood Resulted From Russo-Finnish Peace Pact," *Daily Times-Bulletin*, March 23, 1940, 5.

[18] Douglas W. Churchill, "Screen News Here and in Hollywood," *New York Times*, March 9, 1940, 22.

barbarians.[19] With revisions in place, filming resumed and concluded in early April, with general release on May 10, 1940. Curiously, Universal steadfastly declined to discuss the identity of the conflict during the film's production, and would give no reason for their refusal. Regardless, it was obvious to everyone else who and what the film was all about, and while not stated in the finished film, it might as well have been.[20]

Ski Patrol is a terrific little film, or at least in the realm of B movies. Admittedly, it is full of clichés and situations geared toward manipulating the audience's emotions, but as a brink-of-war piece it delivers the goods, and in an entertaining package. As far as the inclusion of stock footage goes, this film has perhaps the most intelligent, well-integrated utilization of some really spectacular footage of any of Pivar's films. And there's a whole lot of it.

The film opens with the 1936 Winter Olympics, following the progress of the eighteen-kilometer cross-country ski race. As the competition nears its end, Viktor Ryder (Philip Dorn) of Finland is in first place, Ivan Dubrosky (Reed Hadley) of Russia is in second, and Dick Reynolds (John Arledge) of the USA is in third. As the two leaders ski out of sight of the judges, Dubrosky takes a near-death spill at the edge of a thousand-foot drop. Ryder stops and pulls his competitor to safety, cracking his ski pole while doing so. Dubrosky goes on to win the race and the gold medal, with Ryder close on his heels. In the spirit of camaraderie, Ryder is happy for his opponent's win, and bears no ill feelings. At the medal awards that follow, US Olympic Committee spokesman James Burton (Addison Richards) gives a brotherhood-of-man speech, citing the lessons learned from the previous war and stating flat-out that there will be no future wars. Right.

War breaks out in Europe, and an informative montage summarizes its progress, interspersing footage of troop movements and battles, with close-ups of maps on a country-by-country basis; the maps end with Finland. Russia and Finland are attempting to reach a compromise on an unspecified dispute, but the Finnish troops are amassing on the border just in case.

An engagement party for Paavo Luuki (Edward Norris) and Viktor's sister Lissa Ryder (Kathryn Adams) is in progress, with all of the town's residents in attendance. The festivities are cut short by the arrival of commanding officer Per Vallgren (Samuel S. Hinds), who informs everyone that Russia has commenced bombing without warning, and all able-bodied men are to mobilize. Per's Nobel Prize-winning son Knut (John Ellis) balks, pleading that his important studies must continue, but is finally persuaded by his father to join in. Viktor, a lieutenant, leaves fellow soldier and female friend Julia Engle

---

[19] Douglas W. Churchill, "Around and About Hollywood," *New York Times*, April 7, 1940, 127.

[20] *Ibid.*

The Other Films (1939-1940 season)

(Luli Deste) behind to watch over the town while he assembles his troops, joined by Gustaf Nerkuu (John Qualen), reluctant pacifist Tyko Gallen (Hardie Albright), and Paavo. While Paavo is saying goodbye to Lissa, a Russian plane flies overhead and fires at them, killing Lissa.

With the coming of winter, Viktor's troops dig in at a mountaintop with the task of holding advancing Russian troops at bay. They are joined by crack shot Birger Simberg (Stanley Fields), Jan Sikorsky (Henry Brandon), former American Olympian and old friend Dick Reynolds, and others. After the perimeter is crudely wired and booby-trapped with dangling cans attached to alert them of any advances, the group waits while boredom sets it, their food supply runs low, and tempers flare. Meanwhile, Tyko has taken a Russian prisoner (John Gallaudet) and brings him back to the troops' mountaintop cave. Many argue that he should have killed the Russian instead, but voice-of-reason Viktor disagrees. The prisoner's life is spared, but Simberg berates Tyko for his lack of killer instinct, and continues to do so at later times.

Boredom and a bad set of nerves set in at the Finn's mountaintop cave while waiting for those pesky Russian troops to return. John Qualen (left), John Arledge (third from left, with scarf), Philip Dorn (sitting on table), and Stanley Fields (right) in *Ski Patrol* (1940).

Stop Yellin'

Later, there's a nighttime advance of Russian soldiers, crawling through the snow and snipping away at the wire fence. The rattle of a dropped can alerts the Finnish soldiers, who open fire and drive the Russians back. With this small victory behind them, Viktor orders the mining of the side of the mountain. While the mining is in progress, Russian paratroopers arrive en masse and swarm over the hillside, threatening to surround the small retreating force. Knut makes the altruistic sacrifice of scrambling for the mines' detonator in spite of the impossible odds. He is shot and killed just as he blows up most of the advancing enemy. Per is informed of his son's death.

The Russians realize that they'll never be able to advance as long as the Finns hold the mountaintop. Officer Ivan Dubrosky comes up with a plan: Burrow into the mountain with mining equipment, fill it with explosives, and blow the mountain and its occupants to smithereens. The Russians go to work, and it soon becomes evident to the Finns what their opponents' plan is. When a Finnish supply detachment attempts to reach the mountaintop, the Russians open fire causing an avalanche that buries the helpless Finns.

Viktor decides to risk skiing back to town to alert general headquarters of their now-desperate situation, and barely succeeds in doing so. Once in town, he is reunited briefly with his mother (Leona Roberts) and Julia. He relieves Sorenson (Christian Rub) of his watchtower post and sends him on with the message. Alone with Julia, the two now realize their love for each other, both wishing on an overhead shooting star. Unfortunately, duty calls and Viktor must return to his post, which he does, informing homesick Gustaf that his wife is about to deliver their first child. Later, against Viktor's orders, Gustaf attempts to go AWOL, but is shot dead halfway down the mountain. A shot of his wife's newborn baby cuts back to a fadeout on Gustaf's dead body.

The Finns' Russian prisoner overhears two of them planning to kill him, so he attempts to escape after nightfall. Confronted by Tyko who's on guard duty outside, the prisoner convinces Tyko to let him go. Or so he thinks; Tyko, by now so brainwashed by Simberg's continued taunts, changes his mind and shoots the fellow in the back. Viktor prevents a now-frenzied Tyko from beating the lifeless body with his rifle, firing a sarcastic comment at Simberg. From his reaction, it is evident that Simberg now feels remorse over Tyko's mental collapse.

The drilling finally stops, and the Finns now realize that their time is nearly up. Viktor decides that the only solution is to ski down and blow up the entrance to the Russian's mineshaft before they can fill and detonate it. He assembles a small group of volunteers that includes Simberg, Paavo, Reynolds, Sikorsky and several others, supplying a number of of them with nitro glycerin. The group sets out on what appears to be a suicide mission. The Russians fire upon them, and Jan sacrifices his life by skiing into a machine gun nest, his supply of nitro exploding when he is shot. Before long, most of the other skiers are shot

THE OTHER FILMS (1939-1940 SEASON)

as well, leaving only Viktor and Paavo. Viktor skis on with the remaining nitro, leaving Paavo behind to fend off more Russians. Paavo manages to knife and kill one more attacker before he, too, is shot and killed.

Approaching the mine's entrance, Viktor is shot and wounded. Dubrosky is sent out to capture the intruder. Confronting Viktor, the two old friends recognize each other. Dubrosky says he must take the nitro from Viktor, but will allow him to "escape." When Dubrosky returns, however, he is immediately branded a traitor, and shot dead on the spot. The nitro he has strapped around his neck explodes, achieving the original goal of the Finns.

Much later, Viktor and Julia are reunited, and stand with Per over the graves of Paavo and Lissa. When the two young lovers depart, Per remains and quietly prays aloud: "Forgive them, father, they know not what they've done. The victory is theirs, but they couldn't have realized the cost to them—and to us. The flower of our youth, trampled by their mad ambition. All of them gone, destroyed before their lives had begun, and to what end, O Lord? To what end?"

Ski Patrol was an unofficial reworking of Universal's *The Doomed Battalion* (1932; Cyril Gardner), in which a troop of Austrians find themselves in a similar predicament while fighting the Italians in the Alps during World War I. The remake is a good-looking film, with several handsome sets (specifically the Olympic awards hall filled with a load of healthy-looking extras), excellent nighttime photography, and a lot of great stock footage deftly intercut with the new. The extensive stock footage was culled from Universal's own news division and from other stock libraries, the most rare scenes (costing $25 per foot) showing Russian machinegun units parachuting to earth.[21] The film starts off with a well-executed montage of the Winter Olympic events accompanied by the unseen "announcer" who drones on about the event. Later in the film is some fascinating footage of Finnish troops skiing down a mountainside during the dead of night, illuminated solely by their flares held high.

Bosley Crowther dismissed the film in his *New York Times* review: "Except for a few stock shots of skiers chasing down snowy slopes, the whole picture has the unmistakable artificiality of a studio-made rush job. The manifest irony of former sports rivals fighting one another to the death is given no more than platitudinous point. And the melodramatic action, which should have been tense and exciting, is limp and laboriously contrived. The heroic defense of the Finns certainly deserves a better cinema memorial than this."[22]

Lew Landers' direction suffered somewhat from the production's rushed pace and was singled out for criticism by several reviewers, as was newcomer Huston's final script. Landers managed to offer some nice touches, however: Simberg "notching" his kills by planting spent shell casings in a line in the

---

[21] *Ibid.*

[22] Bosley Crowther, "The Screen," *New York Times*, May 21, 1940, 29.

snow, retrieving one when he realizes he missed; the nighttime advance of the Russian troops crawling through the snow while the only sounds heard are the howling wind and the snips of the wire; and the cool rear-projection shot of Paavo approaching the machine gun nest on skis, heading straight for the Russian fighters in the foreground, and the explosion that follows.

Ski Patrol is notable as perhaps the only film made about the brief Russian-Finnish conflict, and in spite of Crowther's dismissal the film had a lot going for it, not the least of which was the unique setting and the freshness of the topic. Ed Curtiss, the film's editor, made the most of the footage shot by cinematographer Milton Krasner, and integrated the hefty amounts of excellent stock footage to supplement and beef up the on-screen action. The film's biggest asset are the interesting characterizations written by Huston and the solid cast of relative unknowns chosen to portray them, including Samuel S. Hinds, Stanley Fields, Kathryn Adams, John Arledge, John Qualen, Henry Brandon, and Hardie Albright, lured back from the stage after a five-year absence. Unfortunately, Tyko's descent into madness is presented in somewhat of a ham-fisted fashion: Simberg's former verbal imprecations regarding shooting the prisoner are unnecessarily repeated over a close-up of Tyko right before he shoots the escapee, and a later shot of a completely-mad Tyko playing with a knife is gratuitous and almost laughable.

In June 1941, a little over a year after *Ski Patrol*'s release, Finland joined Germany in an attack on the USSR, clouding the viewing public's allegiances and thereby reducing the odds that *Ski Patrol* would ever see a reissue.

Alias the Deacon
(Director: Christy Cabanne; Released May 17, 1940)

The last of Pivar's first six non-series films to be released over a four-month period in 1940 was a return to comedy, this time a remake of a remake of an adapted stage play. *Alias the Deacon*, a comedy co-written by playwrights John B. Hymer and LeRoy Clemens, was a popular three-act play that ran for 277 performances at New York's Harris Theater from late 1925 into 1926, with popular stage star Berton Churchill in the lead. Universal was quick to take note, acquiring the rights, assigning Charles Kenyon and Walter Anthony to adapt it for the screen, and Edward Sloman to direct. Jean Hersholt starred as the deacon in this silent version released in 1927. With the coming of sound, Universal (like so many other studios) looked to their silent properties as possibilities for remake, and *Alias the Deacon*, with its stage origins and proven popularity, was ripe for a revisit. Kurt Neumann was assigned to direct the new version, and original stage star Berton Churchill was hired to reprise his role. *Half a Sinner* was the second go-round's title when released in 1932, with Churchill the most notable aspect of an otherwise sluggish adaption.

The Other Films (1939-1940 season)

Seven years later in mid-1939 Universal once again considered dusting off the play as a vehicle for W.C. Fields,[23] a logical choice for the role of the cardsharp con artist who cozies up to the town's citizens in the guise of a God-fearing deacon. Fields as lead, unfortunately, did not materialize, but Universal plodded forward regardless, assigning the vehicle to executive producer Warren Douglas and associate producer Pivar. *Alias the Deacon* was Pivar's most lavish production to date, given a seventeen-day shooting schedule and comparatively lush budget of $205,000. The remake was scheduled for January 1940, with direction by Richard Wallace and noted comedy writer Nat Perrin scripting.[24] By the time the film actually went before cameras on January 19, 1940, Pivar had reassigned direction to dependable standby Christy Cabanne, with a cast that included Bob Burns in the lead, Peggy Moran and Dennis O'Keefe as the young lovers, Guinn "Big Boy" Williams, Edward Brophy, Jack Carson, Virginia Brissac, Thurston Hall, and Bennie Bartlett.[25] Mischa Auer was a welcome last-minute addition to the cast, a personal appearance tour concluding just in time to squeeze in his part as a barber before moving on to the next "Baby Sandy" film.[26]

Stanley Cortez, a string of films for Universal as director of photography already to his credit, was behind the camera, and Milton Carruth rejoined Pivar as editor following their first collaboration on *Zanzibar*. Richard Wallace, originally assigned and announced as the film's director, was yanked to helm a Gloria Jean production.[27] Or at least that was the official statement; Wallace's relationship with Universal was instead terminated, his last effort for the studio the previous Gloria Jean starrer *The Under-Pup* released back in September 1939.

Studio production chief Charles Rogers had brought in M.F. Murphy back in 1936 as production manager. Murphy's job was to keep tabs on all in-house productions from beginning to end, and issue a weekly report to studio heads on each film's progress and adherence to budget. Impressed by director Cabanne's track record at the studio and his ability to stay within schedule and budget, Murphy was pleased to see the director's assignment to this film; his weekly status reports reflect his admiration for the veteran director. On January 20, 1940: "Their first day out was completed in accordance with our

---

[23] Hedda Hopper, "Fear Rules Producers in Choice of Subjects," *Los Angeles Times*, May 21, 1939) C3.

[24] "'U' Remaking 'Deacon,'" *Boxoffice*, December 2, 1939, 84.

[25] Douglas W. Churchill, "Screen News Here and in Hollywood," *New York Times*, January 19, 1940, 22.

[26] Edwin Schallert, "Auer Returns for 'Alias the Deacon' Role," *Los Angeles Times*, January 31, 1940, 13.

[27] "Hollywood Personnelities," *Boxoffice*, January 13, 1940, 36.

plans and we believe there should be no difficulty in finishing up this show, with the help of Christy Cabanne, right on schedule," and a week later: "This unit with the capable guidance of Christy Cabanne is maintaining their 17-day shooting schedule without difficulty..."[28]

Unfortunately, circumstances beyond the unit's control ultimately worked against the production. Both Bob Burns and Mischa Auer were laid up for several days, but director Cabanne—afflicted with a similar illness—plodded through several days of production in spite of feeling like hell. Considerable rain and cloudy conditions impeded exterior shooting, but it finally cleared and with some night work and second-unit shooting (overseen by assistant director Vaughn Paul), the film wrapped on Saturday night, February 10, just three days over schedule. The first preview on Friday, February 23, revealed some minor deficiencies, resulting in the decision to tweak the editing and take some additional road shots, once again delayed due to inclement weather. The finished film ended up costing $230,000, a hefty $25,000 over the approved budget. *Alias the Deacon* was released to theaters on May 17, 1940.

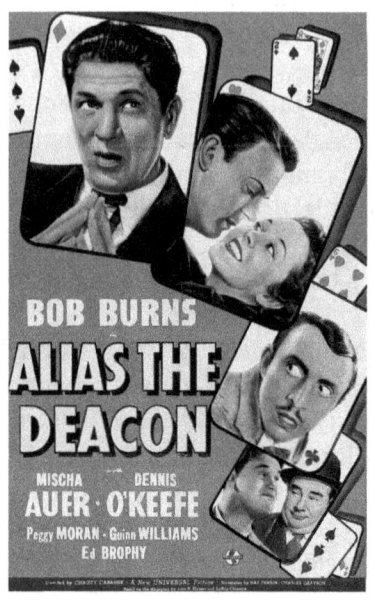

Tumbling from top: Bob Burns; Dennis O'Keefe and Peggy Moran; Mischa Auer; Guinn Williams and Edward Brophy. *Alias the Deacon* (1940). Image courtesy of Heritage Auction Galleries, Ha.com.

Card sharp Deke Caswell (Bob Burns) and his none-too-bright shill Stuffy (Edward Brophy) are run out of the town of Truxton when the sheriff finds them running a bogus game of chance. When his bus is delayed, Deke decides to hitch a ride and sneaks into the back of a truck driven by Johnny Sloan (Dennis O'Keefe). Johnny, meanwhile, flouts company rules by offering a lift to pretty young Phyllis (Peggy Moran). Arriving in the small town of Shelton ("The New Gusher City"), Johnny's boss is annoyed to find Phyllis, but the discovery of Deke seals Johnny's fate; he is fired.

Deke figures that this town is as good as any to chisel some suckers. When Sheriff Tom Yates (Spencer Charters) mistakes him for a deacon and explains that he needs help putting an end to the town's gambling problem, Deke assumes the role and moves into the Clark Hotel. Phyllis gets a job waitressing

---

[28] Universal Studios weekly internal status reports, January 20 and 27, 1940.

The Other Films (1939-1940 Season)

at the hotel as well, and Johnny pursues his dream of purchasing the local run-down garage owned by Ollie. Unfortunately, the remaining payment of $240 and the lack of a paying job to earn it stands in Johnny's way of fulfilling his dream. Romance blossoms between the young couple, but both of them are suspicious of Deke and his ulterior motives.

Deke soon runs afoul of unscrupulous Jim Cunningham (Thurston Hall), the town moneylender attempting to gain possession of Elsie Clark's (Virginia Brissac) hotel by forcing her to default on the mortgage she has with him. Cunningham has similar plans for Ollie, which is why Ollie is so keen on selling his garage. Cunningham is promoting an upcoming prizefight as well, having arranged with manager Sullivan (Jack Carson) to have his fighter Bull Gumbatz (Guinn Williams) duke it out with Knockout Blake. Sheriff Yates assumes the fight will be crooked, and adds that to his list of things to keep an eye on. Cunningham takes an immediate dislike to Deke due to the latter's outspoken disdain for the upcoming match.

Playing the innocent, Deke teams with Elsie in a game of bridge with Mrs. Gregory (Mira McKinney) and her daughter Mildred (Janet Shaw), figuring that the two of them are in cahoots with Cunningham to further impoverish Elsie. He wins big, of course, and turns half of the winnings over to Elsie.

Later, Deke appears before the Ladies' Community League to give a lecture railing against the evils of the upcoming fight, hoping to ingratiate himself with the town's women. Stuffy arrives mid-lecture, and it is all Deke can do to keep the dim-witted loudmouth from blowing his ruse. What Duke doesn't know is that word has come that Knockout Blake has been arrested and won't be able to fight, and that Johnny, in an effort to raise the much-needed final payment, has promoted himself as a fighter; he will receive $150 to fight and another $100 if he lasts ten rounds. Young Willie Clark (Bennie Bartlett) calls Deke out of the lecture hall and informs him of this, so Deke, wanting to help out the young couple, returns and abruptly changes the tone of his lecture, turning it into every woman's patriotic duty to support the fight. The crowd is won over.

The night of the fight arrives, and it is a knock-down, drag-out affair. Johnny is game, though, and barely manages to last the ten rounds. When Cunningham learns that Johnny is not a real boxer, he refuses to pay him. Infuriated, Johnny strikes Cunningham. Later on, when Cunningham finds his wallet missing, he accuses Johnny, who is jailed. Phyllis thinks that Deke stole it, but when she finds the wallet in Johnny's room she now assumes Johnny to be the thief. Heartbroken, she catches the first bus out of town, not wanting to relive an experience that she evidently went through some time earlier back in Truxton with her district attorney father. Deke convinces Elsie to bail Johnny out of jail, but when Johnny hears that Phyllis has fled, he appropriates Ollie's old car. Chasing down the bus, Johnny physically hauls Phyllis into his car and returns to town.

STOP YELLIN'

Deke learns that Cunningham is now demanding full and immediate payment from Elsie, or he is going to assume ownership of the hotel. Once again playing the innocent, Deke mentions possession of $2,500 in parishioners' money and orchestrates both Cunningham and Sullivan into a three-way game of draw poker. Cunningham makes a quick call to the sheriff, telling him to come over and catch the card sharp at work. A marathon game follows, with Deke's two competitors fudging the rules in their favor, only to have Deke use those altered rules to dominate the game and win all of their money. Infuriated, Cunningham blurts out that Deke couldn't possibly have the winning hand he just revealed since Cunningham knew which cards he dealt him. When the sheriff arrives, Sullivan accuses Cunningham of being the card sharp, and Cunningham is arrested.

With his considerable winnings, Deke gives enough money to Elsie to pay off her debt, and pays Ollie for the garage. He also exposes Sullivan as the real thief of Cunningham's wallet, resulting in Sullivan's arrest as well. With Elsie now in full ownership of the hotel, and Johnny receiving the garage as a gift from Deke, things only get better: the presence of oil is discovered under both properties!

Everyone loves Deke now, but the sheriff quietly suggests to him that it would be a good idea to leave town. Deke and Stuffy pack to leave, Deke stating that he promised Stuffy's mother he would return with her son. As they wander down the street, the corner of a Clark Hotel towel is spotted sticking out of Deke's bag.

Two of the film's highlights include the grueling, ten-round fight between O'Keefe and Williams, and the climactic poker game during which the participants' questionable talents are fully employed. Nat Perrin's script (co-written with Charles Grayson) focuses on and emphasizes the original play's comedic elements, resulting in a charming and very amusing film, one of the rare Pivar productions that *New York Times* reviewer Bosley Crowther actually admitted—begrudgingly—to liking ("an undistinguished but thoroughly genial little farce-comedy").[29] *The Hollywood Reporter*'s reviewer was unabashed in his praise, however: "Sticking close to the original plot, but injecting some riotous situations and running gags, scripters Nat Perrin and Charles Grayson have whipped up a well-contrived screenplay ... Christy Cabanne deserves special mention for his swell direction. Associate Producer Ben Pivar has stepped up in class with this production and has delivered a very neat job to Executive Producer Warren Douglas."[30]

Although much of the film's humor derives from Deke's frequent delivery of homespun adages and his straight-faced bilking of others, there are a number

---

[29] Bosley Crowther, "The Screen," *New York Times*, May 14, 1940, 27.
[30] "Bob Burns Tops In Excellent Cast," *Hollywood Reporter*, April 27, 1940, 3.

of other contributors to the overall mirth. Brophy is amusing as Deke's painfully thick plant Stuffy, his good nature turning to belligerence whenever the spirit moves him. Acting as Johnny's ringside man at the boxing match, Stuffy offers him his lucky rabbit's foot, which turns out to be filled with lead! Guinn Williams is hilarious as the ethically challenged, close-to-washed-up pug Bull, and his interplay with Bennie Bartlett's wisecracking teen provides some of the film's heartiest laughs. Mischa Auer is a particular standout as Andre, the high-strung, opera-singing owner of Andre's Tonsorial Parlor ("Coiffures, Shampoos, Turkish Baths, Swedish Rubs"), the town's barbershop and front for back-room stud poker games.

Putting aside any thoughts of what the film might have been with W.C. Fields in the lead,[31] Bob Burns was letter-perfect in the lead. "Bazooka" Bob Burns (1890-1956), as he was commonly referred to at the time, was an extremely popular comedian of the stage, radio, and film. Burns started out at an early age as a musician, and the "Bazooka" appellation derives from the crude trombone-like instrument he pieced together out of plumbers' pipes and a funnel. This musical assemblage became his trademark when popularized in appearances as part of Spike Jones' orchestra on Bing Crosby's *The Kraft Music Hall* radio show in the mid-thirties. Dubbing it a "bazooka," the name supposedly was an original amalgamation of two words, one slang—"bazoo," for a windy individual—and one foreign—the Dutch "bazuin" for "trumpet;" the World War II weapon (and the bubble gum, for that matter) were both named after Burns' creation.[32] (Burns' character Deke is introduced playing his "Bazooka," ostensibly to lure passersby to his street-side game of chance, and a brief opportunity for viewers to see this fabled instrument.) A folksy comedian and humorist known for his homespun hillbilly stories, Burns came to be known as "The Arkansas Traveler," and starred in a handful low-key comedies during the mid- to late-thirties, with a slew of uncredited bits predating these. Dropped from the Paramount contract list in 1939 after

---

[31] It often *feels* like a Fields film, from the opening credit score lifted from Fields' *You Can't Cheat an Honest Man* (1939; George Marshall), to the hotel where much of the action takes place, a set used just two months earlier for Fields' *My Little Chickadee* (1940; Edward F. Cline).

[32] According to Gerald Nachman's *Raised on Radio* (University of California Press, 1998), Burns was also indirectly responsible for what came to be known as the "laugh track." A number of Burns' off-color jokes on one of Crosby's later transcribed radio shows elicited lengthy and hearty laughter, and while the jokes themselves were cut from the show as finally aired, the audience response was saved for future use. These clips were employed at a later date when various guests' jokes fell flat, to enhance or replace tepid audience response.

a long association with that studio, Universal snapped him up for the lead role in *Alias the Deacon*.[33]

Burns' lackadaisical approach to acting differed from his costars, much to the annoyance of director Cabanne, who reportedly confronted him one time during shooting when it was obvious that Burns did not know his lines. Had he studied the script? "Why, no. If I studied my lines, I'd lose my spontaneity."[34] True or not, in this particular film Burns' dry wit and deadpan expressions prove to be sufficiently engaging, and the whole turns out to be enjoyable, if ultimately nondescript, fare. It was, however, a somewhat higher profile release than many of Pivar's efforts.

Alias the Deacon was the second of three Pivar releases in May, all of them reaching theaters over a two-week period; *Deacon* opened on the seventeenth, seven days after *Ski Patrol*, with the sixth film in the Arlen-Devine series, *Hot Steel*, the third release a week later. The series' seventh, *Black Diamonds*, wrapped production in early May as well, freeing up Pivar to commence with the 1940-1941 season's seven entries.

Berton Churchill, for what it is worth, died several months after this final version of *Alias the Deacon*'s release, and, according to one unconfirmed source, had an uncredited bit in this film. If accurate, what Pivar intended as a modest tribute may have been regarded by others as the bittersweet swansong of an artist who'd made the role famous, now relegated to an anonymous bit part.

§

---

[33] Douglas W. Churchill, "Screen News Here and in Hollywood," *New York Times*, March 4, 1941, 20.

[34] Hedda Hopper, "Hedda Hopper's Hollywood," *Los Angeles Times*, February 16, 1940, A15.

8 The Arlen-Devine Series, 1939-1941 (Part 2, the 1940-1941 Season)

In early May 1940, Universal held the first of two regional sales conventions at the Ambassador Hotel in Atlantic City, with the second scheduled to open May 18 in Chicago. William A. Scully, Vice President and Regional Sales Manager, announced plans for the upcoming 1940-1941 season, stating that the company intended to produce more pictures than the previous season, and more with higher budgets. Diminishing foreign returns were given as the primary reason for this up-tick in production, with the goal of increased domestic business.[1] Scully reiterated the company's "flexible" policy which had been put into effect the previous season, wherein additional stars and productions would be added to the announced program as opportunities arose. Scully went on to point out that Marlene Dietrich had been added to the previous season's *Destry Rides Again* in such a fashion. Blumberg, Cowdin, and Work were also in attendance for these announcements by Scully.[2]

The new schedule detailed forty-five features and fourteen "action" films, the latter comprised of seven westerns starring Johnny Mack Brown, Fuzzy Knight, and newcomer stunt-girl Julie Duncan, and seven more Arlen-Devine vehicles from the successful team of Cabanne and Pivar. The pairing of Arlen and Devine had proved to be a winner with audiences, third in popularity only behind MGM's two profitable Andy Hardy and Dr. Kildare series.[3] The Arlen-Devine series formula was described as a blend of adventure, romance, and humor, which was relatively standard for a lot of B's made; paraphrasing an interview with John Stone, a production assistant to Sol Wurtzel at 20th

---

[1] "Universal Plans to Make 59 Films," *New York Times*, May 13, 1940, page unknown.

[2] "59 from 'U' in 1940-1941; More Top Budgets to Offset Foreign Losses," *Motion Picture Herald*, May 18, 1940, 35.

[3] Hedda Hopper, "Hedda Hopper's Hollywood," *Los Angeles Times*, August 13, 1940, 9.

Century-Fox's B unit, Bosley Crowther put it thusly in *The New York Times*: "A general inclination is to make pictures which have the money touches ... the 'just plain folksy' stuff ... which family audiences eat up. Plenty of action ... is essential, as well as plenty of comedy angles; and a substantial underlying plot, no matter how apparent, is an absolute *sine qua non*."[4]

The upcoming series entries were given as *Tall Timber, Leather Pushers, South of the Amazon, Sky Hawks, The Wreck of the Zarago, The Return of the Sheik*, and *Northern Lights*.[5] Only *The Leather Pushers*, based on the popular stories by H.C Witwer, was filmed under the announced title. *Tall Timber* most likely ended up as *Men of the Timberland*, and *Return of the Sheik* was released as *Raiders of the Desert*. Tying the remaining titles to the eventual releases is more of a stretch, leading one to assume that they were abandoned to make way for new subjects.

Although Cabanne was announced as the director for the next seven installments of the series, only *The Devil's Pipeline* ended up in his hands. From 1941 through 1943 Cabanne jumped back and forth between Universal and RKO, where he directed the Scattergood Baines comedies with Guy Kibbee in the lead, and from 1944 through his last picture in 1948 worked primarily for Poverty Row's Monogram where he helmed a number of westerns and a drama, and for PRC on a comedy and a musical. The sole exception during this period was the Lugosi Cinecolor vehicle *Scared to Death* in 1947 for Robert Lippert's Screen Guild Productions.

The Leather Pushers
(Director: John Rawlins; Released September 13, 1940)

The Leather Pushers was the first of the series' second season to go into production, and it started the season with a bang.[6] Larry Rhine and Ben Chapman (later to be joined by Maxwell Shane) were assigned in April 1940 to throw together a workable script retaining Witwer's title, relying heavily on title recognition to lure patrons into the theaters.[7] And why not? Universal had embraced Witwer's original 1920 book twice before with sufficient success, first back in 1922 as a series of twenty-four two-reel silents starring Reginald

---

[4] Bosley Crowther, "How Doth the Busy Little 'B'," *New York Times*, January 2, 1938, 126.

[5] "Universal Plans to Make 59 Films," *op. cit.*

[6] Reviews of this film fluctuated in their spelling of the title, with *The Leatherpushers* and *The Leather-Pushers* appearing as frequently as *The Leather Pushers*. The opening credits give the latter as the spelling, two words, sans hyphen.

[7] Edwin Schallert, "'Leather Pushers' Feature Set at Universal," *New York Times*, April 24, 1940, 26.

The Arlen-Devine Series, Part II (1940-1941)

Denny, and again in 1930 as a series of ten two-reel talkie comedies starring Kane Richmond. Witwer, who was only thirty-nine when he died in 1929, was known primarily for his humorous boxing and baseball stories, written largely in slang. In addition to over 400 stories and magazine articles, he also scripted nearly 125 films and authored a pair of comic strips.[8]

Pivar rehired Astrid Allwyn to co-star, assumedly satisfied with her solid performance three years earlier in *Love Takes Flight*. Her role here is an amalgam of smaller roles portrayed in the first series by Laura LaPlante, Marian Nixon, and "Bubbles" Steiffel. For the first time in the life of the Arlen-Devine series, Cabanne was not behind the megaphone, tied up as he was with another Pivar production, *The Mummy's Hand*. In his stead, former editor John Rawlins was hired to direct,[9] having dabbled on-and-off with direction over the past eight years, demonstrating a sufficient degree of competency and flair. The completed script was ready by June 1940,[10] shooting commenced on Tuesday, July 9, the finished film released on September 13.

Dick Roberts (Richard Arlen) and Andy Adams (Andy Devine) are old buddies whose ongoing money-making plans never seem to pan out. Now Dick is trying to prepare Andy for professional wrestling, and hauls his reluctant pupil over to the gym of J.R. Stevens (Charles D. Brown) for an audition. When Andy's wrestling opponent for the audition throws some cheap punches, an irate Dick leaps into the ring and a huge free-for-all follows; it quickly becomes evident that Dick has some natural ability. Watching from ringside is slimy fight manager Slick Connolly (Douglas Fowley) and *The Journal*'s sports reporter Pat Danbury (Astrid Allwyn), assumed by her readers to be a male. Slick, convinced that he can make some money off Dick, fast-talks him into signing a contract, which Dick naively fails to read.

Twenty-six fights follow in rapid succession against opponents with names like Cyclone Waters, Joe Santoro, and George O'Bannon. Dick—billed as Kid Roberts—is victorious in each. For one fight he is paired with a washed-up fighter named Slugger Mears (Horace McMahon), who unbeknownst to Dick has agreed to take a dive solely to earn some money.

Pat Danbury's late father had the dream of building a camp for former boxers, to give them some honest, money-making work after their retirement from the ring. Pat is now Camp Danbury's driving force, along with a quartet of likable but down-on-their-luck former boxers: Slugger, Sailor McNeill (Shemp Howard), Joe Johnson (George Lloyd), and Pete Manson (Eddie Gribbon). When Slugger hands her the cash and ashamedly explains how he got it, Pat is

---

[8] "H.C. Witwer Dies; A Noted Humorist," *New York Times*, August 10, 1929, page unknown.

[9] "Screen News Here and in Hollywood," *New York Times*, July 10, 1940, 15.

[10] "Hollywood Personnelities," *Boxoffice*, June 22, 1940, 84.

STOP YELLIN'

incensed that he has been taken advantage of, and that ill-gotten gains would be used for the camp. She bangs out an article titled "Connolly Launches Kid Roberts on Tank Town Tour of Phoney Set-ups," and follows this with future articles stating the actual round Roberts' opponents will hit the mat, all based on insider information passed on to her.

When Dick and Andy learn that he has been made a chump, they confront Slick over this and the fact that they haven't yet been paid a cent for any of the fights. Slick promises a big-ticket fight to follow, but behind their backs comes up with a scheme to raffle off Roberts' contract for a dollar a ticket: "See a Fight…and Win a Fighter." Hearing this, Pat dashes off an article predicting the winner will be Slick Connolly himself, or a close relative. When the big night arrives, Slick gets even with her, "gifting" her a raffle ticket and then rigging it so that she wins.

At first Dick balks over being managed by the sportswriter who has taken so many shots at him in print. Pat explains that Slick was her target, and then introduces Dick to her quartet of ex-fighters. She details her camp's mission, and promises that her take in each fight will go directly to the camp. Hearing this, Dick softens and relents. When Pat's editor Frank Mitchell (Charles Lane) delivers her the ultimatum that she is either a sportswriter or sports manager, she quits. Ticked off, Mitchell writes another scathing article about Dick accompanied by an embarrassing illustration, and has it printed under Pat's byline. Thinking that Pat has made an even bigger chump out of him, Dick "fires" her and makes Andy his manager. The misunderstanding is eventually resolved, and Pat gives Dick a tour of the camp-to-be, touting its potential as a training camp for new fighters while giving the ex-fighters employment. A romance between the two quickly blossoms.

Gym owner and fight promoter Stevens still thinks Andy is a phony and refuses to give him a match, so Pat enlists the aid of her former sports writer buddies to put on pressure via the printed word. Annoyed by this, Stevens hatches a plan with Slick. A fight is lined up with a boxer named Givanni (Noble "Kid" Chissel), and the night of the fight a smooth-talking Slick borrows $100 from Pat in the form of a check. The fight is rigged and Givanni takes an obvious dive. The $100 check is offered as "proof" that Pat paid Slick to have Givanni throw the fight. Slick and Givanni disappear, so the fight commissioner (Wade Boteler) goes after Dick and suspends him.

Knowing that Slick and Givanni are the only ones who can prove his innocence, Andy and the four ex-boxers grab Stevens and through a combination of energetic rub-downs and ice treatments finally get the guy to reveal the two crooks' whereabouts. Andy goes after Slick and Givanni for evidence, but they resist and a three-way fight ensues. Andy has the upper hand, but Slick manages to stab him in the back. Dick arrives just in time to rescue Andy.

The Arlen-Devine Series, Part II (1940-1941)

Dick is reinstated, and a fight is quickly set up with the champ, Tim Grogan (Billy McGowan). As a result of his stabbing, Andy needs a blood transfusion the afternoon of the big fight. Dick agrees, putting his friend's wellbeing ahead of his chances of winning. Afterwards, he leaves Pat at the hospital with Andy, saying he is going to go and have the fight postponed. Instead, he goes through with it, which Pat and Andy quickly realize when they turn on the radio. Dick, in a weakened state due to loss of blood, is taking a horrible beating, and Andy is frustrated that he can't be there to talk his buddy through the fight. Hearing this, Joe and Pete head over to the ring and sneak into the control room. They commandeer the loudspeaker system, contact Pat and Andy by phone, then put Andy on the loudspeaker. Dick perks up when he hears his friend's voice, and following Andy's verbal instructions begins to dominate the fight. Andy's command to employ "Davy Jones' Locker"—a one-two-three combination that always seems to work—is heeded by Dick, and results in Grogan's knockout.

Later on, the camp is now finished, and all are happily employed and pleased with its success. When the cook comes to the door and rings the triangle to alert everyone, Joe and Pete respond instinctively to the "bell," knocking Andy to the ground.

This is the first out-and-out comedy of the series, and it is an enjoyable romp. Arlen's character seems a bit dimmer than usual in the earlier scenes, but he soon "matures" into the stalwart Dick audiences had come to expect, and he looks convincing during the various fight sequences. Devine, as usual, has the lion's share of the gags: his oversize bulk filling and eventually destroying a phone booth (perhaps one of the funniest bits in the entire series); making an early morning trek down his rooming-house hall, lifting some milk from one doorstep, a roll from another, a newspaper section from a third; and the bells from an alarm clock, a radio, and finally the cook's triangle all prompting the punch-happy ex-boxers into action, with Andy always the unfortunate recipient of their collective roundhouses.

As washed-up pugilist Sailor McNeill, Shemp Howard is an active, if mute, participant in many of the humorous bits, such as a long, single-take sequence where Andy animatedly regales Shemp with an accounting of a former, fictitious wrestling match. Soon after, Shemp and Andy remove boards from a boarded-up camp window, allowing Shemp full reign to react broadly as one after another of the boards strikes him in the noggin. Later, as each prizefight round ends and another begins, Shemp and Andy have one hell of a time climbing in and out of the ring's corner. And during the climactic fight, Joe and Pete experiment up in the control room in an effort to track down the loudspeaker system, first blaring a John Philip Sousa march to the bewildered fighters and patrons below, followed by several instances of shutting down the lights; Shemp takes the opportunity during these latter blackouts to surreptitiously club rival fighter Grogan over the head with his stool.

Reviewers for a welcome change almost unanimously embraced this series entry. Grace Kingsley, in the *Los Angeles Times*, was particularly effusive: "Surely the fastest and funniest fistic film ever to romp across the screen. So fast that you can't wink without missing a couple of punches, and so funny that the one-a-second laughs mount to a shrieking crescendo at the end. Suffice it to say that there are so many high spots that there's no room for dull ones."[11] The *Brooklyn Daily Eagle* was similarly enthusiastic: "Richard Arlen and Andy Devine, who have been together and so infectiously during the year's film output, are just as appealing—if not more so—in the first of Universal's 1940-41 series of melodramas co-starring them. John Rawlins' direction of this Ben Pivar production has successfully eliminated much extraneous matter...the dialog is crisp and provocative."[12] *The Hollywood Reporter* concurred: "The showmanship injected into this new version of 'The Leatherpushers' should boost the stock of the Richard Arlen-Andy Devine combination immeasurably. It is jam-packed with good clean comedy that will provoke laughs from any audience."[13] *Variety's* Herb Golden put matters in proper perspective by acknowledging *The Leather Pushers'* programmer status: "Because of its story it obviously fits into only the lower half of a dual bill in an action house, and for such a spot it's topnotch. Entertaining and well-produced under budget limitations."[14] And, for a rare occasion, Pivar was singled out for his behind-the-scenes contributions in overcoming the film's budgetary constraints: "Ben Pivar cunningly masked his low production budget with a first-rate cast and a well-knit script;"[15] "Producer Ben Pivar can chalk up a commendable production;"[16] and "Ben Pivar's production is thoroughly sound in all departments."[17]

The cast is uniformly good, with the interaction between Arlen and Allwyn crisp and amusing. Comedian and once-and-future Three Stooges member Shemp Howard is a welcome addition, with support from Eddie Gribbon, George Lloyd, and Horace McMahon as his companions-in-need. Director Rawlins' years of experience as a film editor assumedly influenced his direction of the film, coupled with cinematographer Stanley Cortez's footage and editor Arthur Hilton's assemblage of it, results in a taut, fast-moving comedy that's over in

---

[11] Grace Kingsley, "Fight Feature Previewed," *Los Angeles Times*, August 31, 1940, A7.

[12] A.R., "Dick Arlin (sic), Andy Devine Romp In Fight Film at Boro Strand," *Brooklyn Daily Eagle*, November 15, 1940, 13.

[13] "Arlen and Devine Give Their Best," *Hollywood Reporter*, September 3, 1940, 3.

[14] Herb Golden, "The Leather-Pushers," *Variety*, November 20, 1940, 18.

[15] Ivan Spear, "Spearheads," *Boxoffice*, September 7, 1940, 41.

[16] "Arlen and Devine Give Their Best," *op. cit.*

[17] "The Leatherpushers," *Daily Variety*, September 3, 1940, page unknown.

The Arlen-Devine Series, Part II (1940-1941)

a breathless sixty-four minutes. Their combined efforts shine in particular during the film's climactic fight sequence.

Things were looking up at Universal during this period, with profits on the upswing. Chairman of the Board J. Cheever Cowdin announced that the third quarter of the company's fiscal year, which ended on July 27, 1940, showed net profits for the first thirty-nine weeks amounting to $2,161,804. This compared favorably to the previous year's profits of $989,995 for the corresponding period of time, and a net loss of $773,247 for the corresponding period two years earlier.[18] The popularity of Pivar's low-budget films was a contributing factor to these increased earnings, if only in a small way. Unfortunately, after the high note hit with *The Leather Pushers*, the series went into a gradual decline with only one or two exceptions, hampered by even more juvenile plots and lackluster writing. Coincidence? Perhaps, but it may have had something to do with just how thinly spread Pivar was at this time, responsible for a whopping twelve productions released in 1940 alone; the following year Pivar would oversee a more manageable eight productions, with subsequent years a less stressful average of five credited productions. And perhaps Universal decided it could skimp on the remainder of the series, figuring that it had by now earned a devoted audience who would return based on the teaming, regardless of the gradual deterioration in quality. It did not help matters that Arlen was beginning to grow bored with the ongoing formula and the sameness of the plots, and that alone may have signaled to the powers that the end was nigh.

The Devil's Pipeline
(Director: Christy Cabanne; Released November 1, 1940)

The Devil's Pipeline followed, a quickie cash-in on MGM's *Boom Town* (Jack Conway) and Warners' *Flowing Gold* (Alfred E. Green) involving petroleum engineering and the use of forced labor at a South Pacific oil field. Clarence Upson Young was assigned in June[19] to assist Larry Rhine, Ben Chapman, and Paul Huston in adapting Huston's original *Isle of Missing Men* for the screen, a story having much in common with the previous year's *Tropic Fury*; Christy Cabanne was to direct once again. In spite of what advance publicity had announced, this would be the last of Cabanne's Arlen-Devine vehicles, but by no means his last for Pivar. *The Devil's Pipeline* went before cinematographer Woody Bredell's cameras on August 1, 1940,[20] and was retitled *South of*

---

[18] "Universal Film Earnings Climb," *Los Angeles Times*, September 10, 1940, 23.

[19] "Hollywood Personnelities," *Boxoffice*, June 29, 1940, 22.

[20] "Screen News Here and in Hollywood," *New York Times*, July 25, 1940, 20.

Sumatra[21] by the time shooting completed mid-August[22] and footage was turned over to editor Ed Curtiss;[23] articles and numerous trade ads for Universal's schedule of upcoming releases now referred to it under the new name. Not for long, though; the film had reverted back to its original title by October,[24] and was released as such on November 1. With the conclusion of this film, director Cabanne parted ways with Universal for a couple of years for several projects at RKO.

The plot, which probably sounds better on paper than it looks on the screen, has penniless petroleum engineers Dick Talbot (Richard Arlen) and Andy Jennings (Andy Devine) rehired by Peerless Indies Corporation President R.J. Adams (Emory Parnell). They are to investigate strange messages emanating from the company's oil fields on the East Indies island of Soerleng: secretary Laura Lawson (Jeanne Kelly) has followed her signature on the messages with the shorthand symbol for "Send Help." Dick and Andy accept, and head to Soerleng under the guise of oil workers looking for a job, their goal to track down Laura and get the full story.

In Soerleng, operation head Dowling (James Flavin) tells them there's no work. It doesn't take long for them to find out what's going on down there, however. Sucked into a bogus bar fight, they are arrested on trumped-up charges and sentenced by Gaddi Sang (Francis McDonald, as one of the series' most sinister villains) to two years hard labor at the Peerless oil fields. The scam is that Dowling, along with right-hand man George Butler (John Eldredge), has Gaddi Sang arrest and provide free labor. The trio then pockets the payroll money sent down from the home office in New York. Head guard Molugi (Dick Botiller) keeps the prisoners in line, and any that attempt escape are quickly captured and dealt with by Gaddi Sang's native troops.

An escape is planned, but prisoner Benedict (Eddy Waller) convinces Andy that to join would be foolhardy. Benedict's advice is soon borne out when a mole embedded within the prisoners rats out the plan, resulting in the escapees' deaths. Dowling berates Butler for ordering the escapees shot, saying that laborers are hard to find. The deaths are later attributed to malaria.

Dick finally gets to meet Laura when he is hauled into the office over a fight. He manages to connect with her later on and is filled in on the forced labor scam, Laura helpless to do more as she is a virtual prisoner as well. Lucky for her that Butler has the hots for her; he keeps her on in the hopes of scoring. Prisoner Benedict, having served his trumped-up sentence, is due to be released, so Dick asks him to smuggle out a letter to be mailed back to

---

[21] "Screen News Here and in Hollywood," *New York Times*, August 16, 1940, 11.

[22] "Steady Production Pace Indicated," *Boxoffice*, August 17, 1940, 64.

[23] Some sources erroneously attribute the editing to Ray Curtiss.

[24] "Screen News Here and in Hollywood," *New York Times*, October 31, 1940, 29.

The Arlen-Devine Series, Part II (1940-1941)

the home office explaining the corruption in Soerleng, and that he and Andy are prisoners. Gaddi Sang has no real intention of letting Benedict go, however; Benedict is stopped and killed in transit, and Dick's letter is discovered. Their true identities now exposed, Dick and Andy are jailed. Not for long, though; Dick feigns losing his mind, and they escape when the guard comes to check him out.

Dick takes the first step in a planned uprising, taking possession of the company's supply of nitro glycerin and planting the explosives in key locations for future use. Later on with the backing of their fellow prisoners, Dick and Andy overpower Molugi and his guards. Fellow prisoner Tala Mu (Ray Mala) shoots and kills Butler as he attempts to escape, but Gaddi Sang is successful in avoiding capture, and heads off to gather his native troops. When he returns with his forces,

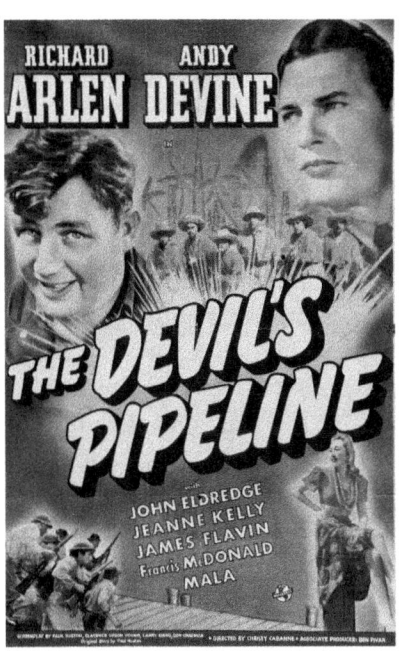

The Devil's Pipeline (1940). Image courtesy of Heritage Auction Galleries, Ha.com.

he is faced with a hastily-erected barricade, armed prisoners firing from beyond. Dick's appropriated nitro glycerin decimates the attacking force, and Gaddi Sang is shot dead. Dowling makes his way to the top of a tall derrick that overlooks the compound, setting up a machine gun and opening fire. Dick topples the tower with some more explosives, and Dowling is killed. All ends happily: Dick is made manager of the Soerleng office, and romance blossoms with Laura. As usual.

Arlen and Devine's banter is more comedic in this film, but frequently falls flat, the jokes thin and humorless. Even Devine's usually-dependable asides miss the mark, although a couple of them warrant some chuckles, such as when he describes a "dream" meal to a rapturous bartender, and his constant kvetching about his need for food. One particular misfire is Devine's "Squeezy, Go Sleepy" routine, wherein a quick pinch to the back of the neck incapacitates his opponent. It is just plain silly, even more so than the usual stomach-bump employed in the two or three donnybrooks per film, and quickly grows old with its repeated use. It is even used as the film's closing gag, Devine accidentally rendering himself unconscious when demonstrating how it is done. I suppose someone found it amusing.

Statuesque actress Jeanne Kelly plays the blindingly blonde, flag-raising secretary, eventually entering into a limp romance with Arlen. A relative newcomer who'd just signed a long-term contract with Universal,[25] Kelly had a handful of minor roles, eventually landing in westerns before her contract expired in 1941 and was not renewed. She married radio writer (and eventual scriptwriter and film director) Richard Brooks,[26] changed her name to Jean Brooks, and went on to star in a number of minor features into the later forties; most memorable of these were the Val Lewton thrillers *The Seventh Victim* and *The Leopard Man* (both 1943). Had she not married and changed her professional name, it might have been interesting to see how MGM would have dealt with its new star Gene Kelly a year later. Any confusion between their sound-alike names would have been dispelled immediately, as there was no mistaking the two: Jeanne was far prettier.

Both Pivar and Cabanne were singled out by several contemporary reviewers for their contributions to the film, and for a refreshing change were reviewed within the context of the modest world of B films, and nothing more. *The Hollywood Reporter* was pleased with the results, stating that "Christy Cabanne did an efficient job of direction, giving the picture excellent pace and balancing its various elements nicely ... Ben Pivar injected more than ordinary production value into the picture, which, in all departments, is well up to the standard set for the series."[27] *Daily Variety* concurred: "Christy Cabanne directed with an eye on movement, injecting sufficient action and comedy in the proceedings to keep the audience interested ... Ben Pivar's production is capable for class of picture."[28]

Arlen demonstrated his patriotism during this period, with action and an open wallet rather than empty words as some others were wont to do. Tapping in to his experience gained serving with the Canadian Royal Air Force back during the First World War, Arlen established and helped equip a training school able to train 300 airplane pilots annually. Six training planes were purchased, hangars built to house them, and sleeping quarters constructed to house the trainees during their stay.[29]

Arlen took a break from his national defense-related efforts to embark on a personal appearance tour following the release in November of *The Devil's Pipeline*. Well-liked and well-received in South America due to several previous films set south of the border, Arlen headed for Rio de Janeiro and surrounding

---

[25] Douglas W. Churchill, "News of the Screen," *New York Times*, September 20, 1940, 26.

[26] "Jeanne Kelly Becomes Bride," *Los Angeles Times*, June 3, 1941, A1.

[27] "New Arlen-Devine Vivid Melodrama," *Hollywood Reporter*, December 5, 1940, 4.

[28] "The Devil's Pipeline," *Daily Variety*, December 5, 1940, 3.

[29] "Would Train Fliers," *Salt Lake Tribune*, August 1, 1940, 9.

The Arlen-Devine Series, Part II (1940-1941)

areas to drum up interest in his newest feature.[30] Devine, meanwhile, stayed close to home, doting on his hundred racing pigeons that occupied so much of his free time.[31]

Lucky Devils
(Director: Lew Landers; Released January 3, 1941)

Lucky Devils came next, with newsreel photographers Dick McManus (Arlen) and his assistant Andy Tompkins (Devine) tangling with saboteurs. Announced in August under the title of *Flying News*,[32] it had acquired the working title of *East of Miami*[33] by the time production was underway in September 1940. Lew Landers, who had adequately helmed Pivar's *Enemy Agent* and *Ski Patrol* the year before, was lured back from Republic to direct after a six-film stint with that studio.

Daredevil newsreel photographers McManus and Tompkins have a reputation for their breathtaking footage, but frequently try the patience of Momsen (Tim Ryan), their long-suffering boss at the Mercury News Reel Co. Dick finagles a lot of hot leads from his fiancée Norma Bishop (Dorothy Lovett), who works in the teletype department at Consolidated News Service. Dick stops at nothing to gain spectacular footage, and frequently breaks the law in order to do so, repeatedly citing the "rights of the citizens." When the duo secretly films the off-limits Phillips Dam, the government threatens to revoke Mercury's photographic permits. There are rumors of plans to sabotage the dam, which would imperil the water supply of millions of people. FBI agent Chandler (William Forrest) is on the case, and he is concerned that Dick and Andy's footage might prove useful to the saboteurs.

When Dick smuggles himself on board a new, pilotless "robot" plane that's about to be demonstrated to the press, he ends up inadvertently causing it to crash. He and Andy are arrested, but Momsen reluctantly agrees to bail them out to get his hands on the spectacular footage Dick managed to shoot. Later, Dick sneaks a document from Norma's desk, an advance report of the upcoming arrival of the Duke and Duchess of Vere. Taking advantage of this insider knowledge, Dick and Andy attend the arrival, and their presence results in a foiled assassination attempt. But while Dick is hailed as a hero, Norma is fired for "leaking" the information to him.

---

[30] Edwin Schallert, "Two Features Announced for Arlen, Devine Team," *Los Angeles Times*, July 24, 1940, 13.
[31] "Hobbies in Hollywood," *Los Angeles Times*, September 22, 1940, C1.
[32] "Screen News Here and in Hollywood," *New York Times*, August 7, 1940, 15.
[33] "Hollywood Personnelities: Scripters," *Boxoffice*, August 31, 1940, 34.

Norma breaks off from Dick, incensed that he always seems to use her solely for self-serving information, and never follows through with his vague promises of marriage. He feels guilty about her firing, though, and arranges for her to become radio station WXEW's news broadcaster on the soon-to-become-popular "Woman's Angle" broadcast. In spite of his efforts, Norma resists Dick's appeals to resume their questionable relationship.

Ritter (Ralf Harolde) and Berko (Dick Terry), a pair of spies from the usual unnamed country, intend to sabotage Phillips Dam. To that end they pose as film producers and attempt to acquire Dick's unauthorized footage of the dam. Undeterred when he refuses, the two break into his office after hours and steal the footage.

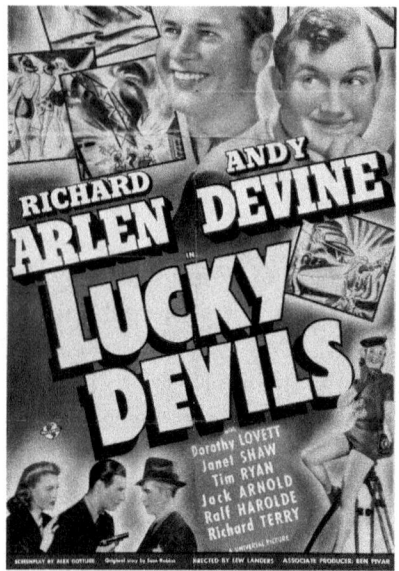

Lucky Devils (1941). Image courtesy of Heritage Auction Galleries, Ha.com.

Deciding to get even with Dick's past trickery, Norma fools him into thinking the dam has been blown up. Realizing that they no longer have the "before" footage of the dam, Andy sneaks into the 1939 New York World's Fair and "borrows" the model exhibit of the dam, ostensibly for some repairs. He takes it back to the barn at his aunt's farm to obtain some footage. Mopey (Robert Winkler), a little kid who flies model airplanes with Andy as a hobby, thinks the footage would be more spectacular with an explosion, so while Andy is otherwise occupied, Mopey turns on the camera and blows up the model. Andy takes the footage and has it rushed into theaters as an "exclusive," but it is quickly revealed as a hoax. FBI agent Chandler links the model's theft to Dick and Andy, and to the planned sabotage. He intends to arrest them.

Meanwhile, Ritter and Berko have been led to believe that Dick has incriminating footage that will reveal them as the intended saboteurs, so they trick Norma into leading them to the two photographers at the barn location. Elsewhere, agent Chandler confronts Andy's girl Gwendy (Janet Shaw) and demands to know the duo's whereabouts. Since she is mad with Andy, she agrees to take Chandler to the barn as well. When Chandler arrives, he finds that Ritter and Berko have been overpowered by Andy and Mopey bombarding them from above with model airplanes, and by Dick using his always-reliable fists. The two spies are arrested, and Dick and Andy are hailed as heroes.

THE ARLEN-DEVINE SERIES, PART II (1940-1941)

Later, Norma is fired from her broadcasting position, but doesn't mind; Dick has finally proposed to her. Andy does likewise with Gwendy. Everyone's happy.

Alex Gottlieb's script, from an original story by Sam Robins, is weaker than the usual series entry, and further weakened by a ludicrous climax that compromises all that has gone before. Heavier on humor and some borderline slapstick, and lighter on action, the plot as such is paper-thin and frequently nonsensical. Lapses in logic abound, such as why would everyone be so concerned about the duo's footage of the "off-limits" dam when there is a detailed model of the thing on display at the World's Fair? Regardless, cast and crew make the most of what was handed them, and the film manages to entertain if only sporadically.

One saving grace—and it is a small one—is that given the premise around which the film is based, and all of the newsreel footage shot and shown, there's more of a legitimate excuse for the oodles of stock footage employed. The film's first half-minute is a nicely executed, split-screen montage of the duo surrounded by newsreel images that mimic several contemporary weekly newsreels' openings. Unfortunately, this slick opening is quickly forgotten when followed by some obvious studio inserts of the intrepid photographers intercut with actual newsreel footage; it could have been handled far more effectively by director Lew Landers and his cinematographer Charles Van Enger. Too bad it was not.

Dorothy Lovett makes a good romantic foil for Arlen in the role of his frustrated fiancée. Comparatively new to film, Lovett had appeared in a handful of uncredited bits before landing at RKO as co-star in the "Dr. Christian" series featuring Jean Hersholt. Born in Providence, Rhode Island, Lovett had earlier been employed in that same city by radio station WPRO, where she gave fashion news broadcasts. With this radio experience under her belt, Lovett was able to offer some inside tips and suggestions to director Landers to supposedly add some additional verisimilitude to her role.[34]

As Andy's dimwitted, marble-mouthed, bathing beauty-wannabe girlfriend Gwendy, Janet Shaw is inconsistently amusing. Jack Arnold is his usual pompous self as rival newsreel photographer Bradford. Shemp Howard has a brief but humorous unbilled part as an inept pickpocket stuck in a cell with Arlen and Devine. Ralf Harolde and Dick Terry are stick-figure stereotypes as the two saboteurs.

Variety, one of the few papers to review the film, was underwhelmed by the plot ("Cast does well enough with the trite situations, though it's difficult adult entertainment"), but charitable enough to give a modicum of credit where a modicum of credit was due ("General production attributes are there, however,

---

[34] "Radio Newscaster Lands Acting Job," *Charleston Gazette*, September 15, 1940, 24.

with Lew Landers' direction being as good as could be expected under the circumstances").[35] Faint praise, indeed. *Lucky Devils* landed in theaters on January 3, 1941.

A Dangerous Game
(Director: John Rawlins; Released August 22, 1941)

Next to be filmed, but the last of the series to be released, was *A Dangerous Game*. Announced in September with the title *Who Killed Doc Robin?*, Jeanne Kelly was to again co-star along with a solid supporting cast of character actors that included Marc Lawrence, Vince Barnett, and Ed Brophy. This was another Rawlins-directed effort intended as a comedy, but sadly fell somewhat short of that goal. Filmed late 1940, it was released in New York City's Rialto Theater on March 3, 1941,[36] but not nationally until late August of that same year, fifty-one weeks after it had gone into production.

The thundering stock music that accompanies the opening credits for *A Dangerous Game*, while admittedly familiar from previous Universal programmers, promises thrills to come. The film's opening shot reinforces this, with a moody tracking shot following a faceless stranger as he approaches the Fleming Sanitarium on a windswept night, moving forward through the establishment's iron gates. Pan up to a second-floor window as a shadowy figure looms over a man sleeping in bed, interrupted when a female enters the room, silhouetted by the hall light beyond. She takes in the scene, and screams in terror; it is Jeanne Kelly in all her Rubenesque splendor. She flees in terror down the sprawling circular staircase to the hall below where she is confronted by the establishment's two head doctors. Promising stuff, indeed, but it is all downhill from there.

This is one of the weakest entries in the fourteen-film series. The script by Larry Rhine and Ben Chapman, based on their original story and beefed up with contributions from Maxwell Shane, tries far too hard for laughs in what was intended as a mystery laced with humor. Not that there aren't some laughs; there are. But so much of it falls flat, and the added slapstick elements are intrusive and unwelcome. As for the mystery, it is standard B film stuff, and is not so mysterious when viewed with closer scrutiny.

Silas Biggsby (Andrew Tombes, here billed as "Toombes") arrives at the Fleming Sanitarium with a satchel full of the $250,000 he has just inherited. Cab driver Bugs (Edward Brophy) recognizes his penny-pinching customer from an article in the newspaper and remembers the satchel he was carrying,

---

[35] Naka, "Lucky Devils," *Variety*, February 26, 1941, 16.

[36] "Screen News Here and in Hollywood," *New York Times*, March 3, 1941, page unknown.

so he heads off to inform his tough guy boss Joe (Marc Lawrence). In the meantime, sanitarium doctors Robin (Irving Mitchell) and Fleming (Robert O. Davis[37]) confront their hysterical nurse Anne Bennett (Kelly), screaming her head off as a result of the previously described opening sequence. Fleming has told her never to go near perpetually sedated patient Olaf Henderson (George Pembroke), and fires her because she has disobeyed his orders. Biggsby's arrival cuts short her termination, as he is the boss and Bennett is his tiddlywinks-playing companion; he restores her position and reprimands Fleming. Fleming is immediately suspect in the viewer's mind, since he speaks with a heavy German accent.

Joe and Bugs arrive soon after, and with pistols drawn force the sanitarium's occupants onto the floor while they demand to know the whereabouts of the satchel of cash. In addition to Fleming, Robin, Biggsby, and Bennett are male nurse Andy McAllister (Andy Devine), and two patients: flirtatious, heavy-drinking Mrs. Hubbard (Mira McKinney) and poetry-spouting, knife-throwing Mr. Whipple (Richard Kean). Dick Williams (Richard Arlen) arrives unannounced and gains control of the situation, seemingly another hood after the cash. After several face-offs with Joe and Bugs, the three of them agree at a deal where they'll split the cash three ways.

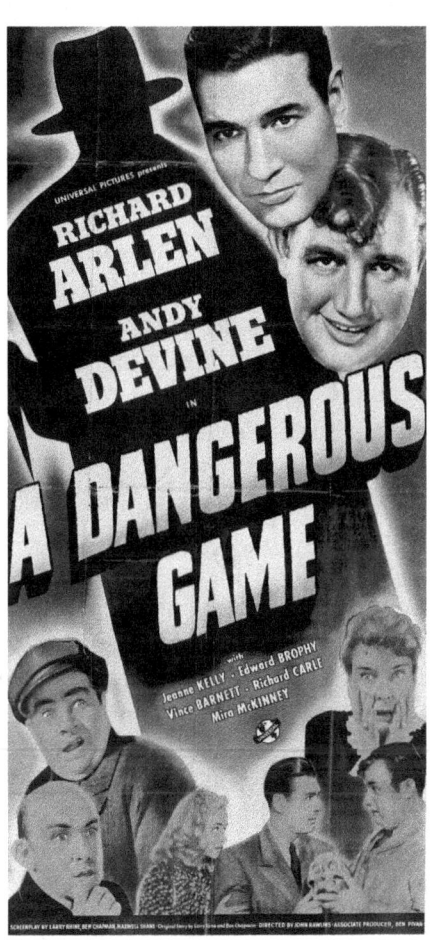

A Dangerous Game (1941). Image courtesy of Heritage Auction Galleries, Ha.com.

The group is joined by another trio of money-hungry crooks, towering Aunt Agatha, who is actually Mooseface Hogarty (Richard Carle) in drag, accompanied by his two henchmen, Clem (Tom Dugan) and Ephriam (Vince Barnett); they claim to be Biggsby's aunt and nephews from Sioux City.

---

[37] The actor formerly known as Rudolf Amendt, and who would soon name-change again to Rudolph Anders.

Even Joe and Bugs do not fall for this, and force the new arrivals to join the others on the floor.

Heavily-drugged Olaf wanders in, moaning something about "poison." Dr. Robin escorts the fellow back upstairs, taking a glass of water and a sedative with him. Robin reappears soon after with a spectacular tumble down the building's huge winding spiral staircase, dead from poisoning. Dick reassumes control, but is just as quickly disarmed. Dick's true identity is found out by Joe and Bugs: he is a supposedly famous private detective. Dick again reassumes control—this back-and-forth grows tiresome—with an assist by Andy, who announces that he is a freshman in the Pinkelton Correspondence School of detection. Dick invites Joe to help him find the murderer, initially assigning him the task of ensuring that no one else leaves the house.

The suspects are numerous, some of them even offering up what turn out to be false confessions: Olaf, because he is nuts and hated Dr. Robin; Biggsby, because everyone's after his money, Dr. Robin included; Nurse Bennett, because Dr. Robin stole the sanitarium from her dad; and Dr. Fleming because, as Andy puts it, he had too much competition from Dr. Robin. Dick grows suspicious of Bennett later on when he catches her trying to sneak out of the place. Andy catches Dr. Fleming attempting to break into the newly-locked medicine cabinet where more poison is stored, and knocks him unconscious. When Fleming regains consciousness, he is offered a restorative drink while Dick grills him. Just as Fleming is about to reveal the murderer's name, he keels over, dead from poisoning.

Biggsby is spotted attempting to retrieve the satchel that's hidden in the fireplace. The lights go out and a painfully humorless chase follows, with all of the sanitarium's inhabitants in a mad scramble for the money-filled satchel. When the lights are restored, Joe and Bugs are convinced that Andy knows its whereabouts, and proceed to give him the third degree. And the fourth degree. And, finally, the fifth degree where they torment him by withholding his favorite foodstuff.

In the meantime, Dick solves the puzzle after discovering some of the sanitarium's records, a stunning achievement since he has been comparatively incompetent up to this point. Olaf and Biggsby had both initially arrived at the sanitarium at the same time, and Olaf, assisted by both Doctors Robin and Fleming, had assumed Biggsby's identity. The real Biggsby has been kept heavily-sedated ever since, and assumed by all to be Olaf Henderson. Olaf had killed for the inheritance of the $250,000, and collected it in the guise of Biggsby. Greed and paranoia had kicked in, resulting in the subsequent murders. Olaf/Biggsby had poisoned each of his two cohorts by the ingenious (?) method of using tiddlywinks to fire the poison tablets into the intended victim's glass. Dick arrests the real Olaf just as Andy is led down the steps by his tormentors, broken by them into offering an obviously false confession.

The Arlen-Devine Series, Part II (1940-1941)

It turns out that the money is no longer in the satchel. Andy, now revealed as Dick's assistant, had previously hidden it in the living room. As the crowd swarms into that room, someone accidentally hits the switch to a fan that blows the money, hidden high up on the fan's shelf, all about the room. As the greedy group stuffs bill after bill into their pockets, Andy follows with a vacuum cleaner and recollects the bills.

Like most of Pivar's films and the Universal B's in general, the film is visually pleasing, with shadowy lighting and effective camera work again supplied by Stanley Cortez, seamless editing by Pivar regular Edward Curtiss, coupled with John Rawlins' workmanlike direction and the ensemble acting of the cast. Devine stands out here in a couple of scenes, one momentarily serious and surprisingly affecting where he thinks he is dying and tearfully comments on his impending demise, and another—the film's highlight—when the assembled hoods torture him (don't worry, it is just with words and bananas—yes, *bananas*) in an effort to find out where he has hidden the cash-filled satchel.

Marc Lawrence has some particularly amusing moments, in general due to his character's lack of intelligence, and during the lovey-dovey phone conversations that follow when he is forced to take calls from his wife Lulu. Jeanne Kelly's secondary role seems intended more as eye candy than any sort of love interest, but as eye candy she is formidable. The rest of the cast is well chosen for their roles, Richard Carle among them in drag for most of the film as bogus Aunt Agatha. I'd like to say it is a shame that Carle died several months after the film's completion and before he could see it when released wide to theaters, but he really did not miss much.

Much of the humor and slapstick falls flat, with several instances just out-and-out silly. Devine has two entrances sliding down the winding staircase's waxed banister, both times accompanied by the sound of screeching tires on the soundtrack. There's another sequence where a potential suspect is given the third degree while sitting in Andy's newly-invented "lie detector" chair, a jerry-rigged wheelchair complete with wired steel helmet and a trio of light bulbs that supposedly determine whether the responder is telling a big lie, a smaller white lie, or a tiny fib (all three bulbs explode when someone tells "a whopper"). The joke, if you want to call it that, is that the contraption's response to the truth is untested and unknown, since (according to Andy) everyone always lies. Inmate Whipple always recites poetry and Shakespeare, Brophy's cab drives off with an explosive backfire and accompanying cloud of smoke, Devine's always tripping over steps and luggage, and of course Carle in drag as the not-terribly-feminine Aunt Agatha. The most excruciating sequence is the overlong chase after the money-filled satchel, with the bag repeatedly changing hands, the involved participants running from room-to-room, door-to-door, all in long shot. It is a scene more suitable to a Jules White two-reel comedy, but painfully out of place in a six-reel feature.

As for the plot gimmick wherein the murderer sneaks a poison pill into his victims' drinking vessels while their backs are turned via a well-placed tiddlywinks shot, while an admittedly novel approach, why not simply drop the pill into the glass by hand? Having said all that, the film (believe it or not) improves with a second viewing, and in spite of the fact that it is overlong even at a brief sixty-three minutes, still has enough good moments to compensate for the not-so-good.

Why the shuffling of the film's release? Hobe Morrison's review in *Variety* a few days after its New York unveiling may have given Universal cold feet: "'A Dangerous Game' is murder. Intended as a comedy-thriller, it is neither comic nor thrilling. It is undoubtedly one of the most strenuous and absurd farce attempts in years. But for all its frantic, deafening slapstick, it remains stubbornly humorless. If there's such a thing as a class D picture this is it. Juve audiences may laugh at it, but anyone over 12 will merely get the fidgets."[38] That review must have thrilled Pivar and his superiors. Whatever the reason, the film did not see wide release for close to six months after it was unveiled in New York, with the final three series entries yet to be filmed all released before it.

Mutiny in the Arctic
(Director: John Rawlins; Released April 18, 1941)

Buck Privates was the next project announced for the team in late September-early October by both *Daily Variety* and *Boxoffice*, with Pivar again named to produce.[39] It is unclear whether or not this was accurate at the time, but by early November the *Los Angeles Times* was naming Bud Abbott, Lou Costello, and the Andrews Sisters—Patti, Maxene, and LaVerne—as the stars lined up for the production. The *Times* cited the past success of the Ritz Brothers as the reason behind the selection of Abbott and Costello to star, and the favorable reception of the Andrews Sisters in the recently released *Argentine Nights* as a factor in the decision to pair the new comedy team with the popular singing group.[40] Audience reaction to the team of Abbott and Costello had yet to be determined, as the release of their maiden vehicle, *One Night in the Tropics*, was still days away. Stubbornly, *Boxoffice* was still citing Arlen and Devine as

---

[38] Hobe Morrison, "A Dangerous Game," *Variety*, March 5, 1941, 16.

[39] "Making 'Buck Privates,'" *Boxoffice*, October 12, 1940, 91; *Daily Variety*, September 25, 1940, 4.

[40] Edwin Schallert, "Universal Plans New Comedy Quintet," *Los Angeles Times*, November 12, 1940, A10.

the leads along with the Andrews Sisters only days before production was to begin.[41]

Arlen, looking for a film project to fill the production breaks at Universal, found just what he needed in late 1940. William H. Pine and William C. Thomas, both former associate producers at Paramount, joined together to form a new production company named Picture Corporation of America. Headquartered at the Fine Arts Studio, Pine served as president and Thomas as executive vice president in charge of production. Arlen hooked up with the new group to film three aviation-based action-adventure films for release through Paramount for the 1941-1942 season.[42] The first of these, *Power Dive*, was to go into production in early January 1941, and finish in time for Arlen's next commitment to Universal, the splendid *Mutiny in the Arctic*.

Director John Rawlins returned to helm *Mutiny in the Arctic*, an arctic-based adventure scripted by Maurice Tombragel and Victor McLeod that went into pre-production in February 1941.[43] "Battling the Fury of Nature and Madmen! A Fight for a Fortune … with Death for the Losers!" screamed the ads upon its release in April. *Mutiny in the Arctic* is an exciting, if somewhat juvenile, adventure following the exploits of radium-hunting explorers in the arctic seas. Anne Nagel costars, here as Devine's sister and, of course, Arlen's love interest. Don Terry, Addison Richards, Oscar O'Shea, and Harry Cording round out the cast.

There was almost another cast member, this one of the four-legged variety, which never came to be. Back in November 1940, Army private Everett Scott left his farm in Kansas and headed to Fort Ord, California, for basic training, leaving his ten-year-old Airedale "Laddie" behind with a friend. Laddie went into a funk over the departure of his master, refused to eat, and lost twenty pounds over the following months. By February, Laddie's condition was in a critical state, and Scott was informed of his pet's worsening condition. His commanding officers were sympathetic, and told Scott that he could keep the dog at the base if he could get him there.

The story had by now become a nationwide canine-interest story, and TWA, offering to fly the dog out to California, built a special crate for him. After some blood transfusions and intravenous injections and feeding, Laddie was flown from Kansas City to San Francisco and reunited with his master.[44]

---

[41] "Wonder About Boxoffice Draw If Defense Films Reach Flood," *Boxoffice*, December 28, 1940, 14.

[42] "Pine, Thomas Form New Company; Para't Outlet," *Boxoffice*, December 7, 1940, 76.

[43] "Republic, Universal Off to Fast Start," *Boxoffice*, January 4, 1941, 70.

[44] "Hungry Only for Love, Laddie is Ready to Die," *Wisconsin State Journal*, March 8, 1941, 1.

Universal had a brainstorm: Since every news wire service in the country had carried the story and everyone knew about Laddie, this dog had the potential to be the next Rin-Tin-Tin! If he recuperated, that is. The Fort Ord vet said that Laddie was showing some improvement, so Pivar scheduled to fly to Camp Ord on the thirteenth to visit the dog and see if he'd pull through. If he did, a plum role in the upcoming production *Mutiny in the Arctic* would be written for the dog.[45] Too bad the Fort Ord vet's prognosis was a bit off, and Laddie ended up dying that same day. A month later, Universal star Deanna Durbin made headlines when she presented Scott with "Mickey," a replacement Airedale, and was dubbed "a lady with a heart."[46] Perhaps, or was the gift orchestrated by Universal to eke out what little publicity they could after their bigger plan fell flat? Call me a cynic.

Explorer Dick Barclay (Richard Arlen) and his aviatrix fiancée Gloria Adams (Anne Nagel) hope to locate the arctic-based Black Mountain, the source of a rich supply of pitchblende her late father had written about years earlier. Armed with a composite map made up of numerous aerial photographs acquired on previous flyovers, the couple approaches her father's old explorer friend Ferguson (Addison Richards) for advice. Together they enlist the aid of Captain Morrissey (Oscar O'Shea), who agrees to pilot them in his ship the S.S. *Astoria* in return for 20% of the profits. Dick and Gloria persuade her bookish brother Andy (Devine) to accompany them, even though he'd prefer to remain behind and study celestial navigation from the comfort of his home. Morrissey refuses to allow Gloria to be part of the voyage, however, citing "bad luck." Disappointed, she agrees to remain behind and monitor their progress via radio reports.

Ferguson is not to be trusted. Scheming with Captain Morrissey's First Mate Cole (Don Terry) and a fellow officer Harmon (Harry Cording), Harmon bumps off Morrissey's right-hand officer so that Cole will be promoted as his replacement. Once at sea, Cole steals the map from Morrissey's quarters, but when he is seen doing so by the mess boy (John Rogers), Harmon kills the mess boy as well. Captain Morrissey is next in line, lured below deck by Harmon and then bludgeoned to death. Cole and Harmon assume control of the ship and have Dick, Andy, and co-conspirator Ferguson locked up as mutineers. Cole orders full speed ahead, in spite of the crew's misgivings due to the thick fog and numerous icebergs.

It is not long before they hit an iceberg (an unconvincing miniature) and start to sink. Cole and Harmon set off in a lifeboat along with the rest of the crew, leaving the imprisoned trio to drown. Dick chops a hole in the wall with

---

[45] Louella O. Parsons, "'Laddie' May Get Part in Movie," *Charleston Gazette*, March 13 1941, 17.

[46] "Laddie is Replaced by Film Star," *Helena Daily Independent*, March 13, 1941, 2.

an ax and they manage to escape, rescuing the ship's cook (Jeff Corey) and the late Captain's husky Mukluk in the process. Cole's boat reaches land and they take refuge in the Eskimo village there. Andy and his group are less fortunate, navigating tiny ice floes to a nearby iceberg and taking refuge in an ice cave. When Mukluk is threatened by an advancing polar bear, Dick springs into action and rescues the dog. Now with only two days' supply of food and the iceberg slowly breaking apart around them, the future looks bleak. Neither Dick nor Andy realizes that Ferguson has been a traitor all along.

Andy Devine and Richard Arlen, set adrift on an ice floe in *Mutiny in the Arctic* (1941).

An S.O.S. was sent as the ship had started to sink, however, and Gloria heard it on her radio. Familiar with the lay of the land in that region, she theorizes that Dick will head for a known Eskimo village, the same village that Cole and his group has stumbled upon. She hops in her seaplane and flies north. Landing in the waters by the village, Cole informs her that Dick and Andy have perished in the sinking ship. Once that news has sunk in, Gloria announces that she is heading back south to arrange a rescue party for the surviving crew.

When Dick sees Gloria's plane flying overhead, he has Andy set fire to their tent to attract her attention. Seeing the flames, Gloria flies low for a closer look, but crashes while doing so. Dick rescues her from the burning wreckage, and her future now looks as bleak as the others.' With the iceberg rapidly disintegrating around them, Ferguson loses it and admits to his treachery and complicity in the crimes of Cole and Harmon. Later, while the others sleep, Ferguson heads after a polar bear in the slim hopes of obtaining some much-needed food. He only manages to wound the bear, and while attempting to swim back to safety is mauled and killed for his futile efforts, now leaving (as the Universal publicity department put it) "Three men, a girl and a dog afloat on an iceberg, at the mercy of tugging Arctic currents which threaten at any moment to overturn their frozen raft and drown them in icy water ..."[47]

In front of their ice cave, fretting over the disintegration of their iceberg. From left: Addison Richards, Jeff Corey, Richard Arlen, Andy Devine. *Mutiny in the Arctic* **(1941).**

Andy's navigation skills now come to good use as he figures that they have now floated in close proximity to land and the Eskimo village. While the others sleep, Dick dives into the frigid waters and swims from ice floe to ice floe, hypothermia be damned, finally arriving at the village. Alerting the Eskimos to his friends' presence on the deteriorating iceberg, they set out in a flotilla of kayaks and rescue Gloria, Andy, the cook, and Mukluk just in the nick of time. The iceberg collapses into the sea as the group paddles back to land.

Meanwhile, Cole and Harmon strong-arm the villagers into taking them up to Black Mountain. The villagers do so reluctantly, warning of the upcoming spring storms. Once they've obtained a load of pitchblende, Cole and Harmon

---

[47] "Arlen-Revine [sic] Find Arctic Adventures," *Big Spring Daily Herald*, June 1, 1941, 2.

make the long trek back to the village through the growing storms. Men, dogs, and supplies are lost along the way, but the survivors finally make it back to safety, along with the pitchblende.

As usual, boys will be boys. Hearing that Dick is there, alive and well (and assumedly very cold), Cole attempts to kill him with a spear, impaling what turns out to be an empty bed. The two engage in a furious fistfight, and when Harmon attempts to knife Dick from behind, one of the villagers harpoons him. Dick emerges victorious, with Cole now his prisoner. The group is taken back home with a rescue party sent out after Gloria. Later, in the comfort of their home, Dick, Gloria, and Andy look over to Mukluk and his new canine mate, and their litter of newborn puppies.

Easily one of the best entries in the fourteen-film series, *Mutiny in the Arctic* has a glossier, higher-budget look than was the norm. Director John Rawlins shows some real flair in his handling of the action, with stylish results. A standout example is Harmon's murder of the mess boy, an extreme point-of-view close-up of Harmon's face as he bludgeons his helpless victim, followed by a shot of the dead mess boy dragged away, the toe of his shoe leaving a long scrape on the deck's surface. The film's two fistfights are effectively staged as well, the first between our two heroes and Cole and Harmon aboard ship, the second a bruising slugfest between Dick and Cole in the Eskimo village.

Happily, Devine gets to play a comparatively straight role, credited for once with a fair degree of intelligence as the studious brother. This is a welcome change of pace from his typical buffoonish character. Arlen starts off as an atypically curt, condescending, almost unlikable character, berating Andy for his booklearning and later accusing him of the theft of a map, and belittling fiancée Nagel for supposedly fogging the negatives she developed; the audience would have cheered if she had slapped the unpleasant son-of-a-bitch. Needless to say, Arlen quickly undergoes a personality change, shifting gears and "reverting" to the two-fisted, altruistic character we've come to expect. Still, those opening sequences leave an unpleasant taste, if only for a few subsequent scenes. Nagel is fine as Arlen's partner in adventure, and she's an actress that grows on you with further exposure. Richards is appropriately heartless as the duplicitous fellow explorer, Terry menacing as the conniving first mate, and Cording cold as the ice around him as Terry's murderous accomplice.

John Boyle's photography is an asset as well, with nicely lit scenes and effective camera placement and movement. The sets are solid looking and convincing, notably the various iceberg hills and caves. Even the participants' beards look real, not usually the case with the hastily applied makeup in some of these low-budget affairs. The abundant stock footage, lifted from Universal's earlier *S.O.S. Iceberg* (1933; Tay Garnett), includes some spectacular, edge-of-the-seat stuff. The awesome "birth of an iceberg" sequence of massive ice walls tumbling into the seas, avalanches threatening nearby human life, huskies plummeting to their apparent deaths and daredevil leaps and swims from one ice floe to another keep your eyes riveted to the screen. Pivar must have spent untold months holed away in a Universal projection room reviewing miles of stock footage for potential plot ideas for the series' films, and this one ranks among the series' best for the integration of previously filmed footage that provides the backbone of the story being told.

Budgeted at $81,000, *Mutiny in the Arctic* went before Boyle's cameras on Friday, March 7, the first of a scheduled ten-day shooting schedule. Workdays were long back then, as the hours spent on this production illustrate. There were 8:00 a.m. calls every day but one, with Friday ending at 6:45 p.m., Saturday at 7:40 p.m., Monday the tenth at 7:35 p.m., Tuesday at 6:05 p.m., Wednesday at 10:30 p.m., Thursday ("late" 8:30 a.m. call) at 10:50 p.m., Friday at 7:00 p.m., Saturday at 7:15 p.m., Monday the seventeenth at 7:30, and Tuesday, the tenth day of shooting, at 7:50 p.m.

Mutiny in the Arctic (1941). Image courtesy of Heritage Auction Galleries, Ha.com.

The first four days were spent filming interiors and on the process stage, covering thirty-seven-and-a-half pages of the script's eighty-two-and-a-half page total with ninety different camera setups. The fifth and sixth days were spent primarily on the Eskimo village set, but it was the seventh day when production started to bog down. Shooting in the ice cave interior, Rawlins was plagued with the technical difficulty of keeping the set sufficiently iced up. Production plodded along, completing the ice cave and iceberg shots on the eighth and ninth days, and it quickly became apparent that an additional eleventh day would be necessary. After a tenth day spent attempting to catch up with various interiors and pickup shots, the eleventh and final day was reserved for the least comfortable shooting. This took place on the process stage with rear-projected footage of ice floes and icebergs, while several cast members were required to swim in the foreground clad in their bulky fur garments. Bound and determined to wrap up the film on this extra day, Rawlins kept cast and crew working until 12:10 a.m. the following morning, more than a sixteen-hour day.[48]

Surprisingly, reviewers were not overly impressed by the finished film. *Variety* took note of the climactic fight: "Arlen and Devine handle their roles

---

[48] Universal Pictures *Daily Committee Meeting* notes, March 6-20, 1941.

The Arlen-Devine Series, Part II (1940-1941)

well, though the final fisticuffing, in which Arlen is involved with Don Terry, spoils the illusion of combat since both are obviously pulling their punches." Not so. As for Nagel, *Variety* provided somewhat of a backhanded compliment: "Anne Nagel is in more or less of a minor role as the sister of Devine and the sweetheart of Arlen. She doesn't impress as an actress though a looker."[49]

Boxoffice was unimpressed with both the plot and, in this case, what it felt was a less than adequate usage of stock footage: "Universal has what is certainly the wildest, and probably the weakest, of its Richard Arlen-Andy Devine series in 'Mutiny in the Arctic.' Strictly for the Jack Armstrong-Saturday matinee trade, it may encounter trouble getting by with the more exacting of that class due to an abundance of mixed-up stock shots."[50] Picky, picky, picky; while the back-and-forth cuts between new and stock footage is readily apparent, this is a minor quibble; the stock footage is that good.

Which brings us back to Laddie: The potential part that Pivar had in mind for the ill-fated soldier's dog must have been that of Mukluk's mate briefly seen in the closing shot of the film, since there's no way that an Airedale would match with the stock footage's all-white husky. Or at least one hopes that's what he had in mind. Alas, the dog that portrays Mukluk failed to receive onscreen credit, the ultimate indignity for an aspiring canine actor.

Men of the Timberland
(Director: John Rawlins; Released June 6, 1941)

Pivar's next to last film in the series was titled *Men of the Timberland*, adapted by Maurice Tombragel and Griffin Jay from an original story by relative newcomer Paul Jarrico. Rawlins was again assigned to direct, reunited with his *Mutiny in the Arctic* cinematographer (and Pivar regular) John Boyle. Claire Dodd, just signed by Universal to a seven-year contract due to her performance in Albert S. Rogell's *The Black Cat*, was named to star opposite Arlen,[51] but she was quickly yanked to star opposite Abbott and Costello in the film *In the Navy*.[52] Linda Hayes, new to Universal after completing a two-year contract at RKO, was the chosen replacement. Accompanied by a cast that included Francis McDonald, Paul E. Burns, Willard Robinson, Hardie Albright, Roy Harris, and Gaylord Pendleton, the production headed 240 miles north of Hollywood for location shooting in the Alabama Hills, a fringe portion of the

---

[49] Naka, "Mutiny in the Arctic," *Variety*, May 7, 1941, 12.

[50] Ivan Spear, "Spearheads," *Boxoffice*, May 3, 1941, 43.

[51] Edwin Schallert, "Movieland Jottings and Castings," *Los Angeles Times*, March 29, 1941, A9.

[52] Edwin Schallert, "Claire Dodd Signed for Comedy Lead," *Los Angeles Times*, April 1, 1941, 13.

Stop Yellin'

Sierra Nevada Mountains near Lone Pine, California. Shooting commenced late in April 1941.[53]

Unscrupulous lumberman Tim MacGregor (Willard Robertson) wants to clear-cut 20-million-board feet of timber on wealthy debutante Kay Hadley's (Linda Hayes) land up in St. James, Canada. Now living elsewhere, she has no interest in the land and is very interested in MacGregor's money, so she is ready to sign over the timber rights just as soon as she comes back north to Canada. The problem is that the State Forestry Department has strict guidelines on just how much timber can be removed at any given time, and MacGregor wants to circumvent those restrictions and clear out the area, then clear out himself before he gets caught. To that end he has bribed Forestry employee Jim Dudley (Hardie Albright) to falsify the charts to make it appear that there's far less timber than there actually is.

Ranger Dick O'Hara (Richard Arlen) is sent up to St. James when the charts' accuracy is questioned, and confronts Dudley with his concerns. Dudley panics and threatens MacGregor with exposure if he can't take care of O'Hara. MacGregor's thuggish French-Canadian timber boss Jean Collet (Francis McDonald, among the series' most threatening heavies) takes matters in his own hands, and his knife as well, and kills Dudley. Not about to put up with meddler O'Hara's nonsense, MacGregor sends for "Bull of the Woods" Andy Jensen (Andy Devine), the only man who can clear the woods within the two-week time frame. This way the work will be completed before O'Hara can fully check the charts against new surveys and issue a restraining order. O'Hara has old ranger friend Tex (Gaylord Pendleton) and new ranger Withers (Roy Harris) sent up to assist him with the surveying.

When Kay shows up and is about to sign MacGregor's papers, O'Hara intervenes and requests a two-week moratorium on logging so that they can confirm that everything is within legal limits. Unfortunately, O'Hara's approach is somewhat brusque and counterproductive, annoying Kay into signing immediately and undermining O'Hara's toothless authority. O'Hara is now convinced that she is simply a rich bitch interested solely in money, who couldn't care less about the environment. Jensen shows up and discusses the enormity of the challenge with MacGregor. Jensen's old friend and fellow logger Lucky (Paul E. Burns) chimes in and insists it can't be done within two weeks, but Kay sweet-talks and flatters Jensen into accepting the offer and coming up with a workable plan. The loggers go to work, and party-pooper O'Hara is persona non grata on the site.

Later, Collet mistakes Withers for a snooping O'Hara, and crushes the poor fellow with a massive log; Jensen and Kay discover the body. Not content with the current body count, Collet shoots Tex, wounding him in the arm. With one

---

[53] "March Production in Like Lamb," *Boxoffice*, March 1, 1941, 87.

The Arlen-Devine Series, Part II (1940-1941)

man dead, another wounded, and informed that over 12-million-board feet have already been logged, O'Hara takes over the surveying himself, and speeds through the process. Collet and two of his thugs confront O'Hara in the woods, and he tells them that he has finished his surveying. Not about to let him go, the trio attacks O'Hara. Collet is about to stab O'Hara when Jensen arrives and sees what's going on. Fair man that he is, he intervenes and breaks up the fight. A begrudging friendship takes hold between O'Hara and Jensen.

MacGregor panics when he hears that O'Hara has completed his work, and sends Collet to retrieve O'Hara's notes. Knife-happy Collet encounters Tex in O'Hara's office and finishes what he started earlier, killing Tex and grabbing what he erroneously thinks are the notes. When O'Hara finds his friend's body, he heads to the Blue Ox Saloon where he knows he'll find Collet. Collet is there with a bunch of his friends, but so are Jensen, Kay, and Lucky at another table. Collet resists O'Hara, and his friends jump him. O'Hara is overwhelmed, and when Jensen sees Collet pull his knife he decides to get into the act and help O'Hara. During the melee Collet throws his knife at Jensen, but unlucky Lucky steps in the way and is hit; he dies soon after. Distraught at his friend's death, Jensen flips out and destroys the saloon while his fellow loggers get the hell out of his way and flee the place. Jensen carries Lucky's body back to O'Hara's office and asks to leave it there, telling O'Hara he is the only friend he has. Seeing this and hearing of Tex's death, Kay has a change of heart. She joins with O'Hara and Jensen in a plan to expose MacGregor.

Kay feigns complicity with Collet and MacGregor, providing them with O'Hara's survey notes that she tells them Collet overlooked when robbing the office. O'Hara arrives and retrieves the notes at gunpoint, telling the three of them that their scam will soon be exposed. He leaves, and MacGregor orders Collet to follow and kill him. Collet attempts to do so, but Jensen is waiting in the shadows and proceeds to beat the knife-wielding fellow to a pulp. Battered and bruised, Collet rats out MacGregor. Both are arrested and convicted of murder.

Later, Kay makes a complete turnaround and decides to remain in St. James. She forms the Paul Bunyon Lumber Co. and makes herself president, while Jensen becomes general manager. She announces to the loggers that they all still have jobs, but from now on they'll operate within the Forestry Department's guidelines. And, once again, Arlen ends up with a starlet eighteen years his junior.

Perhaps the most outstanding aspect of this film is Devine's role, the straightest of the fourteen-film series. Sure, he is given a few moments of humor, but for the most part he plays a tough, no-nonsense logging boss, the so-called "Bull of the Woods," and plays it well. The film's highlight occurs with his friend Lucky's death, a genuinely touching scene between the two with tough-guy Jensen reduced to tears over his impending loss. The aftermath, with

Jensen's furious rampage within the quickly-demolished saloon, reveals the scary side of Devine as he smashes windows, overturns bars, shatters mirrors, and splinters chairs. Later, entering O'Hara's office with Lucky's limp body in his arms, we are again moved by Jensen's overwhelming sadness over the loss of his long-time friend. It is a wonderful performance, and a nice showcase for Devine's talents, usually hidden behind his mask of buffoonery in this series.

John Boyle's beautiful location photography is a big asset in this film. The opening montage of the mountainside vistas is particularly memorable and sets the mood for the film, one shot dissolving into the next, ending with a slow pan down a towering redwood to O'Hara's tiny car driving past its base. There's a lot of stock footage of the logging operations as well, a nicely executed process shot of a huge log rolling down the hill and crushing Withers in the foreground, and another of a huge felled tree falling toward and landing at the feet of the two in the foreground.

Boxoffice griped about what they felt to be an abundance of stock footage (had they somehow missed this in the eleven films that preceded it?), and for that matter the film in general: "It has action but little else to recommend it. Director John Rawlins and Producer Ben Pivar relied extensively on stock shots of lumber operations to keep things moving."[54] C'mon, Ivan—it is a B movie; what did you expect? *The Hollywood Reporter* viewed all of that stock footage in a different light: "Admittedly many of the logging sequences are from stock, but this is excellently chosen stock that the public will never recognize as expertly matched by John W. Boyle's photography." Acknowledging the series' upcoming demise, the reviewer commented that "[a]lthough the team is about to be split, Associate Producer Ben Pivar has not stinted in production values."[55] *Daily Variety* made a point to mention Pivar as well, saying that his "production supervision is ably evidenced in all the entertainment elements packed into script and carried out by all departments."[56]

Storywriter Jarrico claimed years later that he had actually written a full screenplay for the film, which was rewritten by Tombragel and Jay leaving him with only a story credit. He remembered the plot as "the fight that Richard Arlen, Andy Devine, and some Dead End-type kids in the Civilian Conservation Corps put up against the timber barons. Premature environmentalism!"[57] Jarrico followed with a script for Garson Kanin's *Tom, Dick, and Harry* at RKO, which earned him an Oscar nomination, but his career took a nosedive several years later, a victim of the US House Committee on UnAmerican Activities witch

---

[54] Ivan Spear, "Spearheads," *Boxoffice*, May 31, 1941, 31, page unknown.
[55] "Classy Production For Arlen-Devine," *Hollywood Reporter*, May 26, 1941, 3.
[56] "Men of the Timberland," *Daily Variety*, May 26, 1941, 3.
[57] Patrick McGilligan and Paul Buhle, *Tender Comrades* (New York: St. Martin's Griffin, 1999), 337.

hunt for subversives and the blacklisting that followed. Like several others in his uncomfortable shoes, Jarrico went on to write under an alias, eventually producing the award-winning film *Salt of the Earth* in 1954, an expose of the mistreatment of Mexican-American workers in a US mine. Like the old adage says: "The more things change, the more they stay the same."

Following shooting of *Men of the Timberland*, Arlen went back to work for Pine-Thomas and Paramount. His second for the new producing concern, titled *Forced Landing*, went before cameras on April 17, with *Mr. Boggs Steps Out*'s Gordon Wiles directing, an $80,000 budget, and a twelve-day schedule.[58] Two more projects were announced as potential vehicles for Arlen, tentatively titled *Devil Has Wings*[59] and *Wings of Courage*,[60] but both were shelved.

Raiders of the Desert
(Director: John Rawlins; Released July 25, 1941)

"Thundering Action in the Sahara ... Where Men Live, Love and Fight ... Just for the Thrill of It!" "Revolt in a Sea of Sand ... Where Human Passions Blaze ... and Death Stalks Under a Torrid Sun!" "It's Roaring Adventure ... Under the Sahara Sun ... Where Blazing Guns Spell Out a Message That Means Death!" Whew! Sounds like one rip-roaring sand-and-sandal epic, huh? Universal went all-out with the ad catchlines for *Raiders of the Desert*, the last entry in the series to be filmed but released in August several weeks before the aforementioned *A Dangerous Game*. This would be director John Rawlins' last film for Pivar as well. Scripters Tombragel and McLeod were back on board, with Boyle lensing once more and Wright again piecing the footage together.

The film's working title, *Return of the Sheik*, had first been announced the previous May as one of the 1940-1941 seasons' seven titles, and resurfaced in February 1941 as an upcoming production.[61] Another title—*Salvage*—was announced a month later as the planned follow-up to *Timberland*,[62] but it seems doubtful that these were one and the same film, or that *Salvage* ever came to be. Shooting of *Return of the Sheik* commenced on Saturday, May 31,[63]

---

[58] Philip K. Scheuer, "Town Called Hollywood," *Los Angeles Times*, June 1, 1941, C3.

[59] Edwin Schallert, "Dick Arlen to Play in 'Devil Has Wings,'" *Los Angeles Times*, February 7, 1941, A17.

[60] Edwin Schallert, "'Wings of Courage' Slated as Arlen Film," *Los Angeles Times*, May 27, 1941, 13.

[61] "Boxoffice Barometer," *Boxoffice*, February 22, 1941, 142.

[62] Edwin Schallert, "Wings of Courage Slated as Arlen Film," *Los Angeles Times*, March 27, 1941, 13.

[63] "Douglas W. Churchill, "Screen News Here and in Hollywood," *New York Times*, May 30, 1941, 13.

and if nothing else a solid level of proficiency had been attained in cranking out these juvenile adventures. Too bad the plots had devolved into a mindless mix of comedy and action, with little thought given to logic and plausibility. But if you were a twelve-year-old hopping up and down in your seat while stuffing your face with popcorn or Goobers, the films still delivered.

Love interest Linda Hayes was retained for this film, with smaller roles taken by anyone who could be rounded up with even a hint of "exotic" about them. If Universal's publicity machine was to be believed, these included a Syrian linguist, an Egyptian princess, a washed-up Italian opera singer, a Greek heavyweight fighter, a Mexican dancer, two Sikh ex-policemen, a Turk, a Hindu, and a Central American. Universal's two new exotic contractees, Maria Montez and Turhan Bey[64] ("The Man of Mystery") were among these—he is the Turk, she is the Central American—in smaller roles to lend the film some tiny sense of verisimilitude. The only full-blooded Arabian to appear in the film was Abdullah Abbas, a stuntman who occasionally appeared in bit parts.[65] Andy Devine, for better or worse, was able to show off one of his talents in this film, plucking away at his ukulele and "singing" along as only Devine could. The singing part was a first for him, but he'd appeared in uncredited bits in his first celluloid appearances back in 1926 as a ukulele-strumming, raccoon-coated student in Universal's *The Collegians* series.[66] In *Raiders of the Desert*, he is as usual the film's comedic relief, stumbling about in Arab robes and falling for the local charmer.

Dick Manning (Arlen) and Andy McCoy (Devine) pay a con man $25 to stow them away on a ship supposedly bound for California. Discovered by the ship's brutish mate, they are both put to work and informed that the ship's destination is Arabia rather than California. Dick falls for lovely passenger Alice Evans (Hayes), and when the ship sets anchor, Dick and Andy sneak off. Alice is greeted by a fellow named Hassen Muhammed (Turhan Bey), and the two depart in his car. They are headed to the democratic community of Libertahd where she is to work as secretary to an American philanthropist named Jones (George Carleton), the designer and head of the shining new "city." Dick and Andy hire a cabbie named Abdullah (Lewis Howard) to take them there.

Jones, meanwhile, is visited by Sheik Talifah (Ralf Harolde), who warns Jones to pack up and leave: "Give up this wild scheme of yours, this modern metropolis in the heart of our desert." While he won't admit it, Talifah is worried that his tribesmen will come to see that there are better things in life than he can provide, so he wants to nip it in the bud. Jones refuses to leave.

---

[64] So new, in fact, that the credits bill him as *Turban* Bey

[65] "'Raiders of the Desert' Now at Garden," *Cumberland Evening Times*, February 27, 1942, 14.

[66] "Devine Sings in Latest Picture," *Panama City News-Herald*, September 28, 1941, 3.

The Arlen-Devine Series, Part II (1940-1941)

Hassen, a reformed—and now rather stylish—former "desert bandit," is in cahoots with Talifah. Talifah wants to attack Libertahd and kill everyone inside, but Hassen urges him to kill only Jones instead. Two thugs are sent to do just that, but Andy and Dick, having just arrived, thwart Jones' attackers and capture one of them. The knife wielder is jailed, but murdered in his cell by an unknown assailant before he can be questioned.

Later on, Jones' faithful servant Zeid (Neyle Marx) is poisoned by coffee intended for Jones. Local merchant Ahmed (John Harmon) is suspected, having sold the coffee earlier that day. Dick and Alice decide to visit fortuneteller Suliman (Sig Arno), who had earlier predicted Jones' troubles. Before Suliman can name the traitor in their midst, he too is stabbed and killed.

Jones decides to arm the citizens of Libertahd against attack, and orders a shipment of arms to be delivered. Talifah gets wind of this and has his tribesmen attack and kill the drivers, and take possession of the shipment of weapons. He has some of his men smuggle a load of the weapons into Libertahd, hidden inside large, lumpy coffee bags. They are instructed to incite an uprising the next day, during which Talifah and his men will ride to the "rescue" and assume control of the town. Andy gets wind of this when one of the weighty "coffee" bags drops on his foot, and informs Dick of his suspicions. Later on the two of them sneak in and find the weapons. They are discovered but successfully win another fight (it doesn't hurt that Andy is former Yonkers wrestler Andy "The Hammer" McCoy), and force Talifah's plan from one of their captives. Jones is alerted, and he cables for British troops to come to their aid.

The troops ride to the rescue, intercepting many of Talifah's tribesmen on the way to Libertahd, these encounters padded with lots of atypically ill-matching stock footage. The Brits, of course, are victorious with their overwhelming display of force. Meanwhile, Talifah and some of his tribesmen ride into Libertahd, but are stunned to find everything peaceful. Weapon-bearing citizens appear and surround them, and a spectacular (by B movie standards, anyway) battle erupts within the town's walls. Talifah is shot, and Dick punches Hassen through a window when he discovers him about to shoot Jones; Jones emerges from the gun battle with only a slight wound. The film concludes with Alice leaving with Dick, Andy following close behind. Jones comments that next time around he'll hire a less attractive secretary.

This is one of the series' most comedic entries, with Devine portraying a thicker-than-usual character. Arlen, supposedly the brains of the duo, displays some remarkable naiveté in the earliest scenes, but this lapse in common sense was required to kick-start this brief little adventure. The humor, while broad and unsubtle, permeates the film: Arlen and Hayes' struggle with the collapsing deck chair; Devine's repeated attempts to reassemble his oft-broken ukulele; Devine's dismay when an attacker stabs the ukulele instead of him ("Went right through my G string"); Devine's ongoing—and repeatedly frustrated—pursuit of Abdullah's girl Zuleika (Maria Montez); the duo's escape from the ship in a large hamper, one leg each out holes in its sides propelling them along; and Abdullah's many young female "cousins" who are constantly—and amorously—greeting him. The downside of setting the story in the unnamed mid-eastern country is that Russell Gausman's set decorators had to make do with the Universal back-lot and interior sets, and on the usual miniscule budget. The street scenes are okay, but the interior of Jones' apartment looks more like a Manhattan penthouse, and every non-Arab dresses as if ready for a night out in the big city. As for the "locals," their accents as such are uniformly terrible, and their beards reminiscent of a dime store's Halloween offerings (was Jack Pierce responsible for this?). The plot itself is paper-thin, and devices such as Hassen and company's "secret" person-to-person signals using light reflected off pocket mirrors a hokey device at best, and blatantly obvious to anyone else in proximity who doesn't have his eyes shut. There are a few shots of visual interest, such as the seamless transition from pier to village street as Alice walks behind a large sign, and the matte shot of Libertahd that's used several times. John Rawlins' direction is unremarkable.

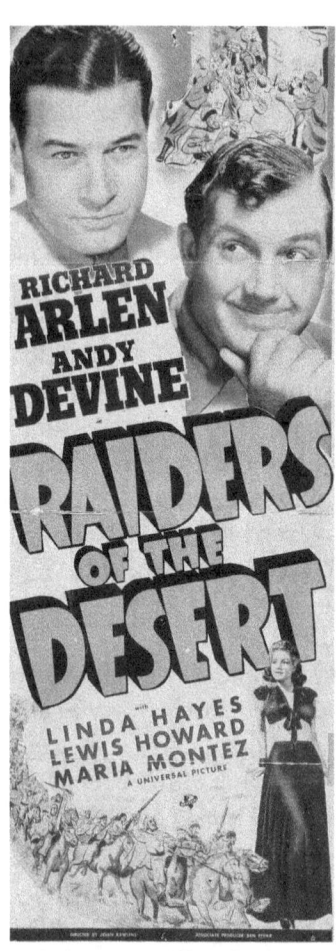

Raiders of the Desert (1941), the last in a tired series. Image courtesy of Heritage Auction Galleries, Ha.com.

Newcomer Maria Montez appears in the small role of Zuleika, the native object of Devine's lust, with Lewis Howard giving a standout comedic performance as the local cabbie increasingly enraged over that same pursuit. Stock footage again helps to pad out the film and save some production dollars, and there's a short clip from 1937's *I Cover the War* with actors John Wayne and Don Barclay visible in a truck.[67] Contemporary reviews—admittedly sparse—were all over the place: "That very happy team, Richard Arlen and Andy Devine, deserts the Far West with its cowboys and crooked sheriffs, for the Far East and its dark-eyed knife-stickers … and the boys are no less entertaining on the hot sands," stated

---

[67] John Cocchi, *Second Feature* (New York: A Citadel Press Book, 1991), 171.

The Arlen-Devine Series, Part II (1940-1941)

the *Los Angeles Times* approvingly,[68] as opposed to Ivan Spear's dismissal in *Boxoffice*: "Limping along in the extreme rear...the co-stars drag their fisticuffs and comparably obtuse humor to distant Arabia to wallow in a story that is heavy on action but extremely skimpy on plausibility."[69]

With the completion of *Raiders of the Desert* and the fulfillment of his contract with Universal, Arlen severed his ties and moved over to the studio of Pine and Thomas where he filmed *Flying Blind* in late June and early July. Pine and Thomas dissolved their Picture Corporation of America after the third film's completion, and reorganized under their own names for future releases. Arlen signed another three-picture contract with what was now Pine-Thomas Productions,[70] and *Torpedo Boat*, a sea-based adventure for a refreshing change, followed in mid-October.[71] Arlen's association with Universal was now history, but the series—albeit in a slightly altered form—would soldier on.

§

---

[68] "Pair Invade Film Desert," *Los Angeles Times*, July 9, 1941, 16.

[69] Ivan Spear, "Spearheads," *Boxoffice*, July 12, 1941, 49.

[70] Douglas W. Churchill, "Screen News Here and in Hollywood," *New York Times*, June 30, 1941, 13.

[71] Edwin Schallert, "Reel Notes Reeled Off Briefly," *Los Angeles Times*, October 4, 1941, A9.

9 The Mummy Returns

Alerted to the renewed interest in films of a horrific nature by the successful August 1938 reissue of *Dracula* and *Frankenstein*, Universal dove back into the genre with both feet and increased the budget for their upcoming sequel *Son of Frankenstein* to $500,000.[1] The release of director Rowland V. Lee's stylish (and ultimately costlier) A-status *Son of Frankenstein* in January 1939 was responsible for the revival in popularity of the horror film, and with its success Universal began to increase its product in this vein. Universal was, after all, the one Hollywood studio most closely associated with the genre, and various attempts by other studios to cash in on the horror film's popularity had little impact in altering that association in the minds of the film-going public at large.

In 1940, two sequels (of sorts) appeared in addition to Arthur Lubin's *Black Friday*: *The Invisible Man Returns* (Joe May) and Pivar's *The Mummy's Hand* (Christy Cabanne). From that time on through 1946, the majority—eighteen—of Universal's horror output was handled by Pivar's B unit, the Mummy series and the Inner Sanctum mysteries included. Larger budgets were reserved for the Frankenstein and Wolf Man series, several more invisible person films, and a few one-shot deals such as Arthur Lubin's *Phantom of the Opera* remake (1943) and George Waggner's *The Climax* (1944), all of these made under the supervision of other producers. A handful of genre B's were made independent of Pivar's unit as well in 1941, including producer Paul Malvern's *The Mad Doctor of Market Street* (Joseph H. Lewis), and producer Jack Bernhard's *Man Made Monster* (George Waggner) and *The Strange Case of Doctor Rx* (William

---

[1] "Rowland Lee to Engineer Return of Frankenstein," *Los Angeles Times*, November 15, 1938, A14.

Nigh). Pivar would soon become the studio's undisputed purveyor of cut-rate horror.

The Mummy's Hand
(Director: Christy Cabanne; Released September 20, 1940)

Given the renewed popularity of the horror film, it was only a matter of time before Pivar would become involved with the genre, one that was new to him and probably a welcome change. His next assignment: Make a sequel to Universal's popular Karloff vehicle of eight years earlier, *The Mummy*, but do it on a B film budget of $80,000. Pivar's first full-fledged venture into the horror film, *The Mummy's Hand* was filmed in June and released in September 1940. Little was retained story-wise from Karl Freund's atmospheric original of 1932. Essentially an inexpensive production, the film looks several notches classier than its three sequels as a result of extensive footage lifted from the original film, and the use of the impressive Incan temple set left over from James Whale's *Green Hell*, filmed in late summer 1939.

The Mummy's Hand (1940). Image courtesy of Heritage Auction Galleries, Ha.com.

Pivar reenlisted the services of both director Christy Cabanne and actress Peggy Moran, who had worked together on *Danger on Wheels*, *Alias the Deacon*, and *Hot Steel*. Griffin Jay was hired to cobble together a workable story with the budget limitations in mind, which he and Maxwell Shane adapted into a shooting script. In order to keep costs down, the original film was revisited with an eye toward reusing footage whenever feasible from that more expensive and lavish production. This impacted cameraman Woody Bredell as well, since he'd need to shoot new footage and insert shots to dovetail with the old footage, which editor Phil Cahn would marry together in as seamless a fashion as possible. Dick Foran and Wallace Ford were hired to star, with an excellent supporting cast that included George Zucco, Cecil Kellaway, and Eduardo Ciannelli. Former cowboy star and Olympic weight-lifting contender Tom Tyler was hired to appear beneath the bandages as the mummy, due in part to a sufficiently acceptable resemblance to the original's Boris Karloff, seen in long shot during the reused footage flashback sequences.

Tyler's mummification was achieved by makeup wizard Jack Pierce, who utilized the same time-consuming techniques used for aging Karloff in the original (and techniques similar to those used, less effectively, on Lon Chaney, Jr. in *Man Made Monster* and on David Bruce in *The Mad Ghoul*). Requiring eight hours to apply (including all bandaging), Pierce arranged to have all close-ups shot on the same day to save time and money, and substituted a rubber mask for all subsequent shots. (By the time Chaney's three sequels rolled around, a mask, as well as a fairly obvious zip-up suit, was employed exclusively.) Filming commenced on Friday, May 31.[2]

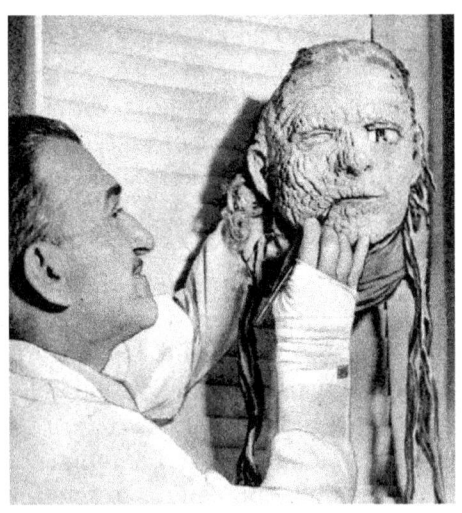

Makeup artist Jack Pierce puts the finishing touches on the mask to be worn by Lon Chaney, Jr., in the subsequent mummy sequels. Photo courtesy of Doug Kennedy.

The muscular, high-adrenaline score that accompanies the opening credits alerts you right out of the gate that this is not your father's *The Mummy*. After a minute's worth of credits, the next nine minutes set the stage and fill us in on what's gone before, admittedly in a revisionist fashion. Andoheb (Zucco) debarks from a train at Cairo's station, the camera following him in tracking close-up through the crowds on the platform. A montage follows of Andoheb trekking through the desert on camelback, a mix of (mostly) stock and new footage, ending up on a grassy hillside that looks more like California than Egypt. Ascending the massive staircase leading to an entrance flanked by carvings that look more Incan than Egyptian, Andoheb enters the temple and is greeted by an elderly high priest (Ciannelli), near death. The high priest hands over the secrets guarded for 3,000 years by the high priests of Karnak and brings Andoheb up to speed, telling him to "Look deep into the waters of Kar." What follows is an evocative minute-and-a-half sequence lifted almost in its entirety from the original film, with long shots of a recognizable Karloff

---

[2] Douglas W. Churchill, "Screen News Here and in Hollywood," *New York Times*, May 29, 1940, 26.

Stop Yellin'

intercut with close-ups of a less-emotive Tyler. In these flashbacks, the Scroll of Toth that Karloff lusted over has been replaced with now-extinct Tana leaves. The high priest explains that the mummy Kharis, buried alive and tongue-less 3,000 years earlier because of his forbidden love of the Princess Ananka, has remained alive—well, sort of—thanks to those Tana leaves. Kharis guards the Princess' tomb and is ready at moment's notice to bring death to whomever defiles Ananka's tomb. Three Tana leaves a day produces enough fluid to keep the mummy's heart beating, which if my math is correct required a whopping 3,285,000 leaves, give or take, over the intervening 3,000 years; there must be a warehouse full of them somewhere. Or is Kharis served this potion only once a month? If so, a more modest supply of Tana leaves would have been needed, roughly 108,000 to date. But then Kharis' assignment is supposedly until the end of time, which really complicates the stockpiling of leaves. At any rate, if needed, nine leaves will give the dormant mummy life and movement, but exceed that number and he'll become an "uncontrollable monster, a soulless demon with a desire to kill, and kill." With that, the high priest turns over the duties to Andoheb and dies.

Archaeologist Steve Banning (Foran) is set to return to the United States due to his ongoing failure to find anything of worth in the deserts of Egypt. He makes an abrupt change in plans when he discovers an ancient piece of pottery adorned with a clue to the location of Princess Ananka's tomb. Accompanied by his buffoonish, wisecracking buddy Babe Jensen (Ford), they head to Cairo's Scripps Museum with hopes of obtaining funding for an expedition. Dr. Petrie (Charles Trowbridge) is thrilled with the discovery, but museum head Professor Andoheb—yeah, the same guy—puts the kibosh on any hopes of museum funding, declaring the pottery a fake, and "accidentally" breaks the fragment in the process. Undeterred, Banning sets out to solicit outside funding, finding success—$2,000 worth—in the deep pockets of "The Great Solvani" (Kellaway), a colorful Irish magician. The expedition sets out, with Petrie, Solvani, and Solvani's cute but highly skeptical daughter Marta (Moran) in attendance, guided by a local named Ali (Leon Belasco). All of this is observed from not-so-afar by a beggar (Siegfried Arno), who works for Andoheb and keeps him informed of the group's progress.

Arriving at the site, workers soon uncover the human remains of a member of one of the two previous expeditions, none of whom have ever returned. Babe's mishandling of some explosives drops a mountainside, exposing the entrance to a tomb bearing the unbroken seal of the seven jackals. When Petrie breaks the seal, this proves to be too much for the superstitious and terrified workers. They flee from the area, thereby reducing the number of extras required for the filming of subsequent scenes. Once inside the tomb, they are disappointed to find only a cave and Kharis' mummified remains; as Solvani puts it "in a cheap casket, at that." Later, Andoheb corners Petrie alone in the tomb with the mummy, revives Kharis with the Tana leaf fluid, and lets Kharis have his way with Petrie.

Petrie's death puts a damper on the expedition's members, but the worst is yet to come. Andoheb has the beggar place a vial of the Tana juice in Ali's tent, then sends Kharis out to retrieve it, Kharis' bad right arm and left leg a decided hindrance in making any sort of speedy progress. Breaking into Ali's tent, Kharis makes short work of the poor fellow. Solvani and Marta discover Ali's body, and Banning vows to send them back to safety.

Kharis in his "cheap casket" in *The Mummy's Hand* (1940).

That plan is cut short when Marta deduces the location of Ananka's tomb, its entrance supposedly guarded by Kharis and his cheap casket. Before they have an opportunity to follow through on this discovery, the beggar places yet-another vial of Tana juice in the Solvanis' tent. Kharis comes calling and strangles Solvani, but fails to kill him. Instead, he hauls a fainted Marta back to Ananka's tomb, a present of sorts for Andoheb. Andoheb, being the red-blooded Egyptian male that he is, decides that both he and Marta shall gain eternal life together as a loving high priest and high priestess couple, via injections of Tana fluid.

Meanwhile, Banning and Babe have discovered a battered Solvani and his daughter's absence. Banning heads inside Kharis' cave to track down the entrance to Ananka's tomb, sending Babe to the other side of the mountain to see if he can find an entrance. And does he! The viewer can't imagine how the group managed to miss the massive staircase and temple entrance up until now, but somehow they did. Anyway, Andoheb, interrupted in his intended sacrifice, sends Kharis to kill Banning. Andoheb confronts Babe at the top of that large staircase and shoots him. Wounded, Babe responds by unloading his revolver into Andoheb, who takes one of those bone-busting tumbles down the entire length of the steps. Inside, Kharis goes after Banning, while Marta, strapped to the sacrificial table, alerts him to the urn full of freshly-cooked Tana fluid. After a one-sided struggle with Kharis, Banning tips and spills the Tana fluid onto the floor. Kharis drops to all fours to try to lap it up, but gets torched by Banning for his efforts.

Stop Yellin'

The finished film has little in common with the original: Im-ho-tep has become Kharis, has had his status changed from high priest to prince, and the life-giving Scroll of Toth has been replaced by the Tana leaves. Foran and Ford are sufficiently likable in the leads, their friendly camaraderie akin to that of Arlen and Devine in their series, and a probable factor in Foran as Pivar's eventual choice as replacement for Arlen in that series' third, somewhat altered season. Cabanne's direction is taut and fast moving, and while lacking the finesse and moody chills of the original, it is by far the best of the sequels. Although Leslie Halliwell, in his *Film Guide*, somewhat overstates the case when saying the "The last half hour is among the most scary in horror film history,"[3] it is quite exciting, and the optically blacked-out eyes (and in one instance, mouth) of the approaching Kharis add a totally satisfying chilling effect to the proceedings. Ultimately, however, the film has the look of a B. Despite some occasionally nice photography by cinematographer Bredell, the film repeatedly makes ineffective use of day-for-night and has its share of static sequences. It is a far cry from Charles Stumar's fluid, roving camerawork of the original, no doubt influenced in part by that film's director—and former photographer—Karl Freund. Bredell manages a few nice shots, however, such as his use of a crane in the intro to Ananka's tomb; it makes the most of the set, slowly moving back until the set's entirety is in frame, resulting in a brief but visually impressive few seconds of film.

Stock footage, as always, is utilized as needed, every time the desert comes into play, the accidental explosion of the mountainside, the use of slowed-down silent footage of a howling wolf for a jackal, and the aforementioned lengthy clips from its more prestigious predecessor (including a stock shot of the Cairo Museum interior lifted from that previous film's stock shot). Some poor dubbing, in one instance coming from a tight-lipped Andoheb, does little to help matters. It is a lot of fun, however, and was successful enough to spawn three more sequels over the next four years. There is one curious aspect regarding the original release print, as reported by *Variety*'s reviewer Hobe Morrison: "[A]pparently with the idea of throwing the creeps into the audience, the sequences taking place in the excavations into early Egyptian remains are shown in green-tinted film."[4]

Dick Foran, a solid 6' 2" with red hair and matinee idol good looks, was known in part for his musical abilities. New Jersey-born and the son of a state senator, Foran attended Princeton University where he focused as much on football and student musicals as his studies. Upon graduating from Princeton, Foran formed a band. His Hollywood debut was as Nick Foran singing (and co-

---

[3] Leslie Halliwell. *Halliwell's Film Guide*. New York: Granada Publishing, 1977, 512.
[4] Hobe Morrison, "The Mummy's Hand," *Variety*, September 21, 1940, 15.

The optically blacked-out eyes of Kharis in *The Mummy's Hand* (1940).

starring with Shirley Temple) in Fox's *Stand Up and Cheer* (1934; Hamilton MacFadden), then on to Warners as Dick Foran in 1935 where he starred in a variety of programmers. These included a series of western musicals as a singing cowboy (*Song of the Saddle* and *Treachery Rides the Range* in 1936, *California Mail*, *Cherokee Strip*, *Prairie Thunder*, *Devil's Saddle*, and *Empty Holsters* in 1937, and so on). In 1938, he was in Lloyd Bacon's *Boy Meets Girl*, where he spoofed himself and Hollywood as fictitious cowboy star Larry Toms. But in spite of a return to non-western roles, it was as the open-plains, under-the-stars warbler that he was most closely identified.

Hoping to break free from the boots-and-saddles association, Foran signed with Universal in 1939 and was immediately placed in two films, director Eddie Cline's W.C. Fields-Mae West parody *My Little Chickadee* (a western of sorts, but a comedy first and foremost), and director Joe May's brooding *The House of the Seven Gables*. Then Universal stuck him in two B westerns before Pivar offered him the lead in *The Mummy's Hand*. This was a decided change of pace for the western-weary Foran, a straight horror film, and sequel to one of the studio's most popular horrific offerings of a decade earlier. His performance here is uneven and adequate at best, ranging from natural and relaxed to stiff and stilted.

Moran, as the crack-shot daughter of Cecil Kellaway's magician, is a pleasant addition to the cast, twin dimples and all. Her frustrated interaction with her father, whom she at first believes to be the victim of Foran's swindle, is utterly convincing, and she is a likeable presence. How she gets thirteen shots out of her six-shooter when blasting a "heart" in Foran's door is a mystery, however, and ditto for why she persists with wearing seamed stockings in the wilds of the Egyptian desert. But why quibble about minor details like these when there's a 3,000-year-old mummy stumbling about? As Marta, Moran is lusted after by Zucco's Andoheb rather than by Tyler's mummy, a switcheroo from the original where Princess Anck-es-ens-Amon, reincarnated as Helen Grosvenor, is the object of Karloff's character's irrepressible desire. Zita Johann, with her oversized Campbell's Soup Kid's head, censor-baiting outfits, and exotic demeanor, was the polar opposite of perky Moran.

Dick Foran getting the worst of it from Kharis (Tom Tyler) in *The Mummy's Hand* (1940).

George Zucco, fifteen years Pivar's senior and a fellow native of Manchester, England, had a sizable career in vaudeville and the British stage before entering the film industry, relocating to the United States in the mid-thirties where he played character roles in numerous high-profile films. *The Mummy's Hand* was a turning point of sorts in Zucco's career, where he became increasingly associated with this type of film into the forties. Pivar's *The Mummy's Tomb* (1942), *The Mummy's Ghost* (1944), and *The Mad Ghoul* (1943), PRC's *Dead Men Walk*, *The Black Raven* (both 1943), and *Fog Island* (1945), and numerous others followed; heaven knows he was born to play these roles. It is for these later, lesser efforts that he is most remembered today, but in actuality Zucco continued to take small roles in a wide variety of films and genres up until his retirement in the early fifties.

As Foran's Brooklyn-born buddy Babe, England-born Wallace Ford gets most of the laughs, with Cecil Kellaway only occasionally managing to upstage him. A middle-aged forty-two when the film was shot, Ford was settling in to smaller character roles such as this after a decade's worth of work in more than fifty films. Another twenty-five years in the industry was to follow, with a large body of work in television in his later years. Ford would reappear in this film's sequel as well.

Makeup artist Pierce, long a staple in Universal's makeup department and responsible for most of that studio's horrific creations, was born in Greece in 1889 and came to the United States around the turn of the century. A former semi-pro shortstop on Chicago's Logan Square Team until 1908, Pierce came to California hoping to break into Coast League baseball, but became a projectionist instead. He managed theaters for Harry Culver and served a short stint producing pictures with Native-American producer Young Deer for Kay Bee before going to work at Universal in 1914 as an actor and assistant cameraman. He was with Fox briefly in 1926 where he created his first horrific makeup for Jacques Lerner in Raoul Walsh's *The Monkey Talks*. Pierce became head of Universal's Makeup Department in 1928, and was the creative force behind the iconic makeups for Karloff as both Frankenstein's monster and the mummy, Lon Chaney, Jr.'s Wolf Man, Bela Lugosi's Ygor, and numerous others.

Pierce's base of operations at the studio was Dressing Room No. 5, a one-room bungalow with a shower bath built back in 1922. Void of any furniture except for two wooden kitchen chairs, a barber's chair used when applying makeup, a wardrobe, and an iron cot, the unimposing little structure had, over time, taken on the rather charming nickname "The Bugaboudoir." Tyler would show up at 4:00 a.m. each morning and sit patiently, clad only in a bathing suit, while Pierce spent the next six hours "mummifying" his face and hands. This involved successive applications of collodion and cotton, after which he was wrapped in a reported—and likely exaggerated—1,500 yards of bandages pre-rotted with acid.[5] The results were well worth the effort, and while not quite as effective as that for Karloff's brief appearance years earlier, far and away superior to the stream-lined makeup to be cobbled together for the three subsequent Chaney sequels. Pierce soldiered on until his dismissal in 1946 as part of the Universal-International purge. He worked sporadically in film and television through 1962's *Creation of the Humanoids* and the *Mister Ed*

---

[5] "Haven of the Ghouls," *New York Times*, September 8, 1940, page unknown.

talking-horse television series, a rather sad and anticlimactic swansong to an otherwise impressive career.

Pivar would follow this horror offering with a second genre film within a half-year, and a sequel to this sequel two years later. But it would be several more years before Pivar was to work exclusively on horror films and psychological thrillers, the films that he'd ultimately be remembered for.

§

10 An Unexpected "Horror"

The success of *The Mummy's Hand* opened the door for Pivar to take another shot at the genre. With the ongoing Arlen-Devine series occupying so much of his time, however, it would be another ten months before he had the opportunity to do so. His second genre effort, while not an out-and-out horror film, is a reasonably successful pastiche of comedy, mystery, and haunted house-type thrills. The results are even more impressive in that it was made on a schedule that was daunting even by B film standards.

Horror Island
(Director: George Waggner; Released March 28, 1941)

Horror Island is a handsome film, and demonstrates once again how Pivar, backed by the excellent craftsmen employed by Universal, could produce good-looking results within the confines of a shoestring budget. Woody Bredell's cinematography is typically dark and atmospheric, with effective lighting and judicious camera movement that never draws attention to itself but goes a long way toward enhancing the mood of the piece; the entire opening sequence on the docks and the deck of the *Skiddoo* are an excellent example of this. Director George Waggner was still fairly green, helming films only since 1938 and coming off a string of westerns, but his work here is assured and he would soon come to prominence with films such as Chaney's *The Wolf Man* later in 1941 and Karloff's *The Climax* in 1944. As for the cast, Dick Foran and Peggy Moran were reteamed, and a pleasant pairing it is since the two of them seem so comfortable with each other. Fuzzy Knight supplies the comic relief this time around, stuttering his way through a part that could just as well have been handed to Devine or Wallace Ford. Leo Carrillo, sporting a peg leg and thick accent, is so darn likeable in his first role for Pivar that it is no small wonder Pivar would reuse him in a string of films over the next year. The rest of the cast, drawn primarily from Universal's grab bag of contract players, is equally fine. Too bad the story is so silly.

Bill Martin (Foran) and his buddy Stuff Oliver (Knight) are up to their necks in debt, dodging creditors and the bill collectors hounding them for money owed on their small office and boat they've named *Skiddoo*. Witnessing a dockside struggle, they come to the rescue of one of the fellows thrown into the drink, pulling him to safety. He is "Skipper" Tobias (Carrillo), a peg-legged seaman who quickly explains that he has half of a map pointing to a $20-million-dollar gold treasure somewhere in a castle on Morgan Island, the other half just stolen by his attacker. Tobias is looking for the island's owner, Bill Martin, and is surprised to find that he is talking with him. Martin was left the island and its castle by his grandfather and, unable to unload it, has been stuck with it ever since. Tobias offers Martin half of the treasure if Martin and Stuff will take him out on their boat and assist him in locating the loot, somewhat of a challenge since they now only have half of the map.

They take the map to Professor Jasper (Hobart Cavanaugh) for authentication, but he dismisses it as a forgery. This gives Martin another of his get-rich-quick schemes, and together with Stuff and Tobias they organize "Buried Treasure, Inc.," offering weekend trips by boat out to Morgan Island, a two-night stay in the supposedly haunted castle, and the opportunity to search for hidden treasure—all this for $50 a head. Stuff is assigned the task of "haunting" the castle via hidden microphones, phony skulls, and the like.

"Skipper" Tobias (Leo Carrillo) tries to drum up business for weekend trips to Morgan Island, aka *Horror Island* (1941).

An Unexpected "Horror"

The weekend arrives and the trio has seven paying customers: wealthy Wendy Creighton (Moran), who had earlier crashed into Martin and has agreed to help him drum up business so he can afford to pay for damages to her car; Wendy's snooty companion Thurman Coldwater (Lewis Howard); timid thrill-seeker Professor Jasper; Martin's sleazy cousin George (John Eldredge), who for some unknown reason wants to buy the island for $20,000; a skeptical private investigator named McGoon (Walter Catlett); and the suspicious-looking couple Rod Grady (Ralf Harolde) and wife Arleen (Iris Adrian, in a role originally planned for Anne Nagel[1]). McGoon had earlier tried to deliver a cease-and-desist order to squelch Martin's ad claims regarding ghosts on the island, but was sidetracked when convinced by Martin he should attend the weekend's events; he can determine for sure that there aren't—or are—ghosts out there. A bomb intended for delivery to the boat explodes harmlessly in the water, providing an ominous sendoff.

Once the group is unpacked and settled in at the castle, Martin tries to entertain his guests while Tobias searches for the treasure and Stuff goes to work attempting to spook the assembled group. Strange things begin to happen courtesy of a mysterious cloaked phantom, resulting in some near-fatal accidents when a crossbow is fired at Tobias and a suit of armor falls and almost crushes Wendy. Martin takes Stuff to task thinking him responsible, but Stuff professes ignorance.

And then the killings start. First, Rod—in reality notorious bank robber Killer Grady—is shot when he and Arleen attempt to sneak out and steal Martin's boat. Later, another crossbow arrow intended for Tobias misses him, killing the individual hiding behind a curtain next to him. It is the so-called phantom, and Tobias recognizes him as a former fellow shipmate named Panama Pete who was present when Tobias originally found the treasure map. Martin puts two and two together and "solves" the mystery: Panama Pete had the other half of the map and wanted to scare everyone else away from the castle so he could search for it himself, unchallenged; his death by his own booby-trapped crossbow was accidental. A good theory, but it falls apart when Wendy disappears and cousin George is found dead in a suit of armor soon after.

During all of this Professor Jasper repeatedly reappears, sleepwalking. Clever guy that Martin is, he notices that Jasper always has his slippers on when sleepwalking, a step that a genuine sleepwalker would not take. Martin confronts Jasper, who drops his milquetoast front, admits knowing about the treasure for years, and pulls a .38. After a scuffle, Martin ends up in a subterranean chamber with Stuff and the missing Wendy. Tobias rescues them,

---

[1] Edwin Schallert, "Streamlined Impressions of the News," *Los Angeles Times*, February 27, 1941, 12.

but Jasper reappears and holds them at gunpoint. Demanding the map's other half, he finds the answer to opening the hidden chamber. When he tries to enter the chamber, however, he winds up dead, clobbered by a booby-trapped mallet hanging over the door. The treasure chest is opened, but there's no gold in it, only a rotted, centuries-old corpse.

The Phantom. And, no, it isn't John Carradine; it's Foy Van Dolsen. *Horror Island* (1941).

The film concludes with the usual happy ending: The Navy wants to purchase the island for use as a base (that's why cousin George wanted to buy it), and Martin is now eager to sell. Martin snuggles up to a receptive Wendy, and Thurman, observing this, opens his little black book, makes note that she is no longer available, and settles into a chair with the dejected look of a loser at love.

Based on Alex Gottlieb's original story *Terror of the South Seas* and adapted for the screen by Maurice Tombragel and Victor McLeod, *Horror Island* is a step in the right direction as far as low-budget horror offerings are concerned, in spite of an overabundance of painfully familiar haunted house-type spook stuff. Foran's performance here is breezy and relaxed, which makes one suspect that his rough spots in *The Mummy's Hand* might perhaps have been more attributable to Christy Cabanne's direction and a hurried schedule than any particular thespian shortcomings on Foran's part. Moran is as perky and charming as usual, and has adequate opportunity to demonstrate her admirable screaming abilities. Foy Van Dolsen, a bit player with only a handful of credits on his resume, is delightfully cadaverous as the so-called phantom,

An Unexpected "Horror"

Panama Pete. Lewis Howard, as the bored cynic Thurman Coldwater, steals the show, with Walter Catlett's McGoon a close second. As for the sixty-year-old Carrillo, this was his first for Universal in an exclusive three-year contract that would team him repeatedly with Devine and/or Foran in a number of Pivar productions, as well as a large number of other B westerns and adventures. Poor Peggy Moran, though; it was announced that this was to be her last B as a result of a successful grooming for A's, but *Flying Cadets* (Erle C. Kenton), *Double Date* (Glenn Tryon), *Hello, Sucker* (Edward Cline; all 1941), *Treat 'Em Rough* (Ray Taylor), and *Drums of the Congo* (Christy Cabanne; both 1942) were the comparative disappointments that followed.

Filmed in late February-early March[2] and rushed into theaters later that same month, *Horror Island* was met with indifference by contemporary reviewers. *Variety* trashed it, calling it "a fourth-rate, low-budget mystery-and-adventure flapdoodle, poorly written, sloppily produced and directed."[3] *Boxoffice*'s Ivan Spear was a tad more charitable: "... a treasure-hunting yarn, struggling with a hackneyed story that has been bolstered through the addition of enough trapdoors, clutching hands, phantom killers and the like to qualify it as an average entry in the thriller category ... productional details as supplied by Ben Pivar are adequate."[4] To each his own, but the film is much better and far more enjoyable than their reviews would lead one to believe.

Dick Foran tries to redirect sleepwalking Hobart Cavanagh in *Horror Island* (1941).

---

[2] Douglas W. Churchill, "Screen News Here and in Hollywood," *New York Times*, February 27, 1941, 23.

[3] Char., "Horror Island," *Variety*, April 2, 1941, 16.

[4] Ivan Spear, "Spearheads," *Boxoffice*, April 5, 1941, 37.

A *New York Times* article listing what the author felt to be the year's ten worst pictures resulted in a humorous written response, one that invokes the name of *Horror Island*. Arthur L. Mayer, the letter's writer, was director of New York City's Rialto Theatre, located at 42nd Street and Seventh Avenue, known at this time as a purveyor of low-budget films of all ilks:

Window card poster for *Horror Island* (1941). Ticket prices have increased somewhat over the past seventy years. Image courtesy of Heritage Auction Galleries, Ha.com.

It seems to me grossly unfair to confine your list of the year's ten worst pictures to million-dollar pictures, thus automatically barring the Rialto from this memorable competition.

We have conclusively demonstrated that an indomitable producer without a large expenditure of money can turn out pictures devoid of all traces of literacy, dramatic value, directorial skill and histrionic talent. The powerful first-run circuit houses have made notable inroads in the field of bad pictures, but we proudly believe that week in and week out, the Rialto has maintained this undisputed supremacy.

This season, with products like 'Chinese Den,' 'Man Made Monster,' 'Flying Wild,' 'Horror Island' and 'Invisible Ghost,' we thought we had surely maintained our glorious traditions. To make assurances doubly sure, we had hoped, prior to New Year's Day, to show our next attraction, 'The Mad Doctor of Market Street,' which, incredible though it may seem to you, will make all other holiday offerings along Broadway appear works of unforgettable genius.

At an early date I trust THE TIMES will try to right the injustice it has done and devote some space to the superlatively bad pictures produced even with low budgets in 1941.[5]

Overstated, perhaps, but there were a lot of inept productions released to bolster Mayer's tongue-in-cheek case.

---

[5] "Noted for the Record," letter from Arthur L. Mayer, *New York Times*, January 4, 1942, X4.

An Unexpected "Horror"

Film historian William K. Everson, in revisionist mode, had no such qualms about the film when he presented it at New York's New School more than forty-five years later. In his program notes, Everson commented on Universal's horror films of this era in general—"Universal turned them out to a slick and enjoyable formula: good musical scores, handsome production values, and thrills that weren't rugged enough to really scare anyone but managed to be exciting and lively"—and *Horror Island* in particular—"an expert little film of its kind ... [that] gets under way immediately with no wasted time, and even the comic byplay is punctuation rather than padding ... it's unpretentious, good fun and well-crafted."[6] It is a shame Everson was not reviewing films decades earlier.

With the completion of *Horror Island*, Pivar returned to the Arlen and Devine series. His brief two-film fling with the genre yielded mixed but enjoyable results, and it would be another year-and-a-half and nine more films before he'd reacquaint himself with Kharis and the horror film in general.

§

---

[6] "William K. Everson, Film Series 55: Program #5," New School program notes, March 13, 1987, 2.

11 The Arlen-Devine Series — Sans Arlen, 1941-1942

The fiscal year ending November 1, 1941, had been another good one for Universal, with a net profit of $2,332,742, a profit comparable to that of the previous year.[1] Universal was not about to let Richard Arlen's departure get in the way of a money-making formula. Pivar went to work retooling the series, retaining the predominate elements of stalwart and dependable leading man, comedy-relief sidekick, and plenty of action all wrapped around a paper-thin plot. The result—on paper, at least—was to be a seven-film western series. "[E]arly American yarns laid around the Mexican border," as *Variety* put it, this time with a trio of leads. Devine was the one constant, with character actor Leo Carrillo brought on as backup and to add some "authenticity" as the series' resident ethnic, Pancho. Dick Foran, who'd settled in at Universal and had proved his worth to Pivar in both *The Mummy's Hand* and *Horror Island*, filled Arlen's absence. Foran was to play a character named Kansas.

William A. Scully, Universal's general sales manager, announced the new series early in February 1941, at Universal's annual sales convention in Chicago. Sixty-one productions were planned for the 1941-1942 season, twenty-three of them A pictures; a combined budget in the range of $16,000,000 to $18,000,000 was projected. Fourteen films would be "outdoor and action pictures,"[2] seven of them the Foran-Carrillo-Devine series. Another seven would be the perennial Johnny Mack Brown westerns, again with Fuzzy Knight and Nell O'Day, who had ended up in the roles announced a year earlier for stunt-girl Julie Duncan. Additionally, four serials—two of them tailored "especially for adult audiences"—and sixty-nine reels of short subjects were thrown into the mix. The tentative titles given for the new Foran-Carrillo-

---

[1] "Film Profits Show Gain," *Los Angeles Times*, January 25, 1942, A14.

[2] "23 'A' Productions On Universal List," *Boxoffice*, February 15, 1941, 16.

Devine series were *Beyond the Pampas*; *In Old Monterey*; *Viva, Pancho*; *Sunset on the Sierras*; *Dons of San Marcos*; *The Fighting Padre*; and *The Americanos*.[3] Unlike the tentative titles previously announced for each of the two seasons of the Arlen-Devine series, only one of these—*The Americanos*—would actually make it to film, and with a new title.

The Kid from Kansas
(Director: William Nigh; Released September 19, 1941)

Pivar used a new director for the first in the series, still titled *The Americanos* when it went into production in late June. Fifty-nine-year-old William Nigh was a veteran of the industry, starting as an actor back in 1911, dabbling with direction three years later, with a sole concentration on direction by the mid-twenties. This was a prolific period for Nigh, working at a number of different studios and responsible for dozens of features, Lon Chaney's *Mr. Wu* (1927) for MGM among them. By the time sound came into play, however, Nigh's career was headed southward, with more than seventy low-budget films to his credit before he retired in 1948. Most of these were for the Poverty Row studios Monogram and PRC, with four random productions for Universal in the mid-thirties. *The Americanos* was the first of a renewed six-film association with Universal in the early forties, the aging director by now in the twilight of his career. The fellow knew how to stick to a budget, though, and could knock these things out in his sleep. Too bad the results sometimes looked that way.

Universal placed a full-page ad in a July issue of *Boxoffice* now referring to the series' initial release as *Sumatra*, but that seems odd given the film's South American setting; the two following films were now advertised as *The Sonora Kid* for November 21 release, and *Zambezi* for December 26 release.[4] A month later the film had taken on its upcoming September 19 release title of *The Kid from Kansas*.[5] Ann Doran and Marcia Ralston assumed the female leads, with Antonio Moreno adding a touch of reality to the South America-based story, and American-born "ethnic" Nestor Paiva rounding out the cast. The uncredited bit part of Rosita was played by Carmella Cansino,[6] an actress with a short, unremarkable career; whether or not she was related in some

---

[3] "Universal Plans 61 Films in Season," *New York Times*, February 11, 1941, page unknown.

[4] Universal ad, *Boxoffice*, July 19, 1941, 21.

[5] Douglas W. Churchill, "News from Hollywood," *New York Times*, August 23, 1941, 7.

[6] "Douglas W. Churchill, "Screen News Here and in Hollywood," *New York Times*, June 24, 1941, 17.

fashion or another to *The Dancing Cansinos* and their daughter Margarita—aka Rita Hayworth—is unknown.

In spite of a title that would suggest a western, *The Kid from Kansas* is set at a banana plantation on the mythical South American island of Toalango. Pancho Garcia (Leo Carrillo) and his fellow banana plantation owners are in trouble: Acts of sabotage have been cutting into their businesses, making it increasingly difficult to meet payroll and cover expenses. When local (and sole) buyer Lee Walker (James Seay), a Great Northern Fruit representative, offers an insulting 58¢ per hundred-weight for the newest crop, Pancho reveals that he has taken it upon himself to contact another buyer and line up a far better deal. The new concern's boat is to arrive in several days to pick up the shipment.

A stranger named Kansas (Dick Foran) wanders into town and befriends Pancho's foreman Andy (Andy Devine) when he corrects him on an obvious miscount. The night before the boat is scheduled to arrive, Kansas and Andy sit dockside, allowing Foran to warble his first song, "Red River Valley," while "accompanied" by Andy on concertina. Alerted by the smell of kerosene, the two interrupt a small group of saboteurs in the midst of ruining the shipment of bananas, and prevail in the fight that follows. Just as Andy is about to question one of the gang, the fellow is stabbed in the back and killed. Toalango's chief of police (Antonio Moreno) arrives and places Andy and Kansas under arrest for murder. Pancho secures the pair's release, assuring the chief that they'll be present for the far-off trial.

Toalango's chief of police has our heroes in jail, unjustly of course, in *The Kid from Kansas* (1941). Left to right: Leo Carrillo, Antonio Moreno, Dick Foran, Andy Devine.

STOP YELLIN'

Kansas goes to work for Pancho in spite of the fact that there's no money for payroll, looking only for "a place to sleep and three squares a day." There is dissention among the plantation's workers over the fear of withheld wages, egged on by employee Cesar (Francis McDonald). After a major scuffle, Cesar is knocked cold, but Pancho later announces that the troublemaker can retain his job.

Pretty young Georgette Smith (Ann Doran) arrives at the plantation, and Pancho's delighted that the "G. Smith" he was expecting is a female. Smitty, as she comes to be known, is an agricultural chemist sent down by the Atlantic Research Company, and quickly goes to work testing the crop. That night while both Pancho and Andy spruce up for the young lady, Kansas beats them to the punch; a romance soon blossoms between Kansas and Smitty. She does her job, though, and soon finds that a portion of the crop has been infected with Bahama Fungus, smuggled in from elsewhere. The infected section is isolated, the diseased crop burned, and the soil alkalized.

As money woes mount, Pancho and several other plantation owners visit Toalango Fruit Exchange president John Russell (Wade Boteler), asking for loans to be backed up by their crops now ready for shipping. Russell refuses, a first, citing their recent troubles as the reason. Plantation owner Roy York (Leyland Hodgson) gives up and sells his property to Russell for a measly $5,000, far less than the property is worth.

Pancho throws a farewell party for York, Lee Walker and his wife Linda (Marcia Ralston) among the attendees. Pancho suggests to York that he invest his $5,000 in Pancho's plantation and use the eventual returns to buy back his property. York refuses and leaves, but Kansas follows, returning later with the $5,000 and says that York has changed his mind. When York turns up dead, however, Kansas is arrested for murder and thrown back in jail. Not for long, though; a mysterious stranger sneaks a loaded pistol into Kansas' cell, which Kansas uses to escape. Kansas makes his way back to the plantation where his friends hide him from the law.

Linda Walker arrives and announces that her husband has now agreed to pay top dollar for future shipments of bananas. Later while taking a walk, Kansas and Linda spot some saboteurs planting explosives under the train tracks used to ship the bananas. Kansas tracks the saboteurs back to a hut, which he intends to search later on. Smitty has grown jealous of Linda, suspecting that the married woman has her eyes on Kansas. Learning of this, Kansas responds, "Don't believe anything you didn't see." He takes Smitty along to search the hut where they find a large spray canister filled with the dreaded fungus. Cesar breaks in and attempts to stab Kansas, but Pancho arrives and shoots the fellow, wounding him. Informed of the explosives planted under the tracks, Pancho decides to ship the bananas by barge.

Later, Smitty overhears Linda telling her husband everything by phone, including escapee Kansas' presence at the plantation and the new plans for shipping. Confronted by a suspicious Smitty, Linda assures her that her husband can be trusted, just as she can. Smitty is skeptical, and informs Kansas.

The saboteurs, headed by a rival plantation owner named Jamaica (Nester Paiva), are now aware of the change in plans and plant dynamite in the river. The chief of police arrives at the plantation and re-arrests Kansas, and insists that Pancho, Andy, and Walker all accompany him on his trip back to Toalango. Walker balks when he learns that the trip is to be made on the barge with the banana shipment, but the chief insists. As their trip proceeds down the river, Walker grows increasingly nervous. Fearful for his life, Walker breaks down and insists they stop the trip, revealing the plan to blow up the barge. The saboteurs are spotted on the shore and a gun battle follows. Kansas is wounded in the left arm, but tough guy that he is manages to beat Jamaica to a pulp using only his right. Back at the plantation, a catfight between Smitty and Linda breaks out, and Smitty prevails: "Get tough with me, will you?"

Leo Carrillo, Andy Devine, and Antonio Moreno shoot it out with the bad guys in *The Kid from Kansas* (1941).

The plot's loose ends are tied up in a somewhat perfunctory manner when Kansas confronts Russell, armed with some information provided by Walker, who refuses to be the fall guy. With a minimum of coaxing it is revealed that Russell had plans to take over all of the island's plantations, and to that end had both Walker and Jamaica on his payroll to assist in achieving that goal; Jamaica is named as York's killer.

With the bad guys all under arrest, Kansas is revealed to be an undercover operative of Great Northern Fruit, sent down to investigate Walker whom they suspected of misquoting prices to the local plantation owners and pocketing the difference. Toalango's chief of police was in on this investigation from the beginning, and was the mysterious stranger who had provided Kansas with a pistol when he was in jail.

The wrap-up scene has Kansas once-again correcting Andy's miscounting. Much to the consternation of rival suitors Pancho and Andy, the chief of police wins over the young lady they both had their eyes on.

Foran, Carrillo, and Devine make a very likeable trio, a nice transition from—and perhaps an improvement over—the former Arlen-Devine pairing. Foran handles the macho stuff nicely, throws a punch convincingly, and is relaxed and comfortable with the comic interplay with his partners. Devine does Devine once again, and does it well. Carrillo is a delight, relishing his opportunity to flaunt his affected Spanish accent while mangling the English language. There's an evident fondness between the trio in spite of the constant bickering, Pancho's insults directed at Andy, and even some Stooges-like slapping between the two. Foran is not totally immune from these occasional broad displays of physicality; he is the recipient of a swift kick to the butt at the end of one scene.

Technically, the film is as well crafted as its brethren. William Nigh's direction is workmanlike, as is John Boyle's photography, particularly in the nicely lit nighttime shots. Stock footage is employed more sparingly here, first in an opening montage of the workings of the plantation, a later montage of the isolation and destruction of the infected plants, and finally as background and filler shots during the barge ride down river. Look real hard and you might actually spot James Cagney in a snippet of stock footage from *Torrid Zone*, a Warner Brothers release from the previous year. *The Hollywood Reporter* had this to say about the film's use of stock footage: "Ben Pivar produced and some of the stock shots he dug up for the film are more interesting than the story," a story the reviewer dismissed as "[b]elow average in its bracket."[7]

There's the occasional rushed-production sloppiness, most evident with Foran's undershirt which disappears and reappears with distressing regularity.

---

[7] "Story Rambles Over Too Much Ground," *Hollywood Reporter*, September 16, 1941, 3.

The Arlen-Devine Series — Sans Arlen, 1941-1942

Reaction to the film was mixed (as usual), with Jimmie Fidler optimistically calling it the "First step in a stairway of action mellers that should mount to a popular high."[8] The reviewer for *Boxoffice* was less optimistic but just as succinct, commenting on the new trio replacing the Arlen-Devine duo, the screenplay by Griffin Jay and David Silverstein, Nigh's direction, and the prospects for the new series in general, all in one fell swoop: "While the reorganization might eventually mean an improvement, it has little opportunity here under the handicap of an acutely bad screenplay and complicated heavy-handed direction."[9] *Daily Variety* was more forgiving, calling it "a pleasing bit of blood and thunder … William Nigh directed and can take credit for a job that is up to his usual standard. Production by Ben Pivar is ably handled." The reviewer's final assessment? "It probably won't break any records, but it will more than return its investment."[10] Fair enough.

Universal's fortunes continued on the upswing, and stockholders were paid their first dividends since October 1932. Nate Blumberg, Cliff Work, and Matthew "Matty" Fox—none of whom had any previous experience with film production prior to their placement in charge of same back in 1938 during the company's restructuring—were singled out as being largely responsible for the turnaround. *The New York Times* offered a back-handed compliment for their achievements: "Although they have not revolutionized the character of the pictures, they rescued the company from virtual bankruptcy …"[11]

A pair of lawsuits had been filed in Manhattan Supreme Court the previous October that had put on public display the dissension among Universal Pictures' directors. One charged board chairman J. Cheever Cowdin and nineteen other defendants with conspiracy and the "looting and wasting" of assets,[12] and a second charged much of the same group with "fraud, conversion of assets, and mismanagement."[13] This internal squabbling had been resolved by mid-1941, the company's future now looking to be on solid ground.

William Nigh was announced as director for producer Ben Pivar's upcoming production *North of the Klondike*,[14] but that never came to be. The production was reassigned to Paul Malvern, the direction switched to Erle C. Kenton, and

---

[8] Jimmie Fidler, "Jimmie Fidler in Hollywood," *Los Angeles Times*, September 23, 1941, A9.

[9] "The Kid from Kansas," *Boxoffice*, September 27, 1941, 177.

[10] "The Kid From Kansas," *Daily Variety*, September 16, 1941, 3.

[11] Douglas W. Churchill, "Hollywood Changes," *New York Times*, July 6, 1941, X3.

[12] "Stockholders Sue Universal Films," *New York Times*, October 5, 1940, page unknown.

[13] "Universal Film Fight Broadens," *Los Angeles Times*, October 23, 1940, 18.

[14] "Hollywood Personnelities," *Boxoffice*, August 30, 1941, 36.

the film released early 1942 as *North to the Klondike*. Nigh took it in stride, squeezing in nine more features before directing the series' fourth entry—*Escape from Hong Kong*—a mere eight months later.

Road Agent
(Director: Charles Lamont; Released December 19, 1941)

For whatever reason, Pivar decided to abandon the "South of the Border" theme for the series, and the "Kansas" character along with it. The result was *Road Agent*, an out-and-out western penned by Pivar favorite Maurice Tombragel, with an assist by Morgan Cox and Arthur Strawn. Shooting commenced on Friday, October 17, at the Iverson family ranch, a popular location frequented by the industry since 1912. Jerome Ash handled the camerawork, a position he'd filled on several of Pivar's earlier films at Universal.

Road Agent has a typically solid cast, with Anne Gwynne and Anne Nagel handling the female roles, and Morris Ankrum as the film's heavy. Foran was back in the saddle as Duke Masters, and was required to dust off his windpipes in order to warble two more songs, the old Mexican standard "Cielito Lindo" by Quirino Mendoza y Cortés, and "Ridin' Home," written by Jimmy McHugh and frequent collaborator Harold Adamson. McHugh, for the record, wrote the theme music that accompanied the Universal globe logo at the beginning of each film since the later thirties, unimaginatively titled "Universal Pictures Fanfare."[15]

Direction was handled by Charles Lamont, another veteran who had started in the industry in 1919, moving behind the camera several years later where he spent the bulk of the twenties and early thirties directing two-reel comedy shorts for Grand Asher, Century, Lupino Lane Comedies, Jack White and Educational Pictures, and Christie Studios. Moving into feature direction in 1934, Lamont cranked out a lot of lower-budget fare primarily for Chesterfield and Grand National, finally settling in at Universal in 1939 and sticking with them until his retirement in 1956. The fifties saw his return to comedy direction, handling Abbott and Costello's later (and lamer) films, as well as the last of the *Ma and Pa Kettle* series. Lamont's direction had grown tired by 1941, but he too could deliver the goods, on schedule, within budget, with workmanlike results.

Along with Duke Masters are Pancho (Carrillo) and Andy (Devine), seemingly a trio of latter-day Robin Hoods. After the stagecoach headed to the town of Calliope is robbed and its driver and sheriff guard are killed, Duke and friends confront the robbers, relieve them of their ill-gotten loot, and send them on their way. After helping themselves to a small reward of 10% ($4,000!),

---

[15] Michael Feinstein, "Jimmy McHugh" <www.jimmymchughmusic.com> (December 30, 2010)

Duke returns the rest of the money to the bank in Calliope along with a note identifying himself and claiming the $4,000 as reward money. Jackson, the lone survivor of the coach robbery, arrives in town with the stage and victims' corpses, and says he'd be able to identify the robbers. Some of the more skeptical townspeople, Tom Martin (Richard Davies) included, suspect Duke of the robbery, but Lola (Anne Nagel), an old flame of Duke's, defends him in no uncertain terms.

Anne Nagel at her prettiest in a posed shot for *Road Agent* (1941).

Watching from a nearby rooftop, Duke spots Lola and hears her impassioned defense of him. He follows her into the saloon of a shady fellow named Shayne (Reed Hadley) where she works as a singer. Lola, who is now married, introduces Duke to her husband Steve (John Gallaudet). Duke recognizes Steve as one of the three unsuccessful stage robbers, and Steve, in turn, is shocked to see the man who had relieved him of his ill-gotten gains. Both Duke and Steve act as if they'd never met one another. Meanwhile, Jackson is murdered before he can identify any of the robbers, and Duke is pegged as his killer, sight unseen.

Having learned that Lola is no longer available, Duke now sets his sights on Patricia Leavitt (Anne Gwynne), the attractive daughter of Calliope Exchange Bank owner Sam Leavitt (Samuel S. Hinds). In a reckless attempt to meet her, Duke poses as "Douglas," a cattle rancher from nearby Red Rock, and introduces Andy and Pancho as his ranch foreman and manager, respectively. Duke deposits their $4,000 in Leavitt's bank, and orchestrates an invitation to a big party at Leavitt's home that night where he will be able to meet other influential townspeople.

Later on at the party, Patricia falls head over heels for Duke, much to the annoyance of Tom Martin, who happens to be her jealous former beau. Someone recognizes Duke for who he is, and a posse is organized to arrest him for the murder of Jackson. Patricia warns Duke, but he and his two friends are arrested before they can escape. Duke is scheduled to hang the next morning.

Not so fast, though. Lola steps forward and informs the mob that Duke was in the saloon with her when Jackson was killed. As additional proof, she has her reluctant husband Steve corroborate her claims. The trio is released, and Duke is asked why he came to town in the first place. His response: To even a score with Big John Morgan (Morris Ankrum), the corrupt rancher who has the town paralyzed with fear. Unbeknownst to the town's citizens, both Shayne and Steve work for Big John, who is behind the latest coach robbery and the others that preceded it. In a staggering gesture of good will, Duke is offered the position of town sheriff—and accepts! With Carrillo and Devine as his deputies, his first order of business is the banning of firearms; anyone within the town limits must turn over their guns, to be returned upon their departure. This, of course, doesn't sit well with hot-headed Shayne, who pulls a derringer on Duke when he attempts to disarm him. A huge fight breaks out, but terminates when Andy arrives with a cannon aimed at the saloon's front door. Shayne is arrested and jailed.

Duke's new law and willingness to follow through with it result in a quieting of the town. With a renewed sense of security, the town's citizens once again resume banking with Leavitt, and his safe is soon filled with their cash. Rumors abound that Big John is coming to town to confront Duke, however, and this has Patricia worried. Big John finally shows up and there's a face-off with Duke in the saloon. Duke stands his ground and asks for $50 bail for Shayne's release, and Big John reluctantly agrees.

Big John confronts Leavitt, who it turns out has been working with him behind the scenes. Big John notes that the bank's holdings are swelling, and will soon be worth stealing. Leavitt responds that he wants to go straight, but Big John will have nothing of it. Later, Big John comes up with a plan to lure Duke to Leavitt's home, having word get to Duke that Big John is planning to kidnap Patricia and hold her for ransom. Once Duke is out of town, Big John and his gang will rob the bank unimpeded. But Duke is too clever for them, and "robs" the bank before heading out to the Leavitt home, and deposits the bank's holdings there. When Big John and his boys arrive at the bank to rob it, they find that there is no longer any money to rob; Duke has beaten them to the punch. Furious, they head for the Leavitt home to kill Duke and confiscate the money. Meanwhile, word has gotten out that sheriff Duke has robbed the town bank, and under Martin's supervision a posse is formed and heads for Leavitt's home as well.

In a climactic confrontation between the good guys and the bad guys, padded with mucho stock footage lifted from 1940's *Trail of the Vigilantes* (Allan Dwan), Duke shoots Big John, Pancho shoots Steve, Andy shoots Shayne, and the arriving posse shoots everyone else not wearing a white hat. Our heroic trio emerges triumphant and bids adieu to the town, leaving the "borrowed" bank money along with a note revealing themselves as agents for Wells-Fargo Express. What a surprise.

Standard cowboy stuff, no better or worse than much of what Universal's cowboy unit was cranking out, but competently handled. The three leads are likable as always, Carrillo perhaps mangling the English language even more than usual. If you like singing cowboys, Foran won't disappoint, crooning to piano-playing Nagel in Shayne's saloon, a not illogical place to do so, but more awkwardly so while dancing with Gwynne at the big party while belting out "Cielito Lindo" (you know: the old "Aye, Aye, Aye Aye..." ditty). Devine, in jail, gets to rattle the bars once again, but unlike *The Devil's Pipeline* where he yanked the whole door off and marched around, door in hand, continuing to shout for the guard, here he manages merely to bring the ceiling down.

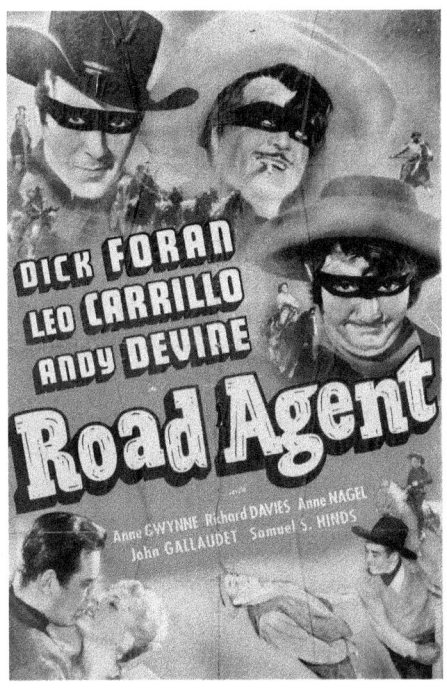

No, they aren't really robbers. *Road Agent* (1941). Image courtesy of Heritage Auction Galleries, Ha.com.

With the completion of *Road Agent*, Foran called it quits with the series, fed up with being dumped back into the horse operas from which he had hoped to distance himself with his departure from Warners. He remained with Universal through 1943, however, primarily in B's and as occasional love interest in Abbott and Costello comedies. He broke with the studio after starring in Eddie Cline's *He's My Guy*, and was out of work for well over a year, during which time his (second) wife of less than two years, aspiring-but-none-too-successful actress Carole Gallagher, sued for divorce.[16] In spite of the usual allegation of "cruelty," Foran's career doesn't seem to have been adversely affected, as he was signed shortly after to costar opposite Claudette Colbert in Sam Wood's *Guest Wife* (1945).[17]

Road Agent was released on December 19, 1941, less than two weeks after Japan's shocking attack on Pearl Harbor. A month later, Universal announced

---

[16] "Dick Foran's Wife Sues," *Los Angeles Times*, September 26, 1944, A1.

[17] Philip K. Scheuer, "A Couple of Prodigal Sons Return," *Los Angeles Times*, November 28, 1944, 11.

its earnings for the thirteen-week period ending January 31, 1942, a net of $1,518,315, more than double the previous year's comparable time period of $703,795. It was observed that the industry's experience was closely following that of England after the outbreak of war there back in 1939: an initial slump in attendance as the populace was caught up in the developing war news, followed by a quick recovery. Chairman of the Board J. Cheever Cowdin offered his two cents: "In war times motion pictures have proved the ideal form of entertainment because they are convenient, they are inexpensive, they afford relaxation."[18] And cheaper looking, too; by mid-year a $5,000-per-picture limitation had been imposed on the cost of new materials for set construction,[19] not that this would have much of an affect on Pivar's already-cut-rate productions.

By the end of April, the company's twenty-six-week net had grown to $3,741,634, more than double the previous year's net of $1,759,534 for the comparable time period.[20] With the outbreak of war weighing heavily on the minds of everyone, it proved to be a boon for the film industry as it drove patrons into the theaters for a night of sheer escapism, providing the various production companies with steadily mounting profits for the duration of the conflict. The five vertically integrated companies that controlled exhibition along with production and distribution—Paramount, MGM, 20th Century-Fox, Warner Brothers, and RKO—fared best, while the three smaller companies—Universal and Columbia with only production and distribution, and United Artists with distribution only—fared less well, but still saw unprecedented profits. Even the tiny Poverty Row studios of Monogram and PRC benefited from the wartime influx of patrons.

Two More, But Not By Pivar

Neither the third nor fourth films in the Devine-Carrillo series, *Unseen Enemy* and *Escape from Hong Kong*, have Pivar's name in the credits. Pivar was spread too thinly during this period, a result of Foran's departure and the change in direction for the series' storylines, compounded by the ramping up of pre-production work on a number of non-series films that would include *The Mummy's Tomb* and *Eyes of the Underworld*. With the outbreak of war, a patriotic fervor engulfed the nation, and the industry responded with a rash of military-themed films. Westerns, for the time being at least, took a back

---

[18] "Universal Net for 13 Weeks is $1,518,315," *Motion Picture Herald*, March 21, 1942, 48.

[19] "40% of Features in Work Have War as Theme," *Motion Picture Herald*, June 20, 1942, 12.

[20] "Universal, Columbia Profits Increase," *Motion Picture Herald*, June 20, 1942, 24.

seat, especially in light of the need to quickly develop scripts that would reflect recent world developments, if only on the most superficial of levels.

Columbia's timing could not have been better—or worse, one would suppose—with the already-filmed Lupe Velez-starrer *Honolulu Lu* (Charles Barton) released only four days after the attack on Pearl Harbor. While it had nothing whatsoever to do with the war, it did have name recognition with the presence of "Honolulu" in its title; given the light nature of the film, it probably proved more of a hindrance than asset. MGM was second out of the gate with February's *A Yank on the Burma Road* (George B. Seitz), and March's *Two Yanks in Trinidad* (Gregory Ratoff) and *Nazi Agent* (Jules Dassin). Already in the works when the attack occurred, some after-the-fact additional footage and verbal references to Pearl Harbor provided the tenuous links to the war. 20th Century-Fox's *Secret Agent of Japan* (Irving Pichel) followed on their heels, in theaters by the beginning of April and most likely the first from the majors fully written after the events of December 11. The Poverty Row studios were more flexible, of course, and could knock out a sensationalized script, film it, and have it released in record time. Monogram rushed *Black Dragons* (William Nigh) into theaters in early March, a far-fetched Lugosi starrer with Japanese spies cosmetically altered to assume the roles of some prominent Americans. PRC followed later that same month with their Nazi spies-on-the-loose drama *The Dawn Express* (Albert Herman).

Universal was not about to be left out in the cold, resulting in the immediate rethinking of the upcoming films in the Carrillo-Devine series, with war-themed films placed on the fast track. The production pace was sufficiently tight that Marshall Grant was brought in as associate producer for the next two films, allowing Pivar some breathing room to work up the remaining three series entries as well as some other unrelated film projects. Given Pivar's close association with the ongoing series, however, it is likely he had some minor involvement with these two films as well, thereby warranting brief mention here.

Unseen Enemy went before John Boyle's cameras in February, with John Rawlins directing and Grant overseeing production. Based on a script pounded out by Roy Chanslor and Stanley Rubin shortly after the Japanese attacked Pearl Harbor from an "idea" by George Wallace Sayre, the San Francisco-based plot involves a German naval officer, recently escaped from a Canadian prisoner-of-war camp. He ambitiously plans to hijack a Japanese freighter, arm it, and use it to raid coastal Pacific shipping. With Foran's departure from the series, brawny action star (and fellow redhead) Don Terry was brought in, having given an adequate performance a year earlier in Pivar and Rawlin's *Mutiny in the Arctic*, and currently attracting attention in the studio's just-released serial *Don Winslow of the Navy*. Foran's sudden absence from the series caught exhibitors off-guard, and one of them griped to *Boxoffice*: "I thought this series was sold as starring Dick Foran, Leo Carrillo, and Andy Devine. I don't see anything of Foran in this!"[21]

In Hollywood from the beginning of the sound era, Don Terry was somewhat of a B film staple as a result of starring roles in a continuous series of action-adventure films and serials such as *The Secret of Treasure Island* (Columbia, 1938; Elmer Clifton) and *Overland Mail* (Universal, 1942; Ford Beebe and John Rawlins). Terry plays undercover Canadian intelligence officer William "Bill" Flynn, whom we think for two-thirds of the film is escaped Nazi prisoner of war Wilhelm Roering. Devine is San Francisco cop Sam Dillon, this time in a humor-free straight role. Carrillo is Schooner Club owner Nick Rand, who may or may not be on our side. Irene Hervey plays his songstress daughter Gen Rand, required to sing an updated version of Franz Schubert's "Who Is Sylvia?" each and every one of the umpteen times a Nazi agent enters the nightclub. Turhan Bey has another tiny role, here as Ito, the enemy agent of indeterminate origin.

Everyone looks grim when our nation's safety is at stake. *Unseen Enemy* (1942). Image courtesy of Heritage Auction Galleries, Ha.com.

John Rawlins, whose direction was wildly uneven from B film to B film, here delivers some stylishly effective orchestration of several action sequences. Photographer John Boyle delivers as well, with well-chosen camera placement and lighting in several nighttime scenes, most memorably the opening escape from the prison camp. Released in April 1942, the film is a genuine curiosity in that it has no opening title or credits, all of them instead appearing at the film's end. One of the leads gets killed off as well, a first—and last—for the series. And, no, Don Terry can't dance.

Escape from Hong Kong followed in March, this one with William Nigh back as director, Woody Bredell behind the camera, Marshall Grant still filling Pivar's shoes, and again based on a Roy Chanslor script. Marjorie Lord was the female lead, and she topped poor Terry in billing. Based in Hong Kong shortly before the Japanese attacked Pearl Harbor, the three male leads here are a

---

[21] "What the Picture Did for Me," *Boxoffice*, August 8, 1942, 52.

vaudeville act billing themselves as "The Three Sharpshooters," decked out in western garb and playing a local theater. Rusty, Pancho, and Blimp—I'll let you guess who played each part—find themselves tangling with Japanese spies, with Leyland Hodgson as undercover Nazi Von Metz posing as British Major Reeves. Marjorie Lord, on the other hand, is British spy Valarie Hale posing as a Nazi agent in an attempt to uncover the intelligence leak. It gets confusing, especially for our bull-headed trio who always seem to be in the right place at the right time, but with the wrong intentions. Everything is cleared up by film's end, Terry catching on with evidence that would leave most others scratching their head. The film's climax is one of those jaw-droppers where our heroes, aboard a fast-moving speedboat, manage to shoot down two attacking Jap planes using only their rifles, hurling colorful but by-now politically incorrect epithets as they do so, and with much gusto I might add. Sharpshooters, indeed!

Woody Bredell's camerawork is the chief asset here, and for a low-budget B the film is visually stunning. While it would be charitable to assign director Nigh some of the credit for the film's glossy look, roving camera work and chiaroscuro lighting, I strongly suspect this is primarily Bredell's doing. The opening sequence, seemingly a campfire-based song and shootout that turns out to be a stage performance, followed by a genuine shootout between a Nazi spy and the British military, promises good things that never really come. Set decorator Russell Gausman tries his hardest to make the Universal back lot look like Hong Kong, but is only occasionally successful. As Von Metz, however, Hodgson is perfectly chilling.

It's going to take some slick shooting to down that thing! *Escape from Hong Kong* **(1942). Image courtesy of Heritage Auction Galleries, Ha.com.**

Soon after *Escape from Hong Kong*'s release in May, associate producer Marshall Grant signed on with the Army as a lieutenant in the Signal Corps, heading off to Camp Crowder for training in June.[22] Pivar resumed full charge of the series.

---

[22] "Kansas City," *Boxoffice*, June 27, 1942, 55.

Top Sergeant
(Director: Christy Cabanne; Released June 12, 1942)

Showdown began filming on Monday, March 9, 1942.[23] With the completion of *Unseen Enemy* and *Escape from Hong Kong*, both William Nigh and John Rawlins had made their last films for Pivar and his action series; dependable standby Christy Cabanne was brought back to help finish off two of the three remaining films. Iron-jawed Don Terry suffered with fourth-place billing behind pretty Universal starlet Elyse Knox, but this time only on the posters; he'd moved up to third place in the film's credits. Don Porter, Roy Harris (soon to undergo a name change to Riley Hill), Addison Richards, and Alan Hale, Jr., co-star in this Army camp-based action piece. Newcomer Porter, with some stage work and only one other film credit (and an uncredited bit) on his resume, gives a standout performance as the film's heavy. Knox, a former model and beauty contest winner, was brought to Hollywood in 1937 for Fox's *Wake Up and Live* (Sidney Lanfield), appearing in a handful more films for that studio before a brief sojourn with Republic and Hal Roach Studios in 1941. Starring roles followed in Universal B's from 1942 through 1944, finishing her short career at Monogram; demonstrating once again that looks will only get you so far. Shoehorned into the plot as the requisite love interest, she is lovely to look at but thespically-challenged; *Boxoffice* dismissed her performance with the curt "Elyse Knox gives feeble feminine support."[24]

Poor Don Terry keeps getting billed below budding starlets. *Top Sergeant* (1942). Image courtesy of Heritage Auction Galleries, Ha.com.

The film still bore the working title of *Showdown* when production wrapped in late March, but within a week was retitled *Top Sergeant*.[25] Monogram had released the popular Army-themed comedy *Top Sergeant Mulligan* a half year earlier, which may or may not have influenced the title change at Universal. Coincidentally, Jean Yarbrough, who would himself be teamed with Pivar several years later, directed *Top Sergeant Mulligan*.

Frenchy Devereaux (Carrillo) and Andy Jarrett (Devine), a pair of loosely disciplined

---

[23] "Screen News Here and in Hollywood," *New York Times*, March 6, 1942, 17.

[24] "Top Sergeant," *Boxoffice*, October 3, 1942, 370.

[25] "Screen News Here and in Hollywood," *New York Times*, April 1, 1942, 27.

corporals in charge of new recruits at military training Camp Amhurst, are demoted once again for listening to a football game when they should have been taking part in field maneuvers. Dick "Rusty" Manson (Terry), their sergeant and old buddy, chews out his younger brother Jack (Gene Garrick) for taking part, and tells him to clean up his act. Later as the bunch of them head back to base, a speeding car cuts off their truck. In it is a hood named Balzer and his gang, fleeing from their robbery of the Brownsville Bank. With the soldiers in pursuit, the gang holes up in an abandoned house and a gunfight erupts. Balzer and most of the gang are shot, but one crook, Al Bennett (Don Porter), shoots and kills young Jack Manson, and steals his uniform. Bennett escapes in the guise of a soldier, taking the bank's cash with him. Dick Manson is devastated by his younger brother's murder, and vows revenge.

Trapped in town, Bennett decides to hide out by enlisting, and coincidentally ends up in Manson's unit. Bennett's cockiness rubs a number of the others the wrong way, Jarrett and Manson in particular, but they have no suspicions regarding his guilt in the robbery and murder. Bennett has a secret partnership in a roadhouse cafe with a hood named Tony Gribaldi (Bradley Page). He sneaks off base to make some final arrangements with Gribaldi, then hitchhikes back with hopes of reentering the camp unseen. Bennett is given a lift by Helen Gray (Elyse Knox), daughter of Colonel Gray (Addison Richards), and Dick Manson's girl. When Manson discovers that Helen is attempting to smuggle smooth-talking Bennett back into the camp hidden in her car, his annoyance with Bennett deepens.

Later, when Manson finds Helen with Bennett, Frenchy, and Jarrett at a nearby roadhouse, he insists that Helen return to base with him. Bennett objects, and soon a huge fight breaks out. As a result, Colonel Gray demotes Manson, who has refused to fess up to the reason for the fight. Helen sets things straight with her father, and Manson is restored to his former rank.

Bennett has grown sweet on Helen, and presents her with a necklace. When some of the $20 bills he used to purchase the jewelry are later identified as having come from the robbed bank, the store's owner Mr. Todd informs the authorities that it was a soldier who made the purchase. Figuring that it was one of the new recruits who passed the bill, Manson pushes for a lineup so that Todd can identify the culprit. Bennett overhears this, and murders Todd before the lineup can take place. When Manson visits Helen and sees the necklace in a Todd jewelry case, she tells him it was a gift from Bennett. Manson puts two and two together and reports his suspicions of Bennett to his superiors, but he is told to leave the investigation to the authorities. Seemingly off the hook, Bennett taunts Manson for his ineffectuality.

Manson contacts Brownsville Bank, inquiring whether cashier Ansel Jacobs could identify any of the robbers. Jacobs writes back that he could, but Bennett intercepts the letter and, learning that there's another loose end, decides to take action. War games are planned, and Frenchy and Jarrett are assigned to rig a bridge located at the bottom of Lackawanna Pass with smoke pots that represent explosives. Manson and some troops are to lead their pursuers over the bridge, after which the fake explosives will be detonated. When Bennett hears the plan, he sneaks into Jarrett and Frenchy's tent that night and resets Frenchy's watch four minutes ahead. He then replaces the smoke pots with real dynamite. His plan works; Jarrett prematurely and unknowingly detonates the explosives, killing fifteen recruits. The war games are halted as a result of this disastrous "accident."

Soon after, Jarrett and Frenchy are about to be court-martialed when Manson enters with cashier Jacobs in tow. Bennett, who is present at the proceedings, is identified by Jacobs as the bank's robber. Manson tidily ties up loose ends with a quick explanation of Bennett's complicity and guilt. Always the man of action, Bennett jumps out a window and commandeers a truck with a machine gun in back. Manson, Jarrett, and Frenchy take off in hot pursuit. Bennett parks and sets up the machine gun, and wounds Manson in the arm. The two grapple but Bennett gets the upper hand. As Bennett is about to kill Manson, Frenchy shoots and kills Bennett.

Top Sergeant is a decent little film, with Porter's convincing performance as duplicitous crook Bennett its single biggest asset. Christy Cabanne's direction is underwhelming but unobtrusive, although there is one nicely composed shot that takes place in Bennett's hideout after the robbery, the camera focusing on Bennett's feet as he paces back and forth in his room, the off-screen radio blaring details of the ongoing manhunt. The film opens with a close-up of Devine, in uniform, facing the camera and giving one of those early-days-of-the-war patriotic speeches meant to inspire the viewer. One suspects that younger viewers were squirming in their seats during this, impatiently waiting for the action to get underway while Devine droned on with his dedication to our men in uniform. The film has the usual number of fistfights, with the café-based donnybrook a notch better than most. As for stock footage, the film is top-heavy with the stuff, all of it courtesy of the US Army, and some of it visually spectacular at that. With all of the tanks, airplanes, explosions, and mobilization of troops, it gives the film a higher-budget look. It is doubtful, though, that anyone actually thought the footage was shot specifically for the film, if they even thought about it at all.

By April 1942, public attitudes had changed toward war-themed films, and Hollywood took notice. Surveys were conducted back in September 1941 by Dr. George Gallup's Audience Research Institute regarding whether or not newsreels showed too much war-related footage. Only 21% said "not enough" while 35% said "too much." A half-year later in April 1942, four months after the attack on Pearl Harbor and America's subsequent entry into the war, the results reversed: 40% said "not enough" while only 21% said "too much."

What the public said, however, did not always translate in reliable theater attendance. According to *Boxoffice*'s records, only two of the top ten money-makers during the first five months of 1942 had military themes, four others made only passing (and inconsequential to their plots) reference to the war, and the remaining four were pure escapist fare with nary a mention of any conflict. The bottom line in Hollywood was to place people's rears in theater seats and their money in the theater coffers; box-office receipts trumped all during the decision-making process, and by mid-1942 only one in seven productions had the war as the dominant theme.[26] Pivar had two more war-themed scripts in the pipeline, but with their completion most of Pivar's programmers for Universal would be purely escapist fare, with only the occasional passing reference to the conflict and one major exception late in 1943, the sensationally titled *The Strange Death of Adolf Hitler*.

Danger in the Pacific
(Director: Lewis D. Collins; Released July 10, 1942)

Danger in the Pacific went before William Sickner's cameras on Tuesday, March 31.[27] Direction was handled by Lewis D. Collins, who had made his first two films at the studio way back in 1930 and now returned after a twelve-year absence. An old and prolific technician who had cranked out films for studios as diverse as Majestic, Monogram, Republic, Imperial, and others for the better part of the thirties, Collins had spent the last five years at Columbia with eighteen films to show for it. With the completion of this film, Collins would make a smattering of features for Universal over the next four years, his primary involvement with many of the studio's serials, co-handling direction with Ray Taylor on more than a dozen of them.

Tropical disease authority Dr. David Lynd (Don Terry) is approached by Leo Marzell (Leo Carrillo), who offers to sponsor an expedition into the wild jungles of Paragelean. The goal, ostensibly, is a cure for paralysis, but Marzell soon reveals that he is an agent for the British Secret Service. This expedition would be a cover for a real, unspecified purpose, later revealed to be the tracking down a hidden Nazi radio station. Lynd refuses at first, just back from Africa and scheduled to marry his daredevil aviatrix girlfriend Jane Claymore (Louise Allbritton), but soon his patriotic side kicks in and he agrees. He is to tell no one the real reason for the expedition, including his photographer buddy Andy Parker (Devine). Jane wants to join them, but when Lynd says no she takes matters into her own hands, planning to fly over on her own.

---

[26] Bosley Crowther, "Reality or Escape?" *New York Times*, June 14, 1942, SM16.

[27] "Screen News Here and in Hollywood," *New York Times*, April 1, 1942, 27.

STOP YELLIN'

Jane arrives in the town of Copanga before Lynd and his group, and learns that a fellow named Zambesi (Edgar Barrier) is the one most familiar with the jungle and friendly with the natives therein. What no one other than the town's storekeeper (David Hoffman) realizes is that Zambesi is a Nazi agent. Jane approaches him with the request that he refuse to lead Lynd when he eventually shows up. Zambesi, earlier alerted that some "enemy" agents were to arrive and snoop around, readily agrees.

When Lynd and company arrive in Copanga, the commissioner (Holmes Herbert) reluctantly issues a permit to travel into the jungles. He warns the small group of the dangers of doing so, and of the savage natives to be found therein. He suggests that they engage Zambesi as their guide. Zambesi's suspicion that Lynd is a spy is confirmed when Lynd states they are there to photograph wildlife, while earlier Jane had instead cited the paralysis-cure angle. Zambesi refuses to guide them.

Lynd and Marzell decide to press on, and Andy reluctantly joins them; Jane, on the other hand, is told to remain behind, not only because this is "man's work," but also because Lynd is pissed off that she showed up uninvited. Lynd approaches the storekeeper for supplies, porters, and a native guide, and is told that Tagani (Turhan Bey) will lead them. What they do not realize is that Tagani is a Nazi agent as well, and the same fellow who attempted to kill Lynd the night before with a poisoned dart, but just narrowly missed.

The explorers head up river on rafts, but the water eventually becomes too shallow to navigate; they are forced onto land where they build a base camp. Using a lamb, Tagani attracts a tiger which attacks and mauls Marzell, but Lynd intervenes and shoots the tiger before it can do too much harm. Later, Tagani quietly convinces the porters that they should leave, and most of them take off on the rafts. Tagani shoots the several that remain behind, but one of them survives long enough to stab Tagani in the back just as he is getting ready to shoot Lynd.

Now it is just the three of them, and they are quickly overwhelmed by a swarm of attacking natives who haul their new prisoners back to their village and its chief (the uncredited Noble Johnson). They are stunned to see Zambesi there as well, and it now becomes evident that he is a foreign agent unwilling to help them. Eying the shrunken heads adorning a nearby shelf, the three prisoners quickly deduce their fate as they are taken into a hut to be beheaded. Marzell employs some slick judo moves, and their three captors are overpowered. Dressing up (not too convincingly) in their captors' garb, they grab Zambesi as a prisoner and manage to escape the village.

Zambesi leads them to the Nazi encampment in the jungle where they find the radio station, its antenna a retractable affair that can emerge from and retract back into the ground at the throw of a switch. The Nazis overpower them, but Jane hears their voices broadcast over the air when a microphone is accidentally left on. Luckily for them, one of their captors mentions their coordinates as well, and Jane uses her plane's radio to alert the British air command to their whereabouts. The encampment is bombed just as a firing squad is about to dispatch our three heroes, and they are rescued.

Medals are awarded to Lynd, Marzell, and Andy, but Jane is informed that they do not have any medals for women. Lynd announces that with their upcoming marriage Jane can share his with him.

Danger in the Pacific is an engagingly taut little film, enhanced by effective lighting and camera movements courtesy of cinematographer William Sickner, and competently overseen by director Lewis Collins. Typical jungle-based heroics, for sure, but some of the snake footage will have you squirming in your seat. The preparations for Carrillo's intended beheading are decidedly off-putting, especially in these current days where that approach to domination has moved west from the cinematic jungles of the Pacific to the sands of the Mideast.

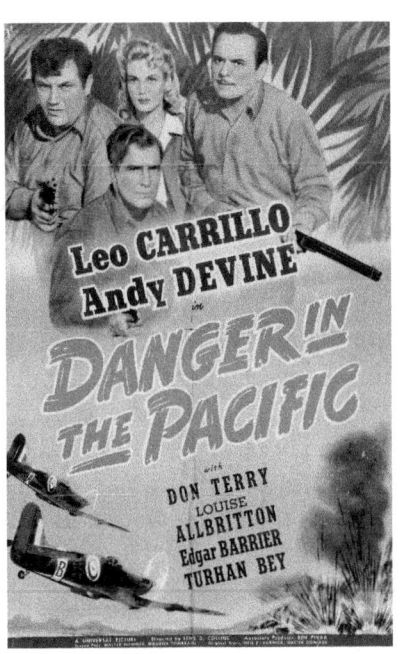

Danger in the Pacific (1942). Image courtesy of Heritage Auction Galleries, Ha.com.

As Dr. Lynd, Don Terry's gruff, bulldog-like demeanor seems somewhat out of character, but he otherwise makes a good, two-fisted hero. Both Carrillo and Devine play their parts straight for a nice change of pace, the former getting to demonstrate some fancy judo moves at the latter's physical expense. Turhan Bey is appropriately bloodthirsty as their duplicitous guide. Dwight Frye, *Dracula*'s Renfield, shows up briefly in a miniscule uncredited part as a Copanga hotel desk clerk.

Co-star Louise Allbritton, a newcomer at Universal with only two Columbia features to her credit (*Parachute Nurse* and *Not a Ladies' Man*, both 1942), provides a feisty girlfriend for Lynd, reveling in her ability to twist him to her will by breaking down his resistance in a hair-raising airplane ride. She had attracted Columbia's attention with her performance in *The Little Foxes* at the Pasadena Community Playhouse,[28] and after her brief stint with that studio had signed with Universal to a seven-year contract. Allbritton remained at

---

[28] Edwin Schallert, "Important Studio News Condensed," *Los Angeles Times*, April 23, 1942, 14.

Universal through 1947, wrapping up her big-screen career with only a handful more films through 1949, settling into television work up into the early sixties.

Danger in the Pacific makes prolific but well-integrated use of stock footage, reportedly using clips from the past Universal jungle-based productions *Green Hell, Sun Never Sets, East of Borneo*, and *Nagana*.[29] *Boxoffice* rendered its opinion of the on-screen results, calling the film "just a program melodrama that will fit in on a dual bill, please the youngsters and possibly attract some customers if the theatre has an air cooling system in working order."[30]

The suits at Universal had some concerns at this time regarding Pivar's name appearing on so many films, and suggested that he acquire a pseudonym for some of his writing credits. Giving it some thought, Pivar pieced together the *nom de plume* Neil P. Varnick, "Neil" taken from his son's first name, and "P. Varnick" an allusion to his father's surname of Pivarnick. "Neil P. Varnick" was credited with writing the original story for *Danger in the Pacific*, and would resurface in the same capacity in the credits for *The Mummy's Tomb* and *Captive Wild Woman* in the months to follow.

At the beginning of June 1942, Universal vice president and general sales manager William Scully announced the studio's planned schedule for the upcoming 1942-1943 season. This consisted of fifty-five features, two of them to be filmed in Technicolor, with studio-saviors Abbott and Costello slated for three and Deanna Durbin slated for two. Fourteen westerns (seven of them reissues), sixty-five shorts, and two newsreels per week were added into the mix.[31] Three of Pivar's so-called "Marquis Productions, the popular series of Universal action dramas"—*Eyes of the Underworld, The Mummy's Tomb*, and *Beast of the East*—were named,[32] although as we'll see only two of these came to fruition.

Timber
(Director: Christy Cabanne; Released August 14, 1942)

The seven-film series concluded with a bang, the surprisingly engaging and action-packed spies-in-a-lumber-camp tale simply titled *Timber*. Filled with lots of rugged action, several atypically well-staged fight sequences, far less forced humor than the norm, a lead actress who could act, some great miniature work, and a plot twist that while naggingly familiar actually works here, *Timber* provided war-era audiences a rousing hour's worth of entertainment with

---

[29] Blackie Seymour, "The Kansas Series," *Classic Images*, No. 381, March 2007, page unknown.
[30] "Review Flashes," *Boxoffice*, August 1, 1942, 41.
[31] "Universal Lists 55 Feature Films," *New York Times*, June 5, 1942, page unknown.
[32] "Universal Has 55 for Year," *Motion Picture Herald*, July 11, 1942, 19.

bad-guy-haul-'em-off-to-justice comeuppance they could sink their collective teeth into.

This action-packed final series entry began filming on Wednesday, April 22,[33] with Cabanne once again calling the shots from a script by Griffin Jay. Jack McKenzie handled the camerawork, a veteran cinematographer with over a quarter century of experience and more than 120 films to his credit. Marjorie Lord was back, with Devine and Carrillo sharing the lead with Dan Dailey, Jr., borrowed from MGM for one last film before going into the military[34] (two, actually; they were able to squeeze him into an Andrews Sisters film as well). Don Terry was off filming the twelve-part serial *Overland Mail* for directors Ford Beebe and John Rawlins, so another big guy was needed. Dailey more than filled the bill, giving a breezy, likeable performance as the two-fisted hero.

Carrillo plays lumber mill operator Quebec, with Devine his logging foreman Arizona. Dan Crowley (Wade Boteler), the lumberyard's owner, is on the Department of National Defense Lumber Division's hot seat. Ever since Crowley was awarded a huge defense contract and dropped all other contracts to focus on it, there's been one problem after another leading to slowdowns and accidents, courtesy of a bunch of stonewalling workers. Crowley is told to solve the problems or shut down, so he heads back to the yard and delivers the ultimatum to Quebec and Arizona. They tell him the only way to do so is to get rid of the slackers and hire some real workers. Their old buddy Kansas (Dailey, and there's that series-bookending name again!) arrives on the scene, so they immediately bring him on board, unaware that he is in reality an undercover agent assigned to unravel the cause of the disruptions.

When Quebec and Arizona fire lead troublemaker Fabian (Nestor Paiva) and his trio of cohorts, the former employees balk and start a fight. Kansas joins in and promptly kicks ass, leaving no doubt as to his prowess as a fighter.

Soon after, Pierre Lacour (Edmund MacDonald) and his knockout sister Yvette (Marjorie Lord) arrive at the camp; they too are hired along with Pierre's devoted friend Bill Cormack (William Hale). It's not long before Kansas is sniffing around Yvette, and the mandatory romance blossoms. We soon learn that Pierre is an undercover agent as well. He informs Kansas that the acts of sabotage are occurring at all of the area's lumber camps and it has been determined—he doesn't say how—that the ringleader must be stationed at Crowley's camp.

---

[33] "Screen News Here and in Hollywood," *New York Times*, April 14, 1942, 17.

[34] Edwin Schallert, "News Clips from Studio Town," *Los Angeles Times*, April 20, 1942, A8.

Stop Yellin'

You could fit three of her into Andy Devine's pants; maybe four. Left to right: Leo Carrillo, Dan Dailey, Jr., Marjorie Lord, Andy Devine. *Timber* **(1942).**

It doesn't take long for Kansas to get a first-hand look at the camp's problems. Trucks haul the huge logs down the mountainside, with sirens blaring to warn on-comers out of the way. This is imperative since it is impossible for the trucks to brake on the steep grade. Local storeowner Pop Turner (Paul Burns) is in reality the chief spy, and he has learned that Kansas is a G-man. Turner tells Fabian to make sure that Kansas has a deadly "accident." When Fabian learns that Kansas is scheduled for truck duty that night, he makes the appropriate arrangements. Kansas and Yvette have a date planned for that night, along with Quebec and his date Ann Barrows (Jean Phillips),[35] one of the company's secretaries. Pierre volunteers to take Kansas' place making the nighttime drive, but probably wishes he hadn't when he sees the lights of an approaching vehicle. He loses control of the truck, and crashes down the mountainside. Miraculously, he is able to relay this story to Arizona before expiring. Arizona tracks down the two couples at Pop Turner's store and informs them of Pierre's death. Turner is shocked when he sees Kansas, realizing that the wrong man was killed.

Bill Cormack is devastated over his friend's death. When he is told that Kansas is responsible, a surprisingly brutal fight takes place between Kansas

---

[35] Known as much for being the late Jean Harlow's double than for her own brief career as an actress; "Action Melodrama Depicts Threat to Vital War Project," *Daily Kennebec Journal*, September 8, 1942, 12.

and Cormack. In spite of Cormack's dirty fighting—he uses a club and ax against his opponent's fists—Kansas emerges victorious. Cormack stumbles off to lick his wounds, vowing to kill Kansas. Kansas decides to find Cormack and convince him of his innocence, but someone gets to Cormack first and kills him. Lumber yard manager Joe Radway (James Seay) is convinced that Kansas is responsible for both the acts of sabotage and Cormack's death, and relays those beliefs to others.

The remaining drivers quit after yet another truck driver loses control and crashes off the side of the mountain. Quebec, Arizona, and Kansas draw cards to sees who's going to drive the next truckload, and Quebec "wins." As Quebec heads out, Kansas finally puts two and two together and figures out the cause of the accidents. Herding Arizona and Yvette into a car, they make a breathless pursuit of Quebec's truck. Kansas climbs out and makes an exciting, high-speed car-to-truck transfer, climbing over the load of logs and crawling to the passenger side of Quebec's cab. When they see approaching headlights, Kansas insists that they drive straight at them. The headlights disappear with the shattering of glass.

Kansas explains the trick to Arizona, Quebec, and Yvette: the "oncoming vehicle" is actually the lumber truck's headlights reflected in a large mirror, activated into position by the truck's siren (a variation on A. Edward Sutherland's *Secrets of the French Police*, a lurid 1932 thriller wherein the rear-projected image of an oncoming vehicle caused a similar panicked reaction). And how did Kansas figure this out? His clues were the discovery of an "Acme Plate Glass and Mirror Co." crate found earlier (shades of Wile E. Coyote), and the small, sound-activated toys made by Pop Turner and sold at his store. And so they connect the crime to Turner. Ann Barrows, actually in cahoots with the saboteurs, overhears this and attempts to alert Turner by phone, resulting in a nifty little catfight between her and Yvette. Yvette emerges victorious, complete with blackened eye. Meanwhile, the trio confronts Turner and his goons, and a donnybrook breaks out with—you guessed it—the trio emerging victorious as well. It is at this point that Kansas is revealed to the others to be a G-man, a last-minute "twist" that by now had grown rather tired in these films.

Released in mid-August, *Timber* leads Carrillo and Devine did their bit for the war effort (and, of course, Universal) by sponsoring a country-wide campaign among school children and civic groups to get out there and plant trees.[36] *Timber* is a handsome little film, with its convincing lumber yard sets and beautiful location photography, a series of well-placed montages serving as a mini-documentary of lumbering activities,[37] some first-rate miniature

---

[36] "'Give Out, Sisters' and 'Timber' a Great Show at the Mohawk," *North Adams Transcript*, December 9, 1942, 5.

[37] In a stunningly impressive display of penny-pinching hubris, Pivar reused an entire

work for the two truck accidents, and a breathtaking process shot of a huge felled tree landing at Arizona and Yvette's feet.

Boxoffice was impressed with the results: "Action and suspense aplenty in this, doubtlessly the best to date in Universal's so-called adventure series. It easily wins that top-of-the-list rating through the presence of several improved production elements. The story is logical and solidly constructed."[38] *Variety* had effusive praise for the film as well: "'Timber' is a compact package of outdoor melodramatics that will provide fast and logical action entertainment as program supporter … Script is crisp throughout, and concentrates on straight-line exposition of the meller aspects. Christy Cabanne's direction unwinds at a fast and constant pace, while exterior backgrounds of the timber country add production values to the moderate budget."[39] *Motion Picture Herald* chimed in with a favorable review: "If you've acquired fixed notions about the series of action films offering Leo Carrillo and Andy Devine as amusing adventures, don't let them cripple your style in presenting this number. This is by wide margin the best of the series, compressing in its hour of running time more melodramatic tension than all the others linked end to end … Production is by Ben Pivar, a good overall job … Not a gigantic or colossal entry in the attractions list, it is nonetheless a triumph within its budget."[40] Too bad it was the last in the official series.

Timber was not alone with the spies-on-the-loose plotline. During the first twelve days of August, twenty-one features were previewed in Hollywood, six of them featuring spies and saboteurs, with another five having the war as background to their plots. These films ranged from Monogram's *Hillbilly Blitzkrieg*, with former diminutive silent comedy star Bud Duncan appearing as the comics' Snuffy Smith, to the more exalted fare of MGM, Warners, and 20th Century-Fox. *Boxoffice* wagged its inky finger at Hollywood, warning that "the geniuses of production had better turn off the spy-saboteur spigot before they find themselves drowned in a resultant flood of public and exhibitor protest."[41] Words of wisdom, sure, but those nasty "Krauts" and "Japs" made such deliciously easy targets. A mere two months later, twenty of the forty-seven films in production were war films, including two at MGM, three at RKO,

---

logging montage from his previous year's *Men of the Timberland*, which had originally used lots of stock footage with Devine's overseeing face superimposed.

[38] "Review Flashes," *Boxoffice*, August 15, 1942, 22.
[39] Walt., "Timber," *Variety*, August 8, 1942, 20.
[40] W.R.W., "Timber," *Motion Picture Herald*, August 15, 1942, 39.
[41] "Ivan Spear, Spearheads," *Boxoffice*, August 22, 1942, 30.

five at 20th Century-Fox, four at Warners, three at Universal, and one each at Paramount, Republic, and another unnamed studio.[42]

In an October interview, Nelson Poynter, Hollywood chief of the Motion Pictures Division of the Office of War Information, clarified that organization's stance on films that would promote hatred of the Japanese and Nazis: "Properly directed hatred is of vital importance to the war effort. The Office of War Information wishes only to insure that hatred will not be directed either at Hitler, Mussolini, Tojo or a small group of Fascist leaders as personalized enemies on the one hand, or at the whole German, Japanese and Italian people on the other hand. Hatred of the militaristic system which governs the Axis countries and of those responsible for its furtherance definitely should be promoted."[43] What? We can drop bombs on Hiroshima and Nagasaki and end the lives of several hundred thousand civilians, but Tojo's a no-no? Adhering to Poynter's directive was quite a balancing act for Hollywood, for sure, and one that would be increasingly ignored as the war dragged on.

Timber ended the official Carrillo-Devine series and Pivar's involvement with it, but the two actors would continue to make the occasional co-starring film for Universal, including *Sin Town* (1942; Ray Enright), *Frontier Badmen* (1943; Ford Beebe), Olsen and Johnson's *Ghost Catchers* (1944; Eddie Cline), and *Bowery to Broadway* (1944; Charles Lamont), as well as cameo appearances in *Crazy House* (1943) along with a host of other Universal "stars" in support of leads Olsen and Johnson. Freed up from the constraints imposed by an ongoing series and the leads attached to it, Pivar could now move on to independent features.

Or so he thought. And then the powers at Universal assigned him to yet-another mummy film.

§

---

[42] William R. Weaver, "U.S. Prefers Less War in Films, More on Effects," *Motion Picture Herald*, October 24, 1942, 21.

[43] William R. Weaver, "Films Fostering Hate for Axis Approved," *Motion Picture Herald*, October 3, 1942, 34.

12 The Mummy Returns Yet Again

Around this time a rather unusual pressure was being exerted on the hapless B. The government was urging the film industry to economize in its use of film stock, the reason being that the chemicals used in making film were also required for the manufacture of explosives. This, of course, was ammo for the ever-present anti-double-feature proponents,[1] but Hollywood hoped to find some means of conservation other than the elimination or curtailment of the production of the B. Several steps were proposed, including the elimination of credits, the condensation or total elimination of trailers, and the reduction of the number of release prints struck for any given film. Dr. George Gallup's American Institute of Public Opinion conducted another poll during the summer; the results showed that now 48% of the public was in favor of the double feature. However, when queried on their reaction to the proposed elimination of the B film until the termination of the war, 71% approved. The most frequent moviegoers still tended to be the most avid supporters of the double bill.

Universal announced plans for fifty-five features for the upcoming 1942-1943 season, five designated as "special releases" by vice president and general sales manager William Scully. "Special" for Universal, at least; two of these would be Technicolor vehicles for the Maria Montez-Jon Hall-Sabu troika *Arabian Nights* (1942; John Rawlins) and *White Savage* (1943; Arthur Lubin), mindless fluff at best and essentially B films with bloated budgets, but undeniably colorful. Scully threw a bone to both Nelson Poynter of the Motion Pictures Division of the Office of War Information and the censorship-happy moralists by stating that "all wartime restrictions will be met in producing

---

[1] The aforementioned Samuel Goldwyn, as well as The National Motion Picture Research Council, The National Education Association, and several others, all of whom were receiving a fair amount of press during this period.

them and the company will respond wholeheartedly to the demand for morale entertainment."[2] With those words, Pivar saw his job get just a little bit more difficult.

Meanwhile, a new "horror" star had appeared at Universal. Lon Chaney, Jr., for years relegated to nondescript roles in an endless succession of B's, westerns, and serials as Creighton Chaney, finally acquiesced during a period of near-starvation in 1937 to change his name to the more marketable Lon Chaney, Jr. After his highly acclaimed role as Lennie in Lewis Milestone's version of Steinbeck's *Of Mice and Men* (1939), Chaney soon appeared in his first semi-horrific role in Hal Roach's *One Million B.C.* (1940). Universal, riding the crest of the newest horror cycle, decided to cash in on the elder Chaney's fame, signing Chaney to a five-year contract and casting him in *Man Made Monster* (1941; George Waggner). The more prestigious *The Wolf Man* (1941; Waggner again) followed shortly thereafter, and Chaney's career was off and running. A succession of sequels to previous financial winners and fan favorites were soon to follow, including the part of the monster in *The Ghost of Frankenstein* (1942; Erle C. Kenton), the wolf man in *Frankenstein Meets the Wolf Man* (1943; Roy William Neill), *House of Frankenstein*, and *House of Dracula* (1944 and 1945, respectively; both Erle C. Kenton), and the vampire Alucard in *Son of Dracula* (1943; Robert Siodmak). During all of this, however, Chaney still found himself cast in numerous potboilers, with bits in westerns, lower-budget horror films, and roles as unglamorous heavies. Ten of these were Pivar-produced horror and psychological thrillers (save one), the first the sequel to the successful *The Mummy's Hand*.

The Mummy's Tomb
(Director: Harold Young; Released October 23, 1942)

Director Harold Young's *The Mummy's Tomb* was the first in the three-film descent in the quality of the series. Henry Sucher was announced to script the film in February 1942,[3] adapting an original treatment by the fabled "Neil P. Varnick" and joined soon after by Griffin Jay. George Robinson handled the camerawork, with Dick Foran, Wallace Ford, and George Zucco reprising their roles from the first Kharis outing; this sequel's story takes place thirty years after the events of *The Mummy's Hand*. The cast is rounded out with lovely Elyse Knox as love interest to actor John Hubbard, with Turhan Bey making another appearance for Pivar, here as the insidious Mehemet Bey. The rest of the cast is filled with an assortment of dependable and solid character actors,

---

[2] "Universal Lists Films for Year," *Los Angeles Times*, June 5, 1942, A10.
[3] "Hollywood Personnelities," *Boxoffice*, February 28, 1942, 82.

including Virginia Brissac, Mary Gordon, Cliff Clark, Paul E. Burns, Emmett Vogan, and Frank Reicher.

The film opens with a page from *Our Age* magazine, focusing on a photo of Stephen Banning, archeologist, seated in an armchair and smoking a pipe. This cleverly dissolves into the real thing, the camera dollying back to reveal the entire living room and the people seated therein. The group includes Banning's doctor son John (Hubbard), John's girlfriend Isobel (Knox) and her mother (Brissac), and Banning's sister Jane (Gordon). Banning (Foran) regales them with a recounting of the horrific events of thirty years earlier, told in flashback, a story his son has no doubt heard dozens of times before. This, not surprisingly, is handled by the cost-expedient method of reusing footage from the earlier film.

Meanwhile, back in Egypt, high priest Andoheb (Zucco)—yes, he is back!—brings his chosen successor Mehemet Bey (Turhan Bey) up to speed, explaining that the bullets he took thirty years earlier

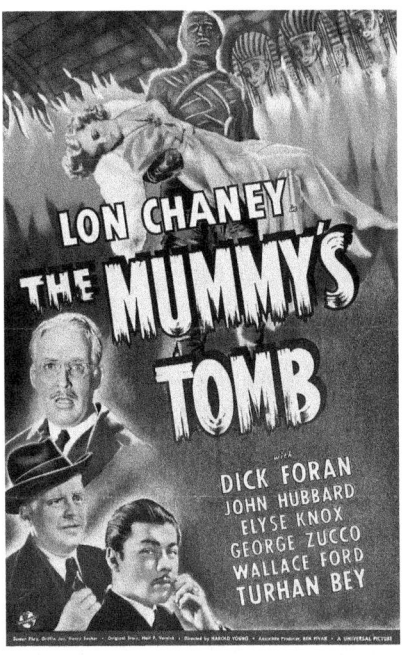

Dick Foran and Wallace Ford in old age makeup, while villainous Turhan Bey twirls his moustache. *The Mummy's Tomb* **(1942). Image courtesy of Heritage Auction Galleries, Ha.com.**

only crushed his arm, and that Kharis merely suffered burns. Kharis "lives" on, his damaged right eye sealed shut and his right hand a burnt, fingerless stump. Andoheb also explains (and gives the viewer a refresher course) about the use of Tana leaves and Kharis' centuries-old job of snuffing out all who would dare enter Princess Ananka's tomb, fortunately a small number as one can pack only so many murders into a sixty-one-minute film. Mehemet Bey is made the new high priest of Karnak, with the assigned task of taking Kharis to the United States and killing off the defilers of Ananka's tomb, and their blood relations for good measure. To that end, Andoheb has somehow managed to obtain a position for Bey as caretaker in the Mapleton Cemetery, right in the heart of Banning's Massachusetts-based hometown. His job done, Andoheb wraps up things by dying.

Bey sails to the United States with Kharis packed away in his unwieldy casket, latter arriving at the cemetery in a horse-drawn coach. (A moment of viewer distraction occurs here when one of the cemetery's solid-looking gravestones waves to-and-fro in a gentle breeze.) Once unpacked, Bey goes to work, feeding Kharis the necessary fluid of nine Tana leaves and sending the reanimated corpse out to kill Banning. Which he does, after climbing a trellis and gaining access to Banning's bedroom; one down, three more victims to go, we are told. Dust samples found on Banning's neck are sent to Professor Norman (Reicher) for analysis, but he is stumped. The town coroner (Vogan) and sheriff (Clark) quickly sum it up as "Just dust" and "Just another one of those fiend murders," much to Dr. John Banning's dismay. Reports by numerous locals of mysterious "shadows" do little to sway the stubborn officials, and given the vagueness of the reports the collective ho-hum reaction of the town officials is understandable, although one would think that generic "fiend murders" would attract somebody's attention.

Bey takes walks around the town, and in convenient B movie fashion always seems to be in the right place at the right time. He spots young lovers John and Isobel together, and immediately falls in love with Isobel in spite of Andoheb's earlier exhortations to avoid any sort of carnal thoughts or involvement. Deaf ears, of course.

When Babe (Ford), Banning's former partner from the previous film (and here inexplicably renamed Hanson from that film's Jensen), hears of his old buddy's death, he travels to Mapleton. Bey carries on with his work, sending Kharis back out to the Banning mansion to kill Banning's sister Jane. Which he does, and in a perfunctory fashion, but not before shocking grounds caretaker Jim (Burns) into a non-responsive state of paralytic shock.

With murder number two, newsmen from across the country descend upon the sleepy little town. Babe, meanwhile, has heard of the dust on the victims' necks and puts two and two together, but the authorities brush him off when he attempts to convince them of a rampaging mummy in their midst. *New York Record* reporter Jake Lovell is more receptive, and the story soon gains some legs in the press. Unfortunate for Babe is Bey's convenient presence in the café where he overhears Babe tell all to Lovell. Babe's days are numbered as a result; he bumps into Kharis on the street while walking home after dark, and meets his maker at the end of a dark alley.

John finds a scrap of bandage and takes it to Professor Norman for analysis. Perceptive scientist that Norman is, he quickly identifies the dust as mold, isolates traces of myrrh (which is only found in Africa), ties the samples to those found on Steve Banning's neck, and quickly deduces that the dust could only have come from a mummy, perhaps a 3,000-year-old mummy; "There's no doubt about it!" And with this pronouncement, the town officials are convinced!

Bey's infatuation with Isobel has grown to such proportions that he comes up with a plan akin to Andoheb's in the earlier film: he and Isobel will gain immortality by drinking Tana leaf fluid, she'll bear him a child to be brought up in the tombs of Karnak, "like I was," and the new family will administer to

Kharis' needs for the rest of eternity. Sounds like a plan. To that end, he sends Kharis out once again, this time for retrieval purposes rather than vengeance. Kharis, it should be noted, is not too keen about this assignment, as it flies in the face of the whole purpose behind his reason for being. Bey attempts to fudge it, though, by explaining to Kharis that "They think there will be a marriage, and an heir to carry on the blood of the Bannings" as the reason behind his co-opting Isobel for his own. By his body language we can tell that Kharis has not been convinced.

Kharis does a double-take when Turhan Bey tells him, "I am going to take unto myself a wife, Kharis. A wife — do you understand that?" *The Mummy's Tomb* (1942). **Image courtesy of Heritage Auction Galleries, Ha.com.**

Like a good soldier, though, Kharis returns with Isobel, and she too gets strapped to a table just like Marta in the previous film. As he is about to administer the Tana fluid—"One day you will thank me for this"—Bey is interrupted when a mob of angry villagers arrive at the cemetery, led by John and the sheriff. Bey attempts to shoot John, but the sheriff beats him to the punch. While this is going on, Kharis has unstrapped Isobel and now carries her back to the Banning mansion. The torch-wielding villagers follow, and after a climactic confrontation at the mansion, John rescues Isobel, the place is torched, and once again we are led to believe that Kharis has perished in the ensuing conflagration. The film ends on the usual happy note, well-wishers seeing newlyweds John and Isobel off on their honeymoon.

The series of flashbacks that open the film, all footage lifted from *The Mummy's Hand*, constitute close to a whopping nine minutes of the film's sixty-one-minute total. This sequence is irritating as well as dull, as Foran's present-day shots are essentially silent other than his dialog, with the action scenes dissolved into for the flashbacks all retaining the original's music. The resulting back-and-forth shift from silence to pounding music without any sort of aural unity is disquieting, to say the least. Aside from this lengthy sequence, the only other stock shots are of several howling dogs and numerous clips of torch-wielding villagers in spirited pursuit, lifted from James Whale's *Frankenstein*.

The Mummy's Tomb has a straightforward, painfully simplistic plot that makes its predecessor look like a masterpiece by comparison. George Robinson's cinematography is effective, if occasionally overlit, with several nice tracking shots, Professor Norman's introduction a notable standout. Milton Carruth's editing is workmanlike, but here too as with its predecessor there's some clumsily handled dubbing that is visually jarring. The film's score, as usual, is all stock music cobbled together from the Universal music library, which is not necessarily a bad thing since the music adds a note of breathless excitement to the visuals. Harold Young, directing since the early thirties but relatively new to Universal, handles those chores here in a straightforward, by-the-numbers fashion, with only a few instances of any sort of visual flare; cameraman Robinson was probably more responsible for these than Young. Makeup artist Jack Pierce's work is more cut-rate than on the previous two films, with Chaney's bandages having the appearance of a hastily applied garment. The old-age makeup for Foran and Ford is adequate.

Foran and Ford's appearances in this sequel are short and sweet, each meeting his death at Kharis' hand much earlier than the viewer would have expected, if expected at all. While it was not generally the custom to do away with young leads during the course of a film, the scriptwriters evidently figured that by aging them thirty years their elimination was now acceptable. Hubbard is unmemorable as the hero of the piece, and his love interest Elyse Knox, while lovely to look at, gives a one-note performance that is equally forgettable. Turhan Bey, on the other hand, imbues his role with equal doses of old-world charm and simmering villainy.

And then there's Chaney, all but unrecognizable buried in his mummy garb, doing as much as possible with a role that only allows him to shuffle about at night and kill off the various participants, his supposedly "useless" right arm snapping to attention when required to haul Knox around and about. Incredibly, Kharis' presence in Mapleton remains a mystery as long as it does, since everywhere he goes he stumbles down the middle of streets and along sidewalks, and nary a person spots him; they only spot his "shadow." Kharis carries out Bey's orders with overweight zest, only to be tracked down by a mob of torch-wielding, too-readily-convinced townspeople who incinerate him in the Banning mansion in a visually convincing conflagration. The film is not particularly good, and Chaney frequently looks rather silly in numerous

A well-fed Kharis has second thoughts after retrieving Isobel for Mehemet Bey in *The Mummy's Tomb* (1942). Image courtesy of Heritage Auction Galleries, Ha.com.

lengthy shots of Kharis shuffling over hill and dale. But it is fun in its own way, and picks up during several of the protracted murders, Babe's entrapment and strangulation in a dead-ended alley in particular.

Released late in October 1942, *Variety* reviewer "Walt" gave an accurate assessment of the finished product: "With no deviation from formula, and obviously on low budget, picture will get by as secondary dualer with audiences not too particular on credulity ... Story is bumpy and cannot stand close analysis, but it will pass with audiences to which it is aimed."[4] And pass it did, sufficiently so that Universal would order an additional two sequels to fill the demand for more films of this type.

One happy note toward the end of the film's production: Pivar's second child, seven-pound, four-ounce daughter Lorie was born at the Cedars of Lebanon Hospital on Sunday night, August 23. In one of the rare instances where Pivar's name actually made it into the press, *Boxoffice* managed to misspell the poor girl's name as Lauraine rather than Loraine.[5]

§

---

[4] Walt., "The Mummy's Tomb," *Variety*, October 12, 1942, 8.

[5] "Cinemarks," *Boxoffice*, August 29, 1942, 65.

13 The Loose Ends of 1943, Adolf Included

Interspersed with his films for the Carrillo-Devine series, the second mummy sequel, and the first in another new horror series yet to be discussed, Pivar managed to fit in another quartet of films of wildly varying genres. Over the fourteen-month period from March 1942 into May 1943, Pivar served as associate producer on a hard-hitting crime thriller, a Dead End Kids and Little Tough Guys dramatic comedy, an absolutely bizarre look at Hitler's Germany, and a minor horror classic. Okay, forget the "classic" part.

Eyes of the Underworld
(Director: Roy William Neill; Released January 8, 1943)

Eyes of the Underworld, filmed in mid-1942 but held back from wide release until the beginning of 1943, is one of Pivar's better productions, a taut crime story helmed by director Roy William Neill. Richard Bryan (Richard Dix) is the tough, no-nonsense, heart-of-gold chief of police in the small city of Lawndale, a position he has held for the three years since arriving in town as a newcomer. Bryan, a widower, has only his young son Mickey (Billy Lee) at home. When the government imposes a moratorium on new car and tire sales to help with the war effort, incidents of vehicle stripping and tire and auto thefts have escalated dramatically; it is clear there is an organized group behind it. Bryan tells his assistant chief Kirby (Joseph Crehan) to track down the crooks, and pronto, not realizing that Kirby is corrupt.

Head crook Lance Merlin (Edward Pawley) hangs out at his low-profile chop shop where serial numbers are removed from engine blocks, cars are repainted, and parts swapped. Most of these end up at the used car business of J.C. Thomas (Lloyd Corrigan), who uses his position as the head of the City Council as a cover for his shady dealings. On-the-take assistant chief Kirby keeps Merlin apprised of what's going on down at the station. Into the mix

Stop Yellin'

enters State Bureau investigator Edward Jason (Don Porter), sent to Lawndale to try to crack the crime ring. He is to keep an eye on Bryan as well, whom his higher-ups think might somehow be involved in the criminal activities. To that end, Jason sets up at Thomas' used car business, revealing his identity and assignment to both Thomas and assistant chief Kirby. Jason poses as that company's sales manager. Kirby is instructed by Jason to keep an eye on Bryan, a task Kirby quickly reveals to Merlin. Merlin immediately sees this as an opportunity to orchestrate Bryan's removal and replace him with Kirby as the new chief.

During all of this Betty Standing (Wendy Barrie), Bryan's secretary, has been making goo-goo eyes at Bryan, and actually seems to like his annoyingly cute son Mickey as well. While most single older guys like Bryan would probably leap at the obvious overtures made by a much-younger woman like Betty, stoical Bryan steadfastly refuses, painfully aware that his hidden past would probably squelch the deal if made known. Jason, meanwhile, has attempted to move in on Betty, figuring that a secretary would know more about her boss' activities than anyone else.

Later, hood Gordon Finch (Marc Lawrence) is apprehended as he attempts to make it out of the city in a hot car, and hauled before Bryan. Which is not a good thing because Finch, now a three-time loser, recognizes Bryan as a fellow inmate from several years back during a stint in prison; he threatens to reveal Bryan's past if Bryan doesn't help him escape. It seems that Bryan had once worked at a bank and unwisely helped himself to some cash, resulting in a three-year term and now a life in the straight-and-narrow. Instead, at a surprise three-year anniversary testimonial dinner thrown for Bryan, Bryan stuns the assemblage by announcing his resignation. He is rebuffed, but intends to follow through the next day. It turns out that Finch's theft and capture was a setup planned by Merlin, and Finch's conversation with Bryan recorded by Kirby. Kirby slips a pistol to Finch and frees him from his cell, resulting in a cop's death during Finch's escape. Kirby reveals the recording of the conversation between Finch and Bryan, and the latter is tossed in the clink on this circumstantial evidence. Kirby is now acting chief.

Betty steadfastly defends Bryan to Jason, and when she mentions the location of the stolen car Finch was driving, Jason takes interest. With a little poking around, Jason quickly ties the stolen car to Thomas' business, and decides to look into this a little deeper. Accompanied by Betty, who by now has learned Bryan's dirty little secret and told him it doesn't matter, Jasper follows Merlin and learns the whereabouts of the chop shop. He and Betty head over to the shop that night and Jason tries to sneak in, but Merlin, Finch, and their gang are waiting for him. They grab Betty as well, and the two are held prisoner until the next day, which sounds like it will be their last.

The Loose Ends of 1943, Adolf Included

Locked in his cell, Bryan confides all that has gone on to his chauffeur-bodyguard Benny (Lon Chaney, Jr.), another former fellow inmate hired by Bryan as part of his rehabilitation. Benny, unfortunately, is not totally rehabilitated, and has a short fuse as well. He offers to "take care of" Merlin, but Bryan nixes that suggestion. Benny heads out into the haunts of the underworld, tapping old acquaintances for any leads, and is finally put on to Merlin's driver, Hub Gelsey (Gaylord Pendleton). Benny grabs Gelsey, ties him to a chair, and tortures the truth out of him. Returning to Bryan with this information, Bryan sends an astounded Benny off to the district attorney (Mike Raffetto) to inform him that Bryan is ready to sign a full confession. It is all part of a plan hatched with two supportive cops, who allow Bryan to "escape" on the ride to the D.A.'s office. Bryan hooks up with Benny, and the two head for the chop shop.

Gaining entrance to the chop shop, the two intruders are spotted and a gunfight breaks out. Merlin shoots Bryan, resulting in Benny "losing it" and breaking Merlin's neck. Jasper gains possession of a gun and shoots some gang members. Benny grabs Finch and strangles him, oblivious to Jasper's commands to stop; it appears that Jasper will have to shoot him as well. Luckily (for Benny), Bryan still has enough strength to tell Benny to stop, which he does.

Bryan recuperates in the hospital, and his future with Betty, to whom he earlier proposed, now looks rosy. Jasper, resigned to his defeat in the quest for Betty's hand, offers Benny a job. Benny balks at this, but when he accidentally enters the hospital's Maternity Ward and hears the cries of all those babies, he realizes what the future with Bryan could hold. He rushes after Jasper, assumedly to accept his offer.

While *Eyes of the Underworld*'s plot may seem a bit familiar and predictable, the film is sufficiently engaging with several sequences that ratchet up the excitement several notches. Visually it is a treat, with George Robinson's photography and lighting a big asset, particularly in the dark and moody nighttime scenes; no day-for-night here. Director Roy William Neill does some admirable work here, guiding both his cast and cameraman to rise above what could have been another flat, routine thriller. An old hand at this stuff with close to a hundred films to his credit since his first in the late teens, Neill would press on for a few more years, inheriting the Sherlock Holmes series and capping off his career in 1946 with his stylish *noir* filming of Cornell Woolrich's *Black Angel*. Frank Gross, cutting film for Universal since 1932, pieced the footage together in a solid fashion, replacing Saul Goodkind who was originally assigned the task.[1] A good-looking film, *Daily Variety* threw a few morsels of

---

[1] "Studio Personnelities," *Boxoffice*, January 16, 1943, 52.

praise in Pivar's direction: "[F]or a budget film Ben Pivar's production values display a high degree of showmanship."²

Star Richard Dix, his career on the wane and pigeonholed of late in B's of this sort, provides a solid performance and some welcome, if somewhat tepid, marquee power. Lon Chaney, Jr., in another variation of his *Of Mice and Men* Lenny characterization (admittedly with a bit more brain power), gives an adequate performance and provides the film with its strongest scene. Having abducted Hub Gelsey and tied him to a chair (in Bryan's living room, no less!), the scene opens shortly after Benny has beaten the stuffing out of the guy, evidently without gaining the information he wants. Then he gets a brainstorm: he'll give the fellow what he refers to as "a Jap manicure," assumedly by pulling out the guy's fingernails. As Benny heads off camera to retrieve a pair of pliers, he announces ominously, "You're gonna live a long time in the next few minutes." Scripters Michael Simmons and Arthur Strawn have thrown a few other tough-as-nails lines into the dialog, but this one's the most memorable, and unsettling.

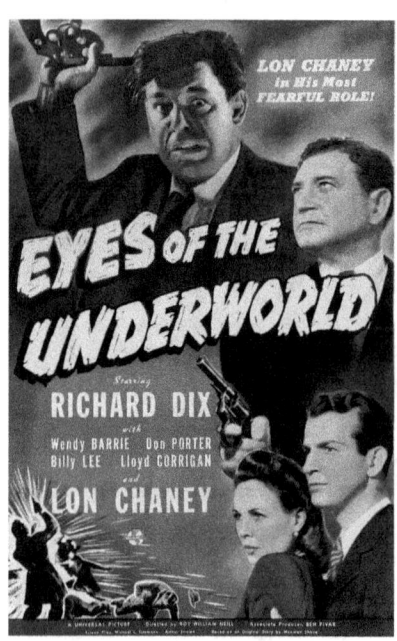

Chaney does crazy in *Eyes of the Underworld* (1943). Image courtesy of Heritage Auction Galleries, Ha.com.

Universal's ad campaign, hoping to cash in on Chaney's growing popularity stemming from his recent performances in *The Wolf Man* and *The Ghost of Frankenstein*, somewhat overstated his role here as "A Stir-Crazy Strangler! Lon Chaney—Running Amuck Against Gangdom's Guns!" Reviewers praised Chaney's performance: "Lon Chaney, Jr., in role of Dix's chauffeur who kills the racketeer downing Dix with a bullet, being singled out for the finest contribution in acting in entire picture;"³ and "Lon Chaney handles the chief's devoted chauffeur for everything the part contains."⁴

As Dix's tepid love interest, Wendy Barrie is the cast's weak link, walking through her part as though bored with it all. Don Porter, with only two previous film roles to his credit, once again gives an assured, likable performance as the

---

² "Eyes of the Underworld," *Daily Variety*, December 30, 1942, 3.

³ *Ibid*.

⁴ "'Underworld' Just Average Program," *Hollywood Reporter*, December 30, 1942, 3.

investigator. Edward Pawley is thoroughly intimidating as the snarling gang leader, perennial gangster Marc Lawrence is oily as ever in the type of role at which he excelled, and Wade Boteler does his Irish cop bit. Child actor Billy Lee, a musical talent in films since he was five, gave one of his last performances as Bryan's kid. He is too cute for comfort in his earliest scenes—must he giggle whenever he speaks?—but manages to rise to the occasion when he gets in a school hall fight with another, bigger kid, and gives him a surreptitious kick to the rear after the brawl has been broken up.

Announced as *Destiny*, Universal's generic title for as-yet untitled films, back in March 1942,[5] the film went into production in April as *Eyes of the Underworld*, freeing up Neill to move on to *Madame Spy*.[6] Once completed, though, Universal sat on and stockpiled this and a number of other finished films with the intention of slowly releasing them over a number of months to come. The reason for this, as mentioned earlier, had to do with the increasing need to conserve film that could otherwise be turned into explosives, much needed now that America was at war.

Lowell Mellett, chief of the Motion Picture Bureau of the Office of War Information, had some time earlier called for the economizing of the use of raw stock by abolishing twin bills. Not only would this lead to a reduction in raw stock, but would also in his opinion "lead to improvement in picture quality and would salvage countless man-hours now wasted by pleasure-cramped audiences on two-feature shows."[7] This call was met with stony silence, not only from the studios but the exhibitors as well. In spite of all the hue and cry in years past regarding the supposedly unpopular double bill, the fact remained that theaters showing dual bills almost always outperformed those showing only a single feature, and bang-for-the-buck audiences had come to expect them.

Given that failure, the War Production Board took another approach, suggesting strongly that Hollywood come up with a voluntary plan to reduce the consumption of raw stock by at least 20% from 1941 footage totals—or else mandatory rationing would be imposed, a Draconian measure in Hollywood's eyes. Seeing the writing on the wall, the studios hastily came up with a plan to reduce each studio's footage based on their previous year's usage and number of film output, with an estimated 200,000,000 feet savings the result. Universal's share would be a reduction of 70 to 100 million feet, but due to their sizable western and serial schedules would be allowed to produce fifty

---

[5] *Boxoffice*, March 28, 1942, 82.

[6] Edwin Schallert, "Reel Notes Reeled Off Briefly," *Los Angeles Times*, April 14, 1942, A8.

[7] Frank S. Nugent, "Double, Double, Toil and Trouble," *New York Times*, January 17, 1943, page unknown.

features as opposed to the larger studios' thirty-six-feature limit. This self-imposed reduction was to take place late in the year.

Proposals to eliminate double features surfaced once again, but "at least two companies are known to be in determined opposition to such a plan and several others were said to have joined them in the opinion that it would not save an amount of film proportionate to possible losses."[8] Universal must have been one of them. As a result, production schedules were beefed up and finished films held back to help provide a backlog in the event that further reductions were to be implemented. This was a growing possibility, as planned savings weren't impacting total usage as much as the studios had anticipated. By November there were fifty features scheduled to start within the next thirty days, and Universal had a stockpile of twenty-five features either completed or nearing completion. Universal also dropped one of its serials previously announced for the 1942-1943 season, thereby freeing up some additional, and increasingly valuable, raw stock.[9] *Eyes of the Underworld* finally went into limited release late in 1942, but it would be another couple of months before it hit theaters nationwide.

Universal had released an earlier film with this same title back in 1929, but it would appear that only the title was reused for this new release. Chaney was now billed simply as Lon Chaney, the "Jr." dropped from the credits for some unknown reason, Universal perhaps thinking the public had by now forgotten about Chaney the elder. They hadn't, and this led to some confusion among filmgoers: the title sounded familiar and Chaney's streamlined billing made it sound like one of his late father's films, repeatedly raising the question whether this was a new film or a reissue of an older film. One glance at posters dominated by junior Chaney's crazed-looking Benny should have been a tip-off to anyone. Evidently it wasn't.

Keep 'Em Slugging
(Director: Christy Cabanne; Released April 2, 1943)

Universal's profits for the fiscal year ending November 1, 1942, were $2,806,952.[10] While comparable to the previous two years' profits, it showed modest improvement, and the studio seemed to be on the right track. Pivar's next assignment during this period of growth was a decided change of pace, a sole entry in the seemingly endless string of "Dead End Kids and Little Tough

---

[8] "Producers Agree on 10-24% Reduction in Raw Stock," *Motion Picture Herald*, August 8, 1942, 12.

[9] "Hollywood Piling Up Production With 50 More Due in November," *Boxoffice*, November 7, 1942, 6.

[10] "Universal Corp. Profits Expand," *Los Angeles Times*, February 5, 1943, 16.

The Loose Ends of 1943, Adolf Included

Guys" adventure-comedies. There was little mention in the trades regarding this production until its release on April 3, 1943, at which time Universal's publicity department launched into its customary maneuver of making a lowly B sound like a mini-epic. Brenda Weisberg's script—her last in a string of them for this series—was strictly routine, with the times dictating the inclusion of the random patriotic comment or speech and a plot very loosely based on the wartime manpower shortage.

Summer in the City and school is out for vacation. Tommy Banning (Bobby Jordan) and his friends Pig (Huntz Hall), String (Gabriel Dell), and Ape (Norman Abbott) are thinking about moneymaking possibilities. A small-time con man named Dugan (uncredited Ernie Adams) approaches them with an offer of summer jobs at seaside concessions, but they know from past experience that this involves illegal activities and a lot of cop dodging. Tommy speaks for his friends when he says that with the war going on, cops have more important things to do than chase after teens like them, and that for once they will be looking for honest, respectable employment. Tommy goes home to his mother's (Mary Gordon) flat and announces his intentions to her and his older sister Sheila (Evelyn Ankers). Both are thrilled with this new display of personal responsibility.

Tommy and his friends quickly sour on the job-hunting process, their juvenile records now coming back to haunt them. One after another, distrustful personnel managers tell them there are no open positions. Sheila works at the National Department Store, and is dating co-worker Jerry Brady (Don Porter) who suggests that she see the store's shipping manager Frank Moulton (Frank Albertson) about a possible position for Tommy in that department. She is turned off when sleazy Moulton suggests a date in return for getting Tommy a job, and tells him so. In spite of this, Tommy soon receives a letter regarding an interview, and Moulton gives him the job. Sheila apologizes to Moulton.

Tommy takes the job seriously, and turns out to be hard working and dependable. One look at jewelry department salesgirl Suzanne Booker (Elyse Knox) has Tommy tripping over his tongue, and he invites her to go to the movies. Tommy's three fun-loving friends tail him there and crash the date, and soon manage to get the bunch of them—Tommy and Suzanne included—thrown out of the theater.

Enlistments are taking their toll on the department store's staff, and when store owner Mr. Carruthers (Samuel S. Hinds) asks for suggestions to make things run more smoothly with the reduced staff, Tommy chimes in: Why not streamline the hiring practice to enable younger men with no past experience or references to fill positions? Carruthers agrees, and soon both String and Ape have jobs in shipping as well. (Tommy had lined up a job for Pig as a parking attendant prior to this.)

It turns out that Moulton is somewhat of a small-time hood, working for mobster Duke Rodman (Milburn Stone), diverting goods from the store onto the black market. Not enough goods to satisfy Duke, however, who lets him know in no uncertain terms his mounting displeasure. Moulton says there's a shipment of linens coming in, and all he needs is a driver. He thinks Tommy might be easily swayed. Sounds good to Duke, so they set up a "chance" encounter between Tommy and sexy Lola LaVerne (Joan Marsh), a singer at Rodman's Ace Café. She lures Tommy to the club for a date, where Duke delivers his proposal to him. Duke is stunned when Tommy turns him down cold, and more so when Tommy says that if any thefts take place at the department store he'll know who was responsible. Duke has Moulton set up Tommy for a fall.

Moulton has Tommy deliver some jewelry to Suzanne, but the boxes are empty. Instead, the jewelry is left on the street where Tommy will find it, which he does. Meanwhile, Suzanne has innocently reported the missing jewelry to Carruthers, and Moulton subtly implicates Tommy. When the cops find Tommy with the jewelry (which he had intended to report as found), Tommy is arrested and put in jail.

Jerry, who, it turns out, is Carruthers' son but hides that fact from fellow workers by adopting his mother's name, is convinced that Tommy is innocent. Suzanne visits Tommy in jail, but the now-bitter youth, convinced that she is responsible for his false imprisonment, sends her packing. His three friends have all lost their jobs as well, in a clear instance of guilt by association.

Bobby Jordan looks happy to see Elyse Knox, and who wouldn't?
Keep 'Em Slugging **(1943).**

The Loose Ends of 1943, Adolf Included

Tommy is bailed out of jail by an unnamed benefactor—Jerry, we later learn. Returning home, his mother asks if he has broken out of jail, and he soon realizes that sister Sheila thinks he is the guilty party as well, and has quit her job as a result. Convinced that no one believes him, Tommy seeks out con man Dugan to accept his shady job offering. Dugan turns him down cold, telling him he is too hot, so Tommy decides to go see Lola and get a job with Duke. He spots her with Moulton, however, and with curiosity aroused follows the two of them to a city garage. (Viewers having seen Pivar's previous release, *Eyes of the Underworld*, will experience a sense of *déjà vu* since the same garage sets were used.)

Sneaking into the garage, Tommy overhears Duke lay out his plans to heist the department store truck full of linens. Tommy goes and recruits his three friends, and they follow the stolen truck into the garage. Tommy sends Ape to get the cops, and soon overhears how the crooks had set him up. His suspicions confirmed, he and the others hold the crooks at bay with a fire hose. The crooks break through and a fight follows, with Tommy winged by a bullet. The cops arrive and arrest the crooks, the stolen goods evidence of their guilt and their fates now sealed. With Moulton in jail, Tommy is made the National Department Store's new shipping manager.

And, of course, the happy ending: Tommy and Suzanne return to the flat with Sheila, who is overjoyed to find boyfriend Jerry and Tommy's trio of buddies there, and a brand-new Oriental carpet on the floor as well. She breaks into tears, and String and Ape follow suit with great big crocodile tears. Pig jokes about it, but when he sees Tommy's mom sniffling, he too breaks out with overly-demonstrative sobbing.

Yet another teaming of "The Dead End Kids and The Little Tough Guys," this film's quartet of "juvenile" actors were the newest incarnation of a lineage that traced back to playwright Sidney Kingsley's mid-thirties Broadway play *Dead End*. After a two-year run, rights were acquired and William Wyler made the film version for producer Samuel Goldwyn, released through United Artists in 1937. Six of the Broadway performers (Billy Halop, Bobby Jordan, Huntz Hall, Bernard Punsley, Gabriel Dell, and Leo Gorcey) were signed to two-year contracts to reprise their roles. With the film's completion their contracts were sold to Warner Brothers, where another six "Dead End Kids" films were made over the next two years.

During this period Universal borrowed a subset of the performers for a film titled *Little Tough Guy* (1938; Harold Young), and then adopted that film's title as a blanket label—"The Little Tough Guys"—for the revolving casts of juveniles who starred in the series of films that followed. With the expiration of the Warners contracts, the label was expanded to "The Dead End Kids and The Little Tough Guys," and remained so for the duration of the series' run. *Keep 'Em Slugging*—pre-production title *Bad Company*—was the last of the

Universal series to be released, although filmed next-to-last. With Jordan, Hall, and Dell as three of the four leads, *Keep 'Em Slugging* could trace its cast's roots back to half of the original group. Fourth cast member Norman Abbott was new to the series and a one-shot addition, his career in film negligible in spite of the fact that he was comedian Bud Abbott's nephew.[11] He was significantly more successful as a director in television, working continuously from 1959 through the 1980s on series that included *Leave It to Beaver*, *The Jack Benny Program*, *Welcome Back, Kotter*, and *The Munsters*.

Keep 'Em Slugging is a routine entry in the series, inoffensive and competently filmed by director Cabanne—his last for Pivar—but immediately forgettable. Jordan, Hall, and Dell had inhabited these roles so many times by now that they were entirely comfortable in them, even though Hall and Dell's characters had evolved into paper-thin comedic parts. Jordan carries most of the film in the lead role, delivering his handful of patriotic speeches with acceptable conviction, and shifting into bitter, nobody-believes-me mode without batting an eye. Along for the ride was actress Evelyn Ankers, Universal's reigning queen of horror films since her signing in 1941, ultimately to be starred in *Hold That Ghost* (1941; Arthur Lubin), *The Wolf Man* (1941; George Waggner), *The Ghost of Frankenstein* (1942; Erle C. Kenton), *Son of Dracula* (1943; Robert Siodmak), and *The Invisible Man's Revenge* (1944; Ford Beebe), as well as Pivar's *The Mad Ghoul*, *Weird Woman*, *The Frozen Ghost*, *Jungle Woman*, and his next in June, *Captive Wild Woman*. As Tommy's sister Sheila, Evelyn Ankers does a lot of heavy sighing and hand-wringing, but doesn't get to scream even once.

Don Porter gives his usual smooth, relaxed, and laid-back performance. Elyse Knox is as lovely as ever, and as much in need of an acting coach as ever. As the head crook Duke Rodman, Milburn Stone is in the sort of role for which he is best suited, tough and intimidating. Shemp Howard is on board as well, adding some little-needed humor as Binky, the exasperated proprietor of the local soda shop. Huntz Hall, of course, is responsible for most of the film's laughs as he smooth-talks and flirts with the female customers at the parking garage. Abbott and Dell have a moderately amusing sequence where the former is forced to dress and pose as a store mannequin after accidentally smashing one while horsing around. When salesgirl Suzanne attempts to adjust his dress, she accidentally pokes him with a pin and he runs shrieking from the store while customers look on in amazement. It is silly, of course, but amusing nonetheless.

A competitive series of sorts began over at Monogram in 1940 when producer Sam Katzman initiated a series of "East Side Kids" comedies. Over time this new series took on some of the original cast members, a process simplified when Universal terminated its series with the release of *Keep*

---

[11] Walt., "Keep 'Em Slugging," *Daily Variety*, February 25, 1943, 3.

'Em Slugging. "The East Side Kids" films ran through 1945 when star Leo Gorcey called it quits over a salary dispute, and Katzman canned the series. The comedies were soon resurrected as "The Bowery Boys," and lived on for another decade with a staggering number of low-budget, low-humor quickies that always managed to do well at the box office, their financial success not as impressive as it might sound since the initial cash outlay for each was so miniscule.

Sales chief William Scully resurfaced in Chicago at Universal's annual sales convention, announcing the company's upcoming 1943-1944 schedule, "with emphasis on the lighter type of film fare." As with the previous season, fifty-five features were planned, five of them so-called "super-specials," another five to be filmed in Technicolor, three more starring Abbott and Costello, and two Deanna Durbin vehicles. Scully commented with his usual stuffiness: "An increased appropriation for production is permitting the acquisition of new and important 'name' producers, directors, writers, and stars to augment Universal's already impressive roster, thus insuring strong boxoffice attractions." Six of Pivar's upcoming productions were named, although others would be piled up on his plate as well.[12] Seven westerns, three thirteen-chapter serials, sixty-seven shorts, and two newsreels per week filled out the program.[13] Oliver Drake was named as producer of the seven westerns, although Pivar would eventually have a hand in those as well.

The Strange Death of Adolf Hitler
(Director: James Hogan; Released October 8, 1943)

Late in 1938 a rumor spread like wildfire throughout Europe and soon trickled over to American shores: Adolf Hitler was actually dead, and had been for some time! This strange account made it into print late in 1938, published by The Macaulay Company of New York under the title of *The Strange Death of Adolf Hitler*. The author's name was suppressed reportedly out of fear of retribution, but it was revealed to have been the work of a soldier of fortune named Maximilian Bauer. The manuscript had been delivered in January by a courier from Switzerland.

According to Bauer's account, he had been arrested by German police back in 1933 due to his physical resemblance to Hitler, but was rescued the next day when the Nazis came into power. Ernst Roehm, head of the feared SA (the *Sturmabteilung*, more commonly known on our shores as the *Stormtroopers*), decided to keep Bauer around, thinking his likeness to Hitler might prove

---

[12] "55 Features, 7 Westerns, 67 Shorts, 104 Newsreels on Universal List," *Boxoffice*, June 19, 1943, 29, 36.

[13] "Universal Plans 55 Feature Films," *New York Times*, June 18, 1943, page unknown.

useful. Bauer would ultimately be one of a group of four men who had the dubious honor of doubling for Hitler when the need arose. In the meantime, Bauer served as Hitler's bodyguard, carefully studying his movements and fine-tuning his mimicry so that he would be totally convincing in the part when finally called upon. Bauer would eventually double for Hitler on numerous occasions, and claimed to have actually delivered a speech following the German occupation of the Rhineland. So convincing was his performance, he claimed, that Hitler had congratulated him on it.

And then in 1938 on the eve of a scheduled meeting with Chamberlain, Mussolini, and Daladier, Hitler met his maker. Bauer said that he had dined that night with Hitler, Goebbels, Von Ribbentrop, and others, and that some officials high up in the Nazi party had poisoned Hitler with an exotic South American drug. Bauer explained in rather melodramatic fashion in his written account:

> He tried to get up from his seat, and he was almost straightened up, but with his features scrunched up and his eyes so narrowed they had disappeared. Then with startling suddenness he slumped back on his chair. "Ach," he half groaned.[14]

After Hitler's death, claimed Bauer, the Nazi officials decided to carry on with the impersonation. Bauer's feet grew increasingly cold as he grew progressively paranoid, fearing a misguided assassination attempt.[15]

World events during the intervening four years suggested rather strongly that Hitler might still be alive, and kicking. Still, the book had sold well, and its title resonated with a war-weary populace who would have liked nothing better than to see Hitler dead. Universal snatched up the rights for $4,000 and assigned it to Pivar, tentatively naming the production *Death of Adolf Hitler*. Pivar in turn went to work organizing what could have been construed as a reunion of Vienna-born Nazi refuges. Émigré Joe May was signed to direct and to collaborate on a treatment with fellow émigré Fritz Kortner. Kortner alone would write the actual screenplay, and casting was scheduled for the beginning of May 1943.[16]

Sixty-two-year-old Vienna-born Joe May was a triple-threat producer-writer-director. One of the founders of the German film industry dating back to 1911, May had fled the country shortly after the Nazis took over. Lured to

---

[14] Anonymous, *The Strange Death of Adolf Hitler* (New York: The Macaulay Company, 1938), 333.

[15] "Fantastic Story of Hitler's Death Circulated Again," *Los Angeles Times*, March 3, 1939, 1.

[16] "May to Direct," *Los Angeles Times*, April 28, 1943, 17.

the U.S. by producer Erich Pommer, yet another German defector, May directed a couple of films for Fox and Warners before settling in at Universal where he directed *The Invisible Man Returns*, *The House of the Seven Gables* (both 1940), and several others. Kortner, also Vienna-born, was first and foremost an actor, with roles dating back to the mid-teens. Kortner had only a few minor writing assignments to his credit, but for whatever reason he was entrusted with the writing of this film. Kortner has a sizable role in the film as well.

The Strange Death of Adolf Hitler was one of seven productions scheduled for June 1943. It was announced on June 9 that shooting was to commence in two weeks with May directing. Within a week, though, May was shown the door and replaced by director James Hogan. A cast was assembled that included Ludwig Donath (yes, another Vienna-born émigré) in the lead, writer Kortner, and a passel of other thick-tongued transplants that included George Dolenz, Ludwig Stossel, William Trenk, Richard Ryen, Rudolf Anders, Hans Schumm, Frederick Gierman, Kurt Kreuger, Trude Berliner, Hans von Twardowsky, and many others.

Donath had fled Berlin right before the Nazis took over, organizing an anti-Nazi underground in Switzerland before eventually making his way to the U.S. He had supplied the voice of Hitler in several previous American films, most recently in *The Moon is Down* (1943; Irving Pichel). William Trenk, yet another Viennese transplant, was a star in his own right, occasionally referred to as the Orson Welles of Europe due to his versatility. As for female lead Gale Sondergaard, it should be noted that in spite of her severe Teutonic looks she hailed from Minnesota, one of the film's few homegrown cast members.

Vienna 1942: Austria is the first to fall under the advance of German troops. Franz Huber (Donath), newly-installed as the District Manager of the Department of Statistics, follows the lead of so many other of his countrymen,

Well, is he? *The Strange Death of Adolf Hitler* (1943). Image courtesy of Heritage Auction Galleries, Ha.com.

keeping a low profile, doing his job, and riding out what is hoped will be a short and relatively painless occupation.

Huber, as it turns out, has a unique talent for being able to imitate the voices of others, with almost instant recall. When fellow employee and friend Graub (Ludwig Stossel) delivers a list of confiscated items of clothing, Huber launches into a word-for-word recital of Hitler's latest speech, and the imitation is flawless. Graub turns out to be the wrong audience for this sort of thing, jealous that Huber was promoted to the position that Graub thought should be his. Graub reports Huber to the Gestapo for mocking *Der Feuhrer*.

Franz Huber (Ludwig Donath) gets a first look at his new face in *The Strange Death of Adolf Hitler* (1943).

That night after work, Huber returns home to his wife Anna (Sondergaard), a decent, religious woman who shares her husband's beliefs that all people should be treated equally, regardless of race, religion, or physical condition. Unfortunately, their two young children Hansl (Merrill Rodin) and Viki (Charles Bates) have fallen under the influence of the Children's Army Youth Leader (Kurt Kreuger), and have taken a distinct disliking for anyone not of German birth and steadfast allegiance to the Nazis. The Hubers' friend Herman Marbach (Dolenz), a Swiss citizen with a business in Austria, has joined them for a schnitzel dinner when the Gestapo agents come and arrest Huber, dragging him away without explanation. Huber is taken to Gestapo headquarters in Berlin.

Huber is grilled by Gestapo agent Mampe (Rudolph Anders, disconcertingly reminiscent of television's Colonel Klink), assisted by fellow agent Profe (Hans Schumm). Huber convinces them that there was no harm intended by his imitation of Hitler, and then astounds them with a repeat performance. He is thrown into a cell, but days later they come and tell him he can go free, only to knock him out cold and haul him off to a surgeon's quarters. Huber awakens to find his face bandaged, and he is told he was in an accident. When the bandages are removed, however, Huber witnesses the surgeon's handiwork: he's now the spitting image of Hitler himself. Huber balks, but is quickly convinced that if he doesn't go along and pose as Hitler's double when needed, his family will be put to death and "we will kill you, postmortem."

Meanwhile, a telegram is sent to Anna stating that her husband has been executed for charges of sedition and high treason. Devastated by the news,

The Loose Ends of 1943, Adolf Included

Anna is comforted by Marbach and another family friend named Bauer (Fritz Kortner). It is revealed to her that both Marbach and Bauer are members of the underground, and she is encouraged to join them should the spirit ever move her to do so.

Under the strenuous tutelage of Colonel von Zechwitz (William Trenk), Huber's brainwashing and assumption of Hitler's mannerisms eventually seem complete. Huber now appears to be a cold, unwavering shell, focusing solely on the furthering of the Nazi cause. Huber is taken back to Vienna to meet Adolf Hitler, who is scheduled to arrive there to give a speech. When Huber arrives, he finds he's now to act as Hitler's double, and readily assumes the role.

An unexpected visit from the amorous Duchess Eugenie (Joan Blair) causes some concern, but Hitler-Huber orders champagne, which he, the Duchess, and von Zechwitz proceed to drink. When Huber appears to have passed out, von Zechwitz and the Duchess retire to a bedroom for a quickie. Huber has feigned drunkenness; he grabs a coat and heads out to go back home and see his wife.

Arriving there, he's confronted by his two Nazi-in-training kids who fail to recognize him. He soon learns that they now despise his memory; both of them convinced long ago that he was a traitor and a coward. Huber doesn't know that his wife Anna also believes him to be dead, and that she and Marbach have gotten married solely to protect her from the billeting of repulsive and sex-crazed soldiers back from the Russian front. Marbach, nice guy that he is, sleeps in a separate bedroom. Huber enters and frightens his just-awakened wife, who screams and awakens the household. Marbach arrives to check out what all the screaming's about, but Huber has by now exited the room. It appears that Anna has had a nightmare, and she is convinced of same. Returning to his bedroom, Marbach is confronted by Huber, who explains all that has happened. Huber says that he is determined to kill Hitler when he meets him after the following day's speech. "My life for the life of a fiend, who's heaped untold misery on the world," exclaims Huber. "My life to atone, for the crime we all committed when we sat back in our smugness and permitted our country to become the symbol of hate for all decent people. How little that is to give." To that end, he convinces Marbach to smuggle a gun into the hotel in which the Nazis are all staying, and to hide it beside an easy chair's cushion in the main lobby.

Anna makes plans to smuggle her children out of the country and into Switzerland. Those plans are cut short when her kids squeal on her to their Youth Leader (are those a pair of Kharis' Tana leaf urns smoking away behind him?), providing as proof the passports she was going to use. The children are taken away from her. Her life in shambles, Anna decides to kill Hitler right after he gives his speech, approaching him with the ruse that she wants to petition him to regain custody of her children. She takes the pistol that Marbach intended to smuggle in to Huber. Bauer thinks this is a bad idea, and unsuccessfully attempts to talk her out of it. Soon after, Marbach goes to retrieve the pistol, finding instead only a goodbye note from Anna revealing her intentions.

Hitler gives his speech to the thousands of people amassed to hear it, or at least they think it is Hitler. Actually, it is Huber, and his performance is totally convincing. When he is finished, he is escorted back to the hotel, but Anna approaches him before he arrives at the door, her pistol hidden in a bouquet of flowers. As the two come eye-to-eye, Huber is thrilled to see his wife, but remains in character. Anna hesitates, a sense of *deju vu* clouding her thoughts. Anna retreats without shooting, but is bewildered by her lack of action. Inside the lobby, Huber-Hitler demands that the petitioning woman be brought in to him, wishing to see her one more time. Bad move. His reluctant handlers agree, if only to avoid a scene. Anna has by now regained her courage, with renewed determination to go through with the assassination; she shoots her husband dead. The handlers in turn shoot Anna dead.

Death by wife. *The Strange Death of Adolf Hitler* (1943).

The Nazi generals, assembled in a room up above, are jubilant that who they think to be Hitler has been killed. They are convinced they can now take over the war, retreat from Russia, and mobilize for attacks on both England and the United States. Their collective jubilation is cut short when the real Hitler arrives, now furious over their words.

Outside, Marbach and Bauer look on with sadness. Bauer observes that it is better that Hitler remain alive and continue to blunder his way into Stalingrad, rather than have the generals in control who would be more likely to win the war. If Hitler was dead, what would be the difference? "We have as many Hitlers as we have generals, officers, and the like," responds Bauer. "The generals, left to their own decision, might have won the war. He won't. There is only one answer—they all have got to go." The patriotic background music swells, and the film comes to an end.

One wonders how this film would have turned out in the hands of a director such as Fritz Lang, who directed the fascinatingly dark anti-Nazi film *Hangmen Also Die!* five months earlier. Director James Hogan did an adequate job on the $166,675 budget, modest by A movie standards but nearly twice what Pivar had to work with on so many of his earlier films. The finished film is rather good, the concept intriguing, the storyline engaging, and the results at times quite moving. Unfortunately, there are numerous instances throughout the film where individual shots or scenes as a whole fall flat, crying out for more assured, stylish direction.

Set decorators Russell Gausman and Edward Robinson have convincingly altered some of Universal's standing sets to visually evoke the Germany and Austria of 1942, although Huber's picket-fenced yard with abandoned wagon and bicycle would look more at home in an Andy Hardy film. (Someone must have realized this, as the clomping of horse hooves has been dubbed into the soundtrack in an attempt to suggest otherwise.) There are Nazi flags everywhere, which don't hurt. The arrival of a fleet of Nazi dignitaries at the Viennese hotel is framed and shot in such a way as to suggest a huge building and massive adoring crowds while actually only showing a small fraction of both. Stock footage of huge audiences, Nazi rallies, and military maneuvers go a long way toward making the film look much grander than it would otherwise without their inclusion. Hogan drops the ball, however, with several poorly framed setups that emphasize the empty boundaries surrounding the small group of assembled extras. This is unfortunate in that it deflates the impression of huge crowds that were so carefully built up in preceding shots and scenes. It is a good-looking film nonetheless, with Universal's typically evocative photography and lighting, and far more fluid camera movements than the norm, all courtesy of Jerome Ash.

Gale Sondergaard delivers the film's best, and most poignant, moments: anguishing over her two sons' growing alienation and hardening; comforting her frantic neighbor who has been raped by a billeted soldier (or two); and herself fighting off another coarse soldier, this one now billeted in her own home. The climactic, tragic confrontation between unrecognizable husband and unsuspecting wife is competently executed for maximum suspense, and it is a downer to put it mildly.

Ludwig Donath really gets into the spirit of things in his dual role as Huber and Hitler, required to give impassioned anti-Nazi speeches in one scene and stomp around stiff-legged issuing gruff commands as *Der Feuhrer* in the next. As the latter it is anyone's guess as to whether or not he sounds at all like the real thing, but the physical resemblance is striking. William Trenk, Rudolph Anders, and the other actors portraying Nazis are the usual collection of haughty, pompous, and cold-blooded sorts typical of war-era films. Ludwig Stossel is a standout as Huber's duplicitous "friend" Graub, and George Dolenz is satisfactory as the Hubers' sympathetic Swiss friend Marbach. Dolenz' primary claim to fame (if you couldn't guess from his name) is as the father of Micky Dolenz of television's *The Monkees*.

One instance of B movie carelessness jumps out at the viewer in the early scene where Huber approaches his house, whistling a happy tune. Cut to the interior as he enters, the whistling still heard on the soundtrack for several seconds, but his mouth is absolutely motionless.

Irishman James Hogan was nearing the end of a lengthy career by this time, having started in the industry back in 1916 as a property man for Mary Pickford following a brief stint playing professional baseball. After a break for World War I, in which he served in the Army Field Artillery and Signal Corps in the Philippines and Siberia—one hopes he packed a change of clothes—he returned to the industry and served as assistant director to both Allan Dwan and Douglas Fairbanks. Stepping up to direction in 1920, Hogan worked at a number of different, smaller studios through the remainder of the silent period.[17] With the advent of sound, Hogan took an extended break from direction to learn the new medium. When he finally returned, he found himself assigned a succession of B films, the "Bulldog Drummond" series for Paramount among them. Admittedly a prolific director, Hogan's output was rather routine, but improved a bit visually during his late-thirties association with Paramount. Hogan's two films for Pivar, this and the follow-up *The Mad Ghoul*, are arguably among his better films.

Hogan's salary for this effort was a flat $2,500, as was Pivar's. Helen McLemore, Pivar's private secretary and confidant, was retained at her usual $500 per picture. $22,950 was allotted for the cast and extras, with Sondergaard receiving a flat $4,000 for her portrayal of the tormented wife, Dolenz a flat $2,500, and Donath receiving $500 per week for three weeks' work in his dual role. Long shots of the Imperial Hotel were made a bit more visually impressive with a matte painting that cost them $350. The ubiquitous stock shots cost another $750, a third of this from Universal's film library, the other $500 from outside sources. The film was scored in a three-hour, twenty-four-man session accounting for another $720 of the film's budget.

Joseph Gershenson, the film's uncredited executive producer, received a flat $1,000 for his efforts. Known as Universal's music department head since 1940, Gershenson was pressed into service as executive producer as well in 1942, with this only his third film. He'd go on to executive produce two more of Pivar's films—*The Mad Ghoul* and *The Mummy's Ghost*—over the next year without credit. Gershenson and his wife Helen lived down the street from Pivar on Valley Spring Lane, and the two couples became fast friends. Gershenson and Pivar would get together for a weekly pinochle game, joined by friends Jack Gross, Murray Melner, and several others, held on a rotating basis at the various participants' homes. In later years Sam Karnes, the husband of Judy's niece Shirley, daughter of Judy's oldest sister Anne, would join them.

---

[17] "James P. Hogan, 52, Director of Films," *New York Times*, November 6, 1943, page unknown.

The Loose Ends of 1943, Adolf Included

Filming began on Tuesday, June 6, 1943, on an eighteen-day shooting schedule that was to wrap on July 6. Various unforeseen delays (such as an afternoon lost on the fourth day due to high winds while attempting to film an exterior street scene) required an additional three days, the film finishing up at 9:15 p.m. on Monday, July 12, 1943.

Joseph I. Breen, film code chief of the Motion Pictures Producers & Distributors of America (MPDA) and perpetual thorn-in-the-side of filmmakers of all stripes, took issue with some of Kortner's lines in the script, finding them far too suggestive. As head of Universal's censorship department, Pivar's brother Murray—still addressed as Maurice in official correspondences—acted as go-between for his younger brother and the all-powerful Hollywood censor-bully Breen. One sticking point was the dialog in the hotel suite scene between Zechwitz, the Duchess Eugenie, and Huber-as-Hitler feigning drunkenness:

> It will be important to avoid any suggestion of illicit sex affair between Zechwitz and the Duchess. To this end, please drop the underlined words: "He's not accustomed to this drinking...<u>and the rest of it</u>." Also, the end of the scene should be shot without any suggestion of a sex affair.

A follow-up scene alluding to the night before came under fire as well:

> Please rewrite the line "...I mean after last night" in order to get away from any possible suggestion that Franz is referring <u>to a sex affair</u>.

Breen concluded with his standard, thinly-veiled threat intended to keep Murray Pivar on his toes, his letter cc'd to brother Ben, director Hogan, executive producer Gershenson, production head Cliff Work, and a trio of others: "You understand, of course, that our final judgment will be based on the finished picture."[18] The changes were made, although the finished film's soundtrack has the first line of dialog as "He's not accustomed to this drinking ... an .... That's genius for you, eh?" revealing that the scene had been filmed prior to Breen's letter. Editor Milton Carruth had cut the sound a moment too late, leaving in a snippet of the offending dialog (part of the first word in the line "and the rest of it").

After an unofficial premiere at Universal on August 25, *The Strange Death of Adolf Hitler* went into limited release on September 10, 1943, with its New York premiere following on October 8. Bosley Crowther, *The New York Times* resident spoilsport, ruined the surprise for potential attendees the next day

---

[18] Letter from Breen to Maurice Pivar, June 23, 1943.

in his review: "Folks who go to the Rialto with high hopes of seeing what it says in Universal's 'The Strange Death of Adolph [sic] Hitler' are due for a disappointment, we're sorry to say. For the fellow who gets the business in this picture is not Der Fuehrer at all, but a poor little man from Vienna who has the misfortune of being able to talk like him and so is compelled to play a 'double' for Hitler, much against his desire."[19] It's too bad that the so-called "Spoiler Alert" was a concept years away.

Variety gave the film a fair assessment, commenting on its box-office potential: "Somewhat unique as to plot, but far from being highly engrossing. 'The Strange Death of Adolf Hitler' is disappointing on the whole. Its title and the exploitation values entailed make for the prime b.o. equation."[20] Perhaps, but while the bevy of transplanted actors lent the film an added measure of verisimilitude, one disappointed exhibitor grumbled, "How do they expect a picture, even with a title like this one, to draw without at least one known actor? It's just a powder keg without a fuse."[21]

An article appeared in numerous papers in late June describing one of Universal's suggested exploitation schemes for the film, and a rather strange one at that. It was reported that Pivar, Hogan, and Kortner had the film's entire script written with one glaring exception: they hadn't figured out how to kill Hitler, and with what weapon. To that end they solicited suggestions from readers in a two-hundred-word letter, to be sent to director Hogan at Universal Studios. The winner of the "How I Would Cause 'The Strange Death of Adolf Hitler'" contest would receive a $100 war bond. "Don't be too gruesome. Don't kill him by degrees, either. And don't kill him too quickly, because the scene is the high point of the picture." The producers would be the sole judge of the entries, and "even if you don't grab the prize, think of all the satisfaction you will have had just cogitating the idea."[22] Universal's publicity campaign was anything but subtle, with one of the film's catch lines shrieking, "Here's the Shock-Crammed Drama of the Ugly Orgies Behind the Hush-hush Stories That All the Swineland Couldn't Suppress!" James Ellroy couldn't do better than that.

Pivar retained screenwriter Fritz Kortner for a follow-up of sorts. Announced in July, Kortner was to come up with an original story centering on

---

[19] Bosley Crowther, "The Screen: Unreasonable Facsimile," *New York Times*, October 9, 1943, 11.

[20] Char., "Strange Death of Adolf Hitler," *Variety*, October 9, 1943, 10.

[21] "The Exhibitor Has His Say," *Boxoffice*, February 26, 1944, 154.

[22] Frederick C. Othman, "Think of Way to Kill Hitler and You'll Get $100 Prize," *Winnipeg Free Press*, June 26, 1943, 19; "Exploitips," *Boxoffice*, September 4, 1943, 138.

Japanese atrocities.²³ The result was titled *Beast of the East*, but it needed some work and a new set of eyes, so Malcolm Stuart Boylan was engaged to revise the script in October.²⁴ The project was eventually shelved.

The Mad Ghoul
(Director: James Hogan; Released November 12, 1943)

Pivar's next assignment was another horror film, more accurately a horror *title* around which a workable script would be written. First announced in January 1943, as *The Mystery of the Mad Ghoul*, writer Hans Kraly was hired to conjure up an original story.²⁵ Born in Hamburg, Germany, in 1884, Kraly—along with Ernst Lubitsch and Emil Jannings—had been a major contributor to that country's film industry since 1911. Lubitsch brought Kraly to the United States in 1922 for what was supposed to be a two-week visit, but Kraly ended up staying. Numerous scripts followed over the next two decades for actresses such as Mary Pickford, Pola Negri, and Vilma Banky, but by 1940 Kraly's career had come to a grinding halt. Universal grabbed him on the way down for this assignment. His task completed by mid-March, Kraly checked off the lot and faded into obscurity, passing on in 1950 with this final work—for better or worse—his swansong.²⁶

Brenda Weisberg adapted Kraly's story to a shooting script,²⁷ making a clean break from her "Little Tough Guys" assignments; Paul Gangelin assisted. James Hogan returned to direct, with filming underway by the end of May. David Bruce, Evelyn Ankers, George Zucco, and Turhan Bey were the leads, with Robert Armstrong, Milburn Stone, Rose Hobart, and Charles McGraw lending support. Hogan reportedly would call for each new take to begin with the long, drawn-out shouted command "Camerawh," then call for its termination with "I'll buy that one!" Greater praise was reserved for particularly good filmed sequences: "Anybody who wouldn't buy that scene doesn't know home cooking when he sees it!"²⁸

"James Hogan directs the yarn in a straightforward manner which reflects his knowledge that the tale is spine-chilling enough without dwelling on the most horrible details," commented *The Hollywood Reporter* the day after

---

²³ Ivan Spear, "Hollywood Report," *Boxoffice*, July 17, 1943, 50.
²⁴ Ivan Spear, "Hollywood Report," *Boxoffice*, October 16, 1943, 24.
²⁵ "Studio Personnelities," *Boxoffice*, January 23, 1943, 46.
²⁶ "Hans Kraly, Film Writer for Three Decades, Dies," *Los Angeles Times*, November 12, 1950, 24.
²⁷ "Studio Personnelities," *Boxoffice*, March 20, 1943, 39.
²⁸ Erskine Johnson, "In Hollywood," *The News*, Frederick, MD, June 12, 1943, 9.

the finished film was previewed in a studio projection room.[29] Universal was sufficiently pleased with the results, rewarding Hogan with a long-term producer-director contract.[30]

Dr. Alfred Morris (Zucco) gives his final lecture to the School of Medicine's chemistry class before the start of spring semester break. He tells the assembled students of his research into an ancient Mayan gas that would reduce its victim to a death-in-life state, one characterized by blind obedience to the perpetrator's commands. Bad enough, granted; but to make matters worse, the only way to return the victim to his former self is with an extract from the heart of a living or recently deceased individual. What historians had thought to be sacrifices to the Gods were in reality rituals to restore life to the affected subjects.

Afterwards, Morris confides in surgical student Ted Allison (David Bruce), telling him that his research is much further along than he led the class to believe, and that he has actually recreated the crystal from which the gas emanates. He invites Ted to join him in his research over the spring break, and Ted enthusiastically accepts. Morris takes Ted to his basement lab where he shows him the result of his experiments, a small monkey named Jocko that appears to be dead, but has a faint heartbeat. Morris explains that the native formula gives "the appearance of emaciation, followed by more marked physical changes, and then by paralysis of the will. This condition inevitably will terminate in death," unless, of course, the action of the gas is reversed with an antidote concocted with the extract from a fresh heart combined with certain herbs. Grabbing a living monkey, Morris goes to work extracting the fluid from the poor simian's heart, with a hesitant assist from Ted. Jocko springs back to chattering life. "I can't help feeling a sense of evil in all this," comments Ted, to which Morris snaps back, "Moral concepts! I'm a scientist. To me there is no good or evil, only true or false. I work with one, discard the other." Uh-oh.

Ted is madly in love with opera singer Isabel Lewis (Evelyn Ankers), and returns with her to Morris' home after dinner to celebrate their success. When Ted heads out of the room to mix drinks, Morris astutely observes that all is not right with Isabel, and correctly surmises that she is no longer in love with Ted; music has opened a new world for her, and she has outgrown him. When she agrees that this is indeed the situation, Morris takes his analysis a quantum leap further: "It's only natural that you should turn to an older man. Someone who knows the book of life, and can teach you to read it." Isabel is too busy fretting over her predicament to pick up on the leering thrust of his comments,

---

[29] "Fresh-robbed Grave Features This One," *Hollywood Reporter*, October 29, 1943, 3.
[30] "Universal Signs Up Hogan On Long-Term Contract," *Boxoffice*, June 5, 1943, 56.

and he is too tangled up with lust to realize the absurdity of his comments. Regardless, Morris quickly hatches a plan to have Isabel all to himself.

George Zucco, getting ready to coo, "It's only natural that you should turn to an older man." Left to right: David Bruce, Evelyn Ankers, Zucco. *The Mad Ghoul* (1943).

Isabel is about to embark on a multi-city concert tour when Morris sends unsuspecting Ted into the gas-filled lab to see the results of the gas on a live human being. Once he has dead-eyed Ted under his power, Morris tells Ted that Isabel no longer loves him. Instead, he explains, she is now in love with "older man" Morris. Later on when he sends Isabel off on her tour, Morris tells her that Ted is too sick to see her off. She frets some more, then leaves, accompanied by her pianist Eric Iverson (Turhan Bey).

That night Morris and zombified Ted make their way to Fairview Cemetery where Ted disinters a deceased lawyer and appropriates his heart (I'll avoid the bad lawyer joke here). Back at the lab, the antidote is whipped up and Ted returned to a normal state. Consciousness now restored, Ted has vague memories of what has transpired, and chalks them up to dreams. He is disappointed that he was not present for Isabel's departure.

Police sergeant Macklin (Milburn Stone) and detective Garrity (Charles McGraw) are assigned to investigate the grave robbery. They are handed their first clue by reporter Ken McClure (Robert Armstrong), who observes the "expert" cutting in the removal of the corpse's heart.

When Jocko collapses, Morris realizes that the effects of the antidote are short-term, and that follow-up administrations will be required to keep the patient alive. He informs Ted that there is more research to be done, but doesn't let on about Jocko. When Ted insists that he is going to follow Isabel on her tour, Morris says he'll accompany him, feigning concern over the fellow's health.

Isabel receives a letter informing her that Ted is on his way, which is troubling since she and her pianist are in love. When Ted arrives and he and Isabel are alone, he proposes to her. Faced with an underwhelming reaction from Isabel, Ted begins to revert back to his altered state. Morris quickly assumes care of Ted before the others realize what a mess he has become. Morris leads the now fully reverted Ted to another cemetery in a quest for another heart, but when the cemetery's caretaker (Gus Glassier) has the misfortune of intervening, he instead becomes the new donor. Restored back to a semblance of normalcy, Ted balks at Morris' suggestion of returning home.

Morris consoles Isabel when she expresses concern with Ted's well-being and erratic behavior. But when she drops the bombshell about her love for Iverson, Morris now realizes he has two annoying rivals for her hand rather than the previously assumed one. Isabel asks Morris, as Ted's doctor, to reveal the truth to Ted, wimpishly explaining that he'll know how to handle it better than she would. Morris agrees and breaks the news to Ted, who once again reverts back to his zombie state. Morris has Ted write a note to Iverson telling him to meet him at the stage door at midnight, and then hands a pistol to Ted and commands him to kill Iverson. In a stylish lead-up to the planned murder, Ted's gun-wielding shadow approaches the unsuspecting Iverson, interrupted at the last moment by Isabel's arrival and well-timed scream. Ted lumbers back to Morris' car and the two beat a hasty retreat.

Over the weeks that follow, a seemingly random series of grave robberies occur in a number of towns and cities. Reporter McClure convinces his editor to give him an expense account to pursue the story. When he runs into fellow reporter Della Elliott (Rose Hobart), who's aware of Isabel's schedule, she makes the off-handed comment that all of the grave robberies have coincided with Isabel's concert tour. McClure latches on to this intriguing piece of information and hightails it to the next town on Isabel's tour schedule. McClure convinces the county's lead mortician Eagen (Andrew Tombes) to help him with a plan to capture the culprits. A bogus obituary is posted and McClure camps out in an open coffin, pistol at his side and hoping to get lucky. Morris and Ted arrive after nightfall, and as they approach the coffin McClure sits up and holds Morris at gunpoint. Unfortunately for McClure, he only sees Morris

Evelyn Ankers better scream, and fast! Left to right: Ankers, Turhan Bey, David Bruce. *The Mad Ghoul* (1943). Photo courtesy of Jerry Murbach at Doctor Macro's High Quality Movie Scans, www.doctormacro.com.

and is unaware that Ted is approaching from behind, scalpel in hand. McClure becomes the next heart donor.

Informed of McClure's death, Della goes to the police and tells all she knows to Macklin and Garrity, who head off and confront Isabel with their newfound suspicions that pianist Iverson is the murderer. She doesn't believe this, but now begins to suspect that Ted may have schizophrenic tendencies; she relays her concerns to Morris. Ted, restored once again by the antidote concocted courtesy of McClure's ticker, overhears this conversation and comes to the realization that he has become a pawn in Morris' hands—his unwitting accomplice. He gives his blessing to Isabel and Iverson's romance and future.

Ted heads to the lab and writes a full confession, then fires up a batch of the lethal crystals before reverting back to his zombie state. Morris enters the lab and delivers his last command to Ted: Isabel is back in town to give a concert that night, and Ted is to go there, kill Iverson, and then kill himself. Ted lumbers off just as Morris realizes he is in a gas-filled room. He screams for Ted to come back, realizing that he too will need assistance with obtaining the materials for the antidote, but Ted's brain is now hard-wired with Morris' most recent command.

Arriving at the concert hall, Ted stumbles on stage with gun in hand. As luck would have it, Macklin and Garrity are both in the audience, and conveniently have front row seats. Garrity shoots and kills Ted before slow-moving Ted can fire a single shot. Meanwhile, Morris is now in the local cemetery, the gas rapidly affecting him. He claws at a new grave hoping to acquire a fresh heart before he falls into a trance and dies. He is not successful.

Needless to say, the film is rather silly, but it does have its suspenseful moments, and the cast pulls it off efficiently. It follows the oft-used B movie formula of the scientist obsessively plugging away at his experiments regardless of the cost to others, sidetracked when he falls head-over-heels for the heroine of the piece, with this new obsession leading to his eventual downfall. Familiar, perhaps, but executed so much more slickly than similar efforts from Poverty Row studios Monogram—*The Corpse Vanishes* (1942; Wallace Fox) and *The Ape Man* (1943; William Beaudine)—and PRC—*The Devil Bat* (1940; Jean Yarbrough) and *The Mad Monster* (1942; Sam Newfield). With Universal's usual solid technical support, workmanlike direction from Hogan, and a uniformly good cast, *The Mad Ghoul* delivered the goods horror fans expected, and in an uncomplicated, straightforward package. Unfortunately for the audience, the film's most eagerly awaited moment wherein Zucco would single-handedly procure a heart and self-administer the antidote, never comes to fruition. *The Mad Ghoul* was released on November 12, 1943, on the bottom half of a double bill with the higher-profile *Son of Dracula* (Robert Siodmak), the headlining Chaney vehicle helping to boost attendance. For the only time in his career, Pivar's name was listed in the credits as the more formal "*Benjamin* Pivar."

After a few small roles at 20th Century-Fox back in the late thirties, Evelyn Ankers was hired by Universal in 1941. Talent scouts caught a performance of the stage play *Ladies in Retirement* and were dazzled by her unique capacity for unleashing impressive, ear-shattering screams, *sine qua non* in the burgeoning field of horror films. Two years and eighteen films later, Ankers found herself placed in a growing number of films of that nature—*The Wolf Man* (1941; George Waggner), *The Ghost of Frankenstein* (1942; Erle C. Kenton), and *Son of Dracula*, for instance—all of which required extensive use of her impressive lung power. *The Mad Ghoul* had promised to be a unique exception: Ankers was assigned the role of the opera singer with the exciting—and potentially door-opening—prospect of doing her own singing in the lead. Studio publicity made a big deal out this: "An innovation in this type of entertainment is the introduction of several attractive musical numbers. Miss Ankers sings for the first time on the screen and her selections include 'All for Love,' 'Our Love Will

The Loose Ends of 1943, Adolf Included

Live' and 'I Dreamt I Dwelt in Marble Halls.'"[31] *Boxoffice* commented on what it saw to be a hindrance rather than an asset: "[The film's] tempo is further slowed through the interpolation of musical interludes, unimpressively supplied by Evelyn Ankers."[32] Universal's publicity blurbs were a slight stretch of the truth, actually; when time and money ran out, Ankers had been forced to lip-synch to library recordings. So much for door-opening.

Turhan Bey gets to play a good guy in this film. After a string of close to two-dozen programmers two-and-a-half years into his contract with Universal, the onslaught of letters from rabid females nationwide had finally convinced Universal that their twenty-four-year-old actor should be advanced up the ladder a rung or two. *The Mad Ghoul* would be his last low-budget role (and his last for Pivar as well), advancing (if you want to call it that) to a role in *Ali Baba and the Forty Thieves* (1944; Arthur Lubin) along with Maria Montez ("The Caribbean Cyclone!") and Jon Hall. Born Turhan Selahettin Schultavey Bey—*Bey* is a Turkish title—in Vienna, Austria, to a well-heeled Turkish father and Czechoslovakian mother, Bey had come to America years before with his divorced mother and grandmother, eventually settling in California due to its mild, Riviera-like climate. Director Arthur Lubin had "discovered" the youth and sent him to Ben Bard's dramatic school. After two small roles in films for Warners, Bey was signed by Universal.[33] In the two-dimensional role of Iverson, Bey manages to give a relaxed performance, oozing Continental charm while delivering his surprisingly almost accent-free lines of dialog.

Newlywed David Bruce handles the dual role of likeable student and unlikeable ghoul adequately, although he probably viewed this part as somewhat of a step down in his career trajectory. After a two-year start with Warners that resulted in small-to-miniscule parts in such high-profile films as *The Sea Hawk* (1940; Michael Curtiz), *Knute Rockne All American* (1940; Lloyd Bacon), *The Sea Wolf* (1941; Michael Curtiz), and *Sergeant York* (1941; Howard Hawks), Bruce was dropped by Warners and picked up soon after by Universal. This move resulted in leads in assembly-line programmers of this sort, but just as many small, supporting parts. Universal cut him loose mid-decade, with random films following for Columbia, Monogram, and several independents before Bruce cut his losses and settled into work for television. A pleasant and competent performer, the Illinois-born actor never really clicked with the film-going public.

---

[31] "'The Mad Ghoul' Tale of Eccentric Scientist," *The Laredo Times*, October 22, 1944, 16.

[32] "The Mad Ghoul," *Boxoffice*, November 6, 1943, 14.

[33] Louella O. Parsons, "Turhan Bey Clicks With the Girls, Has Bright Future," *San Antonio Light*, October 24, 1943, 37.

Zucco, of course, is the film's main attraction as the mad scientist of the piece. In what could have been another over-the-top role, however, Zucco instead imbues his character with a quiet dignity of sorts, sympathetic on the surface while bubbling over inside with madness. Whether this comparatively subdued performance is attributable to Hogan's direction or Zucco's recognition of a script several notches above the usual spook film tripe is arguable; the on-screen results are a pleasure. Robert Armstrong's McClure is the standard fast-talking, wisecracking reporter that audiences had come to expect, and he gives it his best Carl Denham-ish delivery that affords moments of distraction from the rather grim proceedings that dominate the film. Ditto for Andrew Tombes' mortician Eagan, who provides the film's other fleeting moments of humor. As McClure climbs into the coffin to await the grave robbers' appearance, Eagan, seemingly concerned for McClure's well being, dispels that notion with the straight-faced delivery of "Whatever you do, don't mar this coffin." In the small, supporting role of Garrity, tough guy Charles McGraw gives a hint of the type roles he'd soon become known for in such noirs as *Armored Car Robbery* (1950) and *The Narrow Margin* (1952; both Richard Fleischer).

Less than a month after the release of *The Strange Death of Adolf Hitler* and a mere week before *The Mad Ghoul* was to be released, director Hogan died of a heart attack at the age of fifty-two. Coincidentally, the Van Nuys Fire Department inhalator squad that rushed over and unsuccessfully attempted to revive him had just spent the previous hour trying to save the life of one-year-old drowning victim Lou Costello, Jr., unsuccessful at that as well.[34] It was not a good night for any of them.

§

---

[34] "Director James P. Hogan Succumbs in His Home at 52," *Los Angeles Times*, November 5, 1943, A.

14 The Inner Sanctum Mysteries (Part 1, 1943-1944)

Pivar's home on Valley Spring Lane had a badminton court in its backyard. As his fortunes grew, Ben had planned to replace it with an in-ground pool, an addition that was eagerly anticipated by the family. With the drowning death of Costello's son and the presence of their own one-year-old daughter in the household, alternate plans were put into effect. In lieu of the in-ground pool, a shallow aboveground pool was erected. Anticlimactic, but prudent.

Universal announced plans for another fifty-five features for the upcoming 1943-1944 season, plus an additional seven westerns.[1] By this time, Lon Chaney, Jr. had firmly replaced Karloff as the studio's number one horror star, and Pivar, one of the studio's nine associate producers,[2] had demonstrated an affinity for darker, more horrific fare. Deciding to launch a new series of psychological thrillers with Chaney as star, Universal signed an agreement with Simon and Schuster, Inc., publishers of mysteries then being

Pivar and son Neil take a dip, 1942. Photo courtesy of Jan Pivar Dacri.

---

[1] "Universal Plans 55 Features for Coming Season," *Los Angeles Times*, June 18, 1943, 22.

[2] *Daily Variety*, February 9, 1943, 3. Don Brown, Paul Malvern, Bernard C. Burton, Will Cowan, Ken Goldsmith, and Frank Shaw were some of the other associate producers.

adapted for dramatization on the popular *Inner Sanctum* radio show. (There was a forerunner of sorts; in the late thirties Universal had featured a series of "Crime Club" murder mysteries as part of their output, many featuring Preston Foster as detective Bill Crane.) Two mysteries were to be produced per year under the "Inner Sanctum" banner, and since the deal was solely for the use of the name, all stories were to be newly written for the screen.[3] These mysteries were to have supernatural overtones (always logically explained in the denouement), with Chaney as the beleaguered lead and, it was suggested, Gale Sondergaard as his costar. Pivar was to oversee production.

Calling Dr. Death
(Director: Reginald LeBorg; Released December 17, 1943)

The first in the series was an original written by Edward Dein titled *Calling Dr. Death*, purchased a month earlier before the deal with Simon and Schuster had been sealed; Fritz Leiber, Jr.'s novel *Conjure Wife* would follow, to be scripted by Scott Darling.[4] George Dolenz and Isabel Jewell were both slated for supporting roles, but Dolenz was replaced by David Bruce by the time Virgil Miller's cameras rolled on Thursday, October 21; Jewell's character landed on the cutting room floor. Reginald LeBorg was tapped to direct, having just completed filming of *The Mummy's Ghost* (his first of five for Pivar). Paul Sawtell was attached as musical director, a first-time substitute for the ubiquitous Hans J. Salter. Sondergaard was bumped, replaced by Patricia Morison, with J. Carrol Naish, David Bruce, and twenty-four-year-old Ramsay Ames co-starring (at the time promoted as only nineteen). This film, along with four of the five that followed, would open with actor David Hoffman's countenance, encased in a crystal ball on a boardroom tabletop, introducing the film in a sequence supplied by Universal's in-house effects technician John P. Fulton.

> This is the Inner Sanctum. A strange, fantastic world controlled by a mass of living, pulsating flesh—the mind. It destroys, distorts, creates *monsters*—commits *murder*. Yes, even you, without knowing, can commit *murder*.

Neurologist Mark Steele (Lon Chaney, *sans* "Jr.") is a success at what he does, but his marriage to Maria (Ramsay Ames) is a shambles. Returning home after a day's work, Steele finds that Maria is not there, and ends up dining alone—once again. Staring at her portrait that dominates the room, Steele thinks to himself: "Those eyes—mean eyes—selfish. They really portray her soul!" At

---

[3] "Screen News Here and in Hollywood," *New York Times*, June 17, 1943, 17.
[4] "Spook Series Shaped Starring Lon and Gale," *Los Angeles Times*, July 16, 1943, 14.

The Inner Sanctum Mysteries, Part I (1943-1944)

"Yes, even you, without knowing, can commit *murder.*" Crystal ball-encased David Hoffman in the *Inner Sanctum* intros.

which point he smashes some dishes. Steele waits up until 3:00 a.m., only to see Maria arrive home in a convertible driven by another man. Confronting her as she walks through the front door, she mocks him, swearing that she'll never leave him, having grown accustomed to wealth and social standing. "There's nothing you can do," she spits out. "Not murder—you haven't the courage." "I wonder," quietly responds Steele.

The next morning Steele arrives at his office and confronts his nurse assistant Stella Madden (Patricia Morison), professing his love for her. She responds with words that mimic Maria's: "There's nothing we can do about it." Returning home early that Saturday afternoon, Steele is informed by his butler Brian (Holmes Herbert) that Maria has gone away to their cabin for the weekend. Steele takes off in a furious rage, driving like a madman and almost colliding with a passing locomotive.

Monday morning at the office, a sleeping and disheveled, five o'clock shadow-bearing Steele is awakened by Stella. He claims he can't remember anything that happened since Saturday afternoon. Two detectives arrive and inform Steele that Maria has been murdered up at their cabin, and he is to accompany them to identify the body. Stella takes him aside and insists that he use her as a weekend-long alibi.

Steele approaches the cabin in a slick point-of-view tracking shot that leads him through a horde of reporters and up to the front door where he is met by Inspector Gregg (J. Carrol Naish), a no-nonsense cop who doesn't mince with words. Maria's body lies in a trashed bedroom, her skull smashed with a blunt object and her face disfigured with acid. Steele spots a button on the floor and pockets it.

Chaney emotes, or tries to, in *Calling Dr. Death* (1943).

Back in town, Steele shows the button to Stella, and she immediately notices that his suit jacket sleeve is missing that same button. Steele is now convinced that he murdered his wife and has blocked out all memory of it. Gregg calls and informs Steele that they have caught the real murderer, an architect named Robert Duvall (David Bruce) who was Maria's secret lover. Steele goes to the jail and confronts Duvall, who pleads with Steele. He is innocent, he claims, once in love with Maria but annoyed by all her lies, hanging on to her promise to leave Steele. She finally broke it to him up at the cabin that she'd never leave Steele, so Duvall had left her and driven aimlessly all night. Steele believes him and tells him so. Soon after, Gregg, who had listened in on an intercom, tells Steele that he believes Duval, too—because he thinks Steele killed her!

A montage of the Duval trial follows, with the poor sap receiving the death penalty on what is clearly circumstantial evidence. Steele is haunted by voices, convinced of his own guilt and remorseful over the fate that will soon befall Duval. Gregg makes another appearance at Steele's house—doesn't this guy ever knock?—and launches in with another round of mind games: "Can't escape your conscience. It isn't death that frightens men, it's waiting, anticipation, your conscience, haunting you in your sleep, your dreams." He pushes Steele to make a confession, but no dice.

Steele has Stella assist him with self-hypnosis to get at the truth, and has her record his comments while he is in the trance. Which she does, and it would appear that he is innocent until spoilsport Gregg crashes the party once again, listens to the recording, and dismisses it with the assertion that the will to live might affect one's subconscious, and thereby the recording's contents. As icing on the cake, Gregg accuses Stella of being Steele's accomplice.

J. Carrol Naish's Inspector (right) grills Patricia Morison in *Calling Dr. Death* (1943). Image courtesy of Heritage Auction Galleries, Ha.com.

The Inner Sanctum Mysteries, Part I (1943-1944)

Steele visits Duval on death row and probes for more information. Duval confesses that he was penniless, and had gone after Maria solely for money to pay off his gambling debts, a hefty $10,000. He had fallen in love with her, though, and had returned half of the money. Steele presses for the fate of the other half, but Duval clams up. Steele is convinced that he is covering for someone.

When Stella faints in the office, Steele suggests that they go away for the weekend. He will drive her to her folks' home in Malcolm Falls, and then head alone to his cabin in Spring Lake for some fishing. Returning to the office on Monday, the watchman (Alec Craig) informs them that there was a fire. Much of the office was damaged, and the filing cabinets destroyed. Gregg puts in another appearance and quickly deduces the cause of the fire: a vial of acid placed in such a way that the ringing of the telephone would result in the fire. Gregg comments on the coincidence of the use of acid both for this fire and to disfigure Maria's face, and then suggests that perhaps Steele made the phone call from Spring Lake that morning before returning to town.

Duval is to be executed the next day, and Steele tells Stella that he doesn't want to be alone until it is all over. After a joyless night on the town, the two return to his office and before she knows what is happening, Steele hypnotizes her. Her defenses now down, Stella tells the real story, with a lengthy montage of flashback scenes superimposed over her furrowed brow. The plan was all hers, and she convinced Duval to woo Maria and get the money from her. When Duval eventually had a change of heart and asked for Stella's share to be returned, she had refused. When Duval had slapped her, she lost it, following him to the cabin and taking the opportunity of his hasty departure to kill Maria with a poker. She then delivered the acid *coups de grâce*. Returning to the office, she had placed Steele in a hypnotic trance, planting a story in his mind and erasing any conflicting information. When Steele had later suggested that they get some office help with the files, she had set up the fire to destroy any evidence of her cooking the books.

Her "confession" complete, the ever-present Gregg enters the room and arrests her, having heard all. She hisses resistance but doesn't get far when she attempts to escape, fleeing into the arms of the two detectives waiting in the next room. Gregg tells Steele that he never really suspected him, instead using him as bait to catch the real murderer. He calls the warden and has Duval released. Turning to Steele, he tells him he envies him, since he can now return to his life while Gregg will instead pursue the next criminal. "I start with death, I look for life, and then I have to destroy it." Well, it is a dirty job, but somebody has to do it. Fade out on the Hippocratic Oath posted on Steele's wall.

Calling Dr. Death is a relatively interesting, well-crafted mystery, although ultimately quite predictable. Chaney is only slightly more convincing than usual in his uneven performance as the tortured doctor, and director LeBorg should have told him to take the cigarette out of his mouth; Chaney mumbles his way through one nearly unintelligible early scene. Patricia Morison is quite good as Stella, initially sympathetic but turning icy cold without batting an eyelash, her only false note displayed in the closing scene where her histrionics topple over the top. On the stage since 1933, Paramount signed her in 1939 but stuck her in a succession of unspectacular, lower-budget roles. Fed up with her lack of advancement, Morison went freelance in 1942, only to find herself hired by the likes of PRC, RKO, and Monogram for films no better (and many worse) than her previous efforts. *Calling Dr. Death* was yet another film of this ilk.

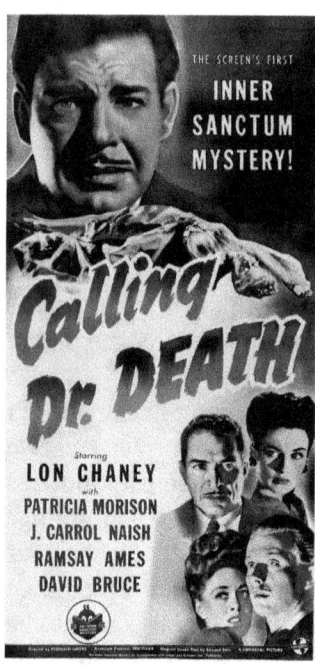

Calling Dr. Death (1943). Image courtesy of Heritage Auction Galleries, Ha.com.

J. Carrol Naish is the film's standout, quietly intimidating with his dogged determination. Fay Helm has a small but effective bit as Duval's wheelchair-bound wife, and David Bruce, returning to a straight role after his mad ghoul, sports a trim little moustache and is convincing as the architect-cum-conman with a conscience. Ramsay Ames delivers a performance worthy of a junior high stage play. This is a surprise since she managed to hold her own in *The Mummy's Ghost*, her previous effort for Pivar and LeBorg that was not released until months after both this film and its "Inner Sanctum" successor. LeBorg must have slacked off when directing her few scenes, and winced when he saw the on-screen results, but Ames gets a pass on looks alone.

Perhaps the most interesting (although bordering on gaudy) aspects of the film are Reginald LeBorg's directorial touches coupled with Virgil Miller's crisp, top-notch photography: beautifully lit nighttime interiors; Steele's approach toward a reclining Maria, hatred welling up in his eyes and murder potentially on his mind, cut short by the screech of their pet cockatiel; the subjective camerawork during Steele's approach to the cabin where his wife's corpse lies; a brief montage during the trial of suspected murderer Duval; the unnerving angles that the camera assumes preceding Steele's hypnotizing of his nurse Stella; and the bizarre, Caligari-esque scenes depicting what the hypnotized Stella relates, culminating in the collapse of the building walls on Steele's wife.

LeBorg, born Heinrich von Grobel, was a forty-year-old native of Austria who came from a moneyed family. Educated at the University of Austria with additional studies at the Sorbonne in Paris, LeBorg entered the family banking

The Inner Sanctum Mysteries, Part I (1943-1944)

business and eventually gravitated to the United States. Deciding that banking was not his calling, he returned to Europe and the stage, where he served as playwright and director of musical comedies and operas. A return to the United States took him to Hollywood where he found employment staging the musical and operatic sequences for films at Columbia, United Artists, and Paramount. LeBorg received his American citizenship papers in mid-July 1937,[5] and after several filmless years was hired by Universal in 1941. He was assigned to direct a slew of musical shorts that kept him busy well into 1943, before the suits advanced him to their B film unit and made him a full-fledged director. *Calling Dr. Death* was only the third of these, and while he appears to have invested his all in its direction, it was clearly a departure from the musically-oriented films that had been his forte.

There are, unfortunately, a number of genuinely irritating aspects to the film, including music director Paul Sawtell's clumsy use of stock music at every moment of mystery or suspense, and Chaney's ear-shattering "whispered" voice-over stream of consciousness that overstays its welcome, and early on. Only minutes into the film are we subjected to a lengthy, plot-advancing soliloquy that bears repeating here, if only for a taste of what the viewer has to suffer through, ad infinitum:

"Hell hath no fury ..."
Patricia Morison wields a poker in *Calling Dr. Death* (1943).

> Neurology, neurology. The results are beyond imagination. To penetrate man's mind intrigues me more and more, even after eight years of practice. It's still fascinating, and there's satisfaction in being successful. Successful—yes, with everyone but myself. My personal life is a failure. After two years of marriage to Maria, it's no-go. We were terribly in love from the moment we met, at least I was. She certainly fooled me. So beautiful—she wore a perfect mask. I couldn't see beyond it. Dr. Mark Steele, neurologist, can't read his own wife's mind. Everybody else could, everybody else did. Even Stella knows it, she probably knew it the day I married Maria. Stella's a fine person. She's not only a nurse; she's my co-worker and confidant. I depend on her more and more. Five o'clock—how I wish the hands would never move. My work keeps me occupied, I don't think of myself. Now I've got

---

[5] "LeBorg Gains Papers," *Hollywood Reporter*, July 16, 1937, 18.

to go home to her. I dread it, but I must face it. It's bad to run away from things you fear. They mustn't be allowed to beat you.

And so on, while we are forced to watch Chaney at his most tortured. Screenwriter Dein later recalled that this voiceover device was implemented primarily because Chaney had difficulty with some of the more complicated dialog, and couldn't effectively deliver it on camera.[6] A more charitable explanation would be that the device was a conscious attempt to evoke the feel of listening to a radio play or reading from a book, where characters are able to reveal their innermost thoughts, something that's lacking in virtually all films. And for good reason, as evidenced here. Contemporary reviewers were quick to pounce on the device: "[T]he stream-of-consciousness soundtrack spiel by the doctor (precisely the kind of thing used too much in radio) is artificial and distracting," complained *Variety*'s Hobe Morrison.[7] "What suspense is attained occasionally is dissipated by Mr. Chaney's sepulchral 'voice' breaking in on the murderer investigation," noted a *New York Times* reviewer.[8] Undaunted by the reviewers' carping, this voice-over device would be used repeatedly throughout the series, although not always as a "whisper."

Fortune finally smiled on Pivar at this time, and Universal rewarded him for his hard work, dedication, and the profitability of his small films. Shortly before shooting commenced on *Calling Dr. Death*, the October 9, 1943, issue of *Boxoffice* announced Pivar's promotion at Universal: "Ben Pivar, who for five years has been an Associate Producer at Universal, has been promoted to a post as one of the studio's Supervising Production Executives. He will have supervision over a number of features, the western output and short subjects."[9]

Calling Dr. Death was Pivar's final credit as associate producer. From then on he was Ben Pivar, Executive Producer, and while the westerns and short subjects were now part of his purview, the films on which he would devote his greatest energies and on which his name would appear would all be of the horror and psychological thriller genres—for a couple of years, at least.

Weird Woman
(Director: Reginald LeBorg; Released April 14, 1944)

Originally announced back in July as *Conjure Wife*, the second "Inner Sanctum" mystery was retitled *Weird Woman* by the time filming begun in December

---

[6] Tom Weaver and John Brunas, "Reginald LeBorg: 50 Years of Horror Filmmaking," *Fantastic Films*, June 1985, #44, 46.

[7] Hobe Morrison, "Calling Dr. Death," *Variety*, December 9, 1943, 8.

[8] A.W., "The Screen," *New York Times*, February 12, 1944, 11.

[9] "Ben Pivar is Promoted to U Supervising Post," *Boxoffice*, October 9, 1943, 39.

The Inner Sanctum Mysteries, Part I (1943-1944)

1943. The first film version of Fritz Lieber, Jr.'s recently-published novel *Conjure Wife*, and the first Universal release with Pivar acting as executive producer (with Oliver Drake as associate), *Weird Woman* arrived on theater screens in April 1944.

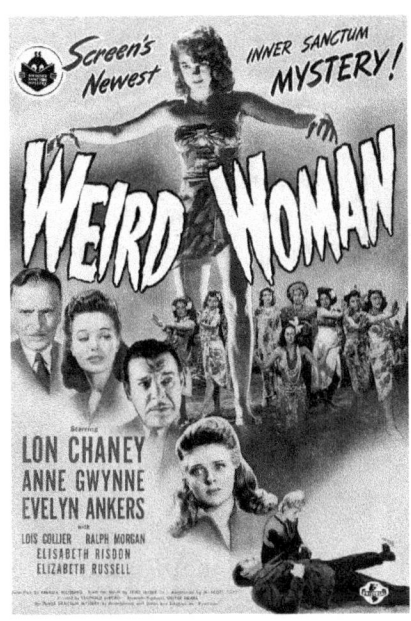

Weird Woman (1944). Image courtesy of Heritage Auction Galleries, Ha.com.

Norman Reed (Chaney), a professor of ethnology at Monroe College, is hard at work late one night writing a book. He thinks to himself (out loud, of course): "Man's struggle upward from his dark past is the struggle of reason against superstition." His thoughts are interrupted by a call from neighbor Evelyn Sawtelle (Elizabeth Russell). She claims she just spotted Norman's wife Paula (Anne Gwynne) returning home, and expresses concern for her wellbeing. Norman is convinced that Paula is in bed asleep, but decides to double-check. She is in bed, all right, but finding some shells near her bed and mud on the steps, he realizes that she had left and returned without his knowing it. "Is she still clinging to the weird pagan rituals of the islands where I first met her?" he wonders, the viewer privy to his thoughts courtesy of the recurring voice-overs. Dissolve to a flashback of explorer Norman arriving at the scene of one of those pagan rituals on some unnamed South Pacific island. They are performing the Dance of Death, performed around a voodoo doll-like figure in a dish of water. Paula is the only white woman there, and she warns Norman against crossing an unseen line that would result in his sacrifice to the gods. When he recognizes her as the freckle-faced kid he remembers from years back, she explains that her nurse brought her here. Norman stupidly crosses the line, and is saved only by the intervention of Paula's former nurse, now a high priestess, who places a Circle of Immunity around him and eventually secures his release.

Norman and Paula, now married, return to his home near the college campus. He takes her to a homecoming party thrown by former flame Ilona Carr (Evelyn Ankers), who throws a private snit when she learns of his marriage. Later, Ilona attempts to cozy up to Norman by requesting to aid him with his research, but when he instead insists on using pretty young student Margaret Mercer (Lois Collier), Ilona is now hellbent to get even with the guy she feels has two-timed her.

Evelyn Ankers (right) turns a cold shoulder to Chaney's new wife Anne Gwynne at his homecoming party in *Weird Woman* (1944).

Norman is the toast of the campus due to the well-received publication of his book *Superstition vs. Reason and Fact*, so much so that he has risen to the top of the list of candidates for the coveted Sociology Chairman position. This doesn't sit well with his ambitious neighbor Evelyn, who is determined to see that her meek husband Professor Millard Sawtelle (Ralph Morgan) gets the position; after all, doesn't he have seniority and his own successful book, *Moral Patterns in Primitive Society*?

Ilona quietly goes to work undermining Norman at every turn. She convinces Evelyn that the position is, by all rights, her husband's, but that Paula's good looks are working in Norman's favor. Aware of Paula's superstitious upbringing, Ilona takes it one step further: "That little doll-faced wife of Norman's is really a witch wife!" Evelyn's mind is now thoroughly poisoned toward the couple. Sophomore David Jennings (Phil Brown), already jealous of his girlfriend Margaret's admiration for Norman, is easily convinced by Ilona that Norman has lascivious intentions.

The big lie is reserved for Millard Sawtelle, however. Ilona knows that his book was really the work of a former student who died mid-term ten years earlier before his thesis could be published. Oozing sympathy, she confronts Millard and tells him that Norman has requested a copy of the student's unpublished paper. He'll no doubt use it, she convinces Millard, to discredit Millard and secure the position of department chairman for himself.

When Norman spots Paula sneaking out late one night, he follows her to the cemetery and catches her mid-ritual. He drags her home along with all of her trinkets and her beloved medallion, and tosses them in the fire. She pleads with him not to, as her rituals were the only thing warding off Norman's enemies, of whom she is convinced there are many. Perhaps he should have listened to her—as the medallion explodes in a shower of sparks, a gunshot is heard next door. Evidently the thought of humiliation was more than Millard could bear, and he shot and killed himself. Evelyn is now in a righteous fury, accusing both Norman and Paula of murder. Norman begins to doubt his own reason and logic.

Later, student assistant Margaret, obsessed with Norman and convinced his feelings are mutual, cozies up to him. He explodes over her "romantic twaddle," and sends her packing. She is devastated, and boyfriend David is convinced that her tears are a result of lascivious actions on Norman's part. He ineffectually confronts Norman, and ends up tossed on his ear.

Paula's grasp on mental stability grows more tenuous after a series of phone calls where she hears the pagan "death chant" at the other end of the line; a nervous breakdown seems imminent. Ilona gloats over the news that the college has hired a professor named Henshaw, luring him there with the promise of the department chairmanship. When she informs Norman of this and he seems to take it in stride, she is even more furious. Norman heads for the gym to clear his mind, but pesky David shows up with a pistol. David is accidentally shot as the two struggle, and hangs on to life by a thread. Norman is jailed, but sympathetic Dean of Women Grace Gunnison (Elisabeth Risdon) bails him out.

Meanwhile, Evelyn has confronted Paula, screaming that Ilona was right, that Paula is a murderer and should go back to the jungle. Norman arrives home to find Evelyn standing over Paula, who has fainted. Evelyn launches into a tirade about the thesis, but when Norman disavows any knowledge of it, it suddenly dawns on Evelyn that Ilona has been playing her all along. Regaining her senses, she admits that Ilona was behind the "death chant" recordings that have been spooking Paula. When Ilona calls Evelyn soon after and tells her that David has died, Evelyn agrees to help Norman expose Ilona.

Evelyn calls Ilona to her house and shows her a "voodoo" doll with pins in its head. She tells her of a dream she had where the doll represented the woman who has spread all the lies that have resulted in two deaths. That woman has thirteen days to live, and will die of strangulation at one minute after midnight. The seed now planted in Ilona's increasingly out-of-kilter mind, Ilona spends the following thirteen days haunted by the thought that death is near, waking up the last day with a classic Ankers scream. Minutes before the thirteenth day is to end, she heads to Evelyn's house and demands the doll—she wants to destroy it. When Evelyn balks, Ilona admits to everything, not realizing that Norman, Paula, Margaret, and Grace are all close by and hear her confession. Confronted by them, she attempts to escape by the window and over a pergola. She loses her footing, and strangles to death from some inconveniently situated vines in the broken trellis work overhead. It is one minute after midnight.

One has to give Chaney credit for trying, but he really is in over his head with this series. The urbane characters he portrays cry out for a more polished actor, but it is Chaney's series and we're stuck with him. Fortunately, he is a likeable lug, so make do with the recurring moments of awkwardness and accept him as the lead, warts and all. As for Evelyn Ankers, this "bitch" role is perfect for her, taking advantage of her below-the-surface hardness and icy demeanor. She seems to revel playing the villain for a change, and rewards us with one of her famously pitch-perfect screams toward the film's end as she awakens from her nightmare. Anne Gwynne is lovely as the superstitious wife Paula, vulnerable and haunted while working behind the scenes for her husband's betterment, and Lois Collier is sufficiently perky as the love-struck student, turning on the tears when her fantasies evaporate before her. It is Elizabeth Russell as the cold and calculating Evelyn Sawtelle who sticks with you after seeing the film, giving a downright frightening, but ultimately sympathetic, performance as the ambitious, domineering wife to Ralph Morgan's timid professor. Incredibly, she was only twenty-seven when this film was made, looking a good twenty years older than that here, and a good match for the book's description of the character ("Her ... angular face, with its shoe-button eyes...").

Elisabeth Risdon rounds out the female-heavy cast, perfect as the no-nonsense, straight-talking Dean of Women. Phil Brown, as ill-fated student David, fares less well, quickly growing tiresome with his all-consuming jealousy and incessant whining; no wonder Margaret is ready to dump him for someone with even a modicum of maturity.

Would you believe twenty-seven? Elizabeth Russell is downright chilling as Evelyn Sawtelle in *Weird Woman* (1944).

As far as adaptations go, *Weird Woman* bears little resemblance beyond the basic premise to the book upon which it was based. Some character and location names were altered (Norman and Paula Reed vs. the book's Norman and Tansy Saylor, Millard Sawtelle vs. Hervey Sawtelle, Grace Gunnison vs. Gulda Gunnison, Monroe College vs. Hempnell College), while others remained unchanged. Perhaps the biggest switcheroo came with the three women, Evelyn Sawtelle, Grace Gunnison, and Ilona (simply "Mrs." in the book) Carr, and their participation in the tale being spun. In *Conjure Wife*, all three of them practice black magic, and are all over poor Tansy when understandably close-minded Norman forces her to abandon her protective white magic. The book's number of "surprises," and its extremely satisfying denouement have all been abandoned for the film's more straightforward tale of jealousy, revenge, and the occult. What is retained, however, and happily so, is the underlying, unresolved question as to whether all of the occult hocus pocus actually works, or is it all simply a function of the characters' minds convincing them that it works. All in all, the book—by now an acknowledged classic tale of horror—is far superior to the film's simplistic reworking of the basic plotline and scriptwriter Brenda Weisberg's altering and combining of author Lieber's more complex characters.

While not a great film, *Weird Woman* is very watchable in its own modest way, and admittedly a hell of a lot of fun. Reginald LeBorg once again delivers the goods as director, if in a somewhat less showy fashion than his previous effort. There are some nicely lit night-for-night shots, and one exterior taken on an atypically chilly California night where you can see Chaney's exhalation in the cold. The montage of Ankers slowly descending into haunted madness over her final thirteen days is nicely executed, her victims both living and dead "speaking" to her, and recurring encounters with numbers that remind her of the days left before her impending doom. Her death by hanging, seen only in shadow, brings a satisfying end to the villainess of the piece. Like its predecessor, the film's plusses are with LeBorg's direction, and the usual competent performances. There are, of course, some unintentionally laughable moments, such as the island-based "Dance of Death" that looks more like a performance for tourists at Hawaii's Oahu-based Polynesian Cultural Center. (We're even treated to a "Spielberg Sky," complete with shooting star!) And as typically slick looking as this production is, there's one visually jarring snippet of stock footage of a college with a Monroe College gate and sign clumsily matted in over it. Another of those inattention-to-detail loose ends that recur with nagging regularity in the B's pops up here: Ankers' character is listed as *Ilona* in the credits, but is spelled *Illona* on the plaque on her office door.

Critics were not overwhelmed by the results, but generally gave it a passing grade. "Picture hits slow pace in early reels to establish characters and foundation for the series of mysterious events, after which it gains momentum and fairly fast clip through directorial efforts of Reginald LeBorg," observed *Variety*.[10] *Boxoffice* was more positive with its assessment: "[T]he film is well handled in every department, and patrons should find it engrossing . . . ."[11] Bosley Crowther, of course, gave another one of his annoyingly condescending reviews in *The New York Times*, wrapping it up with his oh-so clever punch line "Weird, isn't it? And, boy, is it dull."[12] Cute.

Leiber's novel *Conjure Wife* made several subsequent journeys to screens both large and small. The story was presented as *Conjure Wife* on NBC's *Moment of Fear* television series on July 8, 1960. A better, more proper, treatment followed two years later in director Sidney Hayers' 1962 British version *Night*

---

[10] Walt., "Weird Woman," *Variety*, March 30, 1944, 14.

[11] "Feature Reviews," *Boxoffice*, April 8, 1944, 521.

[12] Bosley Crowther, "The Screen," *New York Times*, April 1, 1944, 11.

Stop Yellin'

of the Eagle, scripted by prolific horror and science-fiction writer Charles Beaumont and released in the United States as *Burn, Witch, Burn*. The Teri Garr-Richard Benjamin spoof *Witches' Brew* was the most recent adaptation in 1980, and a rather unfortunate one at that.

The Westerns

While Pivar never received on-screen credit for any of the westerns or shorts that were now part of his charge, a series of Rod Cameron oaters resulted and were released in 1944 and 1945. Pivar served as executive producer, with Oliver Drake receiving credit as associate producer and a revolving set of directors behind the megaphone. Pivar's previous experience over at Columbia a dozen years earlier with the Buck Jones westerns served as preparation for overseeing another low-budget series, this one with new-to-Universal Cameron.

A Realart re-release poster for *Boss of Boomtown* (1944). Image courtesy of Heritage Auction Galleries, Ha.com.

A towering, lanky replacement at the studio for the departed Johnny Mack Brown, Cameron was formerly at different times a stunt double for Buck Jones, a bit player, and serial lead at various studios before Universal signed him for these westerns. All of these (with one exception) co-starred Fuzzy Knight and Eddie Dew. Former vaudevillian and Johnny Mack Brown-sidekick (and no stranger to Pivar) Knight was kept on board for his usual questionable comic relief. Eddie Dew, in mostly uncredited bit roles since the mid-thirties (including Pivar's *Timber*), had been given the lead in Republic's "John Paul Revere" western series in 1943. With Smiley Burnette as his sidekick, Dew failed to click with audiences and was let go after only two films in the failed series; he was picked up by Universal.

The Cameron-Knight westerns executive produced by Pivar included *Boss of Boomtown* (1944; Ray Taylor), *Trigger Trail* (1944; Lewis Collins), *Riders of the Santa Fe* (1944; Wallace Fox), *Beyond the Pecos* (1945; Lambert Hillyer), and *Renegades of the Rio Grande* (1945; Howard Bretherton). Eddie Dew costarred in most of these, with the first—*Boss of Boomtown*—the sole exception. A sixth, *Trail to Gunsight* (1944; Vernon Keays), starred only Dew and Knight, Cameron otherwise occupied with another production at Universal. Typical oaters all, they still had abundant action and the usual slick Universal production values. There was one more in the series, *The Old Texas Trail* (1944; Lewis D. Collins), that co-starred the three of them, but Pivar's name has not yet been connected with this film.

A belated review a year-and-a-half after the initial release of *Beyond the Pecos* summed up Cameron's persona thusly: "Rod Cameron's complete ease and rugged cinematic ways have paid their dividends already, but it is just such a vehicle as this that displays his ability at its solid best. Certainly his mere screen presence practically fulfills the Zane Grey ideal—and is so effortlessly convincing."[13]

While both Cameron and Knight's careers continued with film and television

Eddie Dew looking stern and compact in *Trail to Gunsight* (1944). Image courtesy of Heritage Auction Galleries, Ha.com.

work into the late seventies and sixties, respectively, Dew's career took a different turn. Heading to New York later in 1945, Dew—appearing as Edward Dew—had a small role in the Broadway revival of Victor Herbert's operetta *The Red Mill* ("Edward Dew—a good voice, this last," praised *New York Times* reviewer Lewis Nichols[14]), and followed it with a more prominent role in the musical comedy *If the Shoe Fits* late in 1946. Of this latter role, *New York Times* critic Brooks Atkinson remarked, "Edward Dew, who plays Prince Charming, has an excellent baritone voice."[15] Sandwiched in between these two productions, Dew reportedly headed "South of the Border for a series of Gaucho (Mexican horse opera) films;"[16] whether these actually came to fruition is unknown. Dew resurfaced in the occasional television show and the random film role in the fifties and sixties, his short Broadway career now well behind him.

---

[13] "Beyond the Pecos," *Hollywood Reporter*, March 22, 1946, 3.

[14] Lewis Nichols, "The Play," *New York Times*, October 17, 1945, 27.

[15] Brooks Atkinson, "The Play," *New York Times*, December 6, 1946, 29.

[16] Hedda Hopper, "Looking at Hollywood," *Los Angeles Times*, January 14, 1946, 9.

The budget estimates for the first five confirmed films demonstrate that these westerns were produced in a cookie-cutter approach with standardized fees, schedules, and expectations. $55,000 was the goal cost for each, factoring in the studio's standard 25% overhead. Of the five that Pivar oversaw as executive producer over the three-month period mid-April 1944 into July, the estimated budgets ranged from a low of $53,800 to a high of $55,300. Eight-day shooting schedules were the norm, based on a six-day work week, with 32,000 feet of negative stock allocated for each. Adaptation and continuity for original stories ranged from $1,480 to $1,720. Combined salaries for lead players, supporting cast, and bit players ranged from $9,800 to $11,025 per film, an average of 23½% of the films' direct charges. Directors—and there was a different one for each of the five—were paid a flat fee of $1,000 for the first two films, and $1,050 for the last three figured on a three-week schedule at $350 per week. The cameraman and his assistants were paid a flat $1,600 for the first two and $1,700 last three. Editors received a flat $1,700. Pivar was paid a flat fee of $600 per film to broadly oversee production, and his associate producer, Oliver Drake, a flat fee of $2,600 for doing most of the production grunt work. Pivar's secretary Helen McLemore was paid $150 each for being at Pivar's beck and call. And, of course, in each instance $150 was allocated for Pivar's beloved stock footage.

Beyond the Pecos (1945). Image courtesy of Heritage Auction Galleries, Ha.com.

Music played a part in each of these, with rights to the various songs acquired for $50 per song. Popular twenties ukulele-playing crooner Johnny Marvin (aka "Honey Duke and His Uke") was paid for *Trigger Trail*'s "Long About Sundown," and Ray Whitley (of the singing Bar Six Cowboys) for "Twilight on the Prairie." An outfit named American Music, Inc. was the recipient of the checks for *Riders of the Santa Fe*'s "South of the Rio Grande" and "Bed Down, Bed Down, Little Dogies," and for *Beyond the Pecos*' "Dusty Trail" and "Ridin' High." In each of these instances Pivar was the one to select and approve each song used, and to authorize payment for same.

The Inner Sanctum Mysteries, Part I (1943-1944)

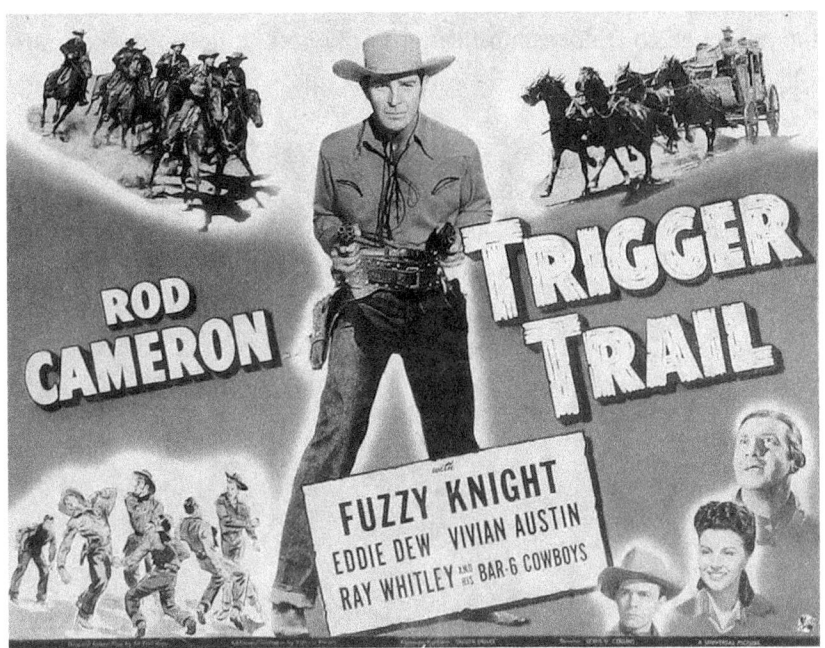

Rod Cameron with six-shooters drawn in *Trigger Trail* (1944).
Image courtesy of Heritage Auction Galleries, Ha.com.

While the plotlines were consistently unremarkable and routine, the films were all fast moving and action-filled. Universal's typical production gloss added immensely to the finished films, with the cinematography of William Sickner and Maury Gertsman a decided asset, in spite of repeated cost-cutting day-for-night sequences. Consistent with most low-budget westerns, a preponderance of the action takes place outdoors, with interior sets kept to a minimum. *Renegades of the Rio Grande*, a typical entry in the series, has only three: the jail, the saloon, and the Rancho Rio Lindo interior. The film's storyline is representative of the series: Buck Emerson (Cameron) spends the film attempting to retrieve a map to the buried $50,000 stolen from the Vista Grande Bank so that he can return it to its rightful owner, lovely Dolores Salezar (Jennifer Holt). Buck's brother Johnny (John James) was part of the gang led by Bart Drummond (Glenn Strange) that robbed the bank, but when Johnny found that the money belonged to his good friend Dolores, he ran off with the loot, buried it, and contacted his brother Buck to help return it. Drummond and his gang pursue them, kill Johnny, and take Buck prisoner thinking he knows where the money is buried. Buck escapes, helped by Rangers Cal Benedict (Dew) and Trigger Bidwell (Knight), but the map is left behind, hidden in Buck's holster that Bart has taken for his own. Bart, of course, doesn't realize this. Five songs and three fistfights later, Buck, Cal, and Trigger overcome Bart, with an assist by quick-to-sing ranch hand Tex Henry (Ray Whitley). Bart is taken prisoner, the map returned to Dolores, and Knight only gets to belt out one marginally amusing song.

Ray Whitley (right) breaks into an obligatory song for Jennifer Holt (left), Rod Cameron (second from left), and Iris Cleve (center).
Renegades of the Rio Grande (1945).
Photo courtesy of Boyd Magers at Western Clippings,
www.westernclippings.com.

Pivar reputedly executive produced over thirty westerns while at Universal, but the ones cited above are the only ones positively linked to him as of this writing. Others will probably come to light in the years to come.

§

15 Cheela Has a Makeover

The suits at Universal wanted some more horror films added to the schedule, and lower-budget ones at that. Pivar had proven himself in both regards, demonstrating time and again that he could function efficiently within the predetermined confines of budget and schedule, and having successfully ushered a pair of mummy sequels to the screen. Whether he was instructed to come up with the new character, or did so on his own is unknown, the result was the same: the saga of Cheela and her humanoid alter ego Paula Dupree.

Captive Wild Woman
(Director: Edward Dmytryk; Released June 4, 1943)

There is some confusion regarding *Captive Wild Woman*'s pedigree. *Captive Wild Woman* was originally named as a feature for the 1941-1942 season,[1] "featuring a new type of star aimed to capture the interest of novelty seekers."[2] Writer Ainsworth Morgan was working on a story with the same title back in April 1941, slated to star Maria Montez.[3] By August the film had undergone a title change to *White Savage*, and had a cast that included Brian Donlevy, Broderick Crawford, and Andy Devine.[4] It was finally released in October as *South of Tahiti*, with newspaper ads still referencing the film's original title:

---

[1] "Universal Plans 61 Films in Season," *New York Times*, February 11, 1941, page unknown.

[2] "'U' Hammers Away on Star Lineup," *Boxoffice*, February 15, 1941, 15-16.

[3] Douglas W. Churchill, "Screen News Here and in Hollywood," *New York Times*, April 26, 1941, 20.

[4] Douglas W. Churchill, "Screen News Here and in Hollywood," *New York Times*, August 25, 1941, 18.

"Captive Wild Woman! Queen of Love . . . of Men and Beasts! Holding the fate of three men in her enchantment . . . in a Pagan Paradise where a white man's love was TABU! SOUTH of TAHITI."

Pivar's *Captive Wild Woman* was announced late in 1942, erroneously tagged by columnist Edwin Schallert as "a sarong picture with mystery thriller motifs," with up-and-coming director Edward Dmytryk borrowed from RKO and signed for those duties.[5] Griffin Jay and Henry Sucher were assigned to write the script back in July 1942,[6] practically a year before the film would hit screens. Adapted from an original story written by Ted Fithian and Pivar (using his *nom de plume* "Neil P. Varnick"), Pivar's brother Murray reportedly took part in structuring the treatment as well, but was conspicuously absent from the credits for what I can only assume was a good reason. Aside from the two mummy sequels that had been successfully entrusted to Pivar's stewardship, it would be Pivar's first all-out horror film, with only a trace of the comic relief present in so many of his previous efforts. *Captive Wild Woman* would be the first in a three-film series attempt to launch yet another horrific creation, and unlike its two rather depressing sequels is quite entertaining and at times quite exciting. Makeup artist Jack Pierce reportedly made a plaster mold of lead actress Acquanetta's body in preparation for developing the half-human appliances required to transform "the screen's first feminine 'horror star'" into the title character,[7] overkill if accurate in that only her hands, feet, and face are ever displayed in the film in their hirsute state.

The poster image would seem to have Cheela picking herself up as Paula Dupree in *Captive Wild Woman* (1943). Image courtesy of Heritage Auction Galleries, Ha.com.

---

[5] Edwin Schallert, "Hither and Yon With Stars," *Los Angeles Times*, December 7, 1942, 24.

[6] "Hollywood Personnelities," *Boxoffice*, June 27, 1942, 37.

[7] Harrison Carroll, "Behind the Scenes in Hollywood," *The Era*, December 22, 1942, 13.

Cheela Has a Makeover

Animal trainer Fred Mason (Milburn Stone), an employee of John Whipple's Circus, returns from Africa with his catch of twenty tigers, twenty lions, six zebras, eleven leopards, and a female gorilla he has named Cheela who seems to be overly fond of her captor. Greeted by his girl (and Whipple's secretary) Beth Coleman (Evelyn Ankers), Beth fills him in during the cab ride home on her sister Dorothy's (Martha MacVicar) health problems. Plagued by a glandular disorder, Beth had taken Dorothy to see Dr. Sigmund Walters (John Carradine) at his Crestview Sanatorium. Walters is a noted scientist, renowned (?) for his "three attempts in racial improvement" and his discovery of vitamin E2, which determines the physical characteristics in all forms of animal life— or something like that. He has had a number of successes improving the appearances of the deformed, but so far success has eluded him in changing the breed and sex of animals. While this litany of past scientific dabblings might scare off the average person, young Dorothy is made of sterner stuff. Walters agrees to keep Dorothy on as a live-in patient.

Invited by Beth to the circus' winter quarters, Walters meets Mason and gets a tour of the place. When he is "introduced" to the caged Cheela, Walters observes that the gorilla is of above-average intelligence, and quickly decides that he wants Cheela for his experiments. To that end he hires Gruen (Paul Fix), a drunken animal handler recently fired for mistreating Cheela, to gorilla-nap her. Gruen does so, but as "payment" Walters hands Gruen over to Cheela who quickly dispatches him off screen. The following day's headlines offer up the sensational "Nails of Beast Press Through Back of Neck Severing Spinal Cord." Now *that's* a headline!

Walters begins his experiments now using Dorothy, who has the misfortune of having a "rare case of a follicular cyst, which induces the secretion of unusual amounts of the sex hormones," as his guinea pig. Multiple blood transfusions follow, with unconscious Dorothy the unwitting donor, and Cheela the recipient. Miss Strand (Fay Helm), Walters' assistant for the past thirteen years, has growing objections to these transfusions, and finally gives voice to them: "I can't have my hands stained with human blood," she pleads. Observing that all of Walters' animal donors have died, she fears that Dorothy will follow suit. Bad move on her part, as Walters makes a spur-of-the-moment decision to kill her and use her cerebrum for a Cheela transplant. As a result of all of Walters' tinkering, Cheela transforms into an exotic beauty he dubs Paula Dupree (Acquanetta). His first order of business with the newly-hatched Paula: introduce her to Mason and see if that deep-seated affection for her captor will bubble up to the surface.

Meanwhile, Mason is planning to beef up his act with the introduction of both lions and tigers into the cage with him at the same time, with killer-lion Nero thrown into the mix. Whipple (Lloyd Corrigan) balks at this, fearing the worst will come to his trainer, but Mason persists and finally breaks the old fellow down. Walters arrives with tight-lipped Paula, whose arrival makes the circus' animals uneasy. Spotting Mason in the ring, a smile cracks on Paula's otherwise immobile face, and it's clear that she is in love with her old "friend."

When Mason's training session goes awry and as he is being mauled by a lion, a fearless Paula steps into the cage and scares off the lion with a bug-eyed stare. Mason is rescued.

Amazed at the unspoken control Paula has over the animals, Mason convinces Whipple to hire her solely to stand just outside the big cage and exert her silent influence over the lions and tigers therein. Whipple reluctantly agrees, and now with Paula's silent presence Mason is able to accomplish amazing feats with his now-cowed beasts, Paula making goo-goo eyes at him all the while.

John Carradine gives Acquanetta a first look at her old boyfriend, and the audience a first look at Acquanetta. *Captive Wild Woman* (1943).

The night of the big dress rehearsal arrives, and Mason gives a rousing performance. The snarling Nero is brought in at the last moment, and much to everyone's surprise. At the performance's conclusion, however, Paula sees Mason and Beth in a loving, celebratory embrace, and Paula's smile turns to jealous anger. She storms into her dressing room and soon realizes that she is reverting to a Paula-Cheela mix.

Fired up with hatred for her unwelcome competitor, Paula-Cheela makes her way over to the boarding house where Beth lives, with murder in mind. Beth's landlady has the misfortune of responding to Beth's screams, and ends up with a severed spinal cord for her efforts. Paula-Cheela heads back to Walters' lab. Walters is incensed by what he sees, and berates her for the regression, informing her that he'll need to perform the transfusions and brain transplant all over again. Beth, shaken by her confrontation, takes Mason into her confidence. She insists that she recognized Paula's face in the beast that attacked her, and somehow or other made the Cheela-Paula connection. Mason scoffs at this, and with good reason.

The first stage in the Paula-to-Cheela regression in *Captive Wild Woman* (1943).

Stage two of the regression. *Captive Wild Woman* (1943).

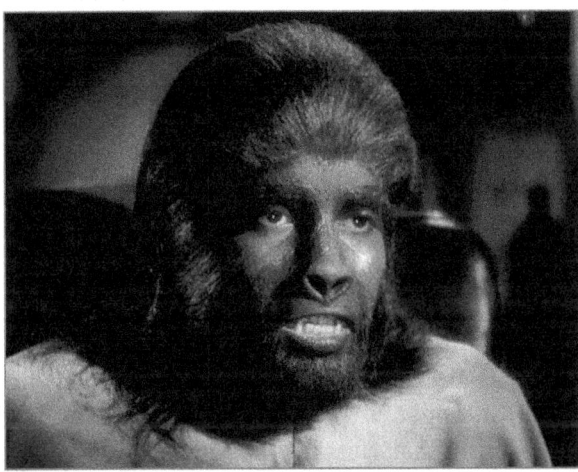

Stage three, but not yet in full-simian mode. *Captive Wild Woman* (1943).

A storm is looming on the night of the circus' reopening, and Whipple is concerned that it might agitate the animals. When Paula fails to show, Whipple's concern prompts him to tell Mason to cancel the act. Mason, trouper that he is, says that the show must go on. Meanwhile, Dorothy, informed that Walters is going to perform another round of procedures, calls Beth in a panic. Walters intervenes and cuts the line, prompting Beth to head over to the sanatorium. This is just what Walters wants, now planning to use Beth's cerebrum for the second transplant into the now fully-regressed and caged Cheela. Beth beats him to the punch, releasing a now fully-regressed Cheela from her cage and freeing Dorothy. Cheela turns her attention to Walters and proceeds to sever spine number three. Cheela leaves the two women behind, and heads back to the circus. Beth and Dorothy follow.

Back at the circus, Mason is giving his lion-and-tiger-taming performance and seems to be getting by without Paula's inert participation. That is, until the storm hits. All hell breaks loose, and the panicking animals break out. While the terrified patrons scramble to get out of the place, Mason and the circus handlers attempt to corral the beasts. Nero gets the best of Mason and begins to maul him when Cheela arrives, scares off the lion and carries Mason to safety. Not recognizing the gorilla for the good Samaritan that she is, a trigger-happy cop shoots Cheela, killing her. Beth and Dorothy arrive, Mason is carried off to have his wounds treated, and the film comes to an atypically abrupt end.

For anyone willing to overlook the absurdities of the premise, and the pseudo-scientific mumbo-jumbo that accompanies it, *Captive Wild Woman* is an enjoyable little film, and heads and tails above its two lifeless successors. Director Dmytryk does some stylish work here, delivering some nicely composed setups and well-chosen camera angles. A former editor, Dmytryk moved into direction of B's at Paramount, Columbia, and RKO, with this his final low-budget film and sole effort for Universal. Dmytryk's fortunes turned as a result of the surprise success of his *Hitler's Children* for RKO, released at the beginning of 1943 during *Captive*'s production. *Tender Comrade* (1943), *Murder, My Sweet* (1944), and *Back to Bataan* (1945; all for RKO) were the bigger-budget films to follow, and Dmytryk never looked back.

Editor Milton Carruth rises to the occasion, piecing together the new footage shot by cinematographer George Robinson with the huge amounts of stock footage. The stock was lifted from Universal's 1933 feature *The Big Cage* (Kurt Neumann), in which famed animal trainer Clyde Beatty appeared as himself and showcased his considerable talents in the caged ring. A lot of this older footage is cleverly integrated into the film as rear-projections for newly-shot foreground action, such as in the scene where Mason, Whipple, and Walters, all in foreground, observe the caged lions and tigers. Every time leading man Stone has to interact with the animals, it is Beatty we see in long shot doing the dirty work. While there are some physical similarities in their dark, wavy hair, in general Stone and Beatty look about as much alike as Abbott and Costello. If you keep your eyes on the animals and go with the flow, however, it all seems to work somehow. It sure doesn't hurt that the old footage is genuinely thrilling, edge-of-your-seat type stuff, and a wise choice for reuse in a B film of this sort. So much footage of Beatty is used, in fact, that the opening credits pause for the shout-out, "We hereby make grateful acknowledgement to Mr. Clyde Beatty for his cooperation and inimitable talent in staging the thrilling animal sequences in this picture." The cooperation probably boiled down to an "okay" and perhaps a small token payment, but without Beatty's footage the film could not have been made. Beatty's impressive accomplishments, unfortunately, are diminished somewhat by the film's premise that it is Paula's presence that keeps the beasts in check rather than the capabilities of a real live human being. Contemporary filmgoers would have to go see him at his circus to get the full impact.

Cheela Has a Makeover

Actor Vince Barnett, who has the bit role of Curley, the not-too-dependable animal feeder, had a role in the former film as well. This further helped tie the new footage together with the old. The B film expedient of using montages to tighten up running time is back, first in a lengthy scene capsulizing Walters' multiple transfusions between Dorothy and Cheela and the first stages of the latter's transformation into something less simian, followed by a later sequence condensing Mason's many training sessions abetted by Paula's wordless presence outside the big cage. George Robinson's new footage is typically effective, with one judiciously employed crane shot over the diners in a nightclub, settling in on Walters pitching the gorilla-heist idea to Gruen.

Acquanetta, born Burnu Acquanetta in 1920, was a former model with little previous film experience. The opening credits read "Introducing Acquanetta," somewhat misleading in that she'd already appeared in several previous Universal films. Her debut as an uncredited harem girl in *Arabian Nights* (1942; John Rawlins) was followed (reportedly) as a member of a circus aerial act in a segment of *Flesh and Fantasy*[8] (1943; Julien Duvivier), and *Rhythm of the Islands* (working title *Isle of Romance*; 1943; Roy William Neill).

For a brief time in 1942, Universal's publicity department was headed by Lou Smith who, prior to his hiring in May 1942, had been involved with the publicity departments of both Columbia and Paramount.[9] Smith was the force behind promoting Acquanetta as "The Venezuelan Volcano," fabricating a more exotic background for her by claiming she was a Venezuelan of Indian descent. The cat was soon out of the bag, however, when she was required to show her passport while registering with the Screen Actors Guild. She couldn't, admitting she was an Indian from Wyoming.[10] (After a brief four months, Smith abandoned Universal for the grander MGM and was replaced by Paramount transplant Terry DeLapp.)[11] Here in her first lead role, Acquanetta gives a silent, one-dimensional performance that requires her to do little more than maintain a blank expression, with only occasional forays into emotion with a slight smile, eye-widened intensity, or a furrowed brow to suggest anger. Her on-screen regression from pretty Paula to a slobbering half-Paula, half-Cheela is effectively presented, her skin first darkening, followed by several dissolves where her hairline lowers and her teeth grow prominent; makeup artist Pierce and director of photography Robinson work well together on this transition. Wisely, Acquanetta has no dialogue in this film and little in its sequel, as I doubt any more than that would have been an asset to either film. Having said that,

---

[8] Edwin Schallert, "Deceptive Burnu Gets Important Film 'Break,'" *Los Angeles Times*, August 10, 1942, 14.

[9] "Smith Heads Universal Studio Publicity," *Boxoffice*, May 9, 1942, 48.

[10] Schallert, *op. cit.*

[11] "DeLapp to Universal; Smith Joins MGM," *Boxoffice*, September 12, 1942, 58.

her dark, exotic, full-figured good looks are a nice fit with this film, and I am sure that adolescents were transfixed whenever the busty actress strode onto the screen in her sequined, two-piece circus attire. Their dads, too.

Giving an adequate, unassuming performance in the lead, Milburn Stone was probably chosen for the role due to his availability, past performances for Pivar, and vague physical similarity to Clyde Beatty. As it turns out, Beatty, in the ubiquitous stock footage, has almost as much screen time as Stone does. Universal rewarded Stone for his efforts, placing him under contract through March 1947. Playing opposite Stone is Evelyn Ankers and, yes, she is a good actress, and, yes, she can scream with the best of them. But as a leading lady she has a tough, almost coarse, edge to her that gets in the way of total audience identification. I have no idea why Lon Chaney, Jr., referred to her not-so-affectionately as Evelyn *Shankers*, but it is a memorable nickname and one that often comes to mind whenever the actress strides on screen. (This may not have been the correct spelling of the meaning that Chaney had intended, but I dutifully report it as spelled in an interview with Chaney's wife Patsy that appeared in *Filmfax*: "He didn't like her. He called her 'Shankers'—Evelyn Shankers.")[12]

This was seventeen-year-old Martha MacVicar's first credited film role, and it is a rather thankless one; she is speechless through most of it, with a good portion of her screen time spent motionless on one of Walters' operating tables. When she is conscious, she is usually sullen and sickly or sobbing into a phone for help. She is adorable, though, and better roles were to come when she eventually wound up at Warner Brothers, changed her last name to Vickers, and appeared as Lauren Bacall's sexpot little sister in Howard Hawks' *The Big Sleep*.

It is Carradine's film, of course, and it is one of those rare instances where he actually underplays his role and keeps his broader tendencies in check. Director Dmytryk should receive credit for reining in Carradine's performance, since it is doubtful that Carradine could ever exercise the self-restraint required left to his own devices. He is perfect here as the scientist with a single-minded obsession, that of "creating a race of super men," delivering his lines and making ridiculously over-the-top speeches with total conviction. Alas, this film marked a turning point of sorts for the unfortunate Carradine. After years of promise in the thirties and early forties in numerous effective supporting roles, Carradine began a slow descent after this film into a plethora of horror and mad doctor roles in which he seemed to be permanently, though not exclusively, typecast up to his death in 1988.

---

[12] Jack Gourley, "A Man, a Myth, and Many Monsters: Lon Chaney, Jr.," *Filmfax*, May 1990, No. 20, 53.

Reviewers dismissed the film as so much hokum, but begrudgingly admitted that it would go over well with lovers of this sort of thing. *Variety* gave its usual matter-of-fact review: "Another horror thriller, packed with the usual implausibilities, 'Captive Wild Woman' is an exploitable picture that should rack up some coin for Universal. While much of the plot is strictly off the cob, this film has enough excitement and strange elements to appease the thrill patrons. Should be a strong secondary attraction on twin bills."[13] *The New York Times* dismissed it, which shouldn't come as a shock: "[T]here are two ways of looking at 'Captive Wild Woman.' Either you decide to meet this bit of scientific hocus-pocus at its own inane level or else you are likely to get hopping mad, since there is nothing to recommend in the story or the performances. It all depends on the mood you're in. The picture as a whole is decidedly bad."[14] The *Los Angeles Times* review was only marginally better, but at least Philip K. Scheuer had something positive to say about the film's new "star": "'Captive Wild Woman' is more of the same, but on a trashier scale. It features Acquanetta—just Acquanetta—who has a lulu of a figure."[15] You look hard enough, you can find something good in most any film.

The most scathing criticism came in an editorial subtitled "HITLER GETS A FREE MOVIE" that appeared in the *California Eagle*, one of California's oldest African-American newspapers founded back in 1879:

> In *Mein Kampf*, that porridge of nonsense and witchcraft which has become the Nazi bible, Hitler screams:
>
> "... It is a criminal absurdity to train a born half-ape, until one believes a lawyer has been made of him ... it is a sin against the will of the eternal creator ..."
>
> And by "half-ape" Hitler makes clear he means all colored people.
>
> You can understand, then, why this columnist is dead against the latest free gift to Hitler's fifth Column, the latest boner from Hollywood, called CAPTIVE WILD WOMAN, just put out by Universal Pictures. In this movie, Universal Pictures peddles Hitler's tripe by showing an ape being turned into a Negro girl by a "scientist." Get it. The Negro is an ape, says smug Universal Pictures.

---

[13] Wear., "Captive Wild Woman," *Variety*, April 28, 1943, 8.

[14] Thomas M. Pryor, "The Screen," *New York Times*, June 7, 1943, 9.

[15] Philip K. Scheuer, "Chaney Meets Lugosi and Reviewer Orders Aspirin," *Los Angeles Times*, July 23, 1943, 15.

MEMO TO UNIVERSAL PICTURES: (address 120 Sixth Avenue, N.Y.C.) Patriotic Americans don't want any of your CAPTIVE WILD WOMAN with its Hitler porridge of racial slander. TAKE IT AWAY AND BURN IT.[16]

Historian Tom Weaver questioned Dmytryk about this controversy several decades later: "I didn't even *think* about that at the time, and neither did anybody else I know of. We got that criticism a little bit—not *too* damn much, but *I* heard it. (I never got any organized thing from any of the black societies; I guess they weren't that well-organized then.) But, the point is, what do you *do*? If you change a gorilla to a human being, gorillas are dark, and unfortunately you have to go through that intermediate stage. Not because blacks are intermediates, not because blacks are the Missing Link—not by *any* means! I think that's going too far, 'political correctness' long before its time."[17]

Jungle Woman
(Director: Reginald LeBorg; Released July 7, 1944)

*Captive Wild Wo*man had added another character to Universal's roster of creatures, and the new addition made money, so a little controversy or accusations of tastelessness was not about to keep Universal from cranking out a sequel. *Jungle Woman* was the result, released in July 1944. This time around J. Carrol Naish stars as Dr. Carl Fletcher, who nurses Cheela the ape back to bone-breaking health. As one would expect, Cheela eventually transforms into exotic Paula Dupree. Acquanetta, Evelyn Ankers, and Milburn Stone recreate their roles from the original, and John Carradine reappears as Dr. Walters in footage lifted from the original for the usual money-saving flashbacks, and when it comes to money-saving flashbacks, this one's packed with them. Pivar served as the film's executive producer, only his second credit as such, with Will Cowan assuming the position of associate producer. Henry Sucher was again signed to script the sequel to his previous effort, announced in the trades as *Jungle Queen*.[18] Filming took place in late February 1944, the film now bearing its release title *Jungle Woman*. Set decorator Russell A. Gausman

---

[16] M. Moran Weston, "I Take the People's Side," *California Eagle*, April 22, 1943, page unknown.

[17] Tom Weaver, *Science Fiction and Fantasy Film Flashbacks: Conversations with Twenty-Four Actors, Writers, Producers, and Directors from the Golden Age* (Jefferson, North Carolina: McFarland & Company, Inc., 1998), 108-109.

[18] Ivan Spear, "Hollywood Report," *Boxoffice*, August 28, 1943, 24. The title *Jungle Queen* was eventually assigned to another Universal release of January 1945, scripted by Morgan Cox, Andre Lamb, and George H. Plympton. Pivar had no involvement with this other film.

finally received his first name credited in full—as Russell A. rather than as R.A.—on this and subsequent films. This change was most likely in recognition for the Academy Award he won for art/set decoration for the previous year's *The Phantom of the Opera* (1943; Arthur Lubin), an award he shared with art directors Alexander Golitzen and John B. Goodman, and fellow set decorator Ira S. Webb.

The film starts out moodily enough. An unidentifiable man trudges through the windswept night, approaching a line of small cottages. A ferocious woman attacks him, and we watch their shadows as she savages him. After much struggle he puts an end to her with a stabbing motion, but it is not at all clear what has just happened.

Cut to a coroner's inquest, where timid Dr. Carl Fletcher (J. Carrol Naish) is grilled by a district attorney (Douglass Dumbrille), under the watchful eye of the coroner (Samuel S. Hinds). In attendance is a jury of six along with four witnesses, the latter group including Fred Mason (Milburn Stone), his fiancée Beth (Evelyn Ankers), Dr. Fletcher's daughter Joan (Lois Collier), and Joan's fiancé Bob Whitney (Richard Davis). Fletcher remains tight-lipped, knowing that the truth is beyond belief, but gives in when urged by his daughter. His story and those of Mason and Beth as well are all shown in flashback.

Fletcher relates how he had been in the audience for the performance that climaxed the previous film. Rushing over to confirm Cheela the ape's demise after she had been shot, he found that she still had a faint pulse and was not dead after all. He had taken Cheela back to his lab and nursed her back to health.

Fred Mason testifies that he had visited Fletcher to see how his old ape buddy was doing, and relates the story of originally finding the affectionate ape in the Belgium Congo, capturing and bringing her back to the States. He also tells of Dr. Walters' introduction of Paula (Acquanetta), her strange control over the wild animals, and her jealousy over his romantic relationship with Beth.

Beth is called to the stand and continues the story, telling about her bedroom encounter with the strange creature that murdered her landlady, and whom she came to be convinced was Paula. Fletcher returns to the stand and completes the story.

Intrigued by the connection with Dr. Walters, Fletcher purchases the Crestview Sanatorium and studies Walters' notes and files. His mentally challenged helper Willie (Edward M. Hyans, Jr.) announces that Cheela has escaped, so the two head out to conduct a search for the ape. Willie instead returns with Paula, and Fletcher takes her in under his care. She is uncommunicative, but displays incredible strength. When Fletcher's daughter Joan arrives with boyfriend Bob, sex-starved Paula quickly forgets about her previous devotion to Mason and zeroes in on the young man. Paula breaks her silence and introduces herself. Nice guy Bob pays attention to her, much to Joan's annoyance and Paula's delight. When the couple leaves, Paula plants herself at her window waiting for her new love's return.

Willie can't leave well enough alone, and makes a pest of himself in his romantic pursuit of Paula. When Joan and Bob return and make the mistake of a romantic embrace and passionate kiss within Paula's view, Paula has one of those Paula moments. While Fletcher takes Bob aside and warns him to steer clear of Paula, Joan is approached by a "hideous shadow" and screams, saved by the return of the two men. Willie has the bad timing of approaching and pestering Paula once more, and is crushed for his efforts. His body is left in the brush.

Paula and Bob go canoeing, not realizing that a submerged Paula follows. Paula yanks the canoe under water from below, but the couple makes it back to the shore. Reporting the incident to Fletcher, Willie becomes the prime suspect. The two men attempt to locate Willie, but return when Joan screams after seeing an animalistic face at her window. Fletcher sees Paula walking away.

Paula confronts Bob, exposing her bare, bruised shoulder, accusing Fletcher of physical abuse. Joan enters without knocking, spots Paula in her partially undressed state, and jumps to what seems like an obvious conclusion; she is now convinced that Bob is romantically interested in Paula. Groundskeeper George (Christian Rub) informs Fletcher that something with great strength has destroyed all of the animal pens and their occupants as well, killing George's German Shepherd for good measure. Fletcher begins to suspect Paula, so he sneaks into her room to retrieve a fingerprint-covered perfume bottle for comparison with prints found on the animal pens. Paula discovers Fletcher in her room and lunges at him in a rage, Fletcher striking her to the floor in self-defense. Bob sees the tail end of this and now believes Paula's accusations of abuse. He takes Paula to Dr. Meredith (Pierre Watkin) to examine her injuries, but Dr. Meredith insists that he take her back to Fletcher.

Fletcher has the fingerprints analyzed, and the results show that they are identical in pattern, but not in size. Furthermore, they aren't human, more like a combination of human and anthropoid. When George and Fletcher's nurse Miss Gray (Nana Bryant) inform Fletcher that they've found Willie's crushed body and that Paula is missing, it finally dawns on Fletcher that Paula is the guilty party. He fills a syringe with a sedative.

When Bob returns to the sanatorium with Paula, she is visibly upset with him and now wants him to leave. Bob insists on staying, adding salt to the wound by confirming his love for Joan. Paula storms out of Bob's car, but soon after she overhears Joan badmouthing her to Bob, which sends her over the edge. In a fury, she stalks Joan as she returns to her cottage on the sanatorium's grounds, snapping limbs left and right in her pursuit. Paula attempts to break into Joan's cottage, but is interrupted by Fletcher's arrival. In their struggle, Fletcher accidentally administers an overdose of the sedative, resulting in Paula's death.

With Fletcher's strange story now concluded at the coroner's inquest, the smirking district attorney thinks he has won. A trip to the morgue puts an end to that, though, as the assembled group views the contents of Paula's drawer. Seeing the monstrosity therein, the district attorney quickly apologizes to Fletcher, the case against him assumedly to be dropped. "The evil that man has wrought shall in the end destroy itself..." reads the closing title.

"Flesh of Beauty! Soul of Satan!" Acquanetta goes out on a limb in *Jungle Woman* (1944). Image courtesy of Heritage Auction Galleries, Ha.com.

This is not a particularly good film, but it is not a particularly bad one, either, with some clever structuring and enough engaging moments to salvage it. The gimmick of presenting the story as a series of flashbacks, while an old device, actually works to this film's advantage. Ankers and Stone are on board only long enough to seamlessly tie in the abundant stock footage from the film's predecessor. Carradine doesn't receive a credit, but they've reused some of his footage as well. Whatever arrangement Universal had made with Clyde Beatty to get him to okay the reuse of his *The Big Cage* footage a year earlier carried through to this film as well, with the opening, "We hereby make grateful acknowledgement to Mr. Clyde Beatty...." title card trotted out once again.

Naish gives a believable—if unenthusiastic—performance as the soft-spoken doctor who gets in way over his head, and for once the film has a decent leading man in Richard Davis, whose film career was surprisingly brief. Collier, attractive in spite of her Pez-dispenser mouth, comes across well as the young love interest, with competent supporting performances by Samuel S. Hinds and Douglass Dumbrille. Ramsay Ames was briefly considered for a role in the film, but it is unclear which part she would have been assigned.[19] The one stunningly bad performance is by Edward M. Hyans, Jr., as dim-witted

---

[19] Edwin Schallert, "Drama and Film," *Los Angeles Times*, November 5, 1943, 14.

Willie, a terrible caricature of a role that director Reginald LeBorg should not have tolerated. One wonders what *The Hollywood Reporter*'s reviewer was smoking when he wrote, "Edward M. Hyans, Jr., does well with the role of the lumbering admirer who pays for his attentions with his life."[20] It must have been something good.

And then there is Acquanetta. I am not an Acquanetta basher, and I think she is actually rather good in this one. Physically she is perfect for the role, stocky enough to believably beat the stuffing out of Naish if she really wanted to, and attractive in a way that sets her apart from most of the budding, cookie-cutter starlets of that era. They even trusted her with dialog, and while it can be labored at times, the viewer should keep in mind that she is, after all, just a retrofitted ape. Given the circumstances, she is rather articulate.

LeBorg makes the most of his modest budget, and provides one really terrific shot in the canoe sequence. As Joan and Bob float in their canoe toward the camera, filmed from overhead, the wake from an underwater pursuer approaches ominously from behind, quickly catching up to and disappearing under their canoe. It is a shot that Val Lewton must have envied, and one of those less-is-more type setups that would reappear time and again, most notably years later in Steven Spielberg's *Jaws*.

There are the usual incongruities, of course. When Mason tells Fletcher about finding Cheela in the jungle, he adds that the natives had told him that Cheela was the handiwork of some far-off doctor, who had turned natives into animals. This revisionist account comes as news to viewers of the first film, not that anyone would really care one way or the other. Later, when Cheela disappears and Paula appears, she is fully dressed, as if Cheela carried a change of clothes around with her. But then this was not the first film to conjure up clothing at a moment's notice, and it surely would not be the last. *Jungle Woman* has the distinction of being the only film of the three where we do not actually see Ms. Dupree in her hairier state until the closing shot where she is laid out dead in the morgue's drawer. Prior to this she is seen only in shadow and silhouette, and this works in the film's favor for the less blood-and-thunder members of the audience, leaving more of the mayhem to the viewer's imagination. Was this a stylistic decision rather than one dictated by budgetary constraints? Director LeBorg claimed years later that it was the former: "If you'd seen the Ape Woman immediately, you wouldn't care about it anymore. The story was so bad, I felt I had to do *something*—if I gave it away in the first reel, I would have no more picture."[21]

Regardless, it was an effective decision.

---

[20] "Jungle Woman," *Hollywood Reporter*, May 22, 1944, 3.

[21] Tom Weaver and John Brunas, "Reginald LeBorg: 50 Years of Horror Filmmaking," *Fantastic Films*, June 1985, #44, 46.

Variety actually gave the film an uncharacteristic *two* reviews, both positive but one more favorable than the other: "Another horror drama with good blend of thrills and suspense for the chiller-minded customers ... Dark-eyed and dark-complexioned Acquanetta is an excellent choice for the ape-girl role ... Direction by Reginald LeBorg is crisp throughout, accenting the suspense and thrill sequences supplied by compact script."[22]

As one would expect, Bosley Crowther disliked the film.

The Jungle Captive
(Director: Harold Young; Released June 29, 1945)

What little *Jungle Woman* had going for it fell by the wayside by the time the third and final entry—*The Jungle Captive*[23]—went into production. The formula had now devolved into the most simplistic of plotlines: Doctor obsessed with restoring life to the ape woman transforms her into a humanoid beauty with some success, but ultimately perishes at the hands of his own creation. Otto Kruger was awarded the role of the misguided villain of the piece, and looks somewhat embarrassed as director Harold Young allows him to occasionally lapse into ham; it is difficult to believe that this is the same actor who was so delightfully and believably menacing in Hitchcock's *Saboteur* a mere three years earlier. Acquanetta, who'd been slated for this third go-round back in mid-1944,[24] had gotten out of her contract with Universal by the time production began in September due to her displeasure with these ape woman roles. She ended up at Monogram where it was reported she was to star in two films for producers Sam Katzman and Jack Dietz, a major step down from her modest work at Universal. The first of these was to have the rip-off title *Jungle Fear*,[25] but never came to fruition. *Tarzan and the Leopard Woman*, produced by Sol Lesser for RKO, was Acquanetta's sole role in 1946.

Dr. Stendahl (Kruger), of the Stendahl Biological Laboratory, successfully restores life to a dead rabbit through administrations of electricity and blood transfusions. Assisting him with his experiments is young Don Young (Phil

---

[22] Walt., "Jungle Woman," *Variety*, May 24, 1944, 10.

[23] While the film itself bears the title *The Jungle Captive* in the opening credits, the trailers shown in theaters gave the title as *Jungle Captive*. The film was also known as *Wild Jungle Captive* when re-released by Realart. The bulk of Universal's product from 1933 to 1943 was re-released in some form or other from mid-1947 through mid-1957 as a result of a ten-year, $3 million-plus lease acquired by Harris-Broder Pictures Corp., with a number of post-1943 productions re-released during this period as well.

[24] "'U' Plans 55 Features; Diversity is Stressed," *Boxoffice*, June 17, 1944, 18.

[25] Ivan Spear, "Shapely Acquanetta to Be Starred In Two New Monogram Pictures," *Boxoffice*, September 9, 1944, 34.

Brown), with nurse assistant and Young's girl Ann Forrester (Amelita Ward) looking on with wide-eyed admiration. Heady with his success, Stendahl has his dimwitted assistant Moloch (Rondo Hatton) go to the city morgue and steal the corpse of the ape woman (Vicky Lane) so that he can continue with his experiments. Ham-fisted Moloch obediently follows Stendahl's orders, but manages to kill the less-than-cooperative attendant in the process. Moloch wrecks his stolen ambulance on the way back to Stendahl's "secret" country cottage and lab, and dumps his surgical smock disguise along with it.

Detective Harrigan (Jerome Cowan) investigates, having retrieved the torn smock from the wreckage. Confronting Don and Ann at Stendahl's lab, Harrigan confirms that the smock's laundry mark is identical to those of Stendahl's lab's smocks. When he finds that the smock fits Don perfectly and learns of the lab's experiments, Don jumps to the top of his suspect list. Unaware of his status as suspect number one, Don proposes to Ann and gives her his fraternity pin. She accepts.

Later, Stendahl lures Ann to the country cottage under the ruse that they are visiting a Dr. Kellogg. Entering the fenced and guard dog-protected grounds, Ann soon finds that she is to become part of Stendahl's experiments, a provider of copious amounts of blood for the ape woman. Moloch assists in strapping her to one of the lab's tables, and as usually happens in these films the

The Jungle Captive (1945). Image courtesy of Heritage Auction Galleries, Ha.com.

beast falls for the beauty. Stendahl successfully restores life to the ape woman via the transfusions and electrical stimulation, and then imprisons her in an upstairs bedroom. Undaunted, the resourceful ape woman escapes through the bedroom window. The guard dog's barking alerts Stendahl to the semi-simian's escape, and he tracks down and subdues her with his trusty whip. Moloch, smitten by the unconscious Ann, takes Don's fraternity pin and places it on his own lapel. Ann wakens, weak from loss of blood, and none too happy about her new status as guinea pig.

Cheela Has a Makeover

Not content with bringing life back to "this hybrid," Stendahl now wants to take it one step further and transform the shaggy creature to the more voluptuous Paula Dupree. To that end he assigns Moloch the task of retrieving Dr. Sigmund Walters' surgical records, now in the possession of Dr. Fletcher. Which Moloch does, this time managing to kill Dr. Fletcher in the process.

Don is concerned about Ann's disappearance, and says as much to Harrigan when the detective visits him and Stendahl at the lab. Harrigan is now even more suspicious of Don, having found out from Ann's mother that Ann had implored her to swear to a false alibi regarding Don's whereabouts the night the morgue attendant was murdered.

Later, using Walters' notes and more of Ann's blood, Stendahl transforms the ape woman into lovely Paula Dupree—lovely, but brain dead, staring vacantly into space and wandering about aimlessly. It's back to the bedroom for her, while Stendahl grabs a "Brain Surgery" book off the shelf as a quick refresher, intending to take Ann's cerebrum and plop it into Paula's skull.

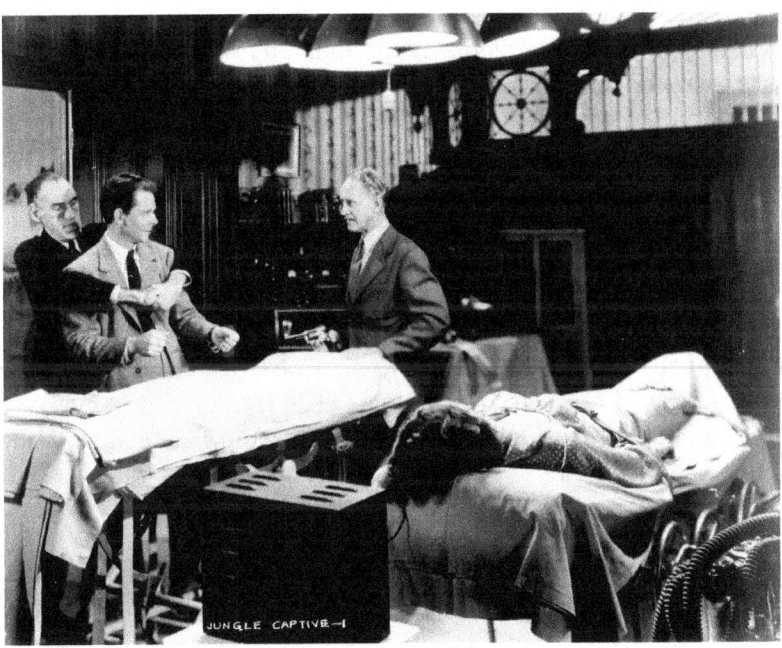

Moloch subdues Don as Stendahl holds him at gunpoint in *The Jungle Captive* (1945). Left to right: Rondo Hatton, Phil Brown, Otto Kruger, Amelita Ward.

While Stendahl is gone, Paula still has enough wits about her to escape once more from the window. When Moloch discovers this, he panics and heads to the City College searching for Stendahl but runs across Don instead. Moloch has never met Don, but Don spots and recognizes his fraternity pin on

Moloch's lapel, so he follows him back to the country cottage. Stendahl and Moloch subdue Don and tie him to a chair in the lab, where Stendahl informs him of his plans for Ann's brain. But first he and Moloch have to track down Paula, still wandering the grounds. Don makes an escape attempt with Ann, but is recaptured and retied to a chair.

Meanwhile, Harrigan and his boys are searching Stendahl's city-based lab. Harrigan admits that he was just "using" Don, and that he really suspects Stendahl. He finds an electric bill for the country cottage property and, remembering that the ambulance was ditched on the road leading to that property, puts two and two together. The cops pack up and head for the property.

Stendahl is about to perform the brain operation on Ann, who is strapped to the operating table, when love-struck Moloch decides to intervene. Advancing menacingly toward Stendahl while Don looks on, the doctor calmly shoots Moloch to death and proceeds with his preparations. His attention diverted, he doesn't realize that Paula has quietly reverted back to the ape woman. She attacks and kills Stendahl, then approaches Ann. Harrigan and company arrive in the nick of time and shoot Paula dead. Don and Ann are rescued.

This is a dreary little film. The script is mindlessly simplistic, the direction perfunctory and unimaginative, and the performances adequate at best. Kruger has the most prominent part, adding a modicum of class to the proceedings while uttering the inane dialog; he walks through his role with little enthusiasm. Amelita Ward, another of Universal's good-looking starlets, gives an amateurish performance when actually called upon to act, spending most of her time in a scripted fog due to loss of blood. Ward was a last-minute replacement for British-born Australian actress Betty Bryant, recently signed to a term contract by Universal due in part to her role in the internationally successful Aussie film *40,000 Horsemen*[26] (1941; Charles Chauvel). Bryant's Hollywood debut fell through when she was taken ill and hospitalized for observation and treatment.[27] Ward's career was a brief one, and if she is remembered today it is as likely due to the fact that she was the third wife (of five) of "Bowery Boy" Leo Gorcey.

Phil Brown makes a "weak" leading man, although his performance here is slightly better than in *Weird Woman*, or at least less annoying. One of the founders of the Actors Laboratory in Los Angeles, his career in film was interrupted when he was blacklisted in the fifties during the Communist scare. Relocating to England, Brown continued in film and television through the

---

[26] Edwin Schallert, "Australian Actress Signed for 'Jungle Captive,'" *Los Angeles Times*, August 31, 1944, 10.

[27] Edwin Schallert, "Amelita Ward Lead in 'Jungle Captive,'" *Los Angeles Times*, September 9, 1944, 5.

nineties, primarily in character roles. Jerome Cowan is doggedly persistent as the pig-headed cop Harrigan, a performance that *The Hollywood Reporter* called "refreshingly real and excellent. He is the one thoroughly credible character."[28]

Eighteen-year-old Dublin-born Vicky Lane assumed the role of Paula Dupree, an inauspicious start in what would prove to be a two-feature career (along with *The Cisco Kid Returns*). The statuesque beauty has no dialog or, for that matter, acting ability, wandering about wordlessly as if a barely-animated department store mannequin. In the several instances where she is required to act menacingly as the ape woman, her exaggerated attempts to appear threatening are little more than laughable. Acquanetta, we miss you!

The film's real "star," for lack of a better word, is raspy-voiced Rondo Hatton as Kruger's moronic assistant Moloch. The fifty-year-old actor was a true screen oddity, suffering from the advanced effects of acromegaly attributed to the inhalation of German poison gas during World War I. Acromegaly is a disease that results in the enlargement and disfiguration of the bones of the head, hands, and feet, caused by the overproduction of growth hormone.

A chance encounter with director Henry King led to a small part for Hatton in the 1930 film *Hell Harbor*, with a number of mostly uncredited bit parts following over the next fourteen years in films such as 20th Century-Fox's *In Old Chicago* (1938; Henry King) and *The Ox-Bow Incident* (1942; William Wellman).

Hatton's fortunes changed when Universal gave him a credited role as the Hoxton Creeper in the Sherlock Holmes entry *Pearl of Death* (1945; Roy William Neill). Pivar was quick to take notice of the actor's rather unique physical attributes, starring him in three of his films; *The Jungle Captive* was the first of these.[29] Rather tastelessly advertised as "The Monster Without Makeup!," Hatton made the best of the hand he was dealt, enduring such lines as the one delivered by Kruger's Dr. Stendahl: "No offense, Moloch, but with that face you're not exactly a Casanova." Hatton's is an awkward presence here, and he is inadvertently responsible for the film's comedic highlights as he barks out his simple-minded utterings in his raspy voice. Hatton alone is the primary reason for sitting through what is otherwise a genuinely miserable finale to the series.

In the interests of full disclosure, it should be noted that one or two generous reviewers actually *liked* the on-screen results, *Daily Variety* one of them. "'Jungle Captive' is first class horror fare [that] develops rapidly, logically,

---

[28] "Cowan Refreshing; Story Line Formula," *Hollywood Reporter*, June 12, 1945, 3.

[29] For an excellent, in-depth biography of Rondo Hatton, see the article "Rondo Hatton: Beneath the Skin" by Fred Olen Ray in *Filmfax*, No. 26, April/May 1991.

and with hysterical suspense ... Harold Young's direction keeps the action well-paced and the scenes convincing."[30] He must have been a Dubliner.

The Jungle Captive was released at the end of June on a double bill with Pivar's fourth "Inner Sanctum" entry, *The Frozen Ghost*. Universal's suggestions to exhibitors for exploitation of the film strongly suggest the audience they had in mind: "[A]im your newspaper ads at children with iron nerves. Dare them to see the picture. Angle at kids who can read current comic books without becoming squeamish."[31] The kids went, all right, but didn't really need to tap into their iron nerves; according to reviewer Grace Kingsley: "Rondo Hatton as the doctor's extremely sinister assistant drew only giggles from the audience kids."[32]

One kid who was not in any of *The Jungle Captive* audiences was Pivar's own, four-and-a-half-year-old Neil. As the cute young son of a Universal executive producer, however, Neil Pivar had what amounted to the world's biggest playground within sight of his house. When he was younger, he would make the two-mile ride over to the studio in his father's brown 1938 Buick Super convertible, sitting on Ben's lap, pretending to drive the car. To an impressionable young kid it felt like he knew or met everyone at the studio, including the front gate guards. Father and son would drive over to Ben's large bungalow office, where Ben's secretary Helen McLemore would greet them. Neil would then have the run of the lot, with the exception of the sets when closed during shooting. High points included "rides" on the various cameramen's booms, "Great fun for a kid." The crew also allowed Neil to watch the film shoots from up on the catwalks where they operated the Kleig lights. "My catwalk excursions ended when my mother found out."[33]

As Neil grew a bit older and became, as he puts it, "an experienced soundstage dweller," cast and crew alike embraced his youthful enthusiasm. As long as he stayed out from under foot and mum, his presence was easily overlooked and quickly forgotten:

> [T]he sets were always busy. I remember after a scene, when the director would say "cut and print it," the place would turn into a madhouse. Everyone would scramble to rearrange things for the next scene. I had to stay out of the way or be trampled.

---

[30] "Jungle Captive," *Daily Variety*, June 13, 1945, 3.

[31] "Exploitips," *Boxoffice*, June 30, 1945, 12.

[32] Grace Kingsley, "Two Thrillers on View," *Los Angeles Times*, September 20, 1945, 11.

[33] Neil Pivar correspondence with author, December 22, 2010.

Cheela Has a Makeover

[T]he best place to be out of the way once the stage was set and ready to shoot was in the seat attached to the camera boom. The director rarely used it. As long as I sat still and kept quiet, no one objected. Probably my dad's idea. Someone alongside would gesture to the trolley and boom operators to move back or forward, or up and down. I mimicked his gestures. How many times did I do this over the years? I have no idea. Perhaps a hundred times, or more. My dad would take me to a soundstage where they were shooting, not necessarily one of his films. I could spend the day there [and] never be bored. As I recall, it was mostly Saturdays when I wasn't in school. I received my introduction to swearing when someone blew their lines during shooting of a scene. [34]

Ben's good friends at the studio became Neil's as well, among them Andy Devine and Lou Costello. Costello was Neil's godfather, or as he put it, his *calabash godfather* (calabash is a colloquial expression of Hawaiian origin for someone who is very close, but not a blood relation. Neil, who lived in Hawaii from 1961 to 1993, would refer to Devine as his *calabash uncle*). Neil used to sit on "Uncle Lou's" lap in the commissary during lunchtime, and Costello, true to form, would joke around to amuse Neil (and himself and others, no doubt) by flipping teaspoons into other people's water glasses.

I remember when I was about six, one day in the commissary; I was sitting on Uncle Lou's lap. He would flip teaspoons across the room, and then point at me. A very large sheriff guy came and arrested me, took me to one of the active western sets, and put me in jail.[35]

And if being jailed at the tender young age of six was not enough of an eye-opener for the youth, one of Neil's more traumatic moments occurred during the filming of one of the three Cheela films. Neil remembers the incident to this day, if not the details:

Sometime in the mid-forties, my dad produced some movies about Cheeta (I believe), an ape or apeman. I remember because one day while I was on the set, a giant ape (a guy in an ape costume) grabbed me and took me up to the catwalks above the set. Scared the s--t out of me... my mother was less than pleased.[36]

---

[34] Neil Pivar correspondence with author, January 8, 2011.

[35] Neil Pivar correspondence with author, November 30, 2009.

[36] Neil Pivar correspondence with author, April 27, 2009.

Stop Yellin'

A reasonable reaction on Judy's part, to say the least, considering that Neil would have been no older than six, and perhaps as young as four-and-a-half.

One of young Neil's favorite places at the studio was the prop department, filled with its eclectic jumble of odds and ends from numerous eras, its contents seemingly shifting from week to week as productions shut down and new ones began. As cool as the prop department was, however, Neil's favorite was the makeup department where he was given the opportunity to help with making masks. Whether this was actual productive work or simply "busy" work to keep the youth out from under foot is unknown, but for a kid no older than eight it must have seemed like heaven.

One of Neil's more pleasurable recollections took place while Ben was still at Universal:

> Can't remember the year, but one day, unbeknownst to me, my dad brought home a live seal from the studio. He put it in the bathtub. He then insisted I take a bath. Imagine my surprise and delight.[37]

It was a young kid in an adult's world, however, so there were the less exciting times as well, especially when it came to the confines of one of Universal's projection rooms. Ben would spend hours viewing the previous day's rushes, and on those days that Neil accompanied him to the studio Neil would be forced to do so as well. Okay, perhaps for a monster scene or a blazing guns shootout, but dialog scenes seemed interminable.

> I [would] sit and watch (boring) dailies at Universal many, many times. I remember thinking that I would much rather be on the backlot watching them shoot westerns. As often as not, Andy Devine would be on the Western sets, and I could sort of hang out with him. I got to shoot their six-guns.[38]

Around this time, Judy's niece Shirley came out to California for a visit. Shirley, then in her early twenties, was Judy's oldest sister Anne's daughter. It was the beginning of a long friendship.

> [Judy] invited me to come to LA in 1942 or 1943. I was glad to go. They had a lovely large house and made me very welcome. The day after I arrived they took me to Musso and Frank's for brunch. I very quickly grew fond of Ben, and we had good times together. Their children were very young, and I was babysitter many evenings. I was in

---

[37] Neil Pivar correspondence with author, August 5, 2010.
[38] Neil Pivar correspondence with author, August 26, 2010.

my early 20s, and they introduced me to a number of people, including setting up blind dates for me. They would have liked me to stay in LA. Ben secured a secretarial job for me at Universal, and I had a great time there. I worked in the editorial department, with Sally Bauer. I met a lot of people when I worked at Universal, and now when I look at the old movies on TV I recognize many names. Joe and Helen Gershenson were particular good friends (a lovely couple) and were very nice to me, too. After several months I returned to New York. About a year later I married a Navy man who was stationed in San Diego. My husband was Sam Karnes, whom I knew since childhood in Brooklyn. We spent free time visiting Ben and Judy. Ben and my husband were instantly good pals. After the war we settled in LA and stayed close to them.[39]

Now firmly entrenched at Universal, Ben could see what this steady employment had yielded—a beautiful house in an upscale neighborhood, a loving wife, an energetic young son, a newborn daughter, and lots of good friends; life was good. These were among the happiest years in the Pivar household.

§

---

[39] Shirley Karnes correspondences with author, January 17-19, 2010.

16 The Mummy Overstays His Welcome

Universal knew how to flog a dying horse, and with the demonstrated acceptance and popularity of the previous two mummy sequels decided to press on with the series. It really didn't seem to matter a whole lot if a subsequent entry proved to be more of the same old thing, just as long as the theater seats were filled and the film made money. Pivar's guidance of the first two had worked out nicely, so he was their man.

The Mummy's Ghost
(Director: Reginald LeBorg; Released July 7, 1944)

The third of the four mummy sequels was announced in February 1943, as *The Mummy Returns*, with Pivar again named as associate producer.[1] Burnu Acquanetta, now a "name" of sorts due to her recent exposure in *Captive Wild Woman*, was chosen for the lead role of the Egyptian transplant, a risky choice due to her lack of experience with dialog. Reginald LeBorg was signed as director, his first effort for Pivar and only his second feature for Universal (although it was released after *Calling Dr. Death* and *Weird Woman*, both of which were filmed subsequent to this). The film went into production in late August, having now acquired its release title, *The Mummy's Ghost*.

Production was halted briefly when Acquanetta was rushed to the Cedars of Lebanon Hospital for treatment of a possible brain concussion. Acquanetta had struck her head on August 25 while rehearsing a fainting scene for the film, and collapsed soon after. She was taken to the hospital after first aid attempts failed to revive her, and placed under a brain specialist's care.[2] She returned

---

[1] "Producer Assignments Doled Out On Half a Dozen New Pictures," *Boxoffice*, February 27, 1943, 24.

[2] "'Horror Queen' of Screen Hurt," *Los Angeles Times*, August 27, 1943, 2.

to work several days later, only to faint once again resulting in a return trip to the hospital. With an eye on a threatened schedule and budget, Pivar quickly replaced the injured actress with Ramsay Ames,[3] whom he was considering for a role in his upcoming production, *Calling Dr. Death*.

When interviewed years later, Acquanetta elaborated on the incident and placed the blame for her injuries on some non-union workers:

> We had scabs on the set. We had a scene where I had to fall, and these scabs had put real rocks down on the path. They were supposed to have papier-mâché rocks but they didn't—these scabs painted real rocks white. I fell and struck my head, and that's all I remember. I woke up in the hospital.[4]

Director LeBorg recalled the incident somewhat at odds with contemporary reports and Acquanetta's account:

> In the morning of the first day of shooting, Acquanetta was on the set at 9:00 but she was walking very awkwardly—she was scared, I think because this was her second or third film. In the second shot, she was supposed to walk from a lawn, up a couple of stairs and into a house. She slipped and fell, and hit her head, and for half an hour she was unconscious. They took her to the dispensary and gave her smelling salts—she was all right, but she had a slight concussion. Pivar didn't want to take any chances, so the role was recast with Ramsay Ames.[5]

The end result was the same: Acquanetta was out, and Ramsay Ames was in. Filming resumed and wrapped in early September, with post-production following. Universal sat on the completed film for a number of months, holding off for a mid-summer release in July 1944.

In Egypt, George Zucco's ancient high priest Andoheb (thought by gullible viewers of the previous film to have died) assigns Yousef Bey (Carradine)

---

[3] Edwin Schallert, "Acquanetta Retires from Thriller Cast," *Los Angeles Times*, September 1, 1943, 13.

[4] Michael Brunas, John Brunas, and Tom Weaver, *Universal Horrors: The Studio's Classic Films, 1931-1946* (Jefferson, NC: McFarland & Company, Inc., 1990), 428. This excellent book is chock full of fascinating information about the production of every one of Universal's horror films during this time period, along with synopses and reviews of the finished product.

[5] Tom Weaver, *Interviews with B Science Fiction and Horror Movie Makers* (Jefferson, North Carolina: McFarland & Company, Inc., 1988), 236.

the task of heading to Mapleton, Massachusetts, to retrieve the mummy Kharis (thought by gullible viewers of the previous film to have been barbecued in the Banning mansion) and the museum-displayed mummy of Ananka. We know he is ancient because he shakes a lot; although that might be due to the frustration of having to repeat this story to so many young initiates who, in the end, consistently refuse to follow orders. Yousef is to return the couple to their rightful tombs so that Kharis can "finish" his assignment of guarding Ananka's resting place 'til the end of time.

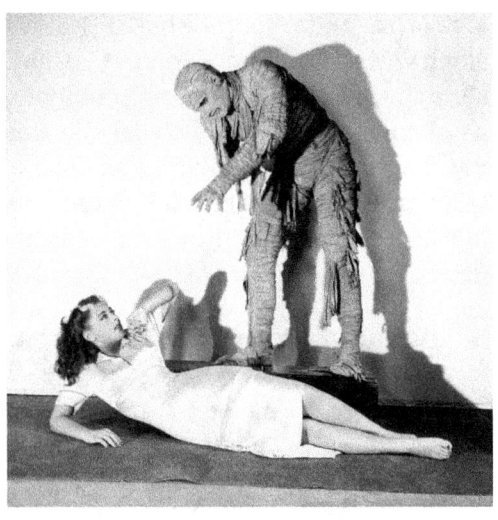

Chaney's Kharis terrorizes Ramsay Ames in this posed studio shot for *The Mummy's Ghost* (1944). Image courtesy of Heritage Auction Galleries, Ha.com.

Cut to Mapleton University where the previous film's Professor Norman (Frank Reicher) relates the story of the mummy's former rampage through town to his skeptical students. The cumulative effect of Andoheb and Norman's spiels is to bring the viewing audience up to date on the backstory, not that it really matters a whole lot. Back to Zucco, who finishes his information session with a rehash of the use of Tana leaves, telling Yousef that if he brews nine of them "Kharis will know, and find it, wherever it is."

University student Tom Hervey (Robert Lowery) heads to the library to see his Egyptian-born girlfriend Amina Mansouri (Ramsay Ames), noticing the book *The Tombs of Ancient Egypt* sitting on her desk. Quirky girl that she is, she is able to read about the old country and take it all in stride, but becomes "jittery" whenever Tom mentions the name "Egypt"; it is a response akin to the one whenever Costello innocently mutters "Niagara Falls." No matter; she is gorgeous, so Tom is not about to let a bad case of nerves get in the way.

Professor Norman works late into the night attempting to decipher the hieroglyphics on a small chest of Tana leaves. Finally meeting with success, he jubilantly informs his wife (Claire Whitney) of this, then sends her to bed so that he can brew up a test batch. Conveniently, it is a full moon, and with the recipe's completion the long-thought-dead Kharis becomes reanimated, and looks no worse than he did in the previous film after the first fire.

Amina, asleep in bed, becomes restless and heads out into the night in a trance. She arrives outside and faints just as Kharis arrives and kills Norman, followed by an invigorating swig of Tana extract. Norman's wife discovers his corpse and calls the sheriff (Harry Shannon), who arrives to investigate along with the coroner (Emmett Vogan). Traces of mold on the victim's throat alert the authorities that the mummy is back! Amina, now awake, disavows any knowledge of how or why she was there, oblivious to the fact that she now has a gray skunk-like streak in her otherwise dark hair. Tom, alerted by a fellow student of the murder and Amina's implication, storms in and offers up himself as an alibi for the previous night. Ineffectually so, says the sheriff, since their date ended hours before the murder.

Professor Norman's view of the approaching Kharis in *The Mummy's Ghost* (1944).]

The townspeople are in a tizzy over the news of the mummy's apparent return, and patrols are formed to roam the streets at night. Yousef, now in Mapleton, brews up a batch of Tana leaves and delivers the first of many incantations to the gods. Getting a long-distance whiff, Kharis bulldozes his way through the brush and makes a beeline for the odoriferous extract. On this journey Kharis manages to brush by Tom and Amina's parked jalopy (although only she notices a strange "shadow"), and kills a farmer whose dog has cornered him in a barn. When the authorities investigate, they once again perceptively recognize Kharis' handiwork.

The Mummy Overstays His Welcome

Professor Norman lies in a heap at the feet of Kharis in *The Mummy's Ghost* (1944).

Yousef and Kharis sneak into the Scripps Museum after dark to visit Ananka's mummy, which is on display in an open casket. Yousef begins another one of his mind-numbing incantations, this time invoking the names of a trio of gods. He is new at this, though, and manages to screw things up; when Kharis touches Ananka's corpse it collapses into a pile of dust, her soul reincarnated into another. Elsewhere, Amina awakens with a scream, so it is rather obvious where Ananka's soul has relocated. Kharis goes on a museum-trashing rampage, enraged that his love has "disappeared" under his touch. The night watchman (Oscar O'Shea) arrives to investigate the ruckus, and ends up dead for his efforts. Yousef laments that the gods have made his job more difficult, stubbornly refusing to acknowledge his part in what has just taken place.

Inspector Walgreen (Barton MacLane) arrives at the Scripps Museum to investigate, and Dr. Ayad (Lester Sharpe) brings him up to speed on all things mummy-related. A quick translation of the hieroglyphics in Ananka's tomb suggests the possibility of reincarnation, and the presence of more mold implicates Kharis. Walgreen, Ayad, and the sheriff head over to Norman's house where Ayad translates as much as he can from the Tana leaf chest, unable to decipher the key parts that reveal the use of nine leaves. Norman's wife provides the missing "nine-leaf" clue, and Walgreen comes up with a plan: lure Kharis to the house with a brewed batch of leaves and catch him in a huge, soon-to-be-dug pit. What they'd do with him after that remains unstated.

Tom announces to Amina that he is going to take her to New York in the morning, away from all of what is happening in sleepy Mapleton that seems to be taking a psychological toll on her. She balks at first, especially since the sheriff had told her to stay put, but smooth-talking Tom convinces her, throwing in a proposal and his little dog Peanuts for good measure. It is her mental health, of course, that he is so concerned about.

Oscar O'Shea's night watchman, in the wrong place at the wrong time, in *The Mummy's Ghost* (1944).

Meanwhile, Yousef implores the gods to provide guidance to the receptacle of Ananka's soul. When a beam of light streams in through the window, Yousef recognizes this as a sign of divine intervention and commands Kharis to follow it. Dutifully, Kharis shuffles off and locates Amina's residence, carrying off the unconscious girl, his one bad arm not so bad that he can't summon it into action to help with the nightgown-clad beauty. Amina's landlady Mrs. Blake, alerted by Peanuts' yapping, calls Tom in a panic. He responds with the obvious: contact the authorities!

Kharis hauls Amina back to the abandoned mine that Yousef has been using as a hideout, and delivers the goods. Tom, led by yappy little Peanuts, follows, with the sheriff and a mob of townspeople close behind. Yousef ties Amina to a table, readying some sort of sacrifice and taking notice of the birthmark of Ananka on her right wrist. Yousef takes one look at Amina, now sporting twin gray streaks, and it is lust at first sight. Following in the footsteps of Andoheb and Mehemet Bey before him in the two preceding films, Yousef makes the spur-of-the-moment decision to administer a dose of Tana extract to both Amina and himself so that the two of them can live on together for eternity—a risky decision at best. Kharis, fed up with this nonsense, quickly terminates Yousef's life by tossing him out a window to his death far below.

Tom arrives but is no match for Kharis, who knocks him silly. The sheriff and the mob arrive, Tom revives, and together they pursue Kharis into the woods. Unconscious Amina is cradled in his arms, her hair now totally white. As he moves into a swamp, we see first her hands and then her feet, both wrinkled with age. The pursuers watch helplessly as Kharis and Amina slowly sink into the swamp, Amina by now a rotting corpse. The pursuers head back home, leaving Peanuts by the swamp, pining for his lost mistress. Zucco's voice is heard over the fadeout: "The fate of those who defy the will of the ancient gods shall be a cruel and violent death."

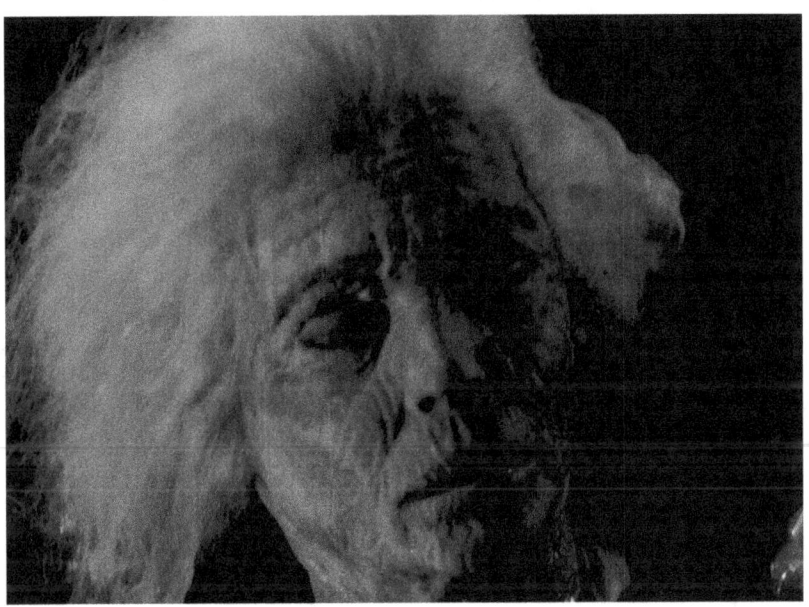

One last look at the rotting Amina before she disappears into the swamp in *The Mummy's Ghost* (1944).

Although more entertaining than its predecessor, writers Griffin Jay and Henry Sucher held slavishly to their former film's storyline, resulting in an unimaginative rehash of *The Mummy's Tomb*'s plot. The film looks thrown together, with LeBorg's direction lackluster for the most part. There are occasional exceptions that stand out, such as Kharis' rampage in the Scripps Museum, ultimately killing the night watchman (off screen, accompanied by loud crunching sounds!), and Kharis' descent into the swamp with the rapidly-aging Amina. William Sickner's photography looks hurried, with flat lighting and lots of cost-cutting day-for-night exteriors instead of sequences shot at night. Much of the outdoor shooting of the former entry in the series has been eschewed for the really poor studio-constructed "outdoor" sets for some shots, complete with "dead" sky and no horizon. There is comparatively little stock footage employed, however, relegated to some opening shots of Egypt, several nighttime skies, and a clip from *The Mummy's Hand* of Zucco ascending the temple steps, here unconvincingly used as a supposed long shot of Carradine. Throw in the overly-familiar library music and a script that feels painfully derivative, and the result is so much more of exactly the same thing.

Carradine plays the role of Yousef Bey in a comparatively subdued, straight-faced fashion, but has little to do throughout except offer up one tiresome entreaty to the gods after another. He does manage to summon up some emotion several times during the story, looking astonished when Ananka's corpse turns to dust under Kharis' touch (why anything would astonish someone who's hanging around with a 3,000-year-old mummy is beyond me), and later as he gives in to his baser instincts when confronted by Ramsay Ames' Amina stretched out before him.

And the film's highlight is Ramsay Ames, one of Universal's most alluring starlets and eye candy for the viewer. LeBorg manages to elicit an acceptable performance from the novice actress, this only her second time before cameras. Mention should be made of designer and Universal mainstay Vera West and her "gowns," specifically the slinky evening gown that adorns Ames in the film's final sequence; it looks as if it was sprayed on. Ames, for the record, was a former model and dancer who became lead singer for a New York-based rhumba band. When the draft decimated her ranks of musicians, "I finally got down to one piano player and he was anemic. So I thought I better give up band leading for the duration and get into something else."[6] B movies, as it turned out.

Barton MacLane is solid but unremarkable as the inspector, and what little his character accomplishes could have easily been assigned to another character. His plan to catch the mummy is quickly forgotten in the chase to catch the lumbering creature, and one senses that its inclusion was more for padding than to advance the plot. Robert Lowery is typically stalwart as the hero of the piece, less bland than many of Universal's B-level leading men, but looks like he should have graduated from the University ten years earlier.

Chaney, by now sick of this ongoing role wrapped in layers of cloth and latex, griped about the costume and script to reporter Frederick Othman (if Othman's reportage is to be believed): "I sweat and I can't wipe it away. I itch and I can't scratch ... If I could just get my hands on the gent who wrote the first

---

[6] Frederick C. Othman, "Mummy Keeps on Suffering As Horror Pictures Roll On," *Charleston Daily Mail*, September 19, 1943, 8.

one of these things, I bet he'd never write another."⁷ Perhaps Griffin Jay and Henry Sucher took notice of Chaney's not-so-thinly-veiled threat; the final film in the series was scripted by another. Othman, incidentally, went on to report that Pivar was present on the set, wearing "a sweater striped like a convict's suit in blue and yellow." Why this particular sartorial selection caught his eye is anyone's guess.

Pivar's promotion to the ranks of executive producer was announced after the film's completion, and shortly before the first "Inner Sanctum" mystery, *Calling Dr. Death*, began shooting. This latter film would be the last to credit Pivar as associate producer, a position to be assumed by others on the films Pivar would oversee for the next several years.

This is probably as good a place as any to comment on the proverbial "800-pound gorilla" in the room, and I'm not referring to Cheela here. Very little has been written over the years about Pivar, but the bulk of it that does exist is in several years-after-the-fact reminiscences by two of his directors, both interviewed by historian Tom Weaver. Pivar's *Captive Wild Woman* director Edward Dymytryk had some marginally dismissive things to say about him, but did acknowledge that "[h]e was a nice-enough guy; he'd invite me to drink after a day's work, but I didn't drink so I didn't accept the invitation."⁸ Much more damaging to Pivar's reputation were the numerous scabrous comments made by director LeBorg, comments that will live on in print and, in the absence of few compensating comments from others and Pivar's obvious inability to defend his reputation, will serve to perpetuate defame Pivar.⁹ I won't bother to reprint them here because my gut feeling is that

Chaney regains the use of his right eye in this poster for *The Mummy's Ghost* (1944). Image courtesy of Heritage Auction Galleries, Ha.com.

---

⁷ Ibid.

⁸ Tom Weaver, *Science Fiction and Fantasy Film Flashbacks: Conversations with Twenty-Four Actors, Writers, Producers, and Directors from the Golden Age* (Jefferson, NC: McFarland and Company, Inc., 1998), 107.

⁹ Michael Brunas, John Brunas, and Tom Weaver, *Universal Horrors: The Studio's Classic Films, 1931-1946* (Jefferson, NC: McFarland and Company, Inc., 1990), 237-238.

it was a case of sour grapes, LeBorg bitter over what he considered work beneath his dignity and taking it out on the fellow who was his boss. And Pivar, long dead when these comments were made, was left defenseless. Perhaps there was an element of truth to some of it, but I prefer to think otherwise.

I contacted Weaver to get his take on this, and he offered a slightly different perspective: "Now that you've gotten me thinking about it, LeBorg did tend to have dismissive comments about a *lot* of people. Thinking back, I don't think he said any of 'em in a *mean* way, but... the same way Hitchcock works in the Truffaut interview, he often put down a number of the people around him on a particular movie, perhaps so the listener will get the idea, 'Hey, I liked that movie... I guess LeBorg was solely responsible for all the good stuff in it, and these other yoyos responsible for all the bad.'"[10]

At any rate, you now have the sources and can pursue this further if the mood strikes you.

The Mummy's Curse
(Director: Leslie Goodwins; Released December 22, 1944)

"Truth will flourish in fantasy, only to wither and die in what you are pleased to call reality." So says Ilzor Zandaab (Peter Coe), the high priest du jour of *The Mummy's Curse*. The series' final installment went into production a few weeks after its predecessor's release in July, arriving in theaters by year's end. Oliver Drake handled the associate producer chores on this one, with direction by Leslie Goodwins. British-born Goodwins was a prolific director who thrived in RKO's B unit for years after a start in the late twenties making two-reel comedies for the ultra-low-budget studio Weiss Brother Artclass Pictures. *The Mummy's Curse* was one of only a handful of films Goodwins directed for Universal over a two-year period in the mid-forties, and one of his rare excursions away from RKO. It would be the only horror film of his lengthy career, the last fifteen years spent in television along with so many others of his B film brethren.

The Mummy's Curse takes up where *The Mummy's Ghost* left off in a rather inexplicable fashion: The swamp in Mapleton, Massachusetts, that Kharis and Ananka sank into twenty-five years earlier has now relocated to the Louisiana Bayous! A construction crew is slated to drain this swamp, and gruff head of engineering Pat Walsh (Addison Richards) is in charge. His superstitious workers are spooked about the project, fearing the unknown and remembering stories about the mummy from years ago; they are quick to verbalize their concerns.

Walsh is not overly thrilled by the arrival of Dr. James Halsey (Dennis Moore) of the Scripps Museum. Halsey has received permission to poke around and attempt to recover the bodies of Kharis and Ananka with the hope

---
[10] Tom Weaver correspondence with author, March 21, 2010.

of returning them to the museum. Egyptian Ilzor Zandaab accompanies Halsey on this mission. Walsh's secretary and niece Betty (Kay Harding) takes an immediate shining to Halsey, and like any healthy leading man Halsey returns the interest. The group is interrupted when Goobie (Napoleon Simpson) bursts in and informs them that worker Antoine has been found dead at the site, a knife in his back. Dr. Cooper (Holmes Herbert) is called in and estimates that Antoine has been dead for twenty-four hours, and then an even more shocking discovery is made: a mummy-shaped hole in the ground and some wrappings that Ilzor identifies as coming from a mummy.

Ilzor, as it turns out, is the latest emissary sent from Egypt on yet-another quest to return Kharis and Ananka to their rightful resting places back in Egypt. Ilzor hooks up with Ragheb (Martin Kosleck), an earlier plant who has infiltrated the crew's workers; Ragheb happens to be Antoine's killer as well. Ragheb leads Ilzor to an abandoned hilltop monastery (a nicely evocative matte painting) where he has Kharis stashed, and explains that he killed the workers who assisted in unearthing Kharis. Ilzor relays the purpose of the Tana leaves, follows with a quick course in Mummy 101 that rehashes the origins of Kharis' eternal plight, and then swears in Ragheb. Ragheb's job is to help Ilzor succeed where Turhan Bey and John Carradine both failed miserably in the two previous outings. Ilzor stimulates Kharis with a dram of Tana extract, and Kharis returns the good deed by strangling Michael (former silent star William Farnum), the monastery's sacristan who has the misfortune of walking in on the proceedings.

With Kharis' rejuvenation, Ananka (Virginia Christine) now rises from the earth, assumedly in the body of *The Mummy's Ghost*'s Amina. She stumbles her muddy way over to a pond where she cleanses the filth from her body while sunlight helps restore her vitality and good looks. Cajun Joe (Kurt Katch), another worker out for a stroll, comes across unconscious Ananka, now wrinkle-free and freshly brunette. He takes her to an upstairs bedroom in the café of Tante Berthe, and then alerts Berthe to the poor girl's plight.

Ilzor sends Kharis after Ananka with instructions to kill anyone who gets in his way. Kharis makes his way to the café and kills Berthe when she puts up a fuss, Ananka taking advantage of this momentary distraction to flee from the area. Halsey and Betty, out together for a pleasant drive through the bayous, rescue Ananka from the side of the road. They drive off just as Kharis arrives, blissfully unaware of his threatening presence. Meanwhile, Dr. Cooper inspects Berthe's corpse and finds traces of that telltale mold on her throat.

STOP YELLIN'

Tante Berthe checks in on Ananka, unaware that Kharis is on her heels. ***The Mummy's Curse*** **(1944). Left to right: Virginia Christine, Ann Codee, Lon Chaney, Jr.**

When Ananka awakens, she remembers nothing of her past or recent events. In a paternalistic gesture, Halsey offers her a job assisting in his lab, and she soon dazzles him when she looks at a piece of Kharis' wrappings under the microscope: "Notice the coarse material, and the number of strands per square inch. This fabric was woven during the dynasty of King Amenophis, and worn by Kharis, Prince of the Royal House." She admits that she is confused by her own knowledge. When Ilzor shows up, he is stunned by her presence, but feigns ignorance of her identity. Ananka, meanwhile, goes into one of her periodic "Kharis"-moaning trances until Halsey snaps her out of it.

Ilzor sends Kharis back out after Ananka, but true to form Kharis only manages to kill Dr. Cooper while Ananka flees once again. Halsey and Cajun Joe set out looking for her, and Ilzor and Ragheb pretend to assist. Conducting his search from his rowboat, Cajun Joe spots Ananka on land and quickly paddles his craft to shore. Instead of finding her, though, Kharis finds him, and another good man meets his maker after ineffectually trying to fend off the beast with blasts from his shotgun.

The Mummy Overstays His Welcome

Kharis strangles Cajun Joe (Kurt Katch) in *The Mummy's Curse* (1944). Image courtesy of Heritage Auction Galleries, Ha.com.

Ananka finds her way back to the workers' campsite and Betty's tent with Kharis close on her heels. Kharis enters the tent uninvited and makes off with Ananka. Betty's screams alert Ragheb who agrees to help her find the others, but in actuality has other plans in mind—the "fate worse than death" kind. Halsey returns and finds Goobie at Betty's trashed tent, some wrappings from the mummy left behind. "The Devil's on the loose, and he's dancing with the mummy!" squeals Goobie, and not for the first time. Halsey sends Goobie after Walsh and others, and sets out on foot following Kharis' dusty tracks.

Kharis returns to the monastery with Ananka cradled in his arms, and places her into an open casket. Ragheb and Betty arrive elsewhere in the structure, and it quickly becomes evident to the poor girl that Ragheb's intentions are not of the virtuous sort. Ragheb's lust-filled approach is cut short by Ilzor's arrival, and Ilzor threatens Ragheb with disfigurement and death for ignoring his oath to the gods. Ragheb is not about to settle for this, and stabs Ilzor. Halsey stumbles onto the scene and struggles with Ragheb, who gets the upper hand and is about to cave in Halsey's skull when Kharis shows up. Kharis, once again displaying his keen sixth sense for high priests and their ilk who wander from the straight and narrow, goes after Ragheb. Ragheb holes up in a stone chamber, Kharis outside smashing at its walls and door. The whole structure collapses, assumedly crushing both Kharis and Ragheb. Ananka, in her open casket, once again bites the dust (both figuratively and literally).

Ananka (Virginia Christine) bites the dust, and this time for good, in *The Mummy's Curse* (1944).

Mercifully, this was the last of a really tired series; not that any one of the films taken individually were terrible; they weren't. But the last three were so similar in concept and execution that, in retrospect, it is difficult to recall which was which. With the events of *The Mummy's Tomb* and *The Mummy's Ghost* taking place thirty years after those of 1940's *The Mummy's Hand*, and *The Mummy's Curse* an additional twenty-five years after, that would place this film's action in 1995! As with *The Mummy's Tomb*, the uninformed viewer is brought up to speed on the backstory via stock footage from both *The Mummy* and *The Mummy's Hand*, here reduced to a manageable three minutes worth.

The Mummy's Curse differs from its predecessors in one small way, however: In the former films willpower did not seem to be a prerequisite for being a high priest. Carradine's Yousef Bey fell for Ramsay Ames' Amina in direct violation of his oath even more readily than George Zucco's Andoheb fell for Peggy Moran's Marta Solvani in *The Mummy's Hand*, and Turhan Bey's Mehemet Bey for Elyse Knox's Isobel Evans in *The Mummy's Tomb*. At least Peter Coe's Ilzor manages to keep any sort of carnal thoughts on a back burner, leaving the more aggressive display of lust to his underling Ragheb.

The Mummy Overstays His Welcome

Kharis is a genuine loose cannon in this film, taking the time to kill anyone with the misfortune of getting in his way during his numerous pursuits of Ananka. The result of these sidetracked killings is that Ananka manages to slip away while Kharis is otherwise occupied choking the life out of someone. And this happens not once, not twice, but three different times, first when he kills Berthe, again when he kills Cooper, and finally when he kills Cajun Joe; you'd think after all these years Kharis would know better—focus!

There are some nice aspects to this film, primary of which is the relocation of the action to the bayous of Louisiana, with its Cajun populace and their colorful patois. This installment is the most visually pleasing of the final three films, and a big step up from the flat *The Mummy's Ghost*. An exciting climax with Kharis bulldozing his way in after Ragheb doesn't hurt either. Atypical of a film of this sort, the opening scene is set in Tante Berthe's Café where Berthe (uncredited actress Ann Codee) belts out the song "Hey, You" in one charming continuous take. The song, incidentally, was co-written by associate producer Oliver Drake and Codee's husband (and former vaudeville costar) Frank Orth, Orth setting the lyrics to Drake's music. While totally unnecessary to the story that follows, it adds a little something extra to what is otherwise another routine horror fest.

"The Monster... That Would Not Die!" Maybe this time. Realart re-release poster for *The Mummy's Curse* (1944). Image courtesy of Heritage Auction Galleries, Ha.com.

The film's highlight, and arguably the strongest scene of any of the four films, is the resurrection of Ananka from the swamp. The crust of moist earth trembles slightly, followed by a hand clawing through, with the mud and slime-covered reanimated corpse finally emerging in a slow, tentative, herky-jerky fashion, stumbling over to a nearby pond to bathe the filth from her body. It is a chilling sequence, and Virginia Christine gives an unforgettable performance; it is her bewildered Ananka who holds the film together. Years later, Christine described the filming conditions to interviewer Gregory Mank:

> They took me out on the back lot, where the grave was dug, right in the soil—not clean, sifted sand! Then they covered me with burnt cork, then they sprayed it with water. Here, I'm lying in the earth, with only

my nostrils open for breathing—and I began to think of all the things that crawl in the earth...

Then, at the last minute, they put the burnt cork (that looked like soil) over my face. I had to get up, and walk—into a stinking, slimy, infested pool, covered with algae, down two or three steps into the pond, and wade in up to my neck...

Well, for the first time in my life, I was ready to scream, "No, I can't do it!" because it's *so* awful to look at! But then I thought, "You wanted to be an actress—let's go![11]

Her misery and perseverance paid off with one of the most memorable scenes of the forties Universal horrors. Goodwins had the good sense to keep the camera rolling while Christine went through her seemingly instinctive physical contortions. If nothing else sticks with the viewer after sitting through this film, this one powerful sequence surely will.

The resurrection of Ananka (Virginia Christine) from the swamp in *The Mummy's Curse* (1944).

Christine commented on her experiences working for Pivar, and on this film in particular: "Ben Pivar was very good to me through the years. I played

---

[11] Gregory Mank, "Virginia Christine and the Mummy's Curse," *Films in Review*, October 1986, 466.

in several of his films. I never regretted making *The Mummy's Curse*."[12] And with good reason; aside from her long-running stint as Mrs. Olson in the Folger's Coffee advertisements, this is arguably the role she is most remembered for today.

In the "lead" roles of the young lovers Halsey and Betty, Dennis Moore and Kay Harding are given little to do, with the bulk of the screen time taken up by the villains and other peripheral characters. This is okay, since former cowboy star Moore lacks any sort of charisma and gives a wooden performance. As for Harding, while pleasant to look at her acting is all over the place and not at all convincing; it is no surprise why her career in film was so short lived.

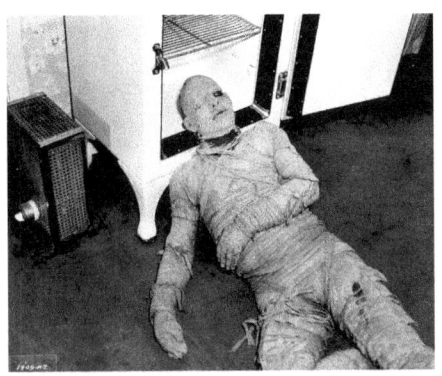

"I sweat and I can't wipe it away." Chaney attempts to cool down between shots. Photo courtesy of Doug Kennedy.

Chaney, wrapped up and unrecognizable in his mummy outfit, had grown to loathe the part, and would whine about it to most anyone who would listen. In the syndicated newspaper column "Hollywood Sights and Sounds," columnist Robbin Coons commented on Chaney's ongoing role, and the rut he was in: "He looks like anybody else of his size and build all wrapped up, and what is embalmed for the moment is actually his career. You take away an actor's face and what has he left? Frustration."[13]

Chaney bemoaned his plight to Coons: "I sit up all night learning my dialogue. My dialogue? What am I talking about? I never say anything. I've no lines, no face. But I have a bet. I've bet that some day one of these pictures will lose money, and then I won't have to do any more. So far, though . . . ."[14]

The Mummy's Curse turned out to be the last of the series, but in another instance of *never say never* Chaney would tackle a similar part fifteen years later in the 1959 Mexican *La Casa Del Terror* (*Face of the Screaming Werewolf* for US release) where he'd play not only a mummy but a werewolf as well. A Halloween segment of the *Route 66* television series ("Lizard's Leg and Owlet's Wing," 1962) would place him in the same roles several years later, with Boris

---

[12] Michael Brunas, John Brunas, Tom Weaver, *Universal Horrors: The Studio's Classic Films, 1931-1946* (Jefferson, NC: McFarland and Company, Inc., 1990), 481.

[13] Robbin Coons, "Hollywood Sights and Sounds," *Niagara Falls Gazette*, September 7, 1944, 23.

[14] *Ibid.*

Karloff co-starring as Frankenstein's monster. While there would be another twenty-five years of active work in the industry ahead of him, the glory days of *Of Mice and Men* and *The Wolf Man* were well behind him by now.

§

17 The Inner Sanctum Mysteries (Part 2, 1944-1945)

Around the mid- to latter part of 1944, there were growing indications that a segment of the film industry planned to get away from double billing. The B units at Warner Brothers, 20th Century-Fox, and Paramount had all been recently eliminated, and there was a marked increase in the production of features with a running time of two hours or more. Several studios increased their short feature production to accompany the longer A films, and there was a generally expressed desire among industry leaders to reduce the overall number of features produced.[1] Universal did not seem to be a part of this trend, however: from a planned high for the 1941-1942 season of sixty-one features, fourteen low-budget westerns and adventures, and four serials, each of the following four seasons saw the planned production of fifty-five features, seven westerns, and three or four serials. Universal's 1945-1946 season's schedule would be one of the heaviest programs announced by any of the major studios,[2] and one that toward season's end resulted in a backlog of unreleased product. It was not until the 1946-1947 season that planned production of features dropped to forty-five; westerns remained at seven, and serials at four.[3]

---

[1] Although mid-1945 showed an increase again in the major companies' B's (now budgeted between $300,000 to $500,000) as a result of the encroachment of shabbier films made by smaller companies; the so-called "super" pictures and top A's could do all right by themselves, but the weaker, less popular A's needed the support of a second feature.

[2] "Universal to Make 55 Feature Films," *New York Times*, June 12, 1944, page unknown; "55 Features Planned," *New York Times*, August 29, 1945, page unknown.

[3] "Universal Releases Set for 45 Pictures," *New York Times*, June 27, 1946, page unknown.

Dead Man's Eyes
(Director: Reginald LeBorg; Released November 10, 1944)

There aren't any supernatural elements in *Dead Man's Eyes*, the intriguingly titled third entry in the "Inner Sanctum" series. It is a mystery, pure and simple, and a love story of sorts. Practically every character in the film is infatuated with another, and not in the healthiest of ways: artist Dave Stuart (Lon Chaney) shares a reciprocal love with fiancée Heather Hayden (Jean Parker); paranoid cad Nick Phillips (George Meeker) is still obsessed with former girl Heather; Stuart's model Tanya Czoraki (Acquanetta) keeps her infatuation with Stuart to herself; and Stuart's good friend (and psychiatrist) Alan Bittaker (Paul Kelly) takes every available opportunity to visit his artist friend so that he can surreptitiously drool over Tanya. Throw Heather's wealthy father Stanley Hayden (Edward Fielding) into the mix, with his man-crush on Stuart and seeming dislike for practically everyone else in the film (he takes every available opportunity to verbally berate and belittle Nick) and you have the underpinnings for the mystery that follows.

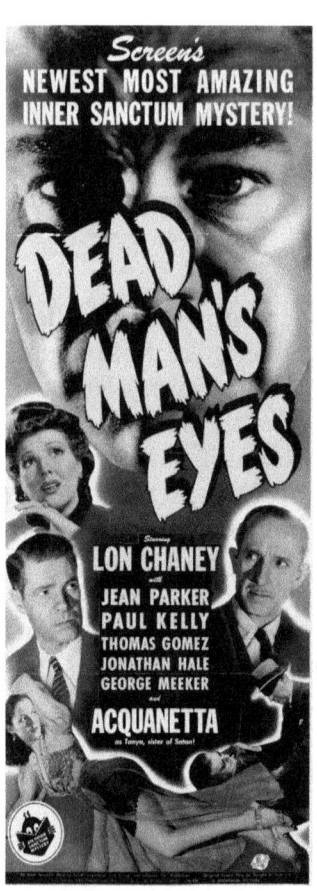

"Acquanetta as Tanya, Sister of Satan!" Sister of Satan? *Dead Man's Eyes* (1944). Image courtesy of Heritage Auction Galleries, Ha.com.

The story is set in motion when Tanya innocently rearranges the bottles on Stuart's shelf while reaching for a box of tissues. When Stuart goes to soothe his weary eyes with some boric acid solution, he instead grabs a misplaced bottle of acetic acid and accidentally blinds himself. "Dad" Hayden calls in eye specialist Dr. Welles (Jonathan Hale), who says that Stuart's only hope is through a corneal transplant that just might restore his vision. The hitch, of course, is finding a donor. "Dad" Hayden steps up to the plate, willing his eyes to Stuart in the event of his death. Hayden makes it a point to threaten Tanya with prosecution for "intentionally" blinding Stuart, thereby adding another potential enemy to the list of people who already hate him.

The Inner Sanctum Mysteries, Part II (1944-1945)

Tanya (Acquanetta) innocently rearranges the bottles in *Dead Man's Eyes* (1944).

Stuart, now short-tempered, self-pitying, and drinking heavily because his career as an artist has been cut short (did he really think his amateurish painting of Tanya would make him famous?), doesn't want to stick Heather with a life of caring for a blind man. He tells her he doesn't love her, and instead loves Tanya. Heather is shattered, and Stuart is now miserable. Tanya, acting as Stuart's nurse, calls in Alan when she hears Stuart crying in his room. Instead of attending to Stuart, however, Alan professes his love to Tanya. She brushes him off and leaves, so with nothing else to do Alan switches into psychiatrist mode and deals with Stuart. He convinces him to patch things up with "Dad" Hayden, with whom Stuart had been rather rough and abrupt previously in his bull-headed approach to being left alone.

Persistent Nick has Heather meet him at a nightclub and tries to convince her that she should stop pitying Stuart, accept that he is blind, and marry him—Nick—instead. This doesn't sit well with her, and she storms out of the place. Heather returns home to find Stuart in her father's library, blood on his hands, her dad dead on the floor with a caved-in skull. Stuart says he found "Dad" that way, but she thinks otherwise. The cops are called and Stuart is arrested. Because of her father's will, Dr. Welles proceeds with the corneal transplant in spite of Heather's objections. On his way to the hospital with his canister of Hayden's eyeballs, Welles gets sidetracked and Tanya makes off with the canister. She figures that if Stuart remains blind he'll never return to Heather. Alan confronts her and convinces her to return the canister, which she agrees to do, successfully and without being seen. The operation takes place but Stuart still can't see when the bandages are eventually removed, the operation seemingly a failure. (Amazingly, the acid-induced scar tissue is now gone!)

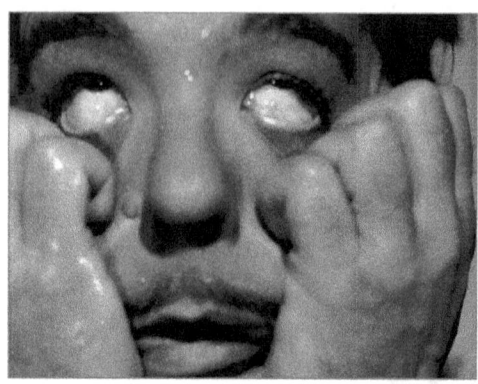

Chaney's acid-filled eyes will soon need a *Dead Man's Eyes* (1944) transplant.

Police Captain Drury (Thomas Gomez) investigates, and while Stuart has the most obvious motive, he doesn't write off Nick or Tanya, either. Heather has come to suspect Nick as well, given his motive and opportunity. Stuart is released from jail, and struggles to recall where the tiny nail he found at the scene of "Dad" Hayden's murder might have come from.

Alan convinces Tanya to meet him for dinner at the Club Royale, where she jealously announces that she hates Heather. Drunken Nick arrives and confronts the couple, ugly words are traded, and the group breaks up. Heading home alone and now resigned to the reality that Stuart doesn't love her and never will, Tanya calls Heather and tells her she knows who killed "Dad" Hayden. In true B movie tradition, she is bludgeoned to death by a shadowy figure right before she can name the killer. Drury returns to confront and grill Stuart over this newest murder, and states outright that he doesn't think Stuart is really blind.

Stuart asks Alan to come to his apartment, and when the shrink arrives Stuart accuses him of the murders. His evidence? The tiny nail missing from the head of Alan's cane, the one Stuart now has in his possession. He theorizes that Alan had wanted Tanya for himself, and had killed "Dad" Hayden to free up his eyeballs, hoping that a successful operation would reunite Stuart and Heather. Alan admits guilt, but before he can add Stuart to his list of victims Drury appears from another room and arrests the fellow, part of a prearranged setup. Stuart reveals that he is

Tanya (Acquanetta), moments before her death, and before she can name the killer, in *Dead Man's Eyes* (1944).

The Inner Sanctum Mysteries, Part II (1944-1945)

no longer blind. His sight had returned days after the bandages were removed, but he'd decided to keep it to himself. He had suspected Tanya of the murders, and thought that would be a way to "secretly" observe her. Stuart and Heather are reunited.

Dead Man's Eyes was the third and final "Inner Sanctum" mystery to be directed by Reginald LeBorg, and his last of five assignments for Pivar. Production took place in March 1944 with Pivar as executive producer and Will Cowan as associate. Prolific pulp writer Dwight V. Babcock was lured into the industry to write the script for this film, his first of seven assignments for Pivar. This was the beginning of a career in low-budget film scripting that lasted through the decade, Babcock moving over to television in the fifties where he spent the next two decades. Veteran photographer Paul Ivano was brought on for this and the next entry in the series, *The Frozen Ghost*, midway through a career that began in the early twenties and would continue unabated through the sixties. The completed film was released in November 1944.

The *Inner Sanctum* logo.

In spite of its great little title, the results are slow going, overly talkative, and unremarkable, the story of barely sufficient interest to hold the viewer's attention for its brief sixty-four minutes. LeBorg seems to have gone through his paces with casual disinterest, although there are a few visually interesting moments such as a rapid dolly in on Heather when she receives the phone news of Stuart's accident, and Stuart's point of view of his room as he goes blind. Chaney's voice-overs are held to a minimum, and that is a welcome change. One moment of apparent sloppiness stands out, when Alan leaves Dave Stuart's apartment and says, "Goodnight, Ed," and no one took the time to loop in the correct name.

Chaney's role is much better suited for him than the previous two "sophisticates" he was required to portray, here more of an everyman whose dream of fame and wealth is cut short by unforeseen circumstances. It starts out as a sympathetic role due to his unfortunate plight, but soon his short fuse kicks in. He yells at whoever has the misfortune of dealing with him, and then apologizes, yells again and apologizes again, ad infinitum. Still, it is one of his better performances. Leading lady Jean Parker, a sort of poor man's Claudette Colbert, is suitably conflicted over her uncomfortable predicament, saddled as she is with a former love gone sour. Parker's career began in the early thirties where she appeared in far more prestigious films such as RKO's *Little Women* (1933; George Cukor) and *The Ghost Goes West* (1936; Rene Clair). By 1944, however, she was on that downhill slide, bouncing from studio to studio for appearances in low-budget efforts at Monogram (the short-lived *Kitty O'Day* series) and PRC. Paul Kelly comes across effectively as Stuart's supposedly sympathetic good friend, and Gomez handles the cookie-cutter cop role with customary coldness. Sixty-nine-year-old character actor Edward Fielding, in-and-out of film since the mid-teens, dropped dead while mowing his lawn a mere two months after the film's release.

And then there's Acquanetta. Her acting abilities haven't improved much in this, her third for Pivar and her fourth credited role at Universal. Still somewhat awkward in her performance, she is given a fair amount of dialog to stumble through. She does so with a strained, single-minded determination, emphatic in her delivery, enunciating every single word, one-by-one. Her performance prompted one of those annoyingly-initialed-only (and uncharitable) reviewers for *The New York Times* to describe her as "... a sloe-eyed lady... who seems to have run a talent for inarticulateness into professional recognition."[4]

Variety's reviewer (Sten? Who in hell is Sten?) was even more negative, trashing the film as a whole: "Filled with stilted dialog, lacking action and suffering from poor performances by most of the cast, 'Dead Man's Eyes' is an Inner Sanctum Mystery that is strictly for the lower dual bills."[5] The reviewer did manage a few words of faint praise, commenting that the "only one who gives out okay is the star, Lon Chaney," and that "direction by Reginald LeBorg keeps an even pace." *Daily Variety* concurred, saying that it "lumbers along heavily most of the way, with dull performances and wooden direction."[6] As if having viewed another picture altogether, *The Hollywood Reporter*'s review positively glowed, asserting that it was "a superior whodunit that should do a lot to sell other Universal program pictures to the trade, for it has been made with all the commercial possibilities thoroughly impregnated and will be a natural for lobby exploitation."[7] One man's meat is another man's poison, I suppose.

In a press release that accompanied the film's release, Chaney (ostensibly) disagreed with the notion that horrific films were a bad influence:

> Horror pictures are often an outlet for pent-up emotions. Far from being harmful, they tend to disperse whatever insane thoughts we may have because we are shown that evil thoughts can become

---

[4] P.P.K., "The Screen," *New York Times*, October 7, 1944, 11.

[5] Sten., "Dead Man's Eyes," *Variety*, September 13, 1944, 10.

[6] "Dead Man's Eyes," *Daily Variety*, September 13, 1944, 3.

[7] "Dead Man's Eyes," *Hollywood Reporter*, September 13, 1944, 3.

monstrosities. By making the characters ridiculous and the crimes hideous, we revolt the minds of movie-goers against evil tendencies.[8]

I'm convinced.

Dead Man's Eyes offered bona fide proof that Acquanetta, while lovely to look at, was not much of an actress. Frustrated by the limited roles she'd been assigned, and in another case of perceived greener grass on the fence's other side, Acquanetta announced in July that she was leaving Universal.[9] Unfortunately for her, it was the aforementioned *Tarzan and the Leopard Woman* that was on the other side. Aside from a few more random films such as *The Sword of Monte Cristo* (1951; Maurice Geraghty) and *Lost Continent* (1951; Sam Newfield), Acquanetta only seemed to resurface in the public eye due to her turbulent private life. A marriage to a Russia-born Mexico City importer in 1946 resulted in a son, but when the couple split and she filed for divorce and child support, it turned out that the marriage was not legal.[10] A marriage to a seventy-one-year-old magazine illustrator (his sixth!) in 1951 ended a year later after an initial divorce suit and follow-up reconciliation,[11] and while this was taking place her four-year-old son died of a gland tumor. The insurance company refused to pay, claiming that she'd failed to give full information regarding his medical history on her application form. She finally won that one,[12] and in the interim she had married an automobile dealer. They had four children before they too divorced in the eighties. Acquanetta died in 2004 after suffering through several years with Alzheimer's.[13]

The Frozen Ghost
(Director: Harold Young; Released June 29, 1945)

What had originally been intended as the third entry in the series ended up as the fourth when a suitable script proved elusive. *The Frozen Ghost* was first announced in the trades in October 1943, stating that Pivar had chosen Harrison Carter and Henry Sucher to write an original story around that title.[14]

---

[8] "Actor Defends Horror Movies," Hagerstown, MD *Morning Herald*, November 16, 1944, 4.

[9] Hedda Hopper, "Looking at Hollywood," *Los Angeles Times*, June 10, 1944, 6.

[10] "Actress Asks $1000 Monthly for Child," *Los Angeles Times*, December 22, 1951, 15.

[11] "Acquanetta Sues Clive for Divorce," *Los Angeles Times*, December 20, 1952, A2.

[12] "Acquanetta Wins Lawsuit Over Death of Her Son," *Los Angeles Times*, November 29, 1955, A5.

[13] "Acquanetta, 83, a Star of B Movies," *New York Times*, August 23, 2004, page unknown.

[14] Ivan Spear, "Hollywood Report," *Boxoffice*, October 30, 1943, 40.

Once that was completed, Bernard Schubert was brought in to adapt the story for the screen.[15] Maurice Tombragel took over from Schubert, but his efforts were cut short when Uncle Sam summoned him for a stint in the military; he was replaced by Luci Ward.[16] Will Cowan was assigned to associate produce the film, with Harold Young directing. Shooting commenced on Monday, June 19, 1944,[17] but the completed film was held back and released a year later in late July 1945, on a limp double-bill with *The Jungle Captive*, also directed by Young.

Famous hypnotist Alex Gregor (Chaney), professionally known as Gregor the Great, is overcome with guilt when the uncooperative and mocking drunk (Arthur Hohl) he has selected from the audience dies on stage ("I could kill him," thinks Gregor, moments before the man collapses). Gregor tries to turn himself in to homicide bureau Inspector Brant (Douglass Dumbrille) for murder, but he is rebuffed when the coroner absolves him of any responsibility. This doesn't sway Gregor, who firmly believes he has the power to "will" people dead. He fires his on-stage hypnotic subject medium (and fiancée) Maura Daniels (Evelyn Ankers) and tells his disbelieving business manager George Keene (Milburn Stone) that he is quitting the business. Gregor writes a note bequeathing all his money and personal property to Maura in the event that anything should happen to him, and gives it to Keene for safekeeping.

The Frozen Ghost (1945). Image courtesy of Heritage Auction Galleries, Ha.com.

Keene shows the note to mutual friend Mme. Valerie Monet (Tala Birell), owner of the Monet Wax Museum and a former lover of Gregor's. Keene suggests that she take Gregor under her wing, let him move into museum quarters, and give him something new and useful to do such as researching the various displays. He tells her that this change of pace may be just what Gregor needs to clear his mind of his own personal demons. Valerie agrees,

---

[15] Ivan Spear, "Hollywood Report," *Boxoffice*, January 15, 1944, 50.

[16] "Studio Personnelities: Scripters," *Boxoffice*, May 20, 1944, 57.

[17] Edwin Schallert, "Film Pact Forecasts Stardom for Da Silva," *Los Angeles Times*, June 16, 1944, A8

and Gregor is talked into the arrangement as well. Keene brings Gregor over to the museum where he is introduced to Rudi (Martin Kosleck), the sculptor who is responsible for creating all of the museum's wax figures' faces. Rudi seems to have a few screws loose, and takes an instant dislike to Gregor. Valerie also introduces Gregor to her niece Nina Coudreau (Elena Verdugo), who lives at the museum as well.

It soon becomes apparent that Gregor is the object of love for every female in the film. Maura still loves him even though she no longer knows where he is, former flame Valerie keeps her passions to herself but wants to keep Gregor close by, and young Nina has a schoolgirl crush on the famous fellow. This annoys hot-head Rudi no end, since he is infatuated with Nina but is shot down every time he makes another obnoxious pass at her. Rudi, as it turns out, was formerly Dr. Rudi Poldan, a renowned plastic surgeon whose career went down in flames when he was blamed for the ruination of a "wealthy dowager's" face.

Rudi convinces Valerie that Gregor is having an affair with her niece, and she goes ballistic. Confronting Gregor, she makes her accusations and proceeds to mock him, which sends poor Gregor off the deep end. Valerie collapses under his stare. When Gregor awakens from a blackout and finds himself on a riverside pier with Valerie's scarf in hand, he thinks he may now be responsible for a second death. He confides his fears to Keene, who insists they go and see Valerie to confirm that she is all right. Arriving at the museum, they are greeted by Inspector Brant, who was summoned to the place by Nina when she found her aunt missing. Rudi and Nina are there as well, and at Brant's request Rudi accompanies him for a look-see through the museum. Valerie's body is stretched out in costume in one of the tableaus, but Rudi manages to hide her from Brant's sight.

Brant is suspicious of Gregor, but he doesn't rule out Maura, either. Visiting her at her home, he grills her and states a possible motive of jealousy. Back at the museum, Nina stumbles across her aunt's body in the tableau, and screams. Rudi, alerted by the screams, pursues her while throwing knife after knife, none of which connect. Nina runs to Gregor's room for help, but when she finds him with her aunt's scarf she screams, "You're both in it" and runs from him. Rudi intercepts her and locks her away in a side room.

It is now revealed that Keene, the trustee of Gregor's estate, is in cahoots with Rudi. His goal is to drive Gregor mad, have him committed, and thereby gain access to Gregor's wealth. Rudi shows Keene how he has used his past medical skills to put both Nina and Valerie into states of suspended animation, and will revive them both once Gregor is out of the way. He blames Gregor for his having to put them both in long-term trances. When Keene discovers that Valerie has actually died, Rudi panics. Keene instructs him to get rid of Valerie's body in the museum's huge furnace, and dump unconscious Nina in there as well while he is at it.

Stop Yellin'

Gregor ponders Nina's accusation, and realizes that by "both" she must have meant Rudi as well. Brant unsuccessfully attempts to arrest Gregor and Maura as they rush to the museum. Keene intercepts them upon their arrival, but Gregor balks when Keene attempts to misdirect them out of the place. Gregor says he is going to put Maura in another trance to find out what she "sees" in a desperate, last-ditch effort to locate Valerie and Nina. Meanwhile, Rudi has consigned Valerie's body to the flames, and now intends to do the same to Nina.

Once Maura is in a trance, she is prompted by Gregor to tell what she "sees" while Keene looks on nervously. She reveals that she "sees" a man standing over Nina's body, but can't identify him. She can, however, identify Keene, and says so. The cat now out of the bag, Keene attempts to escape but is arrested by Brant who has followed the couple to the museum. Maura mentions "seeing" flames, and Gregor now knows what that means. He dashes to the furnace room in time to save Nina. Rudi is less fortunate, backing away from Gregor and, clumsy fellow that he is, falls into the open furnace.

The Frozen Ghost is little more than a dull little mystery, and while the performances are competent, the characters are flat and two-dimensional. There is little sympathy or involvement with the leads, and Chaney's acting—he is playing the tortured soul once again—is forced and mannered throughout. Set in and around a large wax museum, the film does have several effectively handled (and rather grisly) scenes in the wax-melting furnace room, with Kosleck's climactic incineration in the furnace like something out of Grimm's fairy tales. Harold Young's occasional directorial flourishes are heavy-handed, in stark contrast with the bulk of the film that is staged in a perfunctory manner. The opening in the radio studio is distractingly self-conscious, with each subsequent shot filmed at an opposing forty-five-degree angle from the previous shot. And every time Chaney goes to hypnotize someone, his eyes go wide and the camera moves in to an extreme close-up that just about knocks you out of your seat. There's a scene set in an outdoor café with Stone and Birell that positively reeks of artificiality: the rear-projection street scene beyond is a terrible process shot, washed out and constantly twitching out of registry with the foreground action.

The film's plusses are few and far between. The opening is of a poster for "The Fascinating Maura—The Hypnotic Subject of the Mysterious Gregor the Great," its close-up drawing of Maura's face dissolving into the flesh-and-blood Maura, inside the theater and deep in a trance. Several of the interior sets are stunning, no doubt reused from another, higher-budget production; both Gregor's apartment and the museum's office actually have ornate ceilings that Paul Ivano's camera takes pains to keep in view.

Douglass Dumbrille is this film's obstinate detective, somewhat more enjoyable than his predecessors as he fussily goes about each room straightening its picture frames. A noted stage actor of the twenties and thirties, Dumbrille even has the opportunity to recite multiple passages from Shakespeare, if only to Rudi who's more focused on hiding a body than admiring his guest's thespic abilities.

Douglass Dumbrille takes time out from straightening pictures to grill Evelyn Ankers in *The Frozen Ghost* (1945).

As for Kosleck's Rudi, he is a stereotyped though sufficiently sinister character, and chews the scenery at every opportunity. By this time firmly associated in the minds of movie-goers as the preeminent on-screen Nazi, Rudi comes off as yet another hissable war-era German rather than the eastern European his character's last name would suggest—you can take the boy out of his Nazi uniform, but you can't take the Nazi out of the boy. One hopes after seeing Rudi's accuracy with a series of thrown knives that he was a better surgeon than knife thrower. *The Hollywood Reporter* singled out Kosleck for comment: "Kosleck, incidentally, despite the clichés of characterization, is the scariest thing in the film. His malevolence has conviction."[18]

Milburn Stone delivers a solid, believable performance as Gregor's duplicitous business manager, and relative newcomer Elena Verdugo is appropriately perky in only her fourth credited role following on the heels of

---

[18] "Kosleck Best Thing In Lightweight Tale," *Hollywood Reporter*, June 13, 1945, 3.

her performance in *House of Frankenstein* (1944; Erle C. Kenton). Bucharest-born Tala Birell was brought over to Hollywood a dozen years earlier by Universal after several years on the Vienna stage and only a single British film to her credit. In spite of an on again-off again film career, she is quite good as the proprietor of the wax museum, secretly in love with Gregor and consumed by an overpowering jealousy. Birell's film career would last for only a few more films before returning to Germany.

Evelyn Ankers, by now thoroughly fed up with the substandard (in her estimation, at least) roles that she'd been receiving at Universal, had made her displeasure known. Hedda Hopper helped to spread the word, and on the same day that filming commenced.[19] *The Frozen Ghost* would be Ankers' last for the studio, and while she'd continue to make films through the end of the decade, it was for studios such as Republic, PRC, and Columbia, and of similarly modest though non-horrific fare.

Reviews were mixed. "J.R.L." at *The New York Times* panned the film: "When an uninspired cast is coupled with an uninteresting plot, the result is bound to add up to rather unexciting film fare, a fact proved conclusively in 'The Frozen Ghost.'"[20] *The Hollywood Reporter* placed blame on associate producer Will Cowan, stating that he "should have had his scenarists concentrate on motivation and character rather than props and ancient suspense gags."[21] *Variety* was a bit more positive ("Its climax ... is surprising enough to please whodunit fans."[22]), while Grace Kingsley positively gushed over Chaney ("Lon Chaney, without benefit of gargoyle face or crooked limbs and indeed playing a hero role, shows you that he is a fine actor ... He concentrates on the psychological phase of his characterization [and] plays effectively the part of a hypnotist"[23]). They were all, in their own way, right.

Strange Confession
(Director: John Hoffman; Released October 5, 1945)

In 1944, United Artists released the Douglas Sirk-directed *Summer Storm*. While in production, the film had gone through a series of title changes, announced successively as *The Shooting Party*, *The Moon Their Mistress*, *Strange Confession*, and *Goodbye My Love* before acquiring its release title.[24] With *Strange Confession* freed up, Universal grabbed it for the next in the

---

[19] Hedda Hopper, "Looking at Hollywood," *Los Angeles Times*, June 19, 1944, 11.

[20] J.R.L., "The Screen," *New York Times*, July 28, 1945, 7.

[21] *Hollywood Reporter, op cit.*

[22] Sten., "The Frozen Ghost," *Variety*, June 13, 1945, 30.

[23] Grace Kingsley, "Two Thrillers on View," *Los Angeles Times*, September 20, 1945, 11.

[24] Ivan Spear, "Spearheads," *Boxoffice*, May 13, 1944, 45.

The Inner Sanctum Mysteries, Part II (1944-1945)

"Inner Sanctum" series, announced in January 1945. Shooting was underway by February with newcomer John Hoffman at the helm. Filming was delayed slightly when Chaney dislocated a vertebra, the result of a poorly executed sneeze.[25] The finished film was released on October 5, 1945, and for this and all subsequent films made during his tenure at Universal, Pivar's name would appear simply and solely as "Producer."

M. Coates Webster's screenplay was based on Jean Bart's play *The Man Who Reclaimed His Head*, which had an embarrassingly short twenty-eight-performance run in 1932 in Broadway's Broadhurst Theatre after a trial run in Philadelphia. Universal acquired the rights to the play and made it into a film with the same title in 1935, with Claude Rains reprising his role from the stage production and Joan Bennett replacing the stage's Jean Arthur as his wife; Edward Ludwig directed.

The film is better than the poster, honest. *Strange Confession* (1945). Image courtesy of Heritage Auction Galleries, Ha.com.

Strange Confession was a loose reworking of the original film, with Rains' French ghostwriter replaced by Chaney's chemist, and the unscrupulous publisher played in the original by Lionel Atwill enacted here by J. Carrol Naish as the head of a drug manufacturing firm. It is amusing to note that *New York Times* critic Brooks Atkinson commented on Rains' stage performance in 1932 as such: "Claude Rains has acted it with a Lon Chaney make-up and a panting of steam."[26] Senior, no doubt.

Chemist Jeffrey Carter (Chaney), in pain and carrying a heavy satchel, arrives at the elegant home of Brandon (Wilton Graff), a noted attorney and former schoolmate. He begs Brandon to hear him out, and when the attorney hesitates, Carter shows him the contents of his satchel. Stunned by what he sees (and we don't), Brandon sits beside Carter and has him tell his story.

---

[25] Harrison Carroll, "Hollywood," *Evening Independent*, February 14, 1945, 4.

[26] Brooks Atkinson, "The Play: Showmanship and Passion in a Drama Entitled 'The Man Who Reclaimed His Head,'" *New York Times*, September 9, 1932, 17.

Stop Yellin'

Two years earlier Carter worked in the lab of Roger Graham (J. Carrol Naish), owner of the city's largest chemical distributing company. Graham has grown rich reaping the rewards of Carter's past discoveries, hogging the glory all for himself. He even has Carter write the acceptance speech he gives when honored for his achievements. Carter realizes that he is being exploited and underpaid, but he loves his work. His wife Mary (Brenda Joyce) yearns for better things, cooped up in a second-floor walkup with their young son Tommy (Gregory Muradian), making due on her husband's meager salary.

Graham is unscrupulous, and with an eye solely on the money to be made will frequently rush new products into the marketplace before they have been thoroughly tested. When he attempts to pressure Carter into turning over the formula for a medicine still in the testing phase, Carter refuses and resigns. Graham sees to it that Carter is blacklisted within the industry, forcing Carter to go to work as a pharmacist for kindly Mr. Moore (Christian Rub).

A year later on New Year's Eve, Graham pays a visit to Carter in his apartment while Mary is downstairs attending an impromptu party. Graham asks Carter to return to work for him, and to name his own terms. Carter, bitter over his past treatment, politely refuses. When Mary hears of this, she tells him he is stubborn and convinces him to accept. "Take advantage of him this time," she says. She wants the finer things in life, so Carter reluctantly agrees.

Reunited with his affable fellow chemist Dave (Lloyd Bridges), the two resume work on the drug Carter calls Zymurgine,[27] an intended treatment for colds, influenza, and pneumonia. The formula is lacking one item, however: the mold from a plant found only in South America. Graham visits the chemists in their lab and is informed that the drug as it stands is only 75% successful, and that the missing ingredient is essential for its increased efficacy. Graham is shown Carter's typed formula notes and compliments the fellows on their good work. Graham invites Carter and Mary over to dinner at his house, and Mary is thrilled at the news. She now lives in a nice house with a housekeeper, Mrs. O'Connor (Mary Gordon), and has had a taste of the better life. Graham's invitation suggests that even better things are to come.

That night at dinner, Graham announces that he is sending both Carter and Dave down to South America to set up a lab and continue their experiments. Carter is thrilled, but what he doesn't realize is that at that moment Graham's right-hand man Stevens (Milburn Stone) is back in the lab copying Carter's formula. Graham wants Carter out of the way so that he can rush the ineffective Zymurgine onto the market, and needs the formula to do so. Graham also has his eyes on Mary, and thinks he can win her over once Carter is out of the picture.

---

[27] A curious name for a drug, as zymurgy is the art and science of fermentation, as in brewing beer and making wine.

The Inner Sanctum Mysteries, Part II (1944-1945)

Carter and Dave go to work south of the border, oblivious to the fact that Graham is back home approving packaging and advertising for the new product, complete with testimonials from individuals duped into thinking it actually cured them. In the evening, Graham wines and dines Mary at his home, and shows her the bolo knife that Carter has sent to him as a gift, a curved blade affair similar to a machete and used primarily for clearing vegetation. Mary seems pleased with all that Graham does for her, but remains faithful to her husband.

Carter and Dave finally meet with complete success, and find that the active substance in the mold can be made synthetically. Carter cables the formula to Graham, but it is too late; the faulty product is already on the market, and production has been doubled to meet demand due to a new wave of influenza. Graham wants to keep Carter out of his hair for a while longer, assigning the two chemists to additional South America-based experiments. Graham continues his pursuit of Mary, but without the kind of success he hopes for.

When Tommy gets sick with influenza, Mary calls in Dr. Williams (Addison Richards). Knowing of her husband's success and thinking that the Zymurgine on the market is the newest formula, she pushes for its use on her son. The doctor objects, saying that it has not been thoroughly tested, and in his estimation of little use. Undeterred, Mary goes out and buys a bottle, but soon finds that the medicine doesn't work. Meanwhile, Carter and Dave find bottles of Zymurgine on the shelf in a small village store. Checking the ingredients, they find that it consists of the old, ineffectual formula. Carter is outraged, and realizes that Graham has suckered him once again. Having been informed of Tommy's illness, Carter cables Mary, informs her of the bogus product, and tells her that Graham has the real formula. He packs up and heads back home. Mary attempts to contact Graham, but he is out of town. Tommy dies.

When Graham returns from his trip, he contacts Mary and invites her over to his home. She quietly accepts, and packs a revolver in her handbag. When she arrives, Graham makes his big move and professes his love for her. Mary becomes furious, tells him of her son's death and his culpability, and pulls out her pistol. Graham disarms her, but as he attacks her Carter arrives, having been informed by the housekeeper of Tommy's death. Carter grabs the bolo knife he had sent to Graham as a gift, and as he approaches menacingly, Graham shoots him twice. Unfortunately for Graham, his accuracy is poor, and Carter proceeds to hack off his boss' head.

His story finished, the contents of his satchel become evident. Mary arrives at Brandon's home along with the police who had been alerted by Brandon's butler, and Carter is led away. Brandon assures Mary that "I'll do everything I can for him."

The fifth film in the "Inner Sanctum" series came as a welcome surprise, arguably the finest entry to date. Devoid of its predecessors' supernatural overtones, it is a tragedy pure and simple, and light years away from the Grand Guignol overtones that hovered over *The Frozen Ghost*. M. Coates Webster's screenplay is good enough to make one forget about the amateurish script he cranked out for his first Pivar effort, *The Jungle Captive*. Thankfully, Webster avoided the annoying voice-overs that intruded on the earlier films. James Hoffman, new to feature direction, delivers a competent-looking production, his past experience as editor assumedly an assist in choosing camera angles and staging. The sets are typically solid looking and appear lived in, and Maury Gertsman's photography and lighting are consistently effective. One false note creeps in during the final confrontation between Graham and Carter, courtesy of a clumsy sound editor: we hear two gunshots, but it is quite evident visually that Graham has only fired the pistol once.

The performances are uniformly good, both by the leads and supporting actors. Chaney gives a sympathetic and believable performance as the dedicated chemist, with nary a trace of the artifice that frequently would bedevil some of his roles. Naish oozes insincere charm as his duplicitous boss, and the audience can't wait for the slimy bastard to get his comeuppance. Lloyd Bridges is immensely likable as Carter's chemist buddy Dave, breezy and relaxed delivering affectionate banter. His is the kind of effortless performance one wishes more of Universal's B movie leading men would have been capable of, but in many instances weren't. Milburn Stone is back once more as Graham's ethically-challenged right-hand man, and with each new role it becomes increasingly apparent why Pivar would hire him time and again.

As for Chaney's on-screen wife, Brenda Joyce acquits herself satisfactorily. One of the more curious-looking actresses of the era, Joyce had been groomed by 20th Century-Fox for a stardom that proved elusive, resulting in less desirable roles in their B films. Joyce took a break from the industry, but returned a couple of years later as Tarzan's Jane in a series of films made by Sol Lesser for release through RKO. Joyce squeezed in a handful of films for Universal between her jungle-based exploits, including this one and the final "Inner Sanctum" entry, *Pillow of Death*. Her angular good looks usually come across well on the screen, but there's a hardness to her features that dominate in the occasional still shot. It didn't seem to bother Tarzan, though.

Perhaps the finest performance is delivered by Bebe, the thirteen-year-old female South American ringtail monkey who appears in the film as Bridges' south of the border pet. Bebe was a seasoned veteran by the time *Strange Confession* was made, having appeared in various films for the past ten years and earning her trainer Melvin Koontz a cool $3,000 per year for repeat appearances in Dorothy Lamour's tropical pictures at Paramount. Bebe's cut?

The Inner Sanctum Mysteries, Part II (1944-1945)

A bag of peanuts per day, although cast and crew of this latest film reportedly rewarded her with a box of Cracker Jack when her scenes were completed.[28]

Chaney presents a modest gift to wife Brenda Joyce, one of the more curious-looking actresses of the era, in *Strange Confession* (1945).

Strange Confession was virtually impossible to see for many years after its initial release, aside from the Realart rerelease in 1953 under the new title *The Missing Head*. The authors of *Universal Horrors: The Studio's Classic Films, 1931-1946* [29] report that the scuttlebutt regarding the film's lack of availability was due to a legal screw-up on Universal's part. Evidently the original contract with Jean Bart allowed for only one film version of the play to be made, and that *Strange Confession* was an unauthorized remake. As a result, the film was caught up in a legal limbo for decades to follow, and Universal had to withdrawal the film from all theatrical and television distribution. The issue appears to have been resolved, with the film once again available along with the other five "Inner Sanctum" mysteries on Universal's 2006 DVD box set release *Inner Sanctum Mysteries: The Complete Movie Collection*. One would hope that the film's renewed availability will help improve its tattered reputation, one based primarily on word of mouth, supposition, and the handful of lukewarm

---

[28] John Todd, "In Hollywood," *Hammond Times*, March 16, 1945, 11.

[29] Michael Brunas, John Brunas, and Tom Weaver, *Universal Horrors: The Studio's Classic Films, 1931-1946* (Jefferson, NC: McFarland & Company, Inc., 1990), 514.

contemporary reviews from disinterested and dismissive reviewers such as Bosley Crowther.

Pillow of Death
(Director: Wallace Fox; Released December 14, 1945)

Shooting of *Pillow of Death* began on Monday, February 26, 1945, following closely on the heels of *Strange Confession*. The release of this final series entry was equally rushed, arriving in theaters in December 1945, a mere two months after its predecessor. George Bricker's script, adapted from an original story by Dwight V. Babcock, was bloated with dialog; it could easily been mistaken for having its origins on the stage, given that the bulk of the action (or lack thereof) takes place inside several of the Kincaid mansion's rooms. The Chaney voice-over gimmick has once again been dropped, and is not missed, but the viewer is not let off the hook; his character's dead wife's voice is the unwelcome replacement. The trademark opening with David Hoffman's disembodied head giving his little spiel about the Inner Sanctum is missing as well, perhaps a casualty of the film's original overlong running time (variously reported at sixty-seven, sixty-six, and sixty-five minutes, any of these lengths close to "epic" by B film standards).

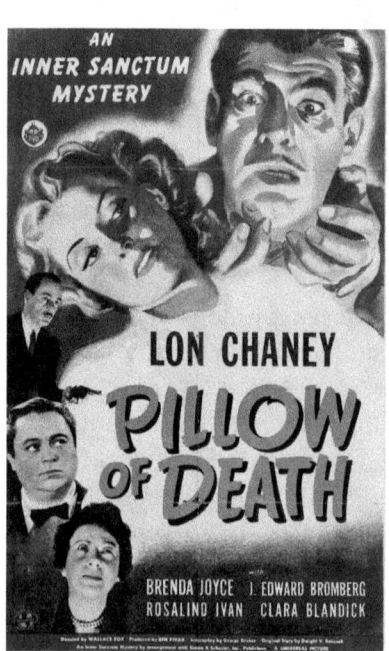

Pillow of Death (1945), the final entry in the Inner Sanctum series. Image courtesy of Heritage Auction Galleries, Ha.com.

Journeyman director Wallace Fox, long a staple at Monogram where he turned out dozens of westerns and "East Side Kids" comedies, was pulled from Universal's B western unit and pressed into service, and then returned just as quickly. Brenda Joyce, signed to a contract with the studio reportedly due to the good work she'd done on *Strange Confession*,[30] reappears here as Chaney's love interest. Befitting her status as departed actress Anne Gwynne's replacement at the studio, Joyce's wardrobe consisted of Vera West leftovers for Gwynne's role in *Weird Woman*. The film's modest (and budget-conscious) cast was rounded out by a dependable assemblage of character actors including

---

[30] Edwin Schallert, "Brenda Joyce Set for 'Pillow of Death,'" *Los Angeles Times*, February 27, 1945, A2.

The Inner Sanctum Mysteries, Part II (1944-1945)

J. Edward Bromberg, Rosalind Ivan, Clara Blandick, George Cleveland, and Wilton Graff. Newcomer Bernard B. Thomas made an appearance as well, which no doubt hastened the demise of his brief career before the cameras.

The Kincaid family has a lot of money, and plenty of time and opportunity to get on each other's nerves. Elderly Belle Kincaid (Clara Blandick) dominates the family, much to the annoyance of her cranky brother Sam (George Cleveland), and niece Donna's (Brenda Joyce) growing dismay. Amelia Kincaid (Rosalind Ivan), a relation from the British branch of the family that "frittered away" their fortune, lives with them as well, pressed into service as a maid of sorts. Donna works as secretary to noted lawyer Wayne Fletcher (Chaney), and their barely-suppressed love for each other is complicated by the fact that Wayne is married—unhappily so—to Vivian. Belle is up in arms over Donna's "relationship" with Fletcher, which she feels is improper and scandalous, and not to be tolerated. She takes every opportunity to let Donna know of her displeasure.

Fletcher returns home to find police Captain McCracken (Wilton Graff) in his home. Vivian has been murdered, apparently suffocated with a pillow. The police had been notified by "psychic investigator" Julian Julian (J. Edward Bromberg), who had gone to the house when Vivian failed to show up for an appointment (he had a "psychic presentiment that something was wrong"). Julian announces that he has been contacted by Vivian's spirit and told that Fletcher wanted Vivian out of the way so that he could hook up with Donna, which is true. Fletcher objects, saying that Vivian, fascinated with the occult, hadn't been herself since she'd first availed herself of Julian's psychic services a year earlier, acting strange and distant, and obsessed with suicide. McCracken hauls Fletcher down to the station when the timing of his alibi appears shaky.

Both Belle and Amelia have used Julian's services many times before, fully convinced of his ability to make contact with long-dead relations on the "other side." Sam, however, has little tolerance for the fellow's claims, and Donna is convinced it is all a sham as well. Later on, lacking anything more than circumstantial evidence on which to hold him, McCracken releases Fletcher. Belle is soon added to his list of suspects when it is learned that she had visited Vivian shortly before she was murdered.

Belle and Amelia arrange a séance with Julian to contact Vivian's spirit, and Sam, Donna, and Fletcher are asked to attend. Julian "summons" Vivian, and her voice is heard; she names Fletcher as her murderer. Fletcher, fed up with this nonsense, accuses Julian of being a fake, and goes after a fellow he spots hiding behind a door whom he states must be Julian's accomplice. It is the Kincaid's young neighbor Bruce Malone (Bernard B. Thomas), who has been hanging around, he claims, to protect Donna from Fletcher, whom he doesn't trust. Bruce spends the entire film sneaking around, peering through windows, and moving about the house via secret passages he'd discovered back when he and Donna were kids.

That night, Fletcher sits up drinking and chain-smoking, agonizing over his wife's death. He hears Vivian's voice, and is lured in a dazed state to the cemetery and the mausoleum where her coffin resides. Fletcher flees when his visit is interrupted by the church sexton. The next morning, Amelia finds Sam in his bed, apparently murdered in the same fashion as Vivian. McCracken interrogates Fletcher, who relays his story of the night before, but says he blacked out after his encounter with the sexton and remembers nothing further. Together they return to the mausoleum and find that Vivian's body is missing. Donna reveals that Sam had been investigating Julian's past, and had discovered that he was a former vaudevillian and ventriloquist. Julian's abilities as a psychic are now more questionable than ever, and provide a potential motive for Sam's death. When Belle is found murdered as well, Julian turns himself in, not to admit guilt but solely to save McCracken the trouble of tracking him down and arresting him.

Psychic investigator Julian Julian (J. Edward Bromberg), in *Pillow of Death* (1945).

Donna, now the heiress to the Kincaid fortune, asks Wayne to stay at the house for added safety, and in spite of Amelia's objections. Julian's incarceration sends Amelia off the deep end, and she manages to lock both Fletcher and Donna in a closet. Convinced that the police will eventually put Julian to death in the gas chamber, she decides to do the same to her captives. Fortunately, Julian is released due to lack of evidence and arrives back at the house in time to save the couple from a premature end.

Donna shows Fletcher one of the secret passageways that persistent Bruce knows about, following it to a basement chamber where they find Vivian's dead body—and Bruce, too; he claims he placed her body there to shock Fletcher into a confession! Fletcher gives Bruce the bum's rush, sends Donna up to bed, and heads into the living room to think things through. Vivian's voice returns, and lures him up to Sam's room where, in a trance, he fesses up to Sam's murder. Donna overhears Fletcher's one-sided conversation, and his confession to Vivian and Belle's murders as well. When Fletcher spots her, he attempts to add her to his list of victims. McCracken and Bruce arrive in the nick of time to rescue her, and Fletcher, out of his mind and lured by Vivian's

The Inner Sanctum Mysteries, Part II (1944-1945)

voice to "join" her, leaps from the bedroom window and to his death. Bruce and Donna are reunited in what one supposes was intended as a happy ending.

Arguably the weakest film of the series, *Pillow of Death* is an overly talkative exercise in tedium that leaves the viewer with more unanswered questions than answered. Wallace Fox's direction is unremarkable at best, although director of photography Jerome Ash provides the film whatever visual distinction it can muster with his moodily effective lighting and several interesting, if somewhat rough, prowling camera movements. Conversely, the optical zoom that opens the film stands out in stark contrast to the physically fluid camera work that one has come to expect from the studio on even its least ambitious B films, if only occasionally. As a mystery, the film is not particularly mysterious, the supernatural mumbo-jumbo merely clouds the issue, and logic seems in short order. Bruce's perpetual slinking about quickly grows to absurd proportions, and his questionable motive suggests that he should be a suspect as well, but that never seems to dawn on McCracken. After Vivian's body is found in the cellar, Fletcher sends Donna to bed and heads into the living room to think, but neither of them seems at all concerned about leaving the missing body where it was found, or body-napper Bruce off the hook. As for Vivian's "voice," what was its source during the séance when everyone in the room heard it rather than just Fletcher? Was it "real," or Julian's handiwork? Not that it really matters.

Chaney and Joyce both give credible performances, with Blandick perfect as Donna's haughty, close-minded aunt. Cleveland is the film's highlight as Donna's consistently complaining uncle ("This is my idea of nothing to do," he snaps at the séance) who has a soft spot for his niece. Ivan is quite good as the unbalanced relation from England, and pudgy, bug-eyed Bromberg sufficiently smug as the quietly self-confident psychic. Graff is okay as the investigator, but he is the least interesting of a long line of police dicks to appear in these films.

As love-struck neighbor Bruce Malone, actor Bernard Thomas is the film's weakest link, a thoroughly personality-less, two-dimensional character who comes across as more of a stalker than a neighbor concerned with Donna's well-being. His repeated intrusion into virtually every scene is at turns laughable and annoying, and the other characters' tolerance for his feeble excuses and explanations defies belief. Thomas, whose former credited claim to fame was several entries in MGM's *Crime Does Not Pay* series, ranks as one of Universal's least charismatic "make-do" wartime actors; it comes as no surprise that any hopes he may have had for stardom were quickly dashed with the war's end.

The film's cast of characters as a whole is one of the most unsympathetic, unlikeable collections of individuals in any of the series' six entries, with only Donna's determined spunk and Sam's caustic asides offering momentary respite from the general dysfunction of the group. The film is notable primarily in that Chaney, the perennial suspect, actually turns out to be the culprit.

With *Pillow of Death*'s release, the "Inner Sanctum" series came to an end with a whimper rather than a bang. Chaney's five-year contract with Universal expired with the completion of the film, and the actor, embittered by the callous treatment he felt he'd received at the hands of the studio, refused to renew. Chaney's next to last at Universal before *Pillow of Death* had been *House of Dracula*, the on-screen results clearly indicating that the Frankenstein, Wolf Man, and Dracula franchises were all running out of steam. Earning less-than-favorable reviews, the worn-out series were all shelved. A nondescript role followed in *The Daltons Ride Again* (1945; Ray Taylor), demonstrating a lack of interest in Chaney on the studio's part. *Pillow of Death* proved to be the proverbial straw.

Chaney, once again playing the tortured soul, in *Pillow of Death* (1945).

Meanwhile, Pivar's children still had the run of the studio, although daughter Lorie at her tender young age needed close monitoring—monitoring that occasionally fell through the cracks. One instance sticks with her, when her youthful exuberance resulted in her unceremonious removal from a western set: "I think it was the Universal backlot. I was about 5 or 6 so I don't remember too many details but I do remember being kicked out and Mom being very mad."[31] If it was Universal, her recollection of her age at the time overshoots the mark. If it was after Universal, the only known western that Pivar was associated with during that period took place in 1948, and may instead be the location for her mishap.

Before Judy had relocated from New York to California she had developed notable skills as a seamstress, a talent passed on from her mother Jennie, who had in turn learned from her mother. Judy's family had discouraged any thoughts about turning those talents into a career, but the talents remained and were put to continuous good use. Young Lorie's clothes were all handmade by Judy, many of them from her own original designs. Dressed up in the latest little outfit, Judy would show off her daughter to friends, neighbors, and Ben's co-workers at Universal. Or, as Lorie puts it, "showing me off like her little toy."[32]

Neil, on the other hand, had become more independent, not unusual in those more innocent, less-paranoid times. Neil and his friends could now head

---

[31] Lorie Pivar Viner correspondence, October 26, 2010.
[32] Lorie Pivar Viner correspondence with author, November 30, 2009.

The Inner Sanctum Mysteries, Part II (1944-1945)

over to the studio, on foot or by bike, unattended. In one instance this led to tragedy.

> Across the golf course, just before Universal, was a river. Shallow enough that I could wade or raft across and go up the bank into Universal's backlot. My friends and I would go quite often. One day when I did not go, one of my friends drowned in the river. Around fourth grade.[33]

More independence for Neil, but parents have a way of intruding on their children's fun. One of Neil's father's little-known talents was described by Andrew Fenady, who collaborated with Ben later in his career in the mid-fifties.

Happier times: Ben and Judy at the beach. Photo courtesy of Jan Pivar Dacri.

> I'll just tell you one thing about Ben now that a lot of people don't know. Are you ready? He was a great little hoofer! The fellow could dance! I saw him dance with professional dancers, and he was better than they were! He could tap dance; he could do all kinds of dances! He really had rhythm. I don't know—I don't know whether he was in vaudeville . . . or what the hell. But somewhere along the line . . . he was damn good![34]

Unfortunately, his son did not share Ben's love of dance. "When I was about ten, my dad forced me to take tap dance lessons from a friend of his named Alan something-or-other. That didn't last long."[35]

Neil's parents enrolled him in the Toluca Boys Club as well, which he described as "kind of an exclusive and convenient after school and weekend dumping ground for movie industry brats." Saturday mornings were spent in North Hollywood's El Portal Theater on Lankersheim Boulevard, enjoying their

---

[33] Neil Pivar correspondence with author, January 8, 2010.

[34] Andrew J. Fenady interview with author, March 22, 2010.

[35] Neil Pivar correspondence with author, March 22, 2010.

all-cartoon shows. In his free time, Neil avoided home as much as possible "to avoid being given chores to do." Boys will be boys.

§

18 The Final Few: Two Noirs, Two Horrors, and One *Horror*

By the end of 1945, Universal's position in the film community was strengthening, slowly but surely. The fiscal year ending November 3 showed a net high of $3,910,928 out of a gross of $51,049,428, compared with the previous year's net of $3,412,701 out of a gross of $51,561,504. A larger net on a smaller gross: clearly the parsimonious studio was doing something right. Expansion plans were announced in late January 1946: in addition to the improvement of Universal City studios, the formation of a new world-wide motion picture distributing concern was planned, as well as the formation of a new major American producing company. As a step toward this goal, Universal planned to acquire half interests in the Leo Spitz-William Goetz-producing company International Pictures Corporation.[1] By the end of the 1945-1946 fiscal year, net profits had grown by nearly 17% to an all-time high of $4,565,219 on a gross of $53,934,865.[2]

The public's interest in horror films was on the wane, but Universal kept cranking them out, albeit in a somewhat disinterested, cost-cutting fashion. The studio's popular "Sherlock Holmes" series, resurrected by Universal in 1942 after 20th Century-Fox had two big-budget goes at the character in 1939 (Sidney Lanfield's *The Hound of the Baskervilles* and Alfred L. Werker's *The Adventures of Sherlock Holmes*), resulted in a twelve-film series that lasted into 1946 under producer-director Roy William Neill's guidance. The studio's two most lavish genre productions, *The Phantom of the Opera* (1943; Arthur Lubin) and *The Climax* (1944; George Waggner), were by now relics of the past, with more modest expenditures the rule for the monster fests *House of*

---

[1] "Film Unit Reports New Profit Peak," *New York Times*, January 29, 1946, page unknown.

[2] "Three New Marks Set By Universal," *New York Times*, January 28, 1947, page unknown.

Stop Yellin'

Frankenstein (1944) and *House of Dracula* (1945; both Erle C. Kenton). The bulk of the remaining product of this sort churned out over the final years of the mid-forties were low-budget affairs, and most of these were assigned to the studio's de facto horror master Ben Pivar. His films were all produced on shoestring budgets and tight schedules, and while none of them ever achieved "classic" status, his four Kharis sequels remain in the public consciousness to this day. They almost always delivered the goods, and rabid fans of this sort of thing flocked to the theaters when each new modest genre production reached the screen. The growing problem, however, was that Universal had beaten its proven characters of Frankenstein, the Wolf Man, Dracula, Kharis, and Invisible people of both genders into the ground, and the public had grown weary of them. The studio also had the occasional annoying habit of attaching horrific-sounding titles to non-genre films, leaving disgruntled patrons miffed at having one pulled over on them, and not for a first time. Some new blood was needed in the increasingly anemic offerings, and to that end in late 1944 Pivar was assigned the task.

Universal issued a press release announcing Pivar's new assignment, and the trades responded with some amusement. Ivan Spear related to his *Boxoffice* readers that "Ben Pivar, Universal film-maker, has been handed what is possibly the toughest chore ever assigned a producer. He has been instructed 'to create and develop an entirely new series of horror characters.' And that at a studio where Frankenstein, Dracula, The Monster, The Mummy and The Mad Ghoul are standard equipment."[3]

Columnist Jimmie Fidler encouraged his readers to submit story suggestions in a tongue-in-cheek open letter:

> Dear Staff: Being the kind of employer who likes to point out opportunities to the hired help, I call your attention to an item in today's trade papers.
>
> At Universal, an associate producer named Ben Pivar has just been assigned a new task. He is to cook up gruesome, shuddery characters for a new horror series—characters that will outdo any hitherto created for the screen. Such a job may seem, at first thought, not too difficult, but I ask you to reflect. Universal produced "The Wolf Man," "The Frankenstein Monster," "The Mummy," "The Mad Ghoul," "The Creeper" and "Dracula." Columbia has three copyrighted horror characters. PRC has a couple and Monogram has one.
>
> I'm afraid poor Mr. Pivar, before his new series is very old, will be in a very receptive mood for suggestions. And you know what Hollywood

---

[3] Ivan Spear, "Spearheads," *Boxoffice*, November 25, 1944, 51.

is willing to pay for suggestions. Why just the other day a chap sold one to Paramount for $28,000 without bothering to put it on paper.

So instead of hounding me for raises, why don't you seize the opportunity while it's knocking at your doors. Eat unpalatable dishes late at night and make notes on your inevitable nightmares. You may be able to ride one to fame and fortune. Spend your weekends in insane asylums and mortuaries; make it a point to attend the best available murder trials. In short, LIVE HORRIBLY, kiddies, and cash in.

Jimmie Fidler, November, 1944[4]

House of Horrors
(Director: Jean Yarbrough; Released March 29, 1946)

In November, Universal's publicity department issued a release stating that production executive Ben Pivar, assigned to develop a new series of horror characters, would introduce "The Creeper" in what they touted as a "top-budget picture" with the tentative title of *The House of Horrors*.[5] The opening credits of *House of Horrors*, the film that eventually reached the screen almost a year-and-a-half later, reiterated that the film was "Introducing Rondo Hatton as The Creeper." This was, of course, somewhat of a stretch, since Hatton had appeared in the Sherlock Holmes film *The Pearl of Death* (1944) as a character called "The Hoxton Creeper," which was both filmed (April 1944) and released (September 1944) before Universal's announcement of this "new" character in November. Hatton had appeared in Pivar's *The Jungle Captive* as Moloch as well, filmed before this announcement (September 1944), but not released until the following year. Pivar's "new" creation was, in reality, simply a retooling of several characters that the hulking Hatton had inhabited over the previous few months. According to a studio blurb commenting on Hatton's role in *The Pearl of Death*, "The resultant flood of fan mail at Universal convinced Producer Ben Pivar that the character was worth an entire series, and so Hatton was signed for the role."[6] It would seem that Pivar did not have to give the issue a whole lot of thought, the character in effect dropped at his feet.

---

[4] Jimmie Fidler, "Fidler in Hollywood," *Nevada State Journal*, November 22, 1944, 4.

[5] "'The Creeper' New Horror for Films," *Brooklyn Eagle*, November 10, 1944, 10.

[6] "House of Horrors," *News-Palladium*, August 17, 1946, 6.

Meet the Creeper! (If you haven't already met him.)
House of Horrors (1946). Photo courtesy of Jerry Murbach
at Doctor Macro's High Quality Movie Scans, www.doctormacro.com.

A decade later when Pivar was working on a syndicated television show with co-worker Andrew J. Fenady, he told of the events surrounding his introduction to Hatton. Fenady recently recounted the story:

> One day his boss called him into his office, and he says: "I want you to meet your new leading man." And he pushes a button and says to his secretary: "Send him in." So in comes this fellow, and it was Rondo Hatton! He says, "You're going to do a series called *The Creeper*." I don't know how many of those he did. It was unfortunate they exploited whatever was wrong with him—he had some kind of a disease, I don't know what the hell it was. It elongated his jaw and it accentuated certain features. Nevertheless, he made a living out of it, so it's better than being unemployed, I guess.[7]

Pivar introduced both of his children to the hulking actor. Son Neil, who would have been only six or seven when he met the actor, recalls Hatton as "a very large, very nice, and very scary-looking man." Daughter Lorie, only three

---

[7] Andrew J. Fenady interview with the author, June 17, 2010.

at the time, doesn't appear to have had any qualms about climbing onto the big fellow's lap in a photo taken at the time.

By December it was announced that the first film of the new series would be *The Brute Man*,[8] the tentative *The House of Horrors* title evidently discarded, if only temporarily. Nothing more was mentioned about this upcoming production while Pivar concentrated on the final two "Inner Sanctum" mysteries, and it was almost a full year later when production of *Murder Mansion* was announced to begin on September 10, 1945.[9] Robert Lowery and Virginia Grey were announced as the romantic leads, with Kent Taylor conflictingly (and erroneously) named to play either "the principal menace role"[10] or the film's requisite detective.[11] Taylor's participation fell through, and radio announcer-cum-actor Bill Goodwin was signed to replace him as the film's indefatigable police dick. The cast was rounded out with Martin Kosleck as the deranged sculptor and, of course, the inimitable Rondo Hatton as "The Creeper." Jean Yarbrough was hired to direct George Bricker's script, his first but far from last for Pivar. *The Brute Man* had, by this time, been rescheduled to follow filming of this newest first entry, even though its script had been co-written by Bricker, M. Coates Webster, and Dwight Babcock earlier in the year.[12]

Three-year-old Lorie Pivar relaxing on the big guy's lap. Photo courtesy of Jan Pivar Dacri.

---

[8] "Screen News," *New York Times*, December 6, 1944, 26.

[9] "Edwin Schallert, "Robert Walker Adult Lead in 'Horses' Film," *Los Angeles Times*, September 1, 1945, A5.

[10] "Virginia Grey Set for Horror Film," *New York Times*, September 8, 1945, 12.

[11] "Kent Taylor in 'Murder Mansion,'" *Boxoffice*, September 22, 1945, page unknown.

[12] "Studio Personnelities," *Boxoffice*, December 16, 1944, 58; Ivan Spear, "Hollywood Report," *Boxoffice*, January 6, 1945, 28.

Stop Yellin'

Pivar has his eyes on lovely Joan Fulton on the *House of Horrors* set. Left to right: Helen McLemore (Pivar's secretary), unidentified, Robert Lowery, Pivar, Joan Fulton. Photo courtesy of Lorie Pivar Viner.

Impoverished sculptor Marcel De Lange (Martin Kosleck) anticipates his upcoming big score that night when deep-pocketed but artistically naive Mr. Samuels is to pay $1,000 for De Lange's latest creation, a modernistic jumble he calls "Surcease from Toil." To De Lange's dismay, however, Samuels brings acid-tongued *Manhattan Magazine* art critic F. Holmes Harmon (Alan Napier) along with him, who outright dismisses the piece as "tripe, pure, unadulterated tripe—with an overtone of lunacy. I loathe it." Outraged, De Lange chases them out of his studio at knifepoint, and then embarks on a fog-bound journey to the pier where he intends to end his life.

Instead, he ends up dragging a waterlogged, nearly-drowned victim from the drink. It is The Creeper (Rondo Hatton), a huge, physically deformed madman previously wanted for a series of spine-snapping murders but now thought dead by the police. The Creeper's bizarre visage immediately inspires De Lange to dispense with suicide and go to work on what he is convinced will be his crowning masterpiece: "Magnifique! The perfect Neanderthal man!"

De Lange's kindness toward The Creeper is returned in kind, and soon the two share a tight bond. De Lange produces a sketch to work from, and the dimwitted Creeper-of-few-words dutifully poses while continuously mauling a small chunk of clay. When The Creeper spots a streetwalker (Virginia Christine) outside their building, however, he can't restrain himself, and trundles after her. Her screams seal her fate ("Stop yellin'," comments The Creeper), and she becomes his newest victim. Police Lieutenant Larry Brooks (Bill Goodwin) is called to the morgue, and remarks to his buddy that the murder looks like the work of the assumed-dead Creeper.

De Lange is no dummy, and he quickly catches on to The Creeper's identity. When he reads Harmon's latest column damning De Lange's work and mocking his abilities, De Lange decides to manipulate The Creeper to exact revenge. Railing on about how Harmon is a "stupid, cruel fool," De Lange states that he'd kill Harmon if he could. The Creeper gets the drift, and asks where Harmon lives. De Lange is quick to provide the address.

Rival art critic Joan Medford (Virginia Grey) confronts Harmon in his apartment over his in-the-works review of an exhibition of the work of commercial artist (and Joan's boyfriend) Steve Morrow (Robert Lowery). Morrow's specialty is girlie paintings for magazine covers, and Joan senses that Harmon's review will be vitriolic, like most of his others. She doesn't get any further with him than to get asked for a date. As soon as Joan leaves, The Creeper enters and murders Harmon.

Lt. Brooks visits Morrow in his studio, where he is painting a shapely model named Stella (Joan Fulton). Morrow is a potential suspect, his anger over Harmon's earlier verbal trashing of his work at the exhibition providing a motive. Joan arrives during Brooks' grilling, and quickly provides a false alibi for Morrow. Brooks says he'll check into it, which he does proving that Joan's claims were bogus, but that Morrow had a different, solid alibi. Morrow states as much as soon as Brooks enters his studio on a return visit. Joan reappears and makes a joking confession to the crime, and all share a nervous laugh.

Virginia Christine's streetwalker hasn't started yet, but The Creeper is about to tell her to "Stop yellin'" in *House of Horrors* (1946).

Back in De Lange's studio, the sculptor comments on Harmon's death. "Are you glad?" asks The Creeper. De Lange answers in the affirmative. "Good. Everybody happy," responds The Creeper as he continues mauling his little chunk of clay.

STOP YELLIN'

Joan pays De Lange several visits at his studio, during which The Creeper hides his oversize bulk behind some shelving. She is friendly toward the starving artist, and supportive of his work. They discuss and have a drink over the "good" news—for the art world, at least—of Harmon's death.

Brooks comes up with a scheme to see if Morrow might have somehow managed to murder Harmon. He convinces Hal Ormiston (Howard Freeman), art critic for the *Daily Chronicle*, to write a scathing review of Morrow's exhibition, to see what happens. Foolishly, Ormiston includes several sentences belittling De Lange's work as well in his column. De Lange reads the piece and gripes to The Creeper, who dutifully makes note of Ormiston's Bagley Terrace address and heads out for another kill. Morrow heads to Ormiston's and confronts him over the review, which is at odds with Ormiston's earlier positive comments while at the exhibition. When Ormiston attempts to call the police, Morrow grabs him. Brooks is waiting in the next room, and intercedes. A shaken Ormiston heads into the kitchen for a drink, encountering The Creeper who makes short work of killing him. Morrow, with Brooks as his witness, is off the hook.

"You happy?" asks The Creeper. "Very happy," responds De Lange. "Ours is a very fortunate alliance, my friend." Like petting a dog.

Joan reappears, but De Lange refuses to show her his latest creation until it is finished (she has already sneaked a peak on an earlier visit). She makes off with his sketch of The Creeper, and takes it to her paper's engraving plant to have a copy made, intending to use it in an upcoming column on De Lange's upcoming work. She hasn't a clue that the picture is of the notorious Creeper, but the fellow at the paper does, and sends her a note asking if she wants it identified as such. Meanwhile, De Lange discovers that the sketch is missing, and The Creeper offhandedly comments that Joan "took something." De Lange panics and psyches up his buddy for dispatching Joan, curiously giving him Morrow's address rather than Joan's. The Creeper puts away his little chunk of clay and sets out once again.

Meanwhile, Brooks has grown fond of model Stella, and calls her at Morrow's for a date. She agrees, and they arrange to meet at Morrow's, the artist finished with her for the day and now gone. The Creeper gets there first, and Stella never gets to go on her date. Brooks arrives later and finds Stella in a lifeless heap.

Meanwhile, Joan revisits De Lange, hoping to quietly return the sketch. He acts oddly cordial at first, but manages several times through various ruses to keep the increasingly nervous woman from leaving. He relays the whole story behind the finished bust that she has now seen, beginning with hauling the fellow from the river. Finally, De Lange announces that she'll never be allowed to leave. She reminds him that his signature was on the sketch she had copied, and the authorities will soon be on to him. He responds that he'll feign ignorance of The Creeper's true identity, and will reap fame and reward from his "crowning achievement" while The Creeper will be put to death for the murders. This doesn't sit well with The Creeper, who has quietly entered the room; he murders his former friend. When he goes after witness Joan, Morrow arrives and attempts to break down the door. Brooks arrives as well and takes the shortcut of simply shooting The Creeper through a closed window, only wounding him so that the fiend can live on for another day, and another movie.

The film was released as one of the studio's four Showman Exploitation Specials on March 29, 1946, as *House of Horrors*, the interim title of *Murder Mansion* discarded for a minor variation of its originally reported title. This was a risky decision in that a film titled *Dr. Terror's House of Horrors* had just made the rounds, a compilation of horrific scenes from a bunch of previously released low-budget independent genre films; Universal ran the risk of potential patrons confusing the two films as one and the same. The opening fanfare that had for years accompanied the spinning Universal globe was now gone, along with the summary credit of the actor names and the roles they played. These cast summaries had followed the opening credits but preceded the film itself through the thirties, but were later moved to the tail-end of the films through the first half of the forties.

House of Horrors' plot is about as simplistic as they come and follows the same general storyline as so many of its predecessors, wherein the obsessed villain has the creature of the piece dispense with a number of individuals before ultimately receiving his comeuppance at the hands of his instrument of death. Regardless, the film is a lot of blatantly perverse fun, and picks up technically for each of The Creeper's murderous rampages. After his distorted silhouette "creeps" across and dominates the screen behind the opening credits, low camera angles maximize his already oversized bulk whenever he switches into killing mode. The Creeper's killing of the first art critic is stylishly executed, when Harmon's fingers, in close-up on the typewriter keys, go fitfully spastic and drop out of frame as the camera pans up to the beginnings of yet another acid-tongued critique. The streetwalker, having first attempted to attract the approaching male, recoils in horror when she gets a better look, disappearing from view as his bulk fills the screen. Ormiston's eyes go wide as he sees what we can't, with a quick cut to the living room where only the shattering of a dropped bottle is heard. Most of the murders take place off-screen, with the occasional shadow play our only glimpse of what's happening, a device common to so many of the films of this era and genre in an unsubtle attempt to placate the fuddy-duddies at the Breen Office. When handled with style, however, the result of leaving the unseen mayhem to the viewer's imagination was often more powerful than if it had been shown.

Romantic leads Robert Lowery and Virginia Grey deliver solid performances, one of Pivar's more likable screen couples. Lowery was lured back to the studio after a year away starring in B films for Pine-Thomas, Columbia, and Monogram, an appropriate choice for the rugged but unflappable commercial artist, quick to rile only when his talents are called into question. Virginia Grey, who appeared in her first film at the tender young age of ten as Eva in Universal's big-budget spectacular *Uncle Tom's Cabin* (1927; Harry Pollard), had made a number of films for MGM and random ones for practically every other studio before her return to Universal in early 1945. She is wonderful in this role with her light-hearted self-assurance, quick with the humorous quip, and equally quick to accept any proffered drink. Virginia Christine, trashily sexy but virtually unrecognizable in her brief but showy bit as the ill-fated streetwalker, makes a good impression.

Martin Kosleck, a surprisingly natural and relaxed actor, is the film's center, and for the sympathetic opening scenes where he "discusses" his plight to his cat Pietro, the film's heart, if only momentarily. One meeting with Napier's Harmon leaves him with a big, critic-induced chip on his shoulder, without which there'd be no film. Napier is stunningly pompous as the condescending critic Harmon, and Goodwin adequate as the cop-of-the-piece, alternating his pursuit of The Creeper with the pursuit of Morrow's sexy model Stella. And as Stella, actress Joan Fulton—who switched back to her real name of Joan Shawlee in the early fifties—is not required to do much acting in this minor part, but she is an eyeful and proves to be a good screamer in her climactic death scene. *The Hollywood Reporter*'s reviewer was smitten with the young lady: "Nothing really vivid commands attention until a certain gorgeous blonde young actress named Joan Fulton is glimpsed. She appears as an artist's model posing in a studio, and wonder of wonders, she has the face and figure to be an artist's model. Her physical attributes would apparently be enough to grace the thoroughly pedestrian vehicle that boasts her presence, whereupon she surprises utterly by delivering a performance in a bit. She hasn't much to do, but that little she does with charming comedy touches. Look for Joan Fulton to start climbing."[13]

I wonder if he got a date out of this review.

Rondo Hatton, with his monosyllabic utterances—"You scared?" "You happy?" "Good. Everybody happy."—makes the film. It is, of course, "politically correct" these days to take Pivar and associates to task for exploiting the actor and his unfortunate affliction, but that was not the case back in the mid-forties. If anything it was Hatton's obvious lack of talent that was commented upon, but these films gave the aspiring actor well-paying work, and roles that steadily grew in prominence from one film to the next. Given his physical appearance, roles for which he was suited were few and far between, and with Pivar's unit he found his niche, and an exploitable character that promised a series

---

[13] "House of Horrors," *Hollywood Reporter*, March 4, 1946, 3.

if successful. Hatton followed his role in *House of Horrors* almost immediately with another in producer Howard Welsch's *The Spider Woman Strikes Back* (1946; Arthur Lubin), with Pivar's *The Brute Man* in production shortly after that film's completion. Hatton died unexpectedly soon after on February 2, 1946, before any of his final three films were released.[14]

Director Jean Yarbrough had his start with Hal Roach, working as assistant director on a string of two-reel comedies in the mid- to late-twenties. Yarbrough worked in a similar capacity for Mack Sennett Comedies in the early thirties and at RKO through the rest of the decade, graduating to full-fledged director knocking out a seemingly endless string of Poverty Row quickies for PRC and Monogram before landing at Universal in early 1943. Yarbrough's fortunes changed slightly when the studio assigned him to direct Abbott and Costello's *In Society* (1944), followed by two more films for the popular duo, *Here Come the Co-Eds* and *The Naughty Nineties* (both 1945). Yarbrough's work on *House of Horrors* is competent and sufficiently stylish given the inherent limitations, and he would quickly become Pivar's favorite director on most of his films to follow, both for Universal and the handful that came after.

Maury Gertsman's camerawork gives the film a visual boost, using his moving camera sparingly but to good advantage, as in the languid dolly movement up to and through De Lange's Greenwich Village-based studio at the film's opening. Another surprising moment comes during De Lange's pier-side flashback to his encounter with Harmon and the latter's dismissive "tripe" comments, when a different camera angle of the action is shown rather than simply reusing the same footage, the latter a familiar B film expedient. George Bricker's screenplay, adapted from yet-another original by Dwight V. Babcock, is routine but sparked with far better dialog than many that came before, and much wittier. The light-hearted banter between the principals is frequently quite amusing, helped in no small part by Grey's note-perfect delivery.

All in all, this is one of Pivar's better efforts of the period, and probably the film that both Hatton and Kosleck are most remembered for today. Contemporary critics were comparatively kind in their reviews. *The New York Times* was uncharacteristically gentle in its review, the writer perhaps keeping in mind what happened to his on-screen counterpart: "If you like this sort of thing, the picture is in the approved shuddery tradition and gets its story told quickly. Rondo Hatton is properly scary as 'the Creeper.'"[15] *Boxoffice* was even more positive: "The feature isn't quite as horrific as its handle indicates. What is lost in chills is more than compensated for by a skillfully conceived screenplay, acceptable performances and, above all, solid direction by Jean Yarbrough. Net

---

[14] "Obituary," *Los Angeles Times*, February 5, 1946, 8.

[15] E.J.B., "The Screen," *New York Times*, February 23, 1946, 20.

result: The film easily qualifies as better than ordinary supporting material."[16] *Daily Variety* gave credit where credit was due, singling out both Pivar and Yarbrough for their efforts: "Production is handled by Ben Pivar with skill that promises well for the future of the series. Materials have been selected and utilized with effective showmanship ... Jean Yarbrough's direction milks the script to the limit for drama and exhibits subtle skill."[17]

The *House of Horrors* prequel *The Brute Man* now moved to the top of the heap, its long-completed script dusted off and set in motion for production. Since the popularity of horror films was on the wane, however, Pivar added some non-genre assignments to his list of potential projects. He assigned the title *Kid Dynamite* to George Bricker to develop and produce,[18] Bricker having been promoted to associate producer on top of his screenwriting chores. Nothing seems to have come of it, and the choice of this title seems odd since it had been used only two years earlier for an East Side Kids film over at Monogram.

Away from the studio, Pivar had settled into an easy existence. Arriving home late in the afternoon, the family would eat dinner together on most days and breakfasts together on the weekends. Judy would frequently cook, but their live-in housekeeper would take over on occasion, and there was always someone else available to wash the dishes and clean the house. As a family they'd attend concerts at The Hollywood Bowl and The Greek Theater, and of course the (in)famous Santa Claus Lane Parade on Hollywood Boulevard, suspended during the war years but resumed in December 1945.

Along with the various housekeepers was a succession of nannies that helped with the young children. In one instance the nanny turned out to be something less than helpful when it was discovered that some household items were missing. Accompanied by the police, Judy and Ben confronted the nanny at her home and found a number of their personal items; Judy's monogrammed guest towels among them. The nanny's employment was short-lived.

Ben and Judy liked to entertain, their closest friends including Charlie and Lucille Gould, Ken and Jean Goldsmith, and Joe (*Uncle* Joe to the kids) and Helen Gershenson. Not too surprisingly, these friendships were born in the workplace: Charlie Gould was an assistant director at Universal who worked with Pivar on *The Mummy's Tomb* and—uncredited—on *Top Sergeant*, *Timber*, and *Calling Dr. Death*; Ken Goldsmith was an associate producer at Universal, and Gershenson was Universal's music department head and uncredited executive producer. And, of course, there were the weekly pinochle games that went on for years.

---

[16] "Feature Reviews," *Boxoffice*, March 9, 1946, page unknown.

[17] "House of Horrors," *Daily Variety*, March 4, 1946, 3.

[18] Ivan Spear, "Hollywood Report," *Boxoffice*, November 24, 1945, 42.

Is there something in Ben's glass? Ben and Judy and friends, partying. Photo courtesy of Jan Pivar Dacri.

The Brute Man
(Director: Jean Yarbrough; Released October 1, 1946)

While *House of Horrors* was still in production (and still known as *Murder Mansion*), another Universal press release was printed verbatim in a slew of papers nationwide, a lighthearted story about his ongoing quest for more stories of a horrific nature: "Someone printed a yarn recently that Universal Producer Ben Pivar was looking for more stories to follow 'Murder Mansion' in his horror series. Now he has a letter from a woman patient in a psychopathic hospital reading: 'For five years I have been having the most horrible dreams which would be perfectly wonderful for murder movies. I'll try to remember some and send them to you.'"[19]

Only three of Pivar's last four films saw release through Universal, and all within little more than a two-month period from mid-April through later-June 1946. *Blonde Alibi* and *Inside Job* were both a return to the mystery-melodrama of several years earlier, and *She-Wolf of London*, while sporting a title guaranteed to lure in the true horror buff, failed to deliver on its promise. But first, the Creeper prequel *The Brute Man* was rushed into production on

---

[19] "A Suggestion to Gene," Dunkirk, N.Y. *Evening Observer*, September 24, 1945, 6.

Monday, November 12, 1945,[20] with Jean Yarbrough back to direct Hatton, Tom Neal, Jan Wiley, and Jane Adams in the leads.

The local populace is in a tizzy over the violent death of Hampton University's Professor Cushman, so when socialite Joan Bemis (Ja Nelle Johnson) meets a similar broken-back death the police are called out en masse. It is the work of The Creeper (Rondo Hatton), the character introduced in the earlier *House of Horrors*, but here in a story that pre-dates its predecessor. Fleeing the approaching horde of cops and trapped in an alley, The Creeper makes his way up a fire escape and into the apartment of blind, piano-playing Helen Paige (Jane Adams). She is not afraid of him—a first due to his lack of good looks—and takes a liking to the fellow. When the cops arrive at her apartment, Helen aides in his escape.

Taking refuge in a pier-side hovel, The Creeper drops off a shopping list at a small grocery store for next-day delivery. Young Jimmy is forced by his disagreeable boss Mr. Haskins to make the delivery, in spite of the boy's concerns that such an odd order might be the work of The Creeper. Curiosity gets the best of the delivery boy, and he becomes The Creeper's next victim. When Jimmy fails to return, Haskins mulls over the poor kid's concerns and contacts the cops.

The murders have been assigned to homicide Captain M.J. Donelly (Donald MacBride) and his partner Lieutenant Gates (Peter Whitney). The public is in an uproar over the murders, so the mayor has delivered an ultimatum to Police Commissioner Salisbury: capture the murderer within twenty-four hours, or hand in your resignation. Accompanied by the mayor's secretary, Parkington, Salisbury passes on the orders to Donelly, along with a thinly-veiled threat.

Donelly and Gates head to the pier-side address given them by Haskins, and there they find Jimmy's dead body. Donelly also finds an old newspaper clipping that provides a potential clue: The Creeper may be Hal Moffat, who was part of a popular Hampton University Class of 1930 trio along with Clifford Scott (Tom Neal) and Virginia Rogers (Jan Wiley). Donelly and Gates visit the now-wealthy Scott, who is now married to Virginia. Scott relates the story of his old friend Moffat:

Roommates Moffat (Fred Coby) and Scott had been rivals both on the football field and for the hand of Virginia, Moffat oblivious to the fact that Joan Bemis was in love with him. When Moffat connives to wrangle a date with Virginia, Scott retaliates by feeding Moffat the wrong formulas for Professor Cushman's chemistry quiz. Exiled to perform some after-class experiments, Scott foolishly taunts the hot-tempered Moffat, resulting in a lab accident that affects Moffat's glands and nerves and leads to eventual disfigurement and

---

[20] Edwin Schallert, "Josephine Hutchinson Persuaded to Do Film," *Los Angeles Times*, November 9, 1945, 11.

mental imbalance. Neither Scott nor Virginia had seen him since he fled from the hospital.

The story now told, Donelly is convinced that Moffat is The Creeper. He assigns a detective to keep an eye on the Scott household, concerned that Scott might become The Creeper's next revenge-fueled victim. Meanwhile, The Creeper, touched by Helen's kindness and lack of fear, heads into a pawnshop to pick up a brooch for her. Not surprisingly, the shopkeeper is frightened by his customer and threatens to call the police, a poorly thought out move that results in yet another murder. The Creeper presents the brooch to a grateful Helen, and only now figures out that the girl is blind. She mentions that a doctor told her that an operation could restore her sight, but she has no chance of affording the two-to-three-thousand-dollar cost. He balks when she wants to touch his face, and heads off to get the money for her. Meanwhile, the Commissioner and Parkington revisit Donelly, but this time the stubborn cop calls their bluff and they back down.

Eluding the guard at the Scott's home, The Creeper enters and confronts Virginia. Recovering from her shock, she finally realizes who the unrecognizable fellow is. "I've changed a little since I last saw you," he says, the understatement of the hour. Her husband returns home, and the three old "friends" are reunited in her bedroom. The Creeper demands money, but Scott says they only have jewelry. He retrieves the jewels from a wall safe, but manages to grab a pistol as well. He shoots and wounds The Creeper, who responds by breaking Scott's back.

The Creeper limps over to Helen's apartment and presents her with the jewelry, telling her to hock the stuff and use the proceeds for her eye operation. When she attempts to do so, however, the pawnshop owner contacts the police, having recognized the items from a previously circulated bulletin. The cops question Helen, and she confesses ignorance of her new friend's deeds, stunned at the news that he is the notorious Creeper. It is not long before newsies citywide are screaming "Blind Girl Tells All." Enraged that Helen has double-crossed him, The Creeper makes his way back to her place and sneaks up behind her while she plays the piano, a murderous glare in his eyes. Donelly anticipated this reaction; the adjacent rooms are filled with cops who pounce on the fellow before he can do any harm to the girl. Helen is miserable over her perfidy, and The Creeper is hauled away, alive and well enough to account for his appearance in *House of Horrors*.

In the tacked-on obligatory happy ending, Donelly informs Helen that it looks encouraging that she'll receive the operation to restore her sight, but doesn't provide any further details. Gates offers to take the blind girl home, and it is obvious that he has romantic designs on the young lady.

Much maligned over the intervening years by do-gooders appalled at the exploitation of Hatton's unfortunate disease and a backstory with unavoidable parallels with Hatton's real-life predicament, *The Brute Man* provides simplistic thrills and shameless fun. It also provided a first lead role for the actor and a correspondingly beefed-up paycheck as well. Hatton's delivery is as labored as ever, but he really gets into the spirit of things, scrambling up fire escapes, trotting down alleys, and snapping spines with untrammeled gusto. We get to see the human side of The Creeper, if only fleetingly (and admittedly awkwardly) in his quieter scenes with Helen.

As the homicide department captain and his leutenant, Donald MacBride and Peter Whitney assume roles similar to ones they would repeat for Pivar a month or so later for *Blonde Alibi*. A tag team of sorts, their characters have been working together long enough that they can finish each other's thoughts, with the mutual goal of solving the crime while keeping the bureaucrats at arm's length. When the commissioner asks if he was clear with his orders, Whitney's character Gates, standing rigidly at attention, responds: "Yes, sir, you were. And I'll pass the bu. . . .—the word right on down the line." MacBride and Whitney are far more amusing here with their casual interplay, Whitney keeping his performance in check and avoiding the broader "comedy" of the sad sack character of his upcoming *Blonde Alibi* role.

Studio portrait of Rondo Hatton, *The Brute Man*. Photo courtesy of Jerry Murbach at Doctor Macro's High Quality Movie Scans, www.doctormacro.com.

Tom Neal gives a quietly restrained performance as Moffat's former college buddy, but newcomer Fred Coby, in one of his first credited roles, is a novice and it shows. Jane Adams spends most of her on-screen time flailing away at the piano keys or staring past Hatton's Creeper, but she pulls off her stock blind-girl character with sufficient conviction. As Moffat's other college buddy and the object of his former lust, Jan Wiley has a small but showy role, particularly memorable in the bedroom scene where her confrontation with The Creeper shifts from initial shock to breathless desperation. Ja Nelle Johnson's primary claim to fame is being the mother of Micky Dolenz of television's *The Monkees*.

The story is sort of a poor man's "beauty and the beast" affair interspersed with the usual string of murders and the lengthy flashback explaining the cause of The Creeper's disfigurement thrown in to pad out the hour's running time. Director Jean Yarbrough and photographer Maury Gertsman once again deliver visually interesting results, although cost-cutting measures continually trip them up. Stock footage is used for police mobilization montages, not just once or twice, but three different times, with several clips used more than once. The final game of Hampton University's football season is composed primarily of stock game footage, but every single insert of player Moffat is shot from high above or from down low, with only the grassy field or the sky above as background, and nary another soul in sight. The intrusion of these barren-looking insert shots is jarring, to say the least. As for the various inserts of newspaper headlines that chronicle the various murders and the ongoing investigation, any viewer bothering to read past the first pasted-on paragraph will be rewarded with a totally unrelated second paragraph. One example falls under the headline "Mayor in Ultimatum to Police," where the first paragraph reads "The mayor has put the police department on the spot by demanding the capture of the Creeper 'or else'" followed by "As to the general outlook in the world of finance, I need not tell you that attempts to look into its future are much more difficult . . . ." in paragraph two. Sloppy.

Still, there are some arresting images, such as when The Creeper ascends the fire escape outside Helen's apartment, shot from directly overhead as The Creeper climbs closer, and later when he convincingly punches, and smashes, his reflection in a small mirror (in stark contrast to Huber's mirror-smashing scene in *The Strange Death of Adolf Hitler*, where it is obviously and unconvincingly faked).

Pivar's *The Brute Man* ended up being sold to Producers Releasing Corporation (PRC) for a reported $125,000[21] and released in October 1946. The reason for this sale has never been adequately explained, although a number of theories have popped up in print over the years. Most likely it was a casualty of the waning interest in films of this nature, coupled with the company's overhaul and shift of focus in July, details of which follow in a few pages. Others have speculated that Hatton's recent death may have been a cause, but that did not stop Universal from releasing two other of his films posthumously. Another risible explanation was the ghastliness of the final product, both in subject matter and quality. *The Hollywood Reporter*'s review of the previously-released *House of Horrors*, one of the less complimentary of the bunch, hinted at this: "[F]ilming has been completed on another 'Creeper' yarn, but if it isn't any better than Ben Pivar's try with this first production, the character is definitely not worth fooling with."[22] Regardless, as a PRC release the film was a stunning achievement in comparison to much of that studio's other offerings. PRC slapped on a new opening title card with a stylized silhouette illustration

---

[21] "PRC Pays 125C for 'Brute Man,'" *Daily Variety*, October 18, 1946, 2.
[22] "House of Horrors," *Hollywood Reporter*, March 4, 1946, 3.

of The Creeper as its background and the PRC name prominent, but left the following credits as filmed by Universal, which unimaginatively reused the same stalking Creeper shadow footage as had previously appeared in *House of Horrors*' opening credits.

Elsewhere at Universal, sixty-eight-year-old Henry MacRae, the longtime supervisor of the studio's serials, passed on at the beginning of October. MacRae was an industry veteran, writing and directing since the early teens, and serving as producer from the mid-twenties on. MacRae's obituaries credited him with all sorts of "firsts," including double exposure, nighttime filming, use of a wind machine (which he was said to have invented), and the use of artificial light on film sets. Clearly a stretch of the truth, but he was there from the medium's infancy and made a number of notable, though perhaps less lofty, contributions. More believable was the claim that he was responsible for designing Universal's half-acre, net-covered "jungle," complete with hidden runway and multiple gates that led from the animal cages and enabled the director to release a lion into any part of the "jungle" as the action dictated. Known as the "King of the Serial Makers," MacRae's four-per-year serials reportedly had profits averaging a half million each, with his first sound serial for Universal, *The Indians Are Coming* (1930), a sensation with more than a million dollar take. "What we give 'em is movies that move, suspense that suspends, and the devil with the talk," stated the no-nonsense filmmaker.[23] And kids nationwide couldn't have been happier. Within a month of MacRae's death, associate producer Morgan B. Cox was promoted to MacRae's now-vacant position, having already assumed some of MacRae's duties in the interim. As production executive of serials, Pivar had overseen MacRae for the past year,[24] but with Cox's promotion was now freed up to devote his energies solely to feature production. *She-Wolf of London* would be the first of these features."[25]

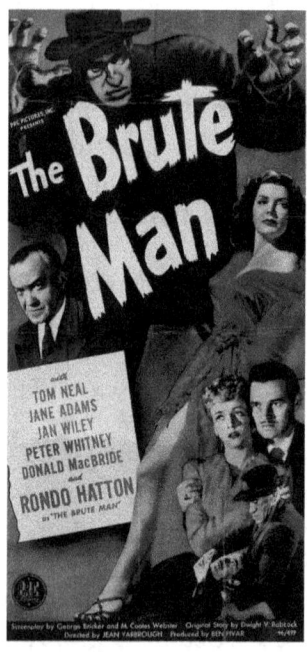

Repackaged as a PRC release: *The Brute Man* (1946). Image courtesy of Heritage Auction Galleries, Ha.com.

---

[23] "Henry M'Rae, 68, Movie Producer," *New York Times*, October 3, 1944, 23; "Henry MacRae, Film Pioneer, Passes at 68," *Los Angeles Times*, October 3, 1944, 7.

[24] "Morgan Cox Heads Universal Serials," *Boxoffice*, November 4, 1944, 66.

[25] Edwin Schallert, "Andrea Leeds' Return Forecast in 'Indians,'" *Los Angeles Times*,

She-Wolf of London
(Director: Jean Yarbrough; Released May 17, 1946)

Pivar's last horror film—and I use the term "horror" loosely here—was the sensationally titled *She-Wolf of London*. As the studio's final film in its long-running horror cycle, the title promised horrors and a wolf woman not to come, and many patrons no doubt felt mislead and cheated; the film was released in Great Britain under the more appropriate title *Curse of the Allenbys*. Screenwriter George Bricker, seemingly joined at the hip to Pivar for the producer's final year at the studio, was once again assigned to give structure to Dwight Babcock's story. The title had been bounced about in the trades nearly a year and a half earlier as an upcoming production,[26] and perhaps at that earlier date a more horrific plotline had been intended. But with the slackening interest in horror films during the interim, Bricker's final script was all tease and no action. Jean Yarbrough was assigned as director in November 1945, with production to start on Monday, December 8. Don Porter and twenty-year-old June Lockhart, daughter of popular character actor Gene Lockhart, were signed as leads, with Sara Haden given the plum role as the scheming aunt. The twelve-day shooting schedule wrapped on Friday, December 21, 1945, the assembled cast and crew making a hasty exit to attend the various Christmas parties already in progress. Everyone that is, except for Lockhart and Porter, who found themselves alone in the suddenly-darkened and vacated process stage. The completed film, brought in at a total cost of $134,890, would not be released for another five months. "The producer, Ben Pivar, was a nice man who was always very encouraging," said Lockhart. "He liked us, 'cause we were on schedule!"[27] And that, of course, was the Holy Grail of the B film.

London at the dawn of the twentieth century, and according to the opening crawl the legend of the Allenby Curse is almost forgotten. Not to worry; we'll soon be reminded of it. Three women are now the sole residents of the Allenby Estate, attended to by their housekeeper Hannah (Eily Malyon). Young, impressionable Phyllis Allenby (June Lockhart) is an orphan, now in the care of her Aunt Martha Winthrop (Sara Haden) whose daughter Carol (Jan Wiley) lives there as well. Phyllis is engaged to Barry Lanfield (Don Porter), a barrister in partnership with his father, Sir Sidney Lanfield. Phyllis and Barry are to be married the following week.

November 1, 1944, 11.

[26] "Universal to Release 55 Features; Diversity of Appeal is Stressed," *Boxoffice*, June 17, 1944, 18, 43.

[27] June Lockhart interview with Tom Weaver, "Interview: June Lockhart on 'She-Wolf of London,'" *Classic-Horror.com* <http://classic-horror.com> (January 3, 2011)

Stop Yellin'

Aunt Martha confides to her daughter Carol that they really are not related to the Allenbys. Martha had been engaged to Phyllis' father Reginald, but had broken it off to marry another. When her husband died and left her penniless, she managed to get a job in the Allenby household as a housekeeper. With Reginald's death she assumed the role of aunt so that she could stay on in the house, but knowing that Phyllis is the sole heir and about to be married, now fears that her ruse will be found out and she will end up without a home.

Meanwhile, there has been a wolf attack in the city park. Scotland Yard detective Latham (Lloyd Corrigan) reports back to Inspector Pierce (Dennis Hoey) that the victim claimed it was a woman in wolf form—or a female werewolf. Pierce scoffs at this, but Latham worries that there may be some truth to the claim. The two head to the park to investigate, and there discuss the case in graphic detail. Barry and Phyllis are horseback riding nearby, and overhear the detectives' conversation; Phyllis becomes worried and distant.

Carol is in love with starving artist Dwight Severn (Martin Kosleck), but Martha forbids her from seeing him. Carol and Martha have a pair of German Shepherds as protection against intruders, and these mutts seem to get along with everyone except for poor Phyllis, who is terrified of them and their constant growling and snapping at her. That night, Phyllis is spooked by the ongoing howling and barking of distant dogs, so she lights a lantern and hangs it in her bedroom window. According to old Scottish superstition, this will drive away evil spirits. Martha enters her room and sees this, but agrees to let her keep it there. Martha brings Phyllis a glass of warm milk to help her sleep. Later, Carol, dressed in a hooded cloak, attempts to sneak out to see Dwight but is intercepted by Martha who sends her back to her room. Housekeeper Hannah witnesses this from afar. Later that same night as police patrol the park, a young boy is attacked and killed, his body mangled. A hooded and cloaked figure returns to the Allenby house, followed by the household's dogs.

The next morning Phyllis awakens from a deep sleep to find blood on her hands and mud on her slippers. She is convinced that the Allenby Curse, which allegedly transforms its victim into a bloodthirsty she-wolf, plagues her—either that or she is going insane. Martha comforts her, and convinces her that she needs rest and should not see Barry. "I feel unclean," moans the increasingly despondent girl. Barry is persistent in his attempts to see her, but Martha, oozing understanding, is adamant that Phyllis is bedridden and needs rest. With Hannah's assistance, Barry gains access to the garden patio where Phyllis is resting. Phyllis offers no encouragement, however, and after he leaves begs Martha to keep him away in the future. She is, after all, damaged goods.

Barry asks Carol to go for a carriage ride with him to discuss Phyllis' condition. This plays right into Martha's hands, since she is scheming to have Barry marry Carol rather than Phyllis, thereby assuring her future. Too bad Carol is not on board, though, since she is madly in love with Dwight and manages to sneak out several times a week for a prearranged rendezvous. Carol suggests to Barry that he be more assertive in his attempts to see Phyllis. Carol approaches Phyllis as well, hoping that the miserable young lady will open up to her. No dice.

That night the park is crawling with Latham's police, with orders to round up all stray dogs, but only Latham seems to put any stock in the possibility of a she-wolf. As Latham pokes about the bushes, the hooded and cloaked figure once again emerges from the Allenby house, the dogs trailing behind. It isn't long before Latham becomes the next victim, managing to choke out something about a she-wolf before keeling over dead. Martha wakens Phyllis the next morning, showing her some bloody clothing and a small, clawed hand tool. She convinces Phyllis to keep this hush-hush, otherwise the police will think her to be nuts and throw her into an asylum.

Barry's attempts to visit Phyllis are repeatedly thwarted, and time after time he ends up only with Carol. Carol finally convinces him to go see Phyllis, regardless of what Martha says. He does so, only to be told by Phyllis that she can no longer marry him. It is the Allenby Curse and her weird dreams of wolves that are getting her down; marriage would be a disaster.

Barry decides to take matters into his own hands. Camping out near the Allenby house that night, he sees the hooded figure emerge and head off to the park where Inspector Pierce has just issued orders to shoot-to-kill anyone who resists arrest. Barry attempts to follow the mysterious figure, but loses her when he responds to screams from nearby. It is Dwight, who while waiting on a bench for Carol's arrival was attacked but not wounded. When Carol arrives in garb identical to the figure he had followed earlier, Barry is convinced she is the culprit.

Later, Barry arrives at the Allenby house and confronts Carol with his suspicions. Carol manages to create some doubt in Barry's mind, unaware that Martha is nearby, listening. When the scheming woman hears that Carol has been meeting Dwight on a regular basis, she loses it. After Barry leaves, Martha confronts Carol and insists that Phyllis is insane. She further insists that she is determined that Carol should marry Barry and forget about Dwight. Once Martha is finished with her tirade and leaves, Carol visits Phyllis in her room and hears firsthand that Phyllis believes herself to be the murderer. Phyllis begs Carol to summon the police to haul her away where she can't do any further harm. Carol agrees and heads out.

Martha visits Phyllis with her daily ration of bedtime milk, which Phyllis dutifully drinks. As Phyllis grows increasingly groggy, Martha tells the helpless girl that she intends to kill her and make it look like suicide. She has been drugging the girl each night, committing the murders herself, and then planting evidence and doubt in the girl's mind to convince her of the curse and her own culpability. Luckily for Phyllis, Hannah is outside the room listening in, and when she intervenes, mad Martha takes after her, large knife in hand. Pursuing Hannah down the staircase, Martha trips and falls, landing on the knife and perishing as a result of her lethal, self-inflicted wound. Carol returns with the police and Barry, having come to realize what Martha was actually up to. Barry and Phyllis are reunited, her mind now cleared of all that Allenby Curse nonsense as a result of Martha's murder-crazed "confession."

Although reasonably atmospheric and suspenseful, and with convincing performances by the leads, the finished product simply does not provide the shameless fun of so many of Pivar's other efforts. The end result is curiously flat, routine, and with a plot that covers some familiar turf. Visually it is a handsome production, or at least in the corner-cutting world of low-budget programmers. Yarbrough's direction is workmanlike, but he is boxed into a corner with a script heavy on dialog and comparatively light on action. Maury Gertsman's photography is typically atmospheric, and there are some nicely staged camera setups and judiciously chosen camera movements. One beautifully composed setup occurs when Martha enters Phyllis' bedroom that first night, standing in the doorway in long shot, framed by the foreground lantern on one side and Phyllis on the other. The climactic scene where Martha forces Phyllis to drink the drugged milk, then casually explains how she intends to murder the helpless young girl as she awaits for her to lose consciousness, is exceptionally well done. Wielding a large kitchen knife, Martha blurs in and out of Phyllis' drug-addled vision, actress Haden perfectly nailing the woman's tip over the edge into madness.

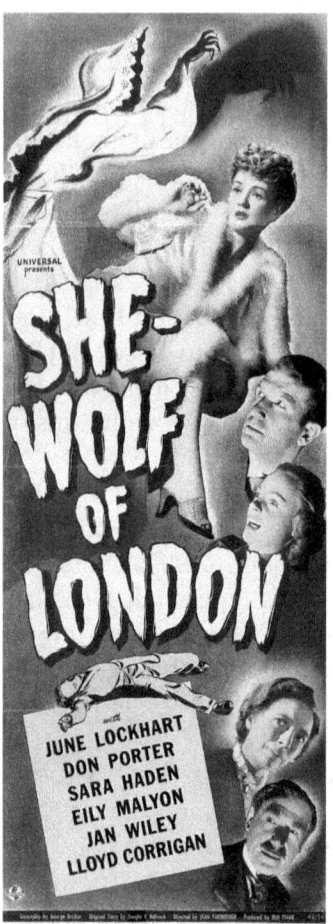

All tease with no payoff: *She-Wolf of London* (1946). Image courtesy of Heritage Auction Galleries, Ha.com.

But there are some sloppily-staged insert shots as well, such as in the aforementioned first bedroom scene where Martha stands in mid-shot, lit from the right with the left half of her face cloaked in shadow. This is followed by a visually jarring close-up where the light source has shifted to the left, the right half of her face now in shadow; this back-and-forth shift is repeated in several subsequent shots. With over fifty previous films to his credit, film editor Paul Landres should have known better; a simple non-Martha cutaway separating the two Martha shots would have masked the on-screen discrepancy. On the plus side, the ever-present London fog pumped out for all of the exterior scenes helps to mask the exterior sets' shortcomings.

In the lead as Phyllis Allenby ("Beauty or Beast? Woman or Monster?" queried the trailer), June Lockhart demonstrates what a capable actress she was at this young age, delivering a sympathetic performance as the tortured young lady. Don Porter gives his usual fine performance, but if that is a British accent he was attempting to mimic, he failed miserably in that regard; dialogue director Raymond Kessler should have had his pay docked. Sara Haden's "Martha" is chillingly stern and overbearing, displaying hollow concern and cordiality and not fooling the viewer one bit. As Phyllis' cousin Carol, actress Jan Wiley gives an acceptable performance in her lesser role, and even manages to imbue her character with moments of warmth when not otherwise occupied with her attempts to sneak out to see Dwight. Older British actress Eily Malyon's severe countenance and gaunt frame give her the appearance of an animated corpse, and she is fine as the Allenby housekeeper who seems to spend most of her time hanging laundry or snooping about. Martin Kosleck is wasted in his two brief scenes, and it is a shame that they did not give the capable young actor more to do. As Inspector Pierce, Dennis Hoey must have felt like he was reprising his overly familiar Inspector Lestrade role from Universal's "Sherlock Holmes" series here, as there's little difference in the two characters. Lloyd Corrigan's bumbling detective is cut from similar cloth, queasily reminiscent of the Holmes series' Watson. Silent comedian and perennial Laurel and Hardy foil James Finlayson has an uncredited bit as one of the constables patrolling the park.

Perhaps the film's weakest aspect is the so-called mystery behind the killings, for while there are several possible suspects it is sufficiently obvious from the deluge of clues just who the real murderer is, and what her motives are. The household dogs do not like Phyllis, so it can't be her they accompany back-and-forth to commit the killings. If it was Carol, why bother to repeatedly hide her face and figure with the hooded cloak (although Yarbrough has planted the red herring seed by having Carol don a hooded cloak in her early attempt to visit Dwight), and what would be her motive? Martha, on the other hand, has already stated a motive for wanting Phyllis out of the way, and within the film's first ten minutes! The killings themselves are dull stuff, with silly and repetitive stalking through the foggy park, the pursued never once hearing the racket made by their pursuer as they both stumble and crash through the thick brush. And while Martha is trying to make the vicious attacks appear to have been committed by a wolf, how on earth does she manage to sound like a wolf when she attacks? If her two attendant mutts have gotten into the act, we sure as hell never see a hint of it on screen. Watching the film, one is reminded more than once of Hitchcock's *Rebecca*, and the sequence where Martha mounts the staircase with tray and glass of milk perched on her outstretched hand screams of Hitchcock's *Suspicion*. If you are going to pilfer, pilfer from someone with visual flair; it is among the finished film's handful of standout shots.

She-Wolf of London was released on May 17, 1946 on a double-bill with Erle C. Kenton's *The Cat Creeps*.

Blonde Alibi
(Director: Will Jason; Released April 12, 1946)

Blonde Alibi is a missed opportunity, an awkward comingling of handsome noir visuals, solid acting, an engagingly convoluted plot, and—unfortunately—painfully unfunny humor. If the makers of this film had only had the confidence to drop the latter, this could have been a very good, if somewhat farfetched, little film.

Blonde Alibi was the next of Pivar's projects to go into production, although it would eventually be released before *She-Wolf of London*. Adapted for the screen by associate producer George Bricker, the original story was written by former newspaperman Gordon Kahn, whose career in the industry would be cut short a few years later when he was blacklisted and canned from his job at Warner Brothers. Originally titled *Killing is Convenient*, the film was retitled *Design for Death* by the time production commenced on Monday, January 7, 1946. Tom Neal returned as the lead, with Martha O'Driscoll co-starring as his love interest. Donald MacBride, Peter Whitney, and Robert Armstrong handled the investigating cop chores, with Samuel S. Hinds, Elisha Cook, Jr., and Marc Lawrence rounding out the cast. Will Jason was hired to direct, having successfully completed his first effort for the studio, the romantic comedy *Idea Girl*. Based on his work on these two films, Universal signed Jason to a long-term contract in February.[28] Shooting wrapped on January 19 at the end of a twelve-day schedule, the completed film released as *Blonde Alibi* in April 1946.

New York City: Dr. Norman Selby stumbles out the front door of his apartment building and into the path of an oncoming cab. Cabbie Sam Collins (Elisha Cook, Jr.) hits the poor fellow before he can slam on his breaks, and takes off in a panic after confirming that the man is dead. Building doorman Pat Tenny (Oliver Blake) calls the cops. When it is discovered that Selby had been shot, homicide Inspector Carmichael (Donald MacBride) investigates, assisted by Lieutenant Melody Haynes (Peter Whitney).

Three pieces of evidence turn up in the dead man's apartment: the revolver that shot him; a woman's glove; and a prescription carbon made out to Selby's last patient, Professor Carl Slater (Samuel S. Hinds). Furthermore, it soon becomes evident that Selby's rare Gutenberg Bible has been stolen. It doesn't

---

[28] Ivan Spear, "Hollywood Report," *Boxoffice*, March 2, 1946, 23.

take long—it is a B movie, after all—to round up a bunch of suspects. Collins is picked up first and held, followed by Selby's fiancée Marian Gale (Martha O'Driscoll), who is on a ship (attempting to skip town?) bound for South America. Pilot Rick Lavery (Tom Neal), a former lover of Marian's, is picked up as well at an airport, also bound for South America. It was Lavery's pistol that was used to kill Selby, although Lavery swears he sold it several months earlier. Marian is released, but Lavery is thrown in the slammer when the alibi that his two friends can provide blows up in his face: the paper reports they were both killed in an air crash a few hours before the murder took place. Professor Slater is picked up and questioned, and identifies Lavery as the man he saw entering Selby's apartment as he left.

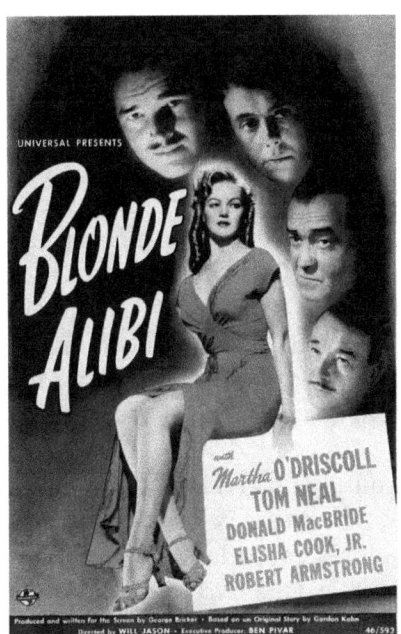

Martha O'Driscoll on prominent display as the *Blonde Alibi* (1946). Image courtesy of Heritage Auction Galleries, Ha.com.

Before Marian leaves the station, she and Lavery are reunited briefly for the first time in two years. She thought he had stood her up two years earlier, but it turns out he was arrested on trumped-up charges and imprisoned for sixteen months; he couldn't contact her. She had recently heard that he was setting up a small air service down in South America, and had tried to follow him there when the cops picked her up over this whole Slater affair. With that bit of backstory out of the way, Carmichael has both Marian and Slater tailed when they leave—just in case.

The Gutenberg Bible was stolen by a two-bit thief named Louie Carney (John Berkes), who is paid a cool $5,000 for his efforts by mobster and art fancier Joe DeLima (Marc Lawrence). Louie is braced by some cops on his walk home, and when they find the wad of cash in his pocket haul him into the station. Detectives Williams (Robert Armstrong) and Lane (Matt Willis) interrogate him repeatedly in an increasingly futile effort to learn the source of the money, but he remains evasive fearing for his life if he squeals on DeLima. When DeLima hears that Louie has been picked up, he dispatches his lawyer to bail him out. Louie, however, doesn't trust DeLima, and fearing for his safety does all he can to stall release and remain in custody.

Marian learns that Slater is almost blind and couldn't possibly have seen Lavery—or anyone else, for that matter—well enough to identify him. When he reveals the self-serving reason behind his false identification, Marian convinces him to go to the station and revise his story for Carmichael. He never makes it, his rotten eyesight allowing him to step out in front of a moving car which hits and kills him. Meanwhile, the apartment building's doorman Pat identifies Lavery as the fellow he saw entering the building, further cooking Lavery's goose.

Carmichael has both Collins and Louie released, but when Louie balks Carmichael has his men take him back to his rooming house by force. As Louie heads up to his room, the building's desk clerk quietly calls DeLima and tells him Louie has returned. Louie reluctantly answers a knock on his door and is confronted by a pistol-wielding DeLima. Just as DeLima is about to kill Louie, however, DeLima is shot and wounded by a pistol fired through the open window. It is Williams and Lane to the rescue, having figured there was a good reason for Louie's panic over being released.

Haynes returns with the lab report on some evidence Carmichael had collected at an undisclosed location. With this in hand, Carmichael approaches Lavery and asks his help with a sting, and Lavery agrees. Putting the plan in action, Lavery confronts the doorman Pat with pistol in hand, claiming he escaped and is now going to kill him if he doesn't fess up to having falsely identified him. Which Pat does, after which Carmichael rushes in and has him arrested.

Back at the station the whole story comes out: Pat had been blackmailing Dr. Selby's patients, and when Selby confronted him over this Pat had shot him with the pistol he'd acquired several months before. Coincidentally, Louie had been interrupted mid-theft and had hidden, but heard the two voices and now confirms that Pat's was one of them. Carmichael's evidence was gathered in Pat's room: metal filings from when Pat had attempted to file off the pistol's serial number and a bank book with annual deposits averaging $20,000 per year, significantly more than a doorman's salary. And why would Selby, mortally wounded, walk past the doorman for help unless the doorman was not there? Louie, for his efforts of identifying Pat as the killer, is still arrested for the Bible's theft, and as a four-time loser his future looks none too bright. Lavery and Marian are reunited.

The decision to release the film with the title *Blonde Alibi* may have been a savvy one, given that this phrase was locked in the public consciousness based on events of the previous fifteen years. Back in 1929, the infamous St. Valentine's Day Massacre had taken place in Chicago, allegedly at the behest of mobster Al Capone. It was widely assumed that Capone gunman "Machine Gun" Jack McGurn had planned the massacre, but the police were unable to pin the killings on him; his girlfriend Louise Rolfe claimed they were together in a hotel at the time of the event. She became known in the press as the "Blonde Alibi," and became Mrs. McGurn soon after. McGurn met a violent end in 1936 when two assassins approached him in a bowling alley and pumped a couple of slugs into his head. In the sensational newspaper accounts of this latter incident, McGurn's widow was still referred to as the "Blonde Alibi."[29]

The film provides a sufficiently enjoyable hour's entertainment, but misses the mark in its ham-fisted attempts to interject humor into the proceedings. The comic interplay between Inspector Carmichael and his curiously-named cohort Lieutenant Melody Haynes is forced and unfunny, and compromises MacBride's otherwise tough-cop demeanor. Peter Whitney's performance is broad and not particularly amusing, and his character of Haynes comes across as a doofus; one marvels at the rare instances when he actually contributes something to the manhunt. The running gag concerning the Narcissus flowers is just plain silly, further demonstrating how dim Lieutenant Haynes actually is, as if we aren't already convinced. This pairing is a variation of their roles in the previously filmed (but not yet released) *The Brute Man*, but far less effective. As outside talent, MacBride and Whitney were paid $1,333 each at $1,000 per week, for one-and-a-third weeks' worth of work.

Neal and the statuesque O'Driscoll make adequate leads, although her illusion of height might be chalked up to a lack thereof among her costars. The film is overly talkative, and too much of the action takes place in the stationhouse. The noirish elements take an unfortunate backseat in what could have been a straightforward, tough-as-nails crime thriller. John Berkes' petty thief Louie Carney provides some chuckles with his increasingly unbelievable explanations to the cops of the source of his pocketful of cash, and noir perennials Elisha Cook, Jr., and Marc Lawrence add to the film's tone in their respective bit parts. As the guilty doorman, Oliver Blake is a standout, and Robert Armstrong, in the role originally slated for actor Joe Sawyer, adds some lighter moments as the increasingly frustrated police interrogator.

O'Driscoll, under contract to Universal, was the film's big salary winner, receiving a flat $5,000 for the film's twelve-day shooting schedule, with another $650 allotted for her wardrobe. Neal fared less well, receiving a modest $1,575 for his efforts; bit players Robert Armstrong and Elisha Cook, Jr., received $1,500 each, with Samuel Hinds topping Neal at $1,900. As executive producer, Pivar's flat rate had by now increased to $5,000, with secretary Helen McLemore tagging along for her usual $500. Director Will Jason received a flat $2,500, scriptwriter George Bricker a total of $2,467, and cameraman Maury Gertsman $350 per week for three weeks' work for a total of $1,050. Stock footage was allocated $500, split evenly between the studio's film library and outside stock footage sources. Scoring required thirty-five musicians for five hours, adding another $1,750 to the budget which came in at a total of $133,500.[30]

---

[29] "Gang War Feared in M'Gurn Killing," *New York Times*, February 16, 1936, 12.

[30] Universal Pictures' *Design for Death: Production Budget*, January 7-19, 1946.

There are far too many coincidences piled into the plot, such as the stunning timing of the death of the two pilots whom Lavery has just named as his alibi, and sight-challenged Slater's death-by-auto on his walk to the station to amend his previous statement; apparently there are a number of careless drivers in this city. As for suspects, practically every one of the cast is under suspicion at one time or another: Collins, for running down and killing the wounded Selby; Slater, the last patient to see Selby alive; Louie, who stole Selby's Gutenberg the night Selby was shot; Lavery, assumedly jealous of Selby's relationship with Marian, and whose pistol was the murder weapon; and Marian (if only briefly), whose glove was found at the scene of the crime. And, of course, all of those "red herrings."

There are, however, some really nice visual elements in this film that stand in stark contrast to the otherwise lethargic plot. The opening shot, filmed from cabbie Elisha Cook's point of view as his car strikes Selby, is an eye-opener. Shortly after, Selby's corpse is filmed through the legs of gawking bystanders, then pans up to the arrival of the police. Lavery and Marian's first encounter after a two-year absence is all shot in tight close-ups and two-shots, an approach that works well to enhance the emotions of the moment. The most effective scene takes place near the film's end, when Joe DeLima enters Louie's room with the intention of murder. Shot from Joe's advancing point of view, Louie backs off pleading, staring the camera straight in the "eye" until gunshots are heard and he crumples into a chair. Effective moments such as these save the film, and would suggest that Will Jason's direction coupled with Maury Gertsman's cinematography was a happy union.

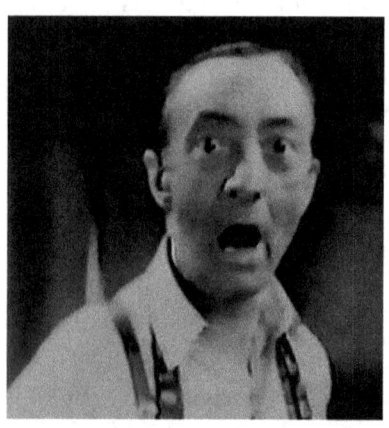

John Berkes recoils in horror from gun-wielding Marc Lawrence in *Blonde Alibi* (1946).

Reviewers were divided over the finished product. *Boxoffice* had nothing but praise for the film: "A compact cops-and-robbers story, ably delineated and expertly directed, qualifies this modestly-budgeted drama as a noteworthy second feature for double bills anywhere. Dialog is sensible, situations are natural and acceptable and the suspense is maintained at top levels until the fadeout ... Performances are exceptionally meritorious, due, obviously, to careful casting which resulted in outstanding contribution by even the lesser members of the Thespic aggregation."[31] *Variety*, on the other hand, trashed it:

---

[31] "Feature Reviews," *Boxoffice*, March 30, 1946, page unknown.

"This routine whodunit hasn't much to commend it ... Situations are trite, with the solution obvious long before the finis. Dialog is pretty pat, and comedy relief weak and juvenile ... cast and director go through the motions, with camera lagging along. Martha O'Driscoll is pretty and static ... while Tom Neal, as the boyfriend, gives the nearest semblance of verity to any performance."[32]

To each his own.

Inside Job
(Director: Jean Yarbrough; Released June 28, 1946)

Evidently pleased with the work he had done on his first few assignments for Pivar, the studio promoted director Jean Yarbrough to associate producer status.[33] His first film in this new capacity (along with his usual directorial duties) was Pivar's next, the crime thriller *Inside Job*. Alan Curtis and Ann Rutherford were signed for the romantic leads, along with Preston Foster as the heavy. Pivar lined up the usual solid cast of supporting actors, with Milburn Stone, Samuel S. Hinds, and Marc Lawrence back for the umpteenth time; John Berkes and Oliver Blake were retained from the just-completed *Blonde Alibi*.

Scripter George Bricker returned to adapt (with an assist by co-scripter Jerry Warner) a story co-written years earlier by horror-thriller director Tod Browning and writer Garrett Fort. The story had been adapted and filmed twice before for Universal, once in 1920 as the silent *Outside the Law* with Lon Chaney, Priscilla Dean, and Wheeler Oakman, and again in 1930 in a sound version of the same title starring Edward G. Robinson. Browning served as director and co-scripter for these earlier versions, but had nothing to do with this newest variation.

Browning's greatest career successes fell primarily during the silent period at MGM with the other Lon Chaney vehicles *The Unholy Three* (1925), *The Road to Mandalay*, *The Blackbird* (both 1926), *The Unknown*, *London After Midnight* (both 1927), and *West of Zanzibar* (1928), and most notably *Dracula* (1931) for Universal during the sound period. Browning had directed his last film in 1939, and would live in obscurity for the next quarter century until his death in 1962.

Garrett Fort's career writing for film was interspersed with playwriting and short stories, with film credits from the early twenties up until his death by his own hand in October 1945, several months before *Inside Job* began filming on Wednesday, February 27, 1946. A "rambling, four-page suicide note" cited poor health as the reason for downing the bottle of sleeping pills.[34]

---

[32] Bron., "Blonde Alibi," *Variety*, March 20, 1946, 26.

[33] "Studio Personnelities," *Boxoffice*, January 12, 1946, 54.

[34] "Actor-Writer Garrett Fort Ends His Life," *Los Angeles Times*, October 27, 1945, 2.

Stop Yellin'

The censors were all over the script, and Joseph Breen fired off a letter to Murray Pivar in Universal's censorship department that left the film's future in doubt:

> [W]e regret to have to inform you that it is in our considered unanimous judgment that this story is completely unacceptable under the provisions of the Production Code for the reason that it is hardly more than a sympathetic treatment of crime, criminals, and criminality. A motion picture following along the lines of this script as now written, could not be approved by us.
>
> This story smacks of the old time crime-gangster story which the Industry, some years back, agreed not to produce. It is the kind of a story, which, if it were to be produced today, would bring down upon your company and the Industry as a whole, widespread, severe condemnation. There are many people who are seriously concerned about the rampant crime conditions throughout the country and who would see in a picture of this kind a definite connection with the growing evil which results in so much juvenile delinquency.
>
> We respectfully recommend that you dismiss from any further consideration, the production of a motion picture based upon this material.[35]

Sounds like it would have made a helluva good film!

Undaunted, Pivar had Bricker and Warner rework the script and resubmitted twenty heavily revised pages for Breen's review on February 22; Breen responded a day later: "This material, as far as it goes, appears to us to be acceptable under the provisions of the Production Code, and to contain little, if anything, that suggests difficulty from the standpoint of political censorship."[36]

But there were other pages still in contention, and after a three-way phone conversation between Breen and the brothers Pivar, Breen dashed off a letter on February 25 with a shopping list of "suggested" changes: ". . . eliminate Bart's line, 'I own a piece of the place';" ". . . find some other business besides that of the cocktail drinking between Bart and Claire;" ". . . eliminate the business of Bart opening the closet and taking out the shoulder holster;" ". . . the business of Claire unwrapping the currency be eliminated;" "We again suggest the possibility of your reducing the amount of money stolen from the department store. Further: please eliminate here all references to fingerprints;" ". . . reconsider Eddie's speech, beginning with the lines, 'Think

---

[35] Correspondence from Joseph I. Breen to Maurice Pivar, dated February 16, 1946.

[36] Correspondence from Joseph I. Breen to Maurice Pivar, dated February 23, 1946.

of the things I'm going to buy your [sic] with this.' It would be good if such a speech could be either dropped entirely, or rewritten with a view to getting away from emphasizing the likely profits from a major crime;" and "We again call your attention to the business of the fingerprints. If possible, this should be eliminated."[37]

Fingerprints? The pettiness of some of these items of contention speaks volumes about the little Napoleons entrenched in the MPDA.

Finally, on the seventh day of filming, Breen signed off on the last of the outstanding issues: "... we are glad to let you know that this material appears to meet the requirements of the Production Code." And I am sure the brothers Pivar were "glad" to have Breen off their collective backs.

Eddie Norton (Alan Curtis) is a man with a past, and his wife Claire (Ann Rutherford) knows nothing about it. Years earlier he was involved in a robbery with Bart Madden (Preston Foster) and ended up taking the rap. After a stay in prison, Eddie had decided to go straight, but soon found that his record was an impediment to getting or keeping a job. It is the Christmas season now, and both Eddie and Claire have taken jobs at a large department store named The Mammoth Store (introduced with a set-extending matte painting by Russell Lawson). Claire works as a model in the French Room, while Eddie, using the alias Eddie Mitchell, poses in the store's window as a crowd-attracting automaton.

It turns out that Madden has done well for himself in this city. Having spotted Eddie in the store window, Madden contacts him and arranges a meeting. He proposes a robbery of The Mammoth Store's Christmas season cash, but when Eddie balks Madden blackmails him with exposure. Eddie reluctantly agrees.

Eddie reveals his criminal past to Claire, and then lures her into his renewed life of crime. He plans to double-cross Madden, commit the robbery himself, and then he and Claire will take off with the haul and live a life of crime-free leisure. Claire goes for it.

As part of Eddie's plan, Claire has an "accidental" run-in with Madden, and soon the mobster is on the hook. Giving her name as Claire Gray, she invites him to that afternoon's fashion show where she is to model creations by Mons. Cordet (William Trenk), including the gown "Moonlight Madness." Madden attends, and then purchases the gown and has it sent to Claire's apartment.

The department store stiffs Claire on expected payment for posing in newspaper ads for the fashion show, so she takes advantage of this to complain to, and then charm, the store's cashier Trent W. Wickle (Howard Freeman). When the lecherous old fellow takes her to dinner and bores her with a bunch of old photos, she realizes that one of them has the combination to the store

---

[37] Correspondence from Joseph I. Breen to Maurice Pivar, dated February 25, 1946.

safe written on the back. She sneaks it out of the pack and later passes the combination to Eddie.

The plan is put in motion. At the end of the work day, Claire punches Eddie's time card while he remains behind hidden in the store. She then heads over to Madden's apartment ostensibly to return the dress, but in actuality to keep Madden busy during the theft. Madden doesn't trust Eddie, however, and has one of his hoods named Freddie (John Berkes) keep an eye on him. Freddie reports that Eddie never left the store, and Madden reveals to Claire that he's on to her and throws her out. Madden heads over to join Freddie in hopes of catching Eddie when he exits the store. Eddie robs the store of $256,723.49 and tosses it out a bathroom window. Claire, dressed as a beggar, grabs the cash, stuffs it in her bag, and makes off with it without Madden recognizing her.

Captain Donovan (Marc Lawrence) investigates the theft, and reports back to District Attorney Sutton (Milburn Stone). They finger Eddie for the theft, and connect both Claire and Madden to him. A warrant is issued for Eddie's arrest. Madden, who thought that Eddie was Claire's boyfriend, is informed that Claire and Eddie are married.

Holed up in their apartment, Claire befriends a neighbor kid named Skipper (Jimmie Moss), aware that his mother is dead but unaware that his father is police Captain Thomas (Joe Sawyer). Eddie thinks this kid will be nothing but trouble, but Claire thinks otherwise, wishing silently to herself for children of her own some day. Eddie promises her that he'll get them both out of town in a day or so, after which she can have anything she wants. She doesn't give voice to her desire for children, but it is evident that is what she wants more than anything else.

Eddie heads to a diner and makes a proposition to a truck driver named Herman (Oliver Blake): $5,000 for transit for two passengers, no questions asked. It's a deal, but later on Herman shoots off his big mouth, and word gets back to Madden that two unnamed people want out, and where they are to be picked up. Madden "knows" who they are, and heads over to grab the stolen cash. Pistol drawn, Madden demands to be let into Eddie's apartment. Captain Thomas arrives back home and encounters Madden, and the two have a shootout. Both are wounded and unconscious. Eddie wants to split, but Claire convinces him that they can't let Captain Thomas die in the hall; they should call a doctor. Eddie reluctantly agrees. Two cops get wind of Thomas' plight and head over to see what is going on. Madden revives long enough to grab the cash, but he trips over the toy hobby horse that Thomas had bought as a Christmas gift for Skipper, and falls down the steps to his death just as the cops arrive. Eddie and Claire are arrested.

Eddie pleads guilty to grand larceny, and is sentenced to prison. He speaks briefly with Claire before he is hauled off to his cell: "Well, beautiful, I guess you'll have to wait a long time for whatever it is you wanted most. You never did tell me what it was." Claire, resigned to her fate, quietly responds: "Never mind, Eddie. Never mind."

Inside Job turned out to be Pivar's last Universal release, and it is a solid, straightforward, humorless noir. Much of Pivar's output at Universal had varying levels of humor, in some instances appropriate and welcome, but in others an action-interrupting impediment. While the varying mix of action and humor of the earlier Arlen-Devine and Devine-Carrillo co-starrers usually worked well in those films' favor, the inclusion of a subsidiary character intended primarily for comic relief in some other films fared less well. The idea, I suppose, was to give the viewer a welcome breather from the action that immediately preceded it, but often as not served simply as an annoying, out-of-place intrusion. There were exceptions, of course, most notably in the sober excursions of *Ski Patrol* and *The Strange Death of Adolf Hitler*, and the dark, sadistic *Eyes of the Underworld*. Even Pivar's earliest horror outings threw in some humorous sidekicks—*The Mummy's Hand*'s wisecracking Babe Jenson, and *Horror Island*'s dim Stuff Oliver—but those were wisely jettisoned for future films when it became apparent what the target audiences wanted, and did not want. Still, humor of questionable value and wit had a way of worming its way into the most inappropriate of films, most notably in the recent *Blonde Alibi* where its absence would have been resoundingly welcomed. *Inside Job* stuck to its grim little story like a thirsty tick, and it is a better film for it. The one minor exception is the little kid's confusion over Eddie's name: he hears Claire call him "Honey," and insists on calling him that through the remainder of the film.

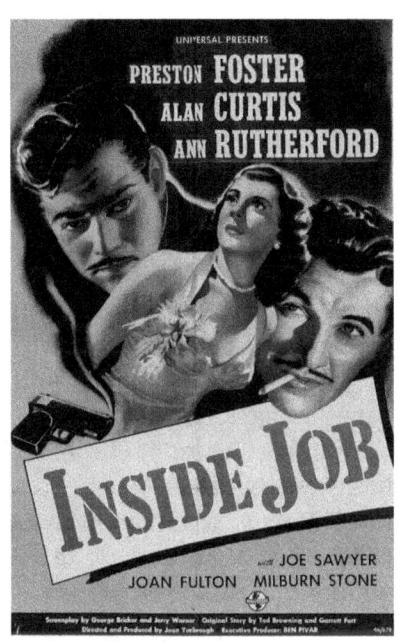

Pivar's best film *noir*, 1946's *Inside Job*. Image courtesy of Heritage Auction Galleries, Ha.com.

Contract player and former commercial artists' model Alan Curtis never cracks a smile as the bitter ex-con goaded back into a life of crime, and is convincing in the role. This would be his last film for Universal in a three-year stint, after which he made a handful of low-budget films and a pair of "Philo Vance" mysteries for PRC before his untimely death at in 1953 from complications following kidney surgery.[38] Preston Foster alternates between charm and menace as Madden, and handles the tough-guy chores with ease. Former MGM starlet and Andy Hardy series regular Ann Rutherford taps into her darker side here, accompanying her husband in a criminal activity without blinking an eye.

The rest of the film's roles are minor ones, providing a number of character actors with a day's work. Joan Fulton is back as Madden's sexy girl Ruthie, and even gets to warble a few lines from a ditty titled "Do You Believe in Love and Honey" (or something like that), and has a surprisingly pleasing voice to accompany her pleasing looks.[39] John Berkes is back and just as twitchy as weaselly two-bit hood Freddie, and Oliver Blake impresses once again as the skeptical truck driver who talks too much. Milburn Stone doesn't have a lot to do as the district attorney, but what little he does he does well. Marc Lawrence looks out of place on the right side of the law. As the department store's cashier Mr. Wickle, Howard Freeman could pass as Robert Benchley. Joe Sawyer takes a bullet and little else but a paycheck as the cop dad, but little Jimmie Moss, who plays his son, is not at all convincing as the annoying kid next door. His dog Slugger is cute, though, and a better actor. Blink and you'll miss Samuel S. Hines' Judge Kinkaid.

Filming began on February 27, on an intended twelve-day shooting schedule budgeted at $200,000. Yarbrough's goal was a nine-page-a-day average for the 109-page script, and the first several days of production took place on a civilized eight-hour working day schedule: Company call at 9:00 a.m., an hour off for lunch midday, and dismissal at 6:00 p.m. (or within a half hour of that to complete setups in progress). This schedule seemed to work for several days, but by the end of the fourth the unit was a day behind schedule, by the eighth day two days behind, falling to three days behind schedule by the end of the tenth day. This growing lag resulted in some extra-long workdays in an attempt to keep the production's head above water, day seven ending at 10:50 p.m., day eight at 11:00 p.m., day thirteen at 11:50 p.m., and the final, fifteenth day at 10:30 p.m. As both director and associate producer, Yarbrough must have been fried by the time shooting wrapped on Friday, March 15, $4,000 over budget.

Scripter George Bricker received $2,800 for his seven weeks' work, with co-scripter Jerry Warner receiving $1,433.35 for the comparable time period. Producer-director Yarbrough earned a flat $3,500, and Pivar his now-standard $5,000 for his executive efforts; secretary Helen McLemore once again received $500 for being at Pivar's beck and call. Cameraman Maury Gertsman

---

[38] "Alan Curtis, Movie actor, Dies in N.Y.," *New York Times*, February 2, 1953, page unknown.

[39] There's a one-hour, $100 line item in the budget for "Voice Doubles," so while it appears to be Fulton singing it may have been a skillful dubbing.

was paid $1,400 for his four weeks' work, with film editor Otto Ludwig earning $1,650 for his ten-week effort to piece the footage into a coherent, acceptable whole. Stock footage played less of a role in this film, $400 worth. Twenty-nine musicians scored the film over a five-hour period, adding another $1,750 to the budget.

The cast and extras accounted for roughly 29% of the film's budget. Contract player Curtis was paid a flat $10,000 for his portrayal of hard guy Eddie, and co-star Rutherford was brought in with a four-week guarantee for a comparable amount. Preston Foster was the big winner here, earning $25,000 for an eight-week guarantee. Milburn Stone earned $600 for two days' work, and Joan Fulton merely $150. Ruby Dandridge, in the uncredited role of Ivory, was paid $500 for her five-and-three-quarters hours of work, with a written agreement that she be released by 4:45 p.m. to accommodate a scheduled radio broadcast. Joe Sawyer earned $1,167 for what ended up as only a few minutes screen time as the cop dad. Slugger the dog earned a whopping $150 (Joan Fulton must have been miffed), which should have kept him in dog biscuits for months to come; his trainer only received $75. Marc Lawrence needed only about nine hours on set for his small role, and Samuel Hinds less than three hours in his tiny role as the judge.

Unseen for years, *Inside Job* finally resurfaced in 2009 for a one-time showing at the 10th Annual Arthur Lyons Film Noir Festival held in Palm Springs, California. Kim Morgan interviewed special guest Ann Rutherford following the screening, Rutherford proving to be quite funny and energetic at age eighty-nine. Rutherford had been married to department store heir David May at the time the film was made, and commented on the plot's department store heist: "Curiously, at the time I made this my husband was in the department store business—he had department stores all over the United States. I must have been out of my gourd to have accepted a part like that, but it was a loan-out." While she had only the dimmest recollections of making the film, she did have some fond memories of her costars—fond and caustic: "The main thing I recall about this was Preston Foster, who was an absolutely delightful gentleman. He had been raised on the West Side of New York, and he could talk in any dialect, and dialog, of anyone. He just filled me full of wonderful Yiddish phrases. I never had a better time in my life working with him." As for Alan Curtis, she said he was "a very nice fellow, and couldn't have been more attractive, and—he should have gone to prison. He was as crooked as a dog's hind leg." One wishes that she had at the time elaborated on that latter comment. As for the rest of the small cast, she offered a generalization: "For me, the joy of seeing this picture was the wonderful faces of the character actors. Under the studio system they all had to have somebody who was always the sheriff, somebody was always the judge, somebody was always one particular thing. To see those glorious, ugly faces—I still love pictures where men wear hats, and they start drinking at ten o'clock in the morning." Interviewer Morgan interjected, "On the set, or just in the movie?" After a pause, Rutherford responded, assumedly with tongue planted firmly in cheek: "Yes. Yup, that too."[40]

Ann Rutherford had remarried in 1953 to television producer William Dozier, and they remained husband and wife up until his death in 1991. When I spoke with her a year after the Morgan interview, she was rather dismissive of the film as a whole, undeservedly so in my humble opinion. "It was a loan-out—I never had a chance to read the script beforehand, or I would have fallen on my face and gotten out of it. They used it last year as a film noir, I don't understand how. I didn't understand why on earth I had to go to Palm Springs to watch them celebrate this dumb movie." When I commented that I thought the film was rather good, she responded, "Well, that's a good thing to hear—maybe it has marinated long enough to be acceptable." I got the distinct impression she'd rather be remembered for her heyday at MGM rather than the later, less-distinguished productions. When asked to elaborate on her comments regarding co-star Alan Curtis, she was shocked when I read them back to her: "I said that? Well, maybe his character. Maybe I wasn't speaking about him personally; I'm sure I was speaking about his character."[41] You be the judge.

Inside Job is a good-looking film given its budgetary limitations. Jean Yarbrough, never the most stylish of directors, rises to the occasion with this film, with Maury Gertsman's dark, shadowy nighttime photography adding to the impending sense of doom that hangs over the film's taut sixty-five minutes. Only the subplot with the kid and the dog slows things down and adds a touch of maudlin to an otherwise cynical plot, but the dog makes up for this in one throwaway bit: We hear Claire's voice and the sounds of bathing coming from the bathroom, and our assumption that it is she who is bathing is turned on its head when she emerges with the just-bathed Slugger.

Several of those B movie lack-of-logic moments occur during the film.

---

[40] Ann Rutherford interview by Kim Morgan at the 10th Annual Arthur Lyons Film Noir Festival in Palm Springs, California, May 30, 2009, after a revival showing of *Inside Job*. <http://www.youtube.com/watch?v=jnvUDgA93-U> (May 23, 2010)

[41] Ann Rutherford interviews with the author, May 27, 2010 and June 3, 2010. Rutherford went on to say that her contract with MGM had been sold to 20th Century-Fox when MGM thought she was stonewalling them over a part in their upcoming *Seven Sweethearts* (1942). In reality, she'd contracted German measles from an enthusiastic—and evidently infected—little kid named Alvin while performing for servicemen. 20th Century-Fox treated her shabbily, loaning her out to any studio willing to pay for her services ("They were just using me to make money"). Loan-outs to Republic, RKO, and United Artists preceded her one loan-out to Universal for *Inside Job* in early 1946.

THE FINAL FEW

Eddie has sent Claire to Madden's apartment to keep him occupied while Eddie robs the department store. Madden reveals that he is on to her and throws her out, and then heads over to the store hoping to intercept Eddie. Soon after his arrival, Claire, dressed as an old woman, scoops up the parcels of cash that Eddie has dumped out a bathroom window and escapes with them right under Madden's nose. One wonders how she would have been available to retrieve the cash if Madden had not earlier thrown her out of his apartment, and had instead taken her to dinner as originally planned. And, at the film's end when the judge sentences Eddie to prison, he acknowledges that the two of them have made full restitution of the stolen cash. Given that the couple was otherwise virtually penniless, one wonders how they managed to pay back the cash spent in the interim, primarily to Herman as down-payment for smuggling them out of town. Not that it really matters.

Music director Frank Skinner's cobbled-together score is at times intrusive, overwhelming the visuals when silence would have been more appropriate and effective. For once Vera West's gowns are the center of attention during the fashion show, the so-called "Moonlight Madness" affair in particular as the back-and-forth gift between Madden and Claire. (Rutherford's wardrobe was budgeted at $1,850, compared to Curtis' and Foster's at a measly $25 and $60, respectively; Milburn Stone had to wear his own suit.)

Daily Variety gave one of its middle-of-the-road reviews that focused primarily on the performers: "Alan Curtis, Preston Foster and Ann Rutherford enact top roles for all parts are worth ... Foster gives rugged impersonation as racketeering chief, but Curtis suffers through indecision of script writers to make him hero or heavy. Miss Rutherford's character, too, is none too clearly cleaved." As for the script and Yarbrough's contributions, "[the story] doesn't always ring true, particularly in case of ex-con's wife agreeing to turn crook with him moment after she learns her husband has prison record ... Yarbrough handled dual chore of producer-director with deft touch."[42]

Exhibitors were all over the place with their reactions to the film, assumedly reacting more to patronage—or lack thereof—than any given film's actual artistic merit. Rivesville, West Virginia, liked it: "This is another picture from Universal that is different from anything that has come out of Hollywood. All the top names in this picture were crooks, which went over big here—and there wasn't the same kind of ending, where the two loved ones kiss." So did Java, South Dakota: "This picture surely filled the bill for midweek. You cannot go wrong on it for this type of picture." Louisburg, North Carolina, was a bit more reserved: "This is an okay program mystery that satisfied on giveaway night." And then there was Harold F. Johnson of the Elberia Theatre in Palisade, Colorado, who clearly had a bone to pick with Universal: "This is one of the

---

[42] "Inside Job," *Daily Variety*, June 14, 1946, 3.

corniest, low-bracket pictures (in my estimation) that was ever put out by any company. Very poorly made, not much of a cast and all this tended to make a truly lousy picture. It will indeed be a pleasure when my present contract with this outfit is completed and I won't have to go hide out when I can't face my patrons after offering them something like this."[43] I guess he didn't like it.

In spite of its Christmastime setting, *Inside Job* was released theatrically on June 28, 1946.

With *Inside Job* in the can, Pivar went to work on his next batch of assignments. The latest wave of horror films had run its course by now, freeing Pivar to concentrate on the taut little crime thrillers he was comfortable churning out on his miniscule budgets. A number of his unit's films were announced in the trades during April, May, and June. The first was *Blind Fury*, to be scripted by newcomer Don Martin,[44] but reassigned to Charles Marion a month later.[45]

The second, tentatively titled *Challenge in the Night*, was to be written by journeyman scriptwriter Arnold Belgard.[46] Leon Barsha was assigned to associate produce, his first project after leaving his production chores at Columbia and joining Pivar's unit at Universal.[47] A former editor from the late twenties who had worked on at least one film with Pivar back at Columbia, Barsha had tried his hand at direction before settling in as a producer at Columbia in the later thirties.

The last two films were to be based on Don Martin originals, a pair of mysteries titled *Once Upon a Crime*[48] and *Lady in Jade*.[49] *Blonde Alibi* director Will Jason, having passed muster on his previous assignment, was slated to direct *Once Upon a Crime* from Arnold Belgard's script. Cameras were scheduled to roll on June 20.[50] Pivar and company were as busy as usual—but not for long. At the end of June Universal announced its tentative schedule for the 1946-1947 season, which included thirty-four features, six of them to be filmed in Technicolor and another two in the less-costly Cinecolor.[51]

---

[43] "The Exhibitor Has His Say," *Boxoffice*, July 27 and November 23, 1946, February 1 and 8, 1947, pages unknown.

[44] "Studio Personnelities," *Boxoffice*, April 20, 1946, 74.

[45] "Studio Personnelities," *Boxoffice*, May 18, 1946, 69.

[46] "Wallace MacDonald Takes Barsha's Columbia Post," *Boxoffice*, May 11, 1946, 28.

[47] "Studio Personnelities," *Boxoffice*, May 18, 1946, 68.

[48] "Studio Personnelities," *Boxoffice*, May 18, 1946, 68, 69.

[49] Ivan Spear, "Hollywood Report," *Boxoffice*, May 25, 1946, 32.

[50] "Henry King to Direct Tyrone Power Opus," *Boxoffice*, June 15, 1946, page unknown.

[51] "34 Features on Universal's Film Schedule," *Los Angeles Times*, June 27, 1946, 9.

The Final Few

At the end of July 1946, however, two announcements were made concerning the future of Universal, both of which rocked the studio. First of all, on the 25th, notice was given to four executive producers that their units were to be dissolved immediately and the twelve productions currently in preparation were to be shelved. The executive producers were Ben Pivar and studio serial supervisor Morgan B. Cox, along with Marshall Grant and Howard Welsch, producers of the bulk of the remainder of the studio's low-budget westerns and melodramas. Along with this action was the termination of employment of the dissolved units' five associate producers, directors, and writers, affecting approximately twenty-five people in total. The reason given for the mass dismissal was the studio's large backlog of B's, and the immediate need for all available stage space for higher-budget productions. According to the Universal spokesman, the decision affected the present year's program only, and that no decision had yet been made regarding future years.[52]

Five days later on the 30th, it was officially announced that Universal Pictures Company and International Pictures Corp. were to merge into a corporation known as the Universal-International Production Company, effective October 1. The merger was put on the fast track, however, going into effect on August 14. United World Pictures Company, Inc., formed back in November 1945 to distribute pictures made by J. Arthur Rank and other international interests,[53] was also to merge with Universal-International, which would be "a wholly owned subsidiary" of Universal Pictures Company. The merger would give Universal-International a stronger position in the industry, with the acquisition of more than a thousand theaters in the world market owned or controlled by the Rank Organization in Great Britain, Canada, Australia, and other British Empire and South American countries, and the planned acquisition of a theater circuit in the United States. From Universal's recently announced 1946-1947 schedule would be the elimination of all B's (including the westerns and serials), and the remaining schedule would be rearranged so that the first year would see the production of "twenty-five pictures of distinction," plus the release of twelve more British Rank-financed features. The reasons behind Pivar's dismissal five days earlier were now crystal clear.

Along with the merger came the usual studio purge. William Goetz and Leo Spitz became president and chairman respectively, positions identical to those previously held by them at International Pictures, putting them in control of studio production activities. Matthew Fox, president of United World Pictures, was elected executive vice president and a director of parent

---

[52] "Universal to Drop Four 'B' Film Units," *New York Times*, July 26, 1946, 16; "Universal Studio Drops Four Production Units," *Boxoffice*, July 27, 1946, 22.

[53] "Film Groups Form New Companies," *Los Angeles Times*, November 28, 1945, 1.

company Universal Pictures.[54] Dan Kelley, head of the talent department and supervisor of high-budget productions, was replaced by William Dozier and Rufus LeMaire. Story department head James Geller was replaced by Ray Crossett, production manager David Garber by James Pratt, casting director Robert McIntire by Jack Murton, and general manager Martin Murphy by John Beck, Jr.; numerous others were affected as well.[55] Pivar's older brother Murray, in charge of Universal's editorial department for the past twenty-five years, was spared the sword and remained in that position with the new company.[56]

Caught off guard by the unexpected turn of events and the receipt of his dismissal notice, Pivar was stunned. He packed his belongings, said goodbye to his fellow employees, climbed into his 1938 Buick convertible and drove home to deliver the devastating news to Judy. For the first time in many years, Pivar found himself without a job, and with no advance warning. It was not the first time, and it would not be the last, but after eight years of dedicated service, advancement within the ranks, a steadily growing salary, and a nice home and lifestyle to show for it, Pivar's world was shaken. No doubt aware of the general decline in interest in the sort of films he was used to making, he must have felt some unease over the prospect of finding a comparably lucrative position within the industry.

The most immediate impact was on his wallet. With the cessation of a steady check, Pivar reluctantly put the Valley Spring Lane house up for rental and moved his family into a much smaller two-bedroom home at 10620 Moorpark Street. 20th Century-Fox actor Mark Stevens assumed possession of the comfortable home, and remained there for several years.

There was one additional factor to add to the family's turmoil. Back in the early forties, Judy and her sister Ina had lured their parents out to California after their father had retired from the butcher business. The elderly couple was put up in a small bungalow at 5640½ Harold Way, between Hollywood Boulevard and West Sunset Boulevard. Leaving a life of toil behind, Wolf and Jennie were finally able to relax and get to know their California-based grandchildren. They lived there for several years in peace and contentment, with annual visits back to Brooklyn for Passover. And now, with Judy concerned over the turn of events affecting her immediate family, one more unexpected issue arose to confront her: her mother Jennie's death on January 4, 1947. Judy's despondent father decided to pack up and return to Brooklyn, where he would live up until his death in 1952.

---

[54] "2 Movie Producers Announce Merger," *New York Times*, July 31, 1946, page unknown.

[55] "Merger Advanced at Film Studios," *New York Times*, August 15, 1946, 30.

[56] "U-I Major Appointments Announced By Executives," *Boxoffice*, September 7, 1946, 51.

The Final Few

With Pivar's production unit eliminated and staff sent packing, recent hires Don Martin and Leon Barsha saw their hopes dashed. Screenwriter Martin looked elsewhere and found sporadic jobs churning out crime stories for PRC, Republic, Eagle-Lion, Columbia, Allied Artists, and even one for Universal-International before settling into television work in the mid-fifties. As for Barsha, with both *Challenge in the Night* and follow-up assignment *Shanghai Lady* now dead and his associate producer position terminated, he gave up production and took a long break from the industry. He eventually returned to filmmaking in the early fifties, once again in the capacity of editor. The final four films announced for Pivar's unit were never made. The abrupt termination of the Universal B units temporarily derailed the careers of many and, in a few sad instances, ended the careers of others.

It was the end of an era for Pivar, his most productive and the period where he was the guiding force behind the films that he is remembered for today. While none of these were great films, and the bulk of them merely routine programmers, there was a handful that stood out as memorable and better than the average low-budget fare. It is the horror films that still have legs—somewhat creaky legs, but legs nonetheless. These latter films are the ones that continue to be re-released every so often on the home video format du jour, with Chaney's Kharis by now an iconic image.

The storylines were frequently the films' weakest aspect, not too surprising given the rushed one-hour formats and Pivar's budget-dictated routine of hiring journeymen writers with little previous experience in scriptwriting or, in some cases, writing in general. Writer Maurice Tombragel's name is ubiquitous in the screenwriting and original story credits, but he'd never written a word for the screen before Pivar engaged him. Larry Rhine, Ben Chapman, and Maxwell Shane's names pop up repeatedly as well, almost always as a trio and frequently along with Griffin Jay, another recurring contributor. M. Coates Webster and former pulp writers George Bricker and Dwight V. Babcock were responsible for a number of the later films' plots, with Brenda Weisberg and Henry Sucher repeat contributors as well. In most instances they were given a pre-selected title around which to build a story and fashion into a workable screenplay. Time was as tight as the budget, and it was a pressure-cooker environment in which only the hardiest wordsmiths could function. Small wonder that what ended up on the screen seemed more like a hastily conceived afterthought than a fully realized scenario.

The acting in Pivar's films was generally good, with the supporting casts of character actors almost uniformly excellent. It was the leads or supporting leads who would tend to fall short, given that these films were the training grounds for the studio's newest and greenest contractees, often with only a handful of previous roles (if any) to their credit, and whose levels of ability were all over the map. For every Don Porter, Tom Neal, and Dan Dailey, Jr., you had a Phil Brown and Edward Hyans, and on the distaff side for every Gale Sondergaard, Peggy Moran, and Virginia Christine, you had a Ramsay Ames, Elyse Knox, and Vicky Lane. And let's not forget Acquanetta and Rondo Hatton, engaged more as eye-catching "objects" rather than for any sort of thespic abilities. Former stars on the downhill slide would fare better, of course, with old-timers such as Richard Arlen, Richard Dix, Noah Beery, and Leo Carrillo engaged for face and name recognition, and to add a modicum of class to otherwise routine films.

It was the combined expertise of the assembled craftsmen at Universal that produced results heads-and-tails above that from poor relation studios such as Monogram and PRC. The photography was almost always excellent, with nighttime shooting favored whenever feasible over the cheaper, more expedient day-for-night. Sets were carefully lit, with Universal's Germanic chiaroscuro lighting a welcome visual treat that predated, but smoothly evolved into, the noir look of the later forties post-war period. Camera movement, while kept to a minimum, was carefully chosen and smoothly executed, and almost always utilized at each film's opening as a means to "guide" the viewer into the story. Cinematographer John W. Boyle's quarter century behind the camera lent an easy assurance to his setups, chosen both for maximum efficiency and storytelling impact; Pivar used him a half-dozen times for his Arlen-Devine and Carrillo-Devine series. Maury Gertsman had spent a number of years previous as assistant cameraman on features and photographer of several studio shorts before Pivar gave him his break. His start in features as director of photography began with several of Pivar's supervised westerns, graduating to the (comparative) big time soon after with seven of Pivar's horror and crime thrillers. Gertsman was a quick learner with a good eye and knack for composition, and was responsible for some of Pivar's most handsome-looking films. Jerome Ash, another old-timer with Universal from the mid-twenties, and a staple of their lower-budget films, lensed another seven films for Pivar spread across all genres. The remainder of Pivar's output was filmed by an array of diverse talents that included William Sickner, Elwood "Woody" Bredell, Milton Krasner, George Robinson, Stanley Cortez, Virgil Miller, Jack MacKenzie, Charles Van Enger, and Paul Ivano. There is not a shabby-looking film in the bunch, although some are far better looking than the others. There was, of course, the occasional camera shadow visible as it dollied forward to a medium- or close-shot, but such were the perils of the breakneck schedules and cost-cutting expediency of B movie filmmaking.

The editing and continuity of these films was usually flawless, with none of the sloppiness and mismatches prevalent in so many other low-budget offerings. Two individuals, Maurice Wright and Milton Carruth, handled well over a third of these films; Wright primarily on the Arlen-Devine series, and Carruth more often than not on the horror flicks. Other frequent contributors included Otto Ludwig and Edward Curtiss with four films each, and Ted Kent, Philip Cahn, Ray Curtiss, and Fred R. Feitshans, Jr. with three films each.

Rare was the instance where a lack of coverage or the necessity to clarify some plot point resulted in some after-the-fact looped-in dialog, but when it was needed it was usually an obvious mismatch in both sound quality and point of origin; *The Mummy's Hand* is a primary offender in this regard. The technicians of Bernard B. Brown's sound department delivered clean and crisp recordings, so it would seem that this dubbed-in dialog was a hastily executed afterthought. Another rarity was the occasional background noise that was not cleaned up in post-production, but it happened, and more than once.

The musical scores for these films are all pastiches of scores from previous Universal A's, cobbled together in most instances under Hans J. Salter's guidance, used and reused one film after another, ad infinitum. While there may be a mind-numbing familiarity to the scores when these films are viewed one after another, the actual schedule where months would pass from one release to the next probably added a note of "freshness" to the scores. Which were, by the way, quite good.

It was the director who was on the firing line for these productions, with Pivar breathing down his neck every step of the way to ensure that everything was kept on schedule and within budget. Only the heartiest and organized of individuals could function within the Draconian constraints imposed; the budgets were parsimonious—*The Mummy's Hand* and *Horror Island* had budgets less than half of the allocation for *The Wolf Man*, and less than a third for *The Invisible Man Returns*—and the shooting schedules a tight ten-to-twelve days. Pivar's bottom line was efficiency, and when he found a director with whom he was fully compatible he'd rehire him time and again. Christy Cabanne provided just that, bringing decades of past experience to the table and the assurance of smooth sailing for each and every production he was assigned to. Pivar and Cabanne made a great team, and Cabanne's efforts contributed in no small part to Pivar's success at Universal. He directed more than a quarter of Pivar's total output, with a staggering ten films (out of thirteen) to his credit in the first two years alone. Jean Yarbrough, another industry vet, provided the bookend to Pivar's tenure at Universal, directing four of Pivar's last five realized productions at the studio, and continuing on elsewhere with several additional productions. Pivar gave Reginald LeBorg, arguably the most stylish director of the bunch, his first real break in an association that lasted for five films. Former editor John Rawlins helmed another four films for Pivar, shoehorned into the middle of a career spent in the lower echelons of the industry. The rest of the directorial credits read like a Who's Who of B film "luminaries," including the likes of Phil Rosen, Lew Landers, William Nigh, Wallace Fox, Charles Lamont, Roy William Neill, George Waggner, Harold Young, and James Hogan. It was the rare occasion when any of these fellows managed to poke his head—if only briefly—above the programmer hordes.

With his termination by Universal, it was the end of a challenging, fruitful, and lucrative era for Pivar. Now he had to go out and find something new.

§

19 Edward Small's Small Reliance Pictures

By mid-1947, as a combined result of rapidly rising production costs and a selling market noticeably restricted by Britain's recently-imposed 75% tax on imported films, production of B's had dropped off precipitously. Labor unions, the perennial whipping boy—oft-times deservedly so—of businesses both large and small, were singled out as a major contributing factor. I.E. Chadwick, president of the Independent Motion Picture Producers Association, a group composed of twenty-nine small studios, testified at a Congressional hearing that union featherbedding threatened the "lessening of production with consequent increase in unemployment." Fifteen association members had already been put out of business, with another fifty films lost to production due to mounting costs. His final volley: "Unless we get protection from Congress we are finished."[1]

A year later Chadwick was sounding a slightly more optimistic note regarding production for the 1948-1949 season, while still bemoaning the increase in costs battering his constituents. He said that over a two- to three-year period, westerns previously costing $15,000 to $18,000 now cost $35,000 to $40,000, and low-budget actioners and serials costing $30,000 to $35,000 now fell in the $80,000 to $100,000 range. Production during the 1947-1948 season had dropped to ninety features, down from the previous season's 150. The segment of the industry Chadwick represented had come to the conclusion that it must have more product to sell if it was to stay in business. As a result, production was ramping up to churn out 150 films, a number comparable to that of the 1946-1947 season.[2]

Hollywood in general was beginning to set forth new plans of operation that included the limited revival of B's. Smaller studios, such as RKO and Universal-

---

[1] "Unions Peril Us, Film Man Says," *Los Angeles Times*, June 19, 1947, 1.
[2] J.D. Spiro, "Hollywood Memos," *New York Times*, September 5, 1948, X3.

International, were able to produce their own, but 20th Century-Fox, with over twice the studio overhead, was not. In September, Fox announced plans to distribute low-budget films produced by independents; they had finalized arrangements (or were about to) for the delivery of at least fifteen films over the next year, with budgets ranging from $100,000 to $200,000. These films, which would be prohibitive at Fox because of their 52% studio overhead, would serve to keep the product flowing in Fox's large distribution and exhibition network. The Fox name and the low budgets virtually guaranteed a profit.[3] Three of the independents who would provide fodder for the 1948 release schedule included Sol M. Wurtzel Productions, Edward L. Alperson's Alson Productions, and Frank Seltzer Productions.[4]

The other independent commissioned by Fox was Bernard Small's Reliance Pictures. Small, the twenty-seven-year-old son of successful independent film producer Edward Small, had gone into the business in mid-1946 when he and partner Lou Appleton, Jr., formed the independent production company Venture Pictures. A deal had been struck with the estate of H.C. McNeile, creator of the popular "Bulldog Drummond" character, to make two Drummond films with an option for six more; arrangements were made for financing and distribution through Columbia Pictures.[5]

The "Bulldog Drummond" character had a long and varied career on film well before Bernard Small acquired the rights, the hero of more than a dozen films since the early twenties. Two silent British versions in 1922 and 1925 were followed by an early sound version starring Ronald Colman in 1929 (*Bulldog Drummond*; F. Richard Jones), who would reprise the role in 1934's *Bulldog Drummond Strikes Back* (Roy Del Ruth). Several other actors tackled the lead, but the role was most recently associated with John Howard who starred in a series of six low-budget offerings from Paramount in the late thirties. After eight years of dormancy, Small resurrected the gentleman adventurer. *Bulldog Drummond at Bay* (1947; Sidney Salkow) and *Bulldog Drummond Strikes Back* (1947; Frank McDonald) were the results; Appleton and Small shared producer credits on these. The partnership was short-lived, however; Venture folded and Appleton departed for not-so-greener pastures.

Small held onto the Drummond option, however, and he and Ben Pivar partnered and reorganized the independent Reliance Pictures unit. Reliance Pictures had been a production company formed back in 1932 by daddy Edward in partnership with Joseph Schenck and Harry M. Goetz, producing a number of films during the thirties for release through United Artists. These

---

[3] Thomas F. Brady, "Hollywood Buzzes," *New York Times*, September 28, 1947, X5.

[4] "20th-Fox Schedules 48 Features For Release During This Year," *Boxoffice*, January 17, 1948, 58.

[5] "Venture to Revive Drummond Series," *New York Times*, June 26, 1946, 19.

films included *I Cover the Waterfront* (1933; James Cruze), *Transatlantic Merry-Go-Round* (1934; Benjamin Stoloff), and *The Last of the Mohicans* (1936; George B. Seitz). Small reorganized in 1938 with Edward Small Productions, releasing through RKO and United Artists into the forties. By the mid-forties Small was releasing through Columbia, producing films under the Edward Small Productions logo—*The Return of Monte Cristo* (1946; Henry Levin)—and through Eagle-Lion as Reliance Pictures—*T-Men* (1947) and *Raw Deal* (1948; both Anthony Mann). Edward Small had a controlling interest in son Bernard's Venture Pictures and the reorganized Reliance Pictures, but remained behind the scenes and off the finished films' credits—for a while, at least. Reliance's offices opened at 846 North Cahuenga Boulevard in Hollywood.

A six-picture distribution deal with 20th Century-Fox was announced in September 1947, with reported budgets of $110,000 per film. Fox vice president Joseph Moskowitz expressed his concerns about oversight of the upcoming productions in a private correspondence with Edward Small, perhaps unconvinced of young Bernard's capabilities. He wanted assurance that Pivar or someone of comparable experience would be in charge. Small responded that "... you know that as long as I am around, I will see that the pictures are properly handled to conform with the spirit of the agreement between Reliance and Fox. If Ben Pivar doesn't produce them, we well secure another Producer equally as competent."[6] Pivar did produce them, for a while at least.[7]

The Challenge
(Director: Jean Yarbrough; Released February 28, 1948)

The first two scheduled films were to continue the "Bulldog Drummond" series.[8] Actor Alan Curtis was named to take the lead in the first of these, tentatively titled *Strange Penalty*,[9] replacing Aussie Ron Randall, star of the first two Columbia Drummonds. Pivar favorite Jean Yarbrough was signed to direct, from a script written by Frank Gruber and Irving Elman; their screenplay was an adaptation of the story *Lady from Shanghai*, recently purchased from Universal.[10] Curtis

---

[6] Edward Small correspondence to Joseph Moskowitz, dated November 11, 1947.

[7] According to a small item in *Daily Variety* (August 27, 1947), Pivar had recently completed a production deal at Columbia. This is the only reference to that production deal uncovered to date.

[8] Thomas F. Brady, "Low-Budget Films Expanding At Fox," *New York Times*, September 23, 1947, 31.

[9] Edwin Schallert, "Alan Curtis Lead in 'Strange Penalty,'" *Los Angeles Times*, October 10, 1947, A9.

[10] Thomas F. Brady, "Van Heflin to Star in Film for Metro," *New York Times*, October 10,

was replaced by former RKO "Falcon" star Tom Conway by the time filming commenced on November 7 at the Motion Picture Center Studios on North Cahuenga Boulevard, with June Vincent costarring. The production had by now been retagged *The Challenge*,[11] the finished film going into release four months later on the bottom half of a double bill with the Clifton Webb comedy *Sitting Pretty* (1948; Walter Lang). Pivar served as executive producer on this and the two films that followed, with Bernard Small serving as (associate) producer. Photographer George Robinson, late of Universal and a veteran of four previous Pivar productions, was brought on to lens these three films as well. As usual, Pivar's trusted secretary Helen McLemore was once again by his side. The completed film came in at $122,954, nearly $5,000 under its budgeted $127,742. Pivar and Bernard Small split the $5,000 "producers" fee.

Tom Conway as the famed adventurer Hugh "Bulldog" Drummond, in *The Challenge* (1948). Image courtesy of Heritage Auction Galleries, Ha.com.

The backstory: Years earlier, Captain Bailey of the schooner *The Flying Dutchman* locates the wreckage of the *Don Pedro*, a Portuguese ship loaded with £2 million in gold bullion, tax revenues collected from the colony of Brazil. Bailey's ship sinks before it reaches home, with only two survivors—first mate Sonnenberg (Houseley Stevenson) and Blinky Henderson (James Fairfax)—making it to shore, and with much of the salvaged gold. Both retire, Blinky setting himself up in a waterfront pub he names The Flying Dutchman, and Sonnenberg adopting the title of "Captain" and moving into a big seaside home with housekeeper Kitty Fyffe (Eily Malyon) at his beck and call. Guilty over absconding with the wealth that rightfully belonged to Captain Bailey, Sonnenberg takes Bailey's orphaned daughter Vivian (June Vincent) under his wing, sending her off to the United States for an education during the war. He has buried the bulk of the treasure nearby at South Rock, and sewn in Morse code the clues to its location in the sail of

---

1947, 32.

[11] Thomas F. Brady, "Studio Will Revise Film for Basehart," *New York Times*, November 4, 1947, 32.

a model of *The Flying Dutchman* that he has built and has on display. Sensing that his end is near, he summons Vivian back to England with a letter that suggests that a "secret" is hidden in the model.

Of course no one knows much of this when the story begins.

Sonnenberg gets shoved off a cliff and dies. Housekeeper Kitty sells the ship model to an auction house for some quick cash. Bulldog Drummond gets involved when his friend Algy Longworth ends up in possession of the auctioned model. Vivian wants to buy it back, but Drummond refuses, curious about her intense interest in the model. Inspector McIver (Stanley Logan) and Sergeant Shubeck (Leyland Hodgson) suspect that Vivian may have played a part in her adoptive father's death. Blinky learns from Vivian that Drummond has the model, and Algy is clubbed when Blinky steals it. Blinky removes and replaces the sails, but is shot to death soon after when the ship is again stolen. Solicitor Jerome Roberts (Pat Aherne) reads Sonnenberg's will: Everything is left to his ne'er-do-well nephew Cliff Sonnenberg (Richard Stapley), and nothing to an enraged Kitty or Vivian, who questions whether there might be a newer will. Vivian returns to her apartment with Drummond, who has befriended her, and is stunned to find the ship model there.

Later, Drummond and Blinky break into dead Blinky's pub and locate the log of the ship *The Flying Dutchman*, and the model's sails that Blinky had earlier removed. Revealed therein is the whole story of the salvaged riches and their eventual fate. Before he can pursue this any further, Drummond is knocked cold and awakens in a warehouse, the prisoner of a thug named Arno (Oliver Blake) and his co-conspirators Kitty, Cliff Sonnenberg, and solicitor Roberts. Vivian is a prisoner as well, and both she and Drummond are beaten until he reveals the whereabouts of the missing sails. Arno forces Drummond to call Seymour and have them delivered, after which Drummond is forced to decipher the Morse-coded directions to the buried treasure. What Arno and his cohorts do not realize is that Drummond has also delivered detailed instructions to Seymour via Morse code (he taps the telephone while they speak), and when the group arrives at the burial site they are met by the police who arrest the gang. Drummond heads off with Vivian, and Algy has to console himself with the return of the ship model he so dearly paid for.

Contemporary reviewers were polite but underwhelmed, giving the modest little film a pass without going overboard. *Motion Picture Daily* was among the more positive, saying that "Pivar and Small produced the film with a gloss which manages to impart some class. There is evident a physical attractiveness that the fragility and commonplaceness of the story may not deserve, although the appeal to the eye does a lot to sell the film."[12] *Film Bulletin*'s credit-less reviewer attempted to put foreign film-adverse patrons'

---

[12] P.E.L., "The Challenge," *Motion Picture Daily*, February 26, 1948, page unknown.

minds at ease: "Good performances by a capable though marquee-weak cast, and an interesting story, lift 'The Challenge' above the average whodunit. Although the soundtrack is heavily loaded with British accent, it is intelligible ..." He (she?) went on to give exhibitors some solid exploitation advice: "Since the name of Bulldog Drummond is not in the title, it should be prominently displayed in all promotional activities."[13] And while *Film Daily* commented on "story material that is resourceful and inventive,"[14] *Independent Film Journal* dismissed the effort as "[m]oderately diverting program fare."[15]

According to a press release circulated at the time, the mostly British cast had decided to forego the customary set party that typically marked a film's completion. Referring to it as a "bit of England's current austerity," the blurb's author went on to say that "[w]hen it came time for the set party, the members of the production, remembering the dire days 'back home,' unanimously agreed that the money meant for the buffet supper be spent instead for food to be sent to Europe."[16] It is unknown whether Pivar initiated or merely went along with this decision, but given his origins in England it must have seemed like a logical, compassionate action to take.

Older brother George was already making generous efforts in this direction. As an importer of fabrics and the like, George had traveled all over Europe before the war and now was doing his bit to help out old friends in heavily-rationed post-war England. There was a Long Island restaurant named Raynor's that specialized in fried chicken. Whenever George would head back to Europe, he would have the restaurant pack up dinner for ten in big boxes filled with fried chicken, muffins, corn fritters, and so forth, kept fresh with dry ice. He would also take instant coffee, tins of sardines and tuna, and deliver them to business and childhood friends, in England and Germany as well, the latter his birthplace back in 1889. The cast and crew's decision followed in the footsteps of George's ongoing generosity, if only in a modest way.

The Challenge is a routine but inoffensive little mystery, set-bound and overly talkative, but with a labyrinthian plot that's sufficiently engaging to make for a painless viewing experience. There are enough Brits in the cast that one could take this for an actual British-made film, and the dearth of exteriors help hide the fact that it was a stateside production. Seaside shots could have been taken anywhere, as could the one London-based sequence with Drummond and compatriots driving a convertible down a busy city street in a poorly executed process shot; all other "exteriors" are interior sets.

---

[13] "The Challenge," *Film Bulletin*, date and page unknown.

[14] "The Challenge," *Film Daily*, February 26, 1948, 6.

[15] "The Challenge," *Independent Film Journal*, February 26, 1948, page unknown.

[16] "Your Campaign Book for The Challenge" promotional booklet, 1948, 1.

Conway is smooth and relaxed as the laid-back adventurer Drummond. John Newland, perhaps best known as the host of the 1959-1961 television series *One Step Beyond*, provides mild comic relief as Drummond's friend Algy. Terry Kilburn's Seymour is instantly forgettable, but Eily Malyon is perfect as the humorlessly sinister housekeeper, with Oliver Blake back in the fold as her most evil of partners in crime. Richard Stapley, in his first film role, has an annoyingly high-pitched voice. Jean Yarbrough's direction is perfunctory with brief moments of inspiration, such as the shockingly unexpected shooting of Blinky as he opens his room's door. George Robinson's photography is overly dark, and hampered visually by high-contrast day-for-night sequences. (Take this comment with a grain of salt, since the problem may have been solely with the print I viewed.) Nonetheless, *The Challenge* is an acceptable mystery, and Conway, Newland, and Kilburn were retained for the second in the series.

13 Lead Soldiers
(Director: Frank McDonald; Released April 24, 1948)

With post-production underway on *The Challenge*, the titles of the other five films in the six-film deal were announced as *13 Lead Soldiers*, *The Cat Man*, *The Creeper*, *Santa Fe Uprising*, and *Killers of the Sea*,[17] seemingly oblivious to the fact that the last two titles had already graced other productions in 1946 and 1937, respectively. *13 Lead Soldiers*, the second in the new Drummond series, was the next in line, starting production in late December 1947,[18] at the Motion Picture Center. Tom Conway returned in the lead, with Helen Westcott borrowed from Warners for his romantic interest;[19] freelance Austria-born actress Maria Palmer rounded out the cast. Frank McDonald, a journeyman director with close to seventy-five films to his credit over the previous twelve years—B's, all of them—was slated to direct; Bernard Small's recent *Bulldog Drummond Strikes Back* was among McDonald's previous efforts. *13 Lead Soldiers* wrapped with a final cost of $126,237, nearly $2,000 less than its $128,117 budget estimate. The finished film was released the following April on the bottom half of a double bill headlined by Victor Mature's *Fury at Furnace Creek* (1948; H. Bruce Humberstone). With the second of the Drummond films once again *sans* the lead character's name in the title, it was clear that Pivar and Small were unconcerned about the public associating the two releases with the popular but perhaps overexposed literary character.

---

[17] Thomas F. Brady, "Windust to Direct Bette Davis' Next," *New York Times*, December 1, 1947, 27.

[18] "Studio Personnelities," *Boxoffice*, December 13, 1947, 66.

[19] "Conway's Lead to Be Helen Westcott," *Los Angeles Times*, December 12, 1947, A9.

Stop Yellin'

Dr. Ashley Stedman (John Goldsworthy) is stabbed to death in his home, and the two lead soldiers and ancient manuscript he had recently acquired are stolen. Soon after, Phillip Coleman (William Stelling) visits Hugh Drummond (Tom Conway) in his home. As Algy Longworth (John Newland) and Seymour (Terry Kilburn) look on, Coleman explains that he has two very similar soldiers, and is fearful for his life because of the threatening fellow who has been stalking him. The soldiers are roughly 900 years old, made of solid lead with a coat of paint, and date back to the days of William the Conqueror. Drummond takes the two soldiers off Coleman's hands and word is spread that he has purchased them, in hopes of flushing out the interested party.

Estelle Gorday (Maria Palmer), ostensibly a reporter for the *Empire Gazette*, shows up to interview Drummond, but mistakes Algy for him. Algy goes along with the misconception, thinking this will give him an easy "in" with the attractive woman. Drummond shows up and goes along with the ruse.

Drummond and Algy visit Stedman's daughter Cynthia (Helen Westcott), and she explains that her father had determined from the manuscript (which she and everyone else refer to as the *palimpsest*) that there are thirteen soldiers in total. She goes on to tell of a stranger—later identified as Edward Vane—who came to the house and demanded to purchase the soldiers. He had left hurling a series of threats when her father refused to sell. Her father had not finished deciphering the manuscript at the time of his death.

Estelle lures Drummond and Algy to her apartment for lunch, while Vane (Harry Cording) steals Coleman's soldiers from Drummond's home. Seymour and Coleman spot Vane and follow him back to his room in Soho above the pub The Cat and Fiddle. Drummond is alerted to this, and he and Algy head to the apartment only to find Vane murdered. Realizing that Estelle set him up, he visits her, feigns lovemaking, and then locks her in her bedroom. A quick search reveals the manuscript in her desk drawer. She admits she was hired by Vane, but professes ignorance of his motives or death, and has no knowledge of the missing soldiers. Drummond returns the manuscript to Cynthia.

Drummond deduces that the thirteen soldiers and manuscript collectively contain the clue to the whereabouts of a 900-year-old treasure, hidden from the advancing troops of William the Conqueror. Having determined that it is somewhere within an antique shop built over an ancient structure, Drummond soon learns from Estelle that the shop's owner is her father, and that her real last name is Prager. Her father has the other nine soldiers and had bought the shop knowing that the treasure was nearby, hiring Vane to acquire the other four soldiers and the manuscript. Drummond and Estelle meet Algy and Seymour at the antique shop and find that her father has been murdered, and Cynthia on the floor out cold. Coleman is found in the next room with all thirteen soldiers and the manuscript, attempting to place them according to the manuscript's guide. They restrain him, summon Inspector McIver, and learn from an awakening Cynthia that Coleman had called her and lured her over with the manuscript. Drummond arranges the soldiers just so on the specified pedestal, and a massive stone door opens in the chamber wall. All enter and find the hidden treasure, while outside McIver and his men arrive. McIver innocently lifts one of the soldiers and the door begins to close. Coleman attempts to escape but is crushed by the closing door. McIver replaces the soldier and goes to help Coleman, and the door reopens, releasing the others back to freedom. When Cynthia, who all along thought Drummond and Algy to be each other, learns their true identities, she is pleased. Algy is not.

13 Lead Soldiers is a perfectly adequate little B mystery, and somewhat better than its predecessor. It suffers some of *The Challenge*'s shortcomings: set-bound without a single exterior, overly talkative, and with Terry Kilburn once again forgettable as Drummond's young male secretary Seymour. It is the mystery itself that adds to the film's interest, given its solid historical context. The gimmick of the properly distributed weight of the thirteen soldiers activating the chamber door is effective if somewhat implausible. John Newland has more to do this time around, taking part in the running joke that is often funnier than it sounds. Algy passes himself off as Drummond with hopes of enticing an attractive prospective client, while an amused Drummond goes along with the subterfuge. Needless to say, it is Drummond the man that the women are all attracted to, rather than the name itself, and a crestfallen Algy eventually comes to that realization as he is repeatedly ignored. The film itself has a lighter tone, with Conway at his most charming as he noodles away at the piano while a gun-wielding Estelle searches his apartment. This all takes an interesting turn of tone with the delightfully grisly climax wherein a shrieking Coleman is crushed in close-up beneath the huge stone door.

With both of the Drummonds in the can at the beginning of 1948, Bernard Small announced that he and Pivar were considering adapting some of James Fenimore Cooper's *Leatherstocking Tales* for the screen as a series of low-budget action films, but not as part of the six-picture arrangement with Fox;[20] this announcement failed to yield any results for the next few years. *The Iroquois Trail* (1951; Phil Karlson), with George Montgomery in the lead, was the only one of these to eventually make it to the screen, a blending of several of the tales produced long after Pivar's departure. A third Drummond film was scheduled to start in February 1948, but neither that film nor any of the other Drummonds ever came to fruition.

While the Reliance Pictures gig was not quite as lucrative as his previous position with Universal, it certainly was not shabby. A level of stability returned to Pivar's life, and the family moved back into the Valley Spring Lane

---

[20] Thomas F. Brady, "Rowland, Ansell Plan New Movie," *New York Times*, January 23, 1948, 27.

home at some point. When he was not working, Pivar continued his weekly pinochle games and would head out to the fights quite often, most likely at the Hollywood Legion Stadium at the corner of Hollywood Boulevard and El Centro. He and Judy liked to go out to restaurants, but excursions to nightclubs were less frequent. When they did go, however, they'd head out to the Clover Club on the corner of Sunset Boulevard and La Cienga, or to the Earl Carroll Theatre or Ciro's on Sunset Boulevard.

Ben (left) and Judy (center) with unidentified admirer "Bill" at the Clover Club, January 20, 1944. Photo courtesy of Jan Pivar Dacri.

"I recall them coming home one night and raving about a brand-new stand-up comedy act they had just seen at a club," reminisced son Neil. "Two guys, Dean Martin and Jerry Lewis. I remember my mother telling me that the skinny guy must have been bruised all over his body because he kept bumping into things, and falling down, a lot."[21] Neil believes that it was Ciro's where they saw the act, but that would have been in 1950. If it truly was a "brand-new" act, it is more likely that it was at Slapsy Maxie's on Wilshire Boulevard, where Martin and Lewis had their west-coast debut in April 1948.

---

[21] Neil Pivar correspondence with author, August 26, 2010.

A distracted Ben and Judy, with Sylvia Reich and her husband
at the Earl Carroll Theatre Restaurant, August 23, 1945.
Photo courtesy of Jan Pivar Dacri.

The Creeper
(Director: Jean Yarbrough; Released September 25, 1948)

Instead of the next Drummond film, Pivar's third for Reliance was the previously announced *The Creeper*, a return to the horror film genre with which he'd had so much success over at Universal. Whether the choice of this title was a cynical attempt to cash in on the character that graced the screen a few years earlier is unknown. Regardless, the connection—if any—is there in title only. Pivar hired his old writing buddy Maurice Tombragel to hammer out a screenplay, their last work together six years earlier on 1942's *Danger in the Pacific*. Jean Yarbrough returned to direct, with production commencing on Saturday, March 7, 1948[22] on a ten-day shooting schedule. Eduardo Ciannelli, Onslow Stevens, June Vincent, and Ralph Morgan headlined the low-wattage cast. The third Reliance production exceeded its estimated budget of $122,208, coming in at $127,638. *The Creeper* was coupled for its initial release in September at Grauman's Chinese with *Apartment for Peggy* (1948; George Seaton).

---

[22] "'Creeper' Shooting as Reliance Opus," *Los Angeles Times*, March 8, 1948, 14.

Dr. Lester Cavigny (Ralph Morgan) and Dr. Jim Bordon (Onslow Stevens) have spent years experimenting with the introduction of phosphorescence into living cell tissue to illuminate internal organs as an aid to surgery. Experiments with cats in the West Indies have resulted in the development of a serum that is shipped back to their lab in Los Angeles. Before departing, however, the wife of cat-wrangler Andre Dussaud (David Hoffman) dies under mysterious circumstances, and Cavigny's daughter Nora (Janis Wilson) catches a fever that leaves her delirious for weeks.

Back in Los Angeles, Bordon and Cavigny discover that all of the vials of serum were destroyed in transit. Cavigny argues for discontinuing the experiments, stating that they were unsuccessful and the serum would release "energies that would only result in mutations, monstrosities, and death." Bordon balks and insists on continuing the experiments, contacting Andre in the West Indies to bring the cats to the States. Unwilling to go along, Cavigny hides his notes and claims that he has mislaid them, forcing Bordon and his young assistant Gwen Runstrom (June Vincent) to recreate the serum from (faulty) memory. Nora, meanwhile, freaks out whenever she sees a cat, her previous delirium leaving her with a crippling neurosis.

Next door to their lab is the lab of Dr. Van Glock (Eduardo Ciannelli) and his young partner Dr. John Reade (John Baragrey). Reade had been lovers with Gwen, but now finds her growing increasingly distant. Instead, he finds himself falling for nervous-wreck Nora, who crumbles each and every time she encounters Reade and Van Glock's cat "Creeper"—or any cat for that matter. Add to that her recurring nightmares filled with hissing and shrieking cats, it is no surprise that some of her acquaintances fear for her mental health.

When Dr. Cavigny is mauled to death, Inspector Fenwick (Richard Lane) investigates, with Nora a suspect due to her mental instability and the dried blood found under her nails. She is arrested, but the coroner's jury determines there is insufficient evidence, and she is released. She moves in with Gwen, Dr. Bordon now her attending physician. There are suspects aplenty: Dr. Van Glock is always snooping around Borden and Cavigny's lab when no one is around; Gwen, increasingly jealous of Reade's growing fondness for Nora, plays mind-games with her, not-so-subtly suggesting that she is mentally unhinged at best, crazy at worst; Dr. Bordon feigns concern for Nora's well-being while probing for the whereabouts of her father's hidden notes, the unstated threat of having her committed bubbling beneath the surface; and, of course, Nora herself.

Andre has in the meantime arrived with his shipment of cats, and is the next to be mauled to death in the lab. Inspector Fenwick makes a return appearance, and both Dr. Bordon and Gwen state that they fear for their lives. Next door, Reade and Van Glock find their lab trashed.

Reade approaches Nora and suggests that she move out of Gwen's apartment, having grown wary of his former lover's motives. Nora says that she intends to move back home, no longer terrified of cats. She now realizes that she subconsciously suspected her father of being responsible for Andre's wife's death in the West Indies, having used her as a "guinea pig" of sorts. She now knows that was not the case, that her father was innocent of that crime. Her neuroses are now gone—in theory, at least.

At home that night, Nora hears the hissing of a cat. Terrified, she grabs a loaded pistol. Reade, having found Gwen mauled to death in her lab and now concerned for Nora's well-being, enters unannounced and frightens her; she shoots him before recognition sets it. Bordon now enters the room and, finding that Nora has burned her father's notes, admits he is the one responsible for the deaths. He is the one who has been scaring her all along with his cat "Creeper," hoping to drive her crazy, have her institutionalized, and then find her father's notes unimpeded. He now injects himself with the serum, and Nora watches in horror as his hand mutates into a heavily-clawed cat-hand. As he is about to maul her, a revived Reade grabs the pistol and shoots Bordon to death. Bordon's hand reverts back to normal before Reade gets a look at it.

The Creeper is a modest little horror thriller, although the "The" in the title seems intended solely to mislead the potential filmgoer into thinking this film to be another entry in the Rondo Hatton series rather than a reference to this film's feline star. The film's three

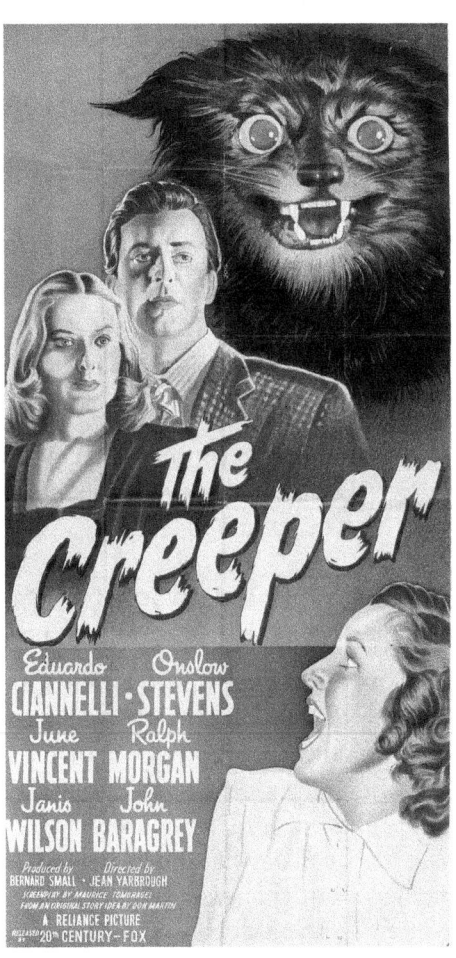

This cat would terrify anyone. *The Creeper* **(1948). Image courtesy of Heritage Auction Galleries, Ha.com.**

swirling, blurred-focus dream sequences, while assembled on a shoestring, have a certain creepiness and power. The film begins promisingly with an atmospheric opening: a black cat walks along a tree branch with the Cavigny mansion beyond,[23] followed by an extended, wordless sequence where sleepwalking Nora enters her dad's library, retrieves a pistol, and wanders back to bed. The direction, lighting, and camera movements here are the best in the film, with what follows tending to be routine and unimaginative.

The performances are acceptable but the characters two-dimensional, and Janis Wilson's Nora wears out her welcome with her all-consuming neuroses and habit of freaking out at the entrance of a cat. The damned things are seemingly everywhere, a Chinese restaurant included. David Hoffman, the film's cat-wrangler, was formerly the disembodied head in the crystal ball in Pivar's "Inner Sanctum" intros. Leading man John Baragrey was a newcomer to film with only a couple of screen appearances before this, and a spotty film career to follow; most of his successes were on the stage and in numerous appearances on television. His performance here is surprisingly natural and relaxed, although what his character sees/saw in these two nutcases, the only two young women in this film's hermetic little world, suggests a lack of good judgment on his part.

Motion Picture Daily decreed it a "hair-raising chiller [that] gets in some telling melodramatic strokes."[24] *Harrison's Reports* dismissed it as "[f]air for those who like horror melodramas, but much below the average for those who don't ... Unsuitable for children and many women."[25] And if you were a woman who didn't like cats ...

Davy Crockett, Indian Scout
(Director: Lew Landers; Released January 6, 1950)

The Creeper turned out to be the final Reliance film released by 20th Century-Fox, the six-film deal terminated prematurely after only three releases. Edward Small signed a new two-picture releasing agreement with United Artists, with Reliance's next production *Indian Scout* to be the first film distributed under this agreement; *Leather Stocking Tales* was to be the second.[26] The story *The Indian Scout* had been named as a possible upcoming production a year earlier,[27] but this was the first official announcement. A portent of things to come was the association in the trades of Edward Small's name with the new production rather than son Bernard's name or that of Bernard's partner.

---

[23] Footage reused from the opening credits of Universal's 1941 comedy-thriller *The Black Cat* (Albert S. Rogell).
[24] "The Creeper," *Motion Picture Daily*, September 1, 1948, page unknown.
[25] "The Creeper," *Harrison's Reports*, October 9, 1948, 162.
[26] "UA and Reliance Sign 2-Picture Deal," *Boxoffice*, July 24, 1948, 7.
[27] Edwin Schallert, "Drama and Film," *Los Angeles Times*, October 10, 1947, A9.

The rare snowfall in Los Angeles. Neil recalls being dared by neighbor Bob Hope to hit him with a snowball. He did. Left to right: Ben, Neil, Lorie, Jan, unidentified. Photo courtesy of Jan Pivar Dacri.

George Montgomery and Ellen Drew, late of Columbia, were signed for the leads.[28] Fifty-nine-year-old Ford Beebe was hired to co-write the screenplay with Pivar associate George Bricker, and to direct the film as well.[29] Beebe, a veteran of the industry since the mid-teens, had become associated with action B films and serials since the beginning of the sound era. Beebe had a long affiliation with westerns and seemed a natural choice for helming a modestly-budgeted oater. Location filming commenced on Monday, June 14, 1948, at Nevada's Red Rock Canyon.[30] Co-starring with Montgomery (who portrays Davy Crockett—not *the* Davy Crockett, rather the famous frontiersman's nephew) and Ellen Drew were Noah Beery Jr., and Philip Reed as an Indian guide, with Addison Richards in a top-supporting role.

A full-page ad appeared in *Boxoffice* in November, this time with Edward Small's name prominent: "EVERY *Edward Small* PRODUCTION BRINGS WITH IT A GREAT BOX-OFFICE HERITAGE! Each Picture INDEPENDENTLY PRODUCED by the EDWARD SMALL Organization." There, at the bottom of a ten-film list was *Indian Scout*, starring George Montgomery and Ellen Drew, produced by Ben Pivar and directed by Ford Beebe. The ad stated that *Indian Scout* was "NOW EDITING."[31] Editing spilled into December,[32] with liberal amounts of

---

[28] Edwin Schallert, "Ellen Drew Lead With George Montgomery," *Los Angeles Times*, May 24, 1948, 17.

[29] Thomas F. Brady, "Disney Set to Film Story On Hiawatha," *New York Times*, May 25, 1948, 33.

[30] "Movieland Briefs," *Los Angeles Times*, June 11, 1948, 22.

[31] "Edward Small Productions" ad, *Boxoffice*, November 20, 1948, 43.

[32] "Grad Sears to Coast for UA Film Deals," *Boxoffice*, December 4, 1948, 46D.

stock footage from Edward Small's bigger-budget *Kit Carson* (1940; George B. Seitz) utilized. Upon the film's eventual release, this stock footage inspired one annoyed Wichita, Kansas-based exhibitor to write in to *Boxoffice* magazine to complain: "'Davy Crockett' was just par filmfare, with a lot of duplicate shots from 'Kit Carson' which didn't fool too many patrons, since it too is playing around town."[33]

Here's where the film's production gets a bit cloudy. Two months later Lew Landers was announced in the trades as the *upcoming* director of *Indian Scout*,[34] and it was Landers' name that appeared in the finished film's credits when released at the beginning of 1950 as *Davy Crockett, Indian Scout*. Richard Schayer was named in the credits as screenwriter, working from a story by Ford Beebe; this was Beebe's sole listing. Grant Whytock and Bernard Small were credited as the film's producers, with Ben Pivar's name nowhere to be found. One can speculate as to what went wrong and why the absence of both Pivar's name as (executive) producer and Beebe's as director and screenwriter, but it would appear that the film as originally shot and assembled in editing proved to be unacceptable, necessitating extensive reshooting under Landers' guidance.

Don't look for Pivar's name anywhere on this poster; you won't find it. *Davy Crockett, Indian Scout* (1950). Image courtesy of Heritage Auction galleries, Ha.com.

It is 1848, a peace treaty between the United States and Mexico opens up the west for settlement, and the Native Americans already there aren't happy about newcomers. A wagon train slowly makes its way to the fort at Great Plains with troop reinforcements, escorting a group of hopeful settlers along the way. Captain Weightman (Addison Richards) is in command, with Davy Crockett (Montgomery) and Cherokee Red Hawk (Reed) as scouts. Indians attack along the way, but they are repelled. The group makes a midway stop at Fort Gardner where they tell Colonel Pollard (John Hamilton)

---

[33] "The Exhibitor Has His Say," *Boxoffice*, October 21, 1950, 3.

[34] Thomas F. Brady, "Ann Blyth Shifts Role At U-I Studio," *New York Times*, February 4, 1949, 31.

of their suspicions of a possible spy in their ranks. Hothead Simms (Erik Rolf) accuses Red Hawk simply because he is an Indian, but Crockett vouches for him. Simms is not convinced.

Pressing on, the presence of a spy is confirmed when Captain Weightman finds that someone has rifled through his dispatch case and learned of his plans to head through either the more distant South Pass or the closer but dangerously narrow Manitou Pass. Red Hawk sets out and discovers that Indian tribes are gathering for an attack, so the decision is made to take the safer route through South Pass in spite of its distance and the parched journey to get there.

Tex (Noah Beery, Jr.), another scout accompanying the wagon train, grows suspicious of pretty young schoolteacher Frances Oatman (Ellen Drew) and her deaf-mute driver Ben (Paul Guilfoyle), both rescued earlier from a band of pursuing Indians and now part of the group. Red Hawk recognizes that Frances has Indian blood and confronts her, and she admits that her dad was a Kiowa and her mother a white woman. Red Hawk agrees to keep her secret. Crockett, on the other hand, has fallen in love with Frances, and is oblivious to the possibility of her being anything other than a good-looking innocent.

Frances and Ben are indeed spies for the Indians, Ben only feigning being deaf and dumb. Crockett grows suspicious of Ben, and follows him when he sneaks out of the camp late that night. The two get into a fight, and Ben is stabbed with his own knife. Ben was a decoy to divert attention from Frances, who now heads off on horseback to warn the gathering tribes of the army's change in plans. She spills all to her father, Kiowa Chief James Lone Eagle (Robert Barrat), the one who has planned the upcoming attacks on both Fort Gardner and the reinforcements heading there at South Pass. Red Hawk has followed her but is caught, strung up with wet rawhide to die slowly in the sun. When Frances learns that her father intends to slaughter everyone, women and children included, she has a change of heart. She orchestrates Red Hawk's escape, and the two of them head back to the wagon train to alert Weightman and Crockett of the planned attack at South Pass. Their story is believed, but the two of them are arrested for being spies. Crockett now thinks the worst of Red Hawk, believing him to be an embedded spy, and says so.

The route is switched to Manitou Pass, and word is sent on to Fort Gardner. The messenger is intercepted, and the Indians regroup. At Manitou Pass, the soldiers leave the settlers behind as they head through the pass to ensure its safety. The Indians attack the soldiers, separating them from the settlers by causing an avalanche that blocks the pass behind them. More Indians attack the poorly defended wagon train. Rising to the occasion, Crockett fills a wagon full of gunpowder and drives it toward the pass' blockage; Red Hawk rides behind, shooting any Indian that threatens Crockett's progress. Crockett leaps from the wagon at the last moment, the powder explodes, and the passage is unblocked.

The troops return to save the beleaguered settlers. Later, Crockett's testimony and good words for Frances and Red Hawk spare them imprisonment. The two of them plan to marry and open the area's first school for Indian children.

Davy Crockett, Indian Scout is a rather standard western, cliché-filled and clumsily written, with a plot that challenges credulity. It is marred somewhat visually by the numerous interior sets and process shots that do not mesh well with the location footage, much of the latter lifted from the aforementioned *Kit Carson*. George Montgomery, while a good-looking, rugged leading man, delivers his lines as if with a mouth full of marbles, and as Crockett's Cherokee pal Red Hawk, Philip Reed is likable but lacks believability as an Indian. Pretty Ellen Drew, her best roles behind her and now exiled to westerns of this sort, handles her role as the duplicitous schoolteacher with ease. Noah Beery, Jr. doesn't have much to do in the bit part of Tex, but what is there adds a note of much-needed lightness. Given that additional scenes were filmed after-the-fact and the film reedited may explain why there are so many dual credits, two each for director of photography, film editing, art direction, set decoration, and wardrobe. Pivar, on the other hand, doesn't receive any credit at all.

There is no doubt that Pivar was involved with the original production, and not only from the numerous mentions in the trades: Pivar's son Neil, ten years old at the time, recalls driving out to the desert-based shooting location in what he thinks was his father's new 1949 Lincoln Cosmopolitan ("I remember he told me it cost almost three thousand dollars. I thought that was an awful lot of money for a car")[35] and seeing lead George Montgomery and visitor Dinah Shore, Montgomery's wife at the time. Father and son spent an overnight there before returning home, son Neil sharing a room with Montgomery. The extent of Pivar's involvement with the final production is unclear, but it is safe to assume that he made numerous contributions to the project. The reasons behind his lack of credit remain a mystery, but one thing is clear: Pivar's involvement with Reliance had come to an end.

Coincidentally, Ben's brother Murray, supervising editor for most of his thirty-two years at Universal, resigned from that position in August 1949.[36] Murray signed with Columbia shortly thereafter in October as editorial supervisor,[37] squeezing in a trip to France during the interim with his wife, his brother Ed, and Ed's wife Ida. He would remain with that studio until his retirement in 1962. While at Columbia, Murray oversaw the editing of hundreds of films that included *High Noon* (1952; Fred Zinnemann) and *On the Waterfront* (1954; Elia Kazan). Neil would visit Murray (whom he called Uncle Mony) in the Columbia editing facilities, receiving hands-on lessons in

---

[35] Neil Pivar correspondence with author, January 8, 2010.

[36] *Daily Variety*, August 8, 1949, 1.

[37] *Daily Variety*, October 24, 1949, 1; "Heartbeats," *Boxoffice*, November 12, 1949, 93.

the use of the Moviolas. When no one was watching, Murray would slip money to Neil for model airplane kits.

With no immediate prospects at hand and a newborn at home (daughter Jan, born on October 5, 1949), Pivar decided to take a stab at independent production. His approach: write a screenplay, form a production company, arrange for financial backing, make the film, and find a distributor. The first step was easy enough, since he'd written enough treatments ten years earlier at Universal, and it was a solitary process he could undertake on his own. The result was tentatively titled *Invasion*, and involved the friendship of two former college roommates—one American and the other Japanese—who find themselves on opposite sides with the outbreak of World War II. Pivar found an interested partner in General Service Studios executive Charles Weintraub, and the two of them organized Quality Films, Inc. to produce the film. An attorney named Max Fink headed to New York to arrange financing for the project, while Pivar started casting and lining up a crew.[38] The project fell through, however, and Pivar and Weintraub had a parting of the ways. Weintraub continued with Quality Films, changing the focus of the business to the distribution of old films to television stations.[39]

Once again Pivar had to scramble to find gainful employment.

§

---

[38] "New Producing Company Formed," *Los Angles Times*, July 31, 1950, 27; "Quality Pictures to Make Debut With 'Invasion,'" *Boxoffice*, August 5, 1950, 20.

[39] "Republic Executive Says No Conspiracy On 16mm," *Boxoffice*, October 15, 1955, 14.

20 The Syndicated Television Shows

Pivar put the Moorpark Street house up for sale in the latter part of 1950 with an asking price of $10,950. A year after the family's return to the Valley Spring Lane home, son Neil had his Bar Mitzvah ceremony. Pivar's Bar Mitzvah present to his son? A practical (but not terribly exciting) power lawnmower to replace the push mower that used to take Neil almost all Saturday to mow his parents' lawn. Neil later added lawn mowing at $2 a lawn to his part-time moneymaking endeavors, an eventual replacement for the newspaper route he'd had for the last few years.

The remainder of Pivar's career was a spotty one, filled with a wide array of short-term successes, aborted projects, and general frustrations. Through all this he managed to keep busy and eke out a reasonably comfortable, if uneven, living. There were

Pivar (center) with Universal music department head Joe Gershenson (second from right) and Neil's tap instructor Alan (second from left). Neil's Bar Mitzvah, 1951. Photo courtesy of Jan Pivar Dacri.

a number of small projects to follow, but some of those that never came to fruition were not mentioned in the trades, and only discussed in passing—if at all—at the dinner table. They are for all intents and purposes lost to time, or at least to memory.

It was becoming increasingly apparent that interest in lower-budget films was rapidly diminishing, and the growth of the television industry was cited as the primary cause. Independent Motion Picture Producers Association head I.E. Chadwick put it bluntly: 1949 had been the poorest year for the association's members, with only ninety pictures made; the poorest year, that is, until 1950, when a mere forty films were produced. His advice to his members: sell your pictures to television just as soon as they have run their course theatrically.[1] The alternative, of course, was to start making product for direct release to television; there had been, after all, more than 4 million TV sets sold in 1950 alone, bringing the total to more than 7 million sets in circulation. After twenty-five years in the film industry, this is the path that Pivar now chose. To that end, Pivar joined the National Society of Television Producers (NSTP), a group formed back in 1950 with the merger of Hollywood's Television Producers' Association (TPA) and New York's Independent Television Producers' Association (ITPA).[2]

One of Pivar's first projects was the stock film library that he ran out of the Hal Roach Studios in Culver City in the early fifties. Set up in November 1951,[3] and called the Independent Film Library, Pivar's business partner in this venture was Norman Cerf, a former film editor who had cut Pivar's *Calling Dr. Death* back in 1943, and had lived several blocks away from him on Valley Spring Lane. The business was positioned to provide stock footage to filmmakers, and heaven knows Pivar knew stock footage intimately by this time. It turned out to be a short-lived affair due to an incompatibility between the partners, with Pivar selling his interest to Cerf in July 1953.[4]

According to some who knew him, Pivar liked to spend money, and spend it as soon as he earned it. "He wasn't that good at money management," said Lorie, "but that's probably true of a lot of people in the film industry."[5] Pivar's nephew Hank Schonzeit, son of Judy's older brother Dave, explained:

> He would get paid for one of his movies and he'd come home with a pile of money, apparently it was a lot of cash—sometimes he got paid in cash—and they would live like kings for a short while until that cash ran out, then they were back not having any money. There were highs

---

[1] Thomas F. Brady, "Some Film-Makers Turn to Television," *New York Times*, December 6, 1950, 56.

[2] "TPA and ITPA To Merge Into NSTP," *Boxoffice*, March 25, 1950, 6.

[3] *Daily Variety*, November 20, 1951, page unknown.

[4] *Daily Variety*, July 16, 1953, page unknown.

[5] Lorie Pivar Viner correspondence with author, August 6, 2010.

and lows; they'd finish a picture, he would get paid, and they just spent the money like crazy, having parties and buying things, then a few months later they didn't have any money.[6]

Daughter Jan described some of the purchases made while Ben was entrenched at Universal, and had the steady income to support them:

[Mom] had great taste in furniture and was an avid collector of antiques. Our house was furnished with magnificent pieces that she bought at auctions and from antique collections. She was adamant that she never did her shopping at "regular stores."[7]

Judy's older sister Libby was more succinct about the couple's spending, as paraphrased by her daughter Bette:

It was on and off. They lived high on the hog, and then they went from the big grand house into the smaller one and then back again.[8]

And now it was time to move, yet again.
Pivar put the Valley Spring Lane home up for sale, and the family relocated in 1952 to a more modest 1,765-square-foot, three-bedroom, two-bath home located at 10720 Hortense Street; "Quite a step down," observed Neil. Even after the move the weekly pinochle games continued with his friends, Ben smoking and having the occasional scotch, while little Lorie would place bets on the games.
Over the years, Pivar possessed a stunningly large number of cars, some of them personally owned, some studio-lent, and a number of others promotional vehicles provided for his use. In addition to the 1938 Buick Super convertible while at Universal, there was a 1937 Plymouth sedan, a 1947 Dodge four-door sedan, the 1949 Lincoln Cosmopolitan sedan, followed by a 1949 Buick Roadmaster four-door sedan after the return to Valley Spring Lane. And now, on Hortense, began a string of autos that included a 1950 Chevrolet convertible (later sold to Kirk Douglas), a 1951 Ford Victoria two-door coupe, a 1952 Buick two-door, a 1953 Jaguar Mark 7 four-door sedan, a 1954 Kaiser four-door sedan, a 1956 DeSoto Sportsman two-door, a mid-fifties Packard concept car known as the Polynesian, a 1952 Cadillac Coupe de Ville, and most likely

---

[6] Hank Schonzeit interview with author, March 11, 2010.

[7] Jan Pivar Dacri, "Judy, Ben and Jules: The Judy Story," in Hank Schonzeit's *A Past Remembered* (Reston, VA: Lorah Publishing, 2001), 186.

[8] Bette Marks correspondence with author, January 15, 2010.

several others now long-forgotten. Son Neil has a long-standing love of cars, the seed sown early on by his father's seemingly endless parade of vehicles. As a newly licensed teenager in 1954, the 1949 Buick Roadmaster was the one he first drove. It also provided the sixteen-year-old his first accident, and the 1953 Jaguar his first speeding ticket.

Ben (standing) with his brother George (seated) in 1956. Son Neil received his first speeding ticket in this 1953 Jaguar Mark 7. Photo courtesy of Carol Pivar Miller.

Vacations had been few and far between in the Pivar household, with an occasional short trek to Las Vegas or Palm Springs. One of the family's rare extended vacations took place late in the summer of 1952 or 1953, during one of Pivar's slow periods and in yet-another of his vehicles. Both Lorie and Neil recall it with fondness, although details have blurred over the intervening years. Their father learned of a huge inventory of polished marble on a ranch out toward San Bernardino. When he went out to look at it in the barn in which it was stored, he spotted a custom-built fifth-wheel trailer underneath a huge tarp. On a whim, he bought both the marble and the trailer, along with the Cadillac that was used to tow the trailer.

The trailer was custom-made for some unnamed celebrity, a good thirty-plus feet in length. Unlike most truck-hauled trailers, it attached to a fifth-wheel mount in the trunk of a custom-built 1939 Cadillac coupe. "It was an amazing ensemble. Everything was custom designed," explained Neil. "The drapes matched the bedding which matched the towels which matched the dishes. The interior upholstery matched the car upholstery."[9]

Pivar took the vehicle back home and went to work on it, accompanied by fifteen-year-old Neil, whose love of all things vehicular remains to this day. As it turned out, this father-and-son project almost led to tragedy just a few days from the planned early June departure. Fortunately, it did not.

> The stove and refrigerator were butane operated. The refrigerator compressor was in the rear compartment of the trailer along with the butane tank, possibly two tanks, and other electrical equipment. Stupid design. Apparently there was a gas leak. A spark from a 12v pump, or something, ignited the leaking gas. I was in front working under the dashboard of the car at the time. I heard a huge explosion, everything shook. The next thing I remember was that I was about a block away running at Olympic gold medal record speed. I stopped and looked back. The sky was raining debris ... The explosion took off about six or more feet of the back of the trailer. The damage was so extensive that there was talk of totaling it. I remember there was a huge battle with the insurance company.[10]

Pivar's sister Dinah was helping load the trailer, and moments before had dropped off a box and was returning to the house when the rig blew. A delay of only a few seconds would have resulted in her premature death.

Instead of totaling the trailer, however, in true Humpty Dumpty style the thing was pieced back together. By mid-August they were ready to hit the road. The first stop was Las Vegas, then on to New Mexico, Utah, Colorado, Wyoming, Idaho, up through Oregon, and back down to Los Angeles. Neil recalls diving off a railroad trestle somewhere in California's Russian River Valley.

Lorie recalls one of the more exciting incidents that took place, most likely near Crystal Lake, Oregon. Exciting, that is, for the observer, less so for the drivers:

> We took the trailer up into one of the mountains ... but there was no place to turn it around. I think they had to back it down, and Neil did

---

[9] Neil Pivar correspondence with author, November 1, 2010.
[10] *Ibid.*

a lot of the driving while my dad was [directing] him, even though Neil was too young to drive . . . . Neil did considerable driving.[11]

Neil's take:

> I remember the road sign that said "No trucks or trailers." My dad insisted we go anyway. Verrrry narrow road, no turnarounds for several miles. I don't recall who drove. I can't imagine that I drove that road. Perhaps I was so traumatized I blocked it out.[12]

Regardless, it was the vacation that brought the family together for an extended period, and the one fondly recalled so many years after the fact.

The Pivar household was never without at least one pet, and quite often more than one, cats and dogs coexisting peacefully. In the early forties there was a Persian cat named Goofus that seemed to be partial to Ben. There was a Cocker Spaniel named Junior, followed by an Alaskan malamute named Husky. "I remember everyone saying this was the smartest dog they had ever seen," recalled Neil. "Husky was run over by the grocery truck that delivered groceries in our neighborhood. Apparently not that smart." Later, on Moorpark Street, they had a German Shepherd named Silver. "One night Silver got out of the backyard. We all went out looking for him. My dad was running around the neighborhood calling out, 'Here Silver, here Silver.' One of our neighbors came out of his house and said to my dad, 'Hey, Lone Ranger, lose your horse?'"[13] And on Hortense Street there was another Cocker Spaniel named Junie who lived with the family throughout the fifties. As for cats, Lorie says, "We never didn't have cats." Aside from Goofus, Pivar's appreciation of the various furry creatures seemed to be benign tolerance. Lorie sums it up thusly: "He was just always there, and they were always there. I didn't see him interact with them. [The animals] were always part of our family."[14]

Along with the cats and dogs, however, were the parakeets that Lorie raised and sold to local pet shops from the tender young age of twelve into her mid-teens. Pivar, who was quite handy and loved to build things, initially built an indoor aviary that sat inside Neil's room by his closet door. As the number of parakeets grew, father and son built a much larger aviary outdoors that ended

---

[11] Lorie Pivar Viner interview with author, October 31, 2010.

[12] Neil Pivar, *op. cit.*

[13] Neil Pivar correspondence with author, March 22, 2010.

[14] Lorie Pivar Viner, *op. cit.*

up with nearly a hundred parakeets. Lorie would continue to breed parakeets until forced to give it up by circumstances outside of her control.

Pivar's interest in building things resulted in a rather impressive playhouse for Lorie as well, which she absolutely loved. A much-scaled down version of a real house, it was complete with shingled roof, hardwood floor, and functional door and sash windows, all kid-size. "He was *good* at building things; he was *really* good at that. He loved to build stuff." And with less work and more free time on his hands, Pivar was able to indulge his interest.

Pivar set up a production company as well at the Roach Studios in June 1952,[15] modestly known as Ben Pivar and Associates. His first venture into the young television industry was to be a syndicated show titled *Bureau of Missing Persons*, with Don Martin

The Pivar family on Moorpark Street, June 1947. Left to right: Judy, Lorie, Ben, Silver, Neil. Photo courtesy of Jan Pivar Dacri.

writing the scripts and Arthur Hilton directing. Twenty-six half-hour shows were planned, to be filmed in rented space at the Hal Roach Studios. The first of these was to be filmed in mid-July 1952, but the project fell through at the last minute.[16]

Working in conjunction with Cascade Pictures of California, Pivar served as production coordinator on at least one *Family Theatre* television episode, the sixth. *Family Theatre* was the video spinoff of Mutual Radio's long-running (1947-1957) show produced by Father Patrick Peyton. Filmed on the Roach lot for Thanksgiving 1952 broadcast, it was adapted from Francis Thompson's *The Hound of Heaven* by screenwriter Fred Niblo, Jr.;[17] Ed Sullivan and Rod O'Connor co-starred.

---

[15] "Vidpix Chatter," *Variety*, June 25, 1952, 26.

[16] "Two Film Craftsmen Enter Television," *Boxoffice*, June 28, 1952, 49.

[17] "Hollywood," *Variety*, November 19, 1952, 22.

His next project, a half-hour television show titled *Big Town*, was broadcast on CBS from 1950 through 1956. Originally a radio series that ran from 1937 through 1952, *Big Town* followed the exploits of newspaper columnist Steve Wilson. Patrick McVey starred from 1950 to 1954, followed by former Pivar tenant Mark Stevens from 1954 to 1956. The show credited producers Jack Gross and Philip N. Krasne for the 1953-1954 season, and star Mark Stevens during his tenure 1954-1956. Pivar served as the show's production coordinator in 1953 into 1954.

In early 1954 the California-based production company of Jack Gross and Philip Krasne acquired the rights to author Louis Joseph Vance's fictional character Michael Lanyard, more popularly known as The Lone Wolf. A gentleman by day and daring thief by night, The Lone Wolf had appeared in eight novels over a twenty-year period from the mid-teens to mid-thirties. The film industry took notice and ended up making thrice that number of films, with Warren William most associated with the character in a nine-film series for Columbia, 1939-1943. Pivar, of course, had associate-produced *The Lone Wolf Returns* for Columbia in 1935, his sole association with the character. Gerald Mohr took over the role for three more entries, followed by former Bulldog Drummond lead Ron Randall in a one-shot deal in 1949. The character then went into hibernation until resurrected by Gross and Krasne.

Ben in a posed publicity shot, early- to mid-fifties. Photo courtesy of Lorie Pivar Viner.

Popular actor Louis Hayward was lined up for the lead, his first for television after having turned down numerous television offers over the preceding two years to concentrate on film work. One of the deciding factors was part-ownership of the series, but his publicly-stated reason had a more artistic bent: "[The role is] the most challenging characterization I've ever tackled … Here is a role I can sink my teeth into, because it's the type of person I can understand. The Lone Wolf is a fellow who doesn't like to follow the beaten path, he's a guy who likes adventure."[18]

---

[18] Walter Ames, "Hayward Tackles Video Role of Choice in New Lone Wolf Film

The Syndicated Television Shows

In association with United Television Programs, Inc., seventy-eight half-hour episodes were to be filmed over the next eighteen months at their California studios. Budgets were to average $35,000 per episode, with playwright William Kozlenko originally named to adapt stories for the screen.[19] One of the unique aspects of this production was the intention of filming the bulk of it on location, with destinations such as San Francisco, New Orleans, Mexico City, and several European capitals named, if not all actually used. Ben Pivar was reassociated with the character when he was hired as production supervisor for the series. Former Joe McDoakes comedy shorts cinematographer Fred Gately was signed as director of photography. Newbie television director Bernard Girard handled the first and another eleven episodes, with Dick Dixon and Louis Germonprez assisting.

The series' first episode started filming on Wednesday, November 18, 1953, on location in Las Vegas. A crew of twenty-eight crammed into the Sands Hotel for much of the episode's scenes.[20] The supporting cast included Henry Slate, Vici (Vicki) Raaf, Lewis Martin, and Eileen Howe, although subsequent episodes would have all-new casts. The first episode of *The Lone Wolf* series, "The Las Vegas Story," premiered on Los Angeles television station KTTV on Sunday evening, April 10, 1954, with nationwide release a month later. Subsequent episodes would, with few exceptions, be similarly titled as *The ... Story*.

In all, only thirty-nine of the projected seventy-eight episodes were filmed and released during the 1954-1955 season. Pivar left the series after a dozen episodes, replaced by newcomer (and assumedly smaller salaried) Donald Hyde. After its one-year run, *The Lone Wolf* went into syndication in the later fifties as *Streets of Danger*.

Pivar claimed in later promotional pieces that he acted as producer on the long-running, arts-centric series *Omnibus*. Hosted by Alistair Cooke, the series ran on CBS from 1952-1956, ABC from 1956-1957, and ABC from 1957-1961. The extent of Pivar's involvement with this show is unknown as well, and may only have been for a handful of episodes. According to his two oldest children, however, Pivar was a regular viewer of the series. Cooke, coincidentally, was born in Pivar's hometown of Salford, Manchester, in 1908, seven years after Ben's arrival in this world.

This brings us to *Confidential File*, the creation of thirty-two-year-old Los Angeles reporter Paul Coates. Born and educated in New York, Coates was a former publicist before relocating to Los Angeles and taking a job at

---

Series," *Los Angeles Times*, April 10, 1954, A5.

[19] Walter Ames, "Hayward to Star as 'Lone Wolf;' Tennis, TV Makes Actor Happy," *Los Angeles Times*, September 24, 1953, 32.

[20] "Hayward 'Lone Wolf' First On Location," *Billboard*, November 21, 1953, 7.

the afternoon tabloid *Los Angeles Mirror* in 1948. His first stint was a column ruminating on area restaurants titled "Well, Medium and *Rare*," which soon evolved into general interest stories. Coates befriended the paper's news editor Jim Peck, and together they moonlighted and wrote several episodes for Jack Webb's television show *Dragnet*.

Over time, the *Mirror* job exposed Coates to the sordid underbelly of society, the petty crooks, hookers, drug addicts, con men, and nut-jobs of all stripes. This gave him the idea of creating a local TV expose-type show with what he called "real realism" and "off-beat journalism." Teaming with Peck, the two promoted and sold the idea to the Times-Mirror Company's local independent television station KTTV, broadcasting on channel 11. The proposed format called for a brief introduction by Coates setting up the evening's topic, followed by a filmed ten-to-fifteen-minute mini-documentary on same narrated by Coates. The final portion of the half-hour show was a live segment where Coates would interview one or more people about the subject du jour.

Peck would produce the show, and write the narration and the interview questions, while Coates would act as host and narrator. USC Film School graduate Irvin Kershner was hired to film the introductory segments, and soon after a young University of Toledo graduate named Andrew J. Fenady was brought on board as a "stooge legman" (his words). Fenady's initial duties included assisting Kershner with the filming of the opening segments, but as time passed he took over the narration writing and eventually ended up as the show's associate producer. The show premiered at 10:30 p.m. on Sunday night, August 30, 1953, luring viewers with the none-too-subtle *Los Angeles Times* ad referring to it as "the lid-lifting, hair-curling, sensational new show."

And sensational it was, dealing with a number of heretofore taboo subjects such as prostitution, child molestation, drug addicts, and sexual deviation, along with comparatively milder subjects such as con men, shoplifting, a first-hand account of a flight on a UFO from New Mexico to New York, loan sharks, and spiritualism. The show was an immediate hit, scoring an ARB (now Arbitron) rating of six in Los Angeles, and winning the award for Best Television Public Affairs Program from the Radio and Television News Club of Southern California in June 1954. Two local Emmy Awards followed in March 1955 when the Academy of Television Arts and Sciences named Coates the "Most Outstanding Male Personality" and *Confidential File* the "Best Cultural Program." Numerous "plaques and medals" were doled out as well from "a dozen women's clubs, a Parent-Teacher Association, [and] the City Council."[21] As KTTV general manager Richard Moore put it in the *Los Angeles Times*, "This program has been something of a 'hot potato' because it pulls no punches in exposing some of the shady goings-on in our community. It appears you

---

[21] Barbara B. Jamison, "Oddities in Person," *New York Times*, May 29, 1955, 59.

approve of this experiment in hard-hitting television ..."[22] Given the show's considerable local popularity, the next logical step was to syndicate it and sell it to markets nationwide.

Ted Ashley Associates put the package together. Guild Films Company, Inc., a producer and distributor of such popular syndicated shows as Betty White's *Life with Elizabeth*, *The Frankie Laine Show*, *Joe Palooka*, and *The Liberace Show*, was brought on board to film the half-hour segments on 16mm for later distribution to subscribers. Ben Pivar was hired by Guild to produce the syndicated show, and paid $1,000 per week for his efforts. Fenady became the show's associate producer, Kershner continued to film the documentaries, and a fellow named Irwin "Irv" Moskowitz was hired to assist Fenady writing the interview questions. Filming of the syndicated series began on Monday, December 13, 1954, with thirty-nine twenty-six-minute episodes filmed in all. The series premiered in New York City on WPIX channel 11 on September 14, 1955, and in Los Angeles on September 23.

Syndicated television series *Confidential File* premiered in Los Angeles on September 23, 1955.

The filmed show followed the same pattern as the local show, with some of the best topics from the local show trotted out for remake. For these the original filmed opening segments were in some instances reused, while in others new footage was shot. Coates' follow-up interviews were all filmed using a three-camera setup, one for two-shots, the other two for medium close-ups of interviewer and interviewee, respectively. This was filmed "live" without retakes, and Coates commented at the time "... if I flub a line, that's the way it will go out. We're aiming for realism—even if I have to turn out to be a very bad actor, as a result."[23]

It would not be fair to call Coates a "bad actor" since he really was not acting at all. His delivery was low-key almost to the point of being non-expressive. A big, solid, lumbering fellow, Coates would look at the camera and deliver his

---

[22] Richard A. Moore, "Open Letter to Our Viewers," *Los Angeles Times*, April 10, 1954, 10.

[23] Jamison, *op. cit.*

opening spiel with a solemnity that was intended to convey conviction and bordered on monotone. His narration of the filmed segment was more of the same, as were the interviews that followed. But if the delivery was leaden, the words contained therein were anything but, frequently consisting of a pseudo-heartfelt diatribe that left no doubt what Coates' feelings were regarding the night's topic. On the effects of comic books on children, and the show's contention that they often led to kid-on-kid violence, for example: "[Kids are] not reading anything constructive. They're reading stories devoted to adultery, to sexual perversion, to horror, to the most despicable of crimes ... Men are getting rich off the comic books that teach kids this kind of activity. I don't know how you like it, but it makes me kind of sick."[24] On so-called medical quacks: "The man who mixed this salve wanted money, and he didn't care how he got it. He's what's generally referred to as a quack doctor, but somehow that term just doesn't cover my feelings on the subject. To me, the term 'murderer' is much more appropriate."[25] Coates stated in an interview with *Time* magazine that "[at] no time do I cast myself in the role of expert. I play the reporter. We carefully use psychiatrists and authorities in any particular field ... Even on crime stuff, I'm just a reporter and let the police and others say why a certain kind of bunko game, for instance, is a danger to the community."[26] A reporter, but with strong opinions, and not shy about making them known.

Pivar guided the production of the show's thirty-nine episodes, keeping them on schedule and within budget. Andrew Fenady had this to say about Pivar's contributions, which provides some insight into Pivar's approach to production:

> I don't know how much money [Ben] was making at Universal. I think when he came on, when Paul said, "This is our new producer," I think he was getting a thousand dollars a week on our show, because before that when Peck was producing it he was getting five hundred, and afterward when I produced it I was getting five hundred. I think Ben was getting a grand.
>
> At any rate, Ben, his philosophy was, "If I'm just sitting at my desk not doing anything, that means I've done my job." He would delegate. He would sit and he would say, "Okay, now let's see...." He rarely knew what the hell we were doing, but he knew how it should be done and

---

[24] *Confidential File* episode "Horror Comic Books" on "the effects of crime and horror comics on youngsters," Los Angeles broadcast October 28, 1955.

[25] *Confidential File* episode "Medical Quacks" on "the oldest racket in the conman's kit," Los Angeles broadcast November 4, 1955.

[26] "Slice of Life," *Time*, August 2, 1954, page unknown.

who should be doing what. And one of the things I must say about Ben was after he was there about three weeks he called me into his office—first of all when he took over he rented us a small building right across the street from Hollywood High School, on Hollywood Boulevard; that became the *Confidential File* office. And Paul, you know, was downtown on the newspaper, he also had an office in that building on the Boulevard, and that was our headquarters. That's where we met, that's where we edited, that's where we did everything while Ben was there. And after Ben left I kept the same headquarters. But he called me in and he said, "Now let's see, how much are you making?" And I said, "Well, you know how much; there's the budget …" and he said, "Okay, from now on your salary is doubled." And I said, "Huh? I didn't ask for any raise." And he said, "You don't have to. As far as I'm concerned you're the most valuable man here next to Paul Coates." He was a shrewd [observer]—I have to admit, not humbly—of who's doing what. He was not a hands-on producer, but he sure as hell had an overview of what was going on and what should be going on. He was on top of everything.

[Ben] said, "Look, I know that I'm doing my job when I don't have anything to do." If there was something that had to be done, he would be on top of it. He was not reluctant to fire somebody because he didn't think he was doing his job, and Ben told me, "Look, the difference between Universal and *Confidential File*, Universal was always budget, budget, budget, money, money, how much is it going to cost, are you going to go over?" That was the pressure that he had from his bosses. So, okay, with us at *Confidential File*, the pressure was the deadline, can we make the show. We knew how much money we had to spend, we didn't have to spend any more than that, but the thing is can we do it on time and do it the way it should be done. [27]

A forerunner of sorts of the long-running CBS *60 Minutes* series, the syndicated run of *Confidential File* tackled such attention-grabbing topics as "Child Molesters," "Lysergic Acid" (aka LSD), "Abortions," "Little People," "Narcotics," "Charity Racketeers," "Pyromania," and the aforementioned "Medical Quacks" and "Horror Comic Books." New York City's premiere episode was "Narcotics," and *The New York Times* critic J.P. Shanley was unimpressed: "The program's approach to a critical subject was superficial, tending to emphasize sensational aspects of the narcotic problem,"[28] an observation that

---

[27] Andrew J. Fenady interview with author, June 17, 2010.

[28] J.P. Shanley, "TV: 'Dumbo' Brightens Kids' World," *New York Times*, September 15, 1955, 67.

could have been made of many of the series' entries. The "Child Molesters" episode that aired a month later drew even more scathing criticism from *The New York Times* reviewer Jack Gould: "Sensationalism under the guise of helpful education now has gone about as far as it can on TV ... TV seldom has stooped so low and so needlessly so."[29]

American-International mogul Samuel Z. Arkoff explained to interviewer Linda May Strawn how filming on 16mm for television broadcast helped to keep budgets down:

> There were no unions effective in those days. IATSE [The International Alliance of Theatrical Stage Employees] represented Hollywood films. The networks were doing everything live in those days, so they were dealing with different unions. They were NABET [The National Association of Broadcast Electronic Technicians] and IBEW [The International Brotherhood of Electrical Workers]. So there was sort of a no-man's land when film started on TV.[30]

With an eye always toward the show's modest budgets, Pivar would utilize any free location or prop that was readily available. For one Kershner-directed episode about teenagers, Pivar's seventeen-year-old son Neil was pressed into service, filmed in part in Ben's home and his 1950 Chevrolet convertible.

> [T]he title was something like "A Day in the Life of a Typical Teenager" ... We always thought that was absurd because being typical was the last thing I would ever have been accused of.... It was about my getting up in the morning and going through my daily 16-year-old teenager routine. I remember standing in front of my dresser mirror, checking my face for zits. It concluded with my sitting in the 1950 Chevy convertible making out with this very cute girl. She was a professional actress. Don't know what they paid her, but if I remember correctly, I got $50 for the show ... At 16 years old, I would have been happy to sit in a car all day long alone for $50. On Saturdays, I used to mow our neighbors lawn for $2.[31]

---

[29] Jack Gould, "For Adults Only," *New York Times*, October 13, 1955, 63.

[30] Samuel Z. Arkoff interview by Linda May Strawn, "Samuel Z. Arkoff," *Kings of the B's* (New York: E.P. Dutton & Co., Inc., 1975), 258.

[31] Neil Pivar correspondences with author, May 8, 2009, August 5 and 6, 2010.

Pivar's daughter Lorie became fast friends with Paul Coates' daughter Joren, who took part for a while in the raising of the parakeets. During this time Lorie would spend every single weekend over at the Coates home in the Valley, where she and Joren would ride horses up into the Hollywood Hills, embarking before dawn and returning late in the day. Lorie and Joren's riding skills advanced to the point where they could abandon the western saddles and ride bareback. As happens with budding teens, the two eventually drifted apart.

After its one-year run, the syndicated version of *Confidential File* came to end, as did Pivar's association with the show; its final Los Angeles broadcast was on September 28, 1956. Kershner and Fenady departed on good terms to make a low-budget feature film:

> I said, "Kersh, we got to quit screwing around and make one for real." He said, "What are you talking about?" I said, "We got to do a feature." He said, "What's it going to be about?" I said "Kersh, what do we know? We know kids, we know the street, we know dope, we know cops, we know Los Angeles." So I sat down and wrote an outline, and then we shot the picture.[32]

Stakeout on Dope Street (1958) was the result. Kershner's career as a director in both film and television lasted into the nineties, with his highest-profile effort the *Star Wars* entry *The Empire Strikes Back* (1980). Kershner passed on in November 2010. Fenady's career flourished as well, a prolific producer, writer, and composer, both in film and television, and the author of numerous novels.

Confidential File's local version, broadcasting on Sunday nights concurrent with the syndicated show's run, plodded on after the syndicated show had run its course. After a move to Monday nights in April 1957, the show returned to Sunday nights in 1958 on competitor KETV channel 6 out of San Diego, its final broadcast four months later in May 1958. Coates' columns were a staple in the *Mirror* up until it folded in 1962, after which he moved over to the *Los Angeles Times*. He continued to write his popular column until a short time before his death of a heart attack in 1968, at the comparatively young age of forty-seven.

Fenady offered this description of Pivar, based on decades-old memory:

> He was a short fellow, but he was kind of dapper, and maybe he was about 5 feet 6 or 7, and he was all white-haired, he had a little pepper in his hair at that time. And his left arm had a tendency to twitch a little

---

[32] Fenady, *op. cit.*

bit, you know. And he drank a lot of Maalox or whatever the hell it was for ulcers.[33]

Pivar's ongoing battle with indigestion may well have been a harbinger of more serious problems to come.

With the end of the syndicated show's run, Pivar once again tried to drum up a new project or attach himself to one already in progress. He was named to the board of directors of the National Society of Television Producers (NSTP) in February 1956,[34] and later that year the NSTP merged with the Screen Producers Guild (SPG), with twenty-six NSTP members—Pivar included—accepted into the SPG.[35]

§

---

[33] Fenady, *op. cit.*

[34] "Video Producers Elect William Self President," *Boxoffice*, February 18, 1956, 57.

[35] "26 NSTP Members Taken Into SPG in Integration," *Boxoffice*, September 22, 1956, 43.

21 The Final Years

One of Pivar's most bitter, previously undocumented, disappointments came about earlier in the mid-fifties. It involved the fellow he had met a quarter century earlier at Columbia, who was there to soundproof two of the studio's stages, the fast-talking fellow who called himself Avrom Goldbogen. He did not go by that name anymore, having Anglicized it years ago. Now he was known as Michael Todd, showman extraordinaire. The man who made—and lost—millions. Lost it through shows that flopped, and through an addiction to gambling as well. And as most anyone in the know would tell you, Todd was not much of a gambler—big stakes, and just as big losses. Survived bankruptcy not once, but twice, and rose Phoenix-like each time to amass new fortunes. And now, after more than a decade and seventeen stage shows of wildly varying success, Todd had grown bored. He now had Hollywood in his sights.

Based on his string of successes, Todd had signed a term contract with Universal in September 1945, to produce films for that organization.[1] Todd was spread too thin; another eight stage shows were to be produced over the next five years, and he was never able to come up with an acceptable script for his first film project, an adaptation of Edna Ferber's *Great Son*. It never came to fruition, and Universal—by now Universal-International—terminated Todd's contract.

It would be close to a decade before Todd would take another stab at the film industry. According to Pivar's two oldest children, Pivar was involved with the pre-production phase of one of Todd's two later film ventures, either

---

[1] "Stage Nabob Mike Todd Allied With Universal," *Los Angeles Times*, October 1, 1945, A2.

Oklahoma! or *Around the World in Eighty Days*. Teen and preteen at the time, details of the incident have faded from their memory, but not the overall impact of its outcome.

Oklahoma!, the film version of Rodgers and Hammerstein's 1943 Broadway musical success, was filmed in 1954 and released in 1955. The film was planned as a showcase for Michael Todd's new Todd-AO process, developed in conjunction with the American Optical Company as an intended improvement over Todd's former company's Cinerama process, the company Todd had been forced out of. Cinerama was a cumbersome affair that involved three cameras and, for exhibition, three projectors; Todd-AO utilized a single camera outfitted with a specially-designed lens, recording its image on newly-developed film stock. Todd was forced out of his creative role well before *Oklahoma!* started filming, ceding the production chores to the musical's authors, Richard Rodgers and Oscar Hammerstein.

Todd followed this disappointment by revisiting a failed project from years earlier, based on Jules Verne's novel *Around the World in Eighty Days*. Originally planned as a stage musical, Todd decided it would make a splendid film, and a visually sumptuous one when filmed in the widescreen Todd-AO process. Filmed globally through 1955 and released in 1956, *Around the World in Eighty Days* was a huge success, both artistically and financially.

Pivar's daughter Lorie has this to say about that time:

> The only time I could remember my dad at work … was much later and not at the TV studio, it was another project. To me he came across as tough and demanding but that might have only been that particular project, it seemed to frustrate him.
>
> [D]ad spent a lot of time and did a lot of work on *Oklahoma!* with a "gentleman's contract," in other words a shake of hands with Mike Todd. He even brought home some short pieces of the film in [Todd-AO]. Their agreement was for money but not his name on the film. When it was finished and he was to get paid, Mike refused. My mother was even angrier than my dad, in fact she was never so angry in her entire life that Mike could use Dad's talents for nothing, not even a thank you. That I remember very clearly.[2]

Lorie's recollection was that Todd had been a longtime best friend of Ben's and a former roommate, and that Todd and Pivar met a number of times at the Beverly Hills Hotel when Todd was in town. When Todd failed to pay for, or even acknowledge, Pivar's considerable contributions to the project, this resulted in some "hateful feelings" toward Todd on the part of Judy. Several

---

[2] Lorie Pivar Viner correspondence with author, May 8, 2009.

The Final Years

years later, when Todd died in a plane crash in March 1958, Judy felt "guilty," as if her feelings had in some fashion contributed to his death.[3]

Lorie later qualified her earlier comments. "I think it was *Around the World in Eighty Days* that Dad helped with. It was one of them."

Pivar's son Neil added his thoughts about Todd and the project:

> I believe my mother may have dated Mike Todd before she moved to California. If not dated, she knew him well. She introduced him to my dad. They became friends. As I recall, from my father's perspective, Mike promised my dad the producer's position on *Oklahoma!* For reasons unbeknownst to me, it didn't happen. That disappointment was about the end of the line for him. Along about that time, my dad became friends with a Los Angeles gangster, Mickey Cohen. Whether or not that had anything to do with my dad not getting *Oklahoma!*, I couldn't say.[4]

Pivar's relationship with Cohen will be discussed shortly.

In all likelihood, Pivar had met Todd a quarter century before when he still went by Avrom Goldbogen, back when Todd was a good friend of Ben's brother Murray, and had soundproofed the two stages at Columbia.[5] Both Ben and Todd had overlapping stays at Universal from later 1945 into 1946, but most of Todd's energies during that period were concentrated on his numerous Broadway shows. If their paths crossed then, it was probably briefly.

Regardless of how Pivar and Todd first met, and whatever their relationship was in the mid-fifties, the fact remains that Pivar did some pre-production work for him, and got stiffed. If it was on *Oklahoma!*, Todd's unexpected removal from the project may have resulted in a lack of funds that directly impacted Pivar. If it was on *Around the World in Eighty Days*, Todd was always scrambling for additional monetary backing for that project, at times without the funds to meet payroll. In the latter case, someone being paid "under the table" probably would have been last in line for monetary obligations to be met. According to Todd's biographer Art Cohn, even though Todd played fast and loose with money he always honored his debts, but not always in a timely fashion. Would Pivar have ultimately been paid if he'd kept after Todd, or if Todd (along with biographer Cohn) hadn't died prematurely in a plane crash in March 1958? We'll never know. The fact remains that Pivar never got paid for his time and effort, and at a time when he really could have used the money.

---

[3] Lorie Pivar Viner correspondence with author, April 27, 2009.

[4] Neil Pivar correspondence with author, May 8, 2009.

[5] Art Cohn, *The Nine Lives of Michael Todd* (New York: Random House, 1958), 43-44, 251.

As for the impact of this debacle on Pivar's marriage, Lorie believes that it "could be the thing ultimately responsible for their separation. That was a hard time for everyone."[6]

Ben and Judy's marriage had begun to deteriorate during the early part of the decade, and it became evident to friends and acquaintances that the two were drifting apart during the production of *Confidential File*. In 1956, Pivar's recently married niece Carol (brother George's daughter) was living up near San Francisco. Her husband was in the Air Force at the time, and the young couple had an eight-month-old baby. They came to the Pivars' for a week-long visit in the fall, their first and last.

> I was just newly married with a baby. That was the first time I ever really spent any time with them, and they were in trouble then, I do remember that. We stayed at Judy and Ben's home, and he was sleeping in like a room that was not hers; they did not live together, they weren't in the same bedroom then. There were real problems, and Neil was away at school, and just the two little girls were there. He was sick too then, he wasn't well at that point. I remember he just was very frail, things were lousy. It was a bad time for us to be visiting there.[7]

Things came to a head. In February 1957, Judy and her two daughters, fourteen-year-old Lorie and seven-year-old Jan, boarded the *El Capitan* and made the four-day, three-night train trip back to New York. The three of them began an extended stay with Judy's sister Debbie and her husband David Siskind in their duplex in Brooklyn. Explained to the children as a visit, it later became apparent that this was a trial separation. Eighteen-year-old Neil stayed behind with his father. Judy and her daughters returned to Los Angeles and the Hortense Street house at the end of August in time for the new school year. She and Ben would coexist under the same roof for the next couple of years, Ben sleeping out on the small porch that they referred to as the *lanai*. Neil moved out soon after in 1958.

One of Pivar's preoccupations was the fear of dying from stomach cancer, just as his father had back in 1937. One of the worthless devices his father had acquired years earlier in a futile attempt to remedy his spreading disease was one of many "quack" remedies and devices foisted upon a desperate and hopeful public. Ben retained this device after his father's death, and son Neil remembers it well:

---

[6] Viner, *op. cit.*

[7] Carol Pivar Miller interview with author, February 2, 2010.

> [Dad] had a black box containing several glass tubes of various shapes and sizes, filled with some sort of inert ionizing gas, probably Argon. You would plug one of the tubes into the cord connected to the box. Plug the power cord into the wall. The gas in the tubes would ionize to a blue color, something like the "lightning" in a Telsa glass ball. If you passed the tube along your body, it would emit sparks onto your skin. This was some sort of early 20th-century cancer treatment. I played with this device many times over the years. Foolish of me not to have kept it.[8]

This phobia, if only on a subconscious level, kept Pivar on the alert for any new treatment that showed promise. One of these that caught Pivar's attention sometime in the mid-fifties was that of a fellow named Harry Hoxsey. Hoxsey did not have a license to practice medicine, but for all intents and purposes did so anyway. Hoxsey ran a clinic in Dallas, Texas, utilizing the various "medicines"[9] passed on to him by his veterinarian father thirty years earlier at the latter's deathbed. By 1956, Hoxsey was treating some eight thousand desperate patients per year, charging $460 a visit for little more than a physical exam and a few pills. He grossed in the neighborhood of $1½ million annually. "We don't believe in slap-happy knife-hacking," exclaimed Dr. Newton Allen, head of Hoxsey's sister clinic in Portage, Pennsylvania;[10] soaking the public would be more like it. The US Food and Drug Administration had Hoxsey in their sights, but weren't able to shut him down until 1960, after which the operation packed up and headed south of the border to sunny Tijuana, Mexico, where it continues to bilk desperately susceptible individuals to this day. Regardless of the growing controversy over Hoxsey's treatment, Pivar believed in it and had made a short film about it sometime earlier.

Pivar was not at all well at this time, and it was beginning to take a toll on him physically. In spite of his compromised state, however, Pivar kept pursuing new projects and opportunities, and would continue to do so right up until his death. One project that never came to fruition was a screenplay Pivar was writing about a huge fireball heading toward the earth. Whether he

---

[8] Neil Pivar correspondence with author, August 5, 2010.

[9] "Ingredients of the mixture are potassium iodide, lactated pepsin, burdock root, red clover blossoms, cascara sagrada, licorice, berberis, poke and echinea roots and prickly ash and buckthorn barks." The recipe was thoughtfully supplied, assumedly for those who might want to whip up a batch in the comfort of their kitchen, by Harry Nelson, "Health Board Adopts Curb on Hoxsey Plan," *Los Angeles Times* (September 22, 1962), 12.

[10] "Things Get Hotter for Hoxsey," *Life*, April 16, 1956, Vol. 40, No. 16, 125-128.

ever finished writing it and, if he did, whether he ever shopped it around is unknown.

Yet another was Pivar's original story *Wind River*, adapted for the screen by Sam B. Melner and Frank Hall, with Kathy Marlowe scheduled to star.[11] Hall's sole previous writing credit was 1957's *The Astounding She-Monster* (Ronald V. Ashcroft), and Melner's former credentials are unknown. As for Marlowe, she had appeared in mostly uncredited bits since the late forties, her most recent credit as a "Venusian Girl" in the Zsa Zsa Gabor space opera *Queen of Outer Space* (1957; Edward Bernds). *Wind River* never got beyond the planning stages, but Marlowe's career peaked soon after with the lead in Ashcroft's *Girl with an Itch* (1958), followed by a sole additional credit in 1960's *Five Bold Women* (Jorge López Portillo).

Meanwhile, at the Hal Roach Studios in Culver City, Hal Roach, Jr., had bought out his father's interests in the studios back in early 1955, but in spite of an ambitious push into television production had failed to make a go of it, and by 1959 was foundering. By late 1958 studio production had dwindled to *The Gale Storm Show*, the Boris Karloff anthology series *The Veil*, the Alan Freed feature *Go, Johnny, Go!*, and a couple of pilots. There were a handful of rental tenants as well,[12] Pivar still occupying space there. The Roach studios ceased production in early 1959, with the final episodes of *The Gale Storm Show* transferred to another production company.[13] Pivar's son Neil has fond memories of this endeavor, but not for reasons one might expect.

> Early in 1959 I believe, [Dad] called me. He said the studio was clearing the backlot. Under a collapsed building front they found an old car. It appeared to be in good condition, and was mine for the taking. My friend Charlie and I went there and retrieved the car. It was an almost new 1947 Buick Century fastback. It was called a sedanette in those days. The car had been bought specifically to be used in a movie. It was purposely crashed into a store, or hotel front, and remained there since 1947 or 1948.
>
> In any case, it had only a few hundred miles on it and was in perfect condition. We compounded and polished the paint. It was gorgeous, and it was fast. I drove it for quite awhile. It was an inline 8 cylinder. 3 speed manual.[14]

---

[11] *Daily Variety*, May 16, 1958, 3.

[12] Richard Lewis Ward, *A History of the Hal Roach Studios* (Southern Illinois University Press, 2005), 153.

[13] *Ibid*, 154.

[14] Neil Pivar correspondence with author, August 27, 2010.

The Final Years

Some time during the later fifties a fellow named Alvin Schoncite came into Pivar's life. Born in New York in 1923, Schoncite, a distant relation of Ben's wife Judy, had relocated to California years earlier. He was somewhat of a "black sheep" of the family, having been involved in several shady deals in the early fifties. In one of these, Schoncite acted as a salesman for the Durastone Co., and would convince homeowners that they could have their homes coated with mastic paint free of charge as models—but they'd first need to sign a contract. The fine print, of course, committed them to pay for the job, resulting in forced payments averaging $1,000. Schoncite, along with another salesman and the company's owner, was found guilty of conspiracy, grand theft, and a handful of other charges, and sentenced to serve one- to fourteen years in prison.[15] This sentence was to be served concurrent with one Schoncite was already serving at Chino State Prison in Riverside County, for the attempted bribery of a sheriff to allow them to open a gambling establishment in Palm Springs.[16]

Schoncite was released several years later, having paid his dues and determined to go straight. Somehow he managed to put together a company he modestly, if perhaps optimistically, named Schoncite International Productions. Pivar, beleaguered with recurring gastrointestinal issues and not a well man by this time, was involved with this company in some capacity or other. Schoncite may have sought out his industry-savvy but now down-on-his-luck distant relative for his practical experience, and Pivar may have been attracted to Schoncite's comparative youth, energy, and ambition, misguided though it was several years earlier. Schoncite's wife Glenda has fond memories of Pivar, saying that she knew him "very well. He was around all the time. He was always a quiet one."[17]

Now working together, Pivar was probably responsible for introducing Schoncite to Los Angeles' most notorious mobster, Mickey Cohen. Involved in the rackets from an early age, Cohen had somehow managed to avoid jail until mid-1951 when he was sentenced for income tax evasion. Released from Washington State's McNeil Island Federal Penitentiary in October 1955, Cohen made a big deal of going straight, if only in word and not deed. Evangelist Billy Graham wanted to "save" him, and author Ben Hecht began a series of interviews with the publicity-hungry Cohen in 1957 for a future biography to be titled *The Soul of a Gunman*. An unnamed film studio wanted to make a film of Cohen's life, tentatively and unimaginatively titled *The Mickey Cohen Story*, but Cohen held out for more money and profit participation.[18] Hecht dropped

---

[15] "Jury Convicts Head of Mastic Paint Concern," *Los Angeles Times*, July 29, 1953, A2; "Prisoner Given Added Sentence," *Los Angeles Times*, August 5, 1953, 12 .

[16] "Three Seek Case Retrial," *Los Angeles Times*, June 9, 1953, 22.

[17] Glenda Goldie Schoncite interview with author, March 11, 2010.

[18] "Chicago Attorney Glad to Stake Mickey Cohen," *Los Angeles Times*, June 9, 1958, 19.

out of his deal with Cohen late in 1959 after Cohen sat for an interview used in an article that appeared in *The Saturday Evening Post*.[19]

Pivar's former *Confidential File* cohort Paul Coates and Cohen were friendly, if not friends, and Coates may have introduced Pivar to Cohen at that time. With the Hecht deal dead, this resulted in a number of meetings over time between Cohen and Pivar, with Pivar now planning to write Cohen's story. Whether he intended this for film or publication is unknown. Pivar even invited his son Neil to go along and meet the man, but Neil declined.

With the proposed film version of Cohen's life foundering, it was announced in early 1959 that Schoncite International Productions had signed both Cohen and his current ex-stripper girlfriend Liz Renay to portray themselves in a film to be titled *The Liz Renay Story*. Shooting was to start in late April 1959. The timing of the announcement was interesting, in that a day earlier Renay had been indicted on five counts of perjury for giving false testimony before a federal grand jury investigating the source of Cohen's income.[20] Pivar's voluminous notes were most likely to be the source of the script for this film.

News of this proposed feature was met with mixed feelings, given the fact that Cohen's reputation was something less than untarnished, and he stood to profit from it. Ivan Spear denounced the film in his *Boxoffice* column:

> Opportunism mixed with a touch of sensationalism has always played a part in the business of producing motion pictures. And most of the time, if it manifests a reasonable amount of good taste, it has proven progressive and profitable.
>
> It is doubted, however, that this can be considered true in the reported plans of Schoncite International Productions to have Mickey Cohen portray himself in a feature titled "The Liz Renay Story," which is to be a biofilm about one of Cohen's former girl friends who will star in the offering.
>
> Such casting—in fact the making of the picture—will do nothing by way of adding dignity to or winning respect for the theatrical screen.[21]

Schoncite's girlfriend at the time, Canadian artist Glenda Goldie, went along to one of the meetings and met the mobster. Was she intimidated? "Actually, it was quite fun ... I wasn't intimidated by anyone in those days. I was quite

---

[19] John Buntin, *L.A. Noir: The Struggle for the Soul of America's Most Seductive City* (New York: Harmony Books, 2009), 249.

[20] "Movies May Portray Cohen as Cohen," *Rhinelander Daily News*, March 14, 1959, 1.

[21] Ivan Spear, "Spearheads," *Boxoffice*, April 6, 1959, W-3.

fresh, Canadian, and full of myself."[22] Schoncite and Glenda married soon after in Las Vegas in 1959, but the film deal fell through. No other film projects were to follow, nor was any biography forthcoming until many years later when Cohen told his story during the last months of his life (1975-1976) to author John Peer Nugent, published as *In My Own Words*. Schoncite International Productions was shut down, but Schoncite and Pivar would reteam for several future projects. Pivar's daughter Lorie recalls that her father conducted some of the later interviews while Cohen was in prison. Cohen was sent off to prison a second time in mid-1961 for income tax evasion, so it is possible that Pivar pursued his interviews with Cohen with some other, future project in mind. Either that, or Cohen had been jailed briefly for some minor infraction of the law while *The Liz Renay Story* was in the planning stages, and that's what she is remembering so many years after the fact.[23]

Pivar's marriage had by this time reached the breaking point, and he and Judy separated in February 1959. Judy sued for divorce in Los Angeles Superior Court on April 8, 1959, alleging the boilerplate, one-size-fits-all "cruelty" as grounds for the action. A financial settlement had been reached between the couple providing support for Judy and the three children.[24] The couple divorced soon after, and Pivar moved to the Twin Palms apartments in Burbank. Lorie and Jan would spend weekends with him there, Lorie driving the two of them in the 1956 Buick given to her by her Uncle Murray. As far as Hollywood marriages were concerned, Ben and Judy's had been one of the longer-lasting, spanning a period of more than two decades.

> They kept [their marital difficulties] as hidden as possible. It was also relatively obvious, even through *Confidential File*, that they weren't close. They were okay, but they weren't real, real close. When they did tell us they were getting a divorce, I don't think that was that much of a shock ... I went to Hollywood High where we grew up, and around the kind of people that we were with, everybody that we knew, the kids, were all from divorced parents. The fact that our parents weren't divorced, we were able to brag about that. And then it happened. They probably stayed together longer than most of them. Personalities. They had different personalities.[25]

Pivar was attached to another film at the end of the decade—the horror thriller *The Leech Woman*—for his old studio, now Universal-International

---

[22] Schoncite, *op cit.*

[23] Lorie Pivar Viner correspondence with author, May 8, 2009, and August 17, 2010.

[24] "Director Ben Pivar Sued for Divorce," *Press-Telegram*, April 9, 1959, A16.

[25] Lorie Pivar Viner interview with author, October 30, 2010.

Pictures. But not as a producer; instead, he was credited solely with the original story idea, co-written with Francis Rosenwald, a former writer at Paramount in the mid-forties who'd spent most of the fifties writing for television. The film's producer was Pivar's old friend Joe Gershenson, so his employment on this film may have been a favor of sorts on the part of Gershenson. Coincidentally, Pivar's son Neil had taken a part-time job at Universal in 1958 in the unionized greens department, which he held well into 1959 concurrent with the film's production.

Produced in early 1959 under the working title *The Leech*, the film would not be released until summer 1960, by which time it had undergone its name change. Screenwriter David Duncan commented on *The Leech Woman* script years later when interviewed by historian Tom Weaver, and did not seem impressed with either his or Pivar and Rosenwald's contributions.

> I wrote [*The Leech Woman*] long after I had done *Thing That Couldn't Die* and *Monster on the Campus*. Apparently someone at Universal liked what I had done on those two, and a producer by the name of Joseph Gershenson re-hired me ... They gave me some material—in fact, I think they gave me a screenplay that had been written by somebody named Ben Pivar. It wasn't a very good screenplay—really, it was unshootable. In redoing it, I suppose I changed the story somewhat. I rewrote it on a two-week assignment and never saw it until a couple of months ago, when I happened to catch it on TV. Isn't it *awful*?[26]

Co-starring Coleen Gray, Grant Williams, and late fifties horror-film regular Gloria Talbott, Pivar's story chronicles the exploits of June Talbot (Gray) who, while accompanying her husband Dr. Paul Talbot (Phillip Terry) to darkest Africa, witnesses rites that transform an elderly woman into a young lady. Obsessed with restoring her own youth, June learns that the mixture used in the ritual includes hormones from the pineal gland of a live human. Devoted spouse that she is, she sets up her callous husband as the unwilling donor, and soon she is rejuvenated into a youthful version of herself. Too bad the hormone donors die in the process, but this frees her from her matrimonial obligations to pursue a younger man.

Returning to the States posing as her own younger cousin Terry Hart, she immediately goes to work enticing her younger attorney Neil Foster (Grant Williams). He falls for her, and hard, to the annoyance of his fiancée Sally (Gloria Talbott). There is a minor hitch, though, that soon comes to June's attention: The effects of the mixture are short-lived, and each time they wear

---

[26] Weaver, Tom. *Interviews with B Science Fiction and Horror Movie Makers* (Jefferson, NC: McFarland and Company, Inc., 1988), 124.

off she finds herself aging rapidly. This won't do, and June embarks on a killing spree to repeatedly restore her youthful looks. When Sally confronts her over the alienation of her fiancé's affections, June kills her as well and stores Sally's pineal glands in her bedroom for safe-keeping.

When the police investigate the string of murders, they soon discover June's fingerprints. Arriving at her home, they begin to question June, thinking her to be her niece. The subterfuge works at first until the cops find Sally's body unceremoniously dumped in the hall closet. June notices the first signs of aging, and makes a beeline for her bedroom and Sally's bottled hormones, the cops hot on her heels. Another hitch: Only the hormones from a human male have the rejuvenation effect, so Sally's don't cut it. Aging rapidly, June rushes from her bedroom and the police, leaping off her balcony. It's too late now, and June crumbles to dust.

A subtle reworking of the plotline of *The Mad Ghoul*, there is a sufficient twist here to make the film watchable, but it is not a rewarding viewing experience. Gray gives a credible performance as the youth-obsessed woman driven to murder, but the film as a whole fails to click. Gray described the problems playing a character whose age bounces around over so many years:

> This is one of the most difficult roles I've ever attempted. Not only because each day of shooting I'd be in a different age bracket with different motivations, but with every age change my mannerisms, gestures and speaking voice had to change also. Some days things became so confusing for me my hands would be trembling like an old woman's, my voice would be a youthful twenty-year-old's and my character would be forty-five ... Each day I would report to makeup and Bud [Westmore] would tell me how old I was going to be. Each morning when I'd wake up at home, I'd put on my own makeup to report to the studio looking as beautiful as I could just to be made old.[27]

Or at least the quotes were credited to her; it may have been one of Universal-International's publicists conjuring up words on her behalf.

Still, it was a paycheck for Pivar, and a project that provided some after-the-fact, ongoing compensation. Somewhat amused by the film's lurid title, Pivar's son Neil recalled that "[f]or many years, until recently, my sisters had been receiving small residual checks for a story my dad wrote. Can't remember the title. I think it was *Snake Lady*, or *Slime Woman*, no, how about *Leech Woman*."[28] Neil's sister Jan elaborated on these modest sums: "They were large enough when I was young that [Lorie and I] would cash them and buy something

---

[27] Universal-International Press Release dated January 29, 1959.
[28] Neil Pivar correspondence with author, March 22, 2010.

for ourselves 'from Dad' or go out to a really nice dinner together with this money."[29]

Jan has fond memories of this period. Ben was more available to her than ever before due to a lack of work, in spite of the fact that he no longer lived in the same house. His health further deteriorated, but he retained his good spirits.

> I just enjoyed [Dad's] company from the time I was ten (after the divorce) while he was living in Twin Palms apartment in Burbank with the Palm Trees in front. I never really knew him before that. He and I became good friends then. He played pinochle sitting out by the pool with people who lived in the building and we watched TV and I stayed with him a lot. I rode my bike around the pool and he gave me all of his pennies to put in little paper sleeves. I just loved him—he showed me how the movies were spliced on that machine with the wheel and the film going around in the studio where he worked, wherever that was. He took me to a ceramics class every weekend that I loved. He came to my school plays and did father-daughter dances with me in Walter Reed Jr. High.
>
> I don't remember much more than that about him. He liked his head scratched and had lovely, slick white hair. I recall the smell of Brylcream! Oh yes, I had a lot of nightmares about mummies while we were living on Hortense—and he snored very loudly, sleeping in that little porch room—and he brought me a red fuzzy bull bank from Tijuana.[30]

Neil was offered the opportunity to set up and supervise a branch office of the aircraft component repair service company he worked for, whose bread and butter were military contracts. He leapt at the offer and relocated to Hawaii in 1961, remaining there until 1993. Judy sold the Hortense Street house soon after, and in 1962 she and Jan moved out to Hawaii as well. Lorie remained behind in Los Angeles, by now finished with high school and employed full time.

Pivar's next project with Alvin Schoncite involved the acquisition of the first feature-length Japanese anime *Hakujaden* made by the Toei Studios back in 1958. With the American rights in hand, they hired actor Marvin Miller (check-distributing "Michael Anthony" on the long-running *The Millionaire* TV series) to narrate the film, along with a number of other actors to dub in the various characters' voices. Pivar and Schoncite produced and adapted the retooling of

---

[29] Jan Pivar Dacri correspondence with author, January 6, 2011.
[30] Jan Pivar Dacri correspondence with author, May 9, 2009.

the story, with actor Robert Tafur hired to "direct" the dubbing. Retitled *Panda and the Magic Serpent* for stateside consumption, the film follows the exploits of Panda the Panda and Mimi the Cat in ancient China, in a land inhabited by a serpent with magical powers. The basis of the story is an ancient Chinese fairy tale more than five thousand years old.

Young Hsu Hsien, having released his pet white serpent years earlier, falls in love with Pai Niang. What he doesn't realize is that his snake was actually a snake goddess, and that a storm has changed her into the human form of Pai Niang. Panda and Mimi and their animal friends know better, and try to keep the two apart. Enter the heavy, magician Fa Hai, and the animals have their paws full trying to protect their master from his evil powers. During the course of the film, Panda helps his master escape from prison, and Panda and Mimi rid the waterfront of a gang of crooks.[31]

The Japanese crew's names were eliminated from the credits for the film's release in July 1961 by Globe Releasing Corp. of Los Angeles; Schoncite was listed as vice president of this concern at the time,[32] and it was his name in the newspaper ads as the film's presenter. "Daddy was so excited about it—it was beautiful and dramatic," recalls youngest daughter Jan, twelve years old when it was released stateside, and no doubt within the target range of the hoped-for audience. Unfortunately, the film failed to live up to its producers' expectations, resulting in another comparative disappointment for Pivar. This would be the only production in color that Pivar would ever be involved with.

With a nod to the horror films he'd been associated with fifteen years earlier, Pivar and Schoncite announced titles for some upcoming productions, including *Werewolf*, *The Mummy Walks*, and *The Moon Creature*. Two additional, non-genre titles were added to the pie-in-the-sky roster, *The Damned Don't Die* and *The Lavender Lie*.[33] None of these appear to have made it much further than the pages of *Daily Variety*. Schoncite's only other film credit was the low-budget crime melodrama *The Choppers* (Leigh Jason), released in November 1961. While Pivar was not involved with this production, it was not the end of their relationship, as we shall soon see.

His health deteriorating, Pivar moved out of Twin Palms and into a small apartment at 11042 Aqua Vista Street in North Hollywood, accompanied by a young Hispanic woman. "She was very good to him, much, much younger than he was," said Lorie. "She took very good care of him."[34] When it became apparent later in 1962 that he needed round-the-clock care, however, he was placed in the Motion Picture Country Home. Established two decades earlier

---

[31] "Chinese Fairy Tale Told in Movie," *Hutchinson News*, October 29, 1961, 6.

[32] *Boxoffice*, June 5, 1961, W-2.

[33] *Daily Variety*, April 7, 1961, 9.

[34] Lorie Pivar Viner interview with author, October 30, 2010.

on Ventura Boulevard in the Woodland Hills district of Los Angeles, the home was initially a retirement community for members of the film industry. The acute-care Motion Picture Hospital was opened in the later forties, and the facilities expanded to include members of the television industry.

Pivar was not about to give in to ill health, though, and was willing to lend his name to most any project or venture that would provide a paycheck and keep his hands in the business, even if from afar. His final endeavor, an ambitious sounding one at the time, was the participation in the formation of a company called Television City Arizona, Inc. Pivar was named president of the new concern, organized in conjunction with David I. Pincus, a veteran film producer of more than forty years of educational and industrial films in his New York-based Caravel Studios. Concurrent with this was the formation of Libra Films, Inc. as its industrial and commercial arm, totally financed by Television City and owner of 80% of its stock; Pincus owned the remaining 20%.

Television City's ambitious plans were to produce industrial and educational films, television pilots and commercials, motion picture features, and children's fantasy films. Foreign films were to be imported and dubbed for US release as well. Pincus, an executive in the firm, was to oversee the construction of a $930,000 nucleus structure in the Valley of the Sun, near Phoenix, Arizona,[35] followed by the acquisition of an estimated $580,000 in equipment. Temporary headquarters were set up in the Arizona Bank Building in Phoenix.[36] Along with Pivar and Pincus, the management team also included "Veteran Motion Picture and TV Producers and Directors" Mitch Leiser, Buddy Bregman, Sidney Kaufman, and Earl Haley. Also involved on some level or other was our friend Alvin Schoncite, along with Kurt Lassen, Gil Ausland, Thomas Pyle, Robert Wolfson, and Bernard Klavir. "Veteran" overstated the case somewhat, as most of them were either lightweights with little previous work to their credit (Leiser, Kaufman, Schoncite) or old-timers who hadn't worked in years (Haley, inactive since the late thirties, was born and raised in Arizona, and knew the state well). Lassen, Ausland, and Pyle were total non-entities, assumedly investors with no previous credited experience in the industry. Bregman stood out from the general pack, with past experience in the music end of the business, and a future producer who remains active to this day. Only Pivar and Pincus had decades of prior experience in their respective fields, and

---

[35] Schoncite's widow Glenda was more specific about the location: "We acquired a movie studio out there, on what they called Superstition Mountain; Apache Land." Interview with author, March 11, 2010.

[36] "TV City, Phoenix, Forms Its Commercial Arm," *Boxoffice*, July 9, 1962, W-5; Chris Dutra, "Hollywood Report," *Boxoffice*, July 30, 1962, 16; "Pincus Named Executive of Television City," *Boxoffice*, August 6, 1962, 6-1.

The Final Years

would be the backbone of the new concern. Stock in the new firm was offered to residents of Arizona at the end of August 1962, terminating on September 8.[37]

Pincus announced the fledgling company's first project scheduled for an early 1963 start, writer-director-producer Earl Haley's *Revolt on the Painted Desert*.[38] Soon after Pivar signed British-born producer Sidney Kaufman to a six-picture co-production deal. Kaufman's first film was to be *Blind Fury*, one of the final projects announced for Pivar back at Universal that never got beyond the planning stages. Scripting was to be handled by Arnold Belgard, formerly associated with Pivar on several of those final, ill-fated productions at Universal. Filming was to take place in northern Arizona in and around Flagstaff and Prescott.[39]

Later that same month Pivar purchased two additional properties for filming. *Shanghai Lady* was to be scripted by Lee Loeb, and *Devil's Melody* by Francis Rosenwald.[40] Another three-picture deal was set up with Wade Preston and John Anderson's Strand Productions. Preston, star of the popular TV series *Colt .45*, was to star in the first, a western set in Arizona in the 1800s; Television City's technical facilities were to be used.[41] In November, Sidney Kaufman acquired the rights to the only western ever written by George Bernard Shaw, *The Shewing-up of Blanco Posnet*.[42] This too was to be filmed at the Television City Studios.

Now all they needed was a studio.

And that never happened. By January, Television City had been placed on the Writers Guild of America's "unfair" list for the alleged failure to pay one of its member writers the $12,500 due him. Guild members were told not to work for the outfit. Pivar, Klavir, Ausland, and Schoncite all had their names added to the "unfair" list as well.[43] Television City Arizona met an early demise before a studio was built, and not a single one of the proposed films made it into production. This would prove to be the ignominious end of Pivar's lengthy career in the industry.

---

[37] "Television City Arizona, Incorporated" full-page ads, *Arizona Daily Sun*, August 29, September 5, 7, 1962, 5.

[38] Dutra, *op. cit.*

[39] "TV City Sets Film in Flag," *Arizona Daily Sun*, August 13, 1962, 3.

[40] "Miscellaneous Happenings Among the Filmmakers," *Boxoffice*, August 27, 1962, 13.

[41] "To Coproduce Three Films," *Boxoffice*, September 24, 1962, W-1.

[42] "G.B.S. Western," *Cumberland Evening Times*, November 8, 1962, 12.

[43] *Daily Variety*, January 28, 1963, 1.

STOP YELLIN'

Hank Schonzeit, author of *A Past Remembered: The History of the Schonzeit Family*, and undisputed authority on the Schonzeit genealogy (and the twenty-five-plus variations of the spelling of the name), recently offered what little he knew about Alvin Schoncite:

> [H]e was always in trouble with the law since a teenager. Alvin had five wives, very successful, little money when he died. He was brilliant, he was one of these turn-around guys who would take a company and turn it around. Had a factory in Hong Kong, and his partners sold the company.[44]

Or at least that's the way he heard it from another relative he interviewed for his book. Alvin Schoncite died in 1994.

Pivar's final months were spent in the Motion Picture Home's hospital. Daughter Lorie, the only one of his three children still living in the vicinity, became his daily visitor. The Motion Picture Home was on her route to-and-from work, and she spent every evening with him. Lorie explains with sadness the burden she had to bear:

> This is what was so difficult. When [Dad] was in the hospital, the doctor told me [Dad] was going to die of cancer, and I couldn't tell anybody. [The doctor said] "And I can't tell your father, and I can't tell anyone else, and I have to tell a family member, so I'm telling you." And I said, "Can I call my mother?" "No, don't call anybody, don't tell anyone yet." And this went on, in those days, until the diagnosis was a hundred percent; you had to keep it to yourself. And the day that he told me that, it was miserable. I went for like two weeks without sleeping. It was awful; I wanted to kill myself. And when I finally did tell my mother, she said, "I'm coming back," which is what made it possible for me to live with that.[45]

Neil remembers it this way:

> In late 1962 or early 1963, my mother was visiting me in Hawaii. She got a call that my dad was in the [hospital]. That was the first I had heard of him having cancer. She left immediately for the mainland.[46]

---

[44] Hank Schonzeit interview with author, March 11, 2010.
[45] Lorie Pivar Viner interview with author, October 30, 2010.
[46] Neil Pivar correspondence with author, August 6, 2010.

The Final Years

The whole, lengthy experience of having to keep her father's worsening condition to herself took its toll on Lorie:

> I had I think [what] you'd call—when she got into town—a nervous breakdown. And I was still just a kid. I stayed home from work and I stayed in bed for like a week, couldn't do anything. It wasn't a few days; it was more like a few weeks, or a couple of months [after Judy came back that he died].[47]

Several weeks later, Neil followed his mother and sister back to Los Angeles.

> I remember, a few weeks later, when I arrived at the hospital, and walked into his room, he was in bed, on the phone trying to put together a deal for a movie. He still believed there was a cure just around the corner.[48]

That deal never came about. Pivar died at 4:00 p.m. on March 28, 1963, a few days after Neil's visit. The cause of death was documented by the attending physician as carcinoma of the stomach with hepatic metastases. Or, in layman's terms, stomach cancer that had spread to his liver. Private services were held on Sunday, March 31, in the Mount Sinai Chapel at the Mount Sinai Mortuary. He was buried immediately following in Mount Sinai Memorial Park, section Canaan 6, lot 2843, space 1, in the Hollywood Hills section of Los Angeles.

Jan put it simply: "I was totally heartbroken."

§

---

[47] Viner, *op. cit.*
[48] Pivar, *op. cit.*

22 Gone, But Forgotten: Pivar's Legacy

The forty-eight films for which Pivar received credit while at Universal are typical examples of the studio's B product. Released over a seven-year period from September 1939 to July 1946, they all display a high degree of competency in most of the technical departments, but occasionally fall short in scripting and with individual performances. This could also be said of the B's from rival studios such as Paramount, Columbia, and 20th Century-Fox, but the B's from Universal tended to be a helluva lot more fun, and unabashedly so.

Art direction was usually adequate, with convincingly dressed sets possessing a look of solidity and an appearance of use. This was in stark contrast to the hastily thrown together, cheap-looking flats of Monogram and PRC, although occasional corner-cutting becomes painfully apparent at Universal into the mid-forties.

Camerawork was crisp and unobtrusively fluid, effectively lit and with forethought given to camera placement. With technicians such as John W. Boyle, Maury Getsman, Jerome Ash, William Sickner, Elwood Bredell, Milton Krasner, George Robinson, Stanley Cortez, Virgil Miller, Jack MacKenzie, Charles Van Enger, and Paul Ivano calling the shots, the Universal B's all looked good, setting them far apart from the visual crapiness of their counterparts from PRC and Monogram.

The musical scores were straight from the Universal library, a patchwork most often stitched together under the direction of Hans J. Salter, but in some instances handled by Paul Sawtell. Although certain pieces were often used and perhaps slightly overworked during the horror cycle (as was Tchaikovsky's "Ballet of Swan Lake" years earlier with *The Mummy*, *Dracula*, *Murders in the Rue Morgue*, and several others), the ones chosen were quite appropriate and effectively integrated, as opposed to the clumsily laid in, frequently out of place and overworked scores of many of the independent B's.

Direction was always adequate, with veteran and comparative newcomer alike providing at the very least workmanlike results, and quite often instilling their work with some effective staging and imaginative bits of business. The decades of experience of a Chrisrty Cabanne would infuse the finished film with solidly traditional, if somewhat stodgy, results that audiences were comfortable with, while the youthful energy of a Reginald LeBorg would occasionally take a film in a modestly different, more stylish direction. The one attribute they all had in common was the ability to keep things moving, and in most instances close to schedule and budget.

The scripts, although generally quite simplistic in terms of plotting and asinine in their idea of humor, were really no worse than most of the drivel spewed forth in the years since on television. The requirements imposed on the journeymen writers, some of whom were comparatively new to this line of work, would cause headaches for even the most seasoned of wordscribes: Here's the title, and here's the list of stock shots that need to be woven into the storyline; Good luck! As for the de rigueur humor, Andy Devine could pull this stuff off in his sleep, but a Fuzzy Knight or Vince Barnett had to work a little harder, and for thinner results. Regardless, the various plotlines were (assumedly) what the majority of the movie-going public wanted in the form of mindless entertainment, and Universal delivered.

The performances of the young leads, while uneven as a result of the newcomers' lack of experience, are usually quite competent; Pivar had the pick of a host of young contract players eager to please and striving for roles in the elusive A's. There were exceptions, of course: Chaney, whose popularity far exceeded his talent, had his ups and downs; Acquanetta and Rondo Hatton, both around for their "looks" rather than their talent, are notable as such, their shortcomings easily overlooked and forgiven.

All in all, Pivar's output at Universal tended to be visually and stylistically indistinguishable from that of his peers in the B unit, and that was the studio's intention. That he was very good at what he did is evidenced by the length of his tenure at the studio, the scope of his output, and the executive producer position to which he was ultimately promoted; Pivar thrived in this sort of pressure-cooker environment, and his prodigious output bears mute testimony to that fact. His films were all competently executed, and by virtue of the fact that his horror offerings have remained consistently popular throughout the decades, Pivar's films were the major portion of the Universal B product to remain accessible for public consumption to this day, via release to television in various "packages," and sporadically on VHS and DVD.

So, crack a beer, put on *Weird Woman*, put your feet up and enjoy. While it's no *Citizen Kane*, it's just as enjoyable. Dare I say moreso?

§

The Films of Ben Pivar

Note: Films are listed in release order, which in a number of instances differs from the order in which they were filmed. All credits beginning with Grand National's *The Gold Racket* in 1937 have been taken directly from the films themselves (with the exception of the Universal westerns, as noted), with each credit listed in the order in which it appeared. Variations of spellings have been retained (e.g. Universal editor Ed Curtis/Curtiss, actors Milburn/Milburne Stone and Turhan/Turban Bey). Pivar's position on each film appears as listed in the credits, with associate producer and executive producers credits sometimes listed simply as producer. Films not viewed by the author (primarily those pre-Grand National) have an asterisk following the title; their credits have been obtained from other sources.

The Early Years: As Editor Primarily at Columbia and Universal (incomplete listing)

The Tigress *
Columbia Pictures
Released October 21, 1927; 6 reels; silent; © November 23, 1927
Cast: Jack Holt, Dorothy Revier, Frank Leigh, Philippe DeLacy, Howard Truesdell, Frank Nelson
Producer: Harry Cohn; Director: George B. Seitz; Screenplay: Harold Shumate; Photography: Joseph Walker; Art Director: Robert E. Lee; Film Editor: Ben Pivar; Assistant Director: Clifford Saum

The Clean-Up Man *
Universal Pictures; a Universal Thrill Feature
Released February 12, 1928; 5 reels; silent; © October 19, 1927
Cast: Ted Wells, Peggy O'Day, Henry Hebert, George Reed, Tom Carter
Presented by Carl Laemmle; Director: Ray Taylor; Story, Continuity: George Morgan and Lola D. Moore; Titles: Gardner Bradford; Photography: John Hickson and Milton Bridenbecker; Art Director: David S. Garber; Film Editor: Ben Pivar

Midnight Madness *
DeMille Pictures Corp./Pathé Exchange, Inc.
Released March 25, 1928; 6 reels; silent; © March 3, 1928
Cast: Jacqueline Logan, Clive Brook, Walter McGrail, James Bradbury, Oscar Smith, Vadim Uraneff, Louis Natheaux, Clarence Burton, Virginia Sale, Frank Hagney, Emmett King
Producer: Hector Turnbull; Director: F. Harmon Weight; Scenario: Robert N. Lee, adapted from the play *The Lion Trap, a Comedy in Four Acts* by Daniel Nathan Rubin; Titles: Edwin Justus Mayer; Photography: David Abel; Art Direction: Stephen Goosson; Film Editors: Harold McLernon and Ben Pivar; Costumes: Adrian

Modern Mothers *
Columbia Pictures
Released May 13, 1928; 6 reels; silent; © June 15, 1928
Cast: Helen Chadwick, Douglas Fairbanks, Jr., Ethel Grey Terry, Barbara Kent, Alan Roscoe, Gene Stone, George Irving
Producer: Harry Cohn; Director: Philip Rosen; Story, Scenario: Peter Milne; Photography: Joseph Walker; Art Director: Joseph Wright; Film Editor: Ben Pivar; Assistant Director: Joe Cook

Name the Woman *
Columbia Pictures
Released May 25, 1928; 6 reels; silent; © June 29, 1928
Cast: Anita Stewart, Huntley Gordon, Gaston Glass, Chappell Dossett, Julianne Johnston, Jed Prouty
Producer: Harry Cohn; Director, Writer: Erle C. Kenton; Continuity: Peter Milne; Adaptation: Elmer Harris; Photography: Ben Reynolds; Art Director: Joseph Wright; Film Editor: Ben Pivar; Assistant Director: Charles C. Coleman

Quick Triggers *
Universal Pictures; a Ranch Rider Western
Released July 15, 1928; 5 reels; silent; © October 20, 1927

Cast: Fred Humes, Derelys Perdue, Wilbur Mack, Robert Chandler, Gilbert "Pee Wee" Holmes, Scotty Mattraw, Dick L'Estrange, Ben Corbett
Presented by Carl Laemmle; Director: Ray Taylor; Story, Screenplay: Basil Dickey; Titles: Gardner Bradford; Photography: Al Jones; Art Director: David S. Garber; Film Editor: Ben Pivar

Greased Lightning *
Universal Pictures
Released July 29, 1928; 5 reels; silent; © October 20, 1927
Cast: Ted Wells, Betty Caldwell, Walter Shumway, Lon Poff, George Dunning, Myrtis Crinley, Victor Allen
Presented by Carl Laemmle; Director: Ray Taylor; Story, Continuity: William Lester; Titles: Gardner Bradford; Photography: Milton Bridenbecker; Art Director: David S. Garber; Film Editor: Ben Pivar

Sinner's Parade *
Columbia Pictures
Released September 14, 1928; 6 reels; silent; © October 8, 1928
Cast: Victor Varconi, Dorothy Revier, John Patrick, Edna Marion, Marjorie Bonner, Clarissa Selwynne, Jack Mower
Producer: Harry Cohn; Director: John G. Adolfi; Adaptation, Continuity: Beatrice Van; Story: David Lewis; Camera: James Van Trees; Art Director: Harrison Wiley; Film Editor: Ben Pivar; Assistant Director: Eugene De Rue

Driftwood *
Columbia Pictures
Released October 15, 1928; 7 reels; silent; © November 8, 1928
Cast: Don Alvarado, Marceline Day, Alan Roscoe, J.W. Johnston, Fred Holmes, Fritzi Brunette, Nora Cecil, Joe Mack
Producer: Jack Cohn; Director: Christy Cabanne; Adaptation, Continuity: Lillie Hayward; Titles: Morton Blumenstock; Photography: Joseph Walker; Art Director: Harrison Wiley; Film Editor: Ben Pivar; Assistant Director: Tenny Wright

Nothing to Wear *
Columbia Pictures
Released November 5, 1928; 6 reels; silent; © January 14, 1929
Cast: Jacqueline Logan, Theodore Von Eltz, Bryant Washburn, Jane Winton, William Irving, Edythe Flynn
Producer: Jack Cohn; Director: Erle C. Kenton; Story, Continuity: Peter Milne; Photography: Joseph Walker; Art Director: Harrison Wiley; Film Editor: Ben Pivar; Assist Director: Tenny Wright

Submarine *
Columbia Pictures
Released November 12, 1928; 93 minutes; © November 15, 1928
Cast: Jack Holt, Dorothy Revier, Ralph Graves, Clarence Burton, Arthur Rankin
Irvin Willat Production; Producer: Harry Cohn; Director: Frank R. Capra; Scenario: Dorothy Howell; Story: Norman Springer; Photography: Joseph Walker; Art Director: Harrison Wiley; Film Editor: Arthur Roberts (and Ben Pivar, not credited)

Restless Youth *
Columbia Pictures
Released November 30, 1928; 7 reels; silent; © February 21, 1929
Cast: Marceline Day, Ralph Forbes, Norman Trevor, Robert Ellis, Mary Mabery, Gordon Elliott, Roy Watson
Producer: Jack Cohn; Director: Christy Cabanne; Story: Cosmo Hamilton; Adaptation: Howard Green; Photography: Joseph Walker; Art Director: Harrison Wiley; Film Editor: Ben Pivar; Assistant Director: Buddy Coleman

Object – Alimony *
Columbia Pictures
Released December 22, 1928; 7 reels; silent; © March 23, 1929
Cast: Lois Wilson, Hugh Allan, Ethel Grey Terry, Douglas Gilmore, Roscoe Karns, Carmelita Geraghty, Dickey Moore, Jane Keckly, Thomas Curran
Producer: Jack Cohn; Director: Scott R. Dunlap; Scenario: Peter Milne; Adaptation: Sig Herzig; Story: Elmer Harris; Photography: Joseph Walker; Art Director: Harrison Wiley; Technical Director: Edward Shulter; Film Editor: Ben Pivar

Behind Closed Doors *
Columbia Pictures
Released February 24, 1929; 6 reels; silent; © May 20, 1929
Cast: Virginia Valli, Gaston Glass, Otto Matisen, Andre De Segurola, Fanny Midgley, Torben Meyer, Broderick O'Farrell
Producer: Harry Cohn; Director: Roy William Neill; Scenario: Howard J. Green; Story: Lillian Ducey and H. Milner Kitchin; Photography: Ted Tetzlaff; Art Director: Harrison Wiley; Film Editor: Ben Pivar; Assistant Director: Tenny Wright

The Eternal Woman *
Columbia Pictures
Released March 18, 1929; 6 reels; silent; © June 14, 1929
Cast: Olive Borden, Ralph Graves, Ruth Clifford, John Miljan, Nina Quartaro, Josef Swickard, Julia Swayne Gordon
Producer: Harry Cohn; Director: John P. McCarthy; Screenplay: Wellyn Totman; Photography: Joseph Walker; Art Director: Harrison Wiley; Film Editor: Ben Pivar; Assistant Director: Charles C. Coleman

Sound Films at Columbia:

The Bachelor Girl *
Columbia Pictures
Released May 20, 1929; 7 reels; sound (talking sequences and music score); © June 18, 1929
Cast: William Collier, Jr., Jacqueline Logan, Edward Hearn, Thelma Todd
Producer: Harry Cohn; Director: Richard Thorpe; Story, Continuity: Jack Townley; Dialogue: Frederic Hatton and Fanny Hatton; Titles: Weldon Melick; Photography: Joseph Walker; Art Director: Harrison Riley; Film Editor: Ben Pivar; Assistant Director: George Rhein

Broadway Scandals *
Columbia Pictures
Released November 10, 1929; 9 reels; sound; © December 17, 1929
Cast: Sally O'Neil, Jack Egan, Carmel Myers, Tom O'Brien, J. Barney Sherry, John Hyams, Charles Wilson, Doris Dawson
Producer: Harry Cohn; Director: George Archainbaud; Dialogue Director: James Seymour and Rufus Le Maire; Scenario: Gladys Lehman; Dialogue: Norman Houston and Howard J. Green; Photography: Harry Jackson; Art Director: Harrison Wiley; Film Editor: Leon Barsha and Ben Pivar; Sound Mixing Engineer: W. Hancock; Assistant Director: C.C. Coleman

Flight
Columbia Pictures
Released September 18, 1929; 12 reels; sound; © December 4, 1929
Cast: Jack Holt, Lila Lee, Ralph Graves, Alan Roscoe, Harold Goodwin, Jimmy De La Cruze
Producer: Harry Cohn; Director: Frank R. Capra; Scenario: Howard J. Green; Dialogue: Frank R. Capra; Story: Ralph Graves; Camera: Joseph Walker and Joe Novak; Assistant Cameraman: Elmer Dyer and Paul Perry; Assistant Director: Harrison Wiley; Film Editor: Ben Pivar, Maurice Wright, and Gene Milford; Technical Sound Engineer: John Livadary; Sound Mixing Engineer: Harry

Blanchard; Assistant Director: Buddy Coleman

As Supervisor/Producer

El Código Penal *
Columbia Pictures
Released February 19, 1931 (Mexico City); March 14, 1931 (San Juan, Puerto Rico); April 10, 1931 (New York); 108 minutes
Cast: Barry Norton, Maria Alba, Carlos Villarias, Manuel Arbó, Maria Calvo, Julio Villarreal, Alfredo del Diestro, Ramon Peón, Jose Soriano Viosca
Supervising Producer: Ben Pivar; Director: Phil Rosen; Screenplay: Fred Niblo, Jr. and Seton I. Miller; based on the play "The Criminal Code" by Martin Flavin; Cinematographer: Joseph Walker

A series of **Buck Jones** westerns came next with Pivar acting as Supervisor, although Pivar's name does not appear in the credits. The series was reportedly turned over to George B. Seitz in 1932. The films that Pivar contributed to are most likely among the following, although none of these has been confirmed:

Branded
Columbia Pictures
Released September 1, 1931; 61 minutes; © June 23, 1931
Cast: Buck Jones (Cuthbert Chauncy Dale, aka "Tom"), Ethel Kenyon (Lou Preston), Wallace McDonald (Stage Robber), Philo McCullough (Mac, Fall City Sheriff), Al Smith (Joe Moore, Manager of Preston Ranch), John Oscar (Ole "Swede" Swanson), Clark Burroughs, Fred Burns (Prestonville Sheriff)
Producer: Harry Cohn; Director: D. Ross Lederman; Story, Dialog: Randall Faye; Photography: Benjamin Kline and Elmer Dyer; Film Editor: Otto Meyer; Production Supervision: Ben Pivar (not credited, unconfirmed)

Border Law *
Columbia Pictures
Released October 15, 1931; 63 minutes; © August 18, 1931
Cast: Buck Jones, Lupita Tovar, James Mason, Frank Rice, Don Chapman, Louis Hickus, F.R. Smith, John Wallace, Lafe McKee
Director: Louis King; Producer: Harry Cohn; Story: Stuart Anthony; Photography: L.W. O'Connell; Film Editor: Otto Meyer; Production Supervision: Ben Pivar (not credited, unconfirmed)

The Films of Ben Pivar

Range Feud *
Columbia Pictures
Released December 1, 1931; 58 minutes; © September 24, 1931
Cast: Buck Jones, John Wayne, Susan Fleming, Ed LeSaint, William Walling, Wallace McDonald, Harry Woods, Frank Austin
Director: D. Ross Lederman; Story: Milton Krims; Continuity: George Plympton; Photography: Benjamin Kline; Film Editor: Maurice Wright; Production Supervision: Ben Pivar (not credited, unconfirmed)

The Deadline *
Columbia Pictures
Released December 3, 1931; 63 minutes; © October 15, 1931
Cast: Buck Jones, Loretta Sayers, Robert Ellis, Edwin J. Brady, G. Raymond Nye, Knute Erickson, George Ernest, Harry Todd, James Curtis, James Farley
Director and Story: Lambert Hillyer; Photography: Byron Haskin; Film Editor: Maurice Wright; Production Supervision: Ben Pivar (not credited, unconfirmed)

Ridin' for Justice *
Columbia Pictures
Released January 4, 1932; 61 minutes; © December 11, 1931
Cast: Buck Jones, Mary Doran, Russell Simpson, Walter Miller, Bob McKenzie, William Walling, Billy Engle, Hank Mann, Silver, the horse
Director: D. Ross Lederman; Story: Harold Shumate; Photography: Benjamin Kline; Film Editor: Maurice Wright; Production Supervision: Ben Pivar (not credited, unconfirmed)

One Man Law *
Columbia Pictures
Released January 11, 1932; 61 minutes; © January 11, 1932
Cast: Buck Jones, Shirley Grey, Robert Ellis, Murdock McQuarrie, Harry Todd, Henry Sedley, Ernie Adams, Richard Alexander
Director and Story: Lambert Hillyer; Photography: Mack Stengler; Film Editor: Harry Marker; Production Supervision: Ben Pivar (not credited, unconfirmed)

South of the Rio Grande *
Columbia Pictures
Released March 5, 1932; 55 minutes; © February 23, 1932
Cast: Buck Jones, Mona Maris, George Lewis, Doris Hill, Philo McCollough, Paul Fix, James Durkin, Charles Stevens, Charles Requa, Harry Semels, Silver, the horse
Director: Lambert Hillyer; Story: Harold Shumate and Milton Krims;

Photography: Benjamin Kline; Film Editor: Maurice Wright; Production Supervision: Ben Pivar (not credited, unconfirmed)

High Speed
Columbia Pictures
Released April 2, 1932; 62 minutes; © March 9, 1932
Cast: Charles (Buck) Jones (Bill Toomey), Loretta Sayers (Peggy Preston), Wallace MacDonald (Tom Corliss), Pat O'Malley (Paul Whipple), Ed LeSaint, William Walling (Preston), Ward Bond (Ham), Dick Dickinson (Walter Kane), Martin Faust, Mickey McGuire (Buddy Whipple; not credited)
Director: D. Ross Lederman; Story: Harold Shumate; Adaptation and Dialogue: Adele Buffington; Photography: Ted Tetzlaff; Film Editor: Harry Marker; Production Supervision: Ben Pivar (not credited, unconfirmed)

Hello Trouble *
Columbia Pictures
Released July 15, 1932; 61 minutes; © June 14, 1932
Cast: Buck Jones, Lina Basquette, Wallace MacDonald, "Spec" O'Donnell, Ruth Warren, Otto Hoffman, Ward Bond, Frank Rice, Russell Simpson, Alan Roscoe, Morgan Galloway, Lafe McKee, Al Smith, Walter Brennan, Silver, the horse
Director and Story: Lambert Hillyer; Photography: Benjamin Kline; Film Editor: Gene Milford; Production Supervision: Ben Pivar (not credited, unconfirmed)

McKenna of the Mounted *
Columbia Pictures
Released August 26, 1932; 62 minutes; © July 15, 1932
Cast: Buck Jones, Greta Granstedt, Walter McGrail, Mitchell Lewis, Niles Welch, Ralph Lewis, James Flavin, Jack Kennedy; Story: Randall Faye; Dialogue and Continuity: Stuart Anthony; Photography: Benjamin Kline; Film Editor: Gene Milford; Director: D. Ross Lederman; Production Supervision: Ben Pivar (not credited, unconfirmed)

White Eagle *
Columbia Pictures
Released October 10, 1932; 65 minutes; © September 7, 1932
Cast: Buck Jones, Barbara Weeks, Robert Ellis, Jason Robards, Ward Bond, Robert Elliott, Bob Kortman, Frank Campeau, Jimmy Howe, Jim Thorpe, Clarence Geldert, Silver, the horse
Director: Lambert Hillyer; Story: Fred Myton; Photography: L. William O'Connell; Film Editor: Gene Milford; Production Supervision: Ben Pivar (not credited, unconfirmed)

King of the Wild Horses *
Columbia Pictures
Released November 10, 1933; 62 minutes; © October 23, 1933
Cast: Rex the Wonder Horse, Lady the Horse, Marquis the Horse, William Janney, Dorothy Appleby, Wallace MacDonald, Harry Semels, Ford West, Art Mix
Production Supervisor: George B. Seitz and Ben Pivar; Director: Earl Haley; Screenplay: Fred Myton; from a story by Earl Haley; Cinematography: Benjamin Kline; Editor: Clarence Kolster

The Fighting Ranger *
Columbia Pictures
Released March 17, 1934; 60 minutes; © March 16, 1934
Cast: Buck Jones, Dorothy Revier, Frank Rice, Bradley Page, Ward Bond, Frank La Rue, Paddy O'Flynn, Mozelle Brittone, Art Mix, John Wallace, Silver the horse
Director: George B. Seitz; Screenplay: Harry O. Hoyt; based on a story by Stuart Anthony; Photography: Sidney Wagner; Film Editor: Gene Milford; Production Supervisor: Ben Pivar (not credited)

Man Trailer *
Columbia Pictures
Released March 23, 1934; 59 minutes; © March 30, 1934
Cast: Buck Jones, Cecilia Parker, Arthur Vinton, Clarence Geldart, Steve Clark, Charles West, Tom Forman, Lew Meehan
Director: Lambert Hillyer; Screenplay: Lambert Hillyer; Photography: Benjamin Kline; Film Editor: Gene Milford; Production Supervisor: Ben Pivar (not credited)

Air Hawks
Columbia Pictures
Released June 1, 1935; 68 minutes; © May 8, 1935
Cast: Ralph Bellamy (Barry Eldon), Tala Birell (Renee Dupont), Wiley Post (Himself), Douglass Dumbrille (Victor Arnold), Robert Allen (Bill Lewis), Billie Seward (Mona Greenwood), Victor Kilian (Tiny Davis), Robert Middlemass (Martin Drewen), Geneva Mitchell (Gertie Dunlap), Wyrley Birch (Holden)
Screenplay: Griffin Jay and Grace Neville; based on the story *Air Fury* by Ben Pivar; Photography: Henry Freulich; Film Editor: Richard Cahoon; Director: Albert Rogell; Production Supervisor: Ben Pivar (not credited)

After the Dance *
Columbia Pictures
Released July 26, 1935; 60 minutes; © July 30, 1935
Cast: Nancy Carroll, George Murphy, Thelma Todd, Jack La Rue, Arthur Hohl, Wyrley Birch, Thurston Hall, Victor Kilian, Robert Middlemass, George McKay, Harry Barris, Virginia Sale
Director: Leo Bulgakov; Screenplay: Harold Shumate and Bruce Manning; based on a story by Harrison Jacobs; Photography: Joseph August; Film Editor: Otto Meyer; Production Supervisor: Ben Pivar (not credited); Producer: Irving Briskin (not credited)

Too Tough to Kill *
Columbia Pictures
Released November 23, 1935; 58 minutes; © November 15, 1935
Cast: Victor Jory, Sally O'Neil, Thurston Hall, Johnny Arthur, Robert Gleckler, George McKay, Robert Middlemass, Dewey Robinson
Director: D. Ross Lederman; Screenplay: Lester Cole and Griffin Jay; based on a story by Robert D. Speers; Photography: George Meehan; Film Editor: Gene Milford; Production Supervisor: Ben Pivar (not credited); Executive Producer: Robert North (not credited)

The Lone Wolf Returns
Columbia Pictures
Released December 31, 1935; 68 minutes; © January 2, 1936
Cast: Melvyn Douglas (Michael Lanyard, aka the Lone Wolf), Gail Patrick (Marcia Stewart), Tala Birell (Liane Mallison), Henry Mollinson (Mallison), Thurston Hall (retired Detective Crane), Raymond Walburn (Jenkins), Douglass Dumbrille (Morphew), Nana Bryant (Aunt Julie), Robert Middlemass (Chief of Detectives McGowan), Robert Emmett O'Conner (Detective Benson)
Screenplay: Joseph Krumgold, Bruce Manning, and Lionel Houser; Story: Louis Joseph Vance; Photography: Henry Freulich; Film Editor: Viola Lawrence; Musical Director: Howard Jackson; Costumes: Samuel Lange; Director: Roy William Neill; Production Supervisor: Ben Pivar (not credited); Executive Producer: Robert North (not credited)

Trapped By Television
Columbia Pictures
Released June 16, 1936; 63 minutes; © June 8, 1936
Cast: Mary Astor, Lyle Talbot, Nat Pendleton, Joyce Compton, Thurston Hall, Henry Mollison, Wyrley Birch, Robert Strange
Director: Del Lord; Screenplay: Lee Loeb and Harold Buchman; Story: *The Big Squawk* by Sherman Lowe and Al Martin; Photography: Allen G. Seigler; Film

Editor: James Sweeney; Special Camera Effects: E. Roy Davidson; Associate Producer: Ben Pivar

Two-Fisted Gentleman *
Columbia Pictures
Released August 15, 1936; 63 minutes; © August 11, 1936; pre-release title *The Fighter*
Cast: James Dunn, June Clayworth, George McKay, Thurston Hall, Gene Morgan, Paul Guilfoyle, Harry Tyler, Muriel Evans, Charles Lane
Executive Producer: Irving Briskin; Producer: Ben Pivar; Director: Gordon Wiles; Screenplay: Tom Van Dycke; Photography: John Stumar; Film Editor: James Sweeney

The Man Who Lived Twice
Columbia Pictures
Released October 13, 1936; 73 minutes; © September 24, 1936
Cast: Ralph Bellamy (Slick Rawley/Dr. James Blake), Marian Marsh (Janet Haydon), Thurston Hall (Dr. Schuyler), Isabel Jewell (Peggy Russell), Nana Bryant (Mrs. Schuyler), Ward Bond (Gloves Baker), Henry Kolker (Judge Treacher), Willard Robertson (Inspector Logan)
Director: Harry Lachman; Screenplay: Tom Van Dycke, Arthur Strawn, and Fred Niblo, Jr.; Story: Tom Van Dycke and Henry Altimus; Photography: James Van Trees; Film Editor: Byron Robinson; Special Effects: Kenneth Wheeler; Associate Producer: Ben Pivar; Executive Producer: Irving Briskin (not credited)

End of the Trail *
Columbia Pictures
Released October 31, 1936; 72 minutes; © September 8, 1936
Cast: Jack Holt, Louise Henry, Douglass Dumbrille, Guinn Williams, George McKay, Gene Morgan, John McGuire, Edward Le Saint, Frank Shannon, Erle C. Kenton (as Theodore Roosevelt)
Producer: Ben Pivar; Director: Erle C. Kenton; Screenplay: Harold Shumate; based on Zane Grey's novel *Outlaws of Palouse*; Photography: John Stumar; Film Editor: Al Clark; Executive Producer: Irving Briskin (not credited)

Come Closer, Folks *
Columbia Pictures
Released November 24, 1936; 61 minutes; © October 21, 1936
Cast: James Dunn, Marian Marsh, Wynne Gibson, George McKay, Gene Lockhart, Herman Bing, John Gallaudet, Gene Morgan, Wallis Clark
Associate Producer: Ben Pivar; Director: D. Ross Lederman; Screenplay: Lee

Loeb and Harold Buchman; based on a story by Aben Kandel; Photography: Henry Freulich; Film Editor: Byron Robinson; Executive Producer: Irving Briskin (not credited)

Grand National Pictures, 1937

The Gold Racket
Condor Productions; Grand National Pictures
Edward L. Alperson Presents a George A. Hirliman Production
Released April 10, 1937; 66 minutes; © April 19, 1937; working title *Gold*
Cast: Conrad Nagel (Alan O'Connor), Eleanor Hunt (Bobbie Reynolds), Fuzzy Knight (Scotty Summers), Frank Milan (Steve Williams), Jack Duffy (Hinckel), Albert J. Smith (Fraser), Warner P. Richmond (Doc Johnson), Charles Delaney (Joe), Karl Hackett (Lefty), William Thorn (McKenzie), Edward Le Saint (agent Dixon)
Associate Producer: Ben Pivar; Director: Louis J. Gasnier; Producer: George A. Hirliman; Supervisor: Sam Diege; Original Story: Howard Higgin; Screenplay: David S. Levy; Photography: Mack Stengler; Supervising Editor: Joseph H. Lewis; Art Director: F. Paul Sylos; Film Editor: Robert Jahns; Sound Recorder: W.C. Smith; Assistant Director: Milton Brown; Producer: George A. Hirliman

Love Takes Flight
Condor Productions; Grand National Pictures
Edward L. Alperson Presents a Condor Production
Released August 13, 1937; 70 minutes; © August 9, 1937
Cast: Bruce Cabot (Neil S. "Brad" Bradshaw), Beatrice Roberts (Joan Lawson), Astrid Allwyn (Diana Audre), John Sheehan (Spud Johnson), Edwin Maxwell (David Miller), Grady Sutton (Donald), Arthur Hoyt (Grey), Harry Tyler (Harry Stone), Gordon Elliott (Bill Parker), William Thorne (Bill Parker Sr.), Elliott Fisher (Tommy Lawson), William Moore (Tex Rice), Brooks Benedict (Eddie), Carol Tevis (Myrtle Johnson), Jack Duffy (Bartender), Reed Howes (radio announcer)
Director: Conrad Nagel; Associate Producer: Ben Pivar; Production Manager: Sam Diege; Original Story: Ann Morrison Chapin; Screenplay: Lionel O. Houser and Mervin Houser; Director of Photography: Mack Stengler; Art Director: F. Paul Sylos; Supervising Editor: Robert Crandall; Film Editor: Tony Martinelli; Musical Supervisor: Abe Meyer; Sound Recorder: William Wilmarth; Assistant Director: Doc Merman; Aerial Technician: Herb White; Produced by George A. Hirliman

Mr. Boggs Steps Out

Zion Myers Productions; Grand National Pictures
Presented by Edward L. Alperson
Released November 12, 1937; 68 minutes; © November 12, 1937; working titles *Face the Facts* and *Mr. Boggs Buys a Barrel*
Cast: Stuart Erwin (Oliver Boggs), Helen Chandler (Oleander Tubbs), Toby Wing (Irene Lee), Tully Marshall (Morton Ross), Spencer Charters (Angus Tubbs), Walter Byron (Dennis Andrews), Harry Tyler (Sam Mason), Milburn Stone (Burns), Otto Hoffman (Jenkins), William Moore (Bob Debrette), Nora Cecil (Widow Peddie), Elliott Fisher (Tommy Mason), Edward Kane (Theatre Manager), Harrison Green (Mr. Pry), Wilson Benge (Butler), Otis Harlan (Abner Katz)
Director: Gordon Wiles; Original Story *Face the Facts* in the *Saturday Evening Post* by Clarence Budington Kelland; Screenplay: Richard English; Production Manager: Harold Lewis; Unit Manager: Sam Diege; Assistant Director: Doc Merman; Art Director: F. Paul Sylos; Interior Decoration: Stanley Murphy; Musical Director: Abe Meyer; Sound Supervision: A.E. Kaye; Film Editors: Gene Milford and Guy V. Thayer, Jr.; Photography: John Stumar; Producer: Ben Pivar

Republic Pictures, 1938

The Great Wall St. Scandal *
Republic Pictures
Associate Producer: Ben Pivar
Screenplay: Alex Gottlieb and Norman Burnstine
(unrealized project)

Love is a Fable *
Republic Pictures
Associate Producer: Ben Pivar
(unrealized project)

Lady Mouthpiece *
Republic Pictures
Associate Producer: Ben Pivar
(unrealized project)

On Official Duty *
Republic Pictures
Associate Producer: Ben Pivar
(unrealized project)

Universal, 1939-1946

Mutiny on the Blackhawk
Universal Pictures
Released August 1, 1939; 67 minutes; © June 28, 1939; working title *In Old California*
Cast: Richard Arlen (Captain Robert Lawrence), Andy Devine ("Slim" Collins), Constance Moore (Helen), Noah Beery (Captain), Guinn "Big Boy" Williams (Mate), Mala (Woni), Thurston Hall (Sam Bailey), Sandra Kane (Tania), Paul Fix (Jock), Richard Lane (Kit Carson), Mabel Albertson (Widow), Charles Trowbridge (General Freemont), Bill Moore (Sailor), Byron Foulger (Coombs), Francisco Maran (General Romero), Eddy Waller (Parson), Mamo Clark (Mamo)
Screenplay: Michael S. Simmons; based on Ben Pivar's Original Story *In Old California*; Director of Photography: John W. Boyle; Art Director: Jack Otterson; Associate: Ralph M. DeLacy; Film Editor: Maurice Wright; Musical Director: Charles Previn; Sound Supervisor: Bernard B. Brown; Technician: William Fox; Gowns: Vera West; Set Decorations: R.A. Gausman; Director: Christy Cabanne; Associate Producer: Ben Pivar

Tropic Fury
Universal Pictures
Released October 13, 1939; 62 minutes; © September 12, 1939
Cast: Richard Arlen (Dan Burton), Andy Devine (Tynan "Tiny" Andrews), Beverly Roberts (Judith Adams/Taylor), Lou Merrill (Scipio), Lupita Tovar (Maria), Samuel S. Hinds (J.P. Waterford), Charles Trowbridge (Dr. Taylor), Leonard Mudie (J.T.M. Gallon), Adia Kuznetzoff (Soledad), Noble Johnson (Hannibal), Frank Mitchell (Amando), Milburne [sic] Stone (Thomas E. Snell)
Screenplay: Michael L. Simmons; based on the original story *Fury in the Tropics* by Ben Pivar (not credited) and Maurice Tombragel; Director of Photography: Jerome Ash; Art Director: Jack Otterson; Associate: Ralph M. DeLacy; Film Editor: Maurice Wright; Musical Director: Charles Previn; Sound Supervisor: Bernard B. Brown; Technician: Jess Moulin; Gowns: Vera West; Set Decorations: R.A. Gausman; Producer: Ben Pivar; Director: Christy Cabanne

Legion of Lost Flyers
Universal Pictures
Released November 3, 1939; 63 minutes; © September 15, 1939
Cast: Richard Arlen (Gene "Loop" Gillan), Andy Devine ("Beef" Brumley), Anne Nagel (Paula), William Lundigan (Ralph Perry), Guinn "Big Boy" Williams (Jake Halley), Ona Munson (Martha), Theodor Von Eltz (Bill Desert), Jack Carson (Larry Barrigan), Jerry Marlowe (Freddy Sims), Leon Belasco ("Frenchy"), David Willock ("Blinkey"), Edith Mills (Bertha), Leon Ames (Smythe), Pat

Flaherty (Sam Bradford), Eddy Waller (Petey)
Screenplay: Maurice Tombragel; Original Story: Ben Pivar; Director of Photography: Jerome Ash; Art Director: Jack Otterson; Associate: Harold M. MacArthur; Film Editor: Maurice Wright; Musical Director: Hans J. Salter; Sound Supervisor: Bernard B. Brown; Technician: Charles Carroll; Gowns: Vera West; Set Decorations: R.A. Gausman; Producer: Ben Pivar; Director: Christy Cabanne

Man from Montreal
Universal Pictures
Released December 8, 1939; 60 minutes; © November 8, 1939
Cast: Richard Arlen (Clark Manning), Andy Devine (Constable "Bones" Blair), Kay Sutton (Myrna Montgomery), Anne Gwynne (Doris Blair), Reed Hadley (Ross Montgomery), Addison Richards (Captain Owens), Joseph Sawyer (Biff Anders), Jerry Marlowe (Jim Morris), Tommy Whitten (Brad Owens), Eddy C. Waller (Old Jacques), Eddy Conrad (Marcel Bircheaux), William Royle (Luther St. Paul), Lane Chandler (Constable Rankin)
Screenplay: Owen Francis; Original Story: Ben Pivar; Director of Photography: Milton Krasner; Art Director: Jack Otterson; Associate: Harold H. MacArthur; Film Editor: Maurice Wright; Musical Director: Hans J. Salter; Sound Supervisor: Bernard B. Brown; Technician: Robert Pritchard; Gowns: Vera West; Set Decorations: R.A. Gausman; Producer: Ben Pivar; Director: Christy Cabanne

Danger on Wheels
Universal Pictures
Released February 2, 1940; 61 minutes; © December 31, 1939
Cast: Richard Arlen ("Lucky" Larry Taylor), Andy Devine ("Guppy" Wexel), Peggy Moran (Pat O'Shea), Jack Arnold (Bruce Crowley), Herbert Corthell ("Pop" O'Shea), Sandra King (June Allen), Landers Stevens (Lloyd B. Allen), Harry C. Bradley (Jones), Mary Treen (Esme), John Holmes (Eddie Dodds), Jack Rice (Parker)
Screenplay: Maurice Tombragel; Original Story: Ben Pivar (*Test Driver*); Director of Photography: Elwood Bredell; Art Director: Jack Otterson; Associate: Harold H. MacArthur; Film Editor: Maurice Wright; Musical Director: H.J. Salter; Sound Supervision: Bernard B. Brown; Technician: Jesse Bastian; Gowns: Vera West; Set Decorations: R.A. Gausman; Producer: Ben Pivar; Director: Christy Cabanne

Framed
Universal Pictures
Released February 23, 1940; 61 minutes; © December 31, 1939; working title *Trouble's My Middle Name*
Cast: Frank Albertson (Henry T. Parker), Constance Moore (Phyllis Sanderson),

Jerome Cowan (Monty de Granville), Robert Armstrong (Skippy), Sidney Blackmer (Tony Bowman), Judith Allen (Gwen Porter), Herbert Rawlinson (Walter Billings), Jack Arnold (Nick), Milburn Stone (Matthew Mattison), Barbara Pepper (Goldie Green)
Original Screenplay: Roy Chanslor, based on his original story *Trouble is My Middle Name*; Director of Photography: Jerome Ash; Art Direction: Jack Otterson; Associate: Ralph M. DeLacy; Film Editor: Otto Ludwig; Music Director: H.J. Salter; Sound Supervisor: Bernard B. Brown; Technician: Charles Carroll; Gowns: Vera West; Set Decorations: R.A. Gausman; Producer: Ben Pivar; Director: Harold Schuster

Double Alibi
Universal Pictures
Released March 1, 1940; 60 minutes; © February 16, 1940; working title *The Devil is Yellow*
Cast: Wayne Morris (Stephen Wayne), Margaret Lindsay (Sue Carey), William Gargan (Walter Gifford), Roscoe Karns (Jeremiah Jenkins), Robert Emmett Keane (Chick Lester), James Burke (Captain Orr), William Pawley (Dan Krally), Eddie Chandler (Patrolman Harrigan), Cliff Clark (Inspector Early), Emmet O'Connor (Patrolman Delaney), Wade Boteler (Bartender)
Screenplay: Harold Buchman, Roy Chanslor, and Charles Grayson; based on Frederick C. Davis' original story *The Devil is Yellow*; Director of Photography: Elwood Bredell; Art Direction: Jack Otterson; Associate: Ralph M. DeLacy; Film Editor: Ted Kent; Musical Director: H.J. Salter; Sound Supervisor: Bernard B. Brown; Technician: Robert Pritchard; Gowns: Vera West; Set Decorations: R.A. Gausman; Associate Producer: Ben Pivar; Director: Philip Rosen

Zanzibar
Universal Pictures
Released March 8, 1940; 70 minutes; © February 26, 1940; working title *The River of Missing Men*
Cast: Lola Lane (Jan Browning), James Craig (Steve Marland), Eduardo Ciannelli (Koski), Tom Fadden (Rhad Ramsey), Clarence Muse (Bino), Samuel S. Hinds (Dale), Robert C. Fischer (The Sultan), Henry Victor (Mate Simpson), Oscar O'Shea (Captain Craig), Abner Biberman (Aba), Lionel Pape (Michael Drayton), Everett Brown (Umboga), Harry Stubbs (Alf), Ray Mala (Mayla)
Original Screenplay: Maurice Tombragel and Maurice Wright; Associate Producer: Ben Pivar; Director of Photography: Milton Krasner; Art Direction: Jack Otterson; Associate: Ralph M. DeLacy; Film Editor: Milton Carruth; Set Decorations: R.A. Gausman; Gowns: Vera West; Musical Director: H.J. Salter; Sound Supervisor: Bernard B. Brown; Technician: William Hedgcock; Producer: Warren Douglas; Director: Harold Schuster

Enemy Agent
Universal Pictures
Released April 19, 1940; 61 minutes; © March 28, 1940
Cast: Richard Cromwell (Jimmy Saunders), Helen Vinson (Irene Hunter), Robert Armstrong (Gordon), Marjorie Reynolds (Peggy O'Reilly), Jack Arnold (Lester Taylor), Russell Hicks (Lyman Scott), Philip Dorn (Dr. Jeffry Arnold), Jack LaRue (Alex), Bradley Page (Francis), Abner Biberman (Baronoff), Luis Alberni (A. Calteroni), Jack Carson (Ralph), Milburn Stone (Meeker)
Screenplay: Sam Robins and Edmund L. Hartmann, based on Sam Robins' original story *Enemy Alien*; Director of Photography: Jerome Ash; Art Direction: Jack Otterson; Associate: Harold H. MacArthur; Film Editor: Ted Kent; Musical Director: H.J. Salter; Gowns: Vera West; Set Decorations: R.A. Gausman; Sound Supervisor: Bernard B. Brown; Technician: William Fox; Associate Producer: Ben Pivar; Director: Lew Landers

Ski Patrol
Universal Pictures
Released May 10, 1940; 64 minutes; © May 9, 1940; remake of *The Doomed Battalion* (1932)
Cast: Philip Dorn (Lt. Viktor Ryder), Luli Deste (Julia Engle), Stanley Fields (Birger Simberg), Samuel S. Hinds (Per Vallgren), Edward Norris (Paavo Luuki), John Qualen (Gustaf Nerkuu), Hardie Albright (Tyko Gallen), John Arledge (Dick Reynolds), John Ellis (Knut Vallgren), Henry Brandon (Jan Sikorsky), Kathryn Adams (Lissa Ryder), Abner Biberman (Commanding Officer), Wade Boteler (Speaker), Addison Richards (James Burton), Reed Hadley (Ivan Dubrosky), Trevor Bardette (Aranoff), John Gallaudet (Prisoner), Jodi Gilbert (Fanni), Christian Rub (Sorenson), Leona Roberts (Viktor's Mother)
Original Screenplay: Paul Huston; Associate Producer: Ben Pivar; Director of Photography: Milton Krasner; Art Direction: Jack Otterson; Associate: Ralph M. DeLacy; Film Editor: Ed Curtis; Musical Director: H.J. Salter; Set Decorations: R.A. Gausman; Sound Supervisor: Bernard B. Brown; Technician: Robert Pritchard; Producer: Warren Douglas; Director: Lew Landers

Alias the Deacon
Universal Pictures
Released May 17, 1940; 75 minutes; © April 15, 1940; remake of *Half a Sinner* (1934)
Cast: Bob Burns (Deke Caswell), Mischa Auer (Andre), Peggy Moran (Phyllis), Dennis O'Keefe (Johnny Sloan), Edward Brophy (Stuffy), Thurston Hall (Jim Cunningham), Spencer Charters (Sheriff Yates), Jack Carson (Sullivan), Guinn Williams ("Bull" Gumbatz), Virginia Brissac (Elsie Clark), Bennie Bartlett

(Willie Clark), Mira McKinney (Mrs. Gregory), Janet Shaw (Mildred Gregory)
Screenplay: Nat Perrin and Charles Grayson, based on the stage play by John B. Hymer and LeRoy Clemens; Associate Producer: Ben Pivar; Director of Photography: Stanley Cortez; Art Direction: Jack Otterson; Associate: Harold B. MacArthur; Film Editor: Milton Carruth; Musical Director: H.J. Salter; Sound Supervisor: Bernard B. Brown; Set Decorations: R.A. Gausman; Technician: Robert Pritchard; Executive Producer: Warren Douglas; Director: Christy Cabanne

Hot Steel
Universal Pictures
Released May 24, 1940; 61 minutes; © May 24, 1940
Cast: Richard Arlen (Frank Stewart), Andy Devine (Matt Morrison), Peggy Moran (Beatrice "Bebe" Morrison), Donald Briggs (George Barnes), Anne Nagel (Rita Martin), Joe Besser (Siggie Landers), Wade Boteler (Joe Farley), William Wayne (Dave Martin), James Flavin (Storm Swenson), Robert Emmet O'Connor (Inspector), Myra McKinney (Elvira Appleby), Dorothy Vaughn (Mrs. Morrison), Edward McWade (Carleton)
Screenplay: Clarence Upson Young and Maurice Tombragel; Original Story: Maurice Tombragel; Director of Photography: William Sickner; Art Director: Jack Otterson; Associate: Richard H. Riedel; Film Editor: Ed Curtiss; Musical Director: H.J. Salter; Sound Supervisor: Bernard B. Brown; Technician: William Hedgcock; Gowns: Vera West; Set Decorations: R.A. Gausman; Producer: Ben Pivar; Director: Christy Cabanne

Black Diamonds
Universal Pictures
Released July 16, 1940; 60 minutes; © July 9, 1940
Cast: Richard Arlen (Walter Norton), Andy Devine (Barney Tolliver), Kathryn Adams (Linda Connor), Paul Fix (Matthews), Mary Treen (Nina Norton), Cliff Clark (Mr. Connor), Pat Flaherty (Johnson), Maude Allen (Mrs. Norton), James Norton (Stacey), Tom Chatterton (Dr. Lukas), Henry Roquemore (Editor), Claire Du Brey (Secretary)
Screenplay: Clarence Upson Young and Sam Robins; Original Story: Sam Robins; Director of Photography: William Sickner; Art Director: Jack Otterson; Associate: Harold H. MacArthur; Film Editor: Ted Kent; Musical Director: H.J. Salter; Sound Supervisor: Bernard B. Brown; Technician: Charles Carroll; Gowns: Vera West; Set Decorations: R.A. Gausman; Producer: Ben Pivar; Director: Christy Cabanne

The Leather Pushers
Universal Pictures
Released September 13, 1940; 64 minutes; © September 11, 1940
Cast: Richard Arlen (Dick), Andy Devine (Andy), Astrid Allwyn (Pat), Douglas Fowley (Slick), Charles D. Brown (Stevens), Horace MacMahon (Slugger), Shemp Howard (Sailor), Charles Lane (Mitchell), Wade Boteler (Commissioner), George Lloyd (Joe), Eddie Gribbon (Pete), Frank Mitchell (Grogan's Manager), Reed Kilpatrick (Commentator), Ben Alexander (Announcer), Billy McGowan (Tim Grogan), Nobel "Kid" Chissel (Givanni)
Screenplay: Larry Rhine, Ben Chapman, and Maxwell Shane; Director of Photography: Stanley Cortez; Art Director: Jack Otterson; Associate: Ralph M. DeLacy; Film Editor: Arthur Hilton; Musical Director: H.J. Salter; Sound Supervisor: Bernard B. Brown; Technician: Hal Bumbaugh; Gowns: Vera West; Set Decorations: R.A. Gausman; Dialogue Director: Maurice Wright; Associate Producer: Ben Pivar; Director: John Rawlins

The Mummy's Hand
Universal Pictures
Released September 20, 1940; 67 minutes; © August 23, 1940; sequel to *The Mummy*
Cast: Dick Foran (Steve Banning), Peggy Moran (Marta Solvani), Wallace Ford (Babe Jenson), Eduardo Ciannelli (High Priest), George Zucco (Andoheb), Cecil Kellaway (Mr. Solvani), Charles Trowbridge (Dr. Petrie), Tom Tyler (Kharis), Siegfried Arno (The Beggar), Eddie Foster (Egyptian), Harry Stubbs (Bartender), Michael Mark (Bazaar Owner), Mara Tartar (Girl), Leon Belasco (Ali)
Screenplay: Griffin Jay and Maxwell Shane, based on an original story by Griffin Jay; Director of Photography: Elwood Bredell; Art Direction: Jack Otterson; Associate: Ralph M. DeLacy; Film Editor: Philip Cahn; Musical Director: H.J. Salter; Sound Supervisor: Bernard B. Brown; Technician: Charles Carroll; Gowns; Vera West; Set Decorations: R.A. Gausman; Producer: Ben Pivar; Director: Christy Cabanne

The Devil's Pipeline
Universal Pictures
Released November 1, 1940; 65 minutes; © October 24, 1940; working title *South of Sumatra*
Cast: Richard Arlen (Dick Talbot), Andy Devine (Andy Jennings), John Eldredge (Butler), Jeanne Kelly (Laura Larson), Francis McDonald (Gaddi Sang), James Flavin (Dowling), Ray Mala (Talamu), Eddy Waller (Benedict), Dorothy Appleby (Stewardess), Emory Parnell (Mr. Adams), Jay Novello (Bandad), Dick Botiller (Molugi), John Rogers (Edwards)

Screenplay: Paul Huston, Clarence Upson Young, Larry Rhine, and Ben Chapman; based on Huston's
original story *Isle of Missing Men*; Director of Photography: John Boyle; Art Director: Jack Otterson; Associate: Harold H. MacArthur; Film Editor: E. Curtis; Musical Director: H.J. Salter; Sound Supervisor: Bernard B. Brown; Technician: Hal Bumbaugh; Gowns: Vera West; Set Decorations: R.A. Gausman; Dialogue Director: Maurice Wright; Producer: Ben Pivar; Director: Christy Cabanne

Lucky Devils
Universal Pictures
Released January 3, 1941; 62 minutes; © December 23, 1940
Cast: Richard Arlen (Dick McManus), Andy Devine (Andy Tompkins), Dorothy Lovett (Norma Bishop), Janet Shaw (Gwendy Wemple), Jack Arnold (Bradford), Gus Schilling (Aloysius Grimshaw), Ralf Harolde (R.W. Ritter), Dick Terry (Berko), Tim Ryan (Momsen), James Morton (Exposition Guard), Gladys Blake (Secretary), William Forrest (Chandler), Robert Winkler (Mopey), Shemp Howard (Pickpocket)
Screenplay: Alex Gottlieb; Original Story: Sam Robins; Director of Photography: Charles Van Enger; Art Direction: Jack Otterson; Associate: Ralph M. DeLacy; Film Editor: Ed Curtiss; Musical Director: H.J. Salter; Dialogue Director: Maurice Wright; Sound Supervisor: Bernard B. Brown; Technician: Hal Bumbaugh; Set Decorations: R.A. Gausman; Gowns: Vera West; Producer: Ben Pivar; Director: Lew Landers

Horror Island
Universal Pictures
Released March 28, 1941; 60 minutes; © April 2, 1941
Cast: Dick Foran (Bill Martin), Leo Carrillo (Tobias), Peggy Moran (Wendy Creighton), Fuzzy Knight (Stuff), John Eldredge (George), Lewis Howard (Thurman Coldwater), Hobart Cavanaugh (Professor Jasper), Walter Catlett (McGoon), Ralf Harolde (Rod "Killer" Grady), Iris Adrian (Arleen), Foy Van Dolsen (The Phantom), Emmett Vogan (The Strangler)
Screenplay: Maurice Tombragel and Victor McLeod; based on Alex Gottlieb's original story *Terror of the South Seas*; Director of Photography: Elwood Bredell; Art Direction: Jack Otterson; Associate: Ralph M. DeLacy; Film Editing: Otto Ludwig; Musical Director: H.J. Salter; Gowns: Vera West; Set Decorations: R.A. Gausman; Sound Supervisor: Bernard B. Brown; Technician: Jess Moulin; A Ben Pivar Production; Associate Producer: Jack Bernhard; Director: George Waggner

The Films of Ben Pivar

Mutiny in the Arctic
Universal Pictures
Released April 18, 1941; 61 minutes; © April 21, 1941
Cast: Richard Arlen (Dick Barclay), Andy Devine (Andy Adams), Anne Nagel (Gloria Adams), Addison Richards (Ferguson), Don Terry (Cole), Oscar O'Shea (Captain Morrissey), Harry Cording (Harmon), Jeff Corey (Cook), Harry Strang (Helmsman), John Rogers (Mess Boy)
Screenplay: Maurice Tombragel and Victor McLeod; Original Story: Paul Huston; Director of Photography: John W. Boyle; Art Director: Jack Otterson; Associate: Ralph M. DeLacy; Film Editor: Ed Curtiss; Musical Director: H.J. Salter; Sound Supervisor: Bernard B. Brown; Technician: Robert Pritchard; Gowns: Vera West; Set Decorations: R.A. Gausman; Dialogue Director: Maurice Wright; Associate Producer: Ben Pivar; Director: John Rawlins

Men of the Timberland
Universal Pictures
Released June 6, 1941; 61 minutes; © June 9, 1941
Cast: Richard Arlen (Dick O'Hara), Andy Devine (Andy Jensen), Linda Hayes (Kay Hadley), Francis McDonald (Jean Collet), Willard Robertson (Tim MacGregor), Paul E. Burns (Lucky), Gaylord Pendleton (Tex), Hardie Albright (Jim Dudley), Roy Harris (Withers), John Ellis (Ranger), Jack Rice (Secretary)
Screenplay: Maurice Tombragel and Griffin Jay; Original Story: Paul Jarrico; Director of Photography: John W. Boyle; Art Director: Jack Otterson; Associate: Ralph M. DeLacy; Film Editor: Milton Carruth; Musical Director: H.J. Salter; Dialogue Director: Maurice Wright; Sound Supervisor: Bernard B. Brown; Technician: Jess Moulin; Set Decorations: R.A. Gausman; Associate Producer: Ben Pivar; Director: John Rawlins

Raiders of the Desert
Universal Pictures
Released July 25, 1941; 60 minutes; © July 16, 1941; working title *Return of the Sheik*
Cast: Richard Arlen (Dick), Andy Devine (Andy), Linda Hayes (Alice), Maria Montez (Zuleika), Lewis Howard (Abdullah), Ralf Harolde (Talifah), George Carleton (Jones), Turban [sic] Bey (Hassen), Harry Cording (Rawlins), Sig Arno (Suliman), Neyle Marx (Zeid), John Harmon (Ahmed)
Original Screenplay: Maurice Tombragel and Victor I. McLeod; Director of Photography: John W. Boyle; Art Director: Jack Otterson; Associate: Harold H. MacArthur; Film Editor: Maurice Wright; Musical Director: H.J. Salter; Sound Supervisor: Bernard B. Brown; Technician: Hal Bumbaugh; Set Decorations: R.A. Gausman; Associate Producer: Ben Pivar; Director: John Rawlins

A Dangerous Game
Universal Pictures
Released August 22, 1941 (NYC release March 3, 1941); 63 minutes; © December 19, 1940
Cast: Richard Arlen (Dick Williams), Andy Devine (Andy McAllister), Jeanne Kelly (Anne Bennett), Edward Brophy (Bugs), Marc Lawrence (Joe), Robert O. Davis (Fleming), Richard Carle (Agatha), Andrew Toombes (Silas Biggsby), Tom Dugan (Clem), Vince Barnett (Ephriam), Mira McKinney (Mrs. Hubbard), Richard Kean (Whipple), Irving Mitchell (Robin), George Pembroke (Olaf Anderson)
Screenplay: Larry Rhine, Ben Chapman, and Maxwell Shane; Original Story: Larry Rhine and Ben Chapman; Director of Photography: Stanley Cortez; Art Direction: Jack Otterson; Associate: Harold H. MacArthur; Film Editor: Ray Curtiss; Musical Director: H.J. Salter; Sound Supervisor: Bernard B. Brown; Technician: Robert Pritchard; Gowns: Vera West; Set Decorations: R.A. Gausman; Dialogue Director: Maurice Wright; Producer: Ben Pivar; Director: John Rawlins

The Kid from Kansas
Universal Pictures
Released September 19, 1941; 60 minutes; © September 11, 1941
Cast: Dick Foran (Kansas), Leo Carrillo (Pancho), Andy Devine (Andy), Ann Doran (Smitty), Francis McDonald (Cesar), James Seay (Walker), Marcia Ralston (Linda), Nestor Paiva (Jamaica), Antonio Moreno (Chief of Police), Leyland Hodgson (York), Wade Boteler (Russell), Guy Usher (Maloney)
Screenplay: Griffin Jay and David Silverstein; Original Story: Griffin Jay; Director of Photography: John W. Boyle; Art Director: Jack Otterson; Associate: Ralph M. DeLacy; Film Editor: Arthur Hilton; Musical Director: H.J. Salter; Sound Supervisor: Bernard B. Brown; Technician: Robert Pritchard; Gowns: Vera West; Set Decorations: R.A. Gausman; Associate Producer: Ben Pivar; Director: William Nigh

Road Agent
Universal Pictures
Released December 19, 1941; 63 minutes; © December 8, 1941
Cast: Dick Foran (Duke Masters), Leo Carrillo (Pancho), Andy Devine (Andy), Anne Gwynne (Patricia Leavitt), Samuel S. Hinds (Sam Leavitt), Richard Davies (Tom Martin), Anne Nagel (Lola), Morris Ankrum (Big John Morgan), John Gallaudet (Steve), Reed Hadley (Shayne), Eddy Waller (Lewis), Ernie Adams and Lew Kelly (Jake and Luke)
Screenplay: Morgan Cox, Arthur Strawn, and Maurice Tombragel; Original Story: Sherman Lowe and Arthur St. Claire; Director of Photography: Jerome

Ash; Art Director: Jack Otterson; Associate: Ralph M. DeLacy; Film Editor: Frank Gross; Musical Director: H.J. Salter; Sound Director: Bernard B. Brown; Technician: Robert Pritchard; Gowns: Vera West; Set Decorations: R.A. Gausman; Associate Producer: Ben Pivar; Director: Charles Lamont; Songs: "Cielito Lindo" by Quirino Mendoza y Cortés, and "Ridin' Home" by Jimmy McHugh and Harold Adamson; both sung by Dick Foran

Unseen Enemy
Universal Pictures
Released April 10, 1942; 61 minutes; © March 16, 1942
Cast: Irene Hervey (Gen Rand), Don Terry (William "Bill" Hancock), Leo Carrillo (Nick Rand), Andy Devine (Sam Dillon), Lionel Royce (Wilhelm Roering), Turhan Bey (Ito), Frederick Gierman (Franz Muller), William Ruhl (Callahan), Clancy Cooper (Davies), Eddie Featherstone (Badger)
Screenplay: Roy Chanslor and Stanley Rubin; Original Idea: George Wallace Sayre; Director of Photography: John W. Boyle; Art Direction: Jack Otterson; Associate: Harold H. MacArthur; Film Editor: Edward Curtiss; Musical Director: Charles Previn; Sound Supervisor: Bernard B. Brown; Technician: William Fox; Gowns: Vera West; Set Decorations: R.A. Gausman; Dialogue Director: Harold Erickson; Associate Producer: Marshall Grant; Director: John Rawlins

Escape from Hong Kong
Universal Pictures
Released May 19, 1942; 60 minutes; © May 8, 1942
Cast: Leo Carrillo (Pancho), Andy Devine (Blimp), Marjorie Lord (Valarie Hale), Don Terry (Rusty), Gilbert Emery (Col. J.A. Crossley), Leyland Hodgson (Major Reeves, aka Von Metz), Frank Puglia (Kosura), Chester Gan (Yamota), Frank Kelly (Sergeant), Paul Dubov (Franz Schuler)
Original Screenplay: Roy Chanslor; Director of Photography: Woody Bredell; Art Direction: Jack Otterson; Associate: Ralph M. DeLacy; Film Editor: Maurice Wright; Musical Director: Charles Previn; Sound Director: Bernard B. Brown; Technician: Paul Neal; Gowns: Vera West; Set Decorations: R.A. Gausman; Associate Producer: Marshall Grant; Director: William Nigh

Top Sergeant
Universal Pictures
Released June 12, 1942; 64 minutes; © June 2, 1942; working title *Showdown*
Cast: Leo Carrillo (Frenchy Devereaux), Andy Devine (Andy Jarrett), Don Terry (Dick Manson), Elyse Knox (Helen Gray), Don Porter (Al Bennett), Addison Richards (Colonel Gray), Bradley Page (Tony Gribaldi), Gene Garrick (Jack Manson), Alan Hale, Jr. (Cruxton), Roy Harris (Roy), Richard Davies (Phil), Emmett Vogan (Prosecuting Officer)

Screenplay: Maxwell Shane and Griffin Jay; Original Story: Larry Rhine and Ben Chapman; Director of Photography: George Robinson; Art Director: Jack Otterson; Associate: Richard H. Riedel; Film Editor: Milton Carruth; Musical Director: H.J. Salter; Sound Director: Bernard B. Brown; Technician: Paul Neill; Set Decorations: R.A. Gausman; Associate Producer: Ben Pivar; Director: Christy Cabanne

Danger in the Pacific
Universal Pictures
Released July 10, 1942; 60 minutes; © July 7, 1942
Cast: Leo Carrillo (Leo Marzell), Andy Devine (Andy Parker), Don Terry (David Lynd), Louise Allbritton (Jane Claymore), Edgar Barrier (Zambesi), Turhan Bey (Tagani), Holmes Herbert (Commissioner), David Hoffman (Storekeeper), Paul Dubov (Manolo), Neyle Marx (Lobo), Dwight Frye (Hotel Desk Clerk; not credited)
Screenplay: Walter Doniger and Maurice Tombragel; Original Story: Neil P. Varnick and Walter Doniger; Director of Photography: William Sickner; Art Director: Jack Otterson; Associate: Harold H. MacArthur; Film Editor: Maurice Wright; Musical Director: H.J. Salter; Sound Director: Bernard B. Brown; Technician: Jess Moulin; Set Decorations: R.A. Gausman; Associate Producer: Ben Pivar; Director: Lewis D. Collins

Timber
Universal Pictures
Released August 14, 1942; 60 minutes; © July 21, 1942
Cast: Leo Carrillo (Quebec), Andy Devine (Arizona), Dan Dailey, Jr. (Kansas), Marjorie Lord (Yvette Lacour), Edmund MacDonald (Pierre Lacour), Wade Boteler (Dan Crowley), Nestor Paiva (Jules Fabian), Paul Burns (Pop Turner), James Seay (Joe Radway), Jean Philips (Ann Barrows), William Hale (Bill Cormack), Walter Sande (Sandy)
Screenplay: Griffin Jay, based on an original story by Larry Rhine and Ben Chapman; Director of Photography: Jack MacKenzie; Art Direction: Jack Otterson; Associate: Ralph M. DeLacy; Film Editor: Otto Ludwig; Musical Director: H.J. Salter; Sound Supervisor: Bernard B. Brown; Technician: Glenn Anderson; Set Decorations: R.A. Gausman; Associate: J. Andrew Gilmore; Associate Producer: Ben Pivar; Director: Christy Cabanne

The Mummy's Tomb
Universal Pictures
Released October 23, 1942; 61 minutes; © August 19, 1942; sequel to *The Mummy's Hand*
Cast: Lon Chaney (Kharis), Dick Foran (Steve Banning), John Hubbard (Dr. John

Banning), Elyse Knox (Isobel Evans), George Zucco (Andoheb), Wallace Ford (Babe Hanson), Turhan Bey (Mehemet Bey), Virginia Brissac (Mrs. Evans), Cliff Clark (Sheriff), Mary Gordon (Jane Banning), Paul E. Burns (Jim), Frank Reicher (Professor Norman), Emmett Vogan (Coroner)
Screenplay: Griffin Jay and Henry Sucher; Original Story: Neil P. Varnick; Director of Photography: George Robinson; Art Direction: Jack Otterson; Associate: Ralph M. DeLacy; Film Editor: Milton Carruth; Musical Director: H.J. Salter; Sound Direction: Bernard B. Brown; Technician: William Schwartz; Set Decorations: R.A. Gausman; Associate: J. Andrew Gilmore; Makeup: Jack Pierce; Gowns: Vera West; Assistant Director: Charles Gould; Associate Producer: Ben Pivar; Director: Harold Young

Eyes of the Underworld
Universal Pictures
Released January 8, 1943; 61 minutes; © May 19, 1942
Cast: Richard Dix (Chief Richard Bryan), Wendy Barrie (Betty Standing), Lloyd Corrigan (J.C. Thomas), Don Porter (Edward Jason), Billy Lee (Mickey Bryan), Lon Chaney (Benny), Marc Lawrence (Gordon Finch), Edward Pawley (Lance Merlin), Joseph Crehan (Kirby), Wade Boteler (Sgt. Clancy), Gaylord Pendleton (Hub Gelsey), Mike Raffetto (District Attorney)
Screenplay: Michael L. Simmons and Arthur Strawn; Original Story: Maxwell Shane; Director of Photography: George Robinson; Art Direction: Jack Otterson; Associate: Harold H. MacArthur; Film Editor: Frank Gross; Musical Director: H.J. Salter; Sound Direction: Bernard B. Brown; Technician: William Hedgcock; Gowns: Vera West; Set Decorations: R.A. Gausman; Associate Producer: Ben Pivar; Director: Roy William Neill

Keep 'em Slugging
Universal Pictures
Released April 2, 1943; 60 minutes; © January 5, 1943; pre-production title *Bad Company*
Cast: Huntz Hall (Albert "Pig" Gumm), Bobby Jordan (Tommy Banning), Gabriel Dell (String), Norman Abbott (Ape), Evelyn Ankers (Sheila), Elyse Knox (Suzanne Booker), Frank Albertson (Frank Moulton), Don Porter (Jerry "Brady" Carruthers), Shemp Howard (Binky), Samuel S. Hinds (Carruthers), Mary Gordon (Mrs. Banning), Milburn Stone (Duke Rodman), Joan Marsh (Lola LaVerne)
Screenplay: Brenda Weisberg; Original Story: Edward Handler and Robert Gordon; Director of Photography: William Sickner; Art Direction: John Goodman: Associate: Ralph M. DeLacy; Director of Sound: Bernard B. Brown; Technician: Paul Neal; Set Decorations: R.A. Gausman; Associate: E.R.

Robinson; Film Editor: Ray Snyder; Musical Director: H.J. Salter; Gowns: Vera West; Associate Producer: Ben Pivar; Director: Christy Cabanne

Captive Wild Woman
Universal Pictures
Released June 4, 1943; 61 minutes; © May 11, 1943
Cast: John Carradine (Dr. Sigmund Walters), Evelyn Ankers (Beth Colman), Milburn Stone (Fred Mason), Lloyd Corrigan (John Whipple), Acquanetta (Paula Dupree), Fay Helm (Miss Strand), Martha MacVicar (Dorothy Colman), Vince Barnett (Curley), Paul Fix (Gruen)
Screenplay: Griffin Jay and Henry Sucher; Original Story: Ted Fithian and Neil P. Varnick (and Maurice Pivar, not credited); Director of Photography: George Robinson; Art Direction: John B. Goodman and Ralph DeLacy; Film Editor: Milton Carruth; Sound Direction: Bernard B. Brown; Technician: William Hedgcock; Musical Director: H.J. Salter; Gowns: Vera West; Set Decorations: R.A. Gausman and Ira S. Webb; Associate Producer: Ben Pivar; Director: Edward Dmytryk; Executive Producer: Jack Gross (not credited)

The Strange Death of Adolf Hitler
Universal Pictures
Released October 8, 1943; 72 minutes; © September 3, 1943
Cast: Ludwig Donath (Franz Huber), Gale Sondergaard (Anna Huber), George Dolenz (Herman Marbach), Fritz Kortner (Bauer), Ludwig Stossel (Graub), William Trenk (Col. Von Zechwitz), Joan Blair (Duchess Eugenie), Ivan Triesault (Hohenberg), Rudolph Anders (Mampe), Erno Verebes (Godeck), Merrill Rodin (Hansl), Charles Bates (Viki), Kurt Katch (Karl), Hans Schumm (Profe), Fred Gierman (Himmler), Richard Ryen (Palzer), John Mylong (General Halder), Kurt Kreuger (Youth Leader), Lester Sharpe (Dr. Kaltenbruch), Trude Berliner (Frau Reitler), Hans von Twardowsky (Judge), Wolfgang Zilzer (Attorney)
Screenplay: Fritz Kortner; Original Story: Fritz Kortner and Joe May; Director of Photography: Jerome Ash; Art Direction: John B. Goodman and Ralph DeLacy; Set Decorations: R.A. Gausman and E.R. Robinson; Film Editor: Milton Carruth; Gowns: Vera West; Director of Sound: Bernard B. Brown; Technician: William Hedgcock; Musical Score: H.J. Salter; Technical Advisor: Ernest Richter; Assistant Director: Joseph A. McDonough; Associate Producer: Ben Pivar; Director: James Hogan; Executive Producer: Joseph Gershenson (not credited)

The Mad Ghoul
Universal Pictures
Released November 12, 1943; 64 minutes; © October 7, 1943
Cast: David Bruce (Ted Allison), Evelyn Ankers (Isabel Lewis), George Zucco (Dr. Alfred Morris), Robert Armstrong (Ken McClure), Turhan Bey (Eric Iverson),

Milburn Stone (Macklin), Andrew Tombes (Eagan), Rose Hobart (Della Elliott), Addison Richards (Gavigan), Charles McGraw (Garrity)
Screenplay: Brenda Weisberg and Paul Gangelin; Original Story: Hans Kraly; Director of Photography: Milton Krasner; Art Direction: John B. Goodman and Martin Obzina; Sound Director: Jess Moulin; Set Decorations: R.A. Gausman and A.J. Gilmore; Musical Director: H.J. Salter; Film Editor: Milton Carruth; Gowns: Vera West; Associate Producer: Benjamin Pivar; Director: James Hogan; Executive Producer: Joseph Gershenson (not credited)

Calling Dr. Death
Universal Pictures
Released December 17, 1943; 62 minutes; © December 10, 1943; an *Inner Sanctum* mystery
Cast: Lon Chaney (Dr. Mark Steele), Patricia Morison (Nurse Stella Madden), J. Carrol Naish (Inspector Gregg), David Bruce (Robert Duval), Ramsay Ames (Maria Steele), Fay Helm (Mrs. Duval), Holmes Herbert (Brian the Butler), Alec Craig (Watchman), Fred Gierman (Father), Lisa Golm (Mother), Charles Wagenheim (Coroner), Mary Hale (Marion), George Eldredge (District Attorney), John Elliott (Priest)
Original Screenplay: Edward Dein; Director of Photography: Virgil Miller; Art Direction: John B. Goodman and Ralph M. DeLacy; Director of Sound: Bernard B. Brown; Technician: William Hedgcock; Set Decorations: R.A. Gausman and A.J. Gilmore; Musical Director: Paul Sawtell; Film Editor: Norman A. Cerf; Gowns: Vera West; Special Photography: John P. Fulton; Associate Producer: Ben Pivar; Director: Reginald LeBorg

Weird Woman
Universal Pictures
Released April 14, 1944; 63 minutes; © March 10, 1944; an *Inner Sanctum* mystery
Cast: Lon Chaney (Norman Reed), Anne Gwynne (Paula Reed), Evelyn Ankers (Ilona Carr), Ralph Morgan (Professor Millard Sawtelle), Elisabeth Risdon (Grace Gunnison), Lois Collier (Margaret Mercer), Elizabeth Russell (Evelyn Sawtelle), Harry Hayden (Professor Septimus Carr), Phil Brown (David Jennings), Jackie Lou Harding (Student)
Screenplay: Brenda Weisberg; Adaptation: W. Scott Darling; from Fritz Lieber, Jr.'s novel *Conjure Wife*; Director of Photography: Virgil Miller; Musical Director: Paul Sawtell; Art Direction: John B. Goodman and Richard Riedel; Director of Sound: Bernard B. Brown; Technician: William Hedgcock; Set Decorations: R.A. Gausman and A.J. Gilmore; Film Editor: Milton Carruth; Gowns: Vera West; Special Photography: John P. Fulton; Associate Producer: Oliver Drake; Director: Reginald LeBorg; Executive Producer: Ben Pivar (not credited)

Boss of Boomtown*
Universal Pictures
Released May 21, 1944; 58 minutes; © May 22, 1944
Cast: Rod Cameron (Sergeant Steve Hazard), Tom Tyler (Sergeant Jim Ward), Fuzzy Knight (Corporal Chatter T. Boxie), Vivian Austin (Dale Starr), Ray Whitley (Sergeant Clark), Jack Ingram (Sam Ridgeway), Robert Barron (Norman Brett), Marie Austin (Minerva Sawyer), Max Wagner (Sergeant Dunne), Sam Flint (Blaine Cornwall), Richard Alexander (Yuma), Forrest Taylor (Captain Hiller), Beverlee Mitchell (Saloon Girl)
Executive Producer: Ben Pivar (not credited); Associate Producer: Oliver Drake; Director: Ray Taylor; Assistant Director: Ralph Slosser; Screenplay: William Lively; Photography: William Sickner; Editor: Ted Kent

Jungle Woman
Universal Pictures
Released July 7, 1944; 54 minutes; © June 14, 1944; sequel to *Captive Wild Woman*
Cast: Evelyn Ankers (Beth), J. Carrol Naish (Dr. Fletcher), Samuel S. Hinds (Coroner), Lois Collier (Joan Fletcher), Milburn Stone (Fred Mason), Douglass Dumbrille (District Attorney), Acquanetta (Paula Dupree), Richard Davies (Bob Whitney), Nana Bryant (Miss Gray), Pierre Watkin (Dr. Meredith), Christian Rub (George), Alec Craig (Caretaker), Edward M. Hyans, Jr. (Willie), Richard Powers (Joe, Fingerprint Man)
Screenplay: Bernard Schubert, Henry Sucher, and Edward Dein; Original Story: Henry Sucher; Director of Photography: Jack MacKenzie; Musical Director: Paul Sawtell; Art Direction: John B. Goodman and Abraham Grossman; Director of Sound: Bernard B. Brown; Technician: Jess Moulin; Set Decorations: Russell A. Gausman and E.R. Robinson; Film Editor: Ray Snyder; Gowns: Vera West; Dialogue Director: Emory Horger; Associate Producer: Will Cowan; Director: Reginald LeBorg; Executive Producer: Ben Pivar (not credited)

The Mummy's Ghost
Universal Pictures
Released July 7, 1944; 61 minutes; © December 31, 1943; sequel to *The Mummy's Tomb*
Cast: John Carradine (Yousef Bey), Robert Lowery (Tom Hervey), Ramsay Ames (Amina), Barton MacLane (Inspector Walgreen), George Zucco (High Priest), Lon Chaney (Kharis), Frank Reicher (Professor Norman), Harry Shannon (Sheriff), Emmett Vogan (Coroner), Lester Sharpe (Dr. Ayad), Claire Whitney (Mrs. Norman), Oscar O'Shea (Watchman)
Screenplay: Griffin Jay, Henry Sucher, and Brenda Weisberg; Original Story:

Griffin Jay and Henry Sucher; Director of Photography: William Sickner; Art Direction: John B. Goodman and Abraham Grossman; Film Editor: Saul Goodkind; Musical Director: H.J. Salter; Sound Director: Bernard B. Brown; Technician: Jess Moulin; Set Decorations: R.A. Gausman and L.R. Smith; Make-Up Artist: Jack Pierce; Gowns: Vera West; Associate Producer: Ben Pivar; Director: Reginald LeBorg; Executive Producer: Joseph Gershenson (not credited)

Trigger Trail *
Universal Pictures
Released July 7, 1944; 59 minutes; © July 28, 1944
Cast: Rod Cameron (Clint Farrel), Fuzzy Knight (Echo), Eddie Dew (Bob Reynolds), Vivian Austin (Ann Catlett), Lane Chandler (Slade), George Eldredge (Rance Hudson), Robert "Buzz" Henry (Chip Kincaid), Davison Clark (Silas Farrel), Michael Vallon (Bender), Richard Alexander (Waco), Jack Rockwell (Joe Kincaid), Budd Buster (Tug Catlett), Bud Osborne (Coach Driver), Jack Ingram (Hogan), Roy Butler (Rancher), Ray Whitley
Executive Producer: Ben Pivar (not credited); Associate Producer: Oliver Drake; Director: Lewis D. Collins; Assistant Director: Scott Beal; Screenplay: Ed Earle Repp; Additional Dialog: Patricia Harper; Photography: William Sickner; Editor: Milton Carruth

Trail to Gunsight *
Universal Pictures
Released August 18, 1944; 57 minutes; © August 30, 1944
Cast: Eddie Dew (Dan Creede), Lyle Talbot (Bill Hollister), Fuzzy Knight (Horatius Van Sickle), Ray Whitley (Barton), Maris Wrixon (Mary Wagner), Robert "Buzz" Henry (Tim Wagner), Marie Austin (Clementine Van Sickle), Sarah Padden (Ma Wagner), Glenn Strange (Duke Ellis), Ray Bennett (Bert Nelson), Charles Morton (Reb Tanner), Michael Vallon (Bartender), Forrest Taylor (Sheriff), Jack Clifford (Sheriff), Terry Frost (John Wagner)
Executive Producer: Ben Pivar (not credited); Associate Producer: Oliver Drake; Director: Vernon Keays; Assistant Director: Scott Beal; Screenplay: Bennett Cohen; Original Story: Jay Karth; Additional Dialog: Patricia Harper; Photography: Maury Gertsman; Editor: Russell Schoengarth

Riders of the Santa Fe *
Universal Pictures
Released October, 1944; 60 minutes; © October 5, 1944
Cast: Rod Cameron (Matt Conway), Eddie Dew (Larry Anderson), Fuzzy Knight (Bullseye Johnson), Jennifer Holt (Carla Anderson), Lane Chandler (Earl Duncan), Earle Hodgins (Ed Milton), Ray Whitley (Hank), George Douglas (Tom

Benner), Dick Alexander (Biff MacCauley), Budd Buster (Otis Wade), Ida Moore (Luella Tucker), Vangie Beilby (Stevenson sister), Patsy O'Byrne (Stevenson sister), Sandra Morgan (Stevenson sister), Al Ferguson (Bartender), Jerome Sheldon (Mayor Henry Daws)
Executive Producer: Ben Pivar (not credited); Associate Producer: Oliver Drake; Director: Wallace Fox; Assistant Directors: Scott Beal and Ira Webb; Screenplay: Ande Lamb; Photography: Maury Gertsman; Editor: Ray Snyder

Dead Man's Eyes
Universal Pictures
Released November 10, 1944; 64 minutes; © October 25, 1944; an *Inner Sanctum* mystery
Cast: Lon Chaney (Dave Stuart), Jean Parker (Heather Hayden), Paul Kelly (Alan Bittaker), Thomas Gomez (Captain Drury), Jonathan Hale (Dr. Welles), Edward Fielding (Stanley Hayden), Acquanetta (Tanya Czoraki), George Meeker (Nick Phillips), Pierre Watkin (Attorney), Eddie Dunn (Policeman)
Original Screenplay: Dwight V. Babcock; Director of Photography: Paul Ivano; Musical Director: Paul Sawtell; Art Direction: John B. Goodman and Martin Obzina; Director of Sound: Bernard B. Brown; Technician: William Hedgcock; Set Decorations: Russell A. Gausman and Leigh Smith; Film Editor: Milton Carruth; Gowns: Vera West; Dialogue Director: Stacy Keach; Special Photography: John P. Fulton; Associate Producer: Will Cowan; Director: Reginald LeBorg; Executive Producer: Ben Pivar (not credited)

The Mummy's Curse
Universal Pictures
Released December 22, 1944; 62 minutes; © November 20, 1944; sequel to *The Mummy's Ghost*
Cast: Lon Chaney (Kharis), Peter Coe (Ilzor Zandaab), Virginia Christine (Princess Ananka), Kay Harding (Betty Walsh), Dennis Moore (Dr. James Halsey), Martin Kosleck (Ragheb), Kurt Katch (Cajun Joe), Addison Richards (Pat Walsh), Holmes Herbert (Dr. Cooper), Charles Stevens (Achilles), William Farnum (Sacristan), Napoleon Simpson (Goobie), Ann Codee (not credited)
Screenplay: Bernard Schubert; Original Story: Leon Abrams and Dwight V. Babcock; Director of Photography: Virgil Miller; Musical Director: Paul Sawtell; Art Direction: John B. Goodman and Martin Obzina; Director of Sound: Bernard B. Brown; Technician: Robert Pritchard; Set Decorations: Russell A. Gausman and Victor A. Gangelin; Film Editor: Fred R. Feitshans, Jr.; Music and Lyrics: Oliver Drake and Frank Orth; Special Photography: John P. Fulton; Associate Producer: Oliver Drake; Director: Leslie Goodwins; Executive Producer: Ben Pivar (not credited)

THE FILMS OF BEN PIVAR

Beyond the Pecos *
Universal Pictures
Released January 1945; 58 minutes; © November 20, 1944
Cast: Rod Cameron (Lew Remington), Eddie Dew (Bob Randall), Fuzzy Knight (Captain Barnacle Pete Finnegan), Jennifer Holt (Ellen Tanner), Ray Whitley (Dan Muncie), Eugene Stutenroth (John Heydrick), Robert Homans (Ed Remingon), Jack Ingram (Steve Grenfels), Frank Jaquet (Ord Tanner), Henry Wills (Arizona), Jack Rockwell (Keno Hawkins), Dan White (Sheriff), Al Ferguson (Deek Surrat), Jerome Sheldon (Sam), Buster Brodie (Baldy), Forrest Taylor (Doc Crane); Merle Travis (Slim Jones)
Executive Producer: Ben Pivar (not credited); Associate Producer: Oliver Drake; Director: Lambert Hillyer; Assistant Director: Scott Beal; Screenplay: Bennett R. Cohen; Original Story: Jay Karth; Photography: Maury Gertsman; Editor: Ray Snyder

Renegades of the Rio Grande
Universal Pictures
Released June 1, 1945; 57 minutes; © November 20, 1944
Cast: Rod Cameron (Buck Emerson), Eddie Dew (Cal Benedict), Fuzzy Knight (Trigger Bidwell), Jennifer Holt (Dolores Salezar), Ray Whitley (Tex Henry), The Bar-6 Cowboys, Glenn Strange (Bart Drummond), Edmund Cobb (Karl Holbrook), Richard Alexander (Pete Jackson), Iris Cleve (Maria), John James (Johnny Emerson)
Original Screenplay: Ande Lamb; Director of Photography: Maury Gertsman; Musical Director: Paul Sawtell; Art Direction: John B. Goodman and Harold H. MacArthur; Director of Sound: Bernard B. Brown; Technician: Glenn E. Anderson; Set Decorations: Russell A. Gausman and Ray L. Jeffers; Film Editor: Edward Curtiss; Associate Producer: Oliver Drake; Director: Howard Bretherton; Executive Producer: Ben Pivar (not credited)

The Jungle Captive
Universal Pictures
Released June 29, 1945; 63 minutes; © December 6, 1944; sequel to *Jungle Woman*; rereleased by Realart as *Wild Jungle Captive*
Cast: Otto Kruger (Dr. Stendahl), Amelita Ward (Ann Forrester), Phil Brown (Donald Young), Jerome Cowan (Harrigan), Rondo Hatton (Moloch), Vicky Lane (Paula Dupree), Eddie Acuff (Bill), Ernie Adams (Jim), Charles Wagenheim (Fred), Eddie Chandler (Motorcycle Cop), Jack Overman (Detective)
Screenplay: M. Coates Webster and Dwight V. Babcock; Original Story: Dwight V. Babcock; Director of Photography: Maury Gertsman; Musical Director: Paul Sawtell; Art Direction: John B. Goodman and Robert Clatworthy; Director of Sound: Bernard B. Brown; Technician: Robert Pritchard; Set Decorations:

Russell A. Gausman and A.J. Gilmore; Film Editor: Fred R. Feitshans, Jr.; Dialogue Director: Willard Holland; Costumes: Vera West; Associate Producer: Morgan B. Cox; Director: Harold Young; Executive Producer: Ben Pivar (not credited)

The Frozen Ghost
Universal Pictures
Released June 29, 1945; 61 minutes; © November 20, 1944; an *Inner Sanctum* mystery
Cast: Lon Chaney (Alex Gregor), Evelyn Ankers (Maura Daniel), Milburn Stone (George Keene), Douglass Dumbrille (Inspector Brant), Martin Kosleck (Rudi Poldan), Elena Verdugo (Nina Coudreau), Tala Birell (Mme. Valerie Monet), Arthur Hohl (Skeptic)
Screenplay: Bernard Schubert and Luci Ward; Original Story: Harrison Carter and Henry Sucher; Adaptation: Henry Sucher; Director of Photography: Paul Ivano; Musical Director: H.J. Salter; Art Direction: John B. Goodman and Abraham Grossman; Director of Sound: Bernard B. Brown; Technician: William Hedgcock; Set Decorations: Russell A. Gausman and Ray L. Jeffers; Film Editor: Fred R. Feitshans, Jr.; Dialogue Director: Edward Dein; Gowns: Vera West; Associate Producer: Will Cowan; Director: Harold Young; Executive Producer: Ben Pivar (not credited)

Strange Confession
Universal Pictures
Released October 5, 1945; 62 minutes; © September 28, 1945; an *Inner Sanctum* mystery; remake of *The Man Who Reclaimed His Head* (1935); pre-production title *The Missing Head*
Cast: Lon Chaney (Jeffrey Carter), Brenda Joyce (Mary Carter), J. Carrol Naish (Roger Graham), Milburn Stone (Stevens), Lloyd Bridges (Dave), Addison Richards (Dr. Williams), Mary Gordon (Mrs. O'Connor), George Chandler (Harper), Gregory Muradian (Tommy Carter), Wilton Graff (Brandon), Frances MacDonald (Hernandez), Jack Norton (Boarder), Christian Rub (Mr. Moore)
Screenplay: M. Coates Webster; based on Jean Bart's play *The Man Who Reclaimed His Head*; Director of Photography: Maury Gertsman; Musical Director: Frank Skinner; Art Direction: John B. Goodman and Abraham Grossman; Director of Sound: Bernard B. Brown; Technician: Jess Moulin; Set Decorations: Russell A. Gausman and Andrew J. Gilmore; Film Editor: Russell Schoengarth; Gowns: Vera West; Dialogue Director: Willard Holland; Producer: Ben Pivar; Director: John Hoffman

Pillow of Death
Universal Pictures
Released December 14, 1945; 67 minutes; © October 3, 1945; an *Inner Sanctum* mystery
Cast: Lon Chaney (Wayne Fletcher), Brenda Joyce (Donna Kincaid), J. Edward Bromberg (Julian Julian), Rosalind Ivan (Rosalind Ivan), Clara Blandick (Belle Kincaid), George Cleveland (Sam Kincaid), Wilton Graff (Captain McCracken), Bernard B. Thomas (Bruce Malone)
Screenplay: George Bricker; Original Story: Dwight V. Babcock; Director of Photography: Jerome Ash; Music Director: Frank Skinner; Art Direction: John B. Goodman and Abraham Grossman; Director of Sound: Bernard B. Brown; Technician: Jess Moulin; Set Decorators: Russell A. Gausman and Leigh Smith; Film Editor: Edward Curtiss; Gowns: Vera West; Dialogue Director: George Bricker; Producer: Ben Pivar; Director: Wallace Fox

House of Horrors
Universal Pictures
Released March 29, 1946; 66 minutes; © March 21, 1946; pre-production title *Murder Mansion*
Cast: Robert Lowery (Steve Morrow), Virginia Grey (Joan Medford), Bill Goodwin (Lt. Larry Brooks), Martin Kosleck (Marcel De Lange), Alan Napier (F. Holmes Harmon), Howard Freeman (Hal Ormiston), Joan Fulton (Stella McNally), Virginia Christine (Streetwalker), Rondo Hatton (The Creeper)
Screenplay: George Bricker; Original Story: Dwight V. Babcock; Director of Photography: Maury Gertsman; Film Editor: Philip Cahn; Music Director: H.J. Salter; Art Direction: John B. Goodman and Abraham Grossman; Director of Sound: Bernard B. Brown; Technician: Robert Pritchard; Set Decorations: Russell A. Gausman and Ralph Warrington; Gowns: Vera West; Make-Up Director: Jack P. Pierce; Producer: Ben Pivar; Director: Jean Yarbrough

Blonde Alibi
Universal Pictures
Released April 12, 1946; 62 minutes; © April 9, 1946; pre-production title *Killing is Convenient*; pre-release title *Design for Death*
Cast: Tom Neal (Rick Lavery), Martha O'Driscoll (Marian Gale), Donald MacBride (Inspector Carmichael), Peter Whitney (Lt. Melody Haynes), Samuel S. Hinds (Prof. Carl Slater), Robert Armstrong (Williams), Elisha Cook, Jr. (Sam Collins), Marc Lawrence (Joe DeLima), Oliver Blake (Pat Tenny), John Berkes (Louie Carney), Matt Willis (Lane)
Produced and Written for the Screen by George Bricker; Original Story: Gordon Kahn; Director of Photography: Maury Gertsman; Film Editor: Edward Curtiss; Musical Director: Edgar Fairchild; Art Direction: Jack Otterson and

Robert Clatworthy; Director of Sound: Bernard B. Brown; Technician: Glenn E. Anderson; Set Decorations: Russell A. Gausman and Ted von Hemert; Gowns: Vera West; Director of Make-Up: Jack P. Pierce; Hair Stylist: Carmen Dirigo; Executive Producer: Ben Pivar; Director: Will Jason

She-Wolf of London
Universal Pictures
Released May 17, 1946; 61 minutes; © April 11, 1946
Cast: Don Porter (Barry Lanfield), June Lockhart (Phyllis Allenby), Sara Hayden (Martha Winthrop), Jan Wiley (Carol Winthrop), Lloyd Corrigan (Latham), Dennis Hoey (Inspector Pierce), Martin Kosleck (Dwight Severn), Eily Malyon (Hannah), Frederick Worlock (Constable)
Screenplay: George Bricker; Original Story: Dwight Babcock; Director of Photography: Maury Gertsman; Film Editor: Paul Landres; Music Director: William Lava; Art Direction: Jack Otterson and Abraham Grossman; Director of Sound: Bernard B. Brown; Technician: Joe Lapis; Set Decorations: Russell A. Gausman and Leigh Smith; Gowns: Vera West; Director of Make-Up: Jack P. Pierce; Dialogue Director: Raymond Kessler; Producer: Ben Pivar; Director: Jean Yarbrough

Inside Job
Universal Pictures
Released June 28, 1946; 65 minutes; © June 6, 1946
Cast: Preston Foster (Bart Madden), Ann Rutherford (Claire Gray Norton), Alan Curtis (Eddie Norton), Milburn Stone (District Attorney Sutton), Samuel S. Hinds (Judge Kinkaid), Joe Sawyer (Captain Thomas), Marc Lawrence (Captain Donovan), John Berkes (Freddie), Jimmie Moss (Skipper Thomas), Howard Freeman (Trent W. Wickle), William Trenk (Cordet), Oliver Blake (Herman), Joan Fulton (Ruth), Harry Brown (Pop Hurley), Joe Kirk (Fenway)
Screenplay: George Bricker and Jerry Warner; Original Story: Tod Browning and Garrett Fort; Director of Photography: Maury Gertsman; Film Editor: Otto Ludwig; Music Director: Frank Skinner; Art Direction: Jack Otterson and Abraham Grossman; Director of Sound: Bernard B. Brown; Technician: Charles Carroll; Set Decorations: Russell A. Gausman and Leigh Smith; Gowns: Vera West; Hair Stylist: Carmen Dirigo; Director of Make-Up: Jack P. Pierce; Executive Producer: Ben Pivar; Producer and Director: Jean Yarbrough

The Brute Man
Universal Pictures
Released October 1, 1946 by Producers Releasing Corp.; 58 minutes; © October 13, 1946
Cast: Tom Neal (Clifford Scott), Jan Wiley (Virginia Rogers Scott), Jane Adams

(Helen Paige), Donald MacBride (Police Captain M.J. Donelly), Peter Whitney (Police Lieutenant Gates), Fred Coby (Young Hal Moffat), Ja Nelle Johnson (Joan Bemis), Rondo Hatton (The Creeper, Hal Moffat)
Screenplay: George Bricker and M. Coates Webster; Original Story: Dwight Babcock; Director of Photography: Maury Gertsman; Film Editor: Philip Cahn; Art Direction: John B. Goodman and Abraham Grossman; Director of Sound: Bernard B. Brown; Technician: Joe Lapis; Set Decorations: Russell A. Gausman and Edward R. Robinson; Gowns: Vera West; Hair Stylist: Carmen Dirigo; Director of Make-Up: Jack P. Pierce; Dialogue Director: Raymond Kessler; Producer: Ben Pivar; Director: Jean Yarbrough

The Later Years: Reliance Pictures 1947 - 1950

The Challenge
Reliance Pictures, Inc.; 20th Century-Fox
Released February 28, 1948; 68 minutes; © February 12, 1948; production title *Strange Penalty*
Cast: Tom Conway (Capt. Hugh "Bulldog" Drummond), June Vincent (Vivian Bailey), Richard Stapley (Cliff Sonnenberg), John Newland (Algernon "Algy" Longworth), Eily Malyon (Kitty Fyffe), Houseley Stevenson (Captain Sonnenberg), Terry Kilburn (Seymour), Stanley Logan (Inspector McIver), Leyland Hodgson (Sergeant Shubeck), James Fairfax (Blinky Henderson), Pat Aherne (Jerome Roberts), Oliver Blake (Arno)
Executive Producer: Ben Pivar; Screenplay: Frank Gruber and Irving Elman; Adapted from the Story by "Sapper;" Director of Photography: George Robinson; Film Editor: Fred Feitshans; Art Direction: Walter Koessler; Set Decoration: Ray [sic] Babcock; Sound Engineer: John Carter; Assistant Director: Eddie Stein; Music: Milton Rosen; Producer: Bernard Small; Director: Jean Yarbrough

13 Lead Soldiers
Reliance Pictures, Inc.; 20th Century Fox
Released April 24, 1948; 66 minutes; © April 6, 1948
Cast: Tom Conway (Capt. Hugh "Bulldog" Drummond), Maria Palmer (Estelle Prager, alias Estelle Gorday), Helen Westcott (Cynthia Stedman), John Newland (Algernon "Algy" Longworth), Terry Kilburn (Seymour), William Stelling (Phillip Coleman), Gordon Richards (Inspector McIver), Harry Cording (Edward Vane), John Goldsworthy (Dr. Ashley Stedman), William Edmunds (unnamed character)
Executive Producer: Ben Pivar; Screenplay: Irving Elman; adapted by Dwight V. Babcock from the original story by "Sapper;" Director of Photography: George Robinson; Film Editor: Saul Goodkind; Art Direction: Walter Koessler;

Set Decorations: Fay Babcock; Sound: Benjamin Winkler; Assistant Director: Eddie Stein; Music Director: Milton Rosen; Producer: Bernard Small; Director: Frank McDonald

The Creeper
Reliance Pictures, Inc.; 20th Century Fox
Released September 25, 1948; 64 minutes; © August 18, 1948; pre-production title *The Cat Man*
Cast: Eduardo Ciannelli (Dr. Van Glock), Onslow Stevens (Dr. Jim Bordon), June Vincent (Gwen Runstrom), Ralph Morgan (Dr. Lester Cavigny), Janis Wilson (Nora Cavigny), John Baragrey (Dr. John Reade), Richard Lane (Inspector Fenwick), Philip Ahn (Ah Wong, Chinese restaurant owner), Lotte Stein (Maidie Halpern, nurse), Ralph Peters (workman), David Hoffman (Andre Dussaud)
Executive Producer: Ben Pivar; Screenplay: Maurice Tombragel; Original Story Idea: Don Martin; Director of Photography: George Robinson; Film Editor: Saul Goodkind; Art Direction: Walter Koessler; Set Decorations: Fay Babcock; Sound: Frank McWhorter; Assistant Director: Eddie Stein; Makeup Artist: Ted Larsen; Music Composed and Directed By: Milton Rosen; Director: Jean Yarbrough

Davy Crockett, Indian Scout
Reliance Pictures, Inc./Edward Small Productions; United Artists
Released January 6, 1950; 71 minutes; © January 7, 1950; production title *Indian Scout*
Cast: George Montgomery (Davy Crockett), Ellen Drew (Frances Oatman), Philip Reed (Red Hawk), Noah Beery, Jr. (Tex McGee), Paul Guilfoyle (Ben), Addison Richards (Capt. Weightman), Robert Barrat (James Lone Eagle), Erik Rolf (Mr. Simms), William Wilkerson (High Tree), John Hamilton (Colonel Pollard), Vera Marshe (Mrs. Simms), Jimmy Moss (Jimmy Simms), Chief Thundercloud (Sleeping Fox), Kenneth Duncan (Sgt. Gordon), Ray Teal (Capt. McHale)
Screenplay: Richard Schayer; Story: Ford Beebe; Directors of Photography: George Diskant and John Mescall; Film Editors: Stuart Frye and Kenneth Crane; Art Direction: Rudolph Sternad and Martin Obzina; Set Decoration: C.I. Steenson and Howard Bristol; Wardrobe: Edward Lambert and Elmer Ellsworth; Assistant Director: Harold Knox; Makeup: Don Cash; Sound: L.J. Meyers; Music: Paul Sawtell; Associate Producers: Grant Whytock and Bernard Small; Director: Lew Landers; Executive Producer: Ben Pivar (not credited)

Syndicated Television Series (incomplete)

The Lone Wolf (aka Streets of Danger)
Produced by United Television Programs, Inc. (syndicated television series)
Released 1954-1955; 39 episodes
Cast: Louis Hayward
Producers: Jack Gross, Philip Krasne; Production Supervisor: Ben Pivar; Cinematographer: Fred Gately

Paul Coates' Confidential File
Produced by Confidential Telepictures, Inc.; Distributed by Guild Films Company, Inc. (syndicated television series)
Released 1955-1956; 39 episodes; 26 minutes each
Producers: Ben Pivar and James Peck; Associate Producer: Andrew J. Fenady; Host/Narrator: Paul Coates; Directors: Irvin Kershner, Ben Pivar; Screenplay: Andrew J. Fenady, Irwin Moskowitz; Cinematographer: Irvin Kershner

Two Last Films; One an Import

The Leech Woman
Universal International Pictures
Released May 1960; 77 minutes; working title *The Leech*
Cast: Coleen Gray (June Talbot), Grant Williams (Neil Foster), Phillip Terry (Dr. Paul Talbot), Gloria Talbot (Sally Howard), John Van Dreelen (Bertram Garvay), Estelle Hemsley (Old Malla), Kim Hamilton (Young Malla), Arthur Batanides (Jerry Lando)
Screenplay: David Duncan; Original Story: Ben Pivar and Francis Rosenwald; Director of Photography: Ellis W. Carter; Art Direction: Alexander Golitzen and Robert Clatworthy; Set Decorations: Russell A. Gausman and Clarence Steensen; Sound: Leslie I. Carey and Joe Lapis; Film Editor: Milton Carruth; Costumes: Bill Thomas; Make-Up: Bud Westmore; Assistant Director: Joe Kenny; Music: Irving Gertz; Music Supervision: Milton Rosen; Producer: Joseph Gershenson; Director: Edward Dein

Panda and the Magic Serpent *
Globe Pictures/Toei Animation Studio Co.
U.S. Release July 8, 1961; 76 minutes (released in Japan as *Hakuja den*, October 22, 1958; 90 minutes)
U.S. Release – Producers: Alvin Schoncite and Ben Pivar; Adapted by Alvin Schoncite and Ben Pivar; Director: Robert Tafur; Narrator: Marvin Miller
Japan Release – Executive Producer: Hiroshi Okawa; Associate Producer:

Hideyuki Takahashi, Koichi Akagawa, and Sanae Yamamoto; Director: Kazuhiko Okabe and Teiji Yabushita; Screenplay: Teiji Yabushita and Shin Uehara; Original Dialog: Seiichi Yashiro; Animation: Yasuo Otsuka and Yusaku Sakamoto; Original Drawings: Akira Daikubara and Yasuji Mori; Background: Kazuo Kusano; Director of Photography: Takamitsu Tsukahara; Art Director: Kazuhiko Okabe and Kiyoshi Hashimoto; Film Editor: Shintaro Miyamoto; Music: Chuji Kinoshita; Sound Recording: Takeshi Mori

Bibliography

Books

Alicoate, Jack, ed. *Film Daily Yearbook of Motion Pictures: 1936, 1942*. Fort Lee, NJ: J.E. Brulatour, Inc., 1937.

Anonymous. *The Strange Death of Adolf Hitler*. New York: Macaulay Company, 1938.

Astor, Mary. *My Story: an Autobiography*. Garden City, NY: Doubleday & Company, Inc., 1959.

Beck, Calvin Thomas. *Scream Queens*. London: Collier MacMillan Publishers, 1978.

Bogdanovich, Peter. *Who the Devil Made It*. New York: Alfred A. Knopf, 1997.

Brunas, Michael, Brunas, John, and Weaver, Tom. *Universal Horrors: The Studio's Classic Films, 1931-1946*. Jefferson, North Carolina: McFarland & Company, Inc., 1990.

Buntin, John. *L.A. Noir*. New York: Three Rivers Press, 2009.

Catalog of Copyright Entries: Cumulative Series; Motion Pictures 1912-39, 1940-49. U.S. Copyright Office, The Library of Congress, 1951

Cocchi, John. *Second Feature*. New York: A Citadel Pressbook, 1991.

Cohn, Art. *The Nine Lives of Michael Todd*. New York: Random House, 1958.

Dick, Bernard F. *The Merchant Prince of Poverty Row: Harry Cohn of Columbia Pictures*. The University Press of Kentucky, 1993.

Dimmitt, Richard Bertrand. *A Title Guide to the Talkies*. New York: The Scarecrow Press, 1965.

Dixon, Wheeler W. *The "B" Directors: A Biographical Directory*. Metuchen, New Jersey: The Scarecrow Press, Inc., 1985.

Drinkwater, John. *The Life and Adventures of Carl Laemmle*. London: William Heinemann Ltd, 1931.

Fenin, George N., and Everson, William K. *The Westerns: From Silents to the Seventies.* New York: Penguin Books, 1973.

Fernett, Gene. *Hollywood's Poverty Row.* Satellite Beach, Florida: Coral Reef Publications, Inc., 1973.

Fitzgerald, Michael G. *Universal Pictures.* New Rochelle, New York: Arlington House Publishers, 1977.

Gevinson, Alan, ed. *The American Film Institute Catalog of Motion Pictures Produced in the United States: Within Our Gates: Ethnicity in American Feature Films, 1911-1960.* University of California Press, 1997.

Gifford, Denis. *A Pictorial History of Horror Movies.* New York: Hamlyn Publishing Group Ltd., 1973.

Halliwell, Leslie. *The Filmgoer's Companion, Fourth Edition.* New York: Hill and Wang, 1974.

_____. *Halliwell's Film Guide.* New York: Granada Publishing, 1977.

Hirschhorn, Clive. *The Universal Story.* New York: Crown Publishers, Inc., 1983.

Kann, Red, ed. *1951-52 International Motion Pictures Almanac.* New York: Quigley Publishing Company, 1952.

Koszarski, Richard. *Universal Pictures: Sixty-five Years.* New York: Museum of Modern Art, 1977.

Lamparski, Richard. *Whatever Became of..., Vol 2.* New York: Ace Books, 1968.

Lee, Walt. *Reference Guide to Fantastic Films,* Vols 1, 2, 3. Los Angeles: Chelsee-Lee Books, 1972.

Martin, Len D. *The Republic Pictures Checklist, 1935-1959.* Jefferson, NC: McFarland & Company, 1998.

McCarty, Todd and Flynn, Charles. *Kings of the Bs.* New York: E.P. Dutton & Co., Inc., 1975.

McGilligan, Patrick, and Buhle, Paul. *Tender Comrades.* New York: St. Martin's Griffin, 1999.

Miller, Don. *B Movies.* New York: Ballantine Books, 1987.

Munden, Kenneth W., Executive Editor. *The American Film Institute Catalog of Motion Pictures Produced in the United States: Feature Films 1921-1930.* New York: R.R. Bowker Company, 1971.

Nachma, Gerald. *Raised On Radio.* University of California Press, 1998.

New York City Directories, 1909, 1910, 1915, 1918.

Okuda, Ted. *Grand National, Producers Releasing Corporation, and Screen Guild/Lippert: Complete Filmographies with Studio Histories.* Jefferson, North Carolina: McFarland & Company, Inc., 1989.

Ramsaye, Terry. *A Million and One Nights.* New York: Simon and Schuster, 1926.

Ramsaye, Terry, ed. *International Motion Picture Almanac, 1939-1940, 1949-1950.* New York: Quigley Publishing Co, 1940, 1950.

Schatz, Thomas. *The Genius of the System.* New York: Pantheon Books, 1988.

Bibliography

Schonzeit, Hank. *A Past Remembered: The History of the Schonzeit Family.* Reston, VA: Lorah Publishing, 2001.
Sennett, Ted. *Warner Brothers Presents.* New York: Castle Books, Inc., 1971.
Slater's Manchester, Salford and Suburban Directory, 1903. Part 1: Topography and Street Directory.
Torrence, Bruce T. *Hollywood: The First Hundred Years.* New York: New York Zoetrope, 1979.
Turok, George D. *A Guide to Historic Coal Towns of the Big Sandy River Valley.* University of Tennessee Press, 2004.
Ward, Richard Lewis. *A History of the Hal Roach Studios.* Southern Illinois Press, 2005.
Weaver, Tom. *Interviews with B Science Fiction and Horror Movie Makers.* Jefferson, North Carolina: McFarland & Company, Inc., 1988.
_____. *Science Fiction and Fantasy Film Flashbacks: Conversations with Twenty-Four Actors, Writers, Producers, and Directors from the Golden Age.* Jefferson, NC: McFarland & Company, Inc., 1998.
Weiss, Ken and Goodgold, ed. *To Be Continued ...* New York: Bonanza Books, 1972.
Zinman, David. *Saturday Afternoon at the Bijou.* New York: Castle Books, 1973.

Newspapers, Periodicals
Altoona Mirror, PA, 1941
Arizona Daily Sun, Flagstaff, AZ, 1962
Big Spring Daily Herald, TX, 1941
Billboard, 1953
Boxoffice, 1936-1962
Brooklyn Daily Eagle, NY, 1933-1944
California Eagle, Los Angeles, CA, 1943
Castle of Frankenstein, 1965-1966
Charleston Daily Mail, WV, 1943
Charleston Gazette, WV, 1940-1941
Classic Images, 2007, 2009
Cumberland Evening Times, MD, 1942, 1962
Daily Kennebec Journal, ME, 1942
Daily Times-Bulletin, Van Wert, OH, 1940
Daily Times-News, Burlington, NC, 1942
Daily Variety, 1933-1963
Evening Independent, Massilon, OH, 1945
Evening Observer, Dunkirk, NY, 1945
Evening Telegram, NY, 1921
Fantastic Films, 1985
Film Daily, 1936-1948

Filmfax, 1990-1991
Films in Review, 1986
Hammond Times, IN, 1945
Harrison's Reports, 1936-1948
Helena Daily Independent, MT, 1941
Hollywood Reporter, 1936-1946
Hutchinson News, KS, 1961
Independent Film Journal, 1948
Life, 1956
Los Angeles Times, 1929-1962
Morning Herald, Hagerstown, MD, 1944
Motion Picture Daily, 1935-1948
Motion Picture Herald, 1939-1942
Nevada State Journal, Reno, NV, 1944
New York Herald Tribune, 1936, 1939
New York Times, 1922-1976
New York World-Telegram, 1936
News-Palladium, Benton Harbor, MI, 1946
Niagara Falls Gazette, NY, 1944
North Adams Transcript, MA, 1942
Panama City News-Herald, FL, 1941
Pasadena Star-News, CA, 1971
Philadelphia Exhibitor, PA, 1936
Press-Telegram, Long Beach, CA, 1959
Rhinelander Daily News, WI, 1959
Rochester Democrat & Herald, NY, 1928
Salt Lake Tribune, UT, 1940
San Antonio Light, TX, 1943
Schenectady Gazette, NY, 1937-1938
Select Motion Picture, 1936
The Era, Bradford, PA, 1942
The Laredo Times, TX, 1944
The News, Frederick, MD, 1943
Time, 1954
Universal Pictures Weekly Internal Status Reports, 1939 – 1940
Universal Pictures Daily Committee Meeting Notes, 1941
Variety, 1930-1952
Watertown Daily Times, NY, *1916*
Winnipeg Free Press, Winnipeg, Manitoba, 1943
Wisconsin State Journal, 1941

Index

13 Lead Soldiers 415-417, 499
20th Century-Fox 87, 89, 112, 145, 165, 228-229, 242, 278, 341, 356, 365, 400, 404, 410-411, 463, 499-500
40,000 Horsemen 316

A

A Dangerous Game 115, 178-182, 486
A Past Remembered: A History of the Schonzeit Family 431, 460, 505
A Star is Born 89
A Yank on the Burma Road 229
Abbas, Abdullah 194
Abbott and Costello 152, 182, 189, 227, 304, 375
Abbott, Bud 182, 262
Abbott, Norman 259, 262, 489
Abel, David 466
Abrams, Leon 494
Academy of Television Arts and Sciences 438
Acquanetta, Burnu 300, 302, 305, 308-309, 311-313, 317, 323-324, 342-344, 346-347, 406, 464, 490, 492, 494

Actors Laboratory 316
Acuff, Eddie 495
Adams, Ernie 259, 471, 486, 495
Adams, Jane 378, 498
Adams, Kathryn 123-124, 126, 154, 158, 482
Adamson, Harold 224, 487
Adolfi, John G. 21
Adrian 466
Adrian, Iris 211, 484
Adventure Series 17
Adventures of Sherlock Holmes, The 365
After the Dance 34, 36-37, 474
Agfa Film Corp. 59
Aherne, Pat 413, 499
Ahn, Philip 500
Air Express 92
Air Fury (story) 34, 473
Air Hawks 34-36, 126, 473
Air Mail 91, 109, 111
Akagawa, Koichi 502
Alba, Maria 470
Alberni, Luis 151, 481
Albertson, Frank 129-132, 259, 479, 489
Albertson, Mabel 98, 478

Albright, Hardie 155, 189-190, 481, 485
Alexander, Ben 483
Alexander, Richard 471, 492-493, 495
Algier, Sidney 65
Ali Baba and the Forty Thieves 279
Alias the Deacon 118-119, 158-164, 200, 481-482
All for Love (song) 278
All Over Town 74
All Quiet on the Western Front 81
All-American, The 89
Allan, Hugh 468
Allbritton, Louise 235, 237, 488
Allen, Dr. Newton 449
Allen, Judith 131, 480
Allen, Maude 482
Allen, Robert 36, 473
Allen, Victor 467
Allied Artists Pictures Corporation 405
Allwyn, Astrid 59-60, 167, 170, 476, 483
Alperson, Edward L. 51-52, 69, 410, 476-477
Alson Productions 410
Altimus, Henry 475
Alvarado, Don 467
American Airlines 59, 61
American Institute of Public Opinion 80, 245
American Madness 91
American Music, Inc. 296
American Mutoscope and Biograph Company 12, 94
American Optical Company 446
Americanos, The 218
Ames, Leon 107, 111, 478
Ames, Ramsay 282, 286, 324-325, 330, 336, 406, 491-492
Anaconda Bend 4

Anders, Rudolph 179, 266, 269, 490
Anderson, Glenn E. 488, 495, 498
Anderson, John 469
Anderson, John Murray 81
Andrews Sisters: Patti, Maxene, LaVerne 182-183
Andrews, Del 25
Andy Hardy series 398
Angels with Dirty Faces 52, 69
Ankers, Evelyn 259, 262, 273-275, 277-279, 289-293, 306, 308-309, 311, 351-352, 489-492, 496
Ankrum, Morris 226, 486
Anthony, Stuart 470, 472-473
Anthony, Walter 158
Apartment for Peggy 419
Ape Man, The 278
Appleby, Dorothy 473, 483
Appleton, Lou, Jr. 410
Arabian Nights 245
Arbó, Manuel 470
Archainbaud, George 23, 469
Argentine Nights 182
Arkoff, Samuel Z. 442
Arledge, John 154-155, 158, 481
Arlen, Richard 38, 85-90, 92-95, 97, 99-102, 104-107, 112, 114, 117, 119, 121-124, 126-127, 129, 165, 167, 169-175, 177, 179, 182-183, 185-187, 189-197, 204, 209, 215, 217-218, 222-223, 397, 406, 478-479, 482-486
Arlen, Rickey 88
Armored Car Robbery 280
Armstrong, Robert 129-130, 133, 147-148, 273, 280, 388-389, 391, 480-481, 490, 497
Arno, Siegfried (Sig) 195, 485
Arnold, Edward 100
Arnold, Jack 115, 132-133, 148, 177, 479-481, 484

INDEX

Around the World in Eighty Days 446-447
Arson Gang Busters 72
Arthur Lyons Film Noir Festival, 10th Annual 399-400
Arthur, Jean 353
Arthur, Johnny 37, 474
Ash, Jerome 150, 224, 269, 463, 478-481, 490, 497
Ashcroft, Ronald V. 450
Associated First National Pictures, Inc. 14, 20
Astor, Mary 41-42, 474, 503
Astounding She-Monster, The 450
Atkinson, Brooks 295, 353
Atwill, Lionel 353
Audience Research Institute 234
Auer, Mischa 89, 106, 159-160, 481
August, Joseph 474
Ausland, Gil 458-459
Austin, Frank 471
Austin, Marie 492-493
Austin, Vivian 492-493
Autry, Gene 71

B

Babcock, Dwight V. 358, 369, 375, 383, 405, 494-495, 497-499
Babcock, Fay 500
Babe Ruth Story, The 126
Baby Sandy series 159
Bacall, Lauren 306
Bachelor Girl, The 23, 469
Back to Bataan 304
Bacon, Lloyd 205, 279
Bad Company 261, 489
Ballad of Cat Ballou, The 134
Ballet of Swan Lake 463
Ballew, Smith 87
Banky, Vilma 273
Bar Six Cowboys 296, 495

Baragrey, John 420, 422, 500
Barclay, Don 196
Bard, Ben 279
Bardette, Trevor 481
Barkas, Geoffrey 87
Barnes, Howard 98-99
Barnett, Vince 178-179, 305, 464, 486, 490
Barrat, Robert 425, 500
Barrie, Wendy 254, 256, 489
Barrier, Edgar 236, 488
Barris, Harry 474
Barron, Robert 492
Barsha, Leon 24, 402, 405, 469
Barsky, Bud 69
Bart, Jean 353, 496
Barth, Gerson "Gus" 59
Bartlett, Bennie 159, 161, 163, 481
Barton, Charles 229
Basquette, Lina 472
Bastian, Jesse 479
Batanides, Arthur 501
Bates, Charles 266, 490
Bauer, Maximilian 263-264
Bauer, Sally 321
Beal, Scott 493-495
Beast of the East 238, 273
Beatty, Clyde 304, 306, 311
Beau Geste 100
Beaudine, William 278
Beaumont, Charles 294
Bebe (ringtail monkey) 356
Beck, John, Jr. 404
Bed Down, Bed Down, Little Dogies (song) 296
Beebe, Ford 230, 239, 243, 262, 423-424, 500
Beery, Noah (Sr.) 94-95, 100, 406, 478
Beery, Noah, Jr. 423, 425-426, 500
Beery, Wallace 100
Beggars of Life 86

Behind Closed Doors 22, 468
Beilby, Vangie 494
Benjamin, Richard 294
Bela Lugosi Meets a Brooklyn Gorilla 74
Belasco, Leon 107, 202, 478, 483
Belgard, Arnold 65, 402, 459
Bellamy, Ralph 35, 44-46, 473, 475
Ben Pivar and Associates 435
Bendix, William 151
Benedict, Brooks 476
Benge, Wilson 477
Bennett, Joan 353
Bennett, Ray 493
Benny, Jack 119
Bergen, Edgar 85
Berkes, John 389, 391-393, 396, 398, 497-498
Berliner, Trude 265, 490
Bernds, Edward 450
Bernhard, Jack XVIII, 199, 484
Besser, Joe 120, 122, 482
Beth David Hospital 7
Beverly Productions 27
Bey, Turhan 194, 230, 236-237, 246-251, 273, 275, 277, 279, 333, 336, 485, 487-490, 492
Beyond the Pampas 218
Beyond the Pecos 294-296, 495
Biberman, Abner 141, 148, 480-481
Big Cage, The 304, 311
Big Sleep, The 306
Big Squawk, The 474
Big Timer, The 43
Big Town 436
Biggers, Earl Derr 85
Billboard 505
Bing, Herman 475
Biograph Company, American Mutoscope and 12, 94
Birch, Wyrley 36, 41, 473-474

Birell, Tala 35, 38-39, 348, 352, 473-474, 496
Black Angel 255
Black Cat, The 189, 422
Black Diamonds 123-127, 164, 482
Black Dragons 229
Black Friday 199
Black Ivory 51
Black Raven, The 206
Blackbird, The 393
Blackmer, Sidney 129-130, 480
Blair, Joan 267, 490
Blake, Gladys 484
Blake, Oliver 388, 391, 393, 396, 398, 413, 415, 497-499
Blanchard, Harry 469-470
Blandick, Clara 359, 361, 497
Blind Date 30
Blind Fury 402, 459
Blonde Alibi XVIII, 377, 380, 388-393, 397, 402, 497-498
Blue Streak Westerns 17
Blumberg, Nate 83, 165, 223
Blumenstock, Morton 467
Blystone, John G. 52, 150
Boehnel, William 49
Bogdanovich, Peter 16, 503
Bond, Ward 30, 44, 472-473, 475
Bondi, Beulah 89
Bonner, Marjorie 467
Boom Town 171
Borden, Olive 22, 469
Border Law 28, 31-32, 470
Borowsky, Yoselia F. 25
Borzage, Frank 118, 126
Boss of Boomtown 294, 492
Boteler, Wade 120, 140, 168, 220, 239, 257, 480, 482-483, 486, 488-489
Botiller, Dick 172, 483
Bowery Boys, The XVIII, 263
Bowery to Broadway 243

Index

Boy Meets Girl 205
Boylan, Malcolm Stuart 273
Boyle, John W. 110, 187-189, 192-193, 222, 229-230, 406, 463, 478, 484-487
Bradbury, James 466
Bradford, Gardner 466-467
Bradley, Harry C. 479
Bradley, Page 473, 481, 487
Brady, Edwin J. 471
Brahm, John 118
Branded 28-29, 470
Brandon, Henry 155, 481
Brandt, Joseph 19-20
Bredell, Elwood "Woody" 117, 138, 171, 200, 204, 231, 406, 463, 479-480, 483-484, 487
Breen, Joseph I. 271, 394-395
Bregman, Buddy 458
Brennan, Walter 472
Bretherton, Howard 294, 495
Bricker, George 358, 369, 375-376, 383, 388, 391, 393-394, 398, 405, 497-499
Bridenbecker, Milton 466-467
Bridges, Lloyd 354, 356, 496
Briggs, Donald 120, 482
Briskin, Irving 31, 34, 43, 51, 474-476
Brissac, Virginia 159, 161, 247, 481, 489
Bristol, Howard 500
British Intelligence 147
Britton, Mozelle 473
Broadway Scandals 23-24, 469
Broadway 81
Bromberg, J. Edward 359-360, 497
Brook, Clive 18, 466
Brooks, Jean 174
Brooks, Richard 174
Brophy, Edward 159-160, 163, 178, 481, 486

Brother Rat 139
Brown, Bernard B. 407, 478-499
Brown, Charles D. 167, 483
Brown, Donald H. XVIII
Brown, Everett 142
Brown, Harry 498
Brown, Howard C. 25
Brown, Johnny Mack 92, 165, 217, 294
Brown, Milton 476
Brown, Phil 290, 292, 313-316, 406, 491, 495
Brown, Rowland 52
Browning, Tod 68, 82, 106, 393, 498
Bruce, David 201, 273, 275, 277, 279, 282-283, 286, 490-491
Brunette, Fritzi 467
Brute Man, The 369, 375-382, 391, 498
Bryant, Betty 316
Bryant, Nana 46, 310, 474-475, 492
Buchman, Harold 48, 134-135, 474, 476, 480
Buck Benny Rides Again 119
Buck Privates 182
Bulgakov, Leo 34, 36-37, 474
Bulldog Drummond 410
Bulldog Drummond at Bay 410
Bulldog Drummond Strikes Back (1934) 410
Bulldog Drummond Strikes Back (1947) 410, 415
Bulldog Edition 74
Bumbaugh, Hal 483-485
Bureau of Missing Persons 435
Burke, James 140, 480
Burn, Witch, Burn 294
Burnett, W.R. 85
Burnette, Smiley 294
Burns, Bob 158, 160, 163-164, 481
Burns, Fred 470

Burns, Paul E. 189-190, 240, 247, 485, 488-489
Burnstine, Norman 72, 477
Burroughs, Clark 470
Burton, Clarence 466, 468
Bushman, Francis X. 94
Business School of the City College of New York 14
Buster, Budd 493-494
Buzzell, Edward 43
Byron, Walter 66, 477

C

Cabanne, Christy 21-22, 92, 94, 99-102, 106-107, 111-112, 114-115, 117, 119, 123, 158-160, 162, 164-167, 171, 174, 199-200, 204, 212-213, 232, 234, 238, 242, 258, 407, 467-468, 478-480, 482-484, 488, 490
Cabot, Bruce 59-61, 476
Cagney, Bill 52
Cagney, Jimmy 52, 69, 119, 222
Cahn, Philip 200, 483, 497, 499
Cahoon, Richard 473
Caldwell, Betty 17, 467
California Mail 205
California Studios 19-20
Call of the Yukon 105
Calling Dr. Death 282-288, 323, 376, 430, 491
Calling of Dan Matthews, The 87
Calvo, Maria 470
Cameron, Rod 294-295, 297-298, 492-493, 495
Campeau, Frank 472
Cansino, Carmella 218
Cansino, Margarita 219
Capone, Al 390
Capra, Frank 20, 22-24, 40, 65, 91-92, 468-469

Captain Calamity 53
Captain Fury 89
Captive Wild Woman 238, 262, 299-308, 323, 331, 490, 492
Caravel Studios 458
Carey, Leslie I. 501
Carle, Richard 179, 181, 486
Carleton, George 194, 485
Carr, Trem 71
Carradine, John 212, 301, 306, 308, 311, 330, 333, 336, 490, 492
Carrillo, Leo 38, 209-210, 217, 219, 221-222, 224, 226-227, 230, 232, 235, 237, 239-241, 397, 406, 484, 486-488
Carroll, Charles 479-480, 482-483, 498
Carroll, Nancy 36-37, 73, 474
Carroll, Vance 69
Carruth, Milton 145-146, 159, 250, 271, 304, 406, 480-482, 485, 488-491, 493-494, 501
Carson, Jack 111, 151, 159, 478, 481
Carter, Ellis W. 501
Carter, Harrison 347, 496
Carter, John 499
Carter, Tom 466
Casa Del Terror, La 339
Cascade Pictures 435
Cash, Don 500
Cat Creeps, The 388
Cat Man, The 415, 500
Catlett, Walter 211, 213, 484
Cavanaugh, Hobart 210, 484
CBC Film Sales Corporation 19
Cecil, Nora 467, 477
Century Film 224
Cerf, Norman A. 430, 491
Chadwick, Helene 21, 466
Chadwick, I.E. 409, 430
Challenge in the Night 402, 405
Challenge, The 411-415, 417, 499

Index

Chamberlain, Neville 264
Chandler, Eddie 140, 480, 495
Chandler, George 496
Chandler, Helen 66, 68, 477
Chandler, Lane 479, 493
Chandler, Robert 467
Chaney, Creighton 246
Chaney, Lon (Sr.) 218, 258, 393
Chaney, Lon, Jr. XIX, 89, 201, 207, 246, 250, 255-256, 258, 278, 281-283, 285-291, 293, 306-307, 325, 330-331, 334, 339, 342, 345-346, 348, 350, 352-353, 356-359, 361-362, 405, 464, 488-489, 491-492, 494, 496-497
Chaney, Patsy 306
Chanslor, Roy 129, 133-135, 229-230, 480, 487
Chapin, Ann Morrison 53, 476
Chapman, Ben 166, 171, 178, 405, 483-484, 486, 488
Chapman, Don 470
Charsky, Boris 25
Charsky, Sonia 25
Charters, Spencer 66, 68, 160, 477, 481
Chatterton, Tom 482
Chauvel, Charles 316
Cherokee Strip 205
Chesterfield Motion Pictures Corporation 224
China Clipper 110
Chinatown Squad 92
Chinese Den 214
Chissel, Noble "Kid" 168, 483
Choppers, The 457
Christie Studios 224
Christine, Virginia 333-334, 336-338, 370-371, 374, 406, 494, 497
Churchill, Berton 158
Ciannelli, Eduardo 141, 200-201, 419-420, 480, 483, 500

Cielito Lindo (song) 224, 227, 487
Cinerama Releasing Corporation 446
Ciro's 418
Cisco Kid Returns, The 317
City College of New York 8
Civic Repertory Theatre 105
Clair, Rene 345
Clark, Al 475
Clark, Cliff 124, 136, 247, 480, 482, 489
Clark, Mamo 95-96, 478
Clark, Steve 473
Clark, Wallis 475
Clatworthy, Robert 495, 498, 501
Clayworth, June 43, 475
Clean-Up Man, The 16-17, 466
Clemens, LeRoy 158, 482
Cleve, Iris 298, 495
Cleveland, George 359, 497
Clifford, Jack 493
Clifford, Ruth 469
Clifton, Elmer 230
Climax, The 199, 209, 365
Cline, Edward F. 163, 205, 213, 227, 243
Clover Club 418
Coates, Joren 443
Coates, Paul 437-441, 443, 452, 501
Cobb, Edmund 495
Coby, Fred 378, 499
Cochrane, Robert H. 83-84
Codee, Ann 334, 337, 494
Coe, Peter 332, 336, 494
Cohen, Bennett R. 493, 495
Cohen, Mickey 447, 451-453
Cohen, Sue (sister-in-law) 12
Cohn, Art 447, 503
Cohn, Harry 33, 465-466, 468-470, 503
Cohn, Jack 19, 467-468
Cohn, Ralph 43, 51
Colbert, Claudette 227, 345

nan, Buddy 468, 470
nan, Charles C. 466, 469
ians, The series 81, 194
r, Lois 289, 309, 311, 491-492
r, William, Jr. 23, 469
is, Lewis D. 235, 237, 294-295,
    88, 493
an, Ronald 410
45 459
nbia Pictures Corporation XV-XVI,
    /III, XXI, 18-49, 51, 65-66, 84,
    ', 91-94, 118, 126, 135, 139-140,
    12-153, 228-231, 237, 294, 304-
    15, 353, 366, 402, 405, 410-411,
    13, 426, 436, 445, 447, 463, 465-
    '6, 503
nbia series 20
Closer, Folks 34, 48-49, 475
oton, Joyce 42, 474
or Productions 51-53, 57, 62-64,
    '6
dential File 437-443, 448, 452-
    i3, 501
dential Telepictures, Inc. 501
re Wife (film) 288
re Wife (*Moment of Fear* TV show
    isode) 293
re Wife (novel) 282, 289, 292-
    13, 491
olly, Walter 89
id, Eddy 479
olidated Film Industries, Inc. 64,
ay, Jack 171
ay, Tom 412, 415-416, 499
, Elisha, Jr. 388, 391-392, 497
  Joe 466
e, Alistair 437
s, Robbin 339
er, Clancy 487
er, Courtney Riley 85
er, Gary 106, 126, 153

Cooper, James Fenimore 417
Cooper, Merian C. 86
Corbett, Ben 467
Cording, Harry 183, 416, 485, 499
Corey, Jeff 185-186, 485
Corpse Vanishes, The 278
Corrigan, Lloyd 253, 301, 384, 387, 489,
    490, 498
Cortés, Quirino Mendoza y 224, 487
Cortez, Stanley 181, 406, 463, 482-483,
    486
Corthell, Herbert 115, 479
Cosgrove, Justice 63
Costello, Lou 125, 281, 319, 325
Costello, Lou, Jr. 280
Cowan, Jerome 129-130, 132-133, 314,
    317, 480, 495
Cowan, Lester 63
Cowan, Will XVIII, 281, 308, 348, 352,
    492, 494, 496
Cowdin, J. Cheever 82-83, 153, 165, 171,
    223, 228
Cox, Morgan B. XVIII, 224, 308, 382, 403,
    486, 496
Craig, Alec 491-492
Craig, James 141-143, 145, 480
Crandall, Robert 62, 476
Crane, Kenneth 500
Crawford, Broderick 89, 299
Crazy House 243
Creation of the Humanoids 207
Creeper, The 415, 419-422, 500
Crehan, Joseph 253, 489
Crime Club series 282
Crime Does Not Pay series 361
Criminal Code, The 26, 470
Crimson Orchid 34
Crinley, Myrtis 467
Crisler, B.R. 138
Cromwell, Richard 147-148, 150, 481
Crosby, Bing 106, 163
Crossett, Ray 404

INDEX

Crowther, Bosley 62, 99, 104, 157, 162, 166, 235, 271-272, 293, 358
Cruze, James 82, 98, 411
Cruze, Julie 55
Cukor, George 345
Culver, Harry 207
Cummings, Constance 43
Cummings, Irving 27
Curran, Thomas 468
Curse of the Allenbys 383-384
Curtis, Alan 393, 395, 397-401, 411, 498
Curtis, Ed 465
Curtis, James 471
Curtiss, Edward 172, 181, 465, 481-482, 484-487, 495, 497
Curtiss, Ray 172, 486
Curtiz, Michael 279

D

D'Ambricourt, Adrienne 24
Daikubara, Akira 502
Dailey, Dan, Jr. 239-240, 405, 488
Daladier, Edouard 264
Daltons Ride Again, The 362
Damned Don't Die, The 457
Dance Charlie Dance 68
Dancing Cansinos, The 219
Dandridge, Ruby 399
Danger in the Pacific 235-238, 419, 488
Danger on Wheels 115-119, 129, 138, 479
Dark Empire 93, 101-102
Darling, W. Scott 282, 491
Darmour, Larry 71
Dassin, Jules 229
Davidson, E. Roy 475
Davies, Richard 225, 309, 486-487, 492
Davis, Bette 106

Davis, Frederick C. 134, 480
Davis, Robert O. 179, 486

Davy Crockett, Indian Scout 422-426, 500
Dawn Express, The 229
Dawson, Doris 469
Day, Marceline 21, 467-468
de Bujac, Etienne Pelissier Jacques 61
De La Cruze, Jimmy 469
De Rue, Eugene 467
Dead End Kids and Little Tough Guys, The 253, 258-259, 261
Dead End Kids, The 261
Dead End 261
Dead Man's Eyes 342-347, 494
Dead Men Walk 206
Deadline, The 471
Dean, Priscilla 393
Death of Adolf Hitler 264
Death on the Diamond 126
Decker, John 43
Dein, Edward 288, 491-492, 496, 501
Del Ruth, Roy 126, 410
DeLacy, Philippe 465
DeLacy, Ralph M. 478, 480-481, 483-491
Delaney, Charles 476
DeLapp, Terry 305
Dell, Gabriel 259, 261-262, 489
DeMille Pictures Corp. 17-18, 466
Design for Death 388, 391, 497
Deste, Luli 153, 155, 481
Destiny 257
Destry Rides Again 146, 165
Detective Crane 94
Deutsche Universal-Film 98
Devil Bat, The 278
Devil Has Wings 193
Devil in Uniform 135

Devil is Yellow, The 134-135, 480
Devil's Melody 459
Devil's Pipeline, The 166, 171-175, 483-484
Devil's Saddle 205
Devine, Andy 38, 85, 88-89, 92-93, 95-96, 98-101, 103-107, 110, 112, 114-115, 117, 119-126, 129, 165, 167, 170-172, 175, 181-184, 186-187, 189-190, 192, 194-196, 204, 209, 213, 217-219, 221-224, 226-227, 230, 232, 234-235, 237, 239-241, 299, 319-320, 397, 406, 464, 478-479, 482-488
Dew, Eddie 294-295, 297, 493, 495
Dewey, Thomas E. 72
Diamond, David 69
Dickey, Basil 467
Dickinson, Dick 472
Diege, Sam 476-477
Diestro, Alfredo del 470
Dietrich, Marlene 165
Dietz, Jack 313
Dirigible 91
Dirigo, Carmen 498-499
Diskant, George 500
Dix, Richard 253, 256, 406, 489
Dixon, Dick 437
Dmytryk, Edward 299-300, 304, 306, 308, 490
Do You Believe in Love and Honey (song) 398
Dodd, Claire 189
Dolenz, George 265-266, 269, 282, 490
Dolenz, Micky 269, 380
Don Winslow of the Navy 229
Donath, Ludwig 265-266, 269, 490
Doniger, Walter 488
Donlevy, Brian 299
Dons of San Marcos 218
Doomed Batallion, The 157, 481

Doran, Ann 218, 220, 486
Doran, Mary 471
DorElaine Apartments 15-16, 24
Dorn, Philip 148, 151, 153, 155, 481
Dossett, Chappell 466
Double Alibi XVIII, 134-140, 480
Double Date 213
Douglas, George 493
Douglas, Kirk 431
Douglas, Melvyn 38-39, 474
Douglas, Warren 153, 159, 162, 480-482
Dozier, William 400, 404
Dr. Christian series 177
Dr. Kildare series 165
Dr. Terror's House of Horrors 373
Dracula (Spanish language version) 26
Dracula 68, 82, 106, 146, 199, 237, 393, 463
Dracula's Daughter 146
Dragnet 438
Drake, Oliver XVIII, 263, 289, 294, 332, 337, 491-495
Drew, Ellen 423, 425-426, 500
Driftwood 21, 467
Drums of the Congo 213
Du Brey, Claire 482
Dubov, Paul 487-488
Ducey, Lillian 468
Duffy, Jack 55, 62, 476
Dugan, Tom 179, 486
Duke Comes Back, The 73
Dumbrille, Douglass 35-36, 38-39, 309, 348, 351, 473-475, 492, 496
Duncan, Bud 242
Duncan, David 454, 501
Duncan, Julie 165, 217
Duncan, Kenneth 500
Dunlap, Scott R. 22, 468
Dunn, Eddie 494
Dunn, James 43, 48-49, 475

INDEX

Dunning, George 467
Durbin, Deanna 83, 86, 184, 238
Durkin, James 471
Dusty Trail (song) 296
Duvivier, Julien 305
Dwan, Allan 226, 270
Dyer, Elmer 29, 469-470

E

Eagle-Lion Films 405, 411
Earhart, Amelia 61
Earl Carroll Theatre 418-419
Earle, Dudley 69
East of Borneo 140, 146, 238
East of Java 140
East of Miami 175
East Side Kids XVIII, 262, 358
Edmunds, William 499
Educational Films 51, 224
Edward Small Productions 64, 411, 423, 500
Egan, Jack 23-24, 469
El Código Penal 25-26, 135, 470
Eldredge, George 491, 493
Eldredge, John 172, 211, 483-484
Ellery Queen series 140
Elliott, Gordon 468, 476
Elliott, John 491
Elliott, Robert 472
Ellis, John 154, 481, 485
Ellis, Robert 468, 471-472
Ellroy, James 272
Ellsworth, Elmer 500
Elman, Irving 411, 499
Emerson Food Packing Company 15
Emery, Gilbert 487
Empire Strikes Back, The 443
Empty Holsters 205
End of the Trail 34, 47-48, 475
Enemy Agent XVIII, 123, 146-153, 175, 481

Enemy Alien (story) 147, 481
Engle, Billy 471
English, Richard 65, 69, 74, 477
Enright, Ray 110, 243
Erickson, Harold 487
Erickson, Knute 471
Ernest, George 471
Erwin, Stuart 64, 66, 68-69, 477
Escape from Hong Kong 224, 228, 230-232, 487
Esmeralda (parrot) 15
Eternal Woman, The 22, 469
Evans, Muriel 43, 475
Everson, William K. 17, 98, 215, 504
Exposed 134
Eyes of the Underworld XVIII, 228, 238, 253-258, 261, 397, 489

F

Face of the Screaming Werewolf 339
Face the Facts (story) 64
Face the Facts 64-66, 477
Fadden, Tom 141, 145, 480
Fairbanks, Douglas (Sr.), 94, 270
Fairbanks, Douglas, Jr. 21, 106, 466
Fairchild, Edgar 497
Fairfax, James 412, 499
Family Theatre 435
Farley, James 471
Farnum, William 333, 494
Farrell, Glenda 106
Faust, Martin 472
Faye, Randall 470, 472
Featherstone, Eddie 487
Feinberg, Ida 7
Feitshans, Fred R., Jr. 494, 496, 499
Fejos, Paul 81
Fenady, Andrew J. XII, 363, 368, 438-441, 443-444, 501
Ferber, Edna 445
Ferguson, Al 494-495

Fidler, Jimmie 223, 366-367
Fielding, Edward 342, 346, 494
Fields, Leonard 73-74
Fields, Stanley 155, 158, 481
Fields, W.C. 86, 100, 159, 163, 205
Fighter, The 43, 475
Fighting Gringo, The 106
Fighting Padre, The 218
Fighting Ranger, The 31-32, 473
Fine Arts Studio 183
Fink, Max 427
Finlayson, James 387
First National Pictures, Inc., Associated 14, 20
Fischer, Robert C. 141, 480
Fisher, Elliott 476-477
Fithian, Ted 300
Five Bold Women 450
Fix, Paul 124, 301, 471, 478, 482, 490
Flaherty, Pat 124, 126, 478-479, 482
Flavin, James 121, 172, 472, 482-483
Flavin, Martin 26, 471
Fleischer, Dave 74
Fleischer, Max 74
Fleischer, Richard 280
Fleming, Susan 471
Fleming, Victor 27, 86, 111
Flesh and Fantasy 305
Flight Command 126
Flight 24-25, 469-470
Flint, Sam 492
Flowing Gold 171
Flying Blind 197
Flying Cadets 213
Flying News 175
Flying Wild 214
Flynn, Edythe 467
Flynn, Errol 106
Fog Island 206

Foran, Dick 17, 200, 202, 204-207, 209-210, 212-213, 217, 219, 222, 227-230, 246-247, 250, 483-484, 486-488
Foran, Nick 204
Forbes, Ralph 21, 468
Forbidden 91
Forced Landing 193
Ford, John 29, 89, 109-110, 150
Ford, Wallace 200, 202, 207, 209, 246-247, 250, 483, 489
Forman, Tom 473
Forrest, William 175, 484
Fort, Garrett 393, 498
Foster, Eddie 483
Foster, Preston 282, 393, 395, 398-399, 401, 498
Foulger, Byron 95, 478
Four Feathers, The 86
Fowley, Douglas 167, 483
Fox Film Corporation 26, 73, 106, 110, 205
Fox, Matthew "Matty" 223, 403
Fox, Wallace 278, 294, 358, 361, 407, 494, 497
Fox, William 478, 481, 487
Foy, Bryan 119
Framed XVIII, 129-134, 479-480
Francis, Owen 112, 479
Frank Seltzer Productions 410
Frankenstein 82, 199, 250
Frankenstein Meets the Wolf Man 246
Frankie Laine Show, The 439
Freed, Alan 450
Freeman, Howard 372, 395, 398, 497-498
Freulich, Henry 473-474, 476
Freund, Karl 82, 200, 204
Friedlander, Louis 151
Frontier Badmen 243
Frost, Terry 493

INDEX

Frozen Ghost, The 262, 318, 345, 347-352, 496
Frye, Dwight 237, 488
Frye, Stuart 500
Fulton, Joan 370-371, 374, 398-399, 497-498
Fulton, John P. 110, 282, 491, 494
Fury at Furnace Creek 415
Fury in the Tropics (story) 102, 478

G

Gable, Clark 93
Gabor, Zsa Zsa 450
Gale Storm Show, The 450
Gallagher, Carole 227
Gallaudet, John 155, 225, 475, 481, 486
Galloway, Morgan 472
Gallup, Dr. George Gallup 80, 234, 245
Gan, Chester 487
Gangelin, Paul 273, 491
Gangelin, Victor A. 494
Garber, David 404
Garber, David S. 466-467
Gardner, Cyril 157
Garfield, John 106
Gargan, William 136, 140, 480
Garnett, Tay 187
Garr, Teri 294
Garrick, Gene 233, 487
Gasnier, Louis J. 52, 54-56, 476
Gately, Fred 437, 501
Gaumont-British Picture Corporation 87
Gausman, Russell A. 196, 231, 269, 308, 478-499, 501
Gay, Frank 63
Gehrig, Lou 87
Geldart, Clarence 473
Geller, James 404

General Service Studios 427
Geraghty, Carmelita 468
Geraghty, Maurice 347
Germonprez, Louis 437
Gershenson, Helen 321, 376
Gershenson, Joseph 270-271, 321, 376, 429, 454, 490-491, 493, 501
Gertsman, Maury 297, 356, 381, 386, 391-392, 398, 406, 493-499
Gertz, Irving 501
Ghost Catchers 243
Ghost Goes West, The 345
Ghost of Frankenstein, The 246, 256, 262, 278
Gibson, Wynne 475
Gierman, Frederick 265, 487, 490, 491
Gilbert, Jodi 481
Gilmore, Andrew J. 488-489, 491, 496
Gilmore, Douglas 468
Girard, Bernard 437
Girl with an Itch 450
Girls' School 118
Gish Sisters, Lillian and Dorothy 94
Glaesel, Theodore 25
Glass, Gaston 466, 468
Glassier, Gus 276
Gleckler, Robert 474
Globe Pictures/Globe Releasing Corp. 457
Go, Johnny, Go! 450
Goebbels, Joseph 264
Goetz, Harry M. 410
Goetz, William 365, 403
Gold Racket, The 52-57, 465, 476
Gold 53, 476
Goldbogen, Avrom XXI, 445, 447
Golden, Herb 170
Goldsmith, Jean 376
Goldsmith, Ken XVIII, 281, 376
Goldstone, Phil 32, 71

Goldsworthy, John 416, 499
Goldwyn, Samuel 80, 245
Goldwyn Studios 94
Golitzen, Alexander 309, 501
Golm, Lisa 491
Gomez, Thomas 344, 346, 494
Gone with the Wind 111
Goodbye My Love 352
Goodkind, Saul 255, 493, 499-500
Goodman, John B. 309, 489-497, 499
Goodwin, Bill 369, 371, 374, 497
Goodwin, Harold 469
Goodwins, Leslie 332, 338, 494
Goosson, Stephen 466
Gorcey, Leo 261, 263
Gordon, Huntley 466
Gordon, Julia Swayne 469
Gordon, Mary 247, 354, 489, 496
Gordon, Robert 489
Gottlieb, Alex 72, 177, 212, 477, 484
Gould, Charlie/Charles 376, 489
Gould, Jack 442
Gould, Lucille 376
Graff, Wilton 353, 359, 496-497
Graham, Billy 451
Grand Asher Films 224
Grand National Pictures XV-XVI, 51-54, 61, 63-64, 66, 68-69, 465, 476-477, 504
Grand National Studio 51
Granstedt, Greta 472
Grant, Marshall XVIII, 229, 231, 403, 487
Graves, Ralph 22, 24, 468-469
Gray, Coleen 454-455, 501
Grayson, Charles 134-135, 162, 480, 482
Greased Lightning 17, 467
Great Barrier, The 87-88
Great Guy 52
Great Son 445

Great Wall Street Scandal, The 71-75, 477
Greek Theater, The 376
Green Hell 145, 200, 238
Green, Alfred E. 171
Green, Harrison 477
Green, Howard J. 466, 468-469
Grey, Shirley 471
Grey, Virginia 369, 371, 373, 375, 497
Grey, Zane 47, 475
Gribbon, Eddie 167, 170, 483
Griffith, D.W. 94
Gross, Frank 487, 489
Gross, Jack 270, 436, 490, 501
Grossman, Abraham 492-493, 496-499
Gruber, Frank 411, 499
Guest Wife 227
Guild Films Company, Inc. 439, 501
Guilfoyle, Paul 425, 475, 500
Gulliver's Travels 74
Gwynne, Anne 113-114, 129, 224-225, 227, 289-290, 292, 358, 479, 486, 491

H

Hackel, A.W. 71
Hackett, Karl 476
Haden, Sara 383, 387, 498
Hadley, Reed 112, 154, 225, 479, 481, 486
Hagney, Frank 466
Hakujaden 466, 501
Hal Roach Studios 232, 435, 450, 505
Hale, Alan, Jr. 232, 487
Hale, Jonathan 342, 494
Hale, Mary 491
Hale, William 239, 488
Haley, Earl 32, 458-459, 473
Half a Sinner 158, 481

INDEX

Hall Room Boys 19
Hall, Frank 450
Hall, Huntz 259, 261-262, 489
Hall, Jon 245, 279
Hall, Thurston 39, 41, 44, 46, 100, 159, 161, 474-475, 478, 481
Halliwell, Leslie 204, 504
Halop, Billy 261
Hamilton, Cosmo 468
Hamilton, John 424, 500
Hamilton, Neil 72
Hamilton, Kim 501
Hammerstein, Oscar 446
Hancock, W. 469
Handler, Edward 489
Hangmen Also Die! 268
Harding, Jackie Lou 491
Harding, Kay 333, 339, 494
Harlan, Otis 68, 477
Harmon, John 195, 485
Harolde, Ralf 176, 194, 211, 484-485
Harper, Patricia 493
Harris, Elmer 466, 468
Harris, Roy 189-190, 485, 487
Hart, William S. 28
Hartmann, Edmund L. 147, 152, 481
Hashimoto, Kiyoshi 502
Haskin, Byron 471
Hathaway, Henry 150
Hatton, Fanny 469
Hatton, Frederic 469
Hatton, Rondo 314-315, 317-318, 367-370, 374-375, 378-381, 406, 421, 464, 495, 497, 499
Havlick, Gene 92
Hawks, Howard 26, 139, 279, 306
Hayden, Harry 491
Hayers, Sidney 293
Hayes, Linda 189-190, 194, 485
Hayward, Lillie 467
Hayward, Louis 436, 501
Hayworth, Rita 219
Hayworth, Vinton 133
He's My Guy 227
Hearn, Edward 469
Hebert, Henry 466
Hecht, Ben 88, 451-452
Hedgcock, William 480, 482, 489-491, 494, 496
Hell Harbor 317
Hello Trouble 28, 472
Hello, Sucker 213
Helm, Fay 286, 301, 490-491
Hemsley, Estelle 501
Henry, Louise 47, 475
Henry, Robert "Buzz" 493
Herbert, Holmes 236, 283, 333, 488, 491, 494
Herbert, Hugh 106
Herbert, Victor 295
Here Come the Co-Eds 152, 375
Herman, Albert 229
Hersholt, Jean 89, 158, 177
Hervey, Irene 230, 487
Herzig, Sig 468
Hey, You (song) 337
Hicks, Russell 148, 481
Hickson, John 466
Hickus, Louis 470
Higgin, Howard 476
High Noon 426
High Speed 28-30, 472
Hill, Doris 471
Hill, Riley 232
Hillbilly Blitzkrieg 242
Hillyer, Lambert 28, 31, 294, 471-473, 495
Hilton, Arthur 170, 435, 483, 486
Hinds, Samuel S. 102, 105, 158, 225, 259, 309, 388, 391, 393, 399, 478, 480-481, 486, 489, 492, 497-498
Hirlacolor 53
His Girl Friday 139
Hit Parade of 1947 100

Hitchcock, Alfred 48, 135, 313, 332, 388
Hitler, Adolf 75, 243, 253, 263-265, 307-308
Hitler's Children 304
Hobart, Rose 273, 276, 491
Hodgins, Earle 493
Hodgson, Leyland 220, 231, 413, 486-487, 499
Hoey, Dennis 384, 387, 498
Hoffman, David 236, 282-283, 358, 420, 422, 488, 500
Hoffman, John 352-353, 496
Hoffman, M.H. 52, 71
Hoffman, Otto 68, 472, 477
Hogan, James 263, 265, 269-274, 278, 280, 407, 490-491
Hohl, Arthur 348, 474, 496
Holland, Willard 496
Hollywood Bowl, The 376
Hollywood Legion Stadium 418
Hollywood Pictures 63
Holmes, Fred 467
Holmes, Gilbert "Pee Wee" 467
Holmes, John 115, 479
Holt, Jack 20, 22, 24, 47-48, 465, 468-469, 475
Holt, Jennifer 297-298, 493, 495
Homans, Robert 495
Honey Duke and His Uke 296
Honolulu Lu 229
Hope, Bob 152, 423
Hopper, Hedda 352
Horger, Emory 492
Horror Island 118, 209-215, 217, 397, 407, 484
Horton, Edward Everett 89
Hot Steel 92, 110, 118-123, 127, 129, 164, 200, 482
Hound of Heaven, The 435
Hound of the Baskervilles, The 365
House of Dracula XVIII, 246, 362, 366

House of Frankenstein XVIII, 246, 352, 365-366
House of Horrors 367-379, 381-382, 497
House of the Seven Gables, The 205, 265
Houser, Lionel O. 474, 476
Houser, Mervin 57
Houston, Norman 469
Howard, John 410
Howard, Lewis 194, 196, 211, 213, 484-485
Howard, Shemp 167, 169-170, 177, 262, 483-484, 489
Howard, William K. 66
Howe, Eileen 437
Howe, Jimmy 472
Howell, Dorothy 468
Howes, Reed 476
Hoxsey, Harry 449
Hoyt, Arthur 476
Hoyt, Harry O. 473
Hubbard, John 246-247, 250, 488
Hudson, Rochelle 90
Humberstone, H. Bruce 415
Humes, Fred 17, 467
Hunt, Eleanor 53-57, 63, 476
Huston, Paul 153, 171, 481, 484-485
Huston, Walter 26
Hyams, John 469
Hyans, Edward M., Jr. 309, 311-312, 406, 492
Hyde, Donald 437
Hyland, Frances 32
Hyman, Amelia "Milly" 3
Hymer, John B. 158, 482

I

I Cover the War 196
I Cover the Waterfront 411

INDEX

I Dreamt I dwelt in Marble Halls (song) 279
I'll Take Romance 65
Idea Girl 388
If the Shoe Fits 295
IMP (Independent Motion Picture Company) 13
Imperial Pictures 235
In My Own Words 453
In Old Arizona 27
In Old California (story, film) 93, 478
In Old Chicago 317
In Old Monterey 218
In Society 152, 375
In the Navy 189
Independent Film Library 430
Independent Motion Picture Company (IMP) 13
Independent Motion Picture Producers Association 409, 430
Independent Television Producers' Association (ITPA) 430
Indian Scout 422-424, 500
Indians Are Coming, The 382
Ingram, Jack 492-493, 495
Ingram, Rex 66
Inner Sanctum series 199, 281, 283, 288, 318, 342, 345-346, 353, 357, 362, 369, 422, 491, 494, 496-497
Inner Sanctum (radio show) 282
Inside Job XII, XVIII, 377, 393-402, 498
International Alliance of Theatrical Stage Employees (IATSE) 442
International Brotherhood of Electrical Workers (IBEW) 442
International Crime 69
International Pictures Corporation 365, 403
Invasion 427
Invisible Enemy 72-73
Invisible Ghost 214
Invisible Man Returns, The 199, 265, 407
Invisible Man's Revenge, The 262
Iroquois Trail, The 417
Irving, George 466
Irving, William 467
Island of Lost Souls 86
Isle of Missing Men (story) 171, 484
Isle of Romance 305
Ivan, Rosalind 359
Ivano, Paul 345, 350, 406, 463, 494, 496

J

Jack Benny Program, The 262
Jackman, Fred 33
Jackson, Harry 469
Jackson, Howard 474
Jacobs, Harrison 32, 37, 474
Jahns, Robert 476
James, John 297, 495
Janney, William 473
Jannings, Emil 273
Jaquet, Frank 495
Jarrico, Paul 189, 192-193, 485
Jason, Leigh 457
Jason, Will 388, 392, 402, 498
Jaws 312
Jay, Griffin 38, 189, 200, 239, 246, 300, 329, 331, 405, 473-474, 483, 485-490, 492-493
Jazz Singer, The 22
Jean, Gloria 159
Jeffers, Ray L. 495-496
Jewell, Isabel 44, 46, 282, 475
Jezebel 150
Jireh (Diabetic)Food Company 6
Joe McDoakes series 437
Joe Palooka 439
Johann, Zita 206
John Paul Revere series 294

Johnson, "Chic" 243
Johnson, Harold F. 401
Johnson, Ja Nelle 378, 380, 499
Johnson, Noble 103, 236, 478
Johnston, J.W. 467
Johnston, Julianne 466
Johnston, W.L. 71
Jolson, Al 106
Jones, Al 467
Jones, Buck 26-28, 30-31, 91, 294, 470-473
Jones, F. Richard 410
Jones, Spike 163
Jordan, Bobby 259-262, 489
Jory, Victor 37-38, 474
Joyce, Brenda 354, 356-359, 361, 496-497
Jungle Captive, The 313-318, 348, 356, 367, 495-496
Jungle Fear 313
Jungle Woman 262, 308-313, 492, 495

K

K.B.S. Productions 32
Kahn, Gordon 388, 497
Kandel, Aben 65, 476
Kane, Edward 477
Kane, Joseph 118
Kane, Sandra 96, 100, 478
Kanin, Garson 192
Karloff, Boris XIX, 147, 151, 200-202, 206-207, 209, 281, 340, 450
Karlson, Phil 417
Karnes, Sam 270, 321
Karnes, Shirley XII, 270, 321
Karns, Roscoe 136, 140, 468, 480
Karth, Jay 493, 495
Katch, Kurt 333, 335, 490, 494
Katzman, Sam 262-263, 313
Kaufman, Sidney 458-459

Kay Bee Pictures 207
Kaye, A.E. 477
Kazan, Elia 426
Keach, Stacy 494
Kean, Richard 179, 486
Keane, Robert Emmett 136, 480
Keays, Vernon 295, 493
Keckly, Jane 468
Keep 'em Flying 152
Keep 'em Slugging 258-263, 489-490
Keighley, William 119, 139
Kelland, Clarence Budington 64-65, 477
Kellaway, Cecil 200, 202, 205, 207, 483
Kelley, Dan 404
Kelly, Anthony Paul 147
Kelly, Frank 487
Kelly, Gene 174
Kelly, Jeanne 172, 174, 178-179, 181, 483, 486
Kelly, Lew 486
Kelly, Paul 342, 346, 494
Kennedy, Jack 472
Kent, Barbara 466
Kent, Ted J. 138, 480-482, 492
Kenton, Erle C. 21, 34, 47-48, 86, 213, 223, 246, 262, 278, 352, 366, 388, 466-467, 475
Kenyon, Charles 158
Kenyon, Ethel 28, 470
Kershner, Irvin 438-439, 442-443, 501
Kessler, Raymond 387, 498-499
Kibbee, Guy 166
Kid Dynamite 376
Kid from Kansas, The 218-223, 486
Kid Galahad 139
Kilburn, Terry 415-417, 499
Kilian, Victor 35, 473-474
Killers of the Sea 415
Killers, The 138

Killing is Convenient 388, 497
Kilpatrick, Reed 483
King Kong 61
King of Hockey 110
King of Jazz 81
King of the Cowboys 118
King of the Wild Horses 32-33, 473
King of the Wild Horses, The 33
King, Emmett 466
King, Henry 112, 317
King, Louis 28, 470
King, Sandra 115, 479
Kingsley, Grace 170, 318, 352
Kingsley, Sidney 261
Kinoshita, Chuji 502
Kirk, Joe 498
Kit Carson 424, 426
Kitchin, H. Milner 468
Kitty O'Day series 346
Klavir, Bernard 458
Kline, Benjamin 29, 470-473
Knight, Fuzzy 54-55, 165, 209-210, 217, 294-295, 297-298, 464, 476, 484, 492-493, 495
Knox, Elyse 232-233, 246-247, 250, 259-260, 262, 336, 406, 487, 489
Knox, Harold 500
Knute Rockne All American 279
Koessler, Walter 499-500
Kolker, Henry 45-46, 475
Kolster, Clarence 473
Koontz, Melvin 356
Korda, Alexander 88
Kortman, Bob 472
Kortner, Fritz 264-265, 267, 272, 490
Kosleck, Martin 333, 349-351, 369-370, 384, 387, 494, 496-498
Koster, Henry 118
Kozlenko, William 437
Kraft Music Hall, The 163
Kraly, Hans 273, 491
Krasne, Philip N. 436, 501

Krasner, Milton 158, 406, 463, 479-481, 491
Kreuger, Kurt 265-266, 490
Krims, Milton 471
Kruger, Otto 313, 315-317, 495
Krumgold, Joseph 474
Kusano, Kazuo 502
Kuznetzoff, Adia 103, 478
Kyne, Peter B. 85

L

L'Estrange, Dick 467
La Rue, Frank 473
La Rue, Jack 36, 474, 481
Lachman, Harry 34, 44, 475
Laddie (dog) 183-184, 189
Ladies in Retirement 278
Ladies of Leisure 91
Lady (horse) 32
Lady in Jade 402, 473
Lady Mouthpiece 74-75, 477
Laemmle Film Service 12
Laemmle, Carl (Sr.), 11-14, 16, 81-83, 466-467, 503
Laemmle, Carl, Jr. 81-83, 89
Laidlaw, Betty 65
Lamb, Ande 494-495
Lambert, Edward 500
Lamont, Charles 224, 243, 407, 487
Lamour, Dorothy 356
Landers, Lew 146-147, 150-152, 157, 175, 177-178, 407, 422, 424, 481, 484, 500
Landres, Paul 498
Lane Sisters, The: Rosemary, Priscilla, Leota, and Lola 145
Lane, Charles 168, 475, 483
Lane, Lola 141-143, 145, 480
Lane, Richard 97, 100, 420, 478, 500
Lane, Vicky 314, 317, 406, 495
Lanfield, Sidney 232

Lang, Fritz 151, 268
Lang, Walter 82, 412
Langdon, Harry 20
Lange, Samuel 474
Lapis, Joe 498-499, 501
LaPlante, Laura 167
Larceny on the Air 74
Larsen, Ted 500
Lassen, Kurt 458
Last of the Mohicans, The 411
Laughton, Charles 93
Lava, William 498
Lavender Lie, The 457
Lawrence, Marc 41, 178-179, 181, 254, 257, 388-389, 392-393, 396, 398-399, 486, 489, 497-498
Lawrence, Viola 474
Le Gallienne, Eva 105
Le Maire, Rufus 404, 469
Le Saint, Edward 471-472, 475-476
Leather Pushers, The 44, 166-171, 483
Leatherstocking Tales 417, 422
Leave It to Beaver 262
LeBorg, Reginald 282, 285-288, 293, 308, 312-313, 323-324, 329-332, 342, 345-346, 407, 464, 491-494
Lederman, D. Ross 28-29, 34, 37, 48, 470-472, 475
Lee, Billy 253, 257, 489
Lee, Lila 24, 469
Lee, Robert N. 466
Lee, Rowland V. 93, 199
Leech Woman, The 453-455, 501
Leech, The 454
Legion of Lost Flyers 91-92, 106-111, 126, 478-479
Lehman, Gladys 469
Leigh, Frank 20, 465
Leiser, Mitch 458
Leopard Man, The 174
Lerner, Jacques 207

Lesser, Sol 27, 74, 86-87, 313
Lester, William 467
Levin, Henry 411
Levine, Nat 71
Levy, David S. 476
Lewis, David 467
Lewis, George 471
Lewis, Harold 65, 477
Lewis, Jerry 418
Lewis, Joseph H. 56, 100, 199, 476
Lewis, Mitchell 472
Lewis, Ralph 472
Lewton, Val 174, 312
Liberace Show, The 439
Liberty Pictures 52, 71
Libra Films, Inc. 458
Lieber, Fritz, Jr. 289, 293, 491
Life of Riley, The 151
Life with Elizabeth 439
Linder, Max 55
Lindsay, Margaret 135-136, 139-140, 147, 480
Lion Trap, a Comedy in Four Acts, The 17, 466
Lippert, Robert 166, 504
Little Foxes, The 237
Little Old New York 112
Little Tough Guy 261
Little Tough Guys, The 261, 273
Little Women 345
Livadary, John 469
Lively, Robert 65
Lively, William 492
Lives of a Bengal Lancer, The 150
Liz Renay Story, The 452-453
Lizard's Leg and Owlet's Wing (*Route 66* TV show episode) 339
Lloyd, George 167, 170, 483
Lockhart, Gene 48, 383, 475
Lockhart, June 383, 387, 498
Loeb, Lee 48, 459, 474

INDEX

Logan, Jacqueline 17, 23, 466-467, 469
Logan, Stanley 413, 499
London After Midnight 393
London, Jack 85
Lone Ranger, The 74
Lone Rider, The 31
Lone Wolf Returns, The 34, 38-40, 436, 474
Lone Wolf, The (TV series) 436-437, 501
Long About Sundown (song) 296
Lord, Del 34, 41-42, 474
Lord, Marjorie 230-231, 239-240, 487-488
Lost Continent 347
Louis B. Mayer Productions 14
Love Before Breakfast 82
Love is a Fable 73-75, 477
Love Takes Flight 53, 57-63, 167, 476
Lovett, Dorothy 177, 484
Lowe, Sherman 474, 486
Lowery, Robert 325, 330, 369-371, 373, 492, 497
Lubin, Arthur 152, 199, 262, 279, 309, 365, 375
Lubitsch, Ernst 118, 273
Lucky Devils 152, 175-178, 484
Ludwig, Edward 353
Ludwig, Otto 480, 484, 488, 498
Lugosi, Bela 151, 166, 207, 229
Lundigan, William 107, 111, 478
Lupino Lane Comedies 224
Lyon, Ben 43

M

Ma and Pa Kettle series 224
Mabery, Mary 468
MacArthur, Charles 88
MacArthur, Harold H. 479, 481-482, 484-489, 495
MacBride, Donald 378, 380, 388, 391, 497, 499
MacDonald, Edmund 239, 488
MacDonald, Frances 496
MacDonald, Wallace 30, 33, 472-473
MacFadden, Hamilton 205
Macintosh, Charles 4
Mack Sennett Comedies 375
Mack, Joe 467
Mack, Wilbur 467
MacKenzie, Jack 406, 463, 488, 492
MacLane, Barton 327, 330, 492
MacLean, Douglas 64
MacRae, Henry 382
MacVicar, Martha 301, 490
Mad Doctor of Market Street, The XVIII, 199, 214
Mad Ghoul, The 201, 206, 262, 270, 273-280, 286, 366, 455, 490-491
Mad Monster, The 278
Madame Spy 257
Majestic Pictures 71, 94, 235
Mala, Ray 95, 97, 101, 141, 173, 478, 480, 483
Malvern, Paul XVIII, 199, 223, 281
Malyon, Eily 383, 387, 412, 415, 498-499
Man from Montreal 92, 106, 112-115, 126-127, 479
Man Made Monster XVIII, 199, 201, 214, 246
Man Trailer 31, 473
Man Who Lived Twice, The 34, 44-47, 475
Man Who Reclaimed His Head, The 353, 496
Manchester New Synagogue and Beth Hamedrash 3
Manchester Ship Canal 5
Mank, Gregory 337
Mann, Anthony 411
Mann, Hank 471

Manning, Bruce 37, 474
Maran, Francisco 99, 478
Marcus, Rabbi Benjamin 58
Marion, Charles 402
Marion, Edna 467
Maris, Mona 471
Mark of Zorro, The 100
Mark, Michael 483
Marlowe, Jerry 478-479
Marlowe, Kathy 450
Marquis (horse) 33, 473
Marquis Productions 238
Marsh, Joan 260, 489
Marsh, Marian 45-46, 48, 106, 475
Marshall, George 100, 163
Marshall, Tully 66-68, 477
Marshe, Vera 500
Martin, Al 474
Martin, Dean 418
Martin, Don 402, 405, 435, 500
Martin, Lewis 437
Martinelli, Tony 62, 476
Marvin, Johnny 296
Marx, Neyle 195, 485, 488
Mascot Pictures 71, 94
Mason, James 470
Matisen, Otto 468
Mattimore, Richard Van 86
Mattraw, Scotty 467
Mature, Victor 415
Maxwell, Edwin 476
May, David 399
May, Joe 199, 264, 490
Mayer, Arthur L. 214
Mayer, Edwin Justus 466
Mayer, Louis B. 61
McCarthy, John P. 22, 469
McCullough, Philo 470
McDonald, Francis 172, 189-190, 485-486
McDonald, Frank 410, 415, 500
McDonald, Wallace 28, 470-471, 483

McDonough, Joseph A. 490
McGill, H.A. 19
McGowan, Billy 169, 483
McGrail, Walter 466, 472
McGraw, Charles 273, 275, 280, 491
McGuire, John 47, 475
McGuire, Mickey 29, 472
McGurn, "Machine Gun" Jack 390-391
McHugh, Jimmy 224, 487
McIntire, Robert 404
McKay, George 474-475
McKee, Lafe 470, 472
McKenna of the Mounted 28, 472
McKenzie, Bob 471
McKenzie, Jack 239, 488, 492
McKinney, Mira/Myra 120, 179, 482, 486
McLaglen, Victor 89
McLemore, Helen 296, 370, 398, 412
McLeod, Victor 183, 193, 212, 484-485
McLernon, Harold 466
McMahon, Horace 170, 483
McManus, George 17
McNeile, H.C. 410
McQuarrie, Murdock 471
McVey, Patrick 430
McWade, Edward 120, 482
McWhorter, Frank 500
Mecca Building 7, 11
Meehan, George 474
Meehan, Lew 473
Meek, Donald 89
Meeker, George 342, 494
Meins, Gus 75
Melford, George 106, 140
Melick, Weldon 469
Mellett, Lowell 257
Melner, Murray 270
Melner, Sam B. 450

Index

Men of the Timberland 166, 189-193, 242, 485
Mendes, Lothar 86
Meredith, Burgess 89
Merman, Doc 476-477
Merrill, Lou 103, 478
Mescall, John 500
Metro Pictures Corporation 94
Metro-Goldwyn-Mayer Inc. (MGM) 14, 23, 61-62, 68, 82, 87, 89, 93, 100, 118, 171, 174, 218, 228-229, 242, 305, 361, 393, 398, 400
Meyer, Abe 476-477
Meyer, Otto 470, 474
Meyer, Torben 468
Meyers, L.J. 500
MGM (Metro-Goldwyn-Mayer Inc. 14, 23, 61-62, 68, 82, 87, 89, 93, 100, 118, 171, 174, 218, 228-229, 242, 305, 361, 393, 398, 400
Mickey (dog) 184
Mickey Cohen Story, The 447, 451-453
Middlemass, Robert 35-36, 39, 473-474
Midgley, Fanny 468
Midnight Madness 17-18, 466
Milan, Frank 476
Milestone, Lewis 81, 246
Milford, Gene 24, 469, 472-474, 477
Miljan, John 469
Miller, Carol Pivar (niece) XI, 2-4, 6-8, 12, 31, 59, 432, 448
Miller, Clinton 64
Miller, David 25
Miller, Marvin 456, 501
Miller, Seton I. 470
Miller, Virgil 282, 406, 463, 491, 494
Miller, Walter 471
Millionaire, The 456
Mills, Edith 110, 478
Milne, Peter 466-468
Mine with the Iron Door, The 87
Ministry of Fear 151
Miracle Woman, The 91
Missing Daughters 90
Missing Head, The 357, 496
Mister Ed 207
Mitchell, Beverlee 492
Mitchell, Frank 478, 483
Mitchell, Geneva 473
Mitchell, Irving 179, 486
Mix, Art 473
Mix, Tom 26, 28
Miyamoto, Shintaro 502
Mkwawa, Chief 140-141, 143-145
Modern Mothers 21, 135, 466
Mohr, Gerald 436
Mollinson, Henry 474
Moment of Fear 293
Monkees, The 269, 380
Monkey Talks, The 207
Monogram Pictures XVIII, 71, 94, 111, 150, 152, 166, 218, 229, 232, 235, 262, 278, 313, 346, 358, 366, 375-376, 406, 463
Monster on the Campus 454
Montez, Maria 194, 196, 245, 279, 299, 484
Montgomery, George 417, 423-424, 426, 500
Moon Creature, The 457
Moon is Down, The 265
Moon Their Mistress, The 352
Moore, Bill 478
Moore, Constance 96, 100, 129, 133-134, 478-479
Moore, Dennis 332, 339, 494
Moore, Dickey 468
Moore, Ida 494
Moore, Lola D. 466
Moore, Richard 438-439
Moore, William 476-477

Moran, Peggy 115, 118-120, 122, 159-160, 200, 202, 205-206, 209, 211-213, 336, 406, 479, 481-484
Moreno, Antonio 218-219, 221, 486
Morgan, Ainsworth 299
Morgan, Frank 89
Morgan, Gene 475
Morgan, George 466
Morgan, Kim 399-400
Morgan, Ralph 290, 292, 419-420, 491, 500
Morgan, Sandra 494
Mori, Takeshi 502
Mori, Yasuji 502
Morison, Patricia 282-284, 286-287, 491
Morris, Wayne 135, 138-139, 480
Morrison, Hobe 204, 288
Morse, Terry 147
Morton, Charles 493
Morton, James 484
Moskowitz, Irwin "Irv" 439, 501
Moskowitz, Joseph 411
Moss, Jimmie/Jimmy 396, 398, 498, 500
Motion Picture Center 412, 415
Motion Picture Country Home 457
Motion Picture Hospital 458
Motion Picture Patents Company 12
Motion Picture Specialty Co. 6, 14
Motion Pictures Division, The Office of war Information 243
Motion Pictures Producers and Distributors of America (MPDA) 271, 395
Moulin, Jess 478, 484-485, 488, 491-493, 496-497
Movietone System 81
Mowbray, Alan 89
Mower, Jack 467

MPDA (Motion Pictures Producers and Distributors of America) 271, 395
Mr. Boggs Buys a Barrel 66
Mr. Boggs Steps Out 64-69, 476-477
Mr. Deeds Goes to Town 65
Mr. Dodds Takes the Air 65
Mr. Wu 218
Mudie, Leonard 102, 478
Mummy Returns, The 323
Mummy Walks, The 457
Mummy, The 82, 146, 200-201, 463, 483
Mummy's Curse, The 332-339, 494
Mummy's Ghost, The XIX, 206, 270, 282, 286, 323-333, 336, 492-494
Mummy's Hand, The 17, 118, 167, 200-209, 212, 217, 246, 249, 330, 336, 397, 407, 483, 488
Mummy's Tomb, The 17, 206, 228, 238, 246-251, 336, 376, 488-489, 492
Munson, Ona 111, 478
Munsters, The 262
Muradian, Gregory 354, 496
Murder in Greenwich Village 87
Murder Mansion 369, 373, 377, 497
Murder, My Sweet 304
Murders in the Rue Morgue 463
Murnau, F.W. 134
Murphy and Co. 14
Murphy, George 36-37, 474
Murphy, Joseph J. 6
Murphy, M.F. 159
Murphy, Martin 404
Murphy, Stanley 477
Murton, Jack 404
Muse, Clarence 141, 145, 480
Mussolini, Benito 243, 264
Mustang Westerns 17
Mutiny in the Arctic 110, 182-189, 229, 485

Mutiny on the Blackhawk 92-101, 127, 478
Mutiny on the Bounty 93
Mutual Film Corporation 94
My Little Chickadee 163, 205
Myers, Carmel 24, 469
Myers, Zion 51, 64, 477
Mylong, John 490
Mysterious Miss X, The 74-75
Mystery of the Mad Ghoul, The 273
Myton, Fred 472-473

N

Nagana 238
Nagel, Anne 108, 110-111, 120, 122, 183-184, 187, 189, 211, 224-225, 227, 478, 482, 485-486
Nagel, Conrad 53-58, 62-63, 476
Naish, J. Carrol 282-284, 308-309, 311, 353-354, 356, 491-492, 496
Name Above the Title, The 92
Name the Woman 21, 466
Napier, Alan 370, 397
Narrow Margin, The 280
Natheaux, Louis 466
National Association of Broadcast Electronic Technicians (NABET) 442
National Education Association 80, 245
National Motion Picture Research Council 79, 245
National Society of Television Producers (NSTP) 430, 444
Naughty Nineties, The 152, 375
Navy Spy 54
Nazi Agent 229
Neal, Paul 487, 489
Neal, Tom 378, 380, 388-389, 391, 393, 405, 497-498
Negri, Pol 273

Neill, Paul 488
Neill, Roy William 22, 34, 38-40, 246, 253, 255, 257, 305, 317, 365, 407, 468, 474, 489
Nelson, Frank 465
Neumann, Kurt 158, 304
Neville, Grace 473
Newfield, Sam 278, 347
Newland, John 415-417, 499
Niblo, Fred, Jr. 435, 470, 475
Nichols, Lewis 295
Nigh, William 199-200, 218, 223-224, 229-232, 407, 486-487
Night of the Eagle 293-294
Ninotchka 118
Nixon, Marian 167
Norris, Edward 154, 481
North of the Klondike 223-224
North, Robert 34, 474
Northern Lights 166
Norton, Barry 26, 470
Norton, James 124, 482
Norton, Jack 496
Not a Ladies' Man 237
Nothing to Wear 21, 467
Novak, Joe 469
Novello, Jay 483
Nugent, Frank S. 43
Nugent, John Peer 453
Nye, G. Raymond 471

O

O'Brien, Pat 119
O'Brien, Tom 469
O'Byrne, Patsy 494
O'Connell, L. William 470, 472
O'Connor, Robert Emmett 38, 120, 136, 140, 474, 480, 482
O'Connor, Rod 435
O'Day, Nell 217
O'Day, Peggy 17, 466

O'Donnell, "Spec" 472
O'Driscoll, Martha 388-389, 393, 497
O'Farrell, Broderick 468
O'Flynn, Paddy 473
O'Malley, Pat 472
O'Neil, Sally 23, 37-38, 469, 474
O'Shea, Oscar 141, 183-184, 327-328, 480, 485, 492
Oakman, Wheeler 393
Object – Alimony 22, 468
Obzina, Martin 491, 494, 500
Of Mice and Men 89, 246, 256, 340
Office of War Information, Motion Pictures Division, The 243
Okabe, Kazuhiko 502
Okawa, Hiroshi 501
O'Keefe, Dennis 159-160, 162, 481
Oklahoma! 446-447
Old Dark House, The 82
Old Texas Trail, The 295
Olsen and Johnson 243
Omnibus 437
On Official Duty 74-75, 477
On the Waterfront 426
Once Upon a Crime 402
One Hour to Live 134
One Man Law 28, 471
One Million B.C. 246
One Night in the Tropics 182
One Step Beyond 415
Only Angels Have Wings 107, 126
Orth, Frank 337, 494
Osborne, Bud 493
Oscar, John 28-29, 470
Othman, Frederick 330-331
Otsuka, Yasuo 502
Otterson, Jack 478-489, 497-498
Our Love Will Live (song) 278-279
Ouspenskaya, Maria 105
Outcasts of Poker Flats, The 100
Outlaws of Palouse (novel) 47, 475
Outside the Law 393
Overland Mail 230, 239
Overman, Jack 495
Ox-Bow Incident, The 317

P

Padden, Sarah 493
Painter in the Sky 64
Paiva, Nestor 218, 221, 486, 488
Palmer, Maria 415-416, 499
Panda and the Magic Serpent 457, 501-502
Pape, Lionel 141, 480
Parachute Nurse 237
Paramount Pictures 14, 23, 64, 82, 86, 89, 110, 119, 123, 150-152, 163, 183, 193, 228, 243, 286, 304-305, 341, 356, 367, 410, 454, 463
Park Avenue Dame 87
Parker, Cecilia 473
Parker, Jean 345, 494
Parnell, Emory 172, 483
Pathé Exchange 18, 466
Pathé Frères 55
Patrick, Gail 39, 474
Patrick, John 467
Paul Coates' Confidential File 437-443, 448, 452-453, 501
Paul, Vaughn 160
Pawley, Edward 257, 489
Pawley, William 480
Pearl of Death, The 317, 367
Peck, James 438, 501
Peck's Bad Boy with the Circus 74
Pembroke, George 179, 486
Pendleton, Gaylord 189-190, 255, 485, 489
Pendleton, Nat 41-42, 474
Peón, Ramon 470
Pepper, Barbara 130-131, 480
Perdue, Derelys 467
Perfection Series 20

INDEX

Perils of Pauline 55-56
Perrin, Nat 159, 162, 482
Perry, Paul 469
Peters, Ralph 500
Peyton, Father Patrick 435
Phantom Lady 138
Phantom of the Opera 199, 309, 365
Phillips, Jean 240, 488
Pichel, Irving 229, 265
Pickford, Mary 270, 273
Picture Art Sales Corp., Inc. 11
Picture Corporation of America 183, 197
Pierce, Jack P. 196, 201, 207, 250, 300, 305, 489, 493, 497-499
Pillow of Death 356, 358-362, 497
Pincus, David I. 458
Pine, William H. 183, 193, 197
Pine-Thomas Productions 197
Pivar & Company 6, 11
Pivar, Adolphus (Adolph) (father) 2-7, 31, 59
Pivar, Ben
  Alvin Schoncite 451-453, 456-460
  Anglicization of name 4-5
  Arlen-Devine series at Universal 81-127, 165-197
  assignment to create new horror series 366-367
  associate producer at Republic Pictures 71-75
  associate producer at Universal 32, 84-127, 129-197, 199-215, 217-229, 231-243, 245-251, 253-288, 299-308, 323-332
  associate producer with Condor Productions, Grand National Films 51-64
  associate producer with Zion Myers Productions, Grand National Films 64-69
  associate producer/supervisor at Columbia 25-49
  bankruptcy petition against Condor Productions 63-64
  Ben Pivar and Associates 435
  birth, early days in Salford, England 2-5
  birth date ambiguity 1
  birth of children: Neil 75-76; Lorie 251; Jan 427
  Buck Jones series at Columbia 26-32
  cancer concerns and Harry Hoxsey 448-450
  Cheela the Ape Woman series at Universal 299-318
  children Neil and Lorie at Universal 318-320, 362-364
  Creeper series at Universal 367-382
  deterioration of marriage, divorce 448, 453
  Devine-Carrillo series at Universal 217-243
  early employment with Motion Picture Specialty Co. and Murphy and Co. 14
  editor at Columbia 20-25
  editor at DeMille Pictures Corp. 17-18
  editor at Universal 15-17
  education at School of Business and Civic Administration, City College of New York 8-9
  Edward Small Productions 422-426
  emigration to New York 5
  executive producer at Reliance 409-417, 419-422
  executive producer at Universal 288-298, 308-321, 332-362, 365-403

533

freelance production coordinator and writer 435-437, 450, 453-456
home life 77, 281, 320-321, 376-377, 417-419, 429-435, 450
ill health, death 456-458, 460-461
impact of war on films 228-229, 242-243, 245
Independent Film Library 430
Inner Sanctum series at Universal 281-294, 342-362
Joseph L. Breen and MPDA 271, 394-395
K.B.S. Productions 32
legacy 463-464
marriage to Judith Schonzeit 58-59
Michael Todd 445-447
Mickey Cohen 451-453
move to Los Angeles 15
Mummy series at Universal 199-208, 245-251, 323-339
Neil P. Varnick pseudonym 238, 300
non-series films at Universal: Adventure 140-146; Comedy 158-164, 258-263; Horror 209-215, 273-280, 382-387; Mystery and Noir 129-140, 146-152, 253-258, 387-402; War Related 152-158, 263-273
outside resistance to B films 79-80, 245
Paul Coates' Confidential File 437-443
Phil Goldstone Productions 32
physical description 331, 443-444
plagiarism suit over *Danger on Wheels* 118-119
Quality Films, Inc. 427
Rod Cameron series at Universal 294-298

secretive nature 1-2
significance to film industry XV-XVI, XVIII-XIX
summary of Universal films 405-408
Television City Arizona, Inc. 458-459
termination at Universal 403-408
youth in New York 5-8
Pivar, Bertha (sister) 3, 5, 30
Pivar, Dinah/Diana (sister) 3, 5, 30, 433
Pivar, Eli/Edward (brother) 3-6, 30, 426
Pivar, Florence (niece) 15
Pivar, Gershon/George (brother) XII, 3-6, 8, 12, 30
Pivar, Hannah (Anna) Marx (mother) 2-3, 31
Pivar, Ida (sister-in-law) 426
Pivar, Jacob/Jack (brother) 3, 5-6, 14-15, 30
Pivar, Jan (daughter) XI, 16, 38, 48, 58, 67, 72-73, 76, 281, 363, 369, 377, 418-419, 423, 427, 429, 431, 435, 448, 453, 455-457, 461
Pivar, Joe (brother) 3, 5, 31
Pivar, Judy/Judith Schonzeit XI-XII, 58-59, 72-73, 76-77, 108, 270, 320-321, 362-363, 376-377, 404, 418-419, 430-431, 435, 446-448, 451, 453, 456, 461
Pivar, Levi/Louis (brother) 3, 5-8, 12, 31
Pivar, Lois (niece) 12
Pivar, Loraine "Lorie" (daughter) XI, 251, 362, 368-370, 423, 430-436, 443, 446-448, 453, 455-457, 460-461

INDEX

Pivar, Morris/Maurice/Murray (brother) XXI, XXII, 3, 5-6, 11-12, 15-16, 25, 30, 84, 92, 271, 300, 404, 426-427, 447, 453
Pivar, Neil (son) XI, 1, 34, 41, 75-77, 281, 318-320, 362-364, 368, 418, 423, 426-427, 429, 431-435, 442, 447-450, 452, 454-455, 460-461
Pivar, Sidney (nephew) 14-15
Pivar, Yetta (sister-in-law) 14
Pivarnickus 7
Plympton, George 471
Poff, Lon 467
Pollard, Harry 374
Pommer, Erich 265
Porter, Don 232-233, 254, 256, 259, 262, 383, 405, 487, 489, 498
Portillo, Jorge López 450
Post, Wiley 36, 473
Power Dive 183
Powers, Richard 492
Poynter, Nelson 243, 245
Prairie Thunder 205
Pratt, James 404
PRC (Producers Releasing Corporation) XVIII, 65, 150, 152, 166, 206, 218, 229, 278, 346, 353, 366, 375, 381-382, 397, 405-406, 498, 504
Preston, Wade 459
Previn, Charles 478, 487
Pride of the Yankees, The 126
Principal Productions 86-87
Pritchard, Robert 479-482, 485-487, 494-495, 497
Private Lives of Elizabeth and Essex, The 106
Producers Releasing Corporation (PRC) XVIII, 65, 150, 152, 166, 206, 218, 229, 278, 346, 353, 366, 375, 381-382, 397, 405-406, 498, 504

Production Code 394-395
Prouty, Jed 466
Puglia, Frank 487
Punsley, Bernard 261
Pyle, Thomas 458

Q

Qualen, John 155, 158, 481
Quality Films, Inc. 427
Quartaro, Nina 469
Queen of Outer Space 450
Quick Triggers 17, 466-467

R

Radabaugh, Melvin 150
Radio and Television News Club of Southern California 438
Radio Patrol 149
Raaf, Vici (Vicki) 437
Raffetto, Mike 255, 489
Raging Rivers 93
Raiders of the Desert 166, 193-197, 485
Rain or Shine 91
Rains, Claude 353
Ralston, Jobyna 87-88
Ralston, Marcia 218, 220, 486
Ralston, Vera Hruba 71
Randall, Ron 436
Range Feud 28, 471
Rank Organization 403
Rank, Arthur J. 403
Rankin, Arthur 468
Ratoff, Gregory 229
Raven, The 151
Raw Deal 411
Rawhide 87
Rawlins, John 166-167, 170, 178, 181-183, 188-189, 192-193, 196, 229, 230, 232, 239, 245, 305, 483, 485-487

Rawlinson, Herbert 129-130, 480
Ready for Love 86
Realart Pictures 294, 313, 337, 357, 495
Rebecca 388
Rebel, The 98
Red Mill, The 295
Red River Valley (song) 219
Reed, George 466
Reed, Philip 423, 426, 500
Reicher, Frank 247-248, 325, 489, 492
Reliance Pictures XV-XVI, 86-87, 409-411, 417, 419, 422, 426, 499-500
Renay, Liz 452
Renegades of the Rio Grande 294, 297-298, 495
Repp, Ed Earle 493
Republic Pictures Corporation XV-XVI, 64, 69, 71-75, 84, 105, 111, 114, 118, 140, 152, 183, 232, 235, 243, 294, 352, 400, 405, 427, 477, 504
Requa, Charles 471
Resistance to B films, industry and public 79-80, 245
Restless Youth 22, 468
Return of Monte Cristo, The 411
Return of the Shiek, The 166, 193, 485
Revier, Dorothy 20-22, 465, 467-468, 473
Revolt on the Painted Desert 459
Rex the Wonder Horse 32, 473
Reynolds, Ben 466
Reynolds, Marjorie 148, 151, 481
Rhein, George 469
Rhine, Larry 166, 171, 178, 405, 483-484, 486
Rhythm of the Islands 305
Rice, Frank 470, 472-473
Rice, Jack 479, 485

Richards, Addison 112, 154, 183-184, 186-187, 232-233, 332, 355, 423-424, 479, 481, 485, 487, 491, 494, 496, 500
Richards, Gordon 499
Richmond, Kane 167
Richmond, Warner P. 476
Richter, Ernest 490
Ride 'em Cowboy 152
Riders of the Santa Fe 294, 296, 493-494
Ridin' Home (song) 224, 487
Ridin' for Justice 28, 471
Ridin' High (song) 296
Riedel, Richard H. 482, 488, 491
Riley, Harrison 469
Rin-Tin-Tin (dog) 184
Ripley, Robert L. 61
Risdon, Elizabeth 291-292, 491
Riskin, Robert 43
Ritz Brothers 182
River Irwell 4-5
River of Missing Men, The 140, 480
RKO Radio Pictures 52, 61, 63, 82-84, 87, 89, 94, 100, 106, 119, 151, 166, 172, 177, 189, 192, 228, 300, 304, 313, 332, 400, 409
Roach, Hal (Sr.) 89, 375
Roach, Hal, Jr. 450
Road Agent 110, 114, 224-228, 486-487
Road to Mandalay, The 393
Robards, Jason 472
Roberts, Arthur 22, 468
Roberts, Beatrice 59, 61-62, 476
Roberts, Beverly 102, 105, 478
Roberts, Leona 481
Robertson, Willard 44, 46, 190, 475, 485
Robertson-Cole Pictures Corporation 94

Robins, Sam 123, 147, 152, 177, 481-482, 484
Robinson, Byron 46, 475-476
Robinson, Dewey 474
Robinson, Edward G. 393
Robinson, Edward R. 269, 489-490, 492, 499
Robinson, George 250, 255, 304-305, 406, 412, 415, 463, 488-490, 499-500
Rockwell, Jack 493, 495
Rodin, Merrill 266, 490
Roehm, Ernst 263
Rogell, Albert S. 34, 189, 422, 473
Rogers, Charles 83-84, 123, 159
Rogers, John 184, 483, 485
Rolf, Erik 425, 500
Rolfe, Louise 390
Rooney, Mickey 29-30
Roosevelt, James 80
Roosevelt, President Franklin D. 80
Roquemore, Henry 482
Roscoe, Alan 466-467, 469, 472
Rosen, Milton 499-501
Rosen, Philip 21, 25-26, 134-135, 138, 407, 466, 470, 480
Rosenwald, Francis 454, 459, 501
Rosmer, Milton 87
Route 66 339
Rowland, Richard 64
Royce, Lionel 487
Royle, William 112, 479
Rub, Christian 156, 310, 354, 481, 492, 496
Rubin, Daniel Nathan 17, 466
Rubin, Stanley 229, 487
Ruhl, William 487
Russell, Elizabeth 289, 292, 491
Russell, Lillian 84-85
Russell, Rosalind 139
Rutherford, Ann XII, 393, 395, 398-401, 498

Ryan, Tim 74, 175, 484
Ryen, Richard 265, 490

S

S.O.S. Iceberg 187
S.O.S. Tidal Wave 114
Saboteur 313
Sabu 245
Sakamoto, Yusaku 502
Sale, Virginia 466, 474
Salford, Borough of 2, 5-6, 437, 505
Salkow, Sidney 410
Salt of the Earth 193
Salter, Hans J. (H.J.) 282, 407, 463, 479-491, 493, 496-497
Salvage 193
Sam Jaffe, Inc. 101
Sande, Walter 488
Sandrich, Mark 119
Santa Claus Lane Parade 376
Santa Fe Uprising 415
Sapper 499
Sarecky, Louis 32
Saturday Evening Post, The 64-65, 452
Saum, Clifford 477
Sawtell, Paul 287, 463, 491-492, 494-495, 500
Sawyer, Joe 112, 391, 396, 398-399, 479, 498
Sayer, George Wallace 229, 487
Sayers, Loretta 30, 471-472
Scared to Death 166
Scattergood Baines series 166
Schallert, Edwin 300
Schayer, Richard 424, 500
Schenck, Joseph 410
Schertzinger, Victor 52
Schilling, Gus 484
Schlom, Herbert 75
Schoedsack, Ernest B. 86

Schoengarth, Russell 493, 496
Schoncite International Productions 451-452
Schoncite, Alvin XII, 451-453, 456-458, 460, 501
Schoncite, Glenda Goldie XII, 452-453
Schonzeit, Anne (sister-in-law) XII, 59, 270, 320
Schonzeit, David (brother-in-law) XII, 59
Schonzeit, Debbie (sister-in-law) 59, 448
Schonzeit, Hank (nephew) XII, 430-431, 460
Schonzeit, Hyman (brother-in-law) 59
Schonzeit, Ina (sister-in-law) 59, 404
Schonzeit, Jennie Weiner (mother-in-law) 59, 362, 404
Schonzeit, Judith (wife) 58-59
Schonzeit, Libby (sister-in-law) XII, 59, 77, 431
Schonzeit, Ruth (sister-in-law) 59
Schonzeit, Sam (brother-in-law) 59
Schonzeit, Wolfe (father-in-law) 59, 75, 404
School of Business and Civic Administration, City College of New York 8
Schubert, Bernard 348, 492, 494, 496
Schubert, Franz 230
Schumm, Hans 265-266, 490
Schuster, Harold 129, 133-134, 140, 144-145, 480
Schwartz, William 489
Schwarzwald, Milton 134
Scott, Everett 183
Scott, Ewing 66
Screen Actors Guild 305
Screen Guild Productions 166
Screen Producers Guild (SPG) 444
Screen Snapshots 19
Scully, William A. 92, 165, 217, 238, 245, 263
Sea Hawk, The (1940) 279
Sea Patrol 93
Sea Wolf, The (1920) 100
Sea Wolf, The (1941) 279
Seaton, George 419
Seay, James 219, 241, 486, 488
Secret Agent of Japan 229
Secret Enemy 147
Secret of Treasure Island, The 230
Secret Valley 87
Secrets of the French Police 241
Sedgwick, Edward 126
Sedley, Henry 471
Segurola, Andre De 468
Seigler, Allen G. 42, 474
Seitz, Daniel D. 25
Seitz, George B. 20, 31-32, 229, 411, 465, 473
Selwynne, Clarissa 467
Selznick International 89
Selznick, David O. 61
Semels, Harry 471, 473
Sennett, Mack 20
Sergeant York 279
Seven Sweethearts 118, 400
Seventh Victim, The 174
Seward, Billie 473
Seward, Edmond 73-74
Seymour, James 469
Shadow Murder Case, The 69
Shane, Maxwell 166, 178, 200, 405, 483, 486, 489
Shanghai Lady 405, 459
Shanley, J.P. 441
Shannon, Frank 475
Shannon, Harry 326, 492
Sharpe, Lester 327, 490, 492
Shaw, George Bernard 459

Index

Shaw, Janet 176-177, 482, 484
Shawlee, Joan 374
She Done Him Wrong 55
Shearer, Norma 106
Sheehan, John 60, 62, 476
Sheldon, Jerome 494-495
Sherlock Holmes series 255, 317, 365, 387
Sherry, J. Barney 469
Shewing-Up of Blanco Posnet, The 459
She-Wolf of London 377, 382-388, 498
Shooting Party, The 352
Shore, Dinah 426
Show Boat 82
Showdown 232, 487
Showman Exploitation Specials 373
Shulter, Edward 468
Shumate, Harold 37, 465, 471-472, 474-475
Shumway, Walter 467
Sickner, William 235, 237, 297, 406, 463, 482, 488-489, 492-493
Siegel, Sol 74
Signals Over 69
Silent Barriers 87
Silver (horse) 471-473
Silverstein, David 223, 486
Silverstein, Elliot 134
Silverstein, Libby Schonzeit (sister-in-law) XII
Silverstein, Paul (brother-in-law) 77
Simmons, Michael L. 99, 102, 256, 478, 489
Simon, Earl Lester "Wild Bill" 118
Simon, S. Sylvan 100
Simpson, Napoleon 333, 494
Simpson, Russell 471-472
Sin Town 243
Sinner Take All 61
Sinner's Parade 21, 467

Siodmak, Robert 246, 262, 278
Sirk, Douglas 352
Siskind, David 448
Siskind, Debbie Schonzeit 448
Sitting Pretty 412
Ski Patrol 151-158, 164, 175, 397, 481
Skinner, Frank 401, 496-498
Sky Hawks 166
Slapsy Maxie's 418
Slate, Henry 437
Slosser, Ralph 492
Small Town Boy 64
Small, Bernard 410-412, 415, 417, 422, 424, 499-500
Small, Edward XV, 410-411, 422-424, 500
Smith, Albert J. 28, 470, 472, 476
Smith, F.R. 470
Smith, Leigh (L.R.) 493-494, 497-498
Smith, Lou 305
Smith, Noel M. 110
Smith, Oscar 466
Smith, W.C. 476
Snuffy Smith 242
Snyder, Ray 490, 492, 494-495
Sol M. Wurtzel Productions 410
Something to Sing About 52
Son of Dracula 246, 262, 278
Son of Frankenstein 199
Sondergaard, Gale 265-266, 282, 406, 490
Song of the Saddle 205
Sonora Kid, The 218
Soul of a Gunman, The 451
Sousa, John Philip 169
South of Sumatra 171-172, 483
South of Tahiti 299
South of the Amazon 166
South of the Rio Grande (song) 296
South of the Rio Grande 28, 471
Spear, Ivan 133, 197, 213, 366

Speers, Robert D. 474
Spider Woman Strikes Back, The 375
Spielberg, Steven 293, 312
Spirit of Notre Dame, The 88-89
Spitz, Leo 365, 403
Springer, Norman 468
St. Claire, Arthur 486
St. Valentine's Day Massacre 390
Stagecoach 89
Stakeout on Dope Street 443
Stand Up and Cheer 205
Standard Capital Company 82-83
Stand-In 65
Stapley, Richard 413, 499
Steel 92
Steenson, Clarence I. 500
Stefanic, Milan 65
Steiffel, "Bubbles" 167
Stein, Eddie 499-500
Stein, Lotte 500
Steinbeck, John 89, 246
Stelling, William 416, 499
Stengler, Mack 56, 62, 471, 476
Sternad, Rudolph 500
Stevens, Charles 471, 494
Stevens, Landers 115, 479
Stevens, Mark 404, 436
Stevens, Onslow 419-420, 500
Stevenson, Houseley 412, 499
Stewart, Anita 21, 466
Stewart, James 146
Stolen Paradise 55-56
Stoloff, Benjamin 411
Stone, Andrew L. 64-65
Stone, Gene 466
Stone, John 165
Stone, Milburn 105, 129-130, 151, 260, 262, 273, 275, 301, 304, 306, 308, 311, 348, 350-351, 354, 356, 393, 398-399, 401, 477-478, 480-481, 489-492, 496, 498
Storm Over the Andes 92

Stossel, Ludwig 265, 269, 490
Strand Productions 459
Strang, Harry 485
Strange Case of Doctor RX, The XVIII, 199
Strange Confession 352-358, 496
Strange Death of Adolf Hitler, The (book) 263-264
Strange Death of Adolf Hitler, The 235, 263-272, 280, 381, 397, 490
Strange Penalty 503
Strange, Glenn 297, 493, 495
Strange, Robert 41, 474
Strawn, Arthur 224, 256, 475, 486, 489
Strawn, Linda May 442
Streets of Danger 437, 501
Stronger Than Desire 100
Stubbs, Harry 480, 483
Stumar, Charles 204
Stumar, John 66, 475, 477
Stutenroth, Eugene 495
Submarine 22-23, 468
Sucher, Henry 246, 300, 308, 347, 492, 496
Suicide Crew (story) 118
Sullivan, Ed 435
Sumatra 218
Summer Storm 352
Sun Never Sets, The 93, 238
Sunrise – A Song of Two Humans 134
Sunset on the Sierras 218
Sunset Studios 33
Supreme Pictures 71
Suspicion 388
Sutherland, A. Edward 241
Sutter's Gold 82, 98, 100
Sutton, Grady 62, 476
Sutton, Kay 112, 479
Sweeney, James 42, 475
Swickard, Josef 469
Swing That Cheer 134

Sword of Monte Cristo, The 347
Sylos, F. Paul 476-477

T

Tafur, Robert 457, 501
Tail Spin 110
Taite, Evelyn 123
Taite, William 122-123
Takahashi, Hideyuki 502
Talbot, Gloria 454, 501
Talbot, Lyle 41-42, 474, 493
Tall Timber 166
Talmud Torah School 3
Tartar, Mara 483
Tarzan and the Leopard Woman 313, 347
Tarzan series 356
Taylor Ranch 13
Taylor, Forrest 492-493
Taylor, Kent 369
Taylor, Ray 16-17, 213, 235, 294, 362, 466-467, 492
Tchaikovsky, Pyotr Ilyich 463
Teal, Ray 500
Ted Ashley Associates 439
Television City Arizona, Inc. 458-459
Television Producers' Association (TPA) 430
Temple, Shirley 205
Tender Comrade 304
Terror of the South Seas (story) 212, 484
Terry, Dick 176, 484
Terry, Don 183, 229-232, 235, 237, 485, 487-488
Terry, Ethel Grey 466, 468
Terry, Phillip 454, 501
Test Driver (story) 115, 479
Teter, Earl "Lucky" 118-119
Tetzlaff, Ted 30, 468
Tevis, Carol 476

Thalberg, Irving 14
Thayer, Guy V. 477
Thing That Couldn't Die, The 454
This Marriage Business 114
Thomas, Bernard B. 359, 497
Thomas, Bill 501
Thomas, William C. 183, 193, 197
Thompson, Francis 435
Thorne, William 476
Thorpe, Jim 472
Thorpe, Richard 23, 469
Three Faces East 147
Thundercloud, Chief 500
Thurn-Taxis, Alexis 65-66
Tiffany Film Corporation 25, 94
Tigress, The 20, 465
Timber 238-243, 294, 376, 488
T-Men 411
Todd, Harry 471
Todd, Michael 445-447, 503
Todd, Thelma 469, 474
Todd-AO 446
Toei Animation 501
Toei Studios 456
Tol'able David 150
Tom, Dick, and Harry 192
Tombes, Andrew 178, 276, 491
Tombragel, Maurice 85, 102, 107, 111, 115, 119, 145, 183, 193, 212, 224, 348, 405, 419, 478-480, 482, 484-486, 488, 500
Too Tough to Kill 34, 37-38
Toombes, Andrew 178, 486
Top Sergeant Mulligan 232
Top Sergeant 232-235, 376, 487-488
Torpedo Boat 197
Torrid Zone 119, 222
Totman, Wellyn 469
Tovar, Lupita 103, 106, 470, 478
Townley, Jack 469
Trail Blazers, The 87
Trail of the Vigilantes 226

Trail to Gunsight 295, 493
Transatlantic Merry-Go-Round 411
Transatlantic 66
Trapped By Television 34, 41-44, 48, 474-475
Travis, Merle 495
Treachery Rides the Range 205
Treat 'em Rough 213
Treen, Mary 123-125, 479, 482
Trenk, William 265, 267, 269, 395, 490, 498
Trenker, Luis 98
Trevor, Norman 468
Triesault, Ivan 490
Trigger Trail 294, 297, 493
Tropic Fury 93, 101-106, 127, 171, 478
Trouble is My Middle Name (story) 129, 480
Trouble's My Middle Name 129
Trowbridge, Charles 97, 103, 202, 478, 483
Truesdell, Howard 465
Truffaut, Francois 332
Trust, the 12-13
Tryon, Glenn 66, 213
Tsukahara, Takamitsu 502
Tumbling Tumbleweeds 71
Turnbull, Hector 466
Twilight on the Prairie (song) 296
Two Sons 32
Two Yanks in Trinidad 229
Two-Fisted Gentleman 34, 43-44, 66, 475
Tyler, Harry 475-477
Tyler, Tom 201, 206-207, 483, 492
Uehara, Shin 502

U

Ulmer, Edgar G. 16-17
Uncle Tom's Cabin 374
Under-Pup, The 159
Unholy Three, The 393
United Artists Corporation 25, 64-65, 86, 89, 228, 352, 400, 411, 422, 500
United States v. Motion Picture Patents Co. 13
United Television Programs, Inc. 437, 501
United World Pictures Company, Inc. 403
Universal City 11, 13, 365
Universal Film Manufacturing Company, The 11, 13
Universal Pictures XI-XII, XV-XVI, XVIII, XXI, 11-14, 16-20, 22, 24-25, 30, 32, 34, 38, 65, 77, 81-86, 88-90, 92, 98-102, 104-106, 109-111, 114, 118-119, 129, 134, 138-140, 145-147, 150-154, 158-160, 164-166, 171-172, 174, 178, 182-184, 187-189, 193-194, 196-197, 199-200, 205, 207, 209-210, 217-218, 223-224, 227-232, 235, 237-238, 241-243, 245-246, 250, 256-259, 261-264, 269, 271-274, 278-279, 281-282, 288, 294-295, 298-299, 304-308, 311, 313, 316-318, 320-321, 324, 330-331, 338-339, 341, 346-347, 352-353, 356-358, 361-363, 365-367, 373-377, 382-383, 387, 393, 397, 401-409, 411-412, 417, 419, 426-427, 429, 431, 440-441, 445, 447, 453, 459, 463-467, 478-498, 503-504, 506
Universal-International Production Company 403, 445, 453, 455, 501
Unknown, The 393
Unseen Enemy 228-230, 232, 487
Uraneff, Vadim 466

INDEX

US Food and Drug Administration 449
Usher, Guy 486

V

Valli, Virginia 22, 468
Vallon, Michael 493
Van Dolsen, Foy 212, 484
Van Dongen, Frits 150
Van Dreelan, John 501
Van Dycke, Tom 43, 475
Van Enger, Charles 177, 406, 463, 484
Van Sloan, Edward 35-36
Van Trees, James 46, 467, 475
Van, Beatrice 467
Vance, Louis Joseph 474
Varconi, Victor 467
Varnick, Neil P. 238, 300, 488, 490
Vaughn, Dorothy 482
Veil, The 450
Velez, Lupe 229
Vengeance of the Deep 86
Venture Pictures 410-411
Verdugo, Elena 349, 351, 496
Verebes, Erno 490
Verne, Jules 446
Vickers, Martha 306
Victor, Henry 141, 145, 151, 480
Villarias, Carlos 26, 470
Villarreal, Julio 470
Vincent, June 412, 419-420, 499-500
Vinson, Helen 147-148, 151, 481
Vinton, Arthur 473
Viosca, Jose Soriano 470
Virginian, The 27, 86
Viva, Pancho 218
Vogan, Emmett 247-248, 326, 484, 489, 492
von Grobel, Heinrich 286
von Hemert, Ted 498

von Ribbentrop, Joachim 264
von Stroheim, Erich 14
von Suppé, Franz 98
von Twardowsky, Hans 265, 490
von Zelewski, Emil 140
von, Eltz Theodore 107, 111, 467, 478

W

Wagenheim, Charles 491, 495
Waggner, George 199, 209, 246, 262, 278, 365, 407, 484
Wagner, Max 492
Wagner, Sidney 473
Wake Up and Live 232
Walburn, Raymond 38-39, 474
Waldorf Series 20
Walker, Joseph 27, 465-470
Wallaby Jim of the Islands 65
Wallace, John 470, 473
Wallace, Richard 159
Waller, Eddy C. 101, 110, 113, 172, 478-479, 483, 486
Walling, William 471-472
Walsh, Raoul 207
Wanger, Walter 89
War Production Board 257
Ward, Amelita 314-316, 495
Ward, Luci 348, 496
Warner Brothers 22, 52, 65, 89, 98, 105-106, 110-111, 119, 139, 147, 150, 171, 205, 222, 227-228, 242, 261, 279, 306, 341, 388, 415, 505
Warner, Jerry 393-394, 398, 498
Warren, Ruth 472
Warrington, Ralph 497
Washburn, Bryant 467
Watkin, Pierre 310, 492, 494
Watson, Roy 468
Way of the West 92-93
Wayne, John 28, 71, 196, 471

Wayne, William 120, 482
We're in the Legion Now 55
Weaver, Tom XII, 308, 331-332, 454, 503-504
Webb, Clifton 412
Webb, Ira S. 309, 490, 494
Webb, Jack 438
Webster, M. Coates 353, 356, 369, 495-496, 499
Webster, Matthew 74
Weeks, Barbara 472
Weight, F. Harmon 18, 466
Weintraub, Charles 427
Weird Woman 114, 262, 288-294, 316, 323, 358, 464, 491
Weisberg, Brenda 259, 273, 293, 489, 491
Weiss Brothers Artclass Pictures 332
Welch, Niles 472
Welcome Back, Kotter 262
Well, Medium and Rare (newspaper column) 438
Welles, Orson 265
Wellman, William 86, 89, 317
Wells, Ted 17, 466-467
Welsch, Howard XVIII, 375, 403
Werewolf 457
Werker, Alfred L. 365
West of Zanzibar 393
West, Charles 473
West, Ford 473
West, Mae 55, 205
West, Vera 330, 358, 401, 478-487, 489-494, 496-499
Westcott, Helen 415-416, 499
Westlake Case, The 94
Westmore, Bud 455, 501
Westward Ho! 71
Wetzel, Albert 63-64
Whale, James 82, 100, 145, 200, 250
Wheeler, Cliff 65
Wheeler, Kenneth 275

White Eagle 28, 472
White Savage 245, 299
White, Betty 439
White, Dan 495
White, Herb 476
White, Jack 224
White, Jules 182
Whiteman, Paul 81
Whitley, Ray 296, 298, 492-493, 495
Whitney, Claire 325, 492
Whitney, Peter 378, 380, 388, 391, 497, 499
Whitney, Richard 72-73
Whitten, Tommy 115, 479
Who Is Sylvia? (song) 230
Who Killed Doc Robin? 178
Whytock, Grant 424, 500
Wilbur, Crane 54
Wilbur, Dr. Ray Lyman 79
Wild Jungle Captive 313, 495
Wiles, Gordon 34, 43, 64, 66-67, 193, 475, 477
Wiley, Harrison 467-469
Wiley, Jan 378, 380, 383, 387, 498
Wilkerson, William 500
Willat, Irvin 468
William, Warren 436
Williams, Grant 454, 501
Williams, Guinn "Big Boy" 47, 94, 97, 99-100, 107, 111, 159-163, 475, 478, 481
Willis, Matt 389, 497
Willock, David 107, 478
Wills, Henry 495
Wilmarth, William 476
Wilnat Films 20
Wilson, Charles 469
Wilson, Janis 420, 422, 500
Wilson, Lois 22, 468
Wind River 450
Wing, Toby 68, 477
Wings of Courage 193

Wings 86-87
Winkler, Benjamin 500
Winkler, Robert 176, 484
Winninger, Charles 85
Winton, Jane 467
Witches' Brew 294
Witney, William 74
Witwer, H.C. 166-167
Wolf Man, The 209, 246, 256, 262, 278, 340, 407
Wolfson, Robert 458
Wood, Sam 126, 227
Woods, Harry 471
Woolrich, Cornell 255
Work, Cliff 84, 271
Worlock, Frederick 498
Worsley, Wallace 14
Wreck of the Zarago, The 166
Wright, Harold Bell 87, 93
Wright, Joseph 466
Wright, Maurice 114, 117, 145, 406, 469, 471-472, 478-480, 483-488
Wright, Tenny 467-468
Writers Guild of America 459
Wrixon, Maris 493
Wurtzel, Sol 110, 165
Wyler, William 16, 150, 261

Y

Yabushita, Teiji 502
Yamamoto, Sanae 502
Yarbrough, Jean 152, 232, 278, 367, 369, 375-378, 381, 383, 386, 393, 398, 400-401, 411, 415, 419, 497-500
Yashiro, Seiichi 502
Yates, George 74-75
Yates, Herbert J. 71
Yellow Cargo 53, 55-56
You Can't Cheat an Honest Man 100, 163
You're Not So Tough 99
Young Deer 207
Young Mr. Lincoln 150
Young, Clarence Upson 119, 123-124, 171, 482, 484
Young, Harold 246, 250, 313, 318, 347-348, 407, 489, 496

Z

Zambezi 218
Zanzibar 140-147, 151, 159, 480
Zeidman, B.F. (Bennie) 51, 69
Zilzer, Wolfgang 490
Zinnemann, Fred 426
Zucco, George 200-201, 206-207, 246-247, 273, 275, 280, 324, 329-330, 336, 483, 489-490, 492

www.ingramcontent.com/pod-product-compliance
Lightning Source LLC
Chambersburg PA
CBHW051331230426
43668CB00010B/1224